Library of Congress Cataloging-in-Publication Data

Names: Uerpmann-Wittzack, Robert, 1966- editor. | Lagrange, Evelyne, editor. | Oeter, Stefan, editor.
Title: Religion and international law : living together / edited by Robert Uerpmann-Wittzack, Evelyne Lagrange, and Stefan Oeter.
Description: Boston ; Leiden : Brill, 2018. | Includes bibliographical references and index.
Identifiers: LCCN 2018034265 (print) | LCCN 2018034400 (ebook) | ISBN 9789004349155 (ebook) | ISBN 9789004349148 (alk. paper)
Subjects: LCSH: Freedom of religion (International law) | Freedom of religion. | Freedom of religion–Europe. | International law and human rights.
Classification: LCC K3258 (ebook) | LCC K3258 .R4355 2018 (print) | DDC 341.4/832–dc23
LC record available at https://lccn.loc.gov/2018034265

Typeface for the Latin, Greek, and Cyrillic scripts: "Brill." See and download: brill.com/brill-typeface.

ISBN 978-90-04-34914-8 (hardback)
ISBN 978-90-04-34915-5 (e-book)

This book is printed on acid-free paper and produced in a sustainable manner.

Religion and International Law

Living Together

Edited by

Robert Uerpmann-Wittzack, Evelyne Lagrange, and Stefan Oeter

BRILL
NIJHOFF

LEIDEN | BOSTON

Religion and International Law

Contents

PART 6
Religion and Other Individual Rights

PART 7
Conclusions

Preface

It is well established that religions and religious antagonisms are not foreign to the building-up of the international legal system. While the contribution of religious institutions – especially that of the Holy See – has been on the wane over the centuries, international law provides a great number of rules and mechanisms for the settlement of disputes rooted in religious antagonisms, the coexistence of different religions and corresponding domestic legal sets of rules, and the protection of the freedom of religion.

Controversies over the comeback of religious passions and the revival of religious identities have gained in importance over the past years. Thus, secularized Western societies feel confronted with orthodox movements and radical Islamism defying liberal values. Against the backdrop of different and sometimes fierce religious convictions, living together peacefully is still at stake.

A German-French forum was particularly promising for an enquiry on how international law can cope with religious challenges since French laicism differs considerably from the German cooperative approach towards religious groups. It was not a surprise that the case *S. A. S. v. France,* where the European Court of Human Rights had to decide on the total ban on face veiling in public space imposed by French law,[1] triggered heated debates between contributors. As a rule, it is up to domestic law to lay down the rules necessary for living together in society. However, even in an international order of mere coexistence, international law, too, is supposed to ensure that states and societies, but also individuals within a given society may live together peacefully despite religious differences.

The present volume seeks to clarify what 'living together' means with regard to religions and, above all, how international law may contribute to the ultimate goal of living together in peaceful societies. The first contributions will explore the historic roots of international law responses to religious challenges. Then, a second part will shift the perspective to the role of religious institutions and religious law. The following parts focus on human rights. Part three takes a cross-sectional approach in analysing the contributions of different human rights bodies, before further parts deal with the international protection of religion, the relationship between religious beliefs and freedom of expression, and the role of other individual rights.

---

1 *S A S v France* (GC) ECHR 2014-III 341.

While scholars from various European countries (beyond France and Germany: Austria, Italy, Poland, Portugal, Belgium, the UK) have contributed, the volume originates from the long-standing cooperation between the German and the French Societies of International Law, who organize joint conferences every two years and alternately in a German- or in a French-speaking country. On 4 and 5 November 2016, both Societies organized a colloquium on 'Religion and International Law' in Regensburg, which was co-funded by the German Research Foundation (Deutsche Forschungsgemeinschaft).

The editors owe a debt of gratitude to all those who have assiduously helped to realize this volume. This is particularly true for Alina Prechtl and Benjamin Manthey in Regensburg.

Robert Uerpmann-Wittzack, Evelyne Lagrange and Stefan Oeter

Notes on Contributors

Nathalie Bernard-Maugiron
is Senior Researcher at the Institut de recherche pour le développement (IRD) and associated Researcher at the Centre Maurice Hauriou pour la recherche en droit public of the Université Paris Descartes, France.

Laurence Burgorgue-Larsen
is Professor of public law at the Université Paris 1 Panthéon-Sorbonne, France.

Władysław Czapliński
is Director of the Institute of Legal Sciences of the Polish Academy of Sciences, Warsaw, and Professor of International Law at the University of Warsaw, Poland.

Ninon Colneric
was Judge of the Court of Justice of the European Communities, Honorary Professor at the University of Bremen, Germany, and European Co-Dean of the China-EU School of Law, Beijing.

Emmanuel Decaux
is Professor emeritus of public law at the Université Paris 2 Panthéon-Assas, France.

Claas Friedrich Germelmann
is Professor of public law and European law at the University of Hannover, Germany.

Sophie Grosbon
is Lecturer in public law at the Université Paris Nanterre and research fellow at the Centre de droit international de Nanterre (CEDIN), France.

Christoph Grabenwarter
is Professor of public law, business law and international law at the Vienna University of Economics and Business and Vice-President of the Austrian Constitutional Court.

Ludovic Hennebel
is Professor of international human rights law and global law at the Université Aix-Marseille, France, and member of the Perelman Centre of the Law School of the Université Libre de Bruxelles, Belgium.

Evelyne Lagrange
is Professor of public international law at the Université Paris 1 Panthéon-Sorbonne, France.

Irmgard Marboe
is Professor of public international law at the University of Vienna, Austria.

Angelika Nußberger
is Professor of constitutional law, public international law and comparative law at the University of Köln, Germany, and Judge at the European Court of Human Rights, Strasbourg, France.

Stefan Oeter
is Professor of public law, European Union law and public international law at the University of Hamburg, Germany.

Paulo Pinto de Albuquerque
is Professor of law at the Catholic University, Lisbon, Portugal, and Judge at the European Court of Human Rights, Strasbourg, France.

Eleni Polymenopoulou
is Lecturer in law at Brunel University, London, United Kingdom.

Dagmar Richter
is Adjunct Professor of law at the University of Heidelberg and the Europa-Institut of the Saarland University, Saarbrücken, Germany.

Jean-Pierre Schouppe
is Professor of canon law at the Pontificia Università della Santa Croce, Roma, Italy.

Andrea Scoseria Katz
was a Robina Human Rights Fellow at the European Court of Human Rights, Strasbourg, France. She received her Ph.D. in Political Science from Yale University, and a J.D. from Yale Law School.

Robert Uerpmann-Wittzack
is Professor of public and international law at the University of Regensburg, Germany.

Antje von Ungern-Sternberg
is Professor of public and international law at the University of Trier, Germany.

Christian Walter
is Professor of public international and public law at the Ludwig-Maximilian-Universität München, Germany.

Stephan Wendehorst
is Coordinator of the Research Cluster "The Jewish Holy Roman Empire", Lecturer for legal history at the University of Vienna, Austria, and part-time lecturer for early modern history at the Justus-Liebig-University Gießen, Germany.

PART 1

Historic Roots

CHAPTER 1

Religious Rights between International Law and Constitutional Law

A System of Communicating Vessels – From Premodern Historical Evidence to a Reassessment of Doctrine

Stephan Wendehorst

In modern times, that is in the Long Nineteenth and the Short Twentieth Century, the religious rights which a citizen enjoyes both as an individual and as a member of a religious community have been seen primarily as the concern of the respective nation state and hence a matter of domestic law. This has, by and large, remained so to this day. As protectors of the liberty of religion the international community and international law have come into sight only rarely. For good reason, so it seems, for European and extra-European history provides ample examples for the disastrous effects of religious interventions. In France and Germany the French Wars of Religion and the Thirty Years' War have discredited interventions on behalf of persecuted co-religionists both in the eyes of contemporary witnesses in the 16th and the 17th century and in the long term. Where religious interventions continued to be practiced in the 18th and the 19th century they were criticized as thinly veiled vehicles of imperialist expansion. The Partitions of Poland in 1772, 1793 and 1795 justified by Prussia and Russia in part on the grounds of the mistreatment of the Dissidents, i.e. Orthodox and Protestant Christians, in Poland-Lithuania and the largely self-arrogated role of Russia as the protector of Orthodox Christians in the Ottoman Empire from the Peace Treaty of Küçük Kaynarca in 1774 are notorious examples. Unless assimilated to a civilizing mission, religion came to be seen more and more as an irritant for international relations, if not an outright tool of agression and, thus, better contained within the state. This assessment was closely mirorred in the history of international law. Wilhelm Grewe in his magisterial, if not unproblematic work *The Epochs of International Law* remarked that the Peace of Westphalia in 1648 put an end to the practice of religion intervention by replacing it with religious minority protection.[1]

1 Wilhelm Grewe, *Epochs of International Law* (translated and revised by Michael Byers, first published in German in 1984, De Gruyter 2000) 181; on Grewe's opus magnum see Bardo Fassbender, 'Stories of War and Peace. On Writing the History of International Law in the "Third Reich" and After' (2002) 13 *European Journal of International Law* 479–512.

 | DOI:10.1163/9789004349155_002

Through the integration of the Westphalian peace settlement into the *Most Recent Imperial Compact* (*Jüngster Reichsabschied* in German, *recessus imperii novissimus* in Latin) of 1654 the extension of official recognition to the adherents of Reformed Christianity and the establishment of parity between the Catholic and Protestant religious parties in the Holy Roman Empire had been enshrined in imperial public law. Henceforth foreign religious intervention, which had been a legitimate, if controversial institute and practice of the early modern law of nations, was superfluous. In combination with the assumption of a wholesale secularization of the law of nations from as early as the Peace of Westphalia this narrative has become so potent that comparatively little is known about the interface of religion and international law post-1648. The unfolding of toleration – or the lack of it – towards the adherents of non-dominant Christian confessions, Jews and Muslims in Europe and the legal underpinnings of this process has been told as part of the legal history of states, nation states and empires and the respective religious groups as minorities within them, not as part of the history of international law.[2]

1 The Argument

This is, very briefly, and, admittedly, with many simplifications the state of the art, from which this contribution starts. It challenges the long time near-axiomatic view that following the Peace of Westphalia religious rights were to be secured internally, within the legal system of a given state and that interventions on behalf of persecuted co-religionists were neither frequent nor legitimate. This contribution claims that the established narrative is not only anachronistic as far as the 17th and 18th century is concerned – and, to a degree, also beyond –, but has, with more dramatic consequences, led to the eclipse of an adequate understanding of the dynamic interaction between international law and constitutional law concerning the protection of religious rights. It argues that, in particular in the early modern period, it was often the law of nations and constitutional law working in tandem, as a system of

2 See, for example Pierre Birnbaum and Ira Katznelson (eds), *Paths of Emancipation. Jews, States and Citizenship* (Princeton University Press 1995); Rainer Liedtke and Stephan Wendehorst (eds), *The Emancipation of Catholics, Jews and Protestants. Minorities and the nation state in nineteenthcentury Europe* (Manchester University Press 1999); Peter Pulzer, *Jews and the German State. The Political History of a Minority, 1848–1933* (Blackwell 1992) and Pierre Birnbaum, *The Jews of the Republic. A Political History of State Jews in France from Gambetta to Vichy* (Jane Marie Todd tr, first published in French 1992, Stanford University Press 1996).

communicating vessels, that guaranteed religious rights and ponders whether the empirical evidence which the early modern period provides for this argument may be put to use not only for a reassessment of the history, but also for reshaping the doctrine of international law in this respect.

The argument is developed in four further steps. Part two of this paper seeks to provide empirical evidence for the protection of religious rights as objects, part three for religious communities as subjects of the early modern law of nations. The examples are drawn from the Jean Dumont's *Corps universel diplomatique du droit des gens*,[3] Mathias Dogiel's *Codex Diplomaticus*

---

3 Jean Dumont (ed), *Corps universel diplomatique du droit des gens, contentant un recueil des traitez d'alliance, de paix, de trève, de neutralité, de commerce, d'échange, de Protection et de Garantie, de toutes les Conventions, transactions, Pactes, Concordates et autres Contrats qui ont été faits en Europe, depuis le Règne de l'Empereur Charlemagne jusque à présent, avec les Capitulations impériales et royales, les Sentences Arbitrales dans les Causes importantes; les Déclarations de guerre, les Contrats de Mariage de Grands Princes, leurs Testament, Donations, Renonciations, & Protestations; les Investitures des grands Fiefs; les Erections des grandes Dignités, celle des grandes Compagnies de Commerce et en général de tous les Titres, sous quelque nom qu'on les désigne, qui peuvent servir à fonder ou justifier les droits et les intérêrets des princes et états de l'Europe. Le tout tiré en partie des Archives de la très Auguste Maison d'Autriche et en partie de celles de quelques Princes et Etats; comme aussi des Protocolles de quelques grands Ministres; des Manuscrits de la Bibliothèque Royale de Berlin; des meilleures Collections, qui ont déjà paru tant en Allemagne qu'en France, en Angleterre, en Hollande et ailleurs; sur tout des Actes de Rymer et enfin le plus estimés, soit en Histoire, en Politique ou on droit; par M.J. Dumont Baron de Carelscroon, Ecuier, Conseiller et historiographe de Sa Majesté Impériale et Catholique*, vols 1,1–8,2 [in the following referred to as Dumont, *Corps Universel Diplomatique du Droit des Gens*, vols 1,1–8,2] (P. Brunel, R. et G. Wetstein, les Ianssons, Waesperge et l'Honoré et Chatelain/P. Husson et Charles Levier 1726–1731); Jean Dumont and Jean Rousset (eds), *Supplement au Corps Universel Diplomatique du Droit des Gens, contentant un recueil des Traitez, D'Alliance, de Paix, de Trève, de Neutralité, de Commerce, de Garantie, des toutes les Conventions, Transactions, Pactes, Concordates & autres Contracts, Capitulations Impériales, & Royales, Donations, Renonciations, Protestations, Testamens, Investitures, et en general de tous les titres, Sous quelque nom qu'on les désigne, Qui ont échapé aux prémieres recherches de Mr. Du Mont Continué jusqu' à présent par Mr. Rousset, Membre des Académies des Sciences de St. Petersbourg & de Berlin*, vols 1,1–3,2 [in the following referred to as Dumont, *Supplement au Corps Universel Diplomatique du Droit des Gens*, vols 1,1–3,2] (Chez Les Jannsons à Waesberge, Wetstein & Smith, & Z. Chatelain/Chez P de Hondt, la Veuve de Ch Le Vier & J Neaulme 1739); Jean Dumont and Jean Rousset (eds), *Le Ceremonial Diplomatique des Cours de L'Europe, Ou Collection des Actes, Mémoires & Relations qui concernent les Dignitez, Titulatures, Honneurs & Prééminences; les Fonctions publiques des Soveraines, leur Sacres, Couronnements, Mariages, Batêmes, Enterremens; lers Ambassadeurs, leur Immunitez & Franchises, leur Démêlez et de Préséance; Et en général tout ce qui a rapport au Cérémonial &*

Poloniae et Magnus Ducatis Lithuaniae,[4] Georg Friedrich Martens's *Recueils*[5] and Johann Ludwig Klüber's *Acten des Wiener Kongresses*.[6] Jean Dumont's collection, published between 1726 and 1739 in 8 regular and 5 supplement volumes, each of them, with the exception of the last two supplement volumes, consisting of two parts, was regarded as 'la collection la plus vaste et la plus connue' by Georg Friedrich Martens as late as 1802[7] and can be considered the most comprehensive collection of the positive premodern law of

à l'Etiquette. Recueilli en partie par Mr. Du Mont. Mis en ordre & considérablement augmenté par Mr. Rousset, Membre des Académies des Sciences de St. Petersbourg & de Berlin, vols 1–2 (Supplement au Corps Universel Diplomatique du Droit des Gens, vols 4–5) [in the following referred to as Dumont, *Supplement au Corps Universel Diplomatique du Droit des Gens*, vols 4–5] (Chez Les Jannsons à Waesberge, Wetstein & Smith, & Z Chatelain/Chez P de Hondt, la Veuve de Ch. Le Vier & J Neaulme 1739).

4 Mathias Dogiel (ed), *Codex diplomaticus Poloniae et Magni Ducatis Lithuaniae, in quo pacta, federa, tractatus pacis, mutuae amicitiae, subsidiorum, induciarum, commerciorum, nec non conventiones, pactiones concordata, transactiones, declarationes, statuta, ordinationes, bullae, decreta, edicta, rescripta, sententia arbitrales, infeudationes, homagia, pacta etiam matrimonialia et dotalia, litterae item reversales, concessionum, libertatis, immunitatis, donationum, oppignorationum, renunciatonum, erectionum, obligationum, venditionum, emptionum, permutationum, cessionum, protestationum aliaque omnis generis publico nomine actorum et gstorum momumenta nun primum ex archivis publicis eruta ac in lucem protracta, rebus ordine chronologico dispositis, exhibentur*, vols 1, 4, 5 (Ex Typographia Regia, et Reipublicae, Collegii Scholarum Piarum 1758–1764).

5 Georg Friedrich von Martens (ed), *Recueil des Principaux Traites d'Alliance, de Paix, de Trêve, de Neutralité, de Commerce, de Limites, d'Èchange etc. conclus par les puissances de l'Europe, tant entre elles qu'avec les puissances et états dans d'autres parties du monde; depuis 1761 jusqu'à présent*, vols 1–7 (Dieterich 1791–1801); idem (ed), *Supplement au Recueil des Principaux Traites d'Alliance, de Paix, de Trêve, de Neutralité, de Commerce, de Limites, d'Èchange etc. conclus par les puissances de l'Europe, tant entre elles qu'avec les puissances et états dans d'autres parties du monde; depuis 1761 jusqu'à présent, précède de traités du XVIIIeme siècle antérieurs à cette époque et qui ne se trouvent pas dans le corps universel diplomatique de Mrs. Dumont et Rousset et autres recueils généraux de traités*, vols 1–4 (Dieterich 1802–1808); idem (ed), *Recueil des Principaux Traites d'Alliance, de Paix, de Trêve, de Neutralité, de Commerce, de Limites, d'Èchange etc. conclus par les puissances de l'Europe, tant entre elles qu'avec les puissances et états dans d'autres parties du monde; depuis 1761 jusqu'à présent*, vols 1–8, (2nd edn, Dieterich 1817–1835).

6 Johann Ludwig Klüber, *Die Akten des Wiener Kongresses in den Jahren 1814 und 1815*, vols 1–7 (Palm & Encke 1815–1817).

7 Georg Friederich von Martens, 'Discours préliminaire sur les differens recueils de traités publiés jusqu'à ce jour' in idem (ed), *Supplement au Recueil des Principaux Traites*, vol 1 (Dieterich 1802) III.

nations to this day.[8] It is not restricted to international law in the sense of inter-state law and, therefore, more representative of the early modern law of nations than modern collections like *The Consolidated Treaty Series* (CTS), the *Oxford Historical Treaties* (OHT) or the *European Peace Treaties of the Pre-Modern Era Online*.[9]

If both, religious rights as objects and religious communities as subjects, existed as regular features of the early modern law of nations, the question arises, how they fitted into it. Part four seeks to provide an answer, first by analyzing key aspects of the early modern law of nations in contradistinction to modern international law and second, by probing five mechanisms instrumental for the law of nations and municipal law operating as a system of communicating vessels concerning the protection of religious rights.

As a conclusion, part five asks for the consequences, if the law of nations is brought back into play, in two respects. First, to which extent has the genesis of early modern religious toleration and the rise of the modern principle of equality in religious matters, both for the individual and for religious communities, to be reassesssed? Second, which repercussions on the extant body of the doctrine of international law may be expected from the historical evidence assembled in parts two and three and the connections made in part four?

2 Religious Rights as Objects of the Early Modern Positive Law of Nations

The collections of Jean Dumont, Mathias Dogiel, Georg Friedrich Martens and Johann Ludwig Klüber demonstrate the continuing relevance of the law of nations for the protection of religious rights post-1648. In these collections religious guarantees can be encountered as part of positive law in various forms, as an integral part of treaties between sovereign princes, in the form of secret clauses or added on communications. To name but a choice of instructive examples, Calvinists benefitted from religious guarantees in Hungary and

8 For the work of Jean Dumont and other exponents of the practical law of nations as providing the basis for a reassessment of the early modern law of nations see Stephan Wendehorst, *Die Geschichte des Hl. Röm. Reichs deutscher Nation als Völkerrechtsgeschichte* and idem (ed), *Positive Early Modern Law of Nations* (forthcoming 2018).

9 Clive Parry (ed), *The Consolidated Treaty Series, 1648–1919*, vols 1–231 (Oceana Publ. 1969–1981); <https://global.oup.com/academic/product/oxford-historical-treaties-9780199363612?cc=at&lang=en&#> accessed 20 October 2017; <www.ieg-friedensvertraege.de/likecms.php?function=set_lang&lang=en> accessed 20 October 2017.

Transsylvania in the treaties of Vienna 1606, Nikolsburg 1622, Vienna 1624, Preßburg 1626 and Linz 1645[10] in Jülich-Cleves-Berg, in Poland[11] and in those parts of Poland ceded to Austria,[12] Catholics in Livonia in the treaty of Oliva 1660,[13] in Podolia in 1672,[14] in Jülich-Cleves-Berg in the religious compromise

10 Pacificatio Viennensis, sive Tractatus Reconciliationis STEPHANI BOCHKAY DE KISMARIA, & sibi Adhaerentium Hungarorum cum Imperatore & Rege RUDOLPHO II. per MATHIAM Archi-Ducem promotae ac sancitae. Viennae die 23. Junii 1606. Cum ACCEPTATIONIBUS & obligationibus compulsorium Magnatum, nomine Ordinem & Statuum tam Regni HUNGARIAE, quam regni BOHEMIAE hoc super hinc inde commutatis. Vienae die 23. & 26. Septembris 1606, Dumont, *Corps universel diplomatique du droit des gens*, vol 5,2, pp 68–73; Diploma Ferdinandi III. universis Statibus & Ordinibus Regni HUNGARIAE concessum, ac deinde publicis Constitutionibus Regni insertum; Quô, in sequelam Pacificationis cum Principe RAGOCKZI initae, omnia Privilegia, & Statuta Regni & Regnicolarum confirmantur, praesertim in puncto liberi Exercitii Religionis. Datum in Arce Lyncea Austriae die 16. (1.) Decembris 1645, Dumont, *Corps universel diplomatique du droit des gens*, vol 6,1, p 331f.

11 Traité entre Sa Majesté le Roi de Prusse & Sa Majesté le Roi & la Republique de Pologne, conclu à Varsovie le 18. Septembre 1773, Art. IX, Martens (ed), *Recueil des Principaux Traites* (n 5), vol 1, pp 486–96, here p 494.

12 Traité entre Sa Majesté le Roi & la Republique de Pologe, & Sa Majesté l'imperatrice Reine de Hongrie & de Bohème signé à Varsovie le 18. Sept. 1773, Art. V, ibid, vol 4, pp 110–25, here p 118.

13 Tractatus Pacis inter Regem Poloniae JOANNEM CASIMIRUM ejusque Foederatos LEOPOLDUM Imperatorem, & Electorem Brandenburgicum FRIDERICUM WILHELMUM ab una, & CAROLUM XI. Sueciae Regem à parte altera conclusae. Quô omnes omnino inimicitiae inter eosdem exortae abolentur, & à Rege Poloniae pro se & Successoribus suis omnibus in Regnum Sueciae Praetensionibus renunciatur Livoniaque Coronae Suedicae ceditur. Actum Olivae 23. April. 3. Maii 1660. Cum Annexis variis DECLARATIONIBUS, & REVERSALIBUS atque MANDATIS. Art. IV, § 2, Dumont, *Corps universel diplomatique du droit des gens*, vol 6,2–3, p 305.

14 Document 50 (16 October 1672). The Polish document of the agreement of Buczacz, in Dariusz Kołodziejczyk, *Ottoman-Polish Diplomatic Relations (15th–18th Century). An Annotated Edition of Ahdnames and Other Documents* (The Ottoman Empire and its Heritage. Politics, Society and Economy, 18) (Brill 2000), Art. 3, p 495; Document 51 (18 October 1672). The Ottoman document of the agreement of Buczacz, ibid, Art. 3, p 499f; Document 52 (23 October 1672). The 'ahdname sent by Mehmed IV to King Michał, ibid, Art. 3, p 509f; Document 53A (14 October 1676). Version of the Polish document of the agreement of Żuranow, which was not enacted, ibid, Art. 4, p 518; Traité de Paix entre JEAN Roi de Pologne & MAHOMET IV. Empereur des Turcs. Fait le 16. d'Octobre 1676, Art. IV, Dumont, *Corps universel diplomatique du droit des gens*, vol 7,1, p 324; Document 54 (17 October 1676). The Ottoman document of the agreement of Żuranow, in Kołodziejczyk, *Ottoman-Polish Diplomatic Relations* (as above), Art. 7, p 526; Document 55 (4–13 April, 1678). The 'ahdname sent by Mehmed IV to King John III, ibid, p 539; Traité de Paix entre

of 1672,[15] in Courland and Semigallia,[16] in Maastricht in the treaty of Nijmegen between the King of France and the Dutch States-General 1678,[17] in Hanover and Celle in 1692,[18] in Nova Scotia and New Foundland in the treaty of Utrecht between the kings of France and England 1713,[19] in those parts of Upper Guelders ceded by the Emperor to the Prussian king in their treaty of Utrecht

---

JEAN SOBIESKI Roi de Pologne & MAHOMET IV. Fait en l'anée 1679, Dumont, *Corps universel diplomatique du droit des gens*, vol 7,1, p 435.

15 Convention Religieuse entre FREDERIC GUILLAUME Electeur de Brandebourg, & PHILIPPE GUILLAUME Comte Palatin du Rhyn, Duc de Neubourg, par lequelle ensuite de l'Accomodement principal fait entr'euex le 9. Septembre 1666 au sujet de la succession de Juliers, Cleves & c. ils conviennent aussi d'une manière fort entenduë & fort specfique de toute ce qui regarde l'état de la Religion & de toutes les choses Ecclesiastiques, savoir en faveur des Catholiques dans le Duché de Cleves, au Comte de la Marck & au Comte de Ravensberg; & en faveur de ceux de la Confession d'Augsburg, & des Reformez, dans les Duchez de Juilers & Berge, sommis au Duc de Neubourg. Fait à Cologne sur la Sprée le 26. Avril 1672. Avec le Traite Separé du même jour, & la Ratification du Duc. Donnée à Dusseldorp le 11. Juin 1672, Dumont, *Corps universel diplomatique du droit des gens*, vol 7,1, pp 171–94.

16 Reversales Jacobi Ducis Curlandiae, quod Religionis Catholicae liberum excecitum in suis Ducatibus sit conservaturus. Dat. Mitaviae d. 13 Febr. An 1677, Dogiel, *Codex Diplomaticus* (n 4), vol 5, p 466; Literae Reversales Friderici Casimiri Ducis de conservatione liberi exercitii Religionis Catholicae Romanae in Ducatibus Curlandiae, & Semigallia. Dat. Mitaviae d. 6. Mart. An. 1683, ibid, p 474f.

17 Traité de Paix entre Louïs XIV. Roi de France, & les Estats Généraux des PROVINCES UNIES des Païs-Bas; portant que chacun demeurera saisi des Païs, Villes, & Places, qu'il possede, à la reserve de la Ville de Mastricht, avec la Comté de Vronof, & les Païs de Fauquemont, Dalhem & Rolleduc, que Sa Majesté T.C. rendera à Leurs Hautes Puissances. Fait à Nimegue le 10. d'Août 1678, Art. IX, Dumont, *Corps universel diplomatique du droit des gens*, vol 7,1, p 351.

18 Pacte d'Union perpetuelle entre la Maison Archi-Ducale D'AUTRICHE & la Maison Electorale de BRUNSWICH-LUNEBOURG, par laquelle outre le Secours reciproquement proms dans tous les cas de necessité, la Maison Electorale de Brunswick s'engage à procurer autant qu'elle pourra à la Couronne de Boheme l'entiere Resitution de l'Exercice de ses Droits Electoraux, & à donner toujours sa Voix aux Prince Aîne de la Maison Archi-Ducale d'Autriche, pour l'Election d'un Empereur des Romains. Fait à Vienne le 22. Mars 1692. Avec un Article Separé par lequel l'Electeur ERNEST AUGUST promet d'accorder aux Catholiques de Hannover & de Cel la liberté d'y bâtir des Eglises & des Ecoles. A Vienne le 22. Mars 1692, ibid, vol 7,2, pp 307–10.

19 Traité de Paix & d'Amitié entre Louis XIV. Roi de France & Anne Reine de la Grande Bretagne établi sur le fondement d'une Separation reélle & perpetuelle des Couronnes de France et d'Espagne par moyen des Renonciation reciproques de Roi PHILIPPE & des Ducs de BERRY & d'ORLEANS qui y sont inserées: et aussi sur la Reconoissance, que le Roi T.C. y fait, de la Succession à la Coronne de la Grande-Bretagne sur la ligne Protestante de HANOVER avec promesse de ne jamais rien faire, ni permettre qu'il soit fait, directement

1713,[20] in Silesia in the treaty of Hubertusburg 1763,[21] in Canada in the treaty of Paris 1763,[22] in those parts of Poland ceded to Prussia and Russia in the partitions of Poland[23] and in the Ottoman Empire and in the Khanate of Crimea[24] and Lutherans in Jülich-Cleves-Berg in 1672,[25] in Strasbourg in 1681 and in 1697,[26] in Silesia in the capitulation of 1621 and the treaty of Altranstädt

ou indirectement, en favour de ceux qui voudroint la troubler. Le Roi T.C. y promet de plus de faire raser DUNKERQUE, & il y cede à la Couronne d'Angleterre, divers grandes Païs dans l'Amerique septentrionale. Fait à Utrecht le 31. Mars 11. Avril 1713, Art. XIV, ibid, vol 8,1, p 341.

20 Traité entre CHARLES VI. Empereur des Romains & Roi Catholique d'une part, & FREDERIC GUILLAUME, Roi de Prusse d'autre part, par lequel Sa Maj. Imp. & Catholique cede et transporte audit Roi, diverses Places, Villes & Lieux situés dans la Duché de Gueldres, Savoir, la Ville et Bailliage de Gueldres: les Villes & Bailliages de Strahlen, Wachtendonck, Middelaer, Walbeck, Aerssen, Afferden, Weel, Racy & le petit Kevelaer, avec le Païs de Kessel pour satisfaction de ses anciennes pretensions a la charge du feu Roi d'Espagne CHARLES II. Moyennant quoi aussi S.M. Prussienne renonce à toutes sesdites pretensions, & se tient pour contente. A Utrecht le 2. Avril 1713, Art. 4–6, ibid vol 8,1, pp 337–39.

21 Traité de paix entre Sa Majesté l'Impératice Reine de Hongrie & de Bohème & Sa Majesté le Roi de Prusse, conclu & signé au Château de Hubertusbourg le 15. Février 1763, Art. XIV, Martens (ed), *Recueil des Principaux Traites* (n 5), vol 1, pp 61–68, here p 67.

22 Traité définitif de paix & d'amitié entre sa Majesté Britannique, le Roi T. Chrétien & le Roi d'Espagne signé à Paris le 10. Févrièr 1763, Art. IV, ibid, pp 33–60, here p 37.

23 Traité entre Sa Majesté le Roi de Prusse & Sa Majesté le Roi & la Republique de Pologne, conclu à Varsovie le 18. Septembre 1773, Art. VIII, Martens, ibid, pp 486–96, here p 494.

24 Johann Jacob Moser (ed), *Der Belgradische Friedens-Schluß zwischen Ihro Römisch-Kayserl. Majestät und der Ottomanischen Pforte mit Beylagen und Anmerckungen, wodurch die Historie so wohl des Passarowizischen Friedens, als auch der Ursachen des lezten Krieges, der Feldzüge und der Friedens-Handlung, so dann der Innhalt der Articul selber erläutert, die Ubereinstimmung und Abweichung dieses und des Carlowiz- auch Passarowizischen Friedens gezeiget und was bey der bevorstehenden Absendung derer Groß-Bothschaffter beeder Kaysere an einander Merckwürdiges fürkommen möchte, vorgestellet wird, mit einer Vorrede von denen dermalen üblichen Gattungen derer Gesandten und anderer öffentlichen Personen* (Jena, Johann Felix Bielcken 1740) 38–40; Document 71 (6 December 1742). The instrument of peace (yarlıq) sent by Khan Selamet II Giry to King Augustus III, in Dariusz Kołodziejczyk, *The Crimean Khanate and Poland-Lithuania. International Diplomacy on the European Periphery (15th–18th Century). A Study of Pace Treaties Followed by Annotated Documents* (The Ottoman Empire and its Heritage. Politics, Society and Economy, 47) (Brill 2011), Art. 3, p 1006.

25 See n 15.

26 Articles proposez par les Preteurs, Consuls & Magistrat de la Ville de STRASSBOURG, & accordez pour la reduction de ladite Ville à l'obeisance du Roi de France LOUIS XIV. le 30. Septembre 1681, Dumont, *Corps universel diplomatique du droit des gens*, vol 7,2, p 15.

1707,[27] in Courland and Semigallia,[28] in Poland[29] and in those parts of Poland ceded to Austria.[30] The Orthodox benefitted from religious guarantees in Polish-Kossack and in the Polish partition treaties.[31] Several Ashkenazi communities in Alsace were indirectly protected by contractual relations between the French kings and imperial estates (*Reichsstände*) of the Holy Roman Empire as well as the Free Nobility of Lower Alsace.[32] The Sephardi and the Greek-Orthodox communities of Vienna benefitted from treaties of Carlowitz, Passarowitz and Belgrade between the Roman and the Ottoman emperors,[33]

---

27 Conditions ausquelles ceux de SILESIE renntrent sous l'obeïssance de l'Empereur, reglées à Dresde le 8. Fèvrier 1621, Art. VIII, ibid, vol. 5,2, p 379; Capitulation accordée par Jean Ernst Electeur de Saxe, au nom de FERDINAND II. Empereur des Romains aux Etats Provinciaux de SILESIE, par laquelle ils se soumettent à l'obéissance de sadite Majesté Imperiale, laquelle, de sa part, leur pardonne tout le passée. Le 18. Fevrier 1621, Part 2, Art. 3, ibid, p 379f; Articuli Conventionis inter Augustissimum Caesarem JOSEPHUM, & CAROLUM XII. Regem Sueciae, in puncto liberi Exercitii Religionis, incolis Silesiae Augustanae Confesssioni addictis concessi, quorum primus in Castris Regiis Alt-Ranstadiensibus, die 11–22. Augusti initus est, reliqui vero eisdem in Castris die 21. August 1 Septembris 1707, ibid, vol 8,1, pp 221–27.

28 Confirmatio Articuli de libero exercitio Religionis Augustanae in Ducatu Curlandiae. Dat. Varsaviae d. 28. Nov. An 1670, Dogiel, *Codex Diplomaticus* (n 4) vol 5, p 454; Confirmatio Articuli libero exercitio Religionis Augustanae, Dat. Varsaviae d. 27. Apr. An. 1677, ibid, p 465f; Confirmatio Articuli de Religione Augustana, Dat. Varsaviae d. 25. Mart. An. 1683, ibid, p 475f.

29 Traité entre Sa Majesté le Roi de Prusse & Sa Majesté le Roi & la Republique de Pologne, conclu à Varsovie le 18. Septembre 1773, Art. IX, Martens (ed), *Recueil des Principaux Traites* (n 5), vol 1, pp 486–96, here p 494.

30 Traité entre Sa Majesté le Roi & la Republique de Pologe, & Sa Majesté l'imperatrice Reine de Hongrie & de Bohème signé à Varsovie le 18. Sept. 1773, Art. V, ibid, vol 4, pp 110–25, here p 118.

31 Traité entre Sa Majesté le Roi de Prusse & Sa Majesté le Roi & la Republique de Pologne, conclu à Varsovie le 18. Septembre 1773, Art. IX, ibid, vol 1, pp 486–96, here p 494; Traité entre Sa Majesté le Roi & la Republique de Pologe, & Sa Majesté l'imperatrice Reine de Hongrie & de Bohème signé à Varsovie le 18. Sept. 1773, Art. V, ibid, vol 4, pp 110–25, here p 118.

32 Lettres-Patents du Roi de France, portant confirmation de Droits en faveur de M. le Duc de Wirtemberg pour ses posssions en Alsace, Juin 1768, Art. 18, ibid, vol 6, p 112; Lettres-Patents du Roi portant Confirmation de Droits et Priviléges du Corps de la Noblesse de la Basse-Alsace; du mois de May 1779, Art. 21, 22, 30, ibid, pp 195, 197.

33 Art. 14 of the Peace Treaty of Carlowitz, Art. 13 of the Peace Treaty of Passarowitz, Art. 11 of the Peace Treaty of Belgrade and Art. 1 of the Commercial Treaty concluded between the Roman and the Ottoman Emperors on 27 July 1718 granted the subjects

the Muslim Lipka Tartars in the Rzeczpospolita from Ottoman-Polish treaty relations.[34]

In the early modern period, religious rights guaranteed by the positive law of nations were broad and, thus, meant considerably more than the mere freedom of conscience. 'Religious rights and liberties' to use the contemporary terminology comprised the possession, use and maintenance of specific places of worship, endowments, social and educational institutions, the right to train and to appoint religious personnel, to enforce communal discipline and could extend as far as the administration of justice in religious matters. Though often restricted to the nobility, religious guarantees could reach the grassroots level and extend to the indidividual. The treaty of Linz 1645 'guaranteed the freedom of religion and conscience even to the Protetant serfs of Catholic lords'.[35]

In the second half of the 18th century, in particular after the French revolution, there is a significant shift. The struggle for equal civil and political rights for the members of non-dominant religious communities gained centre stage. This shift was reflected in the law of nations. The treaties which Napoleon concluded with the Elector of Saxony and several other German princes in Posen in 1806 and in Warsaw in 1807 concerning their accession to the Confederation

---

of both empirers the right to trade. The background and precise meaning of Art. 14 of the last treaty, which restricted the commercial activities of Jewish merchants remains as yet unclear: Johann Jacob Moser (ed), *Der Belgradische Friedens-Schluß zwischen Ihro Römisch-Kayserl. Majestät und der Ottomanischen Pforte* (n 24) pp 44–55. On Greek Orthodox merchants in Vienna as subjects of the Ottoman emperor see Anna Ransmayr, 'Untertanen des Sultans oder des Kaisers: Struktur und Organisationsformen der beiden Wiener griechischen Gemeinden von den Anfängen im 18. Jahrhundert bis 1918', unpublished Ph.D. thesis, University of Vienna 2016.

34 Document 50 (16 October 1672). The Polish document of the agreement of Buczacz, in Kołodziejczyk, *Ottoman-Polish Diplomatic Relations* (n 14), Art. 1, p 494; Document 51 (18 October 1672). The Ottoman document of the agreement of Buczacz, ibid, Art. 1, p 499; Document 52 (23 October 1672). The 'ahdname sent by Mehmed IV to King Michał, ibid, Art. 1, p 509; Document 53 (15 October 1676). The Polish document of the agreement of Żuranow, ibid, Art. 1, p 516; Document 54 (17 October 1676) The Ottoman document of the agreement of Żuranow, ibid, Art. 1, p 525; Document 55 (4–13 April, 1678). The 'ahdname sent by Mehmed IV to King John III, ibid, p 539.

35 *wodurch auch so gar denen unter Catholischen Herrschafften stehenden Bauern die Religions- und Gewissensfreyheit versichert wurde.* Johann Jacob Moser, Kurtze Historie der Religions-Freyheiten und Beschwerden derer Evangelischen in Ungarn und Siebenbürgen, in: *id.*, *Die Religions-Freyheiten und Beschwerden derer Evangelischen in gantz Europa, besonders aber in Teutschland, zum Theil kürtzlich, zum Theil aber ausführlich aus denen Actis publicis und denen besten Scribenten fürgestellt*, part one (Ebersdorff/Vogtland, Vollrath 1741), § 18, p 9.

of the Rhine demanded not only the equality of the Catholic with the Lutheran cult, but also the 'same civil and political rights' for their adherents. Art 5 of the treaty between Napoleon and the Elector of Saxony stipulated:

> Les lois et actes qui déterminaient les droits réciproques des divers cultes établis en Allemagne ayant éte abolis par le fait de la dissolution de l'ancien corps germanique, et n'étant pas d'ailleurs compatibles avec les principes sur lesquels la confédération a été formée, l'exercice du culte catholique sera, dans la totalité du royaume de Saxe, pleinement assimilé à l'exercice du culte luthérien, et les sujets des deux religions jouiront, sans restriction, des mêmes droits civils et politiques, S. M. l'empereur et roi faisant une condition particulière de cet objet.[36]

The treaties with the dukes of Saxony-Weimar, Saxony-Gotha, Saxony-Meiningen, Saxony-Coburg and Saxony-Hildburghausen, with the dukes of Anhalt-Dessau, Anhalt-Bernburg and Anhalt-Köthen, with the princes of Reuss-Greiz and Reuss-Gera, with the princes of Lippe-Detmold and Lippe-Schaumburg, with the prince of Waldeck and with the princes of Schwarzburg-Sondershausen and Schwarzburg-Rudolstadt contained an additional clause guaranteeing the status quo concerning ecclesiastical property: 'sans cependant déroger à la possession et jouissance actuelles des biens des eglises'.[37] A treaty between the archduke grandduke of Würzburg and the duke of

36 Traité de paix entre S.M. l'empereur des Français roi d'Italie et S.A.S. l'électeur de Saxe; signé à Posen le 11 Déce. 1806, Art. 5, Martens (ed), *Recueil des Principaux Traités* (n 5) vol 8, p 553f.

37 Traité de paix entre S.M. l'empereur des Français roi d'Italie et LL. AA. SS. les ducs de Saxe-Weimar, Saxe-Gotha, Saxe-Meinigen, Saxe-Hildburghausen et Saxe-Cobourg portant l'admission de ces princes à la confédération du Rhin: signé à Posen, le 15 Dec. 1806, ibid, pp 556–58; Traité de paix entre S.M. l'empereur des Français roi d'Italie et LL. AA. SS. les ducs de d'Anhalt-Dessau, Bernbourg et Cöthen, portant l'accession de ceux-ci à la confédération du Rhin; signé à Varsovie, le 18 Avril 1807, ibid, p 558f; Traité entre S.M. l'empereur des Français et les princes de Reuss, portant l'accession de ceux-ci à la confédération du Rhin; signé le 18 Avril 1807, ibid, pp 560–62; Traité entre S.M. l'empereur des Français et les princes de Lippe-Detmold et Lippe-Schaumbourg, portant l'accession de ceux-ci à la confédération du Rhin; signé le 18 Avril 1807, ibid, p 562–64; Traité entre S.M. l'empereur des Français et le prince de Waldeck, portant l'accession de ceux-ci à la confédération du Rhin; signé à Varsovie, le 18 Avril 1807, ibid, p 565f; Traité entre S.M. l'empereur des Français roi d'Italie et les princes de Schwarzbourg-Sondershausen et Rudolstadt, portant l'accession de ceux-ci à la confédération du Rhin; en date de Varsovie, le 18 Avril 1807, ibid, pp 566–68; see: Johann Ludwig Klüber, 'VIII. Über Bestimmung der Rechte der katholischen Kirche und der evangelischen Kirchengesellschaften in den teutschen

Saxony-Hildburghausen stipulated that the former would exercice his episcopal rights and ecclesiastical powers vis-à-vis Protestant subjects formerly subordinated to the latter in ecclesiastical matters through a Protestant consistory.[38]

The provisions of the Final Act of the Congress of Vienna concerning the German Federation, the United Kingdom of the Netherlands and the Free City of Cracow contained guarantees for the equaliy of the rights of individuals irrespective of religious affilitation and in the latter two cases also for the rights of religious communities.[39] In the German Federation the prohibition to discriminate against individuals on religious grounds was limited to adherents of the three publicly acknowledged Christian religions,[40] in the Kingdom of the United Netherlands it extended also to Jews.[41]

3 Religious Communities as Subjects in the Early Modern Positive Law of Nations

The early modern law of nations did not only know the rights of religious communities and their members as objects. It also featured religious communities and their representatives as subjects. Overlaps notwithstanding it may be helpful to distinguish between roughly four constellations in which religious communities assumed the status of a subject of the law of nations. First, their very foundation constituted religious communites as subjects of the law of nations. Second, unresolved conflicts about religious rights created religious communities as subjecs of the law of nations, e.g. French Calvinists, Scottish Puritans or Irish Catholics. Hence Dumont included the national convention

---

Bundestaaten' in idem (ed), *Uebersicht der diplomatischen Verhandlungen des Wiener Congresses überhaupt, und insonderheit über wichtige Angelegenheiten des Teutschen Bundes, Abtheilung 3* (Frankfurt-on-Main, Andreä 1816) 397–457, here pp 415f.

38 Traité entre l'archiduc grand-duc de Wurzbourg et le duc de Saxe-Hildbourghausen, au sujet des possessions de Ganerbiat situées dans des baillages Wurzbourgeois; signé le 15 Juillet 1807, Art. 6, ibid, p 578.

39 Bundes-Acte, Wien, den 8. Juni 1815, Art. 16, Johann Ludwig Klüber (ed), *Schluß-Acte des Wiener Congresses, vom 9. Juni 1815 und Bundes-Acte oder Grundvertrag des teutschen Bundes, vom 8. Juni 1815* (2nd edn, Palm and Enke 1818) 159.

40 *Die Verschiedenheit der christlichen Religions-Parteien kann, in den Ländern und Gebieten des teutschen Bundes, keinen Unterschied in dem Genuß der bürgerlichen und politischen Rechte begründen.*, Bundes-Acte, Wien, den 8. Juni 1815, Art. 16, ibid.

41 Traité entre S.M. le Roi des Pays-Bas, et l'Autriche, la Russie, le Grande-Bretagne, et la Prusse; en date de Vienne le 31 mai 1815. Annexe de L'article 8 du traité précédent du 31 mai 1815, Art. 2, Klüber, *Acten* (n 6) vol 6, 21, p 176.

of French Reformed preachers and notables in La Rochelle in 1621,[42] the Scottish Covenants of 1638 and 1643[43] and the Confederation of Kilkenny 1642[44] in his collection. Whenever Protestant gravamina in the Holy Roman Empire could not be resolved within the framework of domestic law, the Corpus Evangelicorum, the association of the Protestant princes of the Holy Roman claimed the right to act as a subject of the law of nations. In a singular case, in 1750, the Corpus Evangelicorum resorted to self-help and asked one of its members, the Margrave of Ansbach, to take military action against the Catholic branches of the house of Hohenlohe.[45] Also conflicts within religious communities could prompt the creation of subjects of the law of nations. The conversion of Hentry IV to the Roman church, his excommunication and reconcillation constituted him as a distinct subject of the law of nations.[46] It was through the contestation of the election of an archbishop that the 'clergy and people of the archdiocese of Cologne'[47] and through its dissolution that the Jesuit order made a prominent appearance in the law of nations.[48]

42 *Réglement & département fait dans l'Assembée de tous les* REFORMEZ *de France, à la Rochelle le 10. Mai, 1621*, Dumont, *Corps universel diplomatique du droit des gens*, vol 4,2 pp 396–99.

43 Confederation, communément appellée le Covenant, faite premierement par les Puritains d'Ecosse en 1638. contre la Hierachie de l'Eglise Anglicane, & contre tout ce qui approche de la Religion Catholique Romaine, & ensuite renouvellée entre les Ecossois & les Anglois Parlementaires, savoir en Ecosse au mois d'Août, & en Angletere au Mois de Septembre 1643, Dumont, *Corps universel diplomatique du droit des gens*, vol 6,1, pp 287–90.

44 Traité de Confederation entre les Catholiques d'Irlande. Fait environ le Mois de Mars, 1642, Dumont, *Corps universel diplomatique du droit des gens*, vol 6,1, p 241.

45 Johann Jacob Moser, 'Von denen Religions-Beschwerden gegen die Fürsten zu Hohenlohe Waldenburg' in idem, *Neue Berichte von Religions-Sachen* (Frankfurt-on-Main, Philipp Heinrich Hutterer 1751), part one, ch 4, pp 53–94, part two, ch 2, pp 125–52 and ch 4, pp 183–88; Jochen Vötsch, 'Die Hohenloher Religionsstreitigkeiten in der Mitte des 18. Jahrhunderts' (1993) 77 *Württembergisch Franken*, pp 361–99.

46 Declaration de HENRI IV. Roi de France a son Avenement à la Couronne, portant Promesse avec serment de maintenir la Religion Catholique, Apostolique & Romaine en son entier, & qu'il ne desire rien davantage que d'estre instruit par un bon, legitime, & libre Concile General, ou National. Donée à St Cloud le 4. Aoust 1589, Dumont, *Supplement au Corps Universel Diplomatique du Droit des Gens*, vol 2,1, p 208.

47 Actes content les Protestations sollennelles publiées au sujet des prétenduës Nullités insoustenables, faites en Cour de Rome, dans la Confirmation de l'Election du Sérenissime Prince JOSEPH CLEMENT Duc de Baviere, & c. Afin de les rendre notoires au Clergé & au Peuple de l'Archevêche de Cologne. Fait à Bonn au Palais Electoral le 13. d'Octobre 1688, Dumont, *Corps universel diplomatique du droit des gens*, vol 7,2, pp 173–75.

48 Bulles du Pape Clement XIV. portant supresssion de l'ordre des Jesuites, en date du 21. Juin 1773, Martens (ed), *Recueil des Principaux Traites* (n 5) vol 4, pp 84–109.

Third, treaties and other contractual arrangements, whose objective was the simultaneous political incorporation or subordination of one of the contracting parties and its collective continuity as a religious community or as a community with a distinct religious constitution. Scotland's retention of a distinct dominant church, the Presbyterian Kirk, despite its dynastic union and subsequent complete political merger with England in 1707 provides the most enduring example of a constituent part of a composite empire possessing a distinct religious constitution.[49] A further, though abortive example is the attempt to turn Poland-Lithuania into an officially three-national and bi-religious polity. In the treaties of Hadiach (1658) and Cudnow (1660) the Orthodox Cossaks sought to exchange their independence for the status of a third, equal nation and for the recognition of Greek Orthodoxy as the established religion within their part of the Rzeczpospolita.[50]

The above cooptions, whether successful or not, were characterized by political asymmetries. Yet, since 'incorporations' and 'unions' were essentially treaties between nations, they implied not only reciprocity, but also a measure of equality. The element of subordination was more pronounced, when a prince, who differed in religion from the dominant religion of the land and his subjects or parts thereof, isssued a religious guarantee in return for political allegiance. Occasions for such a contractual relationship, one of whose objectives was the collective continuity of one of the contracting parties as a religious community, were the conversion of a reigning dynasty, a treaty of protection or the acquisition of jurisdictions by conquest, election, inheritance or redemption of a pledge. When August the Strong, Elector of Saxony, embraced the Roman-Catholic faith in 1697 in order to acquire the Polish Crown he and his heirs assured the 'estates of Electoral Saxony, that the religion of the Augsburg Confession would be left unchanged in the

49 The Kirk is, at least from 1925, the only institution considered to be exempt from the otherwise sovereign parliament of the United Kingdom.

50 Traité de Paix & d'Accommodement entre le Roi & la Republique de POLOGNE d'une part, & GEORGE CHMIELNICKI, General de l'Armée des Cosaques des Zaporouw avec l'Armée même d'autre part, par lequel les Cosaques renoncent à la Protection du Czar de Moscovie, & se soumettent à la Domination de Sa Majesté Polonoise, s'obligeant de plus à delivrer des mains des Moscovites les Places de l'Ukraine. Fait au Camp près de Cudnow le 17. Octobre 1660. Avec les Formules des Serments faits pour l'observation de ce Traité, tant de la part du Roi de Pologne que de la part du Chef, & de l'Armée des Cosaques, 17. Octobre 1660, Dumont, *Corps universel diplomatique du droit des gens*, vol 6,2, p 335f.

Electorate and the other possessions'.[51] When Louis XIV subdued the free imperial city of Strasbourg in 1681, its religious constitution remained by and large intact.[52] Starting with the Peace of Vienna in 1606, the Habsburg emperors and kings repeatedly had to accept Hungarian and Transsylvanian Protestant demands for religious freedoms and liberties.[53] And when the prince-abbot of Fulda recovered the district of Fischberg, which one of his predecessors had pawned to a neigbouring prince who had introduced the Reformation there, he promised his new subjects 'to maintain their rights and privileges, in particular the excercise of religion according to the Confession of Augsburg', in return for an act of homage.[54] The protection of Christians in the Ottoman Empire was interpreted by Jean Dumont in an analogous fashion, as a treaty between the Prophet Mohammed and the Christian communities.[55]

So far we have identified religious communities and their representatives as situational and partial subjects in the early modern law of nations. The fourth type is characterized by a degree of institutionalization. In the context of early modern diplomacy we encounter not only papal nuncios, and as late as the Congress of Vienna a whole array of Catholic representatives,[56] but also Jewish

---

51 Assecuration Iho Königl. Majest. in Pohlen und Churfürtl. Durchl. zu Sachsen Friderici Augusti, denen Land-Staenden von Chur-Sachsen ertheilet/daß die Religion Augspurgischer Confesion ohnveraendert in Dero Churfuerstenthum und Lande solle gelassen werden. Dreßden den 6. May 1718, ibid, vol 8,1, p 512f.

52 Articles proposez par les Preteurs, Consuls & Magistrat de la Ville de STRASSBOURG, & accordez pour la reduction de ladite Ville à l'obeisance du Roi de France LOUIS XIV. le 30. Septembre 1681, ibid, vol 7,2, p 15.

53 See n 10.

54 Lettres d'Assurance accordées par Adelbert Abbé de Fulda à ses Sujets de la Ville de Vieschberg, par lesquelles il promet de les garder & maintenir inviolablement dans leurs Droits & Privileges, & en particulier dans l'Exercise de la Religion, selon la Confession d'Augsburg, comme aussi dans la perception, & usage de leur Revenues, Salaires, Aumones & c. aussi ne seron-ils pas constraints à celebrer avec les Catholiques les Fêtes inacoutumées & particuliers. A Fulde le 6. Avril 1707, Dumont, *Corps universel diplomatique du droit des gens*, vol 8,1 p 215f.

55 Traité d'Alliance ou Privilege du Prophet MAHOMET pour les Chrêtiens habitans de son Païs, par lequel il promet de les proteger & defendre eux, leur Temples, Chapelles & autres Lieux & Biens contre leurs Ennemis, tant ceux du dedans que ceux du dehors. Fait le dernier jour de la Lune du quatrieme mois, l'an quatrieme de l'Hegire, 6 October, 625, Dumont, *Supplement au Corps Universel Diplomatique du Droit des Gens*, vol 1,1, p 7f.

56 Johann Ludwig Klüber, 'VIII. Über Bestimmung der Rechte der katholischen Kirche und der evangelischen Kirchengesellschaften, in den teutschen Bundestaaten' in idem (ed), *Uebersicht der diplomatischen Verhandlungen des Wiener Congresses überhaupt,*

shtadlanim, i.e. representatives of Jewish communities[57] and conferences of the diplomats of Protestant powers. More stable than such meetings and deputations assembled ad-hoc were the conferences of the Protestant Swiss Cantons and, in particular, the conferences of the Corpus Evangelicorum, the association of the Protestant imperial estates.[58] By the 18th century the latter had turned into a permanent institution with regular meetings and decision making procedures at the seat of, but, despite personal overlaps, institutionally and legally distinct from the Permanent Imperial Diet at Regensburg (*Immerwährender Reichstag*).[59] The representative of the Elector of Saxony at the Imperial Diet and his staff provided the institutional backbone of the Corpus Evangelicorum. It mobilized the support of Protestant powers and intervened on behalf of persecuted Protestants in Catholic imperial estates of the Holy Roman Empire including the dominions of the Austrian Hereditary Lands and occasionally outside the Empire.[60] It also mediated between between Calvinists and Lutherans and was instrumental in effecting the adoption of the Gregorian Calender in Protestant Europe.[61]

---

und insonderheit über wichtige Angelegenheiten des Teutschen Bundes, Abtheilung 3 (Frankfurt-on-Main, Andreä 1816) pp 397–457.

57 Unterthänige Vorstellung und Bittschrift der israelitischen Gemeinde zu Frankfurt am Main, an den hohen Congreß zu Wien. Mit drei Beilagen, Uebergeben daselbst am 10. October 1814, Klüber, *Acten* (n 6) vol 6, pp 396–402.

58 Stephan Wendehorst, 'Das Corpus Evangelicorum als Völkerrechtssubjekt', unpublished lecture held as part of the Ringvorlesung: Aus der Werkstatt: Aktuelle rechtshistorische Forschungen am Juridicum on 31 October 2013 at Vienna University.

59 Eberhard Christian Wilhelm von Schauroth (ed), *Vollständige Sammlung aller Conclusorum, Schreiben und anderer übrigen Verhandlungen des Hochpreißlichen Corporis Evangelicorum. von Anfang des jetzt fürwährenden Hochansehnlichen Reichs-Convents bis auf die gegenwärtige Zeiten nach Ordnung der Materien zusammen getragen und herausgegeben von Eberhard Christian Wilhelm von Schauroth*, vols 1–3 (Regenspurg, Heinrich Georg Neubauer 1751–1752); Nikolaus August Herrich (ed), *Sammlung aller Conclusorum, Schreiben und anderer übrigen Verhandlungen des Hochpreißlichen Corporis Evangelicorum. vom Jahre 1753 bis 1786 als eine Fortsetzung des Schaurothischen Werks nach Ordnung der Materien zusammengetragen und herausgegeben von Nikolaus August Herrich* (Regenspurg, Johann Christoph Keyser 1786).

60 Karl R. von Otto, Zwei Memoriale der aus Oberösterreich, Steiermark und Kärnten nach Siebenbürgen transmigrirten Evangelischen an das Corpus Evangelicorum, *Jahrbuch der Gesellschaft für die Geschichte des Protestantismus in Österreich* (1883), pp 181–187.

61 Conclusion prise le 30. Janvier 1723. dans la Conference des ETATS EVANGELIQUES à Ratisbonne, portant qu'en conformité du calcul Astronomique le plus exact, la Fête de Pâques sera célébrée l'année suivante 1724 au 9. Avril, qu'elle sera marquée ainsi dans le Calendrier amélioré, & que toutes les autres Fêtes mobiles de l'année seront reglées sur

If there is such ample empirical evidence for religious gurantees as objects and religious communities as subjects of the early modern law of nations, the question needs to be addressed, how they fitted into it. An attempt to provide answers will be made in the following part.

4 The Law of Nations and Domestic Law as a System of Communicating Vessels

Although early modern treaties guaranteeing religious rights betray analogies to international regimes for the protection national minority rights in the 19th and 20th century, the majority of the above examples does not fit the accustomed patterns of modern international law. This is true, in particular, for religious communities as subjects of the law of nations. The Holy See,[62] the only religious subject which in Europe has survived from the pluriverse of sovereign and half-sovereign, secular and religious, territorial and personal, collective and individual subjects of the early modern law of nations into modern times, does not owe its recognition in modern international law to its claim to a religious basis of its sovereignty, nor does Iran, Saudi-Arabia, Morocco or the Dalai Lama.

Before proceeding to a discussion of five mechanisms, that made the law of nations and municipal law operational as a system of communicating vessels for the protection of religious rights, we need to clarify two specific features of the early modern law of nations in contradistinction to modern internatonal law. Jean Dumont, in particular, will serve as a guide into the enigmatic maze of the early modern law of nations, its relationship with the legal order in general and with constitutional law in particular.

It is already the baroque title of Jean Dumont's monumental collection of pre-modern positive law of nations[63] that makes it unmistakebly clear that the reach of the early modern law of nations was far broader than that of modern international law in the sense of inter-state law and that any attempt to read an understanding of international law limited more or less exclusively to legal relations between sovereign territorial powers back into the early modern period is anachronistic. Dumont's complete title can be read as a catalogue

celle-là. Conclusum in Conferentia Evangelicorum die 30. Januarii Anno 1723, Dumont, *Corps universel diplomatique du droit des gens*, vol 7,2, p 51.

62 See Jean-Pierre Schouppe, Le Saint Siège en tant que sujet et acteur de droit international, in this volume, chapter 3.

63 See n 3.

of the different categories of the positive sources of the early modern law of nations. In addition to the 'traitez d'alliance, de paix, de trève, de neutralité, de commerce, d'échange, de Protection et de Garantie, de toutes les Conventions, transactions, Pactes, Concordates et autres Contrats', the 'Sentences Arbitrales dans les Causes importantes' and the 'Déclarations de guerre', which may be assimilated to modern international law without greater difficulty, there are also categories that clearly would be absent from a modern collection of positive international law, 'les Contrats de Mariage de Grands Princes, leurs Testament, Donations, Renonciations, & Protestations; les Investitures des grands Fiefs; les Erections des grandes Dignités, celle des grandes Compagnies de Commerce' and 'the Capitulations impériales et royales'.

For the puposes of this contribution only Dumont's last entry, 'the imperial and royal capitulations' are of concern. His collection contains several fundamental laws, not only the capitulations of the Emperors of the Holy Roman Empire and the Polish kings, but also the Magna Charta, the Act of Settlement, the Habsburg Pragmatic Sanction to name but the most renown.[64] The early modern law of nations reaching into what, by modern standards, constitutes the core of constitutional law is also manifest in the table of contents of Mathias Dogiel's *Codex Diplomaticus Poloniae et Magni Ducatis Lithuaniae*. Volume one, part one concerned *Bohemia, Hungaria, Austria, Dania, Bavaria, Marchia Brandenburgensis, Respublica Veneta, Saxonica, Gallia, Ducatus Brunswicensis, Hollandia, Transsylvania*, volume one, part two *Provinciae quae olim sub Imperio Polono erant. Silesia, Pomerania, Marchia Nova, Moldavia et Valachia*, volume four *Prussia*, volume five *Livonia*. If realized volume two, part one would have concerned *Rossia, Turcia, Tartaria Crimensis, Suecia*, volume two, part two *Instrumenta ad negotium summarum Reipublicae Neapolitanarum pertinentia*, volume three, part one *Lituania*, volume three, part two *Masovia, Russia, Podolia, Terra Belzensis, Praefectura Secepusiensis, Ducatus Severiae, ducatus Osviecimensis et Zatoriensis*, volume six *Literae Pontificiae ac Ducum et regum Poloniae Concordata, Privilegia, Ordinationes, Statuta, Edicta, Rescripta,*

64 Magna Charta Libertatum à Rege Anglorum JOHANNE, BARONIBUS, omnibusque Liberis Hominibus Regni Angliae concessarum in Prato Rinigemade vocato inter Stones & Windleschoves die 15. Junii 1215, Dumont, *Corps universel diplomatique du droit des gens*, vol 1,1, pp 153–55; Aurea Bulla CAROLI IV. Imperatoris, qua Regimen & Forma Juris publici totius Romano-Germanci Imperii Solemnitates quoque & Ceremoniae in Electione Romanorum Imperatorum adhibendae ordinantur, & constituuntur; Sancita Norimbergae & Metis anno 1356, ibid, vol 1,2, pp 305–14. For further examples for fundamental laws as part of the early modern law of nations see Stephan Wendehorst, *Die Geschichte des Hl. Röm. Reichs deutscher Nation als Völkerrechtsgeschichte* (forthcoming 2018).

Mandata, ad ordinem Spiritualem et Res regni ecclesiasticas pertinentia, volume seven *Iura, libertates et privilegia nec non Statua et antiquae constitutiones Regni aliaque huius generis monumenta, quae nondum in lucem prodierunt*, volume eight, part one *Supplementum codicis Diplomatici* and volume eight, part two *Regestum Chonologicum Codicis dipolmatici, cum Indice rerum in eo contentarum*.[65] Constitutional law as part of the law of nations is one of the key distinctions between premodern law of nations and modern international law. As Johann Wolfgang Textor explicitly pointed out, public law, as long as it was contracted, belonged also to the law of nations.[66]

It is commonly acknowledged that substantial differences existed between the early modern law of nations and 19th and 20th century international law. The terms 'ius gentium inter se', translated as law between nations or inter-state law, and 'ius gentium intra se', translated as law common to all human beings, are often referred to, in order to explain this difference. According to this reading the premodern law of nations, in addition to inter-state law, roughly comparable to modern international law, also contained an element of natural law. While the early modern legal order comprised the 'officia humanitatis', this is not to be mixed up with the 'ius gentium intra se'. One does not have to be an academic neo-Latinist to realize that 'law common to all nations' can hardly pass as a convincing translation for 'ius gentium intra se'. From the French translation of 'ius gentium intra se' in Dumont's definition of the law of nations one can see that rather the contrary was meant:

> Le Droit des Gens selon moi, peut & doit être défini, le Droit respectif des Peuples les uns envers les autres et aussi en eux mêmes, & ce Droit est ou naturel, ou contracté. ... Et le Droit des Gens contracté, qui dérive de celui-là [droit de Gens naturel, S.W.] & qui en tire toute sa force,

65 Mathias Dogiel, 'Prospectus operis in quo continetur eiusdem in tomos distributio. Ad praestantissimos Regni Poloniae, et M.D. Lituaniae cives' in idem (ed), *Codex Diplomaticus* (n 4), reprinted in Georg Friederich von Martens, 'Discours préliminaire sur les differens recueils de traités publiés jusqu'à ce jour' in idem (ed), *Supplement au Recueil des Principaux Traites* (n 5) vol 1, pp III-LXXIII, here table of contents: pp LV–LVI.

66 Johann Wolfgang Textor, *Ius Publicum Caesareum Sive Sacrae Caesareae Majestatis Ius Supremum. Ex Monumentis Legum, Constitutionum Imperii, Capitulationum Caesarearum et Historiarum Publicis ac fide dignis assertum atque declaratum* (Frankfurt-on-Main, Zunner 1693) 7f, on Textor as an international lawyer see Stephan Wendehorst, 'Johann Wolfgang Textor, seine "Zusammenfassung des Völkerrechts" (Synopsis Iuris Gentium) und das Heilige Römische Reich' in Georg Seiderer et al (eds), *Vielfalt fränkischer Geschichte. Gedenkschrift für Gerhard Rechter 1951–2012* (Jahrbuch des Historischen Vereins für Mittelfranken, 104) (Ansbach 2016) 55–73.

> consiste dans les Contracts, Accords, Pactes, Concesssions, Donations et Renonciations, qui les Princes et les Peuples font entre eux, soit pour se garantir d'un mal, qu'ils craignent, soit procurer un Bien, qu'ils désirent, soit pour tout les deux ensemble.[67]

'Le Droit respectif des Peuples … en eux-mêmes', was regarded as that part of the law of nations, which peoples or nations observed among themselves.[68] If the early modern law of nations consisted of two components, one between and one within nations, it was nevertheless considered to form a unity, in marked contrast to the dualistic understanding of international law and domestic law in the 19th and 20th century.[69] Dumont testified to this unity, when he praised his own work above that of the German Johann Christian Lünig (1662–1740) and the English Thomas Rymer (1643–1713), 'whose books belong to the law of nations only because the public law of their own countries constitutes a branch of it'.[70]

The second cardinal difference concerns the source of sovereignty. The pre-modern law of nations operated on the basis of two sources of sovereignty, the people and God. The lex regia was the archetypal treaty for contractual relationships between the prince and the people, the Biblical Covenants for contractual relationships between God and the people,[71] providing a secular, respectively religious basis for sovereignty. There were several variations of these contractual relationships. Until the late Middle Ages cities and merchant companies included God as a citizen respectively as a partner.[72] In early modern legal thought God no longer makes an appeareance as an immediate

67 Jean Dumont, Preface, in idem, *Corps universel diplomatique du droit des gens,* vol 1,1, p I.

68 Stephan Verosta, the only scholar showing an interest in the work of Jean Dumont not as a mere reference tool, but as an original contribution to the law of nations, is silent on this point: Stephan Verosta, 'Jean Dumont und seine Bedeutung für das Völkerrecht' (1934) 14 *Zeitschrift für öffentliches Recht* 371–97.

69 Heinrich Triepel, *Völkerrecht und Landesrecht* (Hirschfeld 1899, reprint Scientia 1958).

70 *Leurs Livres aussi n'apartiennent au Droit des Gens qu'à cause du Droit public de leur propre Païs qui en fait une branche,* in Jean Dumont, Preface (n 78) v.

71 For an illustration see Ann Freeman and Paul Meyvaert, 'The Meaning of Theodulf's Apse Mosaic at Germigny-des-Prés' (2001) 40 *Gesta* 125–40; Elisabeth Revel-Neher, *Le signe de la rencontre. L'arche d'alliance dans l'art juif et chrétien du second au dixième siècles* (Association des Amis des Etudes Archéologiques Byzantino-Slaves et du Christianisme Oriental 1984).

72 Roland Gerber, *Gott ist Burger zu Bern. Eine spätmittelalterliche Stadtgesellschaft zwischen Herrschaftsbildung und sozialem Ausgleich* (Forschungen zur mittelalterlichen Geschichte, 39) (Böhlau 2001) p 13f.

contracting partner. The religious constitution of a given land had replaced immediate treaty relations with God. Since religious guarantees were part of the religious constitution of a given realm, they were also considered part of the law of nations. From there it becomes clear, why in the early modern period even Protestant Hungarian serfs, to whom the religious guarantees of the Habsburgs were explicitly extended in the treaty of Linz 1645,[73] had a standing in the law of nations. According to Dumont not only theologians, but also lawyers interested in the laws concerning religious matters were well advised to consult his collection:

> Les Théologiens seront bien aises d'y rencontrer un grand nombre d'Edits, de Reglements, de Decrets, de Sentences, de Constitutions, de Censures, de Condamnations, d'Excommunications, de Reconciliations, & et d'autres Actes émanés en divers tems de l'autorité des Souveraines Pontifes, des Empereurs, ou des Conciles Generaux, & Particuliers dans les Affaires de Religion qui ont le plus influé sur celles de l'Etat, & qui ont enfin changé toute la Constitution publique de l'Empire, de la France, de l'Angleterre, & des divers autres grands Royaumes, Etats, & Principautés. Ceux qui étudient les Droits respectifs du Sacerdoce, & de l'Empire ne seront pas mal de consulter aussi cette Collection, car j'ai eu une atention particuliere à y faire trouver tout ce que j'ai pû d'Actes principaux sur cette grande matiere.[74]

In sum, two charcteristics, which distinguished the early modern law of nations from modern international law can be derived from Jean Dumont's work. First, the early modern law of nations possessed two components and formed an integral part of the legal order in general. Lacking an established terminology, I suggest defining these two components as 'external' or 'horizontal' and 'internal' or 'vertical'. They were considered to form a unity, in sharp contradistinction to the separation of international law and domestic law in the 19th and 20th century. Although as late as 1789 roughly half the entries in count Hertzberg's *Recueil* [75] can be subsumed under 'internal' or 'vertical' law of nations, so far only a fraction of it has been recognized as belonging to

73 See n 43.

74 Jean Dumont, Preface (n 78) XI.

75 Hertzberg (ed), *Recueil des déductions, manifestes, déclarations, traités. Et autres actes et ecrits publics, qui ont été redigés et publiés pour la cour de Prusse*, vols 1–2 (2nd edn, Unger 1789). See the second volume in particular.

the law of nations.[76] As can be gathered from the later collections of Georg Friedrich von Martens it was only in the last years of the 18th century that the 'internal' or 'vertical' law of nations, as far as Europe was concerned, was excluded from what became international law. The second key characteristic of the premodern law of nations in contradistinction to modern international law was that divine authority, if in a mediated form, continued to serve as a source of sovereignty.

The above analysis of the work of John Dumont has demonstrated both the reach of the law of nations and the unity of public law as features of early modern law, which were necessary preconditions for the law of nations and municipal law working in tandem for the protection of religious rights. The presentation of the following mechanisms situated at the intersection between historical empirical evidence and legal doctrine is intended to show what this meant in practice and to provide food for thought for a discussion of doctrine: First, the law of nations as a 'safety valve' for deficiencies in domestic law or as an '*ersatz* legal regime' for challenges intractable in municipal law, second, 'most favoured religion' status, third, intervention by a third party on behalf of persecuted religious communities, fourth, the 'situational constitution' of religious communities as subjects of the law of nations and fifth, the critical awareness of the 'constitutional price' to be payed for turning the protection of religious rights from a concern of international law into one of domestic law.

The law of nations functioning as a safety valve for deficiencies in domestic law or as an *ersatz* legal regime for challenges intractable in municipal law, appears from time to time in modern international law. In the Republic of Austria e.g. the protection of national minorites, the financial endowment of the religious communities recognized in public ecclesiastical law and, in part, even of fundamental rights has its basis in the peace treaty of St Germain of 1919 and the State Treaty of 1955. The outsourcing of legislation to the European Union that is practiced in some of its member states may be interpreted as a variant of this mechanism. In the early modern period this technique was employed on a regular basis. Several of the religious guarantees listed above would have been difficult or impossible to grant under municipal law or municipal law only because of internal resistance. The law of nations provided the legal basis for the existence of the Sephardi community in Vienna

76 Stephan Wendehorst, 'Johann Jacob Moser: Der Reichspublizist als Völkerrechtler' in idem (ed), *Die Anatomie frühneuzeitlicher Imperien. Herrschaftsmanagement jenseits von Staat und Nation: Institutionen, Personal und Techniken* (bibliothek altes Reich, 5) (Oldenbourg 2015) 303–24.

in the 18th century, favoured by the emperor as archduke of Austria, but contested by the estates of Lower Austria,[77] or for the emancipation of Catholics in the kingdom of Saxony in 1806, probably favourered by the dynasty that was Catholic itself, but not by the estates as the representatives of the land.

In analogy to the most favoured nation status in modern international law, a mechanism existed in the early modern law of nations which, for lack of an established terminology, I suggest to call 'most favoured religion status'. This institute of 'most favoured religion status' had an external and an internal side. In commercial treaties there was a tendency to include the subjects of the contracting partners irrespective of their religious affiliation despite continuing differences between them in domestic law.[78] For the purposes of this contribution the observations are limited to the internal dimension of the institute of 'most favoured religion status'. It or derivative instruments causing a similar dynamic were deliberately employed as part of government policies in port cities like Altona, Trieste or Livorno as well as in landlocked commercial centres like Brody or Marktbreit. Yet in a number of cases an approximation of the religious rights of the non-dominant religions to those of the dominant one took place not as the result of a policy of grand design of religious toleration, but in a pragmatic fashion following the inherent logic of the mechanism of the 'most favoured religion status'. The development of the religious constitution of the united duchies of Jülich-Cleves-Berg is arguably the most telling example. The duchies of Jülich-Cleves-Berg were populated by Calvinist, Catholic and Lutheran inhabitants, with Calvinists, Catholics and Lutherans respectively enjoying a dominant position in the different parts of this composite micro-empire. After the death of the last duke in 1609 the potential heirs competed for the loyalty of the multi-religious population, promising the adherents of the denominations to which they did not belong themselves and which did not constitute the dominant religion in the respective part of

77 So far this is a hypothesis. Clarification depends on archival research on the Emperor as archduke of Austria, the estates of Lower Austria and the Ottoman Porte. For first promising findings see Sebastian Dallinger, Die Friedensschlüsse von Carlowitz 1699 und Passarowitz 1718, die frühe sephardische Gemeinde Wiens und die niederösterreichischen Landstände, unpublished paper presented at the Jour Fixe – Modern Jewish History at the Institute for Legal and Constitutional History of he University of Vienna on 23 November 2017 (see also n 41).

78 See, for example, Art. 14 of the Peace Treaty of Carlowitz, Art. 13 of the Peace Treaty of Passarowitz, Art. 11 of the Peace Treaty of Belgrade and Art. 1 of the Commercial Treaty concluded between the Roman and the Ottoman Emperors on 27 July 1718: Moser (ed), *Der Belgradische Friedens-Schluß* (n 24) 44–55.

the united duchies equal treatment. As a result a dynamic as well as volatile religious landscape developed, notably different from the stable, yet petrified situation we find in religiously mixed imperial citities.[79] To make the institute of 'most favoured religion status' work with a view to legal parity between religious communities or to overall equality in religious matters, two conditions had to be fulfilled: First, a religiously mixed population possessing rights and liberties extending to the exercise of religion and second, contested or divided sovereignty. This was typically given in a 'territorium non-clausum', an open territory, which was not subject to one power, but rather characterized by competing, overlapping or frequently changing jurisdictions. If the duchies of Jülich-Cleves-Berg may be regarded as the ideal type, a comparable dynamic may be seen at work in East Frisia, the Baltic coast from Royal Prussia to Livonia, in Podolia, Transsylvania, Upper Silesia, Lusatia, the condominia of Swiss Cantons and Alsace.

Third party action on behalf of persecuted religious communities abroad was not appreciated by the rulers concerned, but conformed to the early modern law of nations. In the chapter 'On the Rights of a Sovereign in Religious Matters concerning Foreign Subjects'[80] in a textbook Johann Jacob Moser (1701–1785) had written for students of the law of nations, he wrote in § 13:

> A sovereign who intercedes on behalf of the subjects of another sovereign, who share the religion of the former and are oppressed because of that by the latter, acts in conformity with the law of nations in the eyes of the adherents of all religions.[81]

79 Burkhard Dietz and Stefan Ehrenpreis (eds), *Drei Konfessionen in einer Region. Beiträge zur Konfessionalisierung im Herzogtum Berg* (Schriftenreihe des Vereins für Rheinische Kirchengeschichte, 136) (Rheinland-Verlag 1999); Manfred Groten (ed), *Der Jülich-Klevische Erbstreit 1609. Seine Voraussetzungen und Folgen* (Veröffentlichungen der Historischen Kommission für Westfalen. New Series, 1) (Droste 2011); Etienne Francoise, *Protestants et catholiques en Allemagne. Identités et pluralisme Augsbourg, 1648–1806* (Michel 1993); idem, 'Zusammenleben in der Intoleranz: Provence, Irland und Brandenburg als Beispiele. Kommentar und Vergleich' in Heinz Schilling (ed), *Im Spannungsfeld von Staat und Kirche. «Minderheiten» und «Erziehung»* im *deutsch-französischen Gesellschaftsvergleich 16–18. Jahrhundert* (Zeitschrift für historische Forschung, supplement vol 31) (Duncker & Humblot 2003) 167–72.

80 *Von eines Souverains Gerechtsamen in Religions-Sachen in Ansehung fremder Unterthanen*, in Johann Jacob Moser, *Grund-Sätze des jetzt üblichen Europäischen Völcker-Rechts in Fridens-Zeiten* (Hanau 1750) p 423f.

81 *Es ist ferner unter allen Religions-Verwandten Völcker-Rechtens, dass ein Souverain sich eines anderen Souverains Unterthanen, so sich mit ihme zu einerley Religion bekennen*

While this passage reflects the traditional notion of religious intervention in the sense of a prince intervening on behalf of persecuted coreligionists abroad, § 25 indicates that in the 17th and 18th century a development in a more universal direction had taken place: 'It is by no means a novelty that third powers guarantee the rights that have been granted to the members or subjects of a given state in matters of religion'.[82] As the key example he pointed to the Holy Roman Empire, in particular to Saxony, where the Elector, though personally Catholic, as director of the *Corpus Evangelicorum* was obliged to defend the religious rights Protestants enjoyed in Holy Roman Empire, a task delegated to his Protestant councillors.[83] Precondition for religion-blind third party action on behalf of foreign subjects, whose religious rights had been violated was the separation of the defence of religious rights from the religious affiliation of the intervening prince, of the transgressor and of the victim. In the positive law of nations Art. XVII of the Peace Treaty of Osnabrück placing all substantive provisions, including the religious guarantees under the collective guarantee of the contracting powers irrespective of religion was the decisive turning point: 'All and every partner to this treaty is obliged to defend every provision of this treaty against everyone, irrespective of religion'. The signatory powers of the Peace Treaty of Osnabrück were not only the Emperor and the King of Sweden, but also their allies.[84]

In contrast to modern international law the early modern law of nations was not predicated on a more or less static number of sovereign states as its exclusive actors. On occasion of their foundation, fundamental changes in the religious constitution of a nation or in times of crisis religious communities acted as subjects of the law of nations. The most viable early modern example of a religious community as a temporary and partial subject of the law of nations – temporary in the sense of specific situations, partial in sense of being restricted to religious matters – was the *Corpus Evangelicorum*. When the possibilities of conflict resolution under imperial law were exhausted, the association of the Protestant estates of the Holy Roman Empire constituted themselves as a subject of the law of nations. In 1751 the *Corpus Evangelicorum*

---

und um derselbigen willen bedruckt werden, Vorbitts-Weise annehmen könne, in ibid, § 13, p 423.

82 *Es ist auch nichts neues, dass dritte Machten die Garantie der denen Glidern oder Unterthanen eines Staates in Religions-Sachen zugestandenen Gerechtsamen übernehmen.*, in ibid, § 25, p 424.

83 Exempel vom Röm. Reich, besonders von Chur-Sachsen, in ibid, § 26, p 424.

84 Traité de Paix entre l'EMPIRE & la SUEDE, conclu & signé à Osnabruch, le 24. Octobre l'an 1648, Dumont, *Corps universel diplomatique du droit des gens*, vol 6,1, pp 488–90.

passed a formal resolution, as Moser reported, 'that also for the future it was not prepared to renounce the right to self-help, which had its firm basis in Peace of Westphalia'.[85] While the *Corpus Evangelicorum* reserved the right to self-defence, and thus, an option, to act outside the constitutional framework of the Empire, it was careful to stress that this did not constitute a violation of the constitution. This view did not go unchallenged and met with massive critique from the Emperor. The emergence of the *Völkerrecht der Teutschen*, the 'German Law of Nations' or the 'Law of Nations of the Germans'[86] was both a reaction to and a reflection of the constitutional crisis of the Holy Roman Empire in its final decades.[87]

If the actions of the *Corpus Evangelicorum* are paradigmatic for a shift from domestic law, in this case imperial law, to the law of nations as the legal framework for conflict resolution, the deliberations of the Allied Powers before and during the Congress of Vienna concerning the integration of the formerly Austrian Netherlands into the United Kingdom of the Netherlands show international law and constitutional law working as a system of communicating vessels in the reverse direction. The principal victorious allies had made constitutional guarantees for the equality of religious cults and the equality of citizens irrespective of religious affiliation a condition for the establishment

85 *Ferner beliebte das Corpus Evangelicorum diesen 21sten April* [1751, S.W] *daß man von dem einmal eineschlagenen Weg der in dem Westphälischen Friedens-Schluß best-gegründeten Selbst-Hülfe keineswegs abweichen wolle etc.*, Johann Jacob Moser, *Neue Berichte von Religions-Sachen*, parts five and six (Frankfurt-on-Main, Johann August Raspe, 1756), ch 7, § 7, p 67; for the *conclusum* of the *Corpus Evangelicorum* see Eberhard Christian Wilhelm von Schauroth (ed), *Vollständige Sammlung aller Conclusorum, Schreiben und anderer übrigen Verhandlungen des Hochpreißlichen Corporis Evangelicorum. Von Anfang des jetzt fürwährenden Hochansehnlichen Reichs-Convents bis auf die gegenwärtige Zeiten*, vol 1 (Regenspurg, Heinrich Georg Neubauer 1751) 856.

86 Carl Heinrich von Römer, *Das Völkerrecht der Teutschen. Als Lehrbuch bearbeitet* (Halle, Heller 1789); Stephan Wendehorst, '"Das Völkerrecht der Deutschen": Eine Antwort auf die dogmatischen Herausforderungen der Krise des Reichsstaatsrechts in der zweiten Hälfte des 18. Jahrhunderts', unpublished lecture, held as part of the Ringvorlesung 'Aus der Werkstatt. Aktuelle rechtshistorische Forschungen an der rechtswissenschaftlichen Fakultät der Universität Wien' on 17 March 2016.

87 Curiously, neither Berber nor Randeltzhofer, who have suggested to interpret the Holy Roman Empire as a highly integrated regional subsysten of the law of nations seem to have been aware of the *Völkerrecht der Teutschen*, let alone the role of the *Corpus Evangelicorurm* in it. Friedrich Berber, International Aspects of the Holy Roman Empire after the Treaty of Westphalia, (1964) 8 *Indian Yearbook of International Affaires* 174–83; Albrecht Randelzhofer, *Völkerrechtliche Aspekte des Heiligen Römischen Reichs nach 1648* (Schriften zum Völkerrecht, 1) (Duncker & Humblot 1967).

of the United Kingdom of the Netherlands, consisting of today's Netherlands, Belgium and Luxembourg in the *Eight Articles of London*, also known as the London Protocol of 21 June 1814. Although couched in universal language the move was intended to smooth the integration of the population of the Southern Netherlands with its Catholic and French political traditions into the new kingdom and to preclude repercussions on international relations. In article 8 of the treaty with the allied powers the king of the United Kingdom of the Netherlands promised to uphold the eight articles of the London Protocoll:

> S.M. le Roi des Pays-Bas ayant reconnu et sanctionné, sous la date du 21 juillet 1814, comme bases de la réunion des Provinces-Belgiques avec les Provinces-Unies, les huit articles renfermés dans la pièce annexée au présent traité, lesdits articles auront la mème force et valeur, comme s'ils ètoient inserés de mot à mot dans la transaction actuelle. [88]

Crucial were article 1:

> Cette réunion devra être intime et complete, de façon que les deux pays ne forment qu'un seul et même état, régi par la constitution déjà établie en Hollande, et qui sera modifiée, d'un commun accord, d'apres les nouvelles cironstanstances,[89]

and article 2 of the *Eight Articles of London*:

> Il ne sera rien innové aux articles de cette constitution qui assurent à tous les cultes une protection et une faveur ègales, et garantissent l'admission de tous les citoyens, quelle que soit leur croyance religieuse, aux emplois et offices publics.[90]

In mainstream international legal thought the critical awareness that a 'constitutional price' had to be payed for defusing troublesome and potentially explosive religious conflicts was waning in the 19th century. It was as an extraordinary measure and on the Eastern fringes of Europe, in the

88 Traité entre S.M. le Roi des Pays-Bas, et l'Autriche, la Russie, le Grande-Bretagne, et la Prusse; en date de Vienne le 31 mai 1815, in Klüber, *Acten* (n 6) vol 6, 21, Art. 8, p 174.

89 Traité entre S.M. le Roi des Pays-Bas, et l'Autriche, la Russie, le Grande-Bretagne, et la Prusse; en date de Vienne le 31 mai 1815. Annexe de L'article 8 du traité précédent du 31 mai 1815, in ibid, Art. 1, p 176.

90 ibid, Art. 2, p 176.

successor states of the Ottoman, the Habsburg and the Ramonov empires, that the practice to enshrine constitutional guarantees for the benefit of potentially endangered religious and subsequently national groups in international treaties was continued.

5 Consequences for Historiography and for the Doctrine of Iternational Law

Both, the weight which the law of nations possessed for the protection of religious rights and the interaction between the law of nations and domestic law in this respect tend to be downplayed and have in several cases been entirely overlooked. The traditional understanding of a number of early modern institutions, events and proccess needs to be revised, if the law of nations is brought back into the picture. The law of nations and domestic law working in tandem for the protection of religious rights has consequences not only for historiography, but also for the doctrine of modern internartional law, as exemplified by the work of Ernst Flachbarth in the interwar period.

The role, which Napoleonic France played in the emancipation of Catholics in several states of the Confederation of the Rhine, has been addressed neither by legal history nor by general or ecclesiastical history.[91] A number of other historical institutions, events and practices take on a different, some an entirely different appearance, if investigated in the context of the law of nations. The *Corpus Evangelicorum*, e.g., has been explored as part of the constitutional history of the Holy Roman Empire or within the context of decision-making.[92] The Gordon Riots figuring prominently in

91 The impact of French rule on the legal position of German Catholics is not discussed in Beatrix Jacobs, Raymond Kubben and Randall Lesaffer (eds), *In the embrace of France. The law of nations and constitutional* law *in the French satellite states of the revolutionary and Napoleonic age (1789–1815)* (Studies on the History of International Law, 18, Nomos 2008).

92 Klaus Schlaich, 'Corpus Evangelicorum und Corpus Catholicorum. Aspekte eines Parteienwesen im Hl. Römischen Reich Deutscher Nation' (1972) 11 *Der Staat. Zeitschrift für Staatslehre, Öffentliches Recht und Verfassungsgeschichte* 219–30; Martin Heckel, 'Itio in partes. Zur Religionsverfassung des Hl. Röm. Reiches Dt. Nation' (1978) 95 *Zeitschrift der Savigny-Stiftung für Rechtsgeschichte*, Kanonistische Abteilung 64, pp180–308, reprinted in Martin Heckel, *Gesammelte Schriften. Staat – Kirche – Recht – Geschichte*, vol 2 (Jus Ecclesiasticum 38) (Klaus Schlaich ed, Mohr Siebeck 1989) 636–736; Gabriele Haug-Moritz, 'Corpus Evangelicorum und deutscher Dualismus' in Volker Press (ed), *Alternativen zur Reichsverfassung in der Frühen Neuzeit?* (Schriften des Historischen

crowd studies[93] take on a new dimension, if placed in the context of the law of nations. The Josephinian Edicts of Toleration traditionally seen as the result and vehicle of the policy of one of the figureheads of enlightened absolutism, appear in a different light, if interpreted as measures to counter the interventions of Protestant courts on behalf of persecuted Protestant subjects. One can think of many more historical institutions and events, where the law of nations, if written back into history, calls for a reassessment: The capitulations of the Emperors of the Holy Roman Empire and the Kings of Poland,[94] the meaning of the Protestant Cause or 'Protestant interest', Jewish early modern politics, the Tumult of Thorn (Toruń) or the reestablishment of the Jewish community in Prague in 1748 after its expulsion by Maria Thersia.[95]

Kollegs, 23) (Oldenbourg 1995) 189–207; Andreas Kalipke, '"Weitläufftigkeiten" und "Bedencklichkeiten" – die Behandlung konfessioneller Konflikte am Corpus Evangelicorum' in (2008) 35: 3 *Zeitschschrift für Historische Forschung*405–47; idem, *Verfahren im Konflikt. Konfessionelle Streitigkeiten und Corpus Evangelicorum im 18. Jahrhundert* (Verhandeln, Verfahren, Entscheiden, 1) (University of Münster Diss. Phil. 2014) (Aschendorff 2015).

93 George Rudé, 'The Gordon Riots. A Study of the Rioters and Their Victims' (1956) 6 *Transactions of the Royal Historical Society* 93–114, reprinted in idem, *Paris and London in the eighteenth century. Studies in popular protest* (Collins 1970) 268–92; idem, *The Crowd in History. A Study of Popular Disturbances in France and England, 1730–1848* (2nd edn, first published Wiley & Sons 1964, Serif 2005); Nicholas Rogers, *Crowds, Culture and Politics in Georgian Britain* (Clarendon Press 1998) and Ian Haywood and John Seed (eds), *The Gordon Riots: Politics, Culture and Insurrection in Late Eighteenth-Century Britain* (CUP 2012) pay no or little attention to diplomacy and the law of nations.

94 Wolfgang Burgdorf, *Protokonstitutionalismus. Die Reichsverfassung in den Wahlkapitulationen der römisch-deutschen Könige und Kaiser 1519–1792* (Schriftenreihe der Historischen Kommission bei der Bayerischen Akademie der Wissenschaften, 94) (Vandenhoeck & Ruprecht 2015), presents, in a literal sense, a convincing case for the fundamental importance of the imperial capitulations, but is unaware of the intersection between the law of nations and constitutional law, thus, establishes a questionable genealogy of 19th century constitutionalism.

95 Baruch Mevorach, 'Jewish diplomatic activities to prevent expulsion of the Jews from Bohemia and Moravia in 1744–45' (1989) 1. *Binah. Studies in Jewish History, Thought and Culture* 143–58; François Guesnet, 'Textures of Intercession: Rescue Efforts for the Jews of Prague, 1744/1748'*Jahrbuch des Simon-Dubnow-Instituts/Simon Dubnow Institute Yearbook* 4 (2005) 355–75; François Guesnet, 'Negotiating under duress. The expulsion of Salzburg Protestants (1732) and the Jews of Prague (1744)', in idem, Cécile Laborde, Lois Lee (eds), *Negotiating Religion Cross-disciplinary perspectives* (Routledge, Taylor & Francis Group 2017) 47–62 are unaware of the significance of the law of nations. Guesnet

Taking the weight which the law of nations possessed for the protection of religious rights in the early modern period into proper account does not only change the perception of one or the other individual historical case, but has broader implications for our understanding of the overall historical processes of the development of religious toleration and the rise of the modern principle of equality in religious matters, both for the individual and for religious communities. The claimes which religious communities could make on foreign princes or the international community at large in the early modern period in conformity with the law of nations, if their 'rights and liberties' were violated, and the right and duty of a prince called upon to intervene on behalf of foreign subjects in such cases may be, with due reference to the dangers involved, put to the service of contemporary discussions about humanitarian intervention.[96]

The significance of early modern precedents was not lost on modern international lawyers of an earlier generation. Already in the interwar period lawyers who were dissatisfied with classical 19th century international law turned to history in search for answers for contemporary challenges. Ernst Flachbarth, the first volume of whose magisterial work *System of the International Law of Minorities: History of International Minority Protection. Positive Material Law of Minorities* was published in 1937 in the series of the Institute for the Law of Minorities, a Sub-Unit of the Institute of International Law at Budapest University,[97] was a case in point.[98] What Flachbarth and likeminded lawyers were concerned about, was to make

goes as far as suggesting that the very 'absence of a legal framework' may have helped facilitate the return of the Jews to Prague. Ibid, 61.

96 Stephan Wendehorst, *Vom Schutz verfolgter Religionsverwandter zum Schutz der universalen Menschenrechte: Zur Geschichte von Recht und Praxis humanitärer Intervention. Skript* (4th edn, Gießen/Linz/Vienna: Fachbereich Geschichts- und Kulturwissenschaften, Historisches Institut/Internationales Forschungszentrum Kulturwissenschaften (IFK) Kunstuniversität Linz/Universität Wien, Rechtswissenschaftliche Fakultät, Institut für Rechts- u. Verfassungsgeschichte 2015).

97 Ernst Flachbarth, *System des internationalen Minderheitenrechtes: Geschichte des internationalen Minderheitenschutzes. Positives materielles Minderheitenrecht*, Veröffentlichungen des Instituts für Minderheitenrecht an der Budapester Kgl. Ungarischen Péter Pázmány-Universität, Series 1, vol 1 (Gergely 1937).

98 Stephan Wendehorst, 'Ernst Flachbarth and the Turn to History in International Law: The Transformation of Early Modern Religious Guarantees into National Minority Protection in Interwar International Law', unpublished paper given at the Workshop, 'Institutions and International Law in Eastern Europe' organized by the Leibniz Institute for the History and Culture of Eastern Europe (GWZO) at Leipzig University on 28 September 2017.

the protection of national minorities in the successor states of the multinational and multireligious Habsburg, Ottoman and Romanov empires work. The doctrinal separation of state and nation, the limitation of the sovereignty of several states through the so-called minorities treaties and the, however limited, monitoring and intervention tools of the League of Nations did neither sit well with the states concerned, nor with the principles of absolute sovereignty and non-intervention deeply ingrained in classical nineteenth century international law. It was little consolation for Jan Paderewski (1860–1941), the first president of the re-established Polish state, when he was told by his French counterpart Georges Clémenceau (1841–1929) on 24 June 1919 that the Congress of Vienna had imposed similar limitations of sovereignty on the Netherlands in 1814 and the Congress of Berlin on the successor states of the Ottoman Empire in South-East Europe in 1878 in return for international recognition and territorial expansion.[99] While Flachbarth saw positive law as the primary line of defence – some 400 pages of his book are devoted to positve minority rights – it is precisely such historical precedents, which he also uses to support effective minority protection. The 65 page long history of international minority protection which preceds the 400 page long collection of international minority law deals with religious guranteees for Protestants in the Holy Roman Empire and Hungary in the 16th and 17th centuries, for Christians in the Ottoman Empire from the Middle Ages, for Jews im Romania and for Muslims in the successor states of the Ottoman empire in South-East Europe. By highlighting that religious guarantees were part of the law of nations, that their contents were broadly defined, analogous to modern national minority rights, that they were personal rather than territorial and that they extended to the individual, including even serfs,[100] Flachbarth turned the protection of religious rights in the early modern law of nations into a model for modern international law. There is a significant tension in his work. One the one hand Flachbarth emphasized positive substantative national minority rights, [101] a clear indication of his accceptance

99 Quoted from Flachbarth, *System des internationalen Minderheitenrechtes*, p 1.

100 ibid, p 5.

101 For a similar emphasis on positive substantative national minority rights guaranteed by international law see Jacob Robinson, *Das Minoritätenproblem und seine Literatur. Kritische Einführung in die Quellen und die Literatur der europäischen Nationalitätenfrage der Nachkriegszeit unter besonderer Berücksichtigung des völkerrechtlichen Minderheitenschutzes. Allgemeiner Teil*, vol 1, (De Gruyter 1928, Reprint: Beiträge zum ausländischen öffentlichen Recht und Völkerrecht, 6, De Gruyter 2011); the unpublished manuscript of

of the new order established at the Paris Peace conference in 1919 in marked contrast to other lawyers in countries defeated in World War I. On the other hand he simulatenously, on basis of historical precedent, sought to subvert this very order by sketching out an alternative design characterized by an international community possessing rights of supervision and intervention, the conditionalty of state sovereingty and the empowerment of national minorites in international law so as to secure their collective continuity.

Making the protection of national minorities in states that were bound by the so-called minority treaties effective, was a challenge to international law in the interwar period. At the end of the 20th century, the question, whether the international community had a right or even a duty to intervene in the internal affairs of sovereign states against their will, if they are unable or unwilling to guarantee minimum standards of human rights for their own population or parts thereof, has resurfaced on a universal plane. Thus, there may be a lesson or two to be learned from Flachbarth and other international lawyers from the interwar period intent on establishing effective controll of national minority rights through international law and, therefore, forced to challenge the traditional doctrine of state sovereignty. If one follows Flachbarth in his creative use of early modern law, one should, however, be careful not to dismiss, what Flachbarth either did not see or did not wish to see in the early modern law of nations, the dangers involved in the manipulation of the protection of religous rights, the limitation of 'rights and liberties' to specific groups, the reinforcement of existing asymmetries in the religious constitution, the relationship between the individual and 'his' or 'her' community, and, above all, their ineffectivess coupled with the growing consensus to have the state play the key role in the protection of the rights of his subjects respectively citizens.

This said, which consequences may be drawn for the extant body of the doctrine of international law? The conditionality of state sovereignty and the unity of public law are arguably the aspects of the early modern legal order which may be used most productively for a reconceptualization of what sovereignty and international law may mean in an age beyond the classical state and classical international law understood as inter-state law. It was these two aspects which, in principle, allowed the law of nations to operate as a safety

the second volume, completed in 1933 is located in the National Library of Israel, ARC. Ms. Var. 435, Jacob Robinson Collection, 25-12-02-03, AC-1524; on Robinson, the Jewish nation and international law see Omry Kaplan-Feuereisen, 'Im Dienste der jüdischen Nation: Jacob Robinson und das Völkerrecht', (2008) 58: 8/10 *Osteuropa* 279–94. I'm grateful to the author for sharing his discovery of Robinson's manuscript with me.

valve for deficiencies in domestic law or as an *ersatz* legal regime for challenges intractable in municipal law, which gave individuals and communities a position in the law of nations, which allowed for situational subjects of the law of nations and which allocated rights and duties of monitoring and intervention in domestic affairs to what was then the international community. The law of nations and domestic law functioning as a system of communicating vessels was not neccesarily incompatible with a strong state. Jean Bodin (1530–1596), whose political and legal designs were meant as an antidote to failed or failing states, saw intervention as justified, if directed against an inhuman ruler:

> For just as it is right and proper for anyone to take forcible action to defend the honour and life of those who are oppressed unjustly when the law offers no remedy, so it is highly honourable, and befitting a prince, to take up arms in defence of a whole people unjustly oppressed by a cruel tyrant. Such a one was Hercules when he went about the world destroying monsters of tyranny everywhere. For these exploits he was deified. Such also were Dion, Timoleon, and other generous princes who earned the title of scourge of tyrants ... In such a case there is no doubt that a virtuous prince can proceed against a tyrant either by force of arms, diplomatic intervention, or process of law.[102]

By the end of the 18th century a more absolute form of sovereignty than Bodin had imagined, had won the day over looser alternatives of political organization and less clear-cut divisons between the internal and external in politics and law. Yet even as late as the Congress of Vienna one can observe that a basic understanding of international law and constitutional law functioning as a system of communicating vessels was still in place. On the one hand there was, against the background of the disruptive experiences of the past, a commitment to remove the protection of religious rights from international law. On the other hand, it was equally clear that constitutional guarantees had to be introduced in order to compensate for rights, once protected under the law of nations. The constitutional regime of the United Kingdom of the Netherlands and to a lesser degree the German Federation testify to this. A pragmatic awareness of the inverse proportionality of the frequency of foreign intervention on behalf of religious communities to the level of toleration respectively equality enjoyed by them had been responsible for legal change. The awareness of this

102 Jean Bodin, *Six Books on the Commmonwealth* (M.J.Tooley tr, first published in French in 1576, Blackwell 1955) book II, ch 5 available at <www.constitution.org/bodin/bodin_.htm> accessed 20 October 2017.

inverse relationship has not only helped pave the way for religious tolerance in 17th and 18th century Europe. If universalized, the empirical evidence for the law of nations and domestic law working in tandem for the protecction of religious rights in the early modern period, has the potential for a reassessement of the doctrine of intenational law concerning state sovereignty, intervention and human rights.

CHAPTER 2

A Right of Infidels to Establish Their Own State?

Remarks on the Writing of Paulus Vladimiri and Francisco de Vitoria

Władysław Czapliński

The subject in question was posed by two eminent scholars under different circumstances and in a different period. Francisco de Vitoria was born 50 years after the death of Paulus Vladimiri. The Polish scholar developed his views in a context of dispute and wars between the Kingdom of Poland and the Teutonic Order, while Vitoria concentrated his writing on the consequences of a subjugation of America by Europeans. The former was more a lawyer than a theologist, while the latter on the contrary. On the other hand, both of them studied a similar topic: what the scope of a power of Pope and Emperor in respect of pagans (infidels) was, and whether both authorities could deprive the non-Christians of their States. We shall attempt to confront the writings of both scholars.

We start with a short personal presentation. Paweł Włodkowic, known also under a Latin transcription of his name as Paulus Vladimiri (or Paulus, son of Vladimir) of a noble family Dołęga was born between 1370 and 1373[1] in Northern Poland, in the region of Masovia, diocese of Płock. It was close to the boundary of Poland to Prussia and Lithuania, so as a child Paulus must have experienced armed invasions by Lithuanians[2] and Teutonic knights who subordinated pagan Prussians to their rule in the 13th century. He became a bachelor and then a master in liberated arts (1393), and subsequently he continued studying law at the University of Prague and became bachelor of canon law in 1396. He started his career as a clergyman, first in Poznań and then in Płock. In 1403–1411 Paulus studied law in Italy, mostly in Padova; he also served as a royal legate in negotiations with Pope Alexander v. After having returned to Poland, he obtained a doctor's degree in law at the University of Cracow, which he was the rector (president) of in 1414–1415. In that period, the University was financed by a testamentary bequest of the Queen Jadwiga

1 When he was granted the title of a bachelor in arts in 1389, he had to be at least 16, and probably little older than 16.

2 The Kingdom of Lithuania was established in 1253 after the babtism of a local ruler who became king Mindagas. After his death Lithuania returned to heathendom and was babtised again after 1385 (ie after the treaty on the union between Poland and Lithuania).

 | DOI:10.1163/9789004349155_003

Anjou. In 1415–1418, he stayed in Constance as a member of the Polish legation (embassage) to the Council. Interestingly, although being the youngest delegate, he was the main spokesman presenting the Polish position and arguing against the Teutonic Order. After having returned to Poland, he lived in Cracow, probably involved in the academic life of the University. He owned a house which after his death was inherited by the catholic order of Cracow and then rented to the members of an order.[3] Vladimiri died between 9 October 1435 and 5 October 1443, the exact date raises controversies.

Francisco de Vitoria was born in a small Basque town in the Alava province between 1482 and 1486, although some authors shift the date to 1492–93. It is certain that he entered the Dominican Order in Burgos in 1503. From 1505 to 1510 he studied at the Estudio General de Colegio de San Pablo in Burgos. Subsequently he spent some years in Paris, studying with a Flemish master, Petrus Crokaert. After the return from Paris he became professor at the University of Salamanca, where he successfully taught theology since 1521. Since 1538 his health deteriorated gradually, but constantly. He died on the 12 August 1546.

Both scholars wrote their papers in Latin. I have to admit that my personal knowledge of Latin is extremely poor and I was unable to study old legal texts in the original language. However, those works were successfully translated into modern languages by eminent international lawyers: Paulus Vladimiri by Ludwik Ehrlich; Vitoria – into German by Walter Schaetzel, into Spanish by Antonio Truyol Serra, and into English by E. Nys.

The most important writings by Paulus Vladimiri are:

1. *Saevientibus*, presented to the German nation (Germans, Scandinavians, Scots, Czechs, Hungarians and Poles) during the Council of Constance in July 1415, devoted to the validity of papal and imperial privileges invoked by the Order, and a right of pagans to establish their own states;
2. *Opinio Ostiensis*, distributed among all nations (German, Spanish, Italian, English) devoted to polemics with arguments presented by the Teutonic Order, dated July 1415;
3. *Ad aperiendam*, dated 1416–1417 and distributed among all nations, analysed the legal position of the Order and contained glosses to privileges and other documents invoked by it;

3 Chaplains living in the 'magnificent house' founded by Paulus by his own private means were obliged to pay ca 600 g of silver yearly to finance requiem services for the soul of Paulus Vladimiri.

4. *Iste tractatus* and *Quoniam error*, two letters published in 1417 as polemics with the writings by J. Frebach von Bamberg and J. Falkenberg;
5. *Oculi*, a letter to the German Emperor Sigismund of Luxemburg, dated approximately 1420, presenting the Polish position in the dispute against the Teutonic Order, and serving as a basis for the imperial ruling;
6. *Ad vivendum*, appeal regarding the unfavourable judgment by the emperor to the pope (1421);
7. *Letter to the Bishop of Cracow*, written and sent from Padua to Bishop Oleśnicki in 1432; it contains last arguments by Włodkowic in connection with the German attack against Poland in 1431.

A list of writings by Vitoria includes: *Relecciones* (original presentations of dissertations on most important topics), *Lecturas docentes* (considerations and discussions which are a basis for oral presentations at auditorium rooms, often including notices concerning questions and remarks by students), and others.

Releciones morales are particularly interesting ie open lectures on current issues, pronounced once a year in 1527–1543, *in toto* 15 presentations. In June 1534, the emperor Charles V listened to the lecture.

Vitoria applied a scholastic method of reasoning which was universally accepted by the Dominicans. In his searching for the absolute truth, Vitoria posed a thesis, and then presented arguments in favour and against it.

He showed an interest for the Spanish invasion of the New World after 1533, when F. Pizarro subjugated the Inka Empire and executed Atahualpa. The most significant effect of this interest was a special lecture *De Indis noviter inventis*, hold at the end of 1538 or beginning of 1539.[4] A principal question that the author dealt with was whether the Spanish conquerors were entitled to baptise Indian children against the will of their parents. However, the learnt author dedicated his speech also to other problems relating to Indians.

1 Views of Paulus Vladimiri on International Law

The conflict between Poland and the Teutonic Order appeased after the Battle of Grunwald by the first peace treaty of Toruń of 1411, and escalated again in 1414, shortly before the Council of Constance. Teutonic knights wisely used

4 In fact Vitoria included some considerations on Indians into his Releccio of 1537 (*De Temperancia*), but finally decided to remove it before having pronounced his lecture.

the opportunity to present Poland as aggressor, and this view was supported by a thesis that the Great War of 1409–1410 was won by Poland thanks to the help and support by pagans. The argument was extremely important if we remember that Jan Hus was burnt for being a heretic during the Council.

The general political climate was certainly very heavy at that time. The Order requested also the pope to condemn Poland and to confirm earlier privileges granted to the Order by the Holy See. The claims were supported in particular by a pamphlet by J. Falkenberg.[5] On the other hand, Poland defended her position with arguments based upon the universal value of peace, the doctrine of just war and self-defence, including a right of the pagans to establish their own state that could become allied with the Christian rulers. Under these circumstances it was clear that the ordinary boundary dispute was transformed into a deep doctrinal controversy.

From the theoretical perspective of international law of the 15th century, a distinction should be drawn between two kinds of proceedings: *processus iudicialis* and *processus doctrinalis*. The former one concerned a specific problem and could be compared with a contemporary dispute settlement form: fact-finding. On the contrary, the latter was based on general principles of law, and was much more important. The task conferred upon Włodkowic was to elaborate a Polish doctrinal position. The activities of Włodkowic connected with the Council resulted in several works (listed above) which created in fact a coherent system of legal norms dealing both with the origins of law as such, and with the international legal order. The legal opinions of Włodkowic also influenced his position towards a reform of the Catholic Church, presented during the Council of Constance. Papers presented by Paulus Włodkowic were far from being purely procedural, in accordance with requirements of canon law. He based his papers on a variety of sources, including the Corpus iuris canonici, Corpus iuris civilis, Bible, works by the Holy Fathers of the Catholic Church (St. Augustin, St. Ambrosius, Gregory the Great), eminent philosophers and theologians (Aristotle, Cicero, St. Thomas Acquinas, Innocent IV), known lawyers contemporary to him (Ioannes Andreae, Oldradus, Ioannes de Lignano, Henry de Segusio or Hostiensis, Dominicus di San Giminiano, Francesco Zabarella). He analyzed positive legal instruments including treaties, privileges, judicial decisions and documents reflecting legal proceedings. Considered as a whole, the system of the law of armed conflicts was equally complete as the one by Vitoria and Gentili, but preceded them of some 120 years.

5 See his *Satira contra hereses et cetera nephande Polonorum et forum regis Jagel fidelite descripta*.

Before we present a position taken by Włodkowic as to the legal arguments presented in those treatises, there are in fact issues relating to the dispute between Poland and the Teutonic Order. Five factors can be mentioned: 1) territorial disputes relating to the areas occupied by the Order; 2) regular and permanent expeditions organized by the Teutonic knights and supported by Western countries, with a participation of foreign guest knights against pagan neighbours; 3) the particular position of the Teutonic Order; 4) papal and imperial privileges granted to the Order, and invoked by it; 5) Teutonic propaganda against Poland, aimed at justifying a continued activity of the Order. In his arguments, Włodkowic had to oppose the statements by Peter von Wormdith, the prosecutor of the Teutonic Order, and the opinions presented by Falkenberg. As to the former, he accused Poland of aggression against the Order and of winning the battle of Grunwald/Tanneberg thanks to the help of pagan forces. He invoked papal and imperial privileges granted to the Order, allowing for a subjugation of the territories of Lithuania, Ruthenia, etc. The latter, a Dominican monk originating from Krakow but supporting the Order wrote in his *Satira* that Poles rejected the Catholic religion; they respected and glorified king Jagello as God, and consequently became apostates and heretics. Everyone fighting against Poland should be honoured and merited an eternal life in paradise. The majority (if not all) of Poles should be executed. Abstaining from possible help to crusaders against Poland would amount to a mortal sin.

The pope had power to instigate wars against pagans. Also the emperor as a substitute of God on Earth in his secular acts was competent to occupy all the territories inhabited and owned by infidels. The powers of the pope and emperor to this respect were not limited to the Holy Land, but concerned all the other pagan territories. The world was subordinated to the emperor; as the infidels did not recognize his authority, they should be punished, also by means of preventive war. Finally, we have mentioned a treatise by Vrebach that contained 18 arguments: 14 in favour of the legality of the Teutonic Order as based upon papal and imperial authority, and four concerning the legality (or rather illegality) of pagan assistance to the Polish king against Christians.

In order to cope with his task as counsel to the Kingdom of Poland, Włodkowic constructed a coherent system of international law (and of law in general), providing the right to life, dignity, freedom of conscience and due process. This system has been based on the Ten Commandments, natural law and canon law. As the participants to the Council were often specialists in Roman law, he occasionally referred also to that system. It requires a certain unity and hierarchy of norms – that can be seen from the opinions by Włodkowic on the coherence of the legal order and on consequences of non-conformity of certain norms with the higher ones. In order to present this system, we shall refer to passages from different papers by this author. We shall also confront his ideas and views with those by Falkenberg and von Bamberg to show their importance in the context.

Law is strictly connected with morality and it must be subjected to a certain axiology. The structure of the legal order has many layers. Włodkowic makes clear the distinction between different norms:

> Although from the beginning of man all things were common to all, yet by the law of nations, to wit, natural, and human, there have been distinguished dominions of things and therefore those things which have been previously occupied by one, another is not allowed to seize, because natural law prohibits, to wit: 'What thou wouldst not have done to thee do not to another,' and divine law: 'Remove not the landmarks of thy neighbour'.[6]

Divine law (as formulated in the *Decalogue* and *Holy Bible*) is the highest law. It finds its source in God and divine grace, as well as in the fundamental commandment of love, and as such it preceded mankind. It is binding for everyone, as all people (including pagans) are born as subordinated to God. Divine law constitutes a basis for the primary occupation of territory, so it must be universally respected and applicable by the Catholic Church. Alike, property and power are granted also to infidels. 'It is evidently clear that these have been ordained for every reasonable creature by God who maketh His sun rise on the evil and good and feedeth all fowls (Matthew 5 in fine) and giveth food to all flesh.'[7] However, it is not really universal, as it cannot bind upon people who have not accepted it voluntarily. Infidels should not be compelled to Christianity, as free will should constitute a basis for conversion. In light of the divine law legal institutions like occupation of territories, attacks against pagans, killings, violence, jurisdiction of the state, modes of Christianization should be condemned.

On the second level, there was natural law. It is based upon a general commandment: do not do to the others what you do not want others doing to you, which could be formulated also in a positive meaning: do to the others what they are doing to you. Natural law is a basis of inter-human relations, and it can be modified neither by the pope nor by the emperor. It is common to all

6 Ludwik Ehrlich, *Pisma wybrane Pawła Włodkowica/Works of Paul Wladimiri (a Selection) Warszawa 1966–1969* (editions in Polish, Latin and English translated by the editor) vol I, 121.

7 ibid, II, 12.

nations and everyone must observe it. It constitutes a basis of rights of states, property rights, obedience, but also of an opposition to oppression. On the contrary, Włodkowic drew a distinction between natural law as common to all creatures, and its subsystem, ie law of nations. 'And from the law so called branches off the law of nations, as the jurist says. Now, to consider something in regard to what follows from it is proper to reason, and therefore this is natural to man according to natural reason, which dictates this. Hence the jurist [says]: That what natural reason has constituted among all men, is kept in all nations and is called the law of nations.'[8]

Law of nations was the basis of the establishing of the states, property and authority, but also of the obedience by the subordinated subjects and of the right to resistance. Its norms were binding also upon infidels.

Interestingly, Paulus in principle did not refer in his work to Roman law extensively, except some analogies to private law. The reason was that Roman law belonged to the imperial legal system. As such, it had no validity in the territory of the Kingdom of Poland, and therefore it could not be applicable to the dispute between Poland and Teutonic Order.

All the power existing in the world finds its source either in divine law, or in the will of people (consent). State authority cannot be based upon violence and tyranny; obedience of the population is strictly connected with justice. State organs[9] should act in a just way, meaning however also: they should keep legality. According to L. Ehrlich, one can conclude from the writings by Włodkowic that the *ultra vires* acts of the rulers are illegal and the sovereign causing damages to his kingdom should be treated as a private person. Such action would be invalid, as the sovereign is bound by public law and he cannot contradict it.[10] The sovereignty of the rulers does not amount to omnipotence (absolute power), as their competence is limited to jurisdiction and defence, and not to property rights with respect to everything. If the sovereign does not respect the rights of the people, they are entitled to resist against an injustice. Moreover, the sovereign has important obligations towards his population. He is to ensure respect for religion, morality, decency and freedom of conscience. Furthermore, he is obliged to good administration, protection of private

8 ibid, 92.

9 It is interesting that in the 14th century a specific notion of *Corona Regni Poloniae* was formulated in order to make a distinction between the state powers and the personal domain of the monarchs. This legal institution helped Włodkowic in elaborating his opinion on the position and role of the sovereigns.

10 See Ehrlich (n 6) XLII–XLVI; see also Tadeusz Jasudowicz, 'Człowiek, jego prawa i obowiązki w nauczaniu Pawła Włodkowica' (1992) 1 *Toruński Rocznik Praw Człowieka* 139.

property and law enforcement, including maintaining of state territory and protecting rights of all persons living within the borders of the state, including infidels. As the state power has its sources in the will of God if it is legitimate, the population has to respect public authorities.

Włodkowic questioned any power of the pope and the emperor with respect to infidels. He made a distinction between the nature of both authorities: spiritual (eternal) by the Pope and secular (temporal) by the Emperor. However, the world should be governed by only one supreme agent (*principatus*). As the pope governs souls, and the emperor bodies, and the soul dominates the body, it is natural that the Pope is supreme to the Emperor. Infidels can be subjected to the papal power exclusively as far as divine law is concerned and in a manner conforming to divine and natural law. The Pope can only pass orders and decrees ordering the infidels not to molest unjustly their Christian subjects. The Pope cannot force infidels to accept the Christian religion (this would be contrary to the canon law), but he can demand from them to admit missionaries. The Pope's authority is limited to the punishment for very serious offences against the natural law. The power of the Emperor cannot go further than the papal one. In particular the Emperor can exercise his power exclusively with relation to those infidels who accepted his jurisdiction

According to Paulus, in particular, infidels, pagans, and even heretics have a right to establish their own structures. This opinion reflects a general spirit of tolerance. This right is simply the effect and the consequence of the binding force of natural law. As the general natural law is binding upon all the nations, it grants also a right to create an own state to barbarians or pagans. The states should organize their mutual relations on the basis of agreements and treaties, and all the parties should obey those instruments. The parties should be willing to respect their partners. If they are not, treaties are broken and war replaces peace in the mutual relations.

In that situation, it was also clear that no state or any other authority (including the pope and the emperor) is entitled to decide upon matters or territories of another state. From the political point of view this idea is extremely important, as it proves the illegality of territorial privileges granted to the Teutonic Order by Emperor Frederic the Second. The territories granted belonged to pagan states and they were never subjected to the authority of the German Empire. Włodkowic mockingly concludes: How generous was the Emperor, as far as the matter concerned foreign territories (O quam liberalis fuit iste imperator in re aliena).

A ban on war was a cornerstone of his approach to contemporary legal order. Włodkowic explained his idea of peace as an expression of supreme, divine law.

> For war by its nature cannot be the cause of faith, nor conversely, except by accident and indirectly, that is, where faith would be hampered. And since nothing is said these letters [by the Teutonic order] about such hampering, there is here altogether no cause of a just war.[11]

Włodkowic referred to conditions for just war, as formulated by St. Augustine and St. Raymond of Penaforte, and repeated in the *Decretum Gratiani*: a necessity to protect peace by war (war in self-defence), a necessity to recuperate objects or territories occupied by force, a personal condition (clergymen cannot participate in war), an animus (war cannot be waged for revenge or hate) and an authorization to start war, either by the sovereign unable to ensure justice in another way, or by a decree enacted by the pope (or Catholic Church in general), like in the case of the crusades.[12] All those conditions must be present in every conflict and cannot be presumed. The Teutonic Order never fulfilled any of those conditions. Even if the Teutonic knights pretended that the wars waged by them were just,

> [a]nd although it is pretended here that the aim is spread of the Faith, as is gathered from the abovementioned letters and articles, since however it is impossible to attain this end by these means which are contrary to the same end, are evil by themselves, and are prohibited by divine law, namely by acts of violence, wrongs, rapine and unjust wars, and enough has been mentioned and is known about (the use of) these means from the same letters and articles,- therefore it necessarily follows that the said order is actually something different than what is in appearance.

Moreover, Włodkowic concludes: 'And from this it must be inferred that this order or knighthood is heretical'.[13] We could conclude that in the opinion of Włodkowic, war is illegal unless we are able to prove that it is just. If so, Włodkowic rejected a phenomenon of a 'normative force of facts.' Illegal facts cannot become a source of law even if they have been confirmed by consent of the party concerned. The evaluation of the legal position of the parties can be effectuated on the basis of legal proceedings, investigation of circumstances of the act and analysis of proofs.

11 Ehrlich (n 6) vol II, 234.

12 The opinion by Włodkowic with respect to this question was subjected to a certain evolution, but in all his writings three elements of just war can be found: *auctoritas, causa, intentio*.

13 Ehrlich (n 6) vol II, 301.

It is interesting, however, that Włodkowic provides also for the right to self-defence in case of aggression. This right has been based on principles of Roman law. According to the *Codex Iustiniani*, an owner can use force in order to repeal any attack against his possession. Subsequently, the right to self-defence has also been accepted by the legal doctrine of the Catholic Church.[14] Włodkowic accepted it as *ultima ratio* and connected it with another requirement – all other states and sovereigns should be informed by the power referring to self-defence that the action taken belongs to the category of just war. The right to self-defence played an important role in the system created by Włodkowic. The rule formulated by Włodkowic amounts, however, to the right of every person to defend oneself by all possible means, including a judicial proceeding. On the other hand, the right to defence should be guaranteed and respected. It is based upon the natural law, so that no ruler can abolish it by his decision or act. Włodkowic discussed also issues of international responsibility. He concluded that in case of unjust (forbidden) war, all territories and objects occupied or looted should be restituted. No acquisitive prescription was allowed in relation to such a land. The subjects starting the unjust war or the commander in chief of attacking troops are responsible for all the violence and damages and killings committed by their soldiers.[15]

All the writings by Włodkowic were subjected to a political position, concerning the illegality of territorial occupations by the Teutonic Order. We emphasize that Włodkowic conflicted with an official position of the Catholic Church, although he was deeply connected with it. He never criticized the Catholic religion nor took position towards any kind of heresy, ie views critical towards the Church. He also never put in question the position of the pope as the highest moral authority, and he maintained that all rulers in the world should be subordinated to his power. In some way, however, such an approach could be evaluated as instrumental. Włodkowic several times appealed to the pope when the German emperor passed a judgment unfavourable to Poland and stressed that the final ruling by the pope would create justice. He also presented an argument that if the pope does not possess powers to order a war against barbarians, the more such power must be declined to the emperor.[16]

Włodkowic continued by stating that war is also prohibited under the canon law and referred to a declaration of the General Council of Toledo that forbade the use of force to anyone to make him believe. A thesis that the spreading of

14 Włodkowic referred in his argument to a codification of law known as *Decretum Gratiani*, dated 1120 and founded on the earlier works by St. Augustine.

15 Ehrlich (n 6) vol I, 73–75.

16 ibid, vol II, 233, 234.

the Catholic religion should be left to theologians, and not to warriors, was revolutionary in the time of religious wars as it combined law with universal values of morality and justice. The arguments by Włodkowic were based upon the writings of the most eminent lawyers of those times, including Zabarella and Ancarano. Both of them participated in the Council of Constance and could not be opposed by partisans of the Teutonic Order of equal position. Although he realized that the Teutonic Order constituted a part of the Church and was in a way identified with the latter, he also drew a difference between the Church as a whole and the German Order. Włodkowic discussed the position of the pope and bishops with respect to numerous violations of divine and the natural law by the Teutonic knights, and he expected the hierarchy to intervene in order to stop those violations. The Order itself was consequently described as false prophet and in fact heretic body and organization. Its activity damaged the image of the Catholic Church. That picture of the Order was totally different to the one presented by the Order itself in the Western world: 'And since the Brothers Crucifers of Prussia appear dressed up as sheep and in reality show in themselves the rapacious wolf, it must be concluded from the sacred words of the Gospel that they are deceitful men and false prophets of whom Christ bids beware.'[17] This statement is followed by a description of the war of aggression against the Kingdom of Poland in 1431:

> [T]he sacrilegious hand of the same profane men suddenly, without notifying the said [Polish] King, breaking treaties of peace and violating solemn pacts which are being firmly observed under the natural law of nations even by barbarous nations, casting aside an agreement made at one time, and turning it into their habitual and usual discord, hostilely invaded the most Christian Kingdom of Poland and devastated it by their most fearful cruelty, and excessive and more than pagan atrocity, not sparing sex or age.[18]

The description of destroyed cities and burnt churches, presented by the scholar of high personal and academic authority, was disastrous for the image of the Order.

Finally, Włodkowic strongly emphasized that the Teutonic Order is not identical with the German Order of St. Mary Immaculate established in the Holy Land at the end of 12th century, as it turned from a religious to a secular body; neither the Teutonic knights nor the St. John Order should be allowed to

17 ibid, 208.

18 ibid, vol II, 210.

be organized into a territorial state. In his analysis he refers to three elements: 1) the origin of the Teutonic Order (privileges were granted not to the Order as such with a seat in Jerusalem, but to a group of brethren and knights seated at Akkon, and were aimed at the protection of the hospital, providing care to poor and diseased people and finally fighting in defence of the Holy Land; those tasks could not be performed outside Palestine); 2) the legal nature of the Order; 3) the factual conduct of the Order. After having discussed those entire questions in a sophisticated juridical reasoning, Włodkowic concluded that in fact the Teutonic Order became a kind of heresy or sect as it was at that time based on principles contrary to the Catholic religion.[19]

There existed also an analogy between the Teutonic Order and the Templar Order, condemned by the French King Philip. The arguments presented by Włodkowic were based upon the writings of Thomas Aquinus, but also the French lawyer Henry de Bohic, the English writer Occam and Czech Mauritius Rvacka. In that way Włodkowic intended to convince representatives of different nations nominated as members of the Papal Court to decide on the dispute in favour of Poland. The Teutonic Order's lawyers realized this imminent danger which can be seen from the letters sent by their prosecutor to the Great Master of the Order.[20] The eminent Polish human rights lawyer T. Jasudowicz expressed a view that the doctrine of rights of people formulated by Paweł Włodkowic has in fact been the precursory of modern human rights.[21] All human beings in the world (Włodkowic referred several times to Saracens, Jews, infidels and pagans, in different configurations, and mixed those categories seemingly without any deeper purpose) are born free and the human dignity of all them cannot be put into question. Any attack against another person including infidels is not reconcilable with the commandment to love one's neighbour; man can be subordinated to another man exclusively on the basis of his own free decision, and he is bound by such decision. On many occasions, Włodkowic referred to the unconditional right to live:

> Homicide itself, which is of the genus of evils and by its nature is evil and therefore contrary to all law: divine, natural, and human, and hence prohibited. In this respect this rule is stated in law: When something is

19 ibid, vol I, 190, 191.

20 As to details, cf Anna Maria Wesołowska, *Paweł Włodkowic – współczesne znaczenie poglądów i dokonań* [Paweł Włodkowic – Contemporary Importance of his Views and Achievements] (Toruń, 1997) 75–80.

21 Tadeusz Jasudowicz, *Śladami Ludwika Ehrlicha: do Pawła Włodkowica po naukę o prawach człowieka* [On the Traces of Ludwik Ehrlich: Paweł Włodkowic and a Science on Human Rights] (Toruń, 1995) 33f and 89ff.

> negatively expressly promulgated, or ordered, or forbidden, it is understood to be always prohibited unless it be found to be permitted by law.[22]

The scope of the right to life is extremely wide and covers not only the ban on arbitrary killing, but also the one on every kind of violence, cruel and inhuman treatment. The views on freedom of religion, belief and thoughts have been presented above. We have mentioned also some remarks concerning the right of defence. Włodkowic clearly formulated also other rules of judicial process: 'Manifest is that which arises from public and common information and the knowledge of few. But since when it is a matter of condemning someone, that which is manifest must be proved before one be condemned ... therefore, that which is manifest does not suffice here unless it be proved'.[23] This rule of evidence and burden of proof can be found probably in all contemporary criminal codes in the world. Włodkowic discussed also important issues of private law, including the right to property and fundamentals of the law of obligations. He did that, however, in the context of the powers of the sovereign, who is not entitled to transfer the goods belonging to the kingdom. The king in particular is empowered to expropriate, but he can do that 'for a cause which concerns public utility, and after giving compensation, so that justice shall not be outraged; otherwise not'.[24] This sounds very modern again.

2 Stanislaw from Skarbimierz – Forgotten Polish Medieval International Lawyer[25]

Włodkowic was not the only Polish lawyer strongly engaged in the dispute with the Teutonic Order. Stanislaw from Skarbimierz (Scarbimiri) was another one who had important input in the progressive development of international law of that period. We do not know too much about his life – except that he died in

22 Ehrlich (n 6) vol II, 202.

23 ibid, 33.

24 ibid, 239.

25 On the Polish input into the doctrine of international law in 15th to 19th centuries see Ludwik Ehrlich and Jerzy Stefan Langrod, *Zarys historii nauki prawa narodów politycznego i administracyjnego w Polsce*, including a summary in French (Kraków, 1949), and St.Wielgus, *Polska średniowieczna doktryna Ius gentium*, [Polish doctrine of Ius gentium in Middle Ages], Lublin 1996. On Stanisław Scarbimiri in particular cftwo studies by Ludwik Ehrlich, *Paweł Włodkowic and Stanisław ze Skarbimierza* (Warszawa, 1954) and *Polski wykład prawa wojny XV wieku* [Polish Treatise on the Law of War of 15th century] (Warszawa, 1955).

1431 and he was the first rector of the respected University of Cracow in 1400, and again in 1413. He was a professor at the law faculty. One of his sermons concerned the law of war; it is known as *De bellis iustis*. According to L. Ehrlich, political and ideological elements included in the sermon clearly show that the treatise was strictly connected with the position of Poland in the period preceding the Battle of Grunwald. Stanisław from Skarbmierz started with a general statement that all people (including pagans) can establish their own states, public authorities, property. All those states (Christian and pagan) are bound by the same law. He condemned aggressive wars, including the wars to spread the Catholic religion. Clergymen should not take part in the fighting, except for absolution, moral and spiritual support. Just war could be waged exclusively for defending divine law, for love and justice. Killing people during such a just war is justified, in particular by secular belligerents. Private wars should be forbidden and eliminated. Even the sovereign including the emperor cannot start war if reparation for injuries and damages suffered from the opponent is offered. Disputes should be resolved by judicial proceedings, not by the use of force. The self-defence should be accepted and allowed, also to infidels. The author accepts ambushes as a method of conduct of hostilities, but does not discuss the issue of allowed and forbidden weapons. Destruction of enemy property, if the cause is just, is also acceptable. However, reparation for all unjust damages should be granted. The sermon invokes the same authorities as the treatises by Włodkowic; in fact, mutual influence of both scholars is manifest. The sermon discussed a wide range of issues connected with the law of war, including legality of wars, doctrine of just war, effects of just and unjust wars, self-defence, possibility and legality of alliances with infidels, and the position of individuals subjected to the belligerent sovereign with respect to war (in that context the author presented his opinion on a right of individuals to control the legality of war, and a possibility to reject duties of obedience in case of unjust war).

3 Francisco de Vitoria and ius Gentium

Vitoria was theologist and so are also his works. His approach towards legal questions was if they touched issues of conscience either of individual persons or the sovereign conferred with a task to care of their needs. At the beginning of De Indis, Vitoria posed a question who was entitled to discuss the status of the native people. He concluded that this was not the task of lawyers, at least not only lawyers, as jurists specialized in human law, and the relations between Indians and Christians were subjected to divine law.

He started a discussion with rejecting a traditional (medieval) approach to the position of the Pope and his universal authority, paving therefore a road towards new secular international law. Then he adopted natural law as a basis for a universal system, binding equally all subjects, and capable of being enforced. States are not fully independent. In fact they are rather interdependent, constituting *societas naturalis* of States. Moreover, a violation of rights of one of the States involves also violations of rights of other members of the international community. In the name of the international community each state can act and claim reparation for injuries suffered by any State.

As to the first point, the medieval system of inter-state relations in Europe relied upon three bodies of law: divine, human and natural law. Divine law should take precedence over other systems. The authority of the Pope was supreme to other sovereigns and European rulers tried to expand their authority invoking the support by the Pope to their action. Vitoria denied those positions and adopted natural law governed by secular sovereigns. Natural law is defined as norms established by the reason to govern relations between people (*Quod naturalis ratio intern omnes gentes constituit vocatur ius gentium*).[26] Unbelief cannot destroy the right of infidels, as those rights are not governed by divine law, but by human or natural one. The Pope could only exercise his power under divine law (interpreted and applied by him) in respect of catholic societies in Europe. He could not transfer sovereign rights with respect to Indians to the King of Spain (or emperor), as he never had those rights (according to the rule *nemo plus iuris in allium transferre potest, quam ipso habet*).

The emperor could not exercise his power over the infidels, too. As a papal authority any competence as to divine law cannot be granted to him. Additionally, human or natural law can be subjected to the authority of the emperor exclusively as far as the unbelievers were governed by him previously.

Francisco de Vitoria devoted a large part of his work to a theory of just war, a classical topic of philosophers, theologists and lawyers since ancient times.[27] The most important dissertation on the topic was *De Jure Belli Hispanorum in Barbaros*. However, he approached the issue not so much from a perspective of legitimization of the use of force (as we would say nowadays), but from the point of view of peace protection, which was his main interest (he was a true

26 Joseph Barthélemy, 'François de Vitoria' in *Les Fondateurs de droit international* (Paris 2014) 42.

27 On the concept and heritage of just war in the times of Vitoria see Denis Alland, 'Conquête espagnole des Indes, jugements sur les Indiens d'Amérique et doctrine de la guerre juste' (2007) 46 Droits – revue française de théorie juridique 29.

pacifist).[28] He seemed to support a position of individuals in relations to states, the process which was reversed after Vitoria and reached its apogee in the writings of H. Kelsen, identifying law with statehood. Another part of his writings concerned *ius in bello* (a limitation on the modalities of military activities).

The considerations on just war were necessary to formulate important thoughts about the position of Indians under international law. Vitoria was searching for a just title for Spanish conquerors with respect to the subjugation of the New World, ie for the formulation of a moral and legal title for colonial war.[29] There were two possible approaches to the topic. On the one hand, classical (European) international law could be adapted to a new phenomenon of colonialism. On the other hand, a fully new approach reflecting a new nature of relationship between Europeans and Indians could be elaborated and proposed. Vitoria opted for the latter stance and presented his position in the *Releccio on just war*, which is of much bigger importance than mere considerations on a conquest of America.

The works of Vitoria do not tend to consider the relations between Indians and the Spanish Kingdom as based on international law in a contemporary sense, ie as between equal states. They rather discuss theoretical and philosophical questions, like: Who is a sovereign? What are the powers of a sovereign? Are Indians sovereign? What are rights of Indians and Spaniards, and who decides about them? Those questions are important, because Vitoria attempts to find out a title of Spaniards to territory. He rejects the first option of occupation, as terra nullius only can be subjected to occupation. Indians had established a kind of state. Vitoria realized that because of different habits, customs and way of living, it might be difficult to base mutual relations of the two entities on a basis of existing systems. A new system of law should be elaborated to govern those relations.

At the times of Vitoria modern doctrine of sovereignty did not exist yet and that allowed Vitoria to elaborate a doctrine of mutual relations. Sovereignty means for Vitoria a relationship between the ruler (called Prince) and his population, imposing upon this ruler important obligations, but also as a set of rights and powers, including in particular a right to wage war, to acquire territories through military conflict, and to subordinate their population to their powers.

Furthermore, Vitoria rejected any argument of religious nature, ie based upon a notion of sin. He did not mix conscience and law. The Spanish scholastic

28 Ángela Aparisi Miralles, *Derecho a la paz y derecho a la guerra* (Granada 2007) 9.

29 Cf on that issue Marcelino Rodriguez Molinero, *La doctrina colonial de Francisco de Vitoria o el derecho de la paz y de la guerra. Un legado perenne de la escuela de Salamanca,* (Salamanca 1998), edn 2, passim.

school of philosophy and law was based upon justice (as one learned author wrote, the legacy of Greeks was philosophy and ethics, the legacy of Rome was law, and the one of the classical Spain empire was the idea of justice).

The war should be just and the justness must be somehow objectively identifiable. It does not suffice that the sovereign is subjectively convinced that he is right to start war. Vitoria reserves a right to wage war to Christian powers, by emphasizing that infidels ('Saracens') are *ex definitione* not capable to wage just war. They must be considered violators of laws of war, and therefore it is possible to apply in relation to them such methods of conducting war like carrying women and children into captivity and slavery. Moreover, if they are not sovereign, any conflict between Spaniards and Indians turns into war between sovereign and non-sovereign entity.

Finally, contrary to many of his contemporary writers, he did not consider Indians as animals nor any other non-human creatures. That does not mean that he recognized them as fully equal human beings, on equal footings with Christians. The transformation of Indians into a civilized society requires war, and this is the main reason of Vitoria's interest to the laws of war.[30] If the war is just from the perspective of the enemy (including Indians), measures applicable must be moderated and taking account of the requirements of humanity. The ignorant nature of Indians must be taken into account, as they are less developed than Spaniards.

4 On the Authority of the Pope and the Emperor over Infidels (*De potestatis Papae et Imperatoris Respectu Infidelium*)[31]

4.1 *The Views of Paulus Vladimiri*

The Order's advocates during the Council of Constance argued that the infidels possessed unjustly and sinfully the land they cultivated and their dominions. Neither recognizing nor obeying the power and the authority of the Roman Church, they were not fit to have kingdoms, governments, jurisdiction or dominion. Vladimiri opposed to those stances and developed his own theory on an international legal position of infidels. Włodkowic defined infidels as 'pagan nations who have not the faith of Christ.' However, they should be treated as human beings and therefore respected by Christians. Moreover, the friendship with infidels should not be condemned. In effect, the relationship

30 Barthélemy (n 26) 59.

31 We refer here to the title of the first paper by Paulus Vladimiri.

between Christians and non-Christians should be based on justice, which does not make a distinction between believers and non-believers. As the infidels are capable of moral qualities required for social and political life, they are also capable of managing and controlling their own political affairs. As the infidels have the same nature as Christians, they are bound by a divine law principle 'love the neighbour as thyself.' This is particularly true in respect of non-Christians living in peace and quiet neighbourhood, behaving decently.

Being men created by God, as Christians are, infidels have the same right to own material goods, according to the law of nations. All things belong to God, but men can occupy the territory and become owners; the original possessor has the prior right. The infidels should not be deprived of their property without legitimate cause. The violation of their rights is theft and – if carried by force – a robbery. Imperial donations concerning the infidels' land were therefore contrary to natural and divine law. Pagans have the right to defend their rights in international courts of justice in just the same manner as Christians because the right to self-defence is based on natural law. The testimony of a pagan before the court has the same force as the one by a Christian.

It is extremely important that Włodkowic rejected the papal grants to the Teutonic Order as null and void. He also emphasized that although the unbelievers may and should be stimulated to accept the catholic faith, they should not be converted into Christianity by force. A conversive war could not be called 'holy' but unjust or even pagan. Christian sovereigns can wage war against infidels in order to recover territories unjustly taken or to restore any rights violated. The infidels can deserve punishment if they committed crimes; however, a judicial proceeding being a precondition.

4.2 *The Views of Francisco de Vitoria*

Spanish discoveries in America posed a question whether local inhabitants should be qualified as human beings, or as savages (cercanos a su naturaleza a los monos que a seres humanos). They were also referred to as slaves, sinners, heathers, barbarians, minors, lunatics and animals.[32]

According to Vitoria, they should be treated as humans. If they were monos (ie monkeys), they could not be injured – and that was not the case. Therefore, it would be difficult to shrive conquerors from their cruelties and tyranny. Vitoria indicated in particular that Indians had their own magistrates, marriages, legal order, system of exchange involving a use of reason, and finally they had a sort

32 Antony Anghie, 'Francisco de Vitoria and the Colonial Origins of International Law' (1996) 5 Social Legal Studies 325.

of religion. They were governed by an own political system and they possessed institutions which corresponded to the ones of the European order. Moreover, they are treated by Spaniards as equal, as far as commercial exchange is concerned 'by importing thither wares the natives lack and by exporting thence either gold or silver or other wares the natives have abundance'.[33]

The relations between Spaniards and Indians are therefore subjected to the system of natural law (*jus gentium*) as subjected to the use of reason. The system is based upon freedom to travel, under a reservation that it does not lead towards a deprivation of property (Vitoria defines it as *jus communicationis*). Freedom of communication related in particular to domains which were not occupied by any territorial sovereign, like seas and international rivers. That was meant as support for freedom of commerce and Spanish penetration of Indian territories. Commerce is not limited to exchange of material goods, but covers also an exchange of ideas. Indians should be treated fairly and on an equal footing with Spaniards. However, Indians also have specific social conducts[34] which do not correspond to the 'ideal' conduct provided for the humans and Spaniards have a mission to transform their usages to bring them in conformity with the desirable pattern. This transformation is independent of the will of Indians. Moreover, Spaniards are ambassadors of Christianity in America and they are inviolable according to the law of nations; their status must be respected also by the Indians. If the natural right of free communication is denied, just war could be waged. Finally, as the new way to America was discovered by Spaniards, the Pope as a supervisor of a Christian mission should be competent to forbid travelling and communicating with India to other nations.[35]

Vitoria remained coherently and consequently distanced from the acceptance of a subjugation and subsequent annexation of Indian territories in the New World (nominated insular peoples). He wrote that violence applied against Indians combined elements of military, political and economic force. Economic violence consisted mostly upon a deprivation of possessed and cultivated land. Consequently, Indians were turned into slaves. A description of the fate of Indians by Vitoria is surprisingly sincere and full of compassion. Vitoria posed a question whether Indians were true owners of land under private and public law before the arrival of Spaniards. He answered that whatever their status was (and notwithstanding possible eternal punishment and

33 Francisco de Vitoria, De Indis, Section III, para. 389.

34 Vitoria analyzed in a detailed manner ways of living, rituals and customs of Indians, and on the basis of that review he drew conclusions as to the nature of American civilisation.

35 Johannes Thumfurt, 'On Grotius's *Mare Liberum* and Vitoria's *De Indis*, following Agamben and Schmitt' (2009) 30 Grotiana 82.

condemnation after their death), they could not be deprived of their land just because of their religious views.

The author was followed by a number of scholars regrouped in Salamanca who attempted at protecting inalienable rights of the local population in a surprisingly modern way.

Interestingly, those considerations were not only tolerated, but also supported by Spanish monarchs. Some of them considered to abandon an idea of occupying India. However, the presentation by Vitoria of a critical opinion on the rights of Indians and the lack of power of the Emperor was condemned by Charles v, who sent a letter to the prior of the Dominican convent in Salamanca criticizing the writings of Vitoria and other authors, and ordered that similar writings should not be published without a consent of the Court. On the other hand, his successors, Phillip II, enacted a general order for India in 1573. According to the order, a discovery of new territories was not automatically identical with a subjugation of the land. This should be done with maximum charity and compassion.

5 Summing up: Are the Writings by Paulus and Vitoria Still Actual?

The learned authors briefly presented above wrote their papers within the period of nearly 150 years, at the end of Middle Ages and outbreak of the modern era. We do not know whether Vitoria and Gentili read works by Skarbimirius and Paulus Vladimiri. Some ideas expressed by Vitoria remind us treatises by Włodkowic, but no direct quotations nor references can be found. This is comprehensible, as 100 years after the Council of Constance, the interest for a conflict between the Kingdom of Poland and the Teutonic Order was forgotten, in particular as the State of the Order in Prussia was dissolved and did not play any important role in European politics. As to Vitoria, *Releccion de iure belli* inspired not only Spanish followers (de Soto, Molina and Suarez), but also Grotius, Vattel and Pufendorf who further developed Vitoria's ideas. On the other hand, the teaching of Vitoria in respect of just war has not survived. Protection of individuals and vulnerable groups was to a large extent replaced by devastating military activities. The war became asymmetrical, and weaker groups were forced to use terrorism in order to oppose to omnipotent states.[36]

36 See a brilliant analysis of the influence of Vitoria by Peter Haggenmacher, 'La place de Francisco de Vitoria parmi les fondateurs de droit international' in *Actualité de pensée juridique de Francesco de Vitoria* (Bruxelles 1988) 27; Martti Koskenniemi, 'Vitoria and Us' (2014) 22 Rechtsgeschichte 119.

PART 2

Religious Institutions and Religious Law

CHAPTER 3

Le Saint-Siège en tant que sujet et acteur de droit international

Jean-Pierre Schouppe

Si le rôle que le Saint-Siège remplit sur la scène internationale est loin de s'amenuiser[1], notamment grâce à l'envergure et à la personnalité humaine des papes tels François, Benoît XVI ou Jean-Paul II, l'espace qui lui est dévolu dans les manuels de droit international semble, lui, en nette diminution, voire devenu inexistant[2]. C'est le constat que j'ai pu tirer après un passage en revue des ouvrages principalement français. La prise en compte de nouvelles matières du droit international appelant des solutions plus ou moins urgentes et se substituant progressivement à d'autres éléments plus classiques ou pacifiques ainsi que la croissante sécularisation pourraient expliquer cette évolution. Ce constat ne fait qu'ajouter à ma reconnaissance pour l'invitation qui m'a été aimablement adressée par les organisateurs de ce prestigieux colloque. Je tiens à exprimer toute ma gratitude pour l'honneur qui m'a été fait de pouvoir traiter de ce sujet avec vous aujourd'hui.

Plusieurs aspects contribuent à l'intérêt que présente la thématique : non seulement l'importance de la présence du Saint-Siège sur la scène internationale (un activisme qui suscite aussi des détracteurs), mais aussi la singularité de la religion catholique qui est la seule à présenter les traits d'unité hiérarchique, d'universalité et de respect effectif du dualisme (au sens canonique du terme)[3]. De plus, l'extrême diversité des opinions que la littérature juridique

---

1 Voir « La Santa Sede e le Organizzazioni Internazionali 2015 » (in *L'attività della Santa Sede nel 2010*, L.E.V., Cité du Vatican, 2016, pp. 1349–1398).

2 Ainsi P. Fauchille consacrait « au Pape » le livre II de la première partie de son *Traité de droit international public* (Ed. Rousseau, Paris, 1922, pp. 727–756).

3 Le « dualisme chrétien » – entre Dieu et César – ne correspond pas avec la distinction courante en droit international entre monisme et dualisme, qui s'articule sur la nécessité ou non d'une transposition de la norme internationale en droit interne. Le magistère de l'Église catholique et les canonistes ont à cœur de protéger ainsi l'existence de deux « puissances » – Etat et Eglise – et de deux sphères – temporelle et spirituelle –, chacun des deux pouvoirs jouissant d'une autonomie dans sa propre sphère. Le Concile Vatican II y a ajouté une libre coopération entre l'Eglise et l'Etat (Constitution *Gaudium et Spes*, n° 76c). Mais l'ordre canonique admet la prévalence des concordats sur le Code de droit canonique (voir canon 3 CIC 83 et canon 4 CCEO : *pacta sunt servanda*). Concernant l'histoire du dualisme, qu'il me soit permis

 | DOI:10.1163/9789004349155_004

reflète à l'égard du Saint-Siège et de sa personnalité juridique, surtout depuis 1870 et l'annexion des Etats pontificaux, mais aussi suite au Traité du Latran de 1929, appelle un nouvel essai de clarification de la thématique à la lumière de certains éléments appartenant à la période qui a suivi le concile Vatican II mais aussi de faits plus récents survenus sur la scène internationale.

Le Saint-Siège est intimement lié à l'Eglise catholique et à l'Etat de la Cité du Vatican. Le phénomène « trinitaire » – Saint-Siège-Vatican-Eglise catholique – qui se présente au regard de l'observateur soulève d'emblée la question de savoir s'il y existe un, deux ou trois sujets de droit international. Le caractère « *étatique* » ou non de ces sujets éventuels soulèvera une interrogation subsidiaire. Les nombreuses thèses discordantes qui ont vu le jour au XIXe et au XXe siècles et les clairs désaveux que la réalité historique leur a souvent infligés soulignent la nécessité impérative d'accorder une attention suffisante aux *faits* et à la *praxis*, en suivant le principe d'effectivité régissant le droit international. En l'absence d'une autorité *super partes* qualifiée, le recours au principe d'*effectiveness* permet d'établir la subjectivité internationale des entités[4]. Quant au Saint-Siège, il ne s'agit manifestement pas du cas de figure courant consistant à vérifier l'effectivité d'un contrôle exercé par un gouvernement sur un territoire et sur une population – ce test ne peut avoir de pertinence que vis-vis de l'Etat de la Cité du Vatican – mais plutôt d'observer sa présence et son action sur la scène internationale ainsi que le traitement que les autres sujets lui réservent, à commencer par les Etats. Dans le cadre de cette étude, il ne sera guère possible d'aborder systématiquement toute l'activité du Saint-Siège en droit international, bien que le titre de cette étude puisse le laisser supposer, mais sa présence active apparaîtra d'elle-même, comme en filigrane, dans la réponse qui sera apportée à la question des sujets.

Permettez-moi une brève remarque méthodologique préalable. La question des sujets de droit international doit être tranchée par le droit international. Il faudra donc se référer aux paramètres que le droit international prend en compte pour distinguer les sujets et ils devront être examinés à deux niveaux

---

de renvoyer au chapitre Ier de ma thèse : J.-P. Schouppe, *La dimension institutionnelle de la liberté de religion dans la jurisprudence de la Cour européenne des droits de l'homme*, Pedone, Paris, 2015, pp. 27–97.

4 Pour une présentation actuelle du concept d'effectivité qui est loin d'être univoque, voir H. Taki, « Effectiveness », in *Max Planch Encyclopedia of Public International Law* (consultée le 5 juillet 2016). Ledit principe peut notamment servir à justifier par les faits une situation ou un statut en droit international : « *many writers conceive effectiveness so narrowly as to indicate only phenomena in which a factual situation corresponding to legal status and legal rights exists* ».

différents[5]. Au niveau *du droit interne* (ici canonique ou vatican) s'apprécieront les éléments de souveraineté et d'autonomie d'ordre interne, l'auto-organisation des trois pouvoirs classiques, la population et le territoire, etc. Mais ces éléments requis pour la constitution d'un Etat au sens commun du terme ne sont pas des prérequis pour tout sujet de droit international. Ainsi, certaines de ces conditions ne sont pas réunies par un certain nombre de sujets aussi communément admis que l'ONU, la Croix-Rouge ou l'Ordre de Malte[6]. Les aspects les plus décisifs se rapportant à notre thématique relèveront de *l'ordre international* : entreront en ligne de compte la capacité d'entrer en relation avec d'autres sujets de droit international et de réaliser des actes juridiquement valides, l'adhésion aux règles et aux coutumes ainsi que le fait de faire l'objet de normes générales du droit international.

La méthode proposée permettra d'établir trois constats : l'omniprésence du Saint-Siège, la présence discrète de la Cité du Vatican et l'effacement total de l'Eglise catholique sur la scène internationale. En effet, cette dernière n'y intervient pas comme telle mais seulement à travers le Saint-Siège. De nombreux auteurs, n'envisageant même plus cette hypothèse, se bornent à traiter du Saint-Siège et de la Cité du Vatican. D'autres, comme Joe Verhoeven, continuent à évoquer l'Eglise, mais comme si sa personnalité juridique internationale était un futurible plutôt qu'une réalité[7]. Il arrive toutefois, comme c'est le cas en Israël, qu'il soit fait mention de la personnalité juridique de l'Eglise catholique dans un accord bilatéral mais, en l'occurrence, il s'agit d'une reconnaissance de la personnalité juridique de droit interne[8]. La question des sujets de droit international se jouera donc à deux.

---

5 V. Buonomo, « The Holy See in the Contemporary International Community : A Juridical Approach According to the International Law and Practice », *Civitas et Iustitia*, 2 (2004/1), pp. 7–40 spéc. pp. 12–13 ; *id.*, « Considerazioni sul rapporto Santa Sede-Comunità internazionale alla luce del diritto e della prassi internazionale », *Ius Ecclesiae*, 8 (1996), pp. 3–33 spéc. p. 8.

6 Voir E. Tawil, « La personnalité internationale de l'ordre souverain de Malte », *Annuaire Droit et religions*, t. 4, 2009–2010, pp. 475–482.

7 Voir J. Verhoeven, *Droit international public*, Larcier, Bruxelles, 2000, p. 269. Un certain nombre de canonistes ont soutenu ou continuent à défendre la thèse de la personnalité juridique internationale de l'Eglise catholique dans le cadre de la conception dualiste des rapports entre Eglise et Etat, mais il ne faut pas perdre de vue que la question des sujets de droit international est du ressort du droit international et pas du droit interne. Par ailleurs, le dualisme peut parfaitement s'accommoder de la seule personnalité juridique du Saint-Siège.

8 Voir Accord du 10 novembre 1997 entre le Saint-Siège et l'Etat d'Israël sur la personnalité juridique des institutions catholiques, dont l'article 2 dudit Accord prévoit la personnalité juridique des entités catholiques en Israël (*A.A.S.* 91 [1999], pp. 490–574).

1 Le Saint-Siège

Au-delà de la diversité d'opinions qui a traversé la doctrine juridique[9], un large consensus international a été atteint quant à la personnalité juridique du Saint-Siège, du moins à partir de la moitié du siècle dernier approximativement[10]. Il s'agit d'une personnalité juridique pour laquelle la possession d'un territoire et des autres éléments constitutifs d'un Etat n'est pas requise. Certains auteurs ont estimé devoir lier la personnalité internationale du Saint-Siège à l'existence d'une souveraineté temporelle et donc à un territoire et ils ont dès lors refusé de reconnaître la personnalité juridique internationale du

9 Une vision d'ensemble systématique de ces diverses théories est présentée dans H. Wagnon, *Concordats et droit international*, Duculot, Gembloux 1935, pp. 33 et s. ; *id.*, « La personnalité juridique du Saint-Siège en droit international. Les faits – Les doctrines », *Studia diplomatica*, 30 (1977/4) pp. 321–342.

10 Voir H. Wagnon, *Concordats et droit international*, *op. cit.*, p. 45 ; P.A. D'Avack, « Santa Sede », *Novissimo Digesto Italiano*, vol. XVI, Unione Tipografico, Torino, 1969, pp. 496–526 ; H.E. Cardinale, *The Holy See and the International Order*, Colin Smythe, Gerards Cross, 1976 ; S. Ferlito, *L'attività internazionale della Santa Sede*, Giuffrè, Milan, 1988 ; J.-B. d'Onorio, « Le Saint-Siège et le droit international », *in* J.-B. d'Onorio (dir.), *Le Saint-Siège dans les relations internationales*, Cerf – Cujas, Paris, 1989, pp. 17–18 ; G. Cheli, « La place et le rôle du Saint-Siège dans les organisations internationales », *ibid.*, p. 90 ; J.-Y. Rouxel, *Le Saint-Siège sur la scène internationale*, Th. Droit, Université de Rennes I, 1994, p. 37 ; M.-P. Lanfranchi, « L'accord fondamental du 30 décembre 1993 signé entre le Saint-Siège et Israël », *Annuaire Français de Droit international*, 40 (1994), pp. 328–329 ; G. Arangio-Ruiz (« junior »), « On the Nature of the International Personality of the Holy See », *Revue belge de droit international*, 29 (1996/2), pp. 354–369 ; C. García Martín, « El estatuto jurídico de la Santa Sede en las Naciones Unidas », *Ius Canonicum*, 38/75 (1998), pp. 247–289 ; G. Barberini, *Le Saint-Siège. Sujet souverain de droit international*, Cerf, Paris, 2003, p. 35 ; V. Buonomo, « The Holy See in the Contemporary International Comunity ... », *op. cit.*, pp. 7–40 ; K. Martens, « The Position of the Holy See and Vatican City State in International Relations », *University of Detroit Mercy Law Review*, 83 (2006), pp. 729–760 ; G. Westdickenberg, « Holy See », in *Max Planck Encyclopedia of Public International Law*, publié en juin 2006 (consulté le 5 juillet 2016) ; C. Walter, « Subjects of International Law », in *Max Planck Encyclopedia of Public International Law*, publié en mai 2007 (consulté le 18 juillet 2016) ; E. Tawil, « Eglise catholique, Saint-Siège et Etat de la Cité du Vatican : une, deux ou trois personnes juridiques de droit international? », *Folia Canonica*, 11 (2008), spéc. pp. 126–129 ; J. Combacau et S. Sur, *Droit international public*, 8e éd., Montchrétien-Lextenso, Paris 2008, p. 85 ; P. Daillier, M. Forteau et A. Pellet, *Droit international public*, 8e éd., L.G.D.J. – Lextenso, Paris 2009, pp. 505–508 ; J. González Ayesta, « La personalidad internacional de la Santa Sede : algunas claves de aproximación a un problema complejo », *in* M. Rodríguez-Blanco et J. González Ayesta (dir.), *Derecho internacional*, UNIR-Comares, Grenade, 2013, pp. 127–154.

Saint-Siège pendant l'éclipse étatique résultant de la *debellatio* (1870–1929). Cela les a conduits à orienter la solution de la *question romaine* vers l'octroi d'un support territorial sur lequel la souveraineté du Saint-Siège allait pouvoir s'exercer.

Le Saint-Siège – notion prise ici au sens strict de l'office du souverain pontife[11] – n'a pas attendu la création de l'Etat de la Cité du Vatican pour exercer une souveraineté sur le continent européen ; sa subsistance n'est pas tributaire de ce dernier. Faut-il rappeler que l'Evêque de Rome était déjà représenté au Ve siècle à la cour impériale de Constantinople par des *apocrisarii*[12]? Depuis lors, le Saint-Siège s'est signalé non seulement comme un précurseur mais aussi comme un acteur significatif de la diplomatie moderne ; et ce, bien avant que la *Respublica christiana* ait fait place à la communauté internationale résultant des traités de Wetsphalie conclus en 1648 entre Etats-parties de diverses confessions chrétiennes. Dans ce nouveau contexte, le Saint-Siège continuait d'exister comme sujet souverain mais avec un tout autre statut : il renonça à sa prééminence et à son rang de sujet supra-étatique pour s'accommoder du principe de l'égalité souveraine entre Etats. Depuis lors, le Saint-Siège n'a cessé de faire l'objet d'un traitement analogue à celui d'un Etat, même si, depuis la fin des Etats pontificaux en 1870, il a abdiqué le statut de puissance temporelle qui fut le sien depuis les lointaines donations territoriales de Pépin le Bref. En 1929, les Pactes du Latran lui ont restitué une souveraineté temporelle, certes symbolique, mais effective. Outre l'avènement d'un nouvel équilibre, la *question romaine* a démontré que sa souveraineté spirituelle suffisait à conserver la personnalité juridique internationale du Saint-Siège, ce qui donnait définitivement tort aux défenseurs inconditionnels du critère territorial ou d'une souveraineté strictement étatique.

A cet égard, il convient d'apporter quelques précisions. Bien que la souveraineté originaire du Saint-Siège découle de sa mission spirituelle, celle-ci fut historiquement liée à sa souveraineté temporelle dans le cadre pluriséculaire des Etats pontificaux. Le fait que, pendant le laps de temps correspondant à la *question romaine*, la souveraineté purement spirituelle d'un pape à la fois libre et « prisonnier » dans ses palais, ait suffi à maintenir la souveraineté du Saint-Siège ainsi que l'exercice de toutes ses activités sur la scène internationale apporte une preuve tangible de ce que la souveraineté spirituelle constitue bien l'élément principal et qu'elle peut être distinguée, voire détachée de toute souveraineté temporelle. Si la dimension temporelle

11 Cf. canon 331 C.I.C. 1983.

12 Voir notamment M. Cantori, *La diplomazia pontificia. Aspetti ecclesiastico-canonistici*, Tau Editrice, Todi 2016, pp. 31–35.

de la souveraineté a contribué à mettre en perspective l'indépendance de la papauté recherchée, la suspension de toute souveraineté temporelle, puis sa réapparition en 1929 sous une forme minimaliste et fonctionnelle, ont sans doute accru la crédibilité du dualisme revendiqué et augmenté l'autonomie pastorale effective des papes ainsi que leur prestige moral. Ceci dit, le droit international s'attache à la lecture des faits juridiques et se borne à constater de manière binaire l'existence ou l'absence d'une souveraineté *tout court*.

Mais, se demandera-t-on, pourquoi est-il question d'un « Etat » s'il s'agit d'un office personnel du pape? Le Saint-Siège a obtenu le statut d'observateur permanent à l'ONU en qualité d'« Etat observateur », c'est-à-dire d'Etat non membre, en vertu d'une résolution de 2004[13] qui a entériné le statut d'observateur permanent qu'il possédait déjà depuis le 6 avril 1964. Cette qualification induit à son tour une double explication.

Il convient tout d'abord de pointer du doigt l'ambiguïté du concept d'« Etat » en usage dans le droit international public. Les acteurs y jonglent avec deux acceptions différentes : d'une part, le concept classique de l'Etat composé de certains éléments constitutifs indiqués à l'article 1er du traité de Montevideo[14] ; d'autre part, une acception plus large que l'on observe notamment dans la Convention de Vienne sur le droit des traités de 1969 (article 1er)[15] ou dans le traité sur les immunités juridictionnelles de 2004. Ce dernier concept ne prend nullement en considération l'essence du sujet ou ses éléments constitutifs mais étend la personnalité internationale à des entités qui ne sont pas l'Etat, mais bien ses « organes », ses « composantes » ou ses « établissements » ...[16]. Même si, compte tenu de sa nature spécifique, l'applicabilité de cette situation au Saint-Siège est discutable, l'équivocité du terme « Etat » tel qu'il est utilisé en droit international n'est que trop claire. Si les deux traités susmentionnés parmi d'autres n'excluent pas le Saint-Siège de la catégorie « Etat », c'est seulement pour affirmer qu'il entre en ligne de compte comme destinataire de normes internationales, mais ils n'opèrent aucune qualification juridique du Saint-Siège. Sans être *qualifié* juridiquement d'Etat,

13 Résolution 58/314 de l'Assemblée générale de l'ONU en date du 16 juillet 2004 suivie d'une Note d'interprétation du Secrétariat général (cf. Doc. A/58/871).

14 Voir article 1er de la Déclaration de Montevideo du 27 décembre 1933 sur les droits et devoirs des Etats (V° Conférence panaméenne). Mais les éléments indiqués ne sont pas toujours considérés comme décisifs ou suffisamment précis.

15 Ce traité compte le Saint-Siège parmi les « Etats » destinataires de ces normes.

16 *Convention des Nations Unies sur les immunités juridictionnelles des Etats et de leurs biens* du 2 décembre 2004, article 2.

celui-ci est *traité* comme un « Etat » (*a fortiori* accepté comme un sujet de droit international), sans qu'il lui soit nécessaire de procéder à une analyse préalable de son droit interne.

Lorsque la Commission du droit international des Nations Unies a préparé la Convention sur le droit des traités, elle était parfaitement consciente de cette situation. Les projets de statuts pour le Saint-Siège à l'ONU, élaborés à partir de 1959, avaient envisagé de mentionner des « Etats » et « d'autres sujets de droit international comme des sujets capables de conclure des traités ». Ces spécifications finalement non retenues auraient sans doute permis de remédier à cette ambivalence notionnelle[17].

La seconde explication a trait à la nature spécifique du Saint-Siège et au caractère adéquat du statut d'« observateur permanent ». Alors que la qualification d'« Etat membre » lui aurait ouvert le droit de participation aux votes, le statut actuel permet d'atteindre les finalités spécifiques poursuivies – présence dans les conférences et organisations, participation aux débats, communication des documents, etc. – sans avoir à prendre position dans des questions politiques ou temporelles qui ne correspondraient pas à sa nature spécifique ou à ses engagements internationaux. Ainsi, en cas de guerre, mis à part l'inexistence d'une armée du Vatican faisant le poids, la participation du Saint-Siège à un conflit armé violerait l'obligation de neutralité assumée par celui-ci dans le traité du Latran[18].

L'occupation par le Saint-Siège d'une position « équivalente ou semblable » à celle d'un Etat n'équivaut pas à l'affirmation de son « identité » avec les Etats : la sorte d'autolimitation découlant de sa mission spirituelle et humanitaire, qu'il se doit de respecter et de faire respecter, n'empêche nullement le Saint-Siège d'être traité comme un Etat[19]. S'il est vrai qu'il constitue une *réalité sui generis*, ce serait pour autant une erreur de le réduire au rang d'un *sujet sui generis* : loin d'être un sujet de seconde catégorie, il bénéficie d'une personnalité *pleno iure* de nature gouvernementale[20] ; il est un sujet « primaire », « *non recognoscens superiorem*», l'égal d'un Etat.

Une dernière observation concernant le Saint-Siège. Sa souveraineté et sa qualité de sujet de droit international découlent clairement du traité du Latran et des accords qui ont suivi. Contribuent également à les refléter : de

17 Voir G. Barberini, *Le Saint-Siège. Sujet souverain de droit international*, *op. cit.*, p. 66.

18 Cf. article 24.1 du Traité du Latran.

19 Voir J. González Ayesta, « La personalidad internacional de la Santa Sede … », *op. cit.*, p. 154.

20 G. Barberini, *Le Saint-Siège. Sujet souverain de droit international*, *op. cit.*, p. 68.

nombreux concordats[21], non moins de 185 relations diplomatiques stables[22], des arbitrages et médiations comme la médiation entre l'Argentine et le Chili dans le conflit relatif au Canal de Beagle (1979–1984), ainsi que sa participation active à de nombreuses conférences et organisations internationales qu'il serait trop long d'énumérer ici. Outre ces facteurs qui affirment l'effectivité de sa présence en droit international, en accord avec certains auteurs, il peut être précisé que, du point de vue des sources du droit international, c'est « une norme coutumière le visant spécifiquement » qui a d'abord valu au Saint-Siège la qualité de sujet de droit international[23]. Cette règle coutumière au fondement de son statut, qui « ne pourrait pas être abrogée ou modifiée sans le consentement du Saint-Siège lui-même »[24], représente même la protection la plus solide de sa qualité de sujet de droit international.

2 L'Etat de la Cité du Vatican

La dénomination d'« Etat » ne suffit pas à démontrer par elle-même la qualité étatique d'une entité, à l'instar de certains Etats fédérés, auxquels font défaut certains éléments constitutifs de l'Etat, notamment la souveraineté internationale qui est l'apanage de l'Etat fédéral. Le traité de Montevideo établit quatre éléments constitutifs de l'Etat : population stable, territoire défini, gouvernement souverain et capacité d'entrer en relation avec d'autres Etats[25]. Ces dernières décennies, la praxis de l'ONU accorde davantage d'importance à la

21 Les concordats peuvent être consultés dans A. Mercati, *Raccolta di concordati su materie ecclesiastiche tra la Santa Sede e le Autorità civili*, vol. I, 1098–1914 ; vol. II, 1915–1954, Cité du Vatican, Tipografia Poliglotta Vaticana, 1919 et 1954 ; J.T. Martín de Agar, *Raccolta di concordati, 1950–1999*, Cité du Vatican, Librairie éditrice Vaticane, 2000 ; *id.*, *I concordati del 2000 al 2009*, Cité du Vatican, Librairie éditrice Vaticane, 2010 ; R. Minnerath, *L'Eglise catholique face aux Etats. Deux siècles de pratique concordataire 1801–2010*, Cerf, Paris, 2012.

22 Voir la *Note de la salle de presse du Vatican sur les relations diplomatiques* du 9 janvier 2018 http://fr.zenit.org/articles : dernière consultation le 9 janvier 2018.

23 C. Dominicé, « L'accord de siège conclu par le Comité International de la Croix-Rouge avec la Suisse », *Revue générale de droit international public*, 99 (1995/1), p. 16.

24 E. Tawil, « Eglise catholique, Saint-Siège et Etat de la Cité du Vatican … », *op. cit.*, p. 129.

25 Article 1 « The state as a person of international law should possess the following qualifications : a) permanent population ; b) a defined territory ; c) government ; and d) capacity to enter into relations with the other states.» (http://www.cfr.org/sovereignty/montevideo-convention-rights-duties-states/p15897;dernièreconsultationle23septembre 2016).

capacité d'entrer en relation avec d'autres sujets et à son acceptation par la communauté internationale[26].

S'il est possible de démontrer que ces différents éléments sont présents dans le cas de la Cité du Vatican, c'est au prix d'une interprétation spécifique veillant à considérer la Cité du Vatican en étroite union avec le Saint-Siège[27]. Les critères sont les suivants :

1) Une population d'environ 800 citoyens et de quelques centaines de résidents principalement composée de titulaires de fonctions (*ius officii*) ou des membres de leurs familles ; cette population n'est pas permanente, comme le requiert le critère analysé, mais elle assure une stabilité suffisante pour remplir le but poursuivi ;
2) Un territoire dont l'exiguïté (44 hectares) n'est pas problématique car il existe des micro-Etats et surtout cette superficie réduite, qui a été souhaitée, suffit à la tâche particulière assignée à la Cité du Vatican ;
3) Un gouvernement indépendant : la Cité dispose d'instances législatives, exécutives (*Governatorato*) et judiciaires régies par le droit interne du Vatican et les charges de gouvernement sont confiées à des titulaires différents des autorités de la curie romaine[28]. Mais, s'agissant de la définition d'un Etat souverain, l'autorité gouvernementale doit être souveraine. Or il est permis d'objecter que la Cité du Vatican ne jouit pas elle-même de la souveraineté – elle n'en est pas *dépositaire* – mais bénéficie de la souveraineté du Saint-Siège. L'Etat résultant de telles prémisses fut qualifié d'« Etat atypique » par Jean-Paul II[29]. Abondant dans le même sens, la doctrine a souligné, à l'aide de plusieurs expressions (Etat-patrimoine, Etat-moyen, Etat-fonction…), le caractère organiquement subordonné et instrumental de cet Etat par rapport au Saint-Siège et à la mission ecclésiale.

26 Voir United Nations, *Yearbook of the International Law Commission*, New York, 1949, spec. p. 68.

27 Voir H.E. Cardinale, *The Holy See and the International Order, op. cit.*, 1976, pp. 104–115. C'est également la position défendue par H. Wagnon, *Concordats et droit international, op. cit.*, p. 61 ; J.-B. d'Onorio, « Le Saint-Siège et le droit international », *op. cit.*, pp. 21–35.

28 Voir par exemple la *Loi fondamentale*, entrée en vigueur en 2001, et la *Loi sur les sources* de l'Etat de la Cité du Vatican. Pour un aperçu de l'organisation d'ensemble, voir notamment J.I. Arrieta, *Codice di norme vaticane*, Marcianum Press, Venise, 2006.

29 Jean-Paul II, Lettre *La Sede Apostolica au Cardinal Agostino Casaroli, Secrétaire d'Etat*, 20 novembre 1982 (*A.A.S.* 75 [1983], pars I, n. 2, pp. 119–125).

A l'appui de cette thèse, les articles 3 et 26 du Traité politique conclu au Latran entre l'Italie et le Saint-Siège établissent que la souveraineté sur le Vatican revient au Saint-Siège et nullement au nouvel « Etat » créé comme support de ce dernier. C'est ainsi que « l'Italie reconnaît au Saint-Siège la pleine propriété, le pouvoir exclusif et absolu de la juridiction souveraine sur le Vatican » (article 3). L'article 26 du même traité est on ne peut plus clair : « L'Italie reconnaît l'Etat de la Cité du Vatican sous la souveraineté du Souverain Pontife ». Plutôt qu'un Etat souverain distinct du Saint-Siège, émerge ainsi la souveraineté du Saint-Siège sur le territoire de la Cité du Vatican.

Quant à l'article 24 dudit pacte, il précise que « la Cité du Vatican sera toujours et en tous cas considérée comme un territoire neutre et inviolable ». Certains auteurs ont cru y apercevoir, plutôt qu'un Etat, un territoire à statut international spécial (immunités, extraterritorialité…) destiné à assurer « un service public international » au service du Saint-Siège et sous sa totale dépendance plutôt qu'un Etat[30], mais la volonté des parties au Traité du Latran était indubitablement de constituer un Etat. À l'époque, cette solution était jugée indispensable pour garantir l'indépendance et la souveraineté du Saint-Siège. Mais cet Etat au sens formel du terme a pour finalité d'assurer l'indépendance du Saint-Siège qui exerce sa souveraineté sur ce minuscule territoire[31].

Que faut-il penser des concordats qui reconnaissent expressément une personnalité internationale au Saint-Siège *et* à l'Etat de la Cité du Vatican[32]? La reconnaissance d'Etat est en soi dépourvue de valeur juridique *erga omnes* ; elle donne seulement un signal politique que les autres sujets apprécieront librement parmi d'autres éléments. C'est pourquoi, même si, par cet acte, l'Etat « reconnaissant » s'engage à accorder un traitement d'Etat à une nouvelle collectivité politique dans leurs relations futures, la reconnaissance de la personnalité juridique jouit seulement d'une valeur déclarative et non constitutive en droit international[33].

---

30 Ainsi d'aucuns ne reconnaissent à la Cité du Vatican que « l'apparence d'un Etat » : P. Daillier, M. Forteau et A. Pellet, *Droit international public*, *op. cit.*, p. 506. C. Rousseau rejetait à la fois le caractère étatique et la personnalité juridique internationale de la Cité du Vatican (« Etat de la Cité du Vatican », *Revue générale de droit international public*, 37 [1930], pp. 145–153).

31 Voir V. Buonomo, « Vatican », in *Encyclopedia of World Constitutions* (edited by Gerhard Robbers), Facts on File, New York, 2007, pp. 1006–1011, spéc. p. 1007.

32 Notamment les concordats entre le Saint-Siège et l'Espagne (1953), la République Dominicaine (1954) et le Venezuela (1964).

33 Voir J. Combacau et S. Sur, *Droit international public*, 8e éd., Montchrétien-Lextenso, Paris 2008, p. 289. La position contraire défendue par L. Oppenheim et H. Lauterpacht,

A la différence du Saint-Siège, dont la personnalité juridique est antérieure à l'ordre international lui-même, l'existence de l'Etat du Vatican remonte seulement à 1929. Ce dernier est membre de certaines organisations internationales, notamment de l'Union internationale des communications (UIT) et de l'Union postale universelle (UPU). Ces deux organisations sont devenues des agences spécialisées de l'ONU mais, de manière significative, c'est avec le Saint-Siège que cette dernière organisation est entrée en relation. Par ailleurs, plusieurs dizaines de conventions conclues avec des organismes internationaux concernant la Cité du Vatican ont été signées par le Saint-Siège[34]. Derrière la dénomination « Etat du Vatican », la communauté internationale reconnaît donc communément le Saint-Siège. Un regard sur le recueil des traités de l'ONU suffit pour constater que le Vatican y est considéré comme un synonyme du Saint-Siège[35]. Venons-en au quatrième et dernier élément.

4) La capacité d'entrer en relation avec d'autres Etats, manifeste dans le cas du Saint-Siège, ne peut être affirmée aussi catégoriquement à l'endroit de la Cité du Vatican dans la mesure où les relations de cet Etat atypique avec les autres sujets de droit international se font toujours à travers le Saint-Siège. Le cas échéant, ce dernier interviendra au nom et pour le compte de l'Etat de la Cité du Vatican.

Ainsi, en matière de traités, il est observé que les domaines faisant l'objet d'accords pour le compte du Vatican sont le plus souvent d'ordre temporel ou technique. Ils concernent principalement l'administration du territoire : accords douaniers et monétaires, services postaux, télégraphes et téléphones, chemins de fer, collaboration policière et judiciaire, notification des actes en matière civile et en matière commerciale, etc[36]. Ces questions sont généralement confiées à l'Etat du Vatican, tandis que les sujets religieux ou éthiques, les droits de l'homme ou la recherche de la paix … relèvent prioritairement de la mission dévolue au Saint-Siège. La tendance à accentuer la présence active du Vatican

---

International Law. A Treatise, vol. I : *Peace*, 8e éd., Edinburgh, 1962, p. 12) fut abandonnée après la Seconde guerre mondiale.

34 Voir H. de Riedmatten, « Présence du Saint-Siège dans les organismes internationaux », *Concilium*, 58 (1970), pp. 67–82.

35 Voir <https://treaties.un.org/pages/UNTSOnline.aspx?id=3&clang=_fr> consulté le 21 octobre 2016.

36 Voir, par exemple, la convention monétaire signée entre « la République italienne au nom de la Communauté européenne, et l'Etat de la Cité du Vatican représenté par le Saint-Siège conformément à l'article 3 du Traité du Latran », *Journal Officiel des Communautés européennes*, n° C 299 du 25 octobre 2001, pp. 1–4.

s'explique par une option initiale qui semble se limiter à la période 1929–1932[37]. Par la suite, cette « politique » fut modifiée de façon à mettre en exergue le fait que le sujet de droit international est toujours le Saint-Siège, même lorsque la dénomination employée est celle de la « Cité du Vatican ». Cette relative différenciation des matières (spirituelles ou temporelles) n'autorise nullement une division de la souveraineté du Saint-Siège. En effet, le droit international s'attache à la vérification de la souveraineté correspondant à chaque sujet potentiel, mais il ne s'encombre guère de distinctions entre souveraineté spirituelle et matérielle. La praxis révèle que, lorsque le Saint-Siège prend un engagement international « au nom et pour le compte de » la Cité du Vatican, c'est bien au premier qu'est imputée l'obligation internationale qui en découle[38].

Après avoir constaté que les relations diplomatiques s'effectuent à travers le Saint-Siège[39], il est possible d'analyser l'action de ce dernier en sa qualité de gouvernement de la Cité du Vatican. Procéder de la sorte revient à observer la réalité complexe Saint-Siège et Vatican formant une « union organique » [40], ce qui permet d'établir l'unicité du sujet de droit international[41].

L'affirmation d'un seul sujet de droit international empêche-t-elle de soutenir la thèse selon laquelle l'Etat de la Cité du Vatican jouirait à tout le moins d'une capacité juridique limitée au plan international? La doctrine continue à être divisée à ce sujet. Il paraît toutefois difficile de refuser à la Cité du Vatican

---

37 Voir S. Ferlito, *L'attività internazionale della Santa Sede, op. cit.*, spéc. pp. 144–145.

38 J.-B. d'Onorio, « Le Saint-Siège et le droit international », *op. cit.*, p. 32.

39 « Aucun Etat n'entretient de rapports diplomatiques avec l'Etat du Vatican, afin de respecter son caractère instrumental par rapport au Saint-Siège » (G. Barberini, *Le Saint-Siège. Sujet souverain de droit international, op. cit.*, p. 83). En conséquence, note C. Cardia, « La Cité du Vatican ne saurait avoir de « vie politique autonome » (C. Cardia, *Ordinamenti religiosi e ordinamento dello Stato*, Bologna, 2003, p. 40). Il est néanmoins important que l'Italie se soit engagée à reconnaître l'indépendance de ce territoire aux allures d'Etat et ait même tenu à constitutionnaliser les pactes du Latran (cf. E. Tawil, « Les relations conventionnelles entre l'Etat et les religions en Italie », *Cahiers de la recherche sur les Droits fondamentaux*, 4 (2005), pp. 139–156).

40 L'usage par la doctrine, en ordre dispersé, des notions d'union personnelle, union réelle, Etat vassal ou encore au régime de protectorat se sont avérées tout à fait inadéquates, entre autres parce qu'il ne s'agit pas ici de deux Etats en relation, le Saint-Siège n'étant pas un Etat, au sens commun du terme. L'union organique dont il est question ici est sans correspondant en droit international.

41 Il ne serait pas exact d'escamoter la dimension de sujet revenant depuis toujours au Saint-Siège et de retenir uniquement sa fonction de gouvernement de l'Etat de la Cité du Vatican comme si ce dernier était le sujet souverain (voir A. Bettetini, « Sul titolo giuridico di partecipazione della Santa Sede alle organizzazioni e alle Conferenze interazionali », *Il diritto ecclesiastico*, 1996/3–4, II, pp. 714–734, spéc. pp. 727 et s.).

une certaine capacité juridique internationale mais, dans le même temps, il importe aussi de prendre en considération la dépendance organique de cette dernière par rapport au Saint-Siège. Ferlito a tiré de ce constat des conséquences radicales : vu l'absence de souveraineté et de diplomatie propres ainsi que l'imputation au Saint-Siège des obligations internationales prises au nom et pour le compte de la Cité du Vatican, celle-ci est alors réduite à un simple « organe » du Saint-Siège[42]. S'il semble nécessaire de ne pas ignorer la qualité d'Etat atypique revenant à la Cité du Vatican, ce qui lui permet une certaine participation à la communauté internationale et donc une certaine capacité juridique, il ne saurait toutefois être question d'une pleine capacité juridique équivalente à celle d'un sujet primaire de droit international.

Une solution alternative à l'unicité du sujet est-elle envisageable? Elle consisterait à poser que le Saint-Siège et l'Etat du Vatican, tout en étant réunis par un organe commun (le Saint-Siège), auraient deux personnalités juridiques internationales distinctes. Cette seconde interprétation, soutenue par des auteurs éminents[43], ne semble toutefois pas donner une réponse satisfaisante aux observations qui viennent d'être formulées. Si, comme l'affirme justement García Martín[44], il est exact que l'Etat du Vatican et le Saint-Siège ont tendance à se différencier par leur nature (Etat instrumental *versus* gouvernement de l'Eglise), par leur finalité et domaine d'intervention (service technique local *versus* spirituel et moral universel) ainsi que par leur mode de présence dans les organisations internationales (le plus souvent membre *versus* observateur permanent), il peut sembler peu conforme à la réalité du droit international de considérer celles-ci comme deux personnes juridiques distinctes situées sur le même plan l'une par rapport à l'autre et unies par le Pontife romain comme organe commun.

Dès lors, même s'il est hasardeux de refuser à la Cité du Vatican un certain degré de capacité juridique internationale, le Saint-Siège, comme cela vient

42 S. Ferlito, *L'attività internazionale della Santa Sede*, Giuffrè, Milan, 1988, spéc. pp. 144–145.

43 Notamment H. Wagnon, *Concordats et droit international*, *op. cit.*, pp. 63–64 ; H.E. Cardinale, *The Holy See and the International Order*, *op. cit.*, pp. 115–117 ; C. García Martín, « El estatuto jurídico de la Santa Sede en las Naciones Unidas », *Ius Canonicum*, 38/75 [1998], pp. 262–264. Cela semble aussi être le point de vue de J.C González Ayesta, même s'il doit bien reconnaître que « la présence et la position [de la Cité du Vatican] sont beaucoup moins intenses que celles du Saint-Siège, en raison duquel elle existe et à travers lequel elle agit au plan international » [traduction de l'auteur] (J. González Ayesta « La personalidad internacional de la Santa Sede : algunas claves de aproximación a un problema complejo », *op. cit.*, p. 154).

44 Voir C. García Martín, « El estatuto jurídico de la Santa Sede en las Naciones Unidas », *op. cit.*, pp. 265–266.

d'être montré, est bien le seul sujet *pleno iure* au niveau du droit international, que ce soit pour engager l'Eglise catholique (au nom du Saint-Siège) ou la Cité du Vatican, ou les deux entités à la fois[45]. Le Saint-Siège effectue ces diverses interventions en qualité de « *centre d'imputation* de droits et de devoirs »[46]. Cette personnalité juridique constitutive de la titularité des droits et d'obligations est acceptée tant par le Saint-Siège lui-même que par la communauté internationale[47].

A ce stade de la réflexion, une nuance importante s'impose. Si, du *point de vue des sujets* considérés, le Saint-Siège est bien le seul sujet de droit international *pleno iure*, il n'est pas dit que cette perspective soit la seule envisageable. Il semble également légitime d'appréhender *le phénomène complexe* Saint-Siège uni à la Cité du Vatican. Cette perspective complémentaire (Saint-Siège-Vatican) permet à la Cité du Vatican d'affirmer qu'ainsi (à travers le Saint-Siège) elle est capable de satisfaire aux exigences susmentionnées inhérentes à un sujet de droit international[48]. La Cité du Vatican, sans être elle-même un sujet de droit international, possède à tout le moins une capacité d'agir de droit international analogue à celle d'une entreprise transnationale ou d'un individu qui sont habilités à recourir devant une Cour régionale des droits de l'homme. En revanche, dès qu'entrent en jeu des prérogatives qui sont l'apanage d'un sujet de droit international, comme la conclusion d'un traité ou l'établissement de relations diplomatiques, le Saint-Siège, en sa qualité de sujet, devra intervenir dans une fonction de représentation de la Cité du Vatican.

3 Considérations conclusives sur la souveraineté du Saint-Siège

Le Saint-Siège apparaît clairement comme le sujet qui opère en droit international : c'est au pape (ou, le cas échéant, au secrétaire d'Etat) qu'il revient

45 Par exemple, le Saint-Siège a adhéré le 19 septembre 2016 à la Convention contre la corruption en son nom et au nom de l'Etat de la Cité du Vatican.

46 G. Barberini, *Le Saint-Siège. Sujet souverain de droit international*, *op. cit.*, p. 35.

47 Voir V. Buonomo, « The Holy See in the Contemporary International Community ... », *op. cit.*, p. 16 ; *id.*, « Considerazioni sul rapporto Santa Sede-Comunità internazionale alla luce del diritto e della prassi internazionale », *Ius Ecclesiae*, 8 (1996), p. 11.

48 C'est ainsi que prend tout son sens l'affirmation suivante : « *The Vatican possesses independence and sovereignty not only with reference to its internal powers and domestic jurisdiction, but also in respect of international relations : conclusion of international treaties, relations with other states, participations in international meetings and conferences, and membership in intergovernmental organizations* » (V. Buonomo, « Vatican », in *Encyclopedia of World Constitutions*, *op. cit.*, p. 1008).

d'entrer en relation avec d'autres sujets de droit international ; être destinataire de règles coutumières et conventionnelles au niveau international ; exercer le droit d'envoyer et d'accréditer des représentants diplomatiques (*ius legationis*) ; signer les traités internationaux bilatéraux et multilatéraux (*ius contrahendi*) ; effectuer un arbitrage ou une médiation ; prendre part aux grandes conférences internationales …

Du point de vue de la « réalité complexe » ou unité organique Saint-Siège-Vatican, la praxis du Saint-Siège en matière de traités comporte l'utilisation de la formule : accord signé « entre le Saint-Siège et tel Etat »[49] ou/et « au nom et pour le compte de l'Etat de la Cité du Vatican »[50]. Cette clause revêt une grande valeur interprétative : le Saint-Siège n'agit pas seulement comme représentant ou organe de la Cité du Vatican ou de l'Eglise catholique, mais il s'affirme comme le véritable centre d'imputation des droits et obligations internationales. Dans tous ces cas de figure, loin d'agir simplement comme gouvernement d'un autre sujet, le Saint-Siège réalise des « faits juridiquement propres »[51].

La souveraineté du Saint-Siège n'implique donc nullement l'affirmation de *deux sujets* de droit international : le Saint-Siège et l'Etat de la Cité du Vatican[52]. Le Saint-Siège est le sujet dont la souveraineté rejaillit sur l'Etat du Vatican. Un courant important de la doctrine juridique analyse cette situation en recourant à l'explication suivante : le pape exerce un *double titre de souveraineté* sur deux entités différentes – l'Eglise catholique et la Cité du Vatican – qui poursuivent des finalités harmonisées et complémentaires[53]. Cette souplesse du modèle

49 Cette formule a été utilisée le 1er avril 2015 lors d'une convention entre le Saint-Siège et le Gouvernement de la République italienne en matière fiscale (<www.vatican.va/roman_curia/secretariat_state/2015/documents/rc-seg-st-20150401convenzione-materia-fiscale-italia-testo-definitivo.pdf> consulté le 21 juillet 2016).

50 La seconde a été employée dans l'accord conclu le 10 juin 2015 avec les États-Unis d'Amérique pour favoriser l'observance des obligations fiscales au niveau international et mettre en œuvre la *Foreign Account Tax Compliance Act* (FATCA) <www.vatican.va/roman_curia/secretariat_state/2015/documents/rc-seg-st-20150610_accordo-scv-usa-fatca-comunicato_it.html> consulté le 21 juillet 2016.

51 S. Ferlito, *L'attività internazionale della Santa Sede*, *op. cit.*, p. 53.

52 Comme semble toutefois le suggérer le commentaire figurant sur le site officiel de la Cité du Vatican : « Reconnu comme Etat souverain de droit public international, distinct du Saint-Siège, il est universellement reconnu » <www.vaticanstate.va/content/vaticanstate/fr/stato-e-governo/note-generali.html> consulté le 17 juillet 2016.

53 Outre S. Ferlito, G. Barberini et V. Buonomo, qui ont déjà été cités, soutiennent cette position avec certaines nuances les auteurs suivants : P. Ciprotti, « Le Saint-Siège : sa fonction, sa figure et sa valeur dans le Droit international », *Concilium* 58 (1970), pp. 57–66 ; J.R. Giandurco, *The Holy See as a Juridical Subject « sui iuris » in international* Law, Pontificia

théorique est décelable dans les faits. Elle a notamment permis au Saint-Siège de modifier sans la moindre difficulté le sujet participant à certaines organisations internationales de la constellation ONU[54]. Le droit international gagnerait toutefois en clarté en évitant un « emploi indistinct » des expressions « Saint-Siège » et « Etat de la Cité du Vatican ».

Enfin, je souhaiterais ne pas terminer cette étude sans faire rapport d'un récent arrêt de la Cour d'appel de Gand qui vient corroborer la position préconisée ici. L'affaire tranchée visait à engager la responsabilité civile du Saint-Siège (ainsi que celle des évêques belges concernés). Cette thématique, désormais courante aux Etats-Unis, constitue, à ma connaissance, une « première » en Europe[55]. L'arrêt de la Cour d'appel reprend à son compte la substance de l'argumentation du Tribunal de première instance de Gand. Il s'appuie sur une série d'arrêts rendus aux Etats-Unis depuis une quinzaine d'années qui reconnaissent au Saint-Siège la qualité de « souverain étranger ». C'est à ce titre que l'arrêt belge prononce l'immunité d'Etat au profit du Saint Siège, ce qui implique aussi la jouissance d'une immunité de juridiction[56]. Même si celui-ci

Universitas S. Thomae Romae, 1994, pp. 187–194 ; V. Prieto, *Diritto dei rapporti tra Chiesa e società civile*, Edusc, Roma, 2003, pp. 153–154 ; E. López-Jacoiste Díaz, « Personalidad internacional de la Santa Sede », in *Diccionario general de Derecho canónico*, vol. VI, (J. Otaduy, A. Viana et J. Sedano (dir.)), Universidad de Navarra – Thomson Reuters Aranzadi, Pamplona, 2012, pp. 195–198. G. Westdickenberg (« Holy See », *op. cit.*) est très clair : « *The relationship between the two distinct legal entities can be defined in such a way that the sovereign of both the Vatican State and the Holy See is the Pope and that the Vatican State constitutes the territorial basis for the Holy See, which has unimpeded sovereign powers and jurisdiction over the Vatican State* ».

54 G. Barberini, *Le Saint-Siège. Sujet souverain de droit international*, *op. cit.*, p. 44. Le Saint-Siège effectua en 1960 une rectification du sujet qui conforte le modèle proposé : le remplacement de l'Etat de la Cité du Vatican par le Saint-Siège comme membre fondateur de l'Agence internationale pour l'énergie atomique (AIEA) depuis 1957, lorsque le Saint-Siège fut prié de prendre part aux travaux de cette organisation intergouvernementale liée aux Nations-Unies en tant que ferment de paix. Une modification du même type fut opérée en 1975 dans le cadre de l'Organisation mondiale de la propriété intellectuelle (OMPI).

55 Cour d'appel de Gand (1ère Ch.), *Verschueren et al. c. Saint-Siège, évêques belges et supérieurs religieux*, 25 février 2016, 203/AR/2889, n° 3.3 (dorénavant abrégée *Verschueren c. Saint-Siège*). L'arrêt est définitif et, à ce jour, non publié. Un recours a été intodruit à Strasbourg : *J. C. et 23 autres c. Belgique*.

56 A cet égard, le Saint-Siège est à considérer comme souverain étranger par rapport à la juridiction saisie, en l'occurrence américaine. Il y a lieu de consulter les arrêts *O'Bryan v. Holy See* et *Doe v. Holy See* (*State of the Vatican City*). Ceux-ci prennent en compte le *Foreign Sovereign Immunities Act* (FSIA) approuvé en 1976, qui prive les tribunaux fédéraux de juridiction et de compétence pour être saisis de requêtes concernant des Etats

comporte de nombreuses autres facettes, notamment en matière de responsabilité civile, je me bornerai à synthétiser succinctement quelques aspects du droit international public qui sont en rapport direct avec le sujet traité :

1) La Cour d'appel reconnaît la personnalité juridique du Saint-Siège et sa souveraineté, à « double titre » [57].
2) Elle déclare au profit du Saint-Siège l'immunité de juridiction dont il bénéficie en qualité de « souverain étranger »[58].
3) L'immunité d'Etat – pas simplement l'immunité diplomatique – revient au Saint-Siège en tant que « souverain étranger ayant les mêmes droits et obligations qu'un Etat »[59] ; elle est *ratione personae* et, tout comme la souveraineté, elle est « une et indivisible »[60].
4) L'indivisibilité de la souveraineté implique qu'il n'est pas possible d'accorder au pape une immunité de juridiction en tant que Chef de l'Etat de la Cité du Vatican, tout en la lui refusant en sa qualité de souverain pontife de l'Eglise[61].
5) L'arrêt rejette l'identification de l'Eglise au Saint-Siège[62].
6) La Cour confirme que l'Eglise catholique ne jouit pas de la personnalité juridique, que ce soit dans l'ordre international ou dans l'ordre interne (belge)[63].

étrangers ainsi que leurs « *instrumentalities* », agences et fonctionnaires. Un bon aperçu de cette jurisprudence américaine est disponible dans H. Fox et P. Webb, *The Law of State Immunity*, 3° ed., Oxford International Law 2013, pp. 238 et s. Concernant les affaires dans lesquelles le Saint-Siège était impliqué, voir N. Zambrana Tévar, « La inmunidad de jurisdicción de la Santa Sede frente a las reclamaciones por abusos a menores en los Estados Unidos, *Ius canonicum*, 23 (2013), pp. 125–174.

57 Pour démontrer la reconnaissance de la personnalité juridique du Saint-Siège par la Belgique, les juges se basent notamment sur l'existence d'un concordat signé entre la Belgique et le Saint-Siège en date de 1953 concernant le Congo avant l'indépendance de la République démocratique du Congo survenue en 1960 (*Verschueren c. Saint-Siège, cit.*, n° 3.5.). Le Concordat français de 1801 n'a jamais été applicable au Royaume de Belgique depuis son indépendance en 1830, à la différence du « système concordataire » transmis par le biais de décrets d'application qui n'ont pas été abrogés par le nouvel Etat.

58 *Verschueren c. Saint-Siège, cit.*, n° 3.2.

59 *Verschueren c. Saint-Siège, cit.*, n° 3.2.

60 « Cela concerne en effet un double titre de souveraineté qui est une et indivisible » [traduction par l'auteur de l'original néerlandais] : « *Het betreft immers een dubbele titel van soevereiniteit die één en ondeelbaar is* »), *Verschueren c. Saint-Siège, cit.*, n° 3.3 ; voir aussi n° 3.6.

61 *Verschueren c. Saint-Siège, cit.*, n°3.3.

62 *Verschueren c. Saint-Siège, cit.*, n°3.5.

63 *Verschueren c. Saint-Siège, cit.*, n° 3.5.

CHAPTER 4

Liberté religieuse en islam : l'apostasie dans les pays arabes

Nathalie Bernard-Maugiron

De toutes les libertés reconnues au plan international, la liberté religieuse est l'une de celles qui peinent le plus à s'imposer dans le monde musulman. Chaque année, la Commission américaine sur la liberté religieuse du Département d'Etat américain dresse un bilan particulièrement sombre des restrictions à cette liberté à l'échelle de la planète, où parmi les plus mal notés figurent un grand nombre de pays à majorité musulmane.

La liberté de religion s'y heurte principalement à deux types d'atteintes : l'incrimination de l'apostasie limite la liberté de changer de religion et la liberté religieuse des non-musulmans fait souvent l'objet de restrictions. Ni le Coran[1], parole de Dieu, ni la *Sunna*[2] du Prophète, ensemble des faits et gestes du Prophète Mohammed, ne sont pourtant clairs et univoques à ce sujet. Alors que des versets coraniques semblent interdire toute contrainte en religion[3], ils ont toutefois été généralement interprétés comme posant une simple interdiction de contraindre des non-musulmans à se convertir à l'islam, à la lumière d'autres versets qui interdisent explicitement à un musulman de quitter sa religion[4]. L'islam interdirait donc d'obliger un non-musulman à embrasser l'islam mais ne permettrait pas à un musulman de quitter sa religion.

1 Le Coran est formé de 114 sourates, regroupant des versets. Il contient essentiellement des injonctions d'ordre moral ou éthique ou relatives aux pratiques religieuses.

2 La *Sunna*, ensemble des faits et gestes du Prophète Mohammed tels qu'ils ont été rapportés par une chaîne d'intermédiaires, constitue la deuxième source du droit musulman.

3 « Point de contrainte en matière de religion », sourate II, verset 256 et « Si ton Seigneur le voulait, sûr que les habitants de la terre croiraient tous jusqu'au dernier. Mais toi, peux-tu contraindre les gens à croire? » (Coran X, 99). Tous les versets coraniques cités dans cet article sont repris de la traduction du Coran par J. Berque, *Le Coran : Essai de traduction*, Albin Michel, collection Spiritualités vivantes, 2002.

4 « Or ils s'acharnent à vous combattre pour vous faire apostasier, s'ils le pouvaient, alors que celui des vôtres qui le ferait et mourrait dans la dénégation – et bien! tous ceux-là, leurs actions crèveront en ce monde et dans la vie dernière. Ce sont les compagnons du Feu. Ils y seront éternels » (Coran, II, 217).

 | DOI:10.1163/9789004349155_005

Si l'apostasie est condamnée, le Coran ne précise toutefois pas à quel type de châtiment son auteur s'expose[5] : « s'ils se dérobent, Dieu les châtiera d'un châtiment douloureux en ce monde et dans l'autre ». Il revient donc à Dieu, et non aux hommes, de juger l'apostat. Un *hadith* du Prophète serait cependant venu affirmer : « Celui qui change de religion, tuez-le ». Le manque de concordance entre la *Sunna* et le Coran a entraîné des interprétations divergentes par les savants musulmans et dans les législations nationales actuelles[6].

Les sources religieuses sont également ambiguës en ce qui concerne le statut des non-musulmans. Malgré l'absence de contrainte en religion, le Coran semble prôner la lutte contre les incroyants qui refusent de se soumettre : ils doivent se convertir ou être tués[7]. Les sources sont également ambiguës par rapport aux gens du Livre, c'est-à-dire les chrétiens et les juifs. Si certains versets semblent appeler à la tolérance envers eux[8] en considérant que l'islam se situe dans la continuité de ces deux religions qui l'ont précédé, d'autres semblent exprimer une hostilité à leur égard[9]. En pratique, les gens du Livre se sont vus reconnaître par les autorités musulmanes le statut

5 « Ils jurent Dieu n'avoir pas dit, et pourtant ils l'ont dite, la parole de dénégation! Ils sont devenus dénégateurs après avoir embrassé l'Islam, pour avoir souhaité et n'avoir pas réussi ; et le seul reproche qu'ils peuvent faire, c'est que Dieu (et son Envoyé) les ait enrichis de Sa Grâce. Alors, s'ils se repentent, ce sera pour eux un bien, s'ils se dérobent, Dieu les châtiera d'un châtiment douloureux en ce monde et dans l'autre. Ils ne trouveront sur terre ni protecteur ni secourant » (Coran IX, 74).

6 Pour une étude historique de cette diversité voir notamment M. Garcia-Arenal (dir.), *Conversions islamiques. Identités religieuses en Islam méditerranéen*, Paris, Maisonneuve et Larose, 2001 et H. Bleuchot, *Droit musulman : Tome 1 : Histoire. Tome 2 : Fondements, culte, droit public et mixte*, Aix-en-Provence, Presses universitaires d'Aix-Marseille, 2000. Les modernistes invoquent cette faiblesse des sources religieuses pour s'opposer à la pénalisation de l'apostasie. Voir par exemple M. Charfi, *Islam et liberté, le malentendu historique*, Paris, 1998, Albin Michel, p. 78 et s.

7 « Ceux qui croient combattent sur le chemin de Dieu ; les dénégateurs combattent sur le chemin de l'idole. Combattez les protégés de Satan : impuissante sera leur embûche » (Coran IV, 76) et « Prophète ! Combats les dénégateurs et les hypocrites. Sois rude à leur égard. Qu'ils n'aient d'asile que la Géhenne » (Coran, LXVI-9).

8 « Ceux qui croient, ceux qui suivent le judaïsme, les Chrétiens, les Mandéens, quiconque croit en Dieu et au Jour dernier, effectue l'œuvre salutaire, ceux-là trouveront leur salaire auprès de leur Seigneur. Il n'est pour eux de crainte à nourrir, et ils n'éprouveront nul regret » (Coran II, 62).

9 « Vous qui croyez, ne nouez ni avec les Juifs, ni avec les Chrétiens de rapports de protection. Qu'ils le fassent les uns avec les autres! Quiconque d'entre vous en nouerait avec eux, conséquemment serait des leurs. Dieu ne guide pas un peuple d'iniquité. » (Coran, V, 51).

de « protégés » (*dhimmi*)[10] qui leur permettait de conserver leurs croyances et de pratiquer librement leurs rites tout en étant soumis à leur propre législation en matière de statut personnel. En échange, ils acceptaient de se soumettre à l'autorité musulmane, de payer un impôt particulier – la capitation (*jizya*) – et de respecter des restrictions, notamment dans l'accès aux fonctions publiques. Si le statut de *dhimmi* a disparu des législations nationales contemporaines et que les non-musulmans sont désormais considérés comme des citoyens à part entière, ils continuent souvent à souffrir de discrimination – en fait sinon en droit – et de restrictions dans l'exercice de leur liberté religieuse.

Les pays arabes ne représentent certes qu'une partie du monde musulman, mais leurs systèmes juridiques sont un reflet de la diversité du statut de la liberté religieuse et de sa protection. Même quand leurs constitutions garantissent la liberté religieuse, elles consacrent également la place de l'islam dans le système politique et juridique national. Cette constitutionnalisation à la fois de l'islam et de la liberté religieuse peut sembler antinomique, notamment en ce qui concerne la liberté de changer de religion ou la protection du statut des minorités religieuses et c'est au législateur et au juge qu'il reviendra de tenter de les concilier.

L'étude du droit contemporain des pays arabes permet de mieux saisir l'interprétation qui a été donnée aux principes issus des sources religieuses dans les systèmes juridiques contemporains de ces pays. L'étude de leur position par rapport à la protection internationale de la liberté religieuse et l'analyse de leur législation interne permettra de souligner la diversité de ces interprétations. L'analyse de la jurisprudence du Conseil d'Etat égyptien relative à des requêtes en changement de religion sur des cartes d'identité illustrera le recours par le juge administratif à la notion d'ordre public pour poser des limites à la liberté religieuse.

1 La liberté religieuse dans les constitutions du monde arabe

La plupart des pays du monde arabe ont inséré dans leur constitution des références à l'islam ou à la *charia*, tout en consacrant souvent également la liberté religieuse.

---

10 Pour l'étude du statut de *dhimmi* voir par exemple A. Fattal, *Le statut légal des non-musulmans en pays d'islam*, Beyrouth, Imprimerie catholique, 1958, rééd. coll. Recherches, Dar El-Machreq, Beyrouth, 1995.

1.1 *La religion dans la définition constitutionnelle de l'Etat*

Presque toutes les constitutions actuelles du monde arabe font de l'islam la religion de l'Etat et certaines consacrent également la valeur normative de la *charia* et parfois même d'autres formes de références religieuses.

1.1.1 L'islam religion de l'Etat

L'islam a été consacré religion de l'Etat dans la quasi-totalité des constitutions du monde arabe. Ainsi, la constitution égyptienne de 2014, de même que celles de 2012 et de 1971 qui l'ont précédée, stipule que « l'islam est la religion de l'Etat et l'arabe est sa langue officielle » (art. 2). On trouve une disposition analogue dans les constitutions de l'Algérie (2016, art. 2), de la Jordanie (1952, art. 2), du Koweït (1962, art. 2), d'Oman (1996, art. 2), du Bahreïn (2002, art. 2), du Maroc (2011, art. 3) ou de l'Irak (2005, art. 2). En Mauritanie (1991, art. 5), l'islam est la religion du peuple et de l'Etat. Même la constitution tunisienne de 2014 (art. 1), comme celle de 1959, affirme que « la Tunisie est un Etat libre, indépendant et souverain ; sa religion est l'islam, sa langue l'arabe et son régime la république »[11]. Le Sultanat d'Oman (1996, art. 1), le Bahreïn (2002, art. 1), l'Arabie saoudite (1992, art. 1) et le Yémen (2001, art.1) se définissent comme des Etats islamiques. Dans son préambule, le Royaume du Maroc affirme aussi être un Etat islamique et la Mauritanie est une « république islamique » (2006, art.1). La Syrie est, avec le Liban – Etat multiconfessionnel –, le seul pays arabe contemporain dont la constitution ne fasse pas de l'islam la religion de l'Etat. Elle fait toutefois du *fiqh*[12] islamique une source principale de la législation et exige que le chef de l'Etat soit musulman.

Certaines constitutions interdisent de porter atteinte à l'identité islamique de l'Etat ou à la place de la *charia* par le biais d'amendements constitutionnels. Ainsi, la constitution marocaine (2011, art. 175) interdit d'amender les dispositions constitutionnelles relatives à la religion musulmane. De même, la constitution algérienne (2016, art. 212) interdit toute révision constitutionnelle qui porterait atteinte à l'islam en tant que religion de l'Etat et la constitution du Bahreïn (2002, art. 120) d'amender l'article 2, qui consacre l'islam comme religion de l'Etat et la *charia* comme une source principale de la législation. En théorie, rien n'empêcherait toutefois le constituant d'amender ces

11 Cet article a fait l'objet d'un consensus au sein de la constituante du fait notamment de son ambivalence : fait-il de l'islam la religion de l'Etat ou de la nation ?

12 Le *fiqh* est le droit élaboré par les savants-théologiens à partir du Coran et de la *Sunna*. Il s'agit donc d'une construction humaine, doctrinale, et il existe de grandes différences d'interprétation entre savants quant aux critères et à la sanction de l'apostasie. Voir par exemple R. Peters, G.J.J. De Vries, « Apostasy in Islam », *Die Welt des Islams*, New Series, Vol. 17, Issue 1/4, 1976–1977, pp. 1–25.

mêmes dispositions ou d'adopter un nouveau texte constitutionnel portant atteinte à ces principes.

Dans la plupart des cas, ces dispositions n'ont eu qu'une portée limitée sur l'organisation du pouvoir et des institutions, qui fonctionnent sur le modèle occidental d'une séparation plus ou moins poussée des domaines religieux et étatique. Dans le monde arabe, on ne trouve guère que l'Arabie saoudite pour associer un Comité de grands ulémas à l'exercice effectif du pouvoir.

1.1.2 La valeur normative de la *charia*

Certains textes fondamentaux font référence à la valeur normative de la *charia*, des principes de la *charia*, de l'islam ou du *fiqh* islamique. L'article 1 du statut fondamental saoudien stipule ainsi que le Royaume « a pour constitution le Livre de Dieu et la *Sunna* de son Prophète ». De plus, l'article 7 affirme la supériorité du texte révélé et de la *Sunna* sur tous les autres textes et l'article 67 impose au pouvoir réglementaire de légiférer dans le respect des règles de la *charia*. En Irak, la constitution (2005, art. 2) fait de l'islam une source fondamentale de la législation et interdit la promulgation de toute loi qui serait contraire à ses principes fixes. En Mauritanie, le préambule du texte constitutionnel considère les préceptes de la religion musulmane comme la source unique du droit, mais la portée juridique de cette disposition, insérée dans le préambule et non dans le texte même de la constitution, reste limitée.

D'autres pays ont consacré la normativité de la *charia* en faisant de ses principes une source principale de la législation. C'est le cas des Emirats arabes unis (1971, art. 7), du Koweït (1962, art. 2) ou du Bahreïn (2002, art. 2), où la *charia* islamique « est une source principale de la législation » et à Oman (1996, art. 2) « un fondement de la législation ». Au Qatar (2003, art. 1), « la charia islamique est une source principale de ses lois ». En Syrie (2012, art. 3), c'est le *fiqh* islamique qui constitue cette source principale. Au Soudan, la charia islamique (et le consensus du peuple) constituent des sources de la législation dans les Etats du Nord (art. 5). En Egypte (2014, art. 2), les principes de la *charia* sont « *la* » source principale de la législation et au Yémen (2001, art. 3), elle est « la source de toutes les législations ». Certains Etats ne font toutefois aucune référence à la valeur normative de la *charia* dans leur constitution, comme l'Algérie, le Maroc et la Tunisie.

Du point de vue de l'orthodoxie islamique classique, l'autorité de la *charia* ne dépend pas de l'intervention humaine et le Coran est la seule constitution dont ont besoin les musulmans. Le droit musulman classique ne contient donc aucune disposition relative à la place respective à accorder, au sein de la pyramide des normes, au droit musulman et au droit séculier. En pratique, il est rare que la référence à la valeur normative de la *charia* entraîne son influence réelle sur le droit positif national. Hormis le droit de la famille et parfois le droit pénal, et à l'exception de l'Arabie saoudite et des pays du Golfe, les autres branches du droit ont été partout sécularisées sur le modèle des droits occidentaux.

1.1.3 Autres références religieuses

Certaines constitutions réservent directement ou indirectement les hautes fonctions publiques à des musulmans. En Syrie (2012, art. 3), ainsi, « la religion du président de la République doit être l'islam ». On trouve une disposition analogue dans la constitution tunisienne (2014, art. 74), algérienne (2016, art. 87) ou mauritanienne (1991, art. 23). Quant à la constitution du Qatar (2003, art. 9), elle énonce que l'héritier au trône doit être musulman et de mère musulmane qatarie. En Jordanie (1952, art. 28), au Koweït (1962, art. 4) et à Oman (1996, art. 5), nul n'accédera au trône s'il n'est musulman, de père et de mère musulmans, ce qui exclut les musulmans convertis. Même si d'autres constitutions, comme en Egypte, n'imposent pas expressément que le chef de l'État soit musulman, la candidature et encore plus l'élection d'un non-musulman reste difficilement concevable.

Certaines dispositions invoquent la *charia* islamique pour conditionner l'exercice des droits et de libertés. Ainsi, le statut fondamental saoudien (1992, art. 26) précise que l'Etat protège les droits de l'homme « conformément à la *charia* islamique ». De même, l'article 8 énonce que le régime repose sur les principes de « justice, consultation, et égalité, conformément à la *charia* islamique ». Le principe d'égalité entre l'homme et la femme fait parfois l'objet d'une limitation par une telle référence. Ainsi, la constitution bahreïnie (2002, art. 5) affirme que l'Etat s'efforce de concilier les devoirs de la femme envers sa famille avec son travail au sein de la société et garantit son égalité avec l'homme dans les domaines de la vie politique, sociale, culturelle et économique, « sans préjudice des dispositions de la *charia* islamique ». Selon l'article 31 de la constitution yéménite de 2001, les femmes bénéficient des droits et devoirs « garantis et imposés par la *charia* ».

L'attachement à la religion proclamé au niveau de la constitution est souvent un moyen pour le régime de se réapproprier le référent religieux pour renforcer sa légitimité et reste souvent confiné au symbolique. Il peut toutefois entraîner des tensions, lorsque la constitution consacre également la liberté religieuse ou le principe de non-discrimination sur une base religieuse.

1.2 *Protection constitutionnelle de la liberté religieuse*

La liberté de religion est garantie dans un grand nombre de constitutions du monde arabe, mais en des termes souvent très différents.

A l'exception du Maroc, les nouvelles constitutions adoptées ou révisées après les soulèvements de 2011 ont renforcé la protection de cette liberté. C'est ainsi qu'en Algérie, le nouvel article 42 de la constitution de 2016 affirme que « La liberté de conscience et la liberté d'opinion sont inviolables. La liberté d'exercice du culte est garantie dans le respect de la loi ». La nouveauté réside dans l'ajout de la seconde phrase de l'article, relative à la liberté d'exercice du culte, qui ne figurait pas dans le texte de 1996. Il est encore trop tôt pour évaluer la portée que cet amendement aura sur le statut des minorités religieuses en Algérie et en particulier s'il entraînera l'amendement de l'ordonnance de 2006 qui fixe les règles d'exercice des cultes autres que musulmans[13]. L'article 32 de la constitution relatif au principe d'égalité entre citoyens, quant à lui, ne fait pas mention de la religion : « Les citoyens sont égaux devant la loi, sans que puisse prévaloir aucune discrimination pour cause de naissance, de race, de sexe, d'opinion ou de toute autre condition ou circonstance personnelle ou sociale ».

En Egypte, l'article 64 de la constitution de 2014 affirme que « La liberté de croyance est absolue. La liberté de culte ou d'établissement de lieux de culte pour les adeptes des religions célestes est un droit régi par la loi ». Auparavant, la constitution de 1971 (art. 46) affirmait seulement que « L'Etat garantit la liberté de croyance et de l'exercice du culte ». La constitution de 2014 garantit donc le droit de pratiquer son culte et de construire des lieux de culte, mais le réserve aux seules « religions célestes », c'est-à-dire l'islam, le christianisme et le judaïsme. Les autres confessions, et en particulier les bahaïs, voire les chiites, en sont donc privés. Toute discrimination entre les citoyens en raison de leur religion, croyance, sexe, origine, race, couleur, langue, handicap, classe sociale ou affiliation politique ou géographique est pourtant interdite (art. 53). La constitution autorise également les chrétiens et les juifs à recourir à leurs lois religieuses pour régler les questions de statut personnel et le choix de leurs dirigeants[14]. Conformément à la constitution, qui invitait le législateur à adopter dès sa première législature une loi organisant la construction et la rénovation des églises garantissant aux chrétiens la

13 Cette ordonnance n° 06-03 du 28 février 2006 fixant les conditions et règles d'exercice des cultes autres que musulmans dispose que l'Etat algérien garantit le libre exercice du culte « dans le respect des dispositions de la constitution, de la présente ordonnance, des lois et règlements en vigueur, de l'ordre public, des bonnes mœurs et des droits et libertés fondamentaux des tiers » (art. 2).

14 Art. 3 de la constitution de 2014, qui consacre au niveau constitutionnel une pratique déjà en vigueur et organisée au niveau législatif. Réminiscence du statut de *dhimmi*, cette disposition, incorporée à la demande des Eglises, leur permet de garder le contrôle de la vie religieuse et familiale de leurs fidèles.

liberté de pratiquer leurs rites religieux, le législateur est intervenu pour en organiser l'exercice en août 2016[15].

En Tunisie, l'article 6 de la constitution de 2014 affirme que

> L'Etat protège la religion, garantit la liberté de croyance, de conscience et de l'exercice des cultes. Il assure la neutralité des mosquées et des lieux de culte de l'exploitation partisane. L'Etat s'engage à diffuser les valeurs de modération et de tolérance et à protéger le sacré et empêcher qu'on y porte atteinte. Il s'engage également à prohiber les accusations d'apostasie ainsi que l'incitation à la haine et à la violence et à les juguler.

Cet article est issu d'un compromis entre les différentes parties lors de l'élaboration de la constitution, suite à des menaces contre un élu de gauche. L'opposition laïque a obtenu l'insertion, pour la première fois dans l'histoire constitutionnelle, de la condamnation explicite des campagnes d'accusation d'apostasie. Le contenu vague et parfois contradictoire de cet article devra toutefois être précisé par la Cour constitutionnelle.

En Syrie, le nouveau texte de 2012 (art. 3) affirme que l'Etat respecte toutes les religions et garantit le libre exercice de tous les rites à condition que cela ne perturbe pas l'ordre public. La liberté de culte est également protégée par la loi (art. 42). Les citoyens sont égaux en droits et en devoirs sans aucune distinction, y compris celle fondée sur la religion (art. 33).

La constitution irakienne de 2005 est beaucoup plus précise en ce qui concerne la protection de la liberté religieuse. Elle affirme ainsi que « La constitution garantit l'identité islamique de la majorité du peuple irakien ainsi que tous les droits religieux à la liberté de croyance et au culte religieux de tous les individus, y compris les chrétiens, les yazidis et les mandéens sabéens » (art. 2.2). De plus, « Tout individu dispose de la liberté de pensée, de conscience et de croyance » (art. 42) et « Les adeptes de toutes les religions et confessions sont libres : a) de pratiquer leurs rites religieux, y compris les rites husseinis ; b) de gérer les fondations pieuses (*waqf*), leurs affaires et leurs institutions religieuses, conformément aux dispositions de la loi. 2. L'Etat garantit la liberté de culte et le protection des lieux de culte » (art. 43). Le texte constitutionnel interdit également expressément de discriminer sur la base

---

15 N. Bernard-Maugiron, « Ce que dit la nouvelle loi sur la construction des églises en Egypte », *Newsletter*, Oasis, octobre 2016, en ligne <www.oasiscenter.eu/fr/articles/chr%C3%A9tiens-dans-le-monde-musulman/2016/10/19/egypte-nouvelle-loi-construction-eglises>.

de la religion (art. 14) : « Les Irakiens sont égaux devant la loi, sans discrimination fondée sur le sexe, la race, la nationalité, l'origine, la couleur, la religion, la confession, la croyance, l'opinion, ou le statut économique ou social ».

En Jordanie, selon la constitution (art. 14) « L'Etat protège la liberté de la pratique des religions et des croyances, conformément aux traditions observées dans le Royaume, à moins qu'elle ne porte atteinte à l'ordre public ou aux bonnes mœurs ». La discrimination sur la base de la religion est interdite (art. 6 alinéa 1) : « Les Jordaniens sont égaux devant la loi. Aucune discrimination ne peut être faite entre eux quant à leurs droits et leurs obligations, même s'ils sont différents quant à leur race, leur langue ou leur religion ».

Les constitutions du Golfe sont plus restrictives quant à la protection de la liberté religieuse, ne garantissant généralement que la liberté de culte et invoquant le concept d'ordre public, de coutumes ou de bonnes mœurs pour en limiter l'exercice. La plupart interdisent pourtant la discrimination sur la base de la religion. C'est ainsi qu'au Koweït (1962, art. 35) « La liberté de croyance est absolue. L'Etat protège la liberté de pratiquer les rites religieux conformément aux coutumes établies, à condition qu'elles ne s'opposent pas à l'ordre public et aux bonnes mœurs ». Toutes les personnes sont égales en dignité et dans les droits et devoirs publics devant la loi, sans distinction de race, origine, langue ou religion (art. 29).

A Oman, « La liberté de pratiquer les rites religieux conformément aux coutumes établies est garantie, à condition qu'elle ne s'oppose pas à l'ordre public et ne porte pas atteinte aux bonnes mœurs » (art. 28). La constitution interdit de discriminer sur la base de la religion (art. 17) : « Tous les citoyens sont égaux devant la loi et jouissent des mêmes droits et devoirs publics. Il n'existe aucune discrimination entre eux sur la base du sexe, de l'origine, de la couleur, de la langue, de la religion, de la confession, du lieu de résidence ou du statut social ». Le Qatar garantit lui-aussi la liberté de pratiquer les rites religieux conformément à la loi et aux exigences de maintien de l'ordre public et des bonnes mœurs (art. 50) ainsi que l'égalité des citoyens sans distinction fondée sur la croyance (art. 35) : « Les individus sont égaux devant la loi, sans distinction en raison de la race, du sexe, de la langue ou de la religion ». Aux Emirats arabes unis, la constitution (art. 32) affirme : « La liberté de pratiquer les rites religieux, conformément aux coutumes établies, est protégée, à condition qu'elle ne porte pas atteinte à l'ordre public et aux bonnes mœurs » et interdit de discriminer sur la base de la religion (art. 25) : « Les hommes sont égaux devant la loi. Aucune discrimination parmi les citoyens de la Fédération en fonction de l'origine, du lieu de résidence, de la croyance religieuse ou du rang social ». Au Bahreïn, la constitution de 2002 (art. 22) stipule que « La liberté de conscience est absolue. L'Etat garantit l'inviolabilité des lieux de culte ainsi que la liberté du culte, des processions et réunions religieuses, conformément aux coutumes établies dans le pays ». La constitution (art. 18) interdit également de discriminer sur la base de la religion : « Les hommes sont égaux en dignité humaine. Les citoyens sont égaux devant la loi en droits et en devoirs publics sans discrimination en raison de leur sexe, de leur origine, de leur langue, de leur religion ou de leur croyance ».

Le Liban, quant à lui, affirme (art. 9) que la liberté de conscience est absolue. L'Etat doit prendre des mesures positives pour respecter toutes les confessions ainsi que la protection du libre exercice du culte à condition qu'il ne soit pas porté atteinte à l'ordre public. Le préambule précise que le Liban est fondé sur l'égalité dans les droits et obligations entre tous les citoyens sans distinction ni préférence. La constitution garantit l'égalité des citoyens (art. 7) non seulement devant la loi mais aussi dans la jouissance des droits civils et politiques. Elle repose toutefois sur le principe de la représentation religieuse au sein du parlement et du gouvernement (art. 24 et 95).

Les constitutions du Maroc, de la Mauritanie, de l'Arabie saoudite et du Yémen ne consacrent pas la liberté religieuse. Au Maroc, la constitution de 2011 (art. 3) affirme toutefois que « L'Islam est la religion de l'Etat qui garantit à tous le libre exercice des cultes ». Bien que le projet initial de constitution se référât à la liberté de conscience, les courants conservateurs ont réussi à faire retirer cette disposition du texte finalement adopté et entré en vigueur en 2011. Le préambule énonce cependant que « La prééminence accordée à la religion musulmane dans ce référentiel national va de pair avec l'attachement du peuple marocain aux valeurs d'ouverture, de modération, de tolérance et de dialogue pour la compréhension mutuelle entre toutes les cultures et les civilisations du monde ». Le Maroc s'engage également à « bannir et combattre toute discrimination à l'encontre de quiconque, en raison du sexe, de la couleur, des croyances, de la culture, de l'origine sociale ou régionale, de la langue, du handicap ou de quelque circonstance personnelle que ce soit ».

Si la liberté religieuse fait généralement l'objet d'une garantie dans les textes constitutionnels, les législations nationales viennent souvent en limiter l'exercice à travers l'incrimination de l'apostasie.

2 L'apostasie, limite à la liberté religieuse

La question de la limite à la liberté de changer de religion en islam s'est posée au niveau international ainsi que dans les législations nationales et la jurisprudence de certains Etats à travers le concept d'ordre public.

2.1 *Les Etats musulmans face à la protection internationale de la liberté religieuse*[16]

La question de l'apostasie et de l'interdiction pour un musulman de quitter sa religion a eu des répercussions au plan international. Ainsi, l'Arabie saoudite s'est abstenue lors du vote de la Déclaration universelle des droits de l'homme en 1948, au motif que la reconnaissance du droit de changer de religion dans l'article 18 venait encourager implicitement le prosélytisme. Elle invoqua lors des débats devant la Troisième commission les antécédents historiques des activités des missionnaires : « au cours de l'histoire des missionnaires ont souvent abusé de leurs droits pour devenir les précurseurs d'une intervention politique, entraînant plus d'une fois les peuples, par leurs efforts prosélytes, dans des conflits meurtriers. Ainsi, les croisades, sanglantes et impardonnables, organisées au nom de la religion, avaient pour raison véritable le but économique et politique d'acquérir de l'espace vital pour le surplus de la population de l'Europe »[17]. L'Egypte estima elle aussi que la liberté de changer de religion traduisait « les machinations de certaines missions bien connues en Orient qui poursuivent inlassablement leurs efforts en vue de convertir à leur foi les populations de l'Orient »[18] mais vota quand même en faveur de la déclaration. La non-discrimination dans la conclusion du mariage (art. 16) souleva également les objections des pays musulmans, l'islam n'autorisant pas une musulmane à épouser un non-musulman et un musulman à épouser une femme n'appartenant pas à l'une des trois religions du Livre.

16 M. Al-Midani, « Les Etats islamiques et la Déclaration universelle des Droits de l'Homme », *Le Courrier du GERI*, volume I, n° 3, octobre 1998, pp.179–191.

17 Documents officiels de la troisième session de la Troisième commission de l'Assemblée générale des Nations unies. Comptes rendus analytiques des séances, 9 novembre 1948, 127e séance, pp. 391–392, disponible en ligne <www.un.org/en/ga/search/view_doc.asp?symbol=A/C.3/SR.127> (consulté le 22 février 2017).

18 Documents officiels de la troisième session de l'Assemblée générale des Nations Unies. Comptes rendus analytiques des séances, 10 décembre 1948, A/PV/183, pp. 57–58, disponible en ligne <http://research.un.org/en/undhr/ga/plenary> (consulté le 22 février 2017) : « (…) M. Rafaat (représentant de l'Egypte) fait observer que ce texte ne se borne pas à proclamer le droit à la liberté de pensée, de conscience et de religion, droit que son Gouvernement approuve sans réserve, mais établit également le droit de l'homme de changer de religion ou de conviction. En ce qui concerne ce dernier « droit », la délégation de l'Egypte ne peut l'approuver sans réserve. La foi religieuse ne saurait être changée à la légère. Fort souvent, un homme change de religion sous des influences extérieures ou dans des buts qui ne sont pas recommandables, tels que le divorce. La délégation égyptienne craint qu'en proclamant la liberté de changer de religion ou de conviction, la déclaration encourage – certes sans le vouloir – les machinations de certaines missions bien connues en Orient, qui poursuivent inlassablement leurs efforts en vue de convertir à leur foi les populations de Orient ».

Vingt ans plus tard, lors de l'élaboration du Pacte international sur les droits civils et politiques, les pays de droit musulman s'opposèrent à ce que le droit de changer de religion figure dans l'article 18. Seul le droit de toute personne « d'adopter ou d'avoir une religion de son choix » est donc garanti. Le Comité des droits de l'homme, en charge de superviser la mise en œuvre du Pacte, a toutefois donné une interprétation extensive de cet article, affirmant dans une observation générale en 1993 que la liberté d'adopter ou d'avoir une religion de son choix « implique nécessairement la liberté de choisir une religion ou une conviction y compris, notamment, le droit de substituer à sa religion ou sa conviction actuelle une autre religion ou conviction ou d'adopter une position athée, ainsi que le droit de conserver sa religion ou sa conviction »[19]. Le Pacte a été ratifié par la plupart des pays arabes (Algérie, Bahreïn, Egypte, Irak, Jordanie, Koweït, Liban, Libye, Maroc, Syrie, Soudan, Tunisie, Yémen) et seules certaines réserves concernent directement ou indirectement la liberté religieuse : l'Egypte a formulé une réserve générale indiquant qu'elle devait s'assurer que le Pacte n'était pas incompatible avec les dispositions de la *charia* islamique et le Bahreïn a fait une réserve par rapport à l'article 18.

Adoptée en 1981, la Déclaration sur l'élimination de toutes les formes d'intolérance et de discriminations fondées sur la religion ne mentionne pas le droit de changer de religion ni d'adopter une religion de son choix, à la demande « d'une quarantaine d'Etats islamiques dont le porte-parole a mentionné que le Coran ne permet pas à un musulman de changer de religion et que, par conséquent, ces Etats ne sont pas prêts à accepter l'inclusion explicite d'adopter une religion ou une conviction de son choix »[20]. Une quarantaine d'Etats invoquèrent donc la nécessité de conformité avec la *charia* pour ne pas reconnaître le droit de changer de religion.

Quant aux textes adoptés au niveau régional par des Etats musulmans, ils n'incluent généralement pas le droit de changer de religion et posent des restrictions extensives à l'exercice de la liberté religieuse. Pour la Déclaration islamique universelle des droits de l'homme de 1981, adoptée par le Conseil islamique de Londres, « Toute personne a droit à la liberté de conscience et de culte conformément à ses convictions religieuses » (art. 13). La Déclaration du Caire sur les droits de l'homme en islam, adoptée en 1990 dans le cadre de

---

19 Comité des droits de l'homme, *Observation générale n° 22 sur l'article 18 du Pacte relatif aux droits civils et politiques*, 27 septembre 1993, CCPR/C/21/Rev.1/Add.4.

20 J.A. Walkate, « The Right of Everyone to Change His Religion or Belief », *Netherlands International Law Review*, volume 30, n° 2, août 1983, p.146–160 cité par H. Nadafi, *La liberté de religion dans les Etats de droit musulman*, thèse en droit, Université Jean Monnet-Saint-Etienne, 2013.

l'Organisation de la Conférence islamique, affirme l'égalité en dignité, devoirs et responsabilité de tous les hommes sans distinction de religion (art. 1) mais ne mentionne pas la liberté de religion. Elle se contente d'interdire toute contrainte pour obliger un individu à renoncer à sa religion (art. 10). Pour la Charte arabe des droits de l'homme, adoptée au sein de la Ligue arabe en 1994 puis révisée en 2004 (art. 30) :

> a) Toute personne a droit à la liberté de pensée, de croyance et de religion, qui ne peut faire l'objet d'aucune restriction non prévue par la loi.
> b) La liberté de manifester sa religion ou ses convictions ou de pratiquer individuellement ou collectivement les rites de sa religion ne peut faire l'objet que des seules restrictions prévues par la loi et qui sont nécessaires dans une société tolérante, respectueuse des libertés et des droits de l'homme pour la protection de la sûreté publique, de l'ordre public, de la santé publique ou de la moralité publique ou des libertés et droits fondamentaux d'autrui.

La Charte affirme par ailleurs le principe de non-discrimination sur la base de la religion de façon générale (art. 4) et plus spécifiquement dans l'exercice du droit au travail (art. 34). La Charte arabe reconnaît donc la liberté de religion et le droit de pratiquer les rites religieux, dans certaines limites.

Le code pénal uniforme adopté par le Conseil des ministres arabes de la justice dans le cadre de la Ligue arabe en 1996, quant à lui, condamne l'apostasie en ces termes :

> Art. 162 – L'apostat est le musulman, homme ou femme, qui abandonne la religion islamique par une parole explicite ou un fait dont le sens est indiscutable, insulte Dieu, ses prophètes ou la religion musulmane, ou falsifie sciemment le Coran.
>
> Art. 163 – L'apostat est puni de la peine de mort s'il est prouvé qu'il a apostasié volontairement et qu'il s'y maintient après avoir été invité à se repentir dans les trois jours.
>
> Art. 164 – Le repentir de l'apostat se réalise s'il renonce à ce qui a constitué sa mécréance ; son repentir est inacceptable s'il apostasie plus de deux fois.
>
> Art. 165 – Tous les actes de l'apostat accomplis après son apostasie sont considérés comme nuls, de nullité absolue. Tous les biens qu'il a acquis par ces actes reviennent à la caisse de l'Etat.

Le code adopte donc une interprétation particulièrement stricte de l'interdiction de l'apostasie, punie à la fois sur le plan pénal et civil, conception qui n'a pas été reprise par la plupart des pays arabes.

2.2 *Restrictions à la liberté religieuse des musulmans en droit interne*[21]

Au niveau législatif, la liberté religieuse des musulmans se heurte à un certain nombre de limites, toutes développées par les jurisconsultes après la révélation, pour protéger l'unité de la communauté musulmane naissante[22]. Certaines conduites sont considérées comme constituant des insultes ou un outrage envers Dieu, le Prophète ou la religion[23]. En Egypte, le code pénal (art. 98*f*) réprime « l'exploitation de la religion pour propager par voie orale, écrite, ou par tout autre moyen des idées extrémistes dans le but d'attiser des troubles, avilir l'une des religions célestes ou l'une des communautés en faisant partie ou nuire à l'unité nationale ou à la paix sociale ». La sanction prévue est de six mois à cinq ans de prison et/ou une amende d'un montant maximum de 1 000 LE. Sur la base de cet article, des individus ont été condamnés pour prosélytisme ou des membres de communautés jugées déviantes, comme des chiites ou des soufis, ont été accusés de porter atteinte à la cohésion sociale. Cette disposition a également été utilisée pour sanctionner des conversions de musulmans au christianisme, jugées contraires à la loi islamique[24]. Le blasphème est également pénalisé dans d'autres pays, comme au Qatar[25].

La Mauritanie et le Yémen sanctionnent pénalement l'apostasie, c'est-à-dire le fait de quitter l'islam. En Mauritanie (art. 306 du Code pénal) :

> Tout musulman coupable du crime d'apostasie, soit par parole, soit par action de façon apparente ou évidente, sera invité à se repentir dans un délai de trois jours. S'il ne se repent pas dans ce délai, il est condamné en tant qu'apostat, et ses biens seront confisqués au profit du trésor. S'il se repent avant l'exécution de cette sentence, le parquet saisira la Cour

---

21 S.A.A. Abu Sahlieh, « Le délit d'apostasie aujourd'hui et ses conséquences en droit musulman », *Islamochristiana*, PISAI, Rome, n° 20, 1994, p. 93–116 ; N. Georges, « Les chrétiens dans le monde arabe et la question de l'apostasie en islam », *Maghreb – Machrek*, 3/2011, n° 209, pp. 109–119.

22 Voir H. Nadafi, *La liberté de religion …, op.cit.*, pp. 101 et s.

23 L'Ayatollah Khomeiny avait ainsi émis une fatwa célèbre contre Salman Rushdie réclamant sa mort en 1989 pour son œuvre *Les Versets sataniques*, considérée comme blasphématoire.

24 Voir par exemple Human Rights Watch et The Egyptian Initiative For Personal Right, *Prohibited Identities. State Interference in Religious Freedom*, novembre 2007 (<www.hrw.org/en/reports/2007/11/11/prohibited-identities>)

25 Art. 256 du code pénal qatari de 2004.

> suprême, à l'effet de sa réhabilitation dans tous ses droits, sans préjudice d'une peine correctionnelle prévue au paragraphe 1er du présent article. Toute personne coupable du crime d'apostasie (*Zendagha*) sera, à moins qu'elle ne se repente au préalable, punie de la peine de mort.

En Arabie saoudite, l'apostasie n'est pas sanctionnée en tant que telle par la loi, mais les juges musulmans – les cadis – peuvent se référer directement aux principes du droit musulman classique non codifiés, donc à l'interdiction coranique de quitter la religion musulmane, pour trancher une affaire donnée. La constitution (art. 48) prévoit en effet que « les tribunaux appliquent aux affaires qui leur sont soumises les dispositions de la *chari'a* islamique, conformément à ce qui est indiqué dans le Livre et la *Sunna* et aux règlements pris par le Souverain qui ne sont pas incompatibles avec le Livre et la *Sunna* ».

Plusieurs pays interdisent le prosélytisme lorsqu'il vise à encourager un musulman à quitter sa religion. Au Qatar, ainsi, le code pénal a introduit en 1973 le délit de prosélytisme, puni d'une peine pouvant aller jusqu'à 10 ans d'emprisonnement[26]. En Algérie, l'ordonnance de 2006 (art. 11) qui fixe les conditions et règles d'exercice des cultes autres que musulmans punit d'une peine pouvant aller de deux à cinq ans de prison et d'une amende d'un maximum de 1 000 000 dinars algériens quiconque « incite, contraint ou utilise des moyens de séduction tendant à convertir un musulman à une autre religion, ou en utilisant à cette fin des établissements d'enseignement, d'éducation, de santé, à caractère social ou culturel, de formation ou tout moyen financier. Quiconque fabrique, entrepose, ou distribue des documents imprimés ou métrages audiovisuels ou tout autre support ou moyen qui visent à ébranler la foi d'un musulman ».

Au Maroc, le code pénal (art. 220) prévoit qu'est puni d'un emprisonnement de six mois à trois ans et d'une amende de 100 à 500 dirhams, « quiconque emploie des moyens de séduction dans le but d'ébranler la foi d'un musulman ou de le convertir à une autre religion, soit en exploitant sa faiblesse ou ses besoins, soit en utilisant à ces fins des établissements d'enseignement, de santé, des asiles ou des orphelinats. En cas de condamnation, la fermeture de l'établissement qui a servi à commettre le délit peut être ordonnée, soit définitivement, soit pour une durée qui ne peut excéder trois années »[27].

26 Art. 257 du code pénal qatari de 2004.

27 Bien que cet article ne vise que le prosélytisme, il a été utilisé pour condamner des musulmans convertis au christianisme, dont les actes ou paroles ont été considérés comme destinés à faire naître le doute dans l'esprit des musulmans, voir H. Nadaf, *op. cit.*, p. 110 et s. Le Conseil supérieur des oulémas du Maroc, en février 2017, serait revenu sur une fatwa de 2012 par laquelle il avait estimé, sur la base du hadith du prophète, que les apostats devaient être punis de la peine de mort.

Ailleurs, l'apostat qui quitte l'islam pour une autre religion ne s'expose pas à des sanctions pénales, mais plusieurs pays prévoient la perte de droits sur le plan civil. La déclaration d'apostasie peut ainsi entraîner des modifications du statut personnel : le mariage de l'apostat avec un/une musulman(e) est impossible. C'est le cas en Jordanie[28] et au Yémen[29] où l'apostasie de la femme constitue un empêchement à mariage pour le futur mari. Au Koweït, de même, la déclaration d'apostasie constitue un empêchement à mariage même avec un non-musulman[30].

La dissolution du mariage des convertis est parfois prévue explicitement par la loi, comme au Yémen et en Jordanie si l'un des deux époux renie l'islam[31] ou au Koweït en cas d'apostasie du mari[32]. Jusqu'en 2005, le Code de la famille algérien considérait l'apostasie comme cause de nullité du mariage[33], mais cette disposition a disparu du nouveau code de 2005. Dans les autres pays, la dissolution du mariage peut être prononcée par le juge même si elle n'est pas prévue expressément par la loi. Elle peut en effet être considérée par le juge comme une forme de préjudice rendant impossible la poursuite de la vie commune entre les époux. En Egypte, les juges de la Cour de cassation ont invoqué la *charia* pour contraindre en 1996 un professeur d'université, accusé d'apostasie à cause de ses écrits, à se séparer de son épouse[34].

L'apostat est considéré comme civilement mort et il y aura donc ouverture de sa succession. Tous ses liens familiaux sont rompus et il perd ses droits de

28 Art. 28 du code du statut personnel de 2010.

29 Art. 26 du code de la famille de 1992.

30 Art. 18 du code de la famille de 1984 : « N'est pas conclu le mariage : 1. De la musulmane avec un non-musulman ; 2. D'un musulman avec une non-scripturaire ; 3. De l'apostat ou de l'apostate qui quitte l'islam, même si l'autre conjoint est non-musulman ».

31 Art. 49 du code du statut personnel yéménite de 1992 et art. 142 du code du statut personnel jordanien de 2010.

32 Art. 145 du Code de la famille : « 1. Si le mari apostasie, le mariage est dissous. Mais s'il apostasie après la consommation du mariage et qu'il revient pendant la retraite de la femme, la dissolution est annulée et la vie conjugale est rétablie. 2. Si la femme apostasie, le mariage n'est pas dissous ».

33 Art. 32 du Code de la famille algérien de 1984: « Le mariage est déclaré nul ... si l'apostasie du conjoint est établie ».

34 Sur cette affaire voir B. Dupret, J.-N. Ferrié, « Participer au pouvoir, c'est édicter la norme : sur l'affaire Abu Zayd (Égypte, 1992–1996) », *Revue française de science politique*, vol. 47, n° 6, décembre 1997, pp. 762–775 ; B. Dupret, « L'affaire Abû Zayd, universitaire poursuivi pour apostasie », *Maghreb-Machrek*, vol. 151, 1996, pp. 18 et s. et B. Johansen, « Apostasy as Objective and Depersonalized Fact, Two Recent Egyptian Court Judgements », *Social Research*, 70, 3, 2003.

filiation et le droit de garde de ses enfants (ex. art. 171 code jordanien du statut personnel). Lui-même perd les droits à la succession des membres de sa famille car un non-musulman ne peut hériter d'un musulman.

2.3 *Liberté religieuse et ordre public : l'exemple de l'Egypte*

La supériorité de la *charia* islamique au sein de l'ordre normatif se dégage de la jurisprudence des juges du fond, par le biais de leur recours à la notion d'ordre public, ensemble de valeurs incarnant l'intérêt général suprême d'une société, dont elle a été reconnue comme composante. C'est le cas ainsi en Egypte, pour les juges administratifs du Conseil d'Etat. La place de la *charia* comme composante de l'ordre public y est apparue à l'occasion de litiges de droit administratif touchant à la liberté religieuse, portés devant le Conseil d'Etat. Le juge administratif a en effet affirmé la suprématie sur toute autre norme juridique des principes fondamentaux de la *charia* islamique, à travers le recours à la notion d'ordre public, sur la base notamment de l'article 2 de la constitution.

Le Conseil d'Etat a ainsi été saisi de requêtes en modification de la mention de la religion figurant sur des documents officiels[35] et a invoqué à chaque fois la notion d'ordre public en affirmant la supériorité des principes de la Loi islamique sur toute autre norme du système juridique égyptien.

2.3.1 Anciens chrétiens convertis à l'islam

Le Conseil d'Etat fut amené à examiner des requêtes d'anciens chrétiens, convertis à l'islam, qui souhaitaient revenir au christianisme et modifier la religion et le nom figurant sur leurs papiers officiels. En dehors des cas où la conversion est due à de sincères convictions religieuses, des chrétiens recourent parfois à la conversion à l'islam pour se voir appliquer le droit du statut personnel des musulmans, plus libéral que les lois chrétiennes en matière de divorce[36]. D'autres deviendraient musulmans pour obtenir de meilleures conditions de travail ou un meilleur statut social. Lorsque la conversion est motivée par un mariage ou un divorce, il arrive qu'une fois l'objectif atteint, ces nouveaux convertis cherchent à revenir à leur religion d'origine. S'ils

35 En Egypte, la religion figure sur la carte d'identité, les déclarations de naissance et de décès, les contrats de mariage et les certificats de répudiation.

36 Si le droit égyptien applique le système de la personnalité des lois en matière de statut personnel, la différence de rite entre les époux entraîne l'application de la loi du statut personnel des musulmans et facilite donc la dissolution du mariage. Depuis l'amendement de la loi du statut personnel des coptes orthodoxes en 2008, les membres de cette communauté ne peuvent en effet divorcer qu'en cas de changement de religion du conjoint ou d'adultère.

parviennent à convaincre leurs autorités ecclésiastiques de les réintégrer au sein de leur Eglise, ils doivent alors officialiser leur changement de religion en demandant la modification de l'affiliation religieuse figurant sur leurs papiers officiels. Or, les officiers du département des affaires civiles refusent en principe de procéder à cette modification et les convertis n'ont d'autre solution que de s'adresser au juge administratif pour tenter d'obtenir un jugement en leur faveur.

Entre 2004 et 2007, plus de 200 chrétiens convertis à l'islam auraient fait appel devant le Conseil d'Etat de la décision de refus du département des affaires civiles de modifier leur affiliation religieuse[37]. Si, par une jurisprudence constante, le Conseil d'Etat avait toujours refusé de donner une suite favorable à de telles requêtes[38], il en fut autrement entre avril 2004 et septembre 2006, période pendant laquelle la Cour du contentieux administratif donna raison à 22 demandeurs[39]. Présidée par un juge particulièrement libéral, la Cour affirma que les conversions étaient valables si elles recueillaient l'approbation de l'autorité officielle compétente, c'est-à-dire le patriarcat copte orthodoxe dans le cas de retour au christianisme de coptes orthodoxes convertis. Elle ajouta que la loi de 1994 relative à l'état civil exige que les cartes d'identité reflètent le statut réel des citoyens et qu'autoriser les requérants à changer la religion figurant sur leurs cartes d'identité ne fait que refléter une réalité, sans établir de situation nouvelle. Pour la Cour, le refus du gouvernement de reconnaître le retour de ces citoyens au christianisme devait être considéré comme une ingérence injustifiable et constituait une pression sur le requérant pour le pousser à adopter une certaine foi ou religion contre sa volonté.

Après le départ à la retraite de ce juge, la Cour revint à une position plus traditionnelle, donnant raison au département des affaires civiles contre les requérants[40]. Certes, elle affirma que la liberté de croyance constituait un droit absolu, consacré à la fois par les constitutions égyptiennes et les instruments internationaux relatifs

---

37 Human Rights Watch et The Egyptian Initiative For Personal Rights, *Prohibited Identities. State Interference in Religious Freedom*, novembre 2007. Voir aussi M.A. El Fegiery, « Islamic Law and Freedom of Religion: The Case of Apostasy and Its Legal Implication », *Muslim Word Journal of Human Rights*, vol. 10, n° 1, août 2013, pp. 1–26 et M. Orabi, « Authorizing Religious Conversion in Administrative Courts: Law, Rights, and Secular Indeterminacy », *New Diversities*, vol. 17, n° 1, 2015, pp. 63–76.

38 A.S. Hamad, « Legal Plurality and Legitimation of Human Rights Abuses. A Case Study of State Council Rulings Concerning the Rights of Apostates », *in* B. Dupret, M. Berger, L. Al-Zwaini, *Legal Pluralism in the Arab World*, Kluwer Law International, La Haye, 1999, pp. 219–228.

39 Voir par exemple Cour du contentieux administratif, n° 26103/85, 26 avril 2005.

40 Voir par exemple Cour du contentieux administratif, n° 36075/58, 4 juillet 2007.

aux droits de l'homme, ainsi que par le Coran qui les avaient tous précédés. Mais elle établit une distinction entre la liberté de croyance et la liberté d'expression des croyances religieuses, d'une part, et la liberté de manipuler les croyances et de changer de religion à des fins terrestres et matérielles, d'autre part. Elle ajouta que la religion musulmane repose sur un principe accepté par tous ceux qui choisissent librement d'y adhérer, selon lequel il n'est pas possible de la quitter. Prétendre le contraire serait chercher à manipuler les religions, les croyances et les lois, et violerait les règles impératives qu'imposent l'ordre public et la stabilité de la société, dans un pays où la majorité des citoyens croient en la religion musulmane et où la constitution affirme que la religion de l'Etat est l'islam. Même si la constitution n'impose pas le respect de l'ordre public comme limite à la liberté de croyance, cette limite qui figurait dans les constitutions égyptiennes antérieures[41] et est prévue par le Pacte international sur les droits civils et politiques, est sous-entendue et est présente de façon tacite dans la conscience du législateur et du peuple. L'apostat ne peut donc demander le changement de son affiliation religieuse sur ses papiers d'identité car ce serait contraire à la fois à la loi et à la *charia*. Permettre à un individu de retourner à sa religion initiale après une conversion à l'islam constituerait une attaque contre l'islam.

Si au niveau juridique, rien dans les lois positives actuellement en vigueur en Egypte n'interdit la conversion de musulmans au christianisme, le recours à l'islam comme élément constituant de l'ordre public égyptien permet donc d'introduire cette interdiction. On remarque que la Cour établit une présomption de manque de sincérité des requérants convertis à l'islam qui demandent à retourner au christianisme. La liberté religieuse ne s'applique pas à eux car ils manipulent la religion, ce qui est contraire à l'ordre public.

L'année suivante, la Haute Cour administrative, saisie en appel, autorisa cependant des coptes convertis à l'islam revenus au christianisme à modifier la religion figurant sur leur carte d'identité[42]. Pour la Cour, une telle identification ne constitue en aucune manière une approbation de leur acte mais permet de les identifier et de protéger la société en l'avertissant des éventuels actes frauduleux qu'ils pourraient commettre. Elle ajouta toutefois que la carte d'identité devrait spécifier que son titulaire a été musulman. Cette solution constitue donc une semi-victoire pour les reconvertis car s'ils sont autorisés à

41 Les constitutions égyptiennes antérieures, dès 1923, ont toujours garanti le caractère absolu de la liberté de croyance, mais la liberté de culte devait être exercée en conformité avec les usages en Égypte et à condition qu'ils ne soient pas contraires à l'ordre public et aux bonnes mœurs.

42 Haute Cour administrative n° 13496/53, 9 février 2008.

indiquer « chrétiens » sur leur carte d'identité, la précision « anciens musulmans » risque de les soumettre à des préjugés sociaux et à des discriminations.

2.3.2 Musulmans convertis au christianisme

La notion d'ordre public fut également invoquée pour refuser de modifier l'affiliation religieuse de musulmans d'origine convertis au christianisme[43]. C'est en 2007 que fut soumise la première requête en modification de la mention figurant sur les papiers d'identité d'un musulman de naissance converti au christianisme. Mohammed Ahmed Higazy, devenu Bishoy Armiya Boulos, se vit opposer un refus catégorique par les fonctionnaires du département des affaires familiales[44]. Le 29 janvier 2008[45], la Cour du contentieux administratif confirma le refus, affirmant qu'il serait contraire à l'ordre public de modifier la religion figurant sur la carte d'identité du requérant. Elle réaffirma que la liberté de pratiquer les rites religieux doit s'exercer dans le respect de l'ordre public et des bonnes mœurs, ajoutant que l'ordre public doit être défini en prenant en considération le fait que l'islam est la religion pratiquée par la majorité du peuple égyptien. Or, si l'islam interdit de contraindre un non-musulman à embrasser l'islam, quiconque est entré dans l'islam et a pratiqué ses rites ne peut en sortir car il s'agit du sceau des religions, et ce principe fait partie de l'ordre public. Même si aucun texte législatif ne condamne le crime d'apostasie, le juge administratif est tenu de faire respecter l'ordre public, lequel interdit de porter atteinte à la religion officielle du pays, qui est pratiquée par la majorité du peuple. Dieu a révélé les religions dans un ordre chronologique : le judaïsme, puis le christianisme, puis l'islam. Celui qui croit au judaïsme a vocation à se convertir au christianisme et le chrétien est amené à devenir musulman, mais l'inverse est impossible par la volonté de Dieu et est contraire à l'ordre public.

Maher Ahmed al-Mutasim Billah, devenu Maher al-Gohari, connut le même sort, mais la motivation de la Cour du contentieux administratif fut différente. Dans un arrêt du 13 juin 2009[46], elle refusa de donner valeur juridique à un certificat de conversion que l'Eglise copte orthodoxe avait accepté,

---

43 Si la procédure de conversion à l'islam est bien réglementée, aucun texte ne vient régir la conversion au christianisme.

44 Cette demande d'officialiser la conversion était motivée par le fait que l'épouse du requérant était enceinte et que le couple souhaitait que leur enfant soit enregistré comme chrétien. Voir L. Guirguis, *Les coptes d'Egypte. Violences communautaires et transformations politiques (2005–2012)*, Karthala, collection Terres et Gens d'Islam, 2012, pp. 84 et s. Voir aussi L. Guirguis (dir.), *Conversions religieuses et mutations politiques en Égypte*, Non Lieu, Paris, 2007.

45 Cour du contentieux administratif, n° 35647/61, 29 janvier 2008.

46 Cour du contentieux administratif, n° 22566/63 et 53717/62, 13 juin 2009.

pour la première fois, de remettre à un converti musulman d'origine. La Cour affirma que la liberté de croyance garantie par la constitution, y compris la liberté d'embrasser une autre religion, est une question d'ordre interne, personnelle, qui n'est pas sujette à restrictions. Par contre, la liberté de pratiquer les rites religieux peut être soumise à des limites pour sauvegarder des intérêts supérieurs, comme le respect de l'ordre public et des bonnes mœurs, ainsi que l'avaient reconnu les constitutions égyptiennes successives.

Après avoir rappelé également que la religion officielle de l'Etat est l'islam et que les principes de la *charia* sont la source principale de la législation, elle souligna qu'en Egypte le changement de religion peut avoir des conséquences juridiques significatives, en particulier dans les affaires familiales, comme le mariage, le divorce ou l'héritage, qui diffèrent en fonction de la religion ou de la confession.

Elle invoqua l'article 18 du Pacte international sur les droits civils et politiques, qui reconnaît bien la liberté religieuse, mais précisa que l'Egypte avait émis une déclaration interprétative indiquant qu'elle respecterait le pacte tant qu'il ne viendrait pas en conflit avec les principes de la *charia*. Elle rappela ensuite que, conformément à l'article 47 de la loi de 1994 relative à l'état civil, les demandes de changement d'affiliation religieuse devaient se faire sur la base de jugements ou de documents émanant des organismes compétents. Or, en l'espèce, ajouta la Cour, il n'existait pas de tribunal compétent pour émettre un tel jugement de conversion et le législateur n'avait pas désigné d'autorité administrative compétente pour certifier la conversion d'un musulman vers le christianisme. La Cour refusa de reconnaître la compétence de l'Eglise copte en ce domaine, affirmant qu'aucune disposition législative ne lui attribuait cette faculté. Bien que l'article 47 de la loi sur les affaires civiles acceptât le changement d'affiliation religieuse sans poser de limites, la réalité juridique ne permettait donc pas le changement de religion de l'islam vers une autre religion, conclut la Cour.

On constate que la Cour a fondé sa décision sur le fait que le requérant devait produire un document officiel prouvant sa conversion. Elle invoqua donc des arguments d'ordre strictement juridique (« manque de preuve légale ») et non des arguments religieux (« il n'est pas possible à un musulman de changer de religion »).

2.3.3 Enfants de chrétiens convertis à l'islam

Le Conseil d'Etat fut également saisi de requêtes d'enfants de parents convertis à l'islam : si l'un des parents se convertit, les enfants sont automatiquement considérés comme musulmans eux aussi. Or, bien souvent, c'est le père qui se convertit et les enfants restent vivre avec leur mère, chrétienne, et continuent d'être élevés dans le christianisme. C'est seulement à l'âge de 16 ans, lorsqu'ils font une demande de délivrance de leur première carte d'identité, qu'ils découvrent qu'ils ont été enregistrés comme musulmans, voire que leur nom a été islamisé.

La Cour du contentieux administratif d'Alexandrie a décidé, par un jugement du 3 septembre 2006, que la conversion à l'islam d'un père chrétien entraînait la conversion de ses enfants, même si ces derniers et leur mère chrétienne y étaient opposés. En avril 2009, de même, la Cour du contentieux administratif refusa de donner suite à des requêtes[47] introduites par des mères chrétiennes contre le ministère de l'Intérieur et le directeur de l'office de l'état civil, qui contestaient le changement par l'Etat de l'affiliation religieuse de leurs enfants sur leur carte d'identité. La Cour invoqua le fait que les lois sur le statut personnel des musulmans et des non-musulmans confient au père la tutelle sur ses enfants, et qu'en l'espèce le changement d'affiliation religieuse avait été effectué dans le respect de la loi et des prérogatives du gardien. Les autorités administratives ne pouvaient modifier des informations communiquées par la personne compétente.

Le 30 juin 2009, la Cour du contentieux administratif rejeta un recours présenté par un requérant[48] qui protestait contre le fait qu'il était considéré comme musulman depuis que son père s'était converti à l'islam lorsqu'il avait 6 ans et avait changé son nom en Mohamed Mustafa Mohamed. Ces changements avaient été faits sans son consentement et maintenant qu'il avait atteint l'âge de raison, il demandait à pouvoir revenir à son nom et à sa religion initiale. La Cour rejeta sa requête en affirmant que l'islam, religion de la majorité des Egyptiens, reconnait aux non-musulmans la liberté de choisir la religion révélée de leur choix, mais qu'elle interdit à ceux qui sont entrés dans la religion musulmane et qui ont pratiqué ses rituels de la quitter, car l'islam est le sceau des religions révélées. Ce principe fait partie de l'ordre public et doit être respecté. Bien que les spécialistes religieux soient divisés sur le fait que l'apostasie doive ou non être sanctionnée par la peine de *hadd*[49], il n'en reste pas moins que tous condamnent l'apostasie, ajouta la Cour. L'ordre public est violé chaque fois qu'il est porté atteinte à la religion nationale officielle, qui occupe une place permanente au sein de la majorité du peuple égyptien. Le musulman qui a choisi l'islam ou qui a vécu et intériorisé l'islam ne peut pas le quitter. Le juif est appelé à embrasser le christianisme, qui a été révélé après,

47 Cour du contentieux administratif, n° 27658/62, 14 avril 2009.

48 Court du contentieux administratif, n° 4475/58, 30 juin 2009.

49 Peines légales prévues par le Coran punies par des châtiments corporels ou par la peine de mort.

et le chrétien est appelé à se convertir à l'islam, le sceau des religions. L'inverse n'est pas possible, conformément à l'ordre de révélation par Dieu de ses religions, et conformément à l'ordre public et aux bonnes mœurs. La Cour rejeta donc la requête en affirmant qu'il est de jurisprudence constante au sein des spécialistes du droit musulman que l'enfant suit en religion celui de ses parents qui est musulman et que pour les hanafites[50], il n'est pas nécessaire que l'enfant qui atteint l'âge de maturité réaffirme sa croyance en l'islam car il est déjà considéré comme musulman.

2.3.4 Les minorités religieuses non reconnues

A partir de l'informatisation des cartes d'identité en 1994, les citoyens durent s'adresser au département des affaires civiles pour échanger leur ancienne carte, manuscrite, pour une nouvelle, numérique. Chaque citoyen devait indiquer la religion à faire figurer sur ses papiers, et le système informatique ne donnait le choix qu'entre trois options : musulman, chrétien ou juif. Alors que jusque-là une certaine souplesse avait permis à des adeptes de religions non reconnues, comme les bahaïs, de voir leur affiliation religieuse indiquée sur leurs papiers officiels ou de laisser vide la case « religion »[51], la plupart des officiers du département des affaires civiles refusèrent dès lors d'enregistrer une affiliation religieuse autre que l'une des trois religions reconnues, sous peine de refus de délivrance des documents requis. De nombreux bahaïs choisirent alors de ne pas déposer de demandes de délivrance de carte d'identité et de vivre sans papiers officiels. D'autres attaquèrent le département des affaires civiles devant le Conseil d'Etat. La jurisprudence du juge administratif, longtemps instable, semble maintenant fixée.

Le 4 avril 2006[52], des parents bahaïs obtinrent de la Cour du contentieux administratif le droit d'inscrire leur religion sur les certificats de naissance et les cartes d'identité de leurs trois filles. Les anciens certificats de naissance mentionnant la religion bahaïe avaient été retirés des dossiers administratifs de l'école des enfants et ces derniers étaient menacés d'expulsion s'ils n'en produisaient pas de nouveaux, mentionnant l'une des trois religions reconnues. Cet arrêt, qui venait à l'encontre du refus des responsables du département des affaires civiles de leur délivrer ces documents, reprenait une décision de

50 Le rite hanafite est l'une des quatre écoles sunnites reconnues. C'est le rite officiel en Egypte.

51 Pour le statut juridique des bahaïs en Egypte, voir J. Pink, « A Post-Qurānic Religion between Apostasy and Public Order: Egyptian Muftis and Courts on the Legal Status of the Bahāī Faith », *Islamic Law and Society*, 2003, 10:3, pp. 419 et s.

52 Cour du contentieux administratif, n° 24044/58, 4 avril 2006.

la Haute Cour administrative de 1983[53], affirmant qu'il était dans l'intérêt de l'Etat de reconnaître la véritable affiliation religieuse de ses citoyens, afin que leur statut juridique soit connu et que soient identifiés leurs droits, devoirs et les lois qui leur sont applicables, qui diffèrent de ceux dont bénéficient les musulmans. Pour la Cour, la mention de la véritable affiliation religieuse devait donc permettre de ne pas soumettre ces individus à un régime juridique que leur appartenance religieuse réelle ne justifiait pas. Mais ce jugement fut attaqué par le ministère de l'Intérieur et cassé par la Haute Cour administrative qui décida, en décembre 2006[54] que le gouvernement n'était pas tenu d'autoriser les bahaïs à faire figurer leur religion sur leur carte d'identité. La Cour reprit la distinction entre la liberté religieuse, absolue, et la liberté de culte, conditionnée par le respect de l'ordre public et des bonnes mœurs. Elle considéra le fait d'indiquer sa religion sur les papiers d'identité comme la manifestation d'un rite religieux et accusa la foi bahaïe d'entretenir des liens avec les forces coloniales, et d'avoir établi sa propre loi (*shari'a*), contraire aux règles de l'islam relatives au jeûne, à la prière, au *jihad* ou au droit de la famille. Elle conclut en affirmant que le terme « religion » figurant dans la loi n° 143 de 1994 relative à l'état civil et l'arrêté ministériel n° 1121 de 1995 ne visait que les religions reconnues, qui sont celles dont les constitutions égyptiennes successives ont garanti la liberté d'expression des rites religieux. Quant aux autres religions, comme le bahaïsme, ajouta la Cour, il était interdit de les mentionner dans les documents officiels publics. Les règles juridiques posant cette interdiction devaient être considérées comme faisant partie de l'ordre public et il n'était donc pas possible de les violer dans un pays qui reposait sur la *charia* islamique.

Les bahaïs changèrent alors de stratégie. Puisque la Haute Cour administrative refusait d'inscrire la religion bahaïe sur leurs papiers officiels, ils demandèrent que la case « religion » soit laissée vide. Un étudiant de l'Université de Suez, qui avait vu son inscription suspendue pour ne pas avoir produit de carte d'identité, attaqua le département des affaires civiles pour refus de délivrance de papiers d'identité au nom de sa religion. Le 29 janvier 2008[55], la Cour du contentieux administratif l'autorisa à laisser vide la case « religion », afin de protéger les membres des religions révélées de l'influence néfaste des bahaïs, qu'elle qualifia d'apostats, et qui pourraient essayer de se faire passer pour des chrétiens et des musulmans. Il fallait donc éviter les méfaits qui pourraient

53 Haute Cour administrative, n° 84/31, 29 janvier 1983.

54 Haute Cour administrative, n° 16834 et 18971/52, 16 décembre 2006.

55 Cour du contentieux administratif, n° 12780/61, 29 janvier 2008. Un autre jugement du même jour, dans une autre affaire, confirma la même position (Cour du contentieux administratif, n° 18354/58, 29 janvier 2008).

résulter de leur conduite et des contacts avec eux. La Cour souligna toutefois qu'une telle décision n'entraînait nullement la reconnaissance de la foi bahaïe comme religion et qu'il s'agissait d'une pensée déviante et inadmissible. Elle rappela que la liberté d'expression des rites religieux pouvait être limitée, conformément aux constitutions antérieures, sur la base du respect de l'ordre public et des bonnes mœurs. Si l'ordre public a un contenu différent selon les sociétés, parmi ses éléments constitutifs en Egypte figurait le fait qu'il s'agit d'un pays dont la religion officielle est l'islam, qui est la religion que professe la majorité de la population et que la *charia* islamique est la source principale de la législation. Même si cette disposition juridique s'adresse au législateur, les autres autorités de l'Etat sont elles-aussi tenues de respecter ces principes, notamment dans l'organisation des relations entre les individus et les organes administratifs. La Cour limita toutefois la portée de cette décision aux seuls cas où les documents antérieurs ne mentionnaient pas l'appartenance de l'individu à une des trois religions reconnues, pour protéger le principe de l'interdiction de toute coercition en matière de religion.

Ce jugement reçut un accueil positif de la part de la communauté bahaïe, même s'il confirmait le refus de reconnaissance de cette religion et ne s'appliquait qu'aux cas où des bahaïs avaient obtenu antérieurement la délivrance de papiers d'identité établissant leur appartenance à la religion bahaïe (ou tout au moins n'établissant pas leur appartenance à une religion révélée). Il fut confirmé en appel par la Haute Cour administrative en mars 2009[56] et mis à exécution par un arrêté ministériel[57] qui autorisa les citoyens égyptiens ayant déjà été reconnus personnellement ou à travers leurs parents comme n'appartenant pas à l'une des trois religions reconnues ou en exécution d'une décision de justice, à obtenir des cartes d'identité laissant vide la case réservée à la religion. Notons que cette formulation large peut théoriquement s'appliquer également aux adeptes d'autres religions non reconnues.

On constate également que le référent religieux agit comme une contrainte argumentative, même pour ceux qui n'en reconnaissent pas la légitimité, comme les bahaïs dans leur conflit avec les fonctionnaires, qui invoquèrent la tolérance religieuse prônée par le Coran à l'appui de leurs requêtes. Les nombreuses décisions contradictoires des fonctionnaires du service de l'état civil égyptien et des tribunaux, ainsi que les différentes législations du monde arabe, montrent également combien le contenu incertain des sources religieuses peut donner lieu à des décisions contradictoires et parfois même arbitraires.

56 Haute Cour administrative, n° 10831/54, 16 mars 2009.

57 Arrêté ministériel n° 520 du 19 mars 2009 amendant le règlement n° 1121/1995.

3 Conclusion

Malgré les progrès enregistrés, la liberté religieuse dans les pays de tradition musulmane ne peut être comparée à celle qui est consacrée par les textes internationaux. Cette liberté ne s'y entend pas comme la liberté de toutes les religions, mais comme une liberté s'exerçant dans le cadre strict délimité par l'Etat. Même après 2011, la liberté religieuse, comme les autres libertés, peine toujours à s'imposer, face à des régimes arabes parfois plus répressifs et autoritaires qu'avant les soulèvements populaires. La montée de l'intégrisme et des mouvements islamistes fournit à ces régimes une légitimité pour leurs politiques répressives tout en continuant à faire régner un climat d'intolérance.

Dans le présent comme dans le passé, la majorité des dirigeants des Etats musulmans, aidés par les hommes de religion, tirent profit du flou dans les sources religieuses pour légitimer leur pouvoir par la religion. Jouant de l'ambiguïté, des lacunes et des contradictions des sources religieuses, ils en donnent une interprétation qui sert leurs intérêts politiques et leur permet de garder le contrôle de leur population. Faisant de l'islam la religion de l'Etat, liant ainsi le politique et le religieux, ils contribuent à l'islamisation du droit et de la société tout en exacerbant les tensions entre les citoyens.

PART 3

International Human Rights Bodies and Freedom of Religion

CHAPTER 5

Les organes de protection des droits de l'homme des Nations Unies face à la religion

Ludovic Hennebel

Les droits de l'homme ont été consacrés aux Nations Unies dans une certaine forme d'urgence, au lendemain de la Seconde guerre mondiale. Sans doute n'était-ce ni le lieu, ni le moment, de les penser philosophiquement, et de tenter de s'accorder sur une justification rationnelle de ces droits[1]. Et tant N. Bobbio que Ch. Perelman[2], en se fondant sur une argumentation distincte, achèveront plus tard de nous convaincre que la quête d'un tel fondement absolu est inutile et illusoire. Pourtant, l'on ne peut ignorer les efforts de celles et ceux qui s'efforcèrent de trouver un tel fondement. Parmi les fondements proposés, dès les travaux préparatoires de la Déclaration universelle des droits de l'homme, les religions et convictions furent convoquées[3].

Pour certains auteurs, les droits de l'homme trouveraient leurs racines dans les discours religieux, parfois millénaires[4]. Un tel fondement religieux

---

1 Sur ces questions, voy. L. Hennebel et H. Tigroudja, *Traité de droit international des droits de l'homme*, Paris, Pedone, 2016 ; M.A. Glendon, « Foundations of Human Rights: The Unfinished Business », *American Journal of Jurisprudence*, 1999, vol. 44, pp. 1–14, et les réf. citées. Malgré ces remarques, on notera que des débats philosophiques relatifs aux droits de l'homme furent organisés notamment au sein du Comité de l'Unesco sur les Principes Philosophiques des droits de l'homme : Rapport à la Commission des droits de l'homme des Nations Unies, « Les fondements d'une déclaration internationale des droits de l'homme », Paris : 31 juillet 1947.

2 Voy. les articles de ces auteurs portant sur ce thème publiés dans Actes des entretiens d'Aquila, *Le fondement des droits de l'homme*, Institut international de philosophie, 1966, 402 p.

3 Sur ces questions, voy. M.A. Glendon, « Foundations of Human Rights ... », *op. cit.*, pp. 1–14, et les réf. citées. Malgré ces remarques, on notera que des débats philosophiques relatifs aux droits de l'homme furent organisés notamment au sein du Comité de l'Unesco sur les Principes Philosophiques des droits de l'homme : Rapport à la Commission des droits de l'homme des Nations Unies, « Les fondements d'une déclaration internationale des droits de l'homme », Paris, 31 juillet 1947.

4 Voy. par ex. M.C. Green et J. Witte, Jr., « Religion », *in* D. Shelton (éd.), *International Human Rights Law*, Oxford, OUP, 2013, p. 9 : affirmant que « *religious beliefs provide perhaps the most widely accepted foundations on which human rights law has been built* » ; P.G. Lauren, *The Evolution of International Human Rights: Visions Seen*, Philadelphia, University of

 | DOI:10.1163/9789004349155_006

des droits de l'homme permettrait de justifier l'idée de droits supérieurs au droit positif, inhérents à l'homme, et transcendantaux tout en sacralisant l'être humain, en tant que créature divine, doté de droits inaliénables car de source divine. S'il est vrai que l'on peut retrouver dans les discours religieux des points communs avec le discours des droits de l'homme, et minimiser les contradictions, un tel exercice est avant tout opportuniste en ce sens qu'il vise à affirmer l'harmonie de certains aspects choisis des discours religieux avec une certaine conception de l'idée des droits de l'homme. Toutefois, même si des références à la tolérance, à la dignité humaine, à l'égalité et à la justice sont présentes dans la plupart des discours religieux, l'on ne saurait en aucun cas en déduire un fondement absolu des droits de l'homme. Au mieux, on pourrait y trouver un fondement relatif de nature à emporter l'adhésion de certains croyants à l'idée des droits de l'homme, tout en supposant que les valeurs religieuses convergent avec les valeurs des droits de l'homme. Mais l'exercice de rapprochement des deux types de discours trouve rapidement ses limites. Car le droit international des droits de l'homme tel qu'il fut configuré à partir de 1948 a été laïcisé, en ce sens qu'il a été construit sans référence fondatrice à l'univers conceptuel religieux. En un mot, le droit international des droits de l'homme est un droit sans dieu. Aussi n'est-il pas surprenant que le texte de la Charte arabe des droits de l'homme de 2004 dans laquelle des références appuyées sont faites à dieu, à la charia et à l'islam[5] ait été jugé incompatible avec les « standards internationau » en raison d'une série de dispositions dont certaines sont directement influencées par des considérations religieuses ou culturelles (par exemple : la liberté de pensée, de croyance et de religion peut faire l'objet de restrictions prévues par la loi (article 30 *a*) ; l'égalité des hommes et des femmes est garantie sur le plan de la dignité ainsi que « des droits et des devoirs dans le cadre de la discrimination positive instituée au profit de la femme par la charia islamique et les autres lois divines et par les législations et les instruments internationaux » (article 3 *c*)15).

Le thème religieux n'est pas absent des discussions internationales menées au sein des Nations Unies. Il occupe au contraire une place de choix tant cette organisation – et en particulier le Rapporteur spécial et les organes conventionnels – se trouve confrontée à une série de défis portant sur la religion et

Pennsylvania Press, 2011, p. 5 : soutenant que « *All the major religions of the world seek in one way or another to speak to the issue of human responsibility to others* » ; voy. également sur cette question : M.J. Perry, *The Idea of Human Rights: Four Inquiries*, Oxford, New York, OUP, 1998, p. 11.

5 Voy. M. Rishmawi, « The Revised Arab Charter on Human Rights: A Step Forward? », *Human Rights Law Review*, 2005, pp. 361–376.

la liberté de religion et de conscience, auxquels il lui appartient de répondre avec prudence (2). Par ailleurs, la liberté de religion et de conscience est généreusement consacrée et protégée par un ensemble de normes adoptées dans le cadre des Nations Unies (1).

1 La protection de la religion et des libertés religieuses et de conviction dans le cadre normatif des Nations Unies

La religion reste une matière hautement sensible dans les relations interétatiques, à tel point qu'elle apparaît bien souvent comme une matière réservée, qui échappe à la discussion internationale. Pourtant les religions et les croyances ne sont pas en tant que telles protégées en droit international – en raison sans doute de considérations pragmatiques liées à l'hétérogénéité des croyances. Le droit international protège à travers ses instruments de protection des droits de l'homme la liberté – individuelle et collective – de religion et de conviction (1.1)[6]. Malgré cette large protection normative, les désaccords entre Etats ont été exprimés très tôt dans le processus de production normative, comme le montrent les réserves et objections à ces réserves exprimées à l'égard des dispositions consacrant certains aspects de la liberté de religion ou de conviction (1.2).

1.1 *Les fondements normatifs de la liberté de pensée, de conscience et de religion dans le système universel de protection des droits de l'homme*

La liberté de pensée, de conscience et de religion est consacrée par les conventions générales de protection des droits de l'homme tant dans le cadre des Nations Unies qu'au sein des organisations régionales. Prenant sa source dans l'article 18 de la Déclaration universelle des droits de l'homme[7] [ci-dessous DUDH], elle est énoncée en particulier à l'article 18 du Pacte international

---

6 B. Dickson, « The United Nations and Freedom of Religion », *Canadian Journal of Law and Jurisprudence*, vol. 21, n° 2, 2008, pp. 279–320 [cet article examine la pertinence des mécanismes des Nations Unies en vue de protéger la tolérance religieuse] ; J. Dhommeaux, « L'ONU et la liberté religieuse », *Revue des droits fondamentaux*, 2015, numéro spécial : « Religion et Cour européenne des droits de l'homme », Actes du colloque de l'APIDH, pp. 120 et s.; H. Bielefeldt, N. Ghanea, M. Wiener, *Freedom of Religion or Belief: An International Law Commentary*, Oxford, OUP, 2016.

7 Article 18 de la DUDH : « Toute personne a droit à la liberté de pensée, de conscience et de religion ; ce droit implique la liberté de changer de religion ou de conviction ainsi que la liberté de manifester sa religion ou sa conviction seule ou en commun, tant en public qu'en privé, par l'enseignement, les pratiques, le culte et l'accomplissement des rites. »

relatif aux droits civils et politiques[8] [ci-dessous PIDCP] qui consacre notamment le droit de chacun à la « liberté de pensée, de conscience et de religion », laquelle implique non seulement « la liberté d'avoir ou d'adopter une religion ou conviction de son choix », mais aussi la liberté de « manifester sa religion ou sa conviction ». Conformément aux autres normes régionales de protection, la liberté de pensée, de conscience et de religion, reflétant la croyance intime et le for intérieur, est considérée comme absolue, tandis que seules sont autorisées les restrictions à la liberté de manifester sa religion ou ses convictions. L'article 18 du PIDCP protège par ailleurs la liberté des parents d'assurer l'éducation religieuse et morale de leurs enfants conformément à leurs convictions, une protection que l'on retrouve dans la majorité des normes régionales.

Remarquons déjà à ce stade qu'en matière de liberté de religion et de conviction, la grande distinction qu'il convient d'opérer pour appréhender le régime juridique de cette liberté est celle qui repose sur la dimension interne (*forum internum*) qui jouit d'une protection absolue (article 18§2 du PIDCP) et celle qui relève de la manifestation (*forum extremum*). Les manifestations peuvent être restreintes à condition de respecter les conditions classiques : elles doivent être prévues par la loi et « nécessaires » à la poursuite d'un but légitime à savoir la protection de la sécurité publique, de l'ordre public, de la santé ou moralité publiques, ou des libertés et droits fondamentaux d'autrui. Elles doivent en outre être proportionnelles en ce sens qu'elles doivent générer une ingérence strictement nécessaire à la poursuite d'un but légitime. Pour le Comité : « les restrictions qui ne sont pas spécifiées dans le paragraphe 3 ne sont pas permises .... Les restrictions ne doivent être appliquées qu'aux fins pour lesquelles elles ont été prescrites et doivent être en rapport direct avec l'objectif spécifique qui les inspire et proportionnelles à celui-ci. Il ne peut être imposé de restrictions à des fins discriminatoires ni de façon discriminatoire »[9].

---

8 Article 18 du PIDCP : « 1. Toute personne a droit à la liberté de pensée, de conscience et de religion ; ce droit implique la liberté d'avoir ou d'adopter une religion ou une conviction de son choix, ainsi que la liberté de manifester sa religion ou sa conviction, individuellement ou en commun, tant en public qu'en privé, par le culte et l'accomplissement des rites, les pratiques et l'enseignement. 2. Nul ne subira de contrainte pouvant porter atteinte à sa liberté d'avoir ou d'adopter une religion ou une conviction de son choix. 3. La liberté de manifester sa religion ou ses convictions ne peut faire l'objet que des seules restrictions prévues par la loi et qui sont nécessaires à la protection de la sécurité, de l'ordre et de la santé publique, ou de la morale ou des libertés et droits fondamentaux d'autrui. 4. Les Etats parties au présent Pacte s'engagent à respecter la liberté des parents et, le cas échéant, des tuteurs légaux de faire assurer l'éducation religieuse et morale de leurs enfants conformément à leurs propres convictions ».

9 Comité DH, Le droit à la liberté de pensée, de conscience et de religion (Article 18), Observation générale n° 22, 1993, § 8.

Bien que les Nations Unies n'aient pas adopté de convention internationale portant spécifiquement sur la liberté de religion[10] ou la protection des religions, outre les dispositions mentionnées ci-dessus, la liberté de religion est également protégée dans les dispositions de certains instruments visant à protéger des catégories particulières de personnes telles que : l'article 14 de la Convention relative aux droits de l'enfant[11]; l'article 12 de la Convention internationale sur la protection des droits de tous les travailleurs migrants et des membres de leur famille[12]. On notera également que l'article 5 de la Convention de l'OIT relative aux peuples indigènes et tribaux (n° 169) fait référence aux valeurs et pratiques « religieuses et spirituelles » de ces peuples.

En sus de la protection articulée de la liberté de religion et de conviction, les normes de protection des droits de l'homme protègent les individus contre les discriminations fondées sur la religion ou la conviction. Telle est déjà l'approche retenue par la Déclaration sur l'élimination de toutes formes d'intolérance et de discrimination fondées sur la religion ou la convention (proclamée par l'Assemblée générale des Nations Unies le 25 novembre 1981, rés. 36/55) – ce

10 R. Clark, « The United Nations and Religious Freedom », *New York University Journal of International Law and Politics*, vol. 11, n° 2, 1978, pp. 197–226 [sur les difficultés liées à la protection normative de la liberté de religion au sein des Nations Unies].

11 Article 14 de la Convention sur les droits de l'enfant : « 1. Les Etats parties respectent le droit de l'enfant à la liberté de pensée, de conscience et de religion. 2. Les Etats parties respectent le droit et le devoir des parents ou, le cas échéant, des représentants légaux de l'enfant, de guider celui-ci dans l'exercice du droit susmentionné d'une manière qui corresponde au développement de ses capacités. 3. La liberté de manifester sa religion ou ses convictions ne peut être soumise qu'aux seules restrictions qui sont prescrites par la loi et qui sont nécessaires pour préserver la sûreté publique, l'ordre public, la santé et la moralité publiques, ou les libertés et droits fondamentaux d'autrui ».

12 Article 12 de la Convention sur les travailleurs migrants : « 1. Les travailleurs migrants et les membres de leur famille ont droit à la liberté de pensée, de conscience et de religion. Ce droit implique la liberté d'avoir ou d'adopter une religion ou une conviction de leur choix, ainsi que la liberté de manifester leur religion ou leur conviction, individuellement ou en commun, tant en public qu'en privé, par le culte et l'accomplissement des rites, les pratiques et l'enseignement. 2. Les travailleurs migrants et les membres de leur famille ne peuvent subir aucune contrainte pouvant porter atteinte à leur liberté d'avoir ou d'adopter une religion ou une conviction de leur choix. 3. La liberté de manifester sa religion ou ses convictions ne peut faire l'objet que des seules restrictions prévues par la loi et qui sont nécessaires à la protection de la sécurité, de l'ordre, de la santé ou de la moralité publics ou des libertés et droits fondamentaux d'autrui. 4. Les Etats parties à la présente Convention s'engagent à respecter la liberté des parents, dont l'un au moins est un travailleur migrant, et, le cas échéant, des tuteurs légaux de faire assurer l'éducation religieuse et morale de leurs enfants conformément à leurs propres convictions ».

texte va d'ailleurs bien au-delà puisqu'il énonce une série de libertés religieuses et de croyances –, mais également par la Convention internationale sur l'élimination de toutes les formes de discrimination raciale – obligeant les Etats à garantir « le droit de chacun à l'égalité devant la loi ... dans la jouissance ... du droit à la liberté de pensée, de conscience et de religion » – et par la plupart des normes générales prohibant les discriminations qui les interdisent notamment lorsqu'elles sont basées sur des motifs religieux (e.g. PIDCP, CEDH, CADH). L'article 27 du PIDCP mentionne enfin les minorités religieuses parmi les trois catégories protégées, à côté des minorités ethniques et linguistiques.

Les traités régionaux de protection des droits de l'homme consacrent également, à l'instar de l'article 18 du PIDCP, la liberté de pensée, de conscience et de religion, retenant des termes et une philosophie largement comparable même si des nuances existent : article 9 de la Convention européenne des droits de l'homme (CEDH) ; article 10 de la Charte des droits fondamentaux de l'Union européenne ; article 12 de la Convention américaine des droits de l'homme ; article 8 de la Charte africaine des droits de l'homme et des peuples ; ainsi que l'article 30 de la Charte arabe. Les analogies sont nombreuses, et notamment dans l'esprit de ces normes qui visent à lutter contre l'intolérance religieuse, à protéger positivement la liberté d'avoir ou d'adopter une religion ou une conviction, ainsi que la liberté de les manifester. On notera toutefois quelques divergences entre ces textes. Ainsi, à l'inverse de la CEDH qui ne retient pas l'article 9 parmi les dispositions indérogeables en cas de circonstances exceptionnelles, le PIDCP – à l'instar de la CADH et de la Charte arabe – érige l'article 18 au rang des dispositions indérogeables même en cas de circonstances exceptionnelles. Cette position met en exergue la valeur que les rédacteurs du PIDCP attachent à cette liberté particulière[13].

---

13 Dans le cadre des travaux préparatoires, la mention de la liberté de religion dans la liste des droits indérogeables fit l'objet de discussions. Selon le représentant du Royaume-Uni, l'exercice de ce droit pouvait être assimilé, dans certains de ses aspects, à l'exercice de la liberté d'expression ou du droit de réunion pacifique, dont les possibilités de dérogation en cas de guerre sont considérées par les Etats, unanimement, comme nécessaires. Certains Etats suggéraient qu'accepter de déroger au droit de manifester sa religion, même en cas de guerre, « laisserait une mauvaise impression ». Finalement, la proposition d'amendement qui visait à exclure le paragraphe 3 de l'article 18 de la liste a été rejetée car cette exclusion a été considérée comme inutile au vu de la clause de limitation que comprenait déjà cet article qui stipule que « la liberté de manifester sa religion ou ses convictions ne peut faire l'objet que des seules restrictions prévues par la loi et qui sont nécessaires à la protection de la sécurité, de l'ordre et de la santé publique, ou de la morale ou des libertés et droits fondamentaux d'autrui ». Voy. NU. Doc. E/CN.4/SR.330, p. 64 ; NU. Doc. E/CN.4/SR.331, p. 4.

1.2 *Les réserves de certains Etats dans le domaine de la reconnaissance de certaines libertés religieuses ou de croyance*

Si l'Arabie Saoudite n'a pas exprimé formellement les raisons ayant motivé son abstention lors du vote de la résolution de l'Assemblée générale des Nations Unies portant Déclaration universelle des droits de l'homme, l'on peut supposer à l'instar de J. Humphrey que cette position s'explique par son refus d'adhérer à l'article 18 de la DUDH reconnaissant le droit de changer de religion[14]. Aussi, dès l'adoption du texte fondateur du droit international des droits de l'homme contemporain, l'on perçoit les désaccords qui peuvent opposer les Etats sur la liberté de religion. Ces désaccords restent nombreux et, pour se limiter à quelques exemples formels, l'on constate que restent nombreuses les réserves des Etats faites à l'égard des articles relatifs à la liberté de religion dans le Pacte international relatif aux droits civils et politiques, la Convention sur l'élimination de toutes les formes de discrimination à l'égard des femmes[15], ou encore la Convention relative aux droits de l'enfant, notamment de la part de plus d'une vingtaine d'Etats tels que l'Arabie saoudite, le Bahreïn, le Maroc, le Bangladesh, la Mauritanie, la Syrie, l'Iran ou encore les Maldives au nom de la charia[16]. Les objections à ces réserves des Etats européens sont systématiques, et même si certains Etats réservataires les retirent (par exemple le Pakistan à l'égard du PIDCP), elles n'en restent pas moins préoccupantes du point de vue de la logique de la liberté de religion telle que protégée en droit international des droits de l'homme.

Pour le surplus, ces « réserves charia » ne posent pas tant de difficultés sur le fond du point de vue du droit international[17]. Il ne s'agit pas de s'y opposer sur le terrain des valeurs ou de contester la possibilité d'invoquer une loi

---

14 J.P. Humphrey, *Human Rights & the United Nations: A Great Adventure*, Dobbs Ferry, NY, Transnational Publishers, 1984, p. 73 : S. Waltz, « Universal Human Rights: The Contribution of Muslim States », *Human Rights Quarterly*, vol. 26, 2004, pp. 814–17.

15 Beaucoup d'Etats qui appliquent la charia islamique ont ainsi émis des réserves à l'encontre des articles 2 et 16 de la CEDAW, soumettant expressément les principes d'égalité et de non-discrimination que ces dispositions affirment au respect de la loi religieuse (voy. les réserves du Bahreïn, de l'Egypte ou encore de l'Arabie saoudite et le Koweït). De la même manière, Israël a émis une réserve, pour des motifs religieux, à l'encontre de l'article 7(b) de la CEDAW concernant l'exercice d'emplois publics, les femmes se voyant refuser le droit de siéger dans des tribunaux religieux.

16 J. Dhommeaux, « L'ONU et la liberté religieuse », *Revue des droits fondamentaux*, 2015, numéro spécial : « Religion et Cour européenne des droits de l'homme », Actes du colloque de l'APIDH, pp. 120 et s.

17 Voy. A. Pellet, Guide de la pratique sur les réserves aux traités, Commentaires, Rapport de la Commission de droit international, 2011, A/66/10/Add.1, pp. 387–388, § 7.

religieuse dans le cadre d'une réserve. En revanche, ces réserves sont généralement jugées trop vagues ou générales, empêchant d'apprécier leur compatibilité avec l'objet et le but du traité.

2 Les principaux défis des Nations Unies face à la religion et à la liberté de religion

Sans doute l'un des sujets les plus sensibles politiquement est-il celui de l'amalgame effectué entre la violence et la religion. Le Rapporteur spécial relève sur ce « phénomène complexe » que la « violence commise au nom de la religion, peut se manifester sous différentes formes : attentats contre des personnes ou de communautés, violences intercommunautaires, attentats-suicides, actes terroristes, répression de l'Etat, politiques ou lois discriminatoires et d'autres types encore de comportements violents »[18]. Les formes de cette violence sont variées, autant que les auteurs – étatiques ou non étatiques –, les victimes – dissidents religieux, convertis, minorités religieuses, voire les membres d'une religion majoritaire. Prudemment, le Rapporteur spécial déconstruit les amalgames en rappelant que le lien entre religion et violence – tellement ancré dans l'histoire des relations internationales et dans l'actualité géopolitique – n'est jamais direct puisqu'il requiert toujours une intervention humaine : des groupes ou des individus qui fabriquent artificiellement ce lien. Cette problématique est centrale dans le cadre des relations internationales notamment, dès lors que la majorité des conflits ont une dimension prétendument religieuse. Elle montre aussi le vaste empire de la religion et la portée des défis des Nations Unies en la matière. Mais, pour se limiter à l'examen de la liberté de religion et de conscience, sans s'aventurer sur le terrain plus spéculatif et politique de la relation entre violence et religion, il convient de souligner les défis auxquels se heurte l'organisation dans son travail d'interprétation de la liberté. On mettra en exergue, dans ce cadre, en particulier le rôle majeur joué par le Rapporteur spécial sur la liberté de religion et de conviction, dont les rapports sont riches tant au point de vue empirique qu'analytique. A cela s'ajoutent encore les travaux du Comité des droits de l'homme des Nations Unies (Comité DH), voire d'autres comités conventionnels, qui a contribué largement à interpréter la liberté de religion et de conviction, tant dans le cadre de ses constatations individuelles que dans celui de son mécanisme sur rapport, le tout étant synthétisé dans une observation générale. Les documents

18 Rapport du Rapporteur spécial sur la liberté de religion et de conviction, 29 décembre 2014, A/HRC/28/66, § 3.

issus de l'examen période universel opéré par le Conseil des droits de l'homme permettent tout au plus de souligner l'actualité d'une pratique ou d'une violation[19], ou les objections de certains Etats aux pratiques défendues par d'autres, sans pour autant offrir une plus-value particulière quant à l'approche juridique de la religion en droit international.

On constate, à la lumière d'une brève analyse empirique, que les organes des Nations Unies sont invités à trancher des controverses hautement sensibles dans le domaine des religions. La diversité culturelle et religieuse qu'offrent les 193 Etats membres permet difficilement d'adopter des normes déterminées et précises de nature à appréhender l'ensemble des questions susceptibles d'être posées. La liberté de religion et de conviction est extrêmement délicate à appréhender dans le cadre pluraliste des Nations Unies, non seulement car elle concerne les croyances, mais aussi et surtout car elle soulève inévitablement des questions controversées sur l'égalité entre les hommes et femmes, l'éducation religieuse et l'enseignement des religions, les pratiques culturelles et parfois pseudo-religieuses considérées comme néfastes, les limites de la liberté d'expression, ou encore les droits de la famille.

Le défi majeur des Nations Unies en la matière consiste donc à déterminer le contenu des normes internationales pertinentes protégeant la liberté de religion et de conviction en affichant sa neutralité tout en s'efforçant d'amender les comportements et pratiques incompatibles avec la vision libérale et pluraliste que l'Organisation défend.

2.1 *L'approche pragmatique au service du pluralisme religieux*

Les termes « religion » ou « conviction » restent relativement indéterminés et les organes de protection semblent peu favorables à les enfermer dans les balises d'une définition. Cela permet d'en retenir une acception large de nature à favoriser le pluralisme religieux. Loin de protéger uniquement les croyants des grandes religions traditionnelles ou celles que l'on pourrait assimiler à de telles religions ou encore les religions d'Etat, officielles ou traditionnelles, l'article 18 du PIDCP protège les convictions théistes, non théistes et athées[20], et repose sur une conception ouverte de la religion et de la conviction. La Rapporteur spécial des Nations Unies sur la liberté de religion ou de conviction ajoute sur ce point : « la liberté de religion ou de conviction englobe également les droits des membres des communautés, petites et grandes, des

19 A titre d'exemple, la France est fortement sollicitée par une série d'Etats relativement à sa politique d'interdiction des signes religieux.

20 Comité DH, Le droit à la liberté de pensée, de conscience et de religion (Article 18), Observation générale n° 22, 1993, § 2.

minorités ainsi que des minorités au sein de minorités, des traditionalistes et des libéraux, des personnes converties et reconverties, des dissidents et autres opposants et enfin – et surtout – des femmes qui, hélas, occupent une place marginale dans la plupart des traditions religieuses »[21].

Par extension, la liberté de conscience et de religion permet de protéger positivement des libertés au-delà de la lettre des normes internationales. A titre d'exemple, elle fonde également le droit des objecteurs de conscience de refuser de faire un service militaire, obligeant l'Etat à offrir un service alternatif dans de telles hypothèses. La position du Comité des droits de l'homme[22], qui a inspiré la Cour européenne des droits de l'homme, est très claire – et très pragmatique – : « Le Pacte ne mentionne pas explicitement un droit à l'objection de conscience, mais le Comité estime qu'un tel droit peut être déduit de l'article 18, dans la mesure où l'obligation d'employer la force au prix de vies humaines peut être gravement en conflit avec la liberté de conscience et le droit de manifester sa religion ou ses convictions. Lorsque ce droit sera reconnu dans la législation ou la pratique, il n'y aura plus de différenciation entre objecteurs de conscience sur la base de la nature de leurs convictions particulières, de même qu'il ne s'exercera pas de discrimination contre les objecteurs de conscience parce qu'ils n'ont pas accompli leur service militaire »[23].

De manière générale, en droit international on ne définit pas la « religion » ou la « conviction », mais on se contente de déterminer si les pratiques observées au

21 Rapport du Rapporteur spécial sur la liberté de religion ou de conviction, 2 août 2016, A/71/269, § 12.

22 Voy. par exemple Comité DH, *Ahmet Hudaybergenov c. Turkmenistan*, constatations du 29 octobre 2015, n° 2222/2012 ; Comité DH, *Yoon et Choi c. République de Corée*, constatation du 21 janvier 2007, communications n° 1321/2004 et n° 1322/2004, §§ 8.3-8.4 ; Comité DH, *Kim et al. c. République de Corée*, constatations du 25 octobre 2012, communication n° 1786/2008, § 7.4 : le Comité y rappelle que le « droit à l'objection de conscience est inhérent au droit à la liberté de pensée, de conscience et de religion » ; Comité DH, *Young-kwan Kim et al. c. République de Corée*, constatations du 15 octobre 2014, communication n° 2179/2012, § 7.5. Devant la Cour EDH, voy. l'important arrêt Cour EDH (GC), *Thlimmenos c. Grèce*, arrêt du 6 avril 2000 : la Cour y examine, au regard de l'article 9 combiné à la clause de non-discrimination, la non-inscription sur le registre des experts-comptables du requérant du fait de sa condamnation pour objection de conscience. Elle y décèle une discrimination indirecte sans pour autant se prononcer sur l'insertion de l'objection de conscience dans les croyances protégées par l'article 9, § 44. Pour un revirement de jurisprudence et la prise en compte explicite et appuyée de la jurisprudence du Comité des droits de l'homme sur ce point, voy. Cour EDH (GC), *Bayatyan c. Arménie*, arrêt du 7 juillet 2011, §§ 98-111.

23 Comité DH, Le droit à la liberté de pensée, de conscience et de religion (Article 18), Observation générale n° 22, 1993, § 11.

nom d'une religion ou d'une conviction sont ou non protégées. Aussi, si le Comité estime qu' « une croyance qui consiste essentiellement ou exclusivement dans le culte et la distribution d'un stupéfiant ne saurait entrer dans le champ d'application de l'article 18 du Pacte »[24], il s'agit ici de l'une des rares occurrences – inédite à notre connaissance – dans laquelle cet organe se prononce sur ce que peut être ou non une croyance. C'est donc plutôt sur le terrain de la manifestation des religions qu'il se place pour déterminer la liberté de religion. A titre d'exemple, il ne nie pas le rastafarisme en tant que religion, même s'il admet dans une affaire *Prince c. Afrique du Sud* que la condamnation pénale d'un croyant pour la consommation de cannabis qu'il justifiait pourtant par une pratique religieuse, ne lui paraît pas disproportionnée et est jugée conforme au PIDCP[25].

Par ailleurs le droit international des droits de l'homme ne vise pas à protéger en tant que tels les systèmes de religion et de conviction, mais plutôt les croyants ou non-croyants[26]. Ce choix de la protection individualiste ne s'explique pas en raison d'une vision anthropomorphique du monde, mais de manière beaucoup plus pragmatique parce que les religions et convictions sont tellement différentes, nuancées, variées, parfois irréconciliables dans leurs projets normatifs ou dans leurs pratiques et enseignements, que le seul dénominateur commun qui en émerge est celui qui pratique ou professe la religion ou la conviction, qu'il s'agisse d'un individu ou d'un groupe[27].

Les actes de manifestation religieuse peuvent être très variés. Le droit de manifester sa religion ou ses convictions peut se concrétiser dans le culte, l'accomplissement des rites, les pratiques et l'enseignement. Le concept de culte comprend « les actes rituels et cérémoniels exprimant directement une conviction, ainsi que différentes pratiques propres à ces actes, y compris la construction de lieux de culte, l'emploi de formules et d'objets rituels, la présentation de symboles et l'observation des jours de fête et des jours de repos ». Les rites

---

24 Comité DH, *M.A.B., W.A.T. et J.-A.Y.T. c. Canada*, constatations du 8 avril 1994, communication n° 570/1993, § 4.2.

25 Comité DH, *Prince c. Afrique du Sud*, constatations du 31 octobre 2007, communication n° 1474/2006. Voy. Comm. afr. dr. h. et p., *Prince c. Afrique du Sud*, décision du 23 novembre-7 décembre 2004, pétition n° 255/02, §§ 40 et s.

26 G. Koubi, « La liberté de religion, une liberté de conviction comme une autre », in *Les défis des droits fondamentaux : universalité et diversité, droit et développement, liberté de religion, statut du juge en Afrique*, Bruxelles, Bruylant, 2000, p. 39. L'auteur met d'ailleurs en garde sur les glissements qui ne sont pas uniquement sémantiques entre la « liberté de religion » qui appartient à la sphère des droits de l'homme et la « liberté religieuse » qu'elle qualifie « d'excroissance » de la liberté de religion.

27 Rapport du Rapporteur spécial sur la liberté de religion ou de conviction, 2 août 2016, A/71/269, § 11.

et pratiques ne se limitent pas aux actes cérémoniels, mais comprennent également des coutumes impliquant le respect de prescriptions alimentaires, le port de vêtements ou de couvre-chefs distinctifs, la participation à des rites d'initiation et l'usage d'une langue particulière communément parlée par un groupe. En outre, les groupes religieux doivent pouvoir choisir leurs responsables religieux, leurs prêtres et leurs enseignants, fonder des écoles religieuses et rédiger, publier et diffuser des textes de caractère religieux[28].

Le droit de manifester sa religion ou sa conviction ne peut faire l'objet que des seules restrictions autorisées par la loi et qui sont nécessaires pour protéger la sécurité, l'ordre et la santé publics ou la morale ou les libertés et droits fondamentaux d'autrui. Ces motifs sont exhaustifs. Le Comité a été invité à se prononcer sur la compatibilité de restrictions fondées sur un ou plusieurs de ces motifs. Dans le domaine de la vie privée et familiale, la liberté de religion occupe une place importante, et les ingérences étatiques doivent être examinées avec prudence, sans pour autant autoriser toute pratique. Ainsi, à titre d'exemple, vu que la réglementation relative aux noms et aux changements de noms relève de l'ordre public, le Comité juge dans l'affaire *Coeriel et Aurik c. Pays-Bas*, que le refus de changement de nom que des personnes souhaitent opérer afin d'accéder à certaines fonctions religieuses hindouistes en Inde est conforme à l'article 18§3 du PIDCP[29].

2.2 *L'enregistrement et la personnalité juridique des groupes religieux*

Si le rapporteur spécial sur la liberté de religion et de conviction remarque que la forme de violation la plus répandue de cette liberté est sans doute liée au harcèlement bureaucratique que subissent certains groupes ou certaines personnes appartenant à des communautés religieuses qui sont traités avec mépris, hostilité et suspicion, cela concerne en premier chef les difficultés auxquelles ces groupes se heurtent lorsqu'il s'agit de s'enregistrer administrativement pour exercer leur religion ou pour obtenir un statut ou une personnalité juridique propre[30]. La discrimination religieuse vise bien souvent, à un niveau structurel, soit l'enregistrement de certains groupes religieux, soit la reconnaissance de leur personnalité juridique.

---

28 Comité DH, Le droit à la liberté de pensée, de conscience et de religion (Article 18), Observation générale n° 22, 1993, §4.

29 Comité DH, *Coeriel et Aurik c. Pays-Bas*, constatations adoptées le 31 octobre 1994, n° 453/1991.

30 Rapport du Rapporteur spécial sur la liberté de religion ou de conviction, 2 août 2016, A/71/269, §§ 47 et s.

A titre d'exemple, le Comité des droits de l'homme constate une violation de l'article 18§3 du PIDCP à l'égard d'un ordre religieux qui s'était vu refuser le droit de se constituer en société au Sri Lanka. Le refus était légal mais disproportionné. L'Etat considérait que l'ordre religieux litigieux offrait des avantages matériels et autres à des personnes vulnérables et dès lors propageait une religion de manière contraignante et inappropriée – ce qui n'était toutefois pas démontré selon le Comité – et il estimait en outre que ce projet « compromettait l'existence même du bouddhisme », ce qui avait fondé la décision de rejet de la juridiction interne – sans pouvoir pour autant justifier cette affirmation[31]. Les minorités religieuses – ou tout groupement religieux – doivent pouvoir obtenir le statut de personnalité juridique collective, un statut qui peut être indispensable pour la pratique de leur religion allant de la construction d'un lieu de culte à la création d'écoles confessionnelles par exemple. Les entraves à de telles reconnaissances sont fréquentes et dénoncées par le Rapporteur spécial des Nations Unies [à titre d'exemple, la Hongrie exige que l'organisation prouve qu'elle fonctionne au moins depuis 20 ans ; en France, le mouvement protestant des frères de Plymouth a subi des restrictions liées à son identification en tant que mouvement sectaire][32].

Dans l'affaire *Malakhovsky contre Bélarus*, les auteurs, membres de la communauté Vaishnava, s'étaient heurtés à de lourds obstacles administratifs lorsqu'ils avaient voulu enregistrer leur groupement en tant qu'association religieuse. En effet, la loi de l'Etat partie distinguait entre communautés et associations religieuses, certaines activités ne pouvant être exercées que par ces dernières. Faute d'avoir obtenu le statut d'association religieuse, les auteurs ne pouvaient inviter des ecclésiastiques étrangers au Bélarus, ni créer des monastères ou des établissements d'enseignement, ce qui affectait leur droit de manifester et de pratiquer leur religion. Le Comité estime que la condition selon laquelle une association religieuse devait, pour pouvoir exercer son droit de mener ses activités à caractère religieux, démontrer que ses locaux satisfaisaient aux normes applicables de santé et de sécurité publiques, était une restriction nécessaire à la protection de la santé et de la sécurité publiques, et proportionnée. Toutefois, il note que l'Etat partie n'avait présenté aucun argument pour expliquer en quoi il était nécessaire, aux fins de l'article 18§3, qu'une association religieuse dispose, pour être enregistrée, d'un siège social agréé satisfaisant non seulement aux normes requises pour le siège administratif de l'association mais aussi aux normes nécessaires à la tenue de cérémonies, rites

31 *Soeur Immaculate Joseph et 80 sœurs enseignantes de la Sainte-Croix du Troisième Ordre de Saint-François d'Assise de Menzingen à Sri Lanka c. Sri Lanka*, 2005, n° 1249/2004, § 7.3.

32 Rapport du Rapporteur spécial sur la liberté de religion ou de conviction, A/HRC/22/51.

religieux et autres activités de groupe. Au regard de ces éléments, et compte tenu de l'impact des restrictions sur la liberté de religion des auteurs, le Comité constate la violation de l'article 18§1 du Pacte[33].

2.3 *Le port de signes religieux*

Si la liberté de manifester sa religion comprend le port de vêtements ou de couvre-chefs religieux ou distinctifs, le port de signes religieux reste hautement problématique et sensible. La Cour européenne des droits de l'homme tend sur cette question à se retrancher derrière la marge nationale d'appréciation[34], tandis que le Comité des droits de l'homme choisit d'affronter plus directement ces controverses et se montre plus protecteur.

Ainsi, pour le Comité des droits de l'homme, le turban de la religion sikhe étant considéré non seulement comme un devoir religieux, mais aussi comme lié à l'identité personnelle, le port du turban doit être considéré comme motivé par la religion. L'obligation légale de paraître tête nue sur les photographies d'un passeport est donc constitutive d'une ingérence dans l'exercice du droit à la liberté de religion, et plus particulièrement du droit de la manifester. Tout en admettant la finalité sécuritaire invoquée par l'Etat, le Comité juge que l'Etat n'a pas expliqué pourquoi le port d'un tel turban laissant le visage clairement visible rend l'identification moins aisée que tête nue, et en quoi cette prohibition permettrait de faciliter l'identification des personnes et à combattre les risques de falsification et de fraude des documents officiels. « Le Comité conclut donc que la réglementation exigeant d'apparaître 'tête nue' sur les photographies de passeport est une restriction disproportionnée portant atteinte à la liberté de religion de l'auteur et constitue en l'espèce une violation de l'article 18 du Pacte »[35]. De même, l'exclusion d'un lycéen pour avoir porté le turban est considérée comme une violation de l'article 18 du PIDCP, l'Etat n'ayant pas démontré qu'en portant son turban l'auteur de la communication présentait une menace pour les droits et libertés des autres élèves ou pour

33 Comité DH, *Malakhovsky c. Bélarus*, 2005, n° 1207/2003, §§ 2.1 et s.

34 Cour EDH, *Dahlab c. Suisse*, décision d'irrecevabilité du 15 février 2001, req. n° 42393/98; Cour EDH (GC), *Leyla Sahin c. Turquie*, arrêt du 10 novembre 2005, § 105 ; Cour EDH, *Dogru c. France*, arrêt du 4 décembre 2008, §§ 68-70 ; Cour EDH, *Kervanci c. France*, arrêt du 4 décembre 2008 ; Cour EDH (GC), *S.A.S. c. France*, arrêt du 1er juillet 2014 ; Cour EDH, *Ebrahimian c. France*, arrêt du 26 novembre 2015 : à propos de l'interdiction du port du voile dans les lieux publics ou sur le lieu de travail/l'école, jugée non contraire à l'article 9 de la CEDH. De même, du reste, que ce qui a trait à l'abattage rituel des animaux (Cour EDH (GC), *Cha'are Shalom Ve Tsedek c. France*, arrêt du 27 juin 2000, §§ 75-88).

35 Comité dr.h., *Shingara Mann Singh c. France*, constatations du 19 juillet 2013, n° 1928/2010, § 9.5.

l'ordre de l'établissement, et en raison de la disproportion de la mesure[36]. Dans une affaire plus ancienne en revanche, le Comité juge que l'obligation faite à un Sikh de porter un casque de protection sur les chantiers, bien qu'incompatible avec son obligation religieuse du port du turban, se justifiait dans le cadre de l'article 18§3 du PIDCP[37].

La position du Comité à l'égard du voile islamique est également différente de celle retenue par la Cour européenne. Dans une affaire contre l'Ouzbékistan, le Comité des droits de l'homme est d'avis que l'interdiction du port du voile dans une université ayant conduit à sanctionner une étudiante de la faculté d'histoire qui avait été renvoyée en application du règlement de l'université, était en l'occurrence incompatible avec l'article 18 du PIDCP. Le Comité rappelle qu'en principe, la liberté de manifester sa religion englobe le droit de porter en public des vêtements ou une tenue conformes à sa foi ou à sa religion. Par ailleurs, il estime que le fait d'empêcher une personne de porter un habit religieux en public et en privé peut constituer une violation du paragraphe 2 de l'article 18, qui interdit toute contrainte qui porterait atteinte à la liberté de la personne d'avoir ou d'adopter une religion. Comme l'indique le Comité dans le paragraphe 5 de son Observation générale n° 22, « les politiques ou les pratiques ayant le même but ou le même effet de contrainte directe, telles que celles restreignant l'accès à l'éducation, sont incompatibles avec le paragraphe 2 de l'article 18 du Pacte »[38]. La position du Comité est ici très directive car il se place sur le terrain du paragraphe 2 qui interdit de manière absolue les contraintes, et non sur celui du paragraphe 3 qui permet de limiter certaines pratiques.

Dans le cadre de ses observations finales, le Comité des droits de l'homme est tout aussi explicite. A l'égard de la France, il « exprime sa préoccupation quant à l'encadrement du port de signes religieux qualifiés d' 'ostensibles' dans les établissements scolaires publics (loi n° 2004-228) et l'interdiction de la dissimulation du visage dans l'espace public (loi n° 2010-1192). Le Comité considère que ces lois portent atteinte à la liberté de manifester sa religion ou sa conviction et qu'elles affectent particulièrement les personnes appartenant à certaines religions et les filles. Le Comité s'inquiète par ailleurs de ce que les effets de ces lois sur le sentiment d'exclusion et de marginalisation de certains groupes pourraient aller à l'encontre des buts recherchés »[39].

---

36 Comité DH, *Singh c. France*, constatations du 1er novembre 2012, n° 1852/2008, § 8.7.

37 Comité DH, *Singh Bhinder c. Canada*, constatations du 9 novembre 1989, n° 208/1986.

38 Comité DH, *Hudoyberganova c. Ouzbékistan*, constatations du 5 novembre 2004, n° 931/2000.

39 Comité DH, Observations finales sur la France, 17 août 2015, CCPR/C/FRA/CO/5, § 22.

Le Rapporteur spécial sur la liberté de religion et de conviction adopte une position proche de celle du Comité[40]. Du point de vue des enfants notamment, ou plus particulièrement des élèves, il considère que la liberté de porter un signe religieux doit être protégée et que toute ingérence dans ce domaine doit respecter les critères de l'article 18§3 du PIDCP et de l'article 14§3 de la Convention sur les droits de l'enfant. Il précise sur ce point que « si des restrictions sont jugées nécessaires pour protéger des élèves des pressions exercées par leurs pairs ou le milieu scolaire pour qu'ils portent des symboles religieux, celles-ci doivent être fondées sur une analyse empirique et normative précise de la situation. Les interdictions générales ou de grande ampleur concernant le port volontaire du foulard ou d'autres symboles religieux par les élèves des écoles doivent rester le dernier recours »[41].

2.4 *Les pratiques traditionnelles néfastes*

La tradition, qu'elle soit culturelle ou religieuse, permet de justifier, parfois sous couvert de relativisme, un nombre conséquent de pratiques néfastes manifestement contraires au projet du droit international des droits de l'homme et affectant le plus souvent les personnes les plus vulnérables[42]. Divers organes des Nations Unies analysent ces pratiques[43] pour tenter de les éradiquer. Le Comité pour l'élimination de la discrimination à l'égard des femmes et le Comité des droits de l'enfant ont adopté une recommandation / observation générale conjointe sur ce thème en notant que si la « nature et la prévalence de ces pratiques varient d'une région et d'une culture à l'autre, toutefois, les plus courantes qui sont bien recensées sont les mutilations génitales féminines, le mariage forcé des enfants, la polygamie, les crimes dits d'honneur et la violence

40 Rapport du Rapporteur spécial sur la liberté de religion et de conviction, 5 août 2015, A/70/286, §§ 51 et s.

41 Rapport du Rapporteur spécial sur la liberté de religion et de conviction, 5 août 2015, A/70/286, § 52.

42 Pour une analyse des abominations commises contre les femmes au nom de la religion, des traditions et de la culture – tout cela étant souvent mélangé –, voy. C. Napoli, *L'ONU face aux « pratiques traditionnelles néfastes » à l'égard de l'enfant africain*, Paris, L'Harmattan, 2013, 462 p. Voy. aussi le rapport annuel du Rapporteur spécial sur la liberté de conscience et de religion du 7 août 2013, A/68/290, spéc. §§ 29 et s.

43 Recommandation générale/observation générale conjointe n° 31 du Comité pour l'élimination de la discrimination à l'égard des femmes et n° 18 du Comité des droits de l'enfant sur les pratiques préjudiciables, 2014. Dans ce texte, les pratiques préjudiciables réunissent les critères suivants : « a) Elles constituent une atteinte à la dignité ou à l'intégrité de l'individu et une violation des droits de l'homme et des libertés fondamentales consacrées dans les deux Conventions ; b) Elles constituent une discrimination à l'égard

relative à la dot »[44]. Sur ce point et après avoir souscrit à une série de recommandations énoncées par ces deux organes conventionnels, le Rapporteur spécial sur la liberté de religion et de conviction remarque que le « fait que les pratiques préjudiciables, ou certaines d'entre elles, sont fondées sur la religion reste généralement contesté entre les différentes communautés religieuses et au sein même de celles-ci ». Pourtant la confusion reste préoccupante et un devoir de clarification lie, selon le Rapporteur, les autorités religieuses[45].

En tout état de cause, aucune de ces pratiques ne peut être légitimée comme une manifestation de la liberté de religion ou de conviction. En une phrase, pour le Rapporteur, la liberté de religion ou de conviction « ne peut jamais servir de prétexte pour légitimer des pratiques cruelles et des violations des droits de l'homme »[46]. Certaines pratiques restent difficiles à appréhender sous cet angle. Tel est le cas de la circoncision masculine des nourrissons, largement pratiquée, et qui est un élément essentiel de l'identité religieuse et de l'initiation religieuse. Sur ce point, le Rapporteur spécial considère que cette pratique doit être respectée à condition qu'elle s'opère avec le consentement des parents, par un praticien qualifié, et dans de bonnes conditions d'hygiène[47].

---

des femmes ou des enfants et sont préjudiciables dans la mesure où elles entraînent des conséquences négatives pour les intéressés en tant qu'individus ou groupes, notamment parce qu'elles leur causent un préjudice physique, psychologique, économique et social ou des violences et limitent leur capacité de participer pleinement à la société ou de se développer pour exploiter pleinement leurs potentialités ; c) Ce sont des pratiques traditionnelles, nouvelles ou qui réapparaissent et qui sont prescrites ou maintenues en place par les normes sociales qui perpétuent la domination de l'homme et l'inégalité des femmes et des enfants sur la base du sexe, de l'âge et d'autres facteurs connexes ; d) Elles sont imposées aux femmes et aux enfants par la famille, la collectivité ou l'ensemble de la société, que la victime donne, ou soit en mesure de donner, ou non son consentement plein, libre et en connaissance de cause ».

44 Recommandation générale/observation générale conjointe n° 31 du Comité pour l'élimination de la discrimination à l'égard des femmes et n° 18 du Comité des droits de l'enfant sur les pratiques préjudiciables, 2014.

45 Voy. à ce sujet les clarifications des points de vue religieux sur les mutilations génitales féminines et les recommandations de la conférence internationale regroupant des intellectuels sur l'interdiction des violations du corps des femmes, tenue au Caire, en 2006, référence sous A/HRC/4/21, § 38, note de bas de page.

46 Rapport du Rapporteur spécial sur la liberté de religion et de conviction, 5 août 2015, A/70/286, § 70.

47 Rapport du Rapporteur spécial sur la liberté de religion et de conviction, 5 août 2015, A/70/286, § 73. La position du Comité des droits de l'enfant est comparable : CRC/C/15/Add.122, § 33.

2.5 *L'enseignement religieux*

Les Etats doivent respecter le droit des parents d'assurer l'éducation religieuse et morale de leurs enfants conformément à leurs convictions. Ce droit, consacré notamment à l'article 18§4 du PIDCP. L'article 14 de la Convention sur les droits de l'homme fait écho à cette disposition mais la nuance en affirmant d'abord et avant tout le droit de l'enfant à la liberté de pensée, de conscience et de religion (§ 1), tandis que le deuxième paragraphe évoque « le droit et le devoir des parents ou, le cas échéant, des représentants légaux de l'enfant, de guider celui-ci dans l'exercice du droit susmentionné d'une manière qui corresponde au développement de ses capacités ». Cette disposition a fait craindre à certaines Parties au traité un risque d'érosion des droits parentaux et de la responsabilité des parents en ce qui concerne la socialisation religieuse de leurs enfants[48], ce qui permet d'expliquer que des réserves aient été émises par de nombreux Etats (dont notamment le Bangladesh, Brunei, Emirats arabes unis, Iraq, Jordanie, Malaisie, Maldives, Maroc, Oman, Qatar, Syrie, Saint Siège, Somalie : certaines de ces réserves ayant fait l'objet d'objection de la part d'autres Etats parties).

Ajoutons que l'article 18§4 du PIDCP n'interdit cependant pas l'enseignement de sujets tels que l'histoire générale des religions et des idées dans les établissements publics à condition que l'enseignement soit dispensé de manière neutre et objective. L'enseignement d'une religion ou d'une conviction particulière dans le cadre de l'éducation publique n'est pas en tant que tel incompatible avec l'article 18§4. Mais il doit comprendre un régime d'exemptions ou d'options qui permettent d'accommoder le programme éducatif aux choix des parents[49]. Ainsi, dans l'affaire *Hartikainen et autres contre Finlande*, le Comité concluait que l'instruction dans un contexte religieux devait respecter les convictions des parents et des tuteurs qui n'avaient aucune religion. C'est en appliquant ce principe que le Comité rend sa décision dans *Leirvåg contre Norvège*[50] jugeant que l'enseignement obligatoire d'une matière sur la connaissance chrétienne et l'éducation religieuse et morale était incompatible avec l'article 18§4 du PIDCP. Dans cette affaire, le Comité émet des doutes sur la question de savoir si l'enseignement litigieux était dispensé de façon neutre

48 Rapport du Rapporteur spécial sur la liberté de religion et de conviction, 5 août 2015, A/70/286, § 12.

49 Comité DH, *Hartikainen et autres c. Finlande*, constatations du 9 avril 1981, n° 40/1978, § 10.4.

50 Comité DH, *Leirvåg c. Norvège*, constatations du 3 novembre 2004, n° 1155/2003. La Norvège a une religion d'Etat et une Eglise d'Etat, à laquelle appartiennent environ 86% de la population. Aussi, la Constitution norvégienne dispose que l'Eglise évangélique

et objective, notamment car l'enseignement de la religion et la pratique religieuse se confondaient, et il fonde son constat de violation par ailleurs sur le système de dispense qui imposait un fardeau considérable aux personnes qui en faisaient la demande.

La Rapporteur spécial sur la liberté de religion et de conviction met en exergue toutes les difficultés auxquelles se heurtent en pratique les droits des enfants et des parents dans le domaine de la liberté de religion. L'exemple extrême qu'il cite est celui de l'enlèvement d'enfants appartenant à une minorité religieuse pour les convertir de force à une religion souvent en association avec un mariage forcé précoce[51]. De telles pratiques violent les droits de l'enfant, mais également le droit des parents d'assurer l'éducation religieuse et morale conformément à leurs convictions.

2.6 *La discrimination fondée sur la religion*

Un aspect majeur, et bien ancré en droit international, de la liberté de religion repose sur l'interdiction de discrimination fondée sur la religion ou la conviction. Au plan normatif, ce fondement discriminatoire est systématiquement mentionné dans les instruments de protection, comme nous l'avons évoqué ci-dessus.

Certaines discriminations sont structurelles, elles reposent sur une distinction illicite entre plusieurs religions. A titre d'exemple, le Comité des droits de l'homme relève qu'au Danemark, l'Eglise évangélique luthérienne jouit d'un traitement plus avantageux que les autres communautés religieuses, étant notamment autorisée à enregistrer les naissances et à célébrer les mariages, sans condition[52]; au

luthérienne est la religion officielle et que « les habitants qui en font profession sont tenus d'élever leurs enfants dans cette religion ». La religion chrétienne est enseignée dans ce pays depuis 1739, année de la mise en place de la scolarité générale obligatoire. Toutefois, depuis l'adoption en 1845 de la loi « de dissidence » ou « de non-conformité », il existe un droit de dispense pour les enfants d'autres confessions. En 1997, le gouvernement norvégien imposa néanmoins l'enseignement d'une nouvelle matière à caractère religieux intitulée « Connaissance chrétienne et éducation religieuse et morale», qui reposait sur l'« objectif chrétien de l'école » et transmettait « une connaissance approfondie de la Bible et du christianisme en tant qu'héritage culturel ainsi que de la foi évangélique luthérienne ». Les auteurs de la communication soumise au Comité dans cette affaire, prétendaient que l'impossibilité d'obtenir une dispense totale de ce cours constituait une violation du Pacte.

51 Rapport du Rapporteur spécial sur la liberté de religion et de conviction, 5 août 2015, A/70/286, § 12.

52 Comité DH, Observations finales sur le Danemark, 15 août 2016, CCPR/C/DNK/CO/6, § 37.

Koweït, les non-musulmans ne peuvent pas obtenir la nationalité koweïtienne et des discriminations existent quant à l'octroi de permis de bâtir des lieux de culte[53]; en Irlande, les établissements scolaires qui appartiennent à des communautés religieuses peuvent discriminer à l'égard des employés et des candidats à un poste pour préserver la conviction religieuse, l'enseignement laïque reste peu développé, et l'accès aux plus hautes fonctions de l'Etat ou de membre du pouvoir judiciaire exige la prestation d'un serment religieux[54].

Le Rapporteur spécial a en outre analysé la problématique particulière des discriminations fondées sur la religion ou la conviction sur les lieux de travail[55] ainsi que la problématique de l'égalité des hommes et des femmes à la lumière de la liberté de religion et de conviction[56]. Sur ce terrain, il regrette en particulier que l'on oppose trop souvent la liberté de religion et de conviction à l'égalité entre hommes et femmes, en particulier, car comme « elle permet aussi l'expression des groupes traditionnellement en butte à la discrimination – dont les femmes et les filles – la liberté de religion ou de conviction peut être le point de référence normatif des projets qui remettent en cause les schémas patriarcaux présents dans pratiquement toutes les traditions religieuses »[57]. Notons enfin que la discrimination prend une dimension particulière lorsqu'elle est assimilable à une forme de persécution[58].

2.7 *La criminalisation de l'apostasie et du prosélytisme*

La liberté de religion implique nécessairement le droit de choisir et de conserver une religion ou une conviction, mais aussi le droit d'en changer ou d'adopter une position athée[59]. Cela explique que l'article 18§2 du PIDCP interdit les contraintes pesant sur la liberté de choisir, de conserver ou de changer sa religion ou conviction. Sont ainsi prohibées tant les contraintes directes qui se

53 Comité DH, Observations finales sur le Koweït, 11 août 2016, CCPR/C/KWT/CO/3, § 38.

54 Comité DH, Observations finales sur l'Irlande, 19 août 2014, CCPR/C/IRL/CO/4, § 21.

55 Rapport du Rapporteur spécial sur la liberté de religion ou de conviction, 5 août 2014, A/69/261.

56 Rapport du Rapporteur spécial sur la liberté de religion ou de conviction, 7 août 2013, A/68/290.

57 Rapport du Rapporteur spécial sur la liberté de religion ou de conviction, 7 août 2013, A/68/290, § 71.

58 Comité DH, *A. et B. c. Danemark*, constatations du 13 juillet 2016, n° 2291/2013 : la preuve de la persécution religieuse invoquée pour faire échec à une expulsion est difficile à apporter. Voir aussi : Comité DH, *R.G. et al. c. Danemark*, constatations du 2 novembre 2015, n° 2351/2001.

59 Comité DH, Le droit à la liberté de pensée, de conscience et de religion (Article 18), Observation générale n° 22, 1993, § 2.

matérialisent par des menaces de recours à la force ou des sanctions pénales en vue de contraindre des choix religieux que les contraintes indirectes visant par exemple à limiter, en fonction de choix religieux, l'accès aux soins de santé, à l'éducation, à l'emploi ou aux droits politiques[60].

Le Rapporteur spécial sur la liberté de religion et de conviction souligne sur ce plan les difficultés que posent les interdictions pénales tant de l'apostasie que du prosélytisme[61]. Si l'apostasie semble concerner exclusivement certains pays à majorité musulmane, les lois punissant le prosélytisme (ou les missions de missionnaires) sont plus répandues et sont adoptées pour protéger différentes religions telles que le bouddhisme, le christianisme, l'hindouisme et l'islam[62]. La condamnation à la peine capitale le 21 avril 2016 d'un Mauritanien pour apostasie rappelle toute l'actualité de cette problématique[63], sachant par ailleurs que des condamnations pénales pour apostasie sont régulièrement dénoncées par les Nations Unies, notamment au Soudan[64] ou en Arabie saoudite.

Tant l'apostasie que le prosélytisme sont traités par le Comité des droits de l'homme dans le cadre de son contrôle sur rapports. A titre d'exemple, il se dit préoccupé par les dispositions législatives en Ouzbékistan qui interdisent le prosélytisme ou toute autre activité missionnaire, tandis que des musulmans pratiquant leur religion en dehors de toute structure officielle seraient arrêtés, détenus, maltraités et condamnés et que des chrétiens et des croyants de minorités religieuses seraient poursuivis pénalement pour « activité religieuse illicite »[65]. Pour le Rapporteur spécial sur la liberté de religion et de conviction, il existerait en droit international un droit de se convertir qui impliquerait le droit de changer sa propre religion ou conviction ; le droit de ne pas être obligé de se convertir ; le droit de tenter de convertir d'autres personnes par des moyens de persuasion non coercitifs ; et les droits de l'enfant et de ses

---

60 Comité DH, Le droit à la liberté de pensée, de conscience et de religion (Article 18), Observation générale n° 22, 1993, § 5.

61 Rapport du Rapporteur spécial sur la liberté de religion ou de conviction, 2 août 2016, A/71/269, §§ 43 et s.

62 Rapport du Rapporteur spécial sur la liberté de religion ou de conviction, 2 août 2016, A/71/269, §§ 43 et s.

63 Haut-Commissariat des Nations Unies aux droits de l'homme, communiqué de presse du 26 avril 2016. Voir aussi : Comité DH, Observations finales sur la Mauritanie, 21 novembre 2013, CCPR/C/MRT/CO/1, § 22.

64 Comité DH, Observations finales sur le Soudan, 19 août 2014, CCPR/C/SDN/CO/4, § 20.

65 Comité DH, Observations finales sur l'Ouzbékistan, 17 août 2015, CCPR/C/UZB/CO/4, § 22.

parents à ces égards[66]. L'expert, après avoir énoncé les violations les plus courantes de ces droits, analyse les arguments des Etats qui s'opposent au droit à la liberté de religion ou de conviction : atteinte à la paix et à l'harmonie ; menace d'érosion de valeurs morales ; ou encore l'argument selon lequel le concept de « choix » est impropre en matière de foi[67].

2.8 *La criminalisation du blasphème et la diffamation religieuse*

L'articulation entre la liberté de religion et la liberté d'expression peut être difficile à cerner. Ces deux libertés seraient perçues comme potentiellement antinomiques laissant penser que « si la liberté d'expression favorise un débat franc et ouvert, y compris des provocations satiriques et des caricatures qui pourraient être insultantes pour certains, la liberté de religion ou de conviction, à l'inverse, serait davantage susceptible d'être invoquée contre une provocation excessive concernant des questions religieuses »[68]. En réalité, plutôt que d'opposer ces deux droits, il est possible de les rapprocher, en soulignant d'abord leur point commun : ils protègent de manière absolue le *forum internum*, tandis que seul le *forum externum* peut faire l'objet de limitations selon des critères très similaires pour les deux droits[69]. Mais au-delà de ce rapprochement rationnel, les deux libertés sont parfois opposées dans la rhétorique de certains Etats.

C'est sur ce terrain que s'analyse la problématique particulière du blasphème[70], de la « diffamation religieuse » ou de la critique religieuse. L'Organisation de la Conférence islamique a relancé après les attentats du 11 septembre 2001 le débat sur l'assimilation entre le racisme et la « diffamation religieuse » spécifiquement tournée contre l'islam, même si le blasphème est loin de ne concerner que l'islam[71]. Certains textes des Nations Unies y font

---

66 Rapport du Rapporteur spécial sur la liberté de religion ou de conviction, 13 août 2012, A/67/303, § 16.

67 *Idem*, §§ 51 et s.

68 Rapport du Rapporteur spécial sur la liberté de religion ou de conviction, 23 décembre 2015, A/HRC/31/18, § 5.

69 Rapport du Rapporteur spécial sur la liberté de religion ou de conviction, 23 décembre 2015, A/HRC/31/18, § 7.

70 Rapport du Rapporteur spécial sur la liberté de religion ou de conviction, 2 août 2016, A/71/269, §§ 43 et s.

71 Comité DH, Observations finales sur l'Irlande, CCPR/C/IRL/CO/4, § 22 : « L'Etat partie devrait envisager de supprimer l'interdiction du blasphème de la Constitution, conformément à la recommandation de la Convention constitutionnelle et compte tenu de l'Observation générale n° 34 (2011) du Comité sur l'article 19 (liberté d'opinion et d'expression) évoquant l'incompatibilité des lois sur le blasphème avec le Pacte, sauf dans les circonstances spécifiques envisagées au paragraphe 2 de l'article 20 du Pacte ».

référence, explicitement ou non, bien qu'elle soit controversée[72]. Les termes de la controverse sont clairs : d'une part, il convient de protéger la liberté d'expression ; et d'autre part, il faut prévenir et lutter contre la haine religieuse. En ce sens, la résolution 16/18 du Conseil des droits de l'homme portant sur la lutte contre l'intolérance, les stéréotypes négatifs, la stigmatisation, la discrimination, l'incitation à la violence et la violence visant certaines personnes en raison de leur religion ou de leur conviction, adoptée par consensus le 24 mars 2011, engage les Etats à lutter contre l'intolérance religieuse en assurant la promotion de la liberté d'expression, de la liberté de religion et de conviction, et du droit à la non-discrimination. Ce texte tente d'établir un équilibre entre la protection de ces libertés d'expression et de religion en condamnant toutefois « tout appel à la haine religieuse qui constitue une incitation à la discrimination, à l'hostilité ou à la violence, par l'intermédiaire de la presse écrite, des médias audiovisuels ou électroniques ou de tout autre moyen » (§ 3).

Pour l'heure, le Comité des droits de l'homme a considéré irrecevable – pour non-épuisement des voies de recours internes – une plainte individuelle soulevant la question de la « diffamation de la religion » sur le terrain de l'incitation à la haine prohibée par l'article 20 du PIDCP en lien avec le contentieux lié aux caricatures du Prophète Mahomet[73]. Le Comité adopte une position claire et affirme explicitement dans son Observation générale n° 34 que « [l]es interdictions des manifestations de manque de respect à l'égard d'une religion ou d'un autre système de croyance, y compris les lois sur le blasphème, sont incompatibles avec le Pacte, sauf dans les circonstances spécifiques envisagées au paragraphe 2 de l'article 20 du Pacte. Ces interdictions doivent en outre respecter les conditions strictes énoncées au paragraphe 3 de l'article 19, et les articles 2, 5, 17, 18 et 26 ». De telles interdictions ne peuvent en tout cas pas viser à « empêcher ou à réprimer la critique des dirigeants religieux ou le commentaire de la doctrine religieuse et des dogmes d'une foi »[74].

---

72 Voy. notamment l'introduction de son Rapport à l'AGNU, Combating Defamation of Religions, A/64/609, 31 juillet 2009, § 1 ; Rapport du 20 septembre 2006, A/HRC/2/3, § 36; Voy. aussi Comité DH, Liberté d'opinion et liberté d'expression (Article 19), Observation générale n° 34, 2011, § 48.

73 Comité DH, *Ahmad et autres c. Danemark*, décision du 1er avril 2008, communication n° 1487/2006 : déclarée irrecevable pour non-épuisement des voies de recours internes. Sur la nécessité cependant de lutter contre la « haine religieuse », voy. le rapport du Rapporteur spécial sur la liberté de conscience et de religion du 26 décembre 2013, A/HRC/25/58.

74 Comité DH, Liberté d'opinion et liberté d'expression (Article 19), Observation générale n° 34, 2011, § 48.

Même si l'article 20§2 du PIDCP oblige les Etats à lutter contre le discours de haine, et en particulier contre la haine religieuse, le Plan d'action de Rabat[75] rappelle que l'application de cet article doit respecter des conditions strictes et que la limitation des discours doit demeurer l'exception. Ce texte critique également les lois sur le blasphème car elles censurent le débat public et les critiques qui sont supposés être constructifs, sains et utiles. Il recommande leur abrogation « car ces lois étouffent l'exercice de la liberté de religion ou de conviction et empêchent un dialogue et un débat sains autour de la religion » (§ 25). Le Rapporteur spécial reconnaît pour sa part que « les propos satiriques sur des questions religieuses ou la représentation de figures religieuses peuvent parfois heurter la sensibilité des croyants ». Toutefois, il se prononce clairement contre la censure préalable, et surtout contre la criminalisation du blasphème[76]. A ces problématiques s'ajoutent encore celles de législations criminalisant ou interdisant les incitations à la haine religieuse qui sont souvent mal définies ou d'application discriminatoire, ce que le Rapporteur spécial condamne[77].

3 Conclusion

Les divers organes de protection des droits de l'homme des Nations Unies ont été confrontés à un nombre important de défis interprétatifs en matière de liberté de conscience et de religion. Les travaux de ces organes s'appuient sur des techniques discursives variées, allant de la discussion diplomatique, à l'enquête et l'analyse experte, à la discussion contentieuse, et cette complémentarité semble fructueuse en la matière. Les solutions proposées aux controverses soumises à ces organes sont dans l'ensemble assez convaincantes, voire avant-gardistes. Ainsi, la jurisprudence du Comité des droits de l'homme portant sur la protection de l'objection de conscience a inspiré les organes régionaux de protection et s'impose désormais comme une norme jurisprudentielle internationale. D'autre part, le Comité se montre plus protecteur, et plus respectueux de l'expression religieuse que la Cour européenne notamment, dans sa jurisprudence relative au port de signes religieux. En retenant une approche pragmatique et en promouvant le pluralisme religieux,

75 A/HRC/22/17/Add. 4, appendice, § 19.

76 Rapport du Rapporteur spécial sur la liberté de religion ou de conviction, 23 décembre 2015, A/HRC/31/18, § 61.

77 Rapport du Rapporteur spécial sur la liberté de religion ou de conviction, 23 décembre 2015, A/HRC/31/18, §§ 62 et s.

les organes des Nations Unies sont en mesure, grâce aux fondements normatifs protecteurs, de faire face à un ensemble de défis complexes en tentant d'y apporter des solutions persuasives à l'échelle internationale. On le voit à la lumière des cas exposés, le chantier reste immense et les défis, sans cesse renouvelés, mais la méthode discursive retenue, l'ouverture pluraliste, et les outils utilisés par les organes des Nations Unies semblent être de nature à faire face à ces controverses.

CHAPTER 6

The European Court of Human Rights and Freedom of Religion

Angelika Nußberger

1 Framework for Judicial Decision-Making on Questions of Freedom of Religion

1.1 *Diversity of Constitutional Traditions*

In souvenir shops in Bosnia-Herzegovina, little wooden cubes are sold.* They are composed of two halves. When opened tiny buildings carved out of wood, tightly squeezed together, pop up. A closer look reveals a mosque together with three churches, an orthodox church, a catholic church and a protestant church. The little cube is the model of a State bound to accommodate four different religions and thus to balance the interests and rights of the respective religious communities. Bosnia-Herzegovina as a young State had to pay a high tribute in order to find such a balance, which remains delicate and unstable. As soon as a little detail is modified, the complex system might not function any more. Heightening the minaret or enlarging the building of the Catholic Church could mean that the two halves of the little cube do not fit together any more. The equilibrium would be lost.[1]

History shows that it has always been extremely difficult to define the equilibrium both between religious institutions and the State and between different religions. Fights for privileges and prerogatives, fights against heretics have left bloody traces throughout the centuries.[2]

---

* The views expressed in the article are personal and do not bind the Court in any way.

1 On the development of Islam in Bosnia-Herzegovina see Dzevada Susko, 'Ein Modell für Europa? Geschichte und Praxis des Islam in Bosnia-Herzegowina' (2017) 4 *KAS Auslandsinformationen* 6–21, <www.kas.de/wf/doc/kas_51227-544-1-30.pdf> accessed 15 January 2018; Xavier Bougarel, 'The role of Balkan Muslims in Building a European Islam' (2005) EPC Issue Paper Nr. 43, European Policy Centre, <www.epc.eu/pub_details.php?pub_id=62&cat_id=2> accessed 15 January 2018.

2 See Angelika Nußberger, 'Die Rechtsprechung des Europäischen Gerichtshofs für Menschenrechte zur Lösung von Konflikten in multireligiösen Gesellschaften' (2017) 62 ZevKR 419–39.

 | DOI:10.1163/9789004349155_007

So every State has its own specific model defining the relationship between State and religious communities. It is formed by the history of the country, by factors that are different in each European State.

In Germany, the year 2017 was the year dedicated to the commemoration of 500 years of Martin Luther. The Reformation started almost immediately with fighting. After the Thirty Years' War it took a long time in order to find a way for living together peacefully based on the principle 'cuius regio eius religio' combined with the 'ius emigrandi'.[3] In France, 'laïcité' was enshrined in the Constitution as a basic principle after a long controversy over the role of the Catholic Church in the State. The roots of this fight for power are to be found in the French Revolution as the downfall of the 'Ancien Régime' had been accompanied with the abolition of Church privileges and the affirmation of universal principles. The continuing influence of the Catholic Church was identified as a major factor threatening the successful implementation of the Republican principles.[4] Secularism was first introduced in Turkey with the 1928 amendment of the Constitution of 1924, which removed the provision declaring that the 'Religion of the State is Islam'. This change was brought about by Turkey's first president Mustafa Kemal Atatürk, who wanted to create a modern, democratic State for which he considered secularism to be an essential element.

The European Court of Human Rights (ECtHR) is therefore faced with a panoply of different constitutional models based on deeply held religious beliefs and compromises often only found under duress. Religious pluralism must thus be the starting point whenever the Court is called upon to decide on questions linked to religion.

Against this background, it comes as a surprise to read the Chamber judgment in the case *Lautsi v Italy*, adopted in 2009:

> The State's duty of neutrality and impartiality is incompatible with any kind of power on its part to assess the legitimacy of religious convictions or the ways of expressing those convictions. In the context of teaching, neutrality should guarantee pluralism.[5]

This apodictic statement was virtually torn apart by legal critique. The most famous voice in the choir of critiques was that of Joseph Weiler:

---

3 See Christoph Schönberger, 'Etappen des Religionsrechts von der Reformation bis heute' (2017) 62 ZevKR 333–47.

4 See on the history of 'laïcité' in France Jean Baubérot, *Histoire de la laïcité en France* (PUF 2013).

5 *Lautsi v Italy* App no 30814/06 (ECtHR 2nd Section, 3 November 2009), para 47.

> What, for example, of a Britain, with its established Church, in which the Monarch is not only the Head of State but the Head of the Church of England, in which schoolchildren might be invited to sing the national anthem (God [oy vey] Save the Queen). Is that very constitutional structure of an Established Church not some kind of judgment that in some way at least Anglicanism is not illegitimate? Would the UK ever be able to comply with this norm? Is the Court intimating that Britain is to become a France on this issue? May Irish schools no longer teach the Irish Constitution to schoolchildren because the Constitution endorses *expressis verbis* in its Preamble the Holy Trinity? Must Denmark, like Sweden, abandon Lutheranism as the official Danish Church or hide this fact from its children?[6]

But even the Court's own judges saw such an apodictic statement as untenable, as shown by the concurring opinion of Judge Bonello, attached to the Grand Chamber judgment in the same case:

> A court of human rights cannot allow itself to suffer from historical Alzheimer's. It has no right to disregard the cultural continuum of a nation's flow through time, nor to ignore what, over the centuries, has served to mould and define the profile of a people. No supranational court has any business substituting its own ethical mock-ups for those qualities that history has imprinted on the national identity. On a human rights court falls the function of protecting fundamental rights, but never ignoring that 'customs are not passing whims. They evolve over time, harden over history into cultural cement. They become defining, all-important badges of identity for nations, tribes, religions, individuals'.[7]

This critique makes clear that the existence of many different models – of which the French model of 'laïcité' (implicitly underlying the Chamber judgment in the Lautsi case) is just one – cannot be ignored in Europe. Speaking in Convention terms, a large margin of appreciation is an important feature in all cases concerning questions of freedom of religion touching about the relationship between religious institutions and State.

6 Joseph Weiler, 'EJIL Editorial: Lautsi: Crucifix in the Classroom Redux' (2010) 21 European Journal of International Law 1, 2.

7 Concurring opinion to the judgment *Lautsi and others v Italy* (GC) ECHR 2011-III 61.

1.2 *Protection of Individual Rights in Different Constitutional Settings*

While human rights treaties such as the ECHR are therefore silent on questions of State organisation, guaranteeing individual rights – on a transnational level – is essential to complement the maybe insufficient protection on national level. The Court emphasises the role of religion both for forming individual identity and for fortifying a democratic society. Already in its early jurisprudence it is clear that not only the 'inner', but also the 'outer' dimension of religion is deemed to be important:

> As enshrined in Article 9, freedom of thought, conscience and religion is one of the foundations of a 'democratic society' within the meaning of the Convention. It is, in its religious dimension, one of the most vital elements that go to make up the identity of believers and their conception of life, but it is also a precious asset for atheists, agnostics, sceptics and the unconcerned. The pluralism indissociable from a democratic society, which has been dearly won over the centuries, depends on it.
>
> While religious freedom is primarily a matter of individual conscience, it also implies, inter alia, freedom to 'manifest [one's] religion'. Bearing witness in words and deeds is bound up with the existence of religious convictions.[8]

This is the background against which the role of the European Court of Human Rights has to be seen. It is confronted with different constitutional models governing relations between States and religious denominations, which it has to accept as given, but at the same time has to provide effective protection to the individual and collective right of freedom of religion. The margin of appreciation thus cannot be unlimited. The central question is how to define the limits. Both the Strasbourg Court and the Luxembourg Court coin general formula for defining their subsidiary supervisory role.

The wording of the Strasbourg Court in *Kokkinakis v Greece*, one of the early cases on freedom of religion, is quite general:

> The Court has consistently held that a certain margin of appreciation is to be left to the Contracting States in assessing the existence and extent of the necessity of an interference, but this margin is subject to European supervision, embracing both the legislation and the decisions applying it, even those given by an independent court. The Court's task is to

8 *Kokkinakis v Greece* (1993) Series A no 260-A, p 17, para 31.

determine whether the measures taken at national level were justified in principle and proportionate.[9]

Advocate General Juliane Kokott in her opinion proposes to define the relevant factors to be taken into account in solving such conflicts, but to let the national courts discretion in deciding the concrete cases:

> In a case such as this, the proportionality test is a delicate matter in the context of which the Court of Justice, following the practice of the ECtHR in relation to Article 9 ECHR and Article 14 ECHR, should grant the national authorities, in particular the national courts, a measure of discretion which they may exercise in strict accordance with EU rules. In this regard, the Luxembourg Court does not necessarily have to prescribe a solution that is uniform throughout the European Union. Rather, it would be sufficient, in my opinion, for the Court to indicate to the national court all of the material factors that it must take into account in carrying out the proportionality test but otherwise to leave to that court the actual task of striking a balance between the substantive interests involved.[10]

2 Diversity of Religious Conflicts in Front of the Strasbourg Court

While the Luxembourg Court has only recently been confronted with conflicts on freedom of religion in private enterprises, the Strasbourg Court has quite a long series of Article 9 cases concerning very different topics. Quite many cases were brought before the Grand Chamber, also in recent years. In *Sindicatul v Romania* (GC)[11] the Court had to decide on the refusal to register a trade union for priests on account of the autonomy of religious communities; it did not find a violation. In *Fernández Martinez v Spain* (GC)[12] a catholic ex-priest complained about the refusal to renew his contract as a teacher of Catholic religion and morals under Article 8 of the Convention. The non-renewal decision had been based on the bishop's veto after the applicant had publicly revealed his position as a married priest. Here, again,

---

9 *Kokkinakis v Greece* (n 8), para 47.

10 Opinion of AG, presented on 31 May 2016, Case C-157/15 *Samira Achbita and Centrum voor gelijkheid van kansen en voor racismebestrijding v G4S Secure Solutions nv*, para 99.

11 ECHR 2013-V 41.

12 ECHR 2014-II 449.

the Court decided in favour of Church autonomy and did not find a violation of the Convention. Likewise, the Court accepted that the Hungarian courts decided not to have jurisdiction to hear the pastor's claim for wrongful dismissal by church. As, under domestic law, there was no 'right' the pastor could have relied on, finding a violation of Article 6 of the Convention would have meant – contrary to the Court's long-standing jurisprudence – creating a new right. The Court thus declared the complaint inadmissible.[13] Not the Grand Chamber, but the Chamber had to decide on the German system of church taxes for mixed couples in which only one partner is member of a Church. While the joint liability for the church fee was found to constitute an interference into the negative right to freedom of religion, it was nevertheless justified by the legitimate aim of guaranteeing the rights of churches and religious communities to levy church taxes. It was also deemed to be proportionate.[14]

With the exception of the last Chamber case all the recent Article 9 cases mentioned were very controversial and decided by tight votes.[15] The dissenting opinions show that the weight of the concept of Church autonomy is not always interpreted in the same way.

The cases on freedom of religion can be divided in three groups.[16]

In the first category fall complaints based on negative freedom of religion: Those who claim to be irreligious feel oppressed by the manifestation of religious belief either by the State or by others, be it only tolerated or even admonished by the State.

These complaints have to be distinguished from those where applicants see themselves as 'religious', but argue that they are hindered or not efficiently protected in exercising their positive freedom of religion.

Third, there are complaints brought to the Court by members of religious communities who want to be protected by the State against their own religious communities. Examples would be Fernandez Martinez who in substance disagrees with the Bishop's veto against the renewal of his contract and thus against the policy of the Catholic Church. The same is true for the Hungarian priest Karoly Nagy who has a conflict with the Protestant Church and wants the State's courts to solve it.

13 *Károly Nagy v Hungary* (GC) App no 56665/09 (ECtHR, 14 September 2017).

14 *Klein and others v Germany* App no 10138/11 (ECtHR, 6 April 2017).

15 *Sindicatul v Romania* by 11:6 votes; *Fernández Martinez v Spain* by 9:8 votes; *Karoly Nagy v Hungary* by 10:7 votes.

16 See on this categorisation *Nußberger* (n 2), p. 130.

The first two categories of cases opposing negative and positive freedom of religion are often focussed on the use of religious symbols in a specific context or under specific circumstances. In modern societies such conflicts are predominant, as also shown by the jurisprudence of the Luxembourg Court, the German Federal Constitutional Court (FCC), and the French Conseil d'Etat. That's why they will be analysed in detail below.

3 Predominance of Conflicts over Religious Symbols

A short overview over recent jurisprudence on conflicts about religious symbols shows that they occur in very different settings. There are cases concerning the exhibition of religious symbols or the use of religious clothes in the public space,[17] in primary[18] and secondary schools,[19] in universities,[20] in courts[21] or hospitals.[22] In employment related cases the employer may be private[23] or public.[24] Some of the prohibitions are general and apply everywhere in the public sphere,[25] others are very case specific such as security controls[26] or the taking of passport photos.[27]

---

17 Eg *S A S v France* (GC) ECHR 2014-III 341.

18 Eg *Dahlab v Switzerland* App no 42393/98 (ECtHR, decision of 15 February 2001).

19 Eg *Lautsi v Italy* (n 5); *Osmanoglu and Kocabas v Switzerland* App no 29086/12 (ECtHR, 10 January 2017); *Köse and others v Turkey* (dec.) ECHR 2006-II 339; *Kervanci v France* App no 31645/04 (ECtHR, 4 December 2008); *Aktas v France* App no 43563/08 (ECtHR, decision of 30 June 2009); *Ranjit Singh v France* App no 27561/08 (ECtHR, decision of 30 June 2009).

20 *Leyla Şahin v Turkey* (GC) ECHR 2005-XI 173; *Kurtulmuş v Turkey* ECHR 2006-II 197.

21 *Hamidović v Bosnia and Hercegovina* App no 57792/15 (ECtHR, 5 December 2017); see also the decision of the German FCC 27 June 2017, 2 BvR 1333/17.

22 *Ebrahimian v France* App no 64846/11 (ECtHR, 26 November 2015).

23 *Eweida and others v UK* App nos 48420/10, 36516/10, 51671/10, 59842/10 (ECtHR, 15 January 2013); Case C-157/15 *Samira Achbita and Centrum voor gelijkheid van kansen en voor racismebestrijding v G4S Secure Solutions nv* (ECJ, 14 March 2017); Case C-188/15 *Bougnaoui and Association de défence des droits de l'homme (addh) v Micropole Univers*, (ECJ, 1 March 2017).

24 *Ebrahimian v France* (n 22).

25 *S A S v France* (n 17); *Belcacemi and Oussar v Belgium* App no 37798/13 (ECtHR, 11 July 2017); *Dakir v Belgium* App no 4619/12 (ECtHR, 11 July 2017); *Ahmet Arslan and Others v Turkey* App no 41135/98 (ECtHR, 23 February 2010).

26 *Phull v France* ECHR 2005-I 409; *El Morsli v France* App no 15585/06 (ECtHR, decision of 4 March 2008).

27 *Mann Singh v France* App no 24479/07 (ECtHR, decision of 13 November 2008).

The central question in all those cases is if the prohibition of the use of religious symbols is justifiable. Under the different legal regimes, the ECHR, EU law, and constitutional law, the results might be different. But the answers given by the courts are always context-specific. Thus, in some cases, the courts found a prohibition incompatible with human rights standards.[28] In other cases the prohibition was seen as justified, either because of a negative influence on others,[29] or because of a generally shared concept of 'living together'.[30] In many cases, the majority's view was contradicted by strong dissenting opinions.[31] Against this background, it has to be asked why so many different solutions are given to the phenomenon of 'symbolic' religious confessions. What tips the balance for adopting one or another solution?

The following analysis of the relevant jurisprudence progresses in five steps. The starting point is the definition of what is a 'religious symbol'. Without clarifying its specific meaning, conflicts arising out of the use of religious symbols cannot be understood (3.1). What might be seen objectively as a religious symbol, might subjectively have many different functions (3.2). Prohibitions of the visible display of religious symbols have to be seen in the light of potential dangers they are associated with (3.3). The proportionality analysis is based on different factors (3.4), but always has to leave a large margin of appreciation to the State concerned (3.5).

28 The German FCC distinguished between an 'abstract' and a 'concrete' danger and deemed an abstract danger not to be sufficient for a prohibition (BVerfGE 138, 296, para 80). The Strasbourg Court referred to the size of the religious symbol and the consistency of the enterprise's policy and did not accept the prohibition of a small cross around the neck of a British Airways stewardess (*Eweida v UK*, n 23). AG Sharpston considered a prohibition of a headscarf because of the customers' wishes discriminatory (Opinion of AG Sharpston, presented on 13 July 2016, Case C-188/15 *Bougnaoui and Association de défence des droits de l'homme (addh) v Micropole Univers*). The Conseil d'État cancelled a decree of a mayor prohibiting the burkini as there was no reason to assume that wearing a burkini could cause a nuisance to public order; see on this case Stéphanie Wattier, 'Le Conseil d'État francais suspend l'interdiction du port du "burkini"' (2017) 110 Rev. trim. dr. h. 407–19.

29 Eg *Dahlab v Switzerland* (n 18); *Ebrahimian v France* (n 22).

30 *S A S v France* (n 17).

31 See eg Francoise Tulkens in *Leyla Şahin v Turkey* (n 20); Siofra O'Leary, Vincent A. de Gaetano in *Ebrahimian v France* (n 22); Angelika Nußberger, Helena Jäderblom in *S A S v France* (n 17); Monika Hermanns, Wilhelm Schluckebier in BVerfGE 138, 296 (dissenting opinion), paras 1ff.

3.1 *Functions and Meanings of Religious Symbols – Objective Approach*

The Court was confronted with different religious symbols in its jurisprudence: the Christian cross respectively the crucifix, the Islamic headscarf, burqa/niqab/hijab, burkini, the turban of the Sikh, skullcaps and, in a very specific case concerning the Aczimendi tarikati group, a turban, a sirwal and a tunic, all in black, together with a baton.[32]

Symbols represent something different from what they are themselves, even if they have, in addition, a function such as hiding or protecting a part of the body. They carry a specific meaning and point to an idea they are to materialise.[33] Religious symbols refer, as a rule, to a religious conviction or indicate the membership in a religious community. They show the link between the 'forum internum' and the 'forum externum' and thus serve the externalisation of ideas. For the Court the forum externum is essential 'because of the value to an individual who has made religion a central tenet of his or her life to be able to communicate that belief to others'.[34]

But the meaning of symbols is never unequivocal, as shown by many cases brought before the Court. Loading a symbol with a specific meaning or denying a specific meaning and generalising it might be decisive for the outcome of a case. The most famous example is the dispute over the meaning of the symbol 'crucifix'. Those defending the use of crucifixes in schools heavily rely on the interpretation of the crucifix as a symbol not only for Christianity, but, more generally, for European civilisation.[35] The opposing view interprets it as the expression of a specific religious confession. Thus the German FCC in its judgment of 1995 denies the character of the cross as a 'general trans-confessional symbol' and calls it a 'symbol of faith per se' ('Glaubenssymbol schlechthin'),

32 *Ahmet Arslan and Others v Turkey* (n 25).

33 See for the understanding of symbols Horst Jürgen Helle, 'Symbol', *Herder Staatslexikon* (7th edn 1989) 405ff.

34 *Eweida v UK* (n 23), para 94.

35 The German administrative court first dealing with the crucifix in Bavarian schools (BayVGH NVwZ 1991, 1099ff) spoke of an 'essential object of the general Christian-occidental tradition and common heritage of the Christian-occidental culture area' (wesentlicher Gegenstand der allgemeinen christlich-abendländischen Tradition und Gemeingut des christlich-abendländischen Kulturkreises); see also the argumentation of the Italian Government in front of the Grand Chamber in *Lautsi v Italy* (n 7), para 36, where it emphasized that the cross as a symbol 'could be perceived not only as a religious symbol, but also as a cultural and identity-linked symbol, the symbol of the principles and values which formed the basis of democracy and western civilisation; it appeared, for instance, on the flags of a number of European countries'.

even a 'symbol of the missionary expansion' of Christianity.[36] This meaning is also the one upheld by the Second Chamber of the European Court of Human Rights ('symbol of a particular faith'), and, even if in a more nuanced form, by the Grand Chamber, which states that the cross is 'a sign which, whether or not it is accorded in addition a secular symbolic value, undoubtedly refers to Christianity'.[37]

The interpretation of the meaning of the Muslim headscarf as well as of the Hijab is likewise in the centre of judicial controversy. The main question is if these symbols are 'only' religious or also political symbols. The second senate of the German FCC accepts in its judgment of 2003 that the practice of wearing a headscarf is a sign of belonging to the Muslim community, but, beyond this basic understanding, refers to two opposite interpretations. Thus, a headscarf could be a 'symbol of cultural separation and social repression of women' as well as of 'individual self-determination and in particular the emancipation of women'.[38]

The ECHR is reluctant to enter into the debate of how to define the exact meaning of headscarf and hijab. In the case *S A S v France*, the third-party interveners emphasize the different meanings of the burqa, being seen by feminists as 'demeaning to women, undermining of their dignity, and the result of patriarchy'.[39] The Court does not delve into this discussion, but accepts the burqa as a symbol of faith.[40]

Thus, it seems impossible to take a specific meaning of a religious symbol for granted. Courts are not in a position to take a stand on such questions, which have to be left to the religious communities themselves.[41] Judges can take into account the debate on different objective meanings, but must not ignore that in concrete cases the concrete subjective meaning of a symbol can be at variance with the objective doctrinal meaning if it exists at all.

36 BVerfGE 93, 1 (19f).

37 *Lautsi v Italy* (n 7), para 71.

38 BVerfGE 108, 282 (304f).

39 See on the feminist discussion Ulrike Spohn, 'Sisters in Disagreement: The Dispute among French Feminists About the "Burqa Ban" and the Causes of Their Disunity' (2013) Journal of Human Rights 145–64.

40 *S A S v France* (n 17), para 56.

41 See the critique of the judgment in the case of *Leyla Şahin* by the Turkish Prime Minister Erdogan: 'The decision about the headscarf is not a matter for a court. One should ask the religious scholars as to its religious significance. The decision cannot be made by the court members.' (quoted in Turan Kayaoglu, 'Trying Islam: Muslims before the European Court of Human Rights' (2014) Journal of Muslim Minority Affairs 346).

3.2 *Functions and Meanings of Symbols – Subjective Approach*

Symbols can be used in very different ways and with very different intentions, be it that they are fixed in the centre of a town or worn around the neck. The spectrum stretches from use for decorative purposes to missionary ends.

3.2.1 Religious Symbols as Part of the Personal Dress Code

It cannot be denied that religious symbols may just have decorative functions without being linked to any idea of expressing a certain (religious or spiritual) identity or any world view. It may be just a question of fashion to wear a Buddha around the neck, to print a half moon on a t-shirt or to tattoo parts of the body with quotations of the Bible or the Koran. In such cases, prohibitions would not concern freedom of religion, but respect for private life as the choice of personal style and the decision on appearance is protected under Article 8 ECHR.[42]

3.2.2 Religious Symbols as Expression of an Inner Conviction or Collective Identity

What might seem on the surface to be the very same attitude of just following a certain fashion changes substantially as soon as it is linked to an inner conviction, to the wish of expressing and communicating a certain world view or religious conviction or of emphasizing the fact of being member of a religious community. Thus, the young woman in the case *S A S v France* explains the motives for wearing the niqab in a nuanced manner:

> The applicant added that she wore the niqab in public and in private, but not systematically: she might not wear it, for example, when she visited the doctor, when meeting friends in a public place, or when she wanted to socialise in public. She was thus content not to wear the niqab in public places at all times but wished to be able to wear it when she chose to do so, depending in particular on her spiritual feelings. There were certain times (for example, during religious events such as Ramadan) when she believed that she ought to wear it in public in order to express her religious, personal and cultural faith. Her aim was not to annoy others but to feel at inner peace with herself.[43]

42 See Juliane Pätzold, 'Artikel 8' in Ulrich Karpenstein/Franz C. Mayer (eds), *EMRK* (2nd edn, 2015), para. 15.

43 *S A S v France* (n 17), para 12.

Wearing religious symbols need not even be linked to religious identity. It can also be seen necessary for preserving another form of collective identity as expressed by Ari Shavit in his reflections on Jewish identity in a secular world:

> In the last third of the twentieth century, Hebrew identity was dulled. In the early years of the twenty-first century, it seems to have disintegrated. ... For better or for worse, the more rigid way of life was replaced by wild pluralism. ... Secular faith weakened, progress weakened, the collective narrative dissolved.[44]

3.2.3 Compulsory use of Religious Symbols

While these quotations make clear that it is a choice to wear or not to wear a specific symbol, the situation changes as soon as it is understood as a religious or cultural duty.[45] Veiling and hiding the female body can be seen as an expression of purity; acting against such long-standing traditions would then be considered and condemned as 'sin'. According to the explanations given by a Muslim Turkish organisation in the procedure before the German FCC[46] Muslim women, starting from puberty, have to cover their body – with the exception of hands, feet, and face – when men are present whom they would be allowed to marry. This is understood as a religious commandment.[47] The binding character of a religious duty is not systematically treated in the courts' jurisprudence. Nevertheless, it is clear that it is an essential underlying factor for the conclusions drawn, such as shown by the opinion of Advocate General Juliane Kokott on the acceptability of strict neutrality policies in private enterprises:

> However, unlike sex, skin colour, ethnic origin, sexual orientation, age or a person's disability, the practice of religion is not so much an unalterable fact as an aspect of an individual's private life, and one, moreover, over which the employees concerned can choose to exert an influence. While

44 Ari Shavit, *My promised land* (New York 2013).

45 The difference between binding and non-binding religious precepts is discussed by the British courts in the case *Eweida v UK* (n 23), para 18. The prohibition is considered not to be discriminatory as 'the visible wearing of a cross was not a mandatory requirement of the Christian faith but Ms Eweida's personal choice'.

46 See the explanation given by DITIB (Turkish-Islamic Union), cited in the judgment of the German FCC (BVerfGE 138, 296, para 74).

47 See on the religious commandment of wearing a skullcap for Salafi Muslims *Hamidović v Bosnia-Hercegovina* (n 21), para 41.

> an employee cannot 'leave' his sex, skin colour, ethnicity, sexual orientation, age or disability 'at the door' upon entering his employer's premises, he may be expected to moderate the exercise of his religion in the workplace, be this in relation to religious practices, religiously motivated behaviour or (as in the present case) his clothing.[48]

3.2.4 Use of Religious Symbols with Missionary Aims

Such an obligation is directed against the woman herself; it is her duty and, if she does not obey, her sin. Nevertheless, she remains passive. This situation has to be distinguished from the one when those wearing or exhibiting religious symbols are actively trying to influence and convince others to change their religious belief. This would be called proselytism.[49] In the case *Lautsi v Italy* the Grand Chamber very much focuses on this distinction in order to justify the result of finding no violation:

> Furthermore, a crucifix on a wall is an essentially passive symbol and this point is of importance in the Court's view, particularly having regard to the principle of neutrality … It cannot be deemed to have an influence on pupils comparable to that of didactic speech or participation in religious activities …[50]

3.2.5 Use of Religious Symbols with the Aim of Domination and Oppression

On the very far end of the spectrum is the wish to dominate and suppress. The most evident example would be the flag of the so-called Islamic State shown as a sign of victory and military conquest. History is full of such examples.[51]

In order to assess the intensity of the interference with human rights it is necessary to distinguish between the different scenarios. A prohibition of

---

48 Opinion of AG Kokott, presented on 31 May 2016, Case C-157/15 *Samira Achbita and Centrum voor gelijkheid van kansen en voor racismebestrijding v G4S Secure Solutions nv*, para. 116.

49 See *Pitkevich v Russia* App no 47936/99 (ECtHR, decision of 8 February 2001), concerning the dismissal of a judge because she had, among other things, proselytised and prayed during court hearings.

50 *Lautsi v Italy* (GC) (n 7), para 72; the same is true for the case *Ahmet Arslan and Others v Turkey* (n 25) where the Court also emphasized that those wearing the religious symbols had not sought to exert inappropriate pressure on others in order to promote their religious beliefs.

51 It may be sufficient just to mention crusaders such as the Teutonic Order using the black cross of the Teutonic Order as insignia for their conquests.

wearing or exhibiting a religious symbol can have very different effects; it can cause a real dilemma for those confronted with the choice of abiding by the law and committing a sin or breaking the law and obeying God. On the contrary, changing a fashionable dress code or removing a decoration will not have far-reaching consequences. The German FCC has to be lauded for being precise in this context when it emphasises that its judgment concerns only teachers 'obeying an obligation to cover the body understood to be a religious constraint'.[52] The impact of the prohibition on the person concerned is, however, not clearly established in all cases; those who sacrifice their career and leave school,[53] university[54] or working place[55] might be driven by the feeling not to have any alternative or might consciously choose this alternative.

The Court discusses the cases under Article 8 ECHR, right to private life, under Article 9 ECHR, religious freedom, or under both guarantees.[56]

The majority of the cases concern the positive aspect of freedom of religion – the right to use or exhibit a religious symbol. But the argument can also be turned around. The use of symbols can be seen as intrusive and thus as an infringement into negative freedom of religion, or, in cases concerning schools, into freedom of education (Article 4 of Protocol No 1). This is obvious in cases of domination, oppression, and proselytism, not, however, in cases of 'passive' use of symbols for self-fulfilment, fashion or on the basis of religious commandments. While the first model constitutes a transgression into the sphere of others – not to be dominated, not to be oppressed, not to be forced to change religion –, the second model can be understood as necessitating nothing but tolerance, a value highlighted as central by the Court: '... pluralism, tolerance and broadmindedness are hallmarks of a "democratic society."'[57]

3.3 *Justification of Restrictions*

Whenever interferences into one of the rights protected by the Convention are found, it is necessary to justify them. Conflicts about religious symbols can

52 BVerfGE 138, 296, headnote no. 1: 'Lehrkräfte ..., [die] einem aus religiösen Gründen als verpflichtend verstandenen Bedeckungsgebot ... genügen'.

53 See eg the girls in the case *Dogru v France* App no 27058/05 (ECtHR, 4 December 2008) who continue their education by distant learning.

54 See eg Leyla Şahin who left Turkey and studied medicine in Vienna.

55 See eg Sevgi Kurtumulus who was suspended from her job as an assistant professor at university and even after an amnesty not reinstated as she failed to ask for it; see also Christiane Ebrahimian whose contract as a social worker was not renewed.

56 See eg *S A S. v France* (n 17), para 106.

57 *Chassagnou and Others v France* (GC) ECHR 1999-III 21.

either arise when the use of a symbol is made mandatory by the State[58] or when it is prohibited, be it directly by the State[59] or by private persons (e.g the employer) and upheld by State courts.[60]

In order to justify such prohibitions and restrictions only specific reasons can be adduced as allowed in Article 8 para. 2 and Article 9 para. 2 of the Convention. While the 'rights and freedoms of others' are of central importance in this context, it is also possible to recur to 'public safety' and 'public order'.[61] The Court follows a context-specific approach and takes into account who uses a religious symbol, who is targeted by a religious symbol and where the confrontation happens.

3.3.1 Use of Religious Symbols in Schools

It is generally accepted that small children are easily influenced by the behaviour and clothing of their teachers, even if the effect is difficult to measure. There do not seem to be clear and univocal scientific analyses. Against this background it is either possible to accept the 'potential' danger as sufficient to justify prohibitions or, on the contrary, to demand a concrete proof of the negative influence in each case. This is the dividing line in the headscarf-cases between the approaches of the ECtHR on the one hand and the German FCC on the other hand.

The ECtHR explains its position in the case *Dahlab v Switzerland* where it does not adopt a judgment, but holds the complaint, even if only by a majority, to be manifestly ill-founded:

> The Court accepts that it is very difficult to assess the impact that a powerful external symbol such as the wearing of a headscarf may have on the freedom of conscience and religion of very young children. The applicant's pupils were aged between four and eight, an age at which children wonder about many things and are also more easily influenced than older pupils. In those circumstances, it cannot be denied outright that the wearing of a headscarf might have some kind of proselytising effect, seeing that it appears to be imposed on women by a precept which is laid down in the Koran and which, as the Federal Court noted, is hard to square with the principle of gender equality. It therefore appears difficult

58 The prototype of such cases is *Lautsi v Italy* (n 7) where public schools were obliged to exhibit crucifixes.

59 A prototype would be *S A S v France* (n 17).

60 A prototype would be *Eweida v UK* (n 23).

61 'Public order' is only mentioned in Article 9 ECHR, not in Article 8.

> to reconcile the wearing of an Islamic headscarf with the message of tolerance, respect for others and, above all, equality and non-discrimination that all teachers in a democratic society must convey to their pupils.[62]

The argumentation is double. First, it is based on the danger of proselytism, a red thread running through the Court's jurisprudence, even if the danger is assessed differently concerning the 'passive' use of symbols such as fixing a cross on the wall (Lautsi) and the 'active' use of symbols such as wearing a headscarf, the distinctive element being personalisation.[63] Second, the danger is seen in Islam, as the Koran obliges only women to wear a headscarf and thus undermines an all-embracing understanding of gender equality.[64] The problem of this second argument is that it may be misunderstood as a negative evaluation of a certain belief; that is one of the reasons why some commentators have criticized the Court as being islamophobic.[65]

Wherever 'laïcité' is a constitutional value, the Court accords a special weight to it as a value to be legitimately preserved:

> The Court also notes that in France, as in Turkey or Switzerland, secularism is a constitutional principle, and a founding principle of the Republic to which the entire population adheres and the protection of which appears to be of prime importance, in particular in schools. …

62 *Dahlab v Switzerland* (n 18).

63 What is meant can be illustrated by the statement of the Alevi Community as a third-party intervener in the headscarf case before the German FCC. They explained that the fact that a school teacher having authority over children wears a headscarf exerts pressure on girls, especially for Alevi girls, for whom wearing a headscarf is not a duty, but a personal choice (see BVerfGE 138, 296, para 68).

64 The argument of gender equality is only taken up in relation to a potentially detrimental effect of symbols on children. On the contrary, when an adult voluntarily decides to use or wear a symbol potentially linked with gender discrimination, this has to be accepted as free choice: 'The Court takes the view, however, that a State Party cannot invoke gender equality in order to ban a practice that is defended by women – such as the applicant – in the context of the exercise of the rights enshrined in those provisions, unless it were to be understood that individuals could be protected on that basis from the exercise of their own fundamental rights and freedoms'. (*S A S v France*, n 17, para 119).

65 See eg *Kayaoglu* (n 41); Ilias Trispoiotis, 'Islamophobia in European Human Rights Law', Working Paper, July 2017 <https://cik.leeds.ac.uk/wp-content/uploads/sites/36/2017/07/2017.07.25-Law-Report-IT-final-1.pdf> accessed 9 January 2018; Yasin Aktay, 'European Values and the Muslim World: Turkish Cases at the European Court of Human Rights' (2008) Global Change, Peace & Security 99–108.

> Having regard to the margin of appreciation which must be left to the member States with regard to the establishment of the delicate relations between the Churches and the State, religious freedom thus recognised and restricted by the requirements of secularism appears legitimate in the light of the values underpinning the Convention.[66]

Thus, even when the prohibition concerned pupils and not teachers and could not cause any danger of proselytism, the Court accepts restrictive measures with the aim of defending the requirements of secularism in public education.

In addition to those general models of justification – upholding constitutional principles as a part of public order and preventing proselytism endangering the rights and freedom of others – case-specific reasons are given for restricting the use of religious symbols, such as reasons of health and safety in sport classes.[67]

It is worth mentioning that the use of a burkini is not considered to pose problems, neither for reasons of secularism, nor for any other reason, as shown by the case *Osmanoglu and Kocabas v Switzerland* (n 19). In considering the proportionality of the compulsory participation in mixed swimming classes for Muslim girls, the Court accepts the permission to use burkinis as counterbalancing measure.[68]

3.3.2 Use of Religious Symbols in Universities

The danger of undue influence on religious self-determination and proselytism is not that relevant in the academic world of universities where adults decide for themselves. Nevertheless, the Court shows openness for negative influences of attitudes questioning gender equality:

> … in the Turkish context, it must be borne in mind the impact which wearing such a symbol, which is presented or perceived as a compulsory religious duty, may have on those who choose not to wear it.[69]

Secularism is deemed to be no less important for universities than for schools. The basic idea behind is to ban all religions from State institutions and thus to

66 *Dogru v France* (n 53), para 72.

67 *Dogru v France* (n 53), para 68; see similar justifications in the context of traffic regulations *X v UK* (1978) 14 dr 234.

68 *Osmanoglu and Kocabas v Switzerland* (n 19), para 101.

69 *Leyla Şahin v Turkey* (GC) (n 20), para 115; this is a quotation of the Chamber judgment which the Grand Chamber upholds.

foster equality between different beliefs. It is equality on the zero-level with the (desired) effect of avoiding conflicts. Such a model was deliberately chosen in States fighting against the disproportionate influence of one specific religion (e.g. Catholicism in France and Islam in Turkey). It presupposes a delimitation of two different spheres and opposes State to Society. The total ban of religion from the realm of the State is counterbalanced by the free exercise of freedom in the social sphere.

It is true, however, that this concept is prone to critique.[70] While State and Society can be put under different regimes, believers and atheists will remain believers and atheists, in whatever sphere they are. Thus, it is not possible to ban religious convictions, but only to make them invisible, to ban their manifestation. Furthermore, in as far as religious symbols are concerned, what seems to be 'neutral' touches different beliefs in different ways.[71] While the headscarf is part of a compulsory dress code for religious Muslim women wearing Christian symbols is voluntary. Therefore the legal debate is focussed on Muslim religious symbols, especially female dress codes.

The Court is willing to interpret the question of religious symbols in the respective political and historical context of the countries concerned. It therefore accepts that the principles of secularism and equality – seen as intrinsically linked – can be understood as defence strategies against extremist movements:

> The Court does not lose sight of the fact that there are extremist political movements in Turkey which seek to impose on society as a whole their religious symbols and conception of a society founded on religious precepts.[72]

In the case *Kurtulmuş v Turkey* the Court emphasizes likewise the 'principle of secularism and its corollary, the principle of a neutral public service'.[73] The

70 See Peter B. Danchin, 'Islam in the Secular Nomos of the European Court of Human Rights' (2011) Michigan Journal of International law 663 <http://repository.law.umich.edu/mjil/vol32/iss4/2> accessed 9 January 2018.

71 The idea that the specific features of different religions must not be neglected has been emphasized for the first time in the case *Hamidović v Bosnia and Herzegovina* (n 21), para 41. The European Court in Luxembourg emphasizes questions of indirect and direct discrimination in this context; see below.

72 *Leyla Şahin v Turkey* (GC) (n 20), para 115; this is a quotation of the Chamber judgment which the Grand Chamber upholds.

73 *Kurtulmuş v Turkey* (n 20).

reference to these principles is more convincing here than in the case of Leyla Şahin as the applicant is employed by the State and thus, unlike Leyla Şahin, who is 'only' a student, a representative of the State. Nevertheless, it is obvious that the notion of 'neutrality' and 'secularism' is a product of century-long fights about the respective role of Church and State in Europe. As Danchin rightly points out transferring these notions to conflicts with Muslim believers does not yield per se satisfactory results.[74]

3.3.3 The Use of Religious Symbols in Court-Rooms

In a very recent, not yet final judgment[75] the Court distinguishes between the use of religious symbols in schools, universities, and other work places on the one hand and the use of religious symbols by witnesses in criminal trials on the other hand. It is stressed that, while witnesses are obliged to appear before the court, they are no officials and have no duty of neutrality. Sanctioning the wearing of a skullcap is considered not to be 'necessary in a democratic society'. While the Court refers to the general principles as outlined in the cases of *S A S v France* and *Leyla Şahin v Turkey* it seems to decide on the basis of a less rigid understanding of the requirements of secularism. It does not follow the idea of achieving equality by banning all manifestations of religious beliefs irrespective of the consequences that might have for the individual concerned, but demands to differentiate between different beliefs and to take into account the compulsory character of religious dress codes. This approach, if it is not changed on the level of the Grand Chamber, would mean modifying or at least nuancing the Court's responsiveness to secularism-oriented arguments.[76]

3.3.4 The Use of Religious Symbols in State Enterprises

In public enterprises the use of religious symbols is treated in the same way as in public schools, although this generalisation is criticized by dissenters.[77] The argumentation in the case of *Ebrahimian v France* repeats the idea of equality on a zero-level. The applicant is employed as a social worker in a public hospital. Prohibiting her to wear the headscarf is seen as a sign of 'strict equality',

---

74 See *Danchin* (n 70).

75 *Hamidović v Bosnia-Hercegovina* (n 21).

76 See the critique of the undifferentiated argumentation on the basis of secularism in the dissenting vote of Siofra O'Leary to the case *Ebrahimian v France* (IV) (n 22).

77 See the critique on this 'extension' of the education-specific argumentation to a general professional context in the dissenting opinion of Judge O'Leary to the case *Ebrahimian v France* (I) (n 22).

concerning not only those working for the State, but also the patients, who have a right to be treated in the same way whatever their religion:

> In the present case the purpose was to ensure respect for all of the religious beliefs and spiritual orientations held by the patients who were using the public service and were recipients of the requirement of neutrality imposed on the applicant, by guaranteeing them strict equality. The aim was also to ensure that these users enjoyed equal treatment, without distinction on the basis of religion.[78]

No explanation is, however, given why the Court assumes that nurses manifesting a specific belief would differentiate between their patients on the basis of religion when treating them. While complaints of patients about the applicant wearing a headscarf are mentioned in the facts of the case, it remains open on what elements the patients' real or potential fear of discriminatory treatment is based, this all the more so as the ban cannot change the religious conviction of the person concerned, but only the outside appearance. Nevertheless, the Court holds:

> ..., the neutrality of the public hospital service may be regarded as linked to the attitude of its staff, and requires that patients cannot harbour any doubts as to the impartiality of those treating them.[79]

Thus, the pillar of the judgment is, once again, a rigorous understanding of secularism.

3.3.5 Use of Religious Symbols in Private Enterprises

In private enterprises the State is not responsible for dress codes or general policies restricting the use of religious symbols. Nevertheless, courts are called upon to decide on ensuing sanctions, especially dismissals, and thus have a positive obligation to protect religious freedom.

Interestingly, the Court's most famous case on the use of religious symbols in private enterprises concerns a cross worn at a necklace, not a headscarf. The difference is a twofold one. First, wearing it is not a special obligation for women and thus does not carry with it any gender stereotyping. Second, a cross worn with a necklace is much less visible than a headscarf. The Court takes

78 *Ebrahimian v France* (n 22), para 53.

79 *Ebrahimian v France* (n 22), para 64.

up the second argument stressing that it is 'very discreet' and could not 'have detracted from [the applicant's] professional appearance'.[80] Furthermore, unlike in the case Ebrahimian the dress code of the enterprise is not based on 'strict equality' as not all religious symbols are banned. While the wish of an enterprise 'to communicate a certain image of the company and to promote recognition of its brand and staff' is considered to be a legitimate aim, the disturbances caused by religious symbols are not seen as important:

> There was no evidence that the wearing of other, previously authorised, items of religious clothing, such as turbans and hijabs, by other employees, had any negative impact on British Airways' brand or image.[81]

In a comparable case decided by the Luxembourg Court, Advocate General Kokott argued in favour of allowing a strict policy of neutrality.[82] In her view customers have a right 'to be served without discrimination'.[83] It is, however, not clear in how far wearing religious symbols could be seen as approaching customers in a discriminatory manner. The Luxembourg Court accepted the idea of the legitimate character of a policy of religious and ideological neutrality, but expected national courts in concrete cases to make sure that such a policy does not lead to indirect discrimination.[84] On the contrary, it held in another case that a dismissal cannot be based on wearing a headscarf only because of customers' wishes. The employer's willingness to take account of such wishes does not constitute 'a genuine and determining occupational requirement' in the sense of Article 4 para. 1 of Directive 2000/78.[85] These nuances show that it is not really clear in how far the wish not to be confronted with religious symbols has to be accepted in professional relationships. The Strasbourg Court says 'yes' for vulnerable people in hospitals fearing unequal treatment,[86] the Luxembourg Court says a somewhat vague 'no' for business relationships; while a consistent internal neutrality policy is legitimate, reacting to wishes of

80 *Eweida v France* (n 23), para 94.

81 *Eweida v France* (n 23), para 94.

82 Opinion of AG Kokott, presented on 31 May 2016, Case C-157/15 *Samira Achbita and Centrum voor gelijkheid van kansen en voor racismebestrijding v G4S Secure Solutions nv.*

83 Ibid, para. 92.

84 *Case C-157/15 Samira Achbita and Centrum voor gelijkheid van kansen en voor racismebestrijding v G4S Secure Solutions nv (ECJ, 14 March 2017).*

85 *Case C-188/15 Bougnaoui and Association de défence des droits de l'homme (addh) v Micropole Univers (ECJ, 1 March 2017).*

86 *Ebrahimian v France* (n 22).

individual customers concerning specific symbols is not.[87] One vision is based on neutrality as a precondition for social peace, the other one on tolerance. The common denominator in the jurisprudence of the courts is not to allow any differentiation between religions. The question remains, however, if general prohibitions are indeed 'neutral'. As implicitly shown by the cases before the Luxembourg Court, indirect discrimination might be more important than direct discrimination.

It goes without saying, that for reasons of health and hygiene prohibitions of religious symbols are allowed.[88]

3.3.6 Use of Religious Symbols in the Public Space

If the manifestation of religious convictions is accepted as part of individual self-fulfilment, it cannot be banned in the public space. Wearing kippas, crosses, and headscarves in the streets is therefore generally accepted in free and pluralist societies. The discussion is centred only on some very specific religious symbols, either because of their – potentially controversial – meaning, or because of their – potentially controversial – form. Courts therefore had to deal mainly with full-face veils[89] and, in the aftermath of islamist terrorist attacks in France, with burkinis.[90] In the full-veil cases the Court focussed on the protection of what it called 'the ground rules of social communication and more broadly the requirements of "living together"'.[91] The main distinguishing feature was seen in the fact that the full-face veil conceals the face and thus renders 'normal' societal interaction very difficult or even impossible. Thus the central argument was the form (and effect) of the religious symbol, not its – potentially discriminatory – meaning. The prohibition of the burkini was, on the contrary, not seen to be justified; the respective conflicts were solved before the French courts and therefore did not reach the ECtHR.

The overview shows that the reasons given for allowing or not allowing the use of religious symbols are manifold and vary according to the context. Religious symbols are treated differently inside and outside State institutions with policies being more restrictive for representatives of the State. Protection

87 See n 85.

88 See the case of Ms. Chaplin, the second applicant in the case *Eweida and others v UK* (n 23). The applicant was a nurse on a geriatric ward. The prohibition of wearing a cross on a chain around the neck was justified by the protection of health and safety in the hospital.

89 See *S A S v France*; *Belcacemi and Oussar v Belgium*; *Dakir v Belgium* (all n 25).

90 Conseil d'État, Ordonnance Ligue des droits de l'homme ea, 26 August 2016.

91 *S A S v France* (n 25), para 153.

against proselytism and undue influence on vulnerable groups, especially minors, is a red thread in the jurisprudence. Secularism and neutrality are accepted as models of regulation as long as they are based on strict equality. But even if these rules are free of cultural bias – a thesis challenged by many observers –, the different weight believers attach or feel compelled to attach to wearing visible religious symbols leads to different patterns of exclusion or inclusion.[92]

3.4 *Proportionality*

It is self-evident that conflicts about the use of religious symbols require balancing the respective interests. In this context it is decisive what is weighed: abstract values such as individual (religious) self-fulfilment against secularism, or concrete disadvantages for the person concerned against the specific rights of others or society as a whole. In the Court's jurisprudence both models are present.

An example of the abstract model is to be found in the case *Ebrahimian v France*. The Court does not explore the applicant's potential dilemma, either following compulsory religious rules or continuing the professional career, but takes a general approach:

> Thus, the Court notes that France has reconciled the principle of the neutrality of the public authorities with religious freedom, thus determining the balance that the State must strike between the competing private and public interests or competing Convention rights …[93]

Similarly, in *Kurtumulus v Turkey*, the loyalty to the State and its secular policy has an overwhelming weight:

---

92 See on the aspect of integration Sascha Sebastian, '"Vivre ensemble" und das Recht ein Außenseiter zu sein – Zur möglichen integrationspolitischen Bedeutung der Entscheidung des EGMR zum Verbot der Vollverschleierung' (2017) ZAR 153–62.

93 *Ebrahimian v France* (n 22), para 65; see the critique on this approach in the partially dissenting opinion of Judge O'Leary in Ebrahimian: 'S'agissant de l'appréciation de la proportionnalité par la chamber …, il apparaît que le caractère abstrait des principes invoqués pour faire échec au droit découlant de l'article 9 tend également à rendre cette appréciation abstraite. Le risque est donc que toute mesure prise au nom du principe de laïcité-neutralité et qui n'excède pas la marge d'appréciation d'un État – elle-même très large car ce sont des choix de société que se trouvent en cause – soit compatible avec la Convention'.

> ... that a democratic State may be entitled to require public servants to be loyal to the constitutional principles on which it is founded.

The abstract proportionality test is not convincing. This is also an important point in the dissent in the burqa case:

> ... [the opinion of the majority] sacrifices concrete individual rights guaranteed by the Convention to abstract principles.[94]

On the other extreme an example of the concrete or individualised model is to be found in the case *Hamidović v Bosnia and Herzegovina* where the individual situation of the applicant, his constraints and choices, are taken into account and held against the idea of secularism in courts:

> The Court sees no reason to doubt that the applicant's act was inspired by his sincere religious belief that he must wear a skullcap at all times, without any hidden agenda to make a mockery of the trial, incite others to reject secular and democratic values or cause a disturbance.[95]

3.5 *Large Margin of Appreciation*

A general feature of all Article 9 cases is the Court's willingness to grant a very large margin of appreciation.[96] Leeway is given to realise the respective national constitutional principles, be it secularism or another model. As a result, only in rare cases violations of the Convention are found. The attitude behind is well illustrated in Judge Ranzoni's dissenting opinion in the case *Hamidović v Bosnia and Herzegovina*:

> Does our Court have the necessary knowledge and competence to call into question the State's choice in regulation this specific and sensitive issue? Is it our role to dictate, from a distance and with hindsight, which policies a State has to pursue in the context of a difficult national situation?[97]

---

94 Dissenting opinion of Judges Nußberger and Jäderblom to the judgment *S A S v France* (n 17), para 2.

95 *Hamidović v Bosnia and Hercegovina* (n 21), para 41.

96 On the margin of appreciation in cases concerning freedom of religion see *Nußberger* (n 2), p. 130

97 Dissenting opinion of Judge Ranzoni to the judgment *Hamidović v Bosnia and Hercegovina* (n 21), para 22.

4 Conclusion

History has shown that religious beliefs can divide people and cause violent conflicts. The danger is all the more real when religious convictions are not only held, but also shown. Religious symbols can therefore be stumbling blocks and cause tensions. Two reactions are possible. Both figure in a famous quotation of the case *Serif v Greece*:

> Although the Court recognises that it is possible that tension is created in situations where a religious or any other community becomes divided, it considers that this is one of the unavoidable consequences of pluralism. The role of the authorities in such circumstances is not to remove the cause of tension by eliminating pluralism, but to ensure that the competing groups tolerate each other ....[98]

Prohibiting the use of religious symbols means removing the cause of tension, but eventually also eliminating pluralism, be it only in a specific context (school environment, hospital, enterprise). On the contrary, ensuring that the competing groups tolerate each other might be the more idealistic, but less realistic approach. Despite lip services pointing in another direction, the cases in which the Court accepts rigid solutions based on secularism and strict neutrality seem to outweigh the cases in which the Court accepts the risk of tension and requests tolerance. The approach to Article 9 cases can thus be said to be more cautious than to Article 10 cases where the Court expects conflicts to be rather fruitful than detrimental to societal peace. It may be said that the heritage of Galileo is taken at its face value, while the heritage of Luther is seen in its historical context. To a certain degree, this might be the effect of lessons learnt. Joseph Weiler warns with good cause:

> There are few legal issues which still manage to evoke civic passion in the wider population. Increasingly, and sometimes for the wrong reasons, the place of religion in our public spaces has become one of them.[99]

The Court therefore should take subsidiarity especially serious in cases of religious conflicts:

98 *Serif v Greece* ECHR 1999-IX 73, para 53.

99 *Weiler* (n 6) 1.

> The ECtHR is simultaneously reflective and constitutive of the European constitutional practices and norms. When there is a diverse constitutional practice among the Convention States – and there certainly is in this area – the Court needs to listen, not only preach, and to be seen to be listening.[100]

Nevertheless, the problems of the Court's approach are obvious. The level of protection of the individual is rather low. As most cases concern the integration of religious Muslims into what is perceived to be a Western world, the Court is reproached of not helping against marginalisation and (partial) exclusion of Muslim religious minorities.[101] There are no convincing answers given to the question of how women wearing a burqa should live in Western societies or how women wearing a headscarf should make a career as teachers, judges or medical doctors.

While this critique is justified, it is also necessary to see the other side of the coin. The Court cannot ignore that conflicts about freedom of religion cannot be solved exclusively on the basis of the European Convention of Human Rights, but must be placed in the national constitutional framework as well. As a European Court, the Court has to guard its equidistance to all the 47 constitutional systems of the Member States; it cannot invent one ideal abstract model outside the historical context. As explained in the introduction with respect to Bosnia-Herzegovina, changing a detail in a complex system might upset the delicate balance found after many difficult years of struggle.

Constitutional models on the interaction between State and religion have developed over centuries. They are not static. Traditional models might not be able to give adequate answers to living religious pluralism in a globalised world where the dividing lines are more between believers and non-believers than between different religions. A completely secular State distancing itself from whatever religious heritage might be a model for some, but not for all. It cannot be ignored that, especially in the Eastern part of Europe, there is a

100 *Weiler* (n 6) 1.

101 According to *Danchin* (see above n 70) the reasons for the difficulties in dealing with the manifestation of Muslim belief are deeply rooted in the European human rights protection system. The liberal traditions on which it is based share 'a conception of the public sphere and public reason on the one hand, and of the right to religious freedom on the other, which were conceived internally to Western Christianity and its complex relationship to the rise of the 'secular' European nation-state'. (p 670). The Court's approach has thus to be understood as 'culturally and historically contingent and neutral towards neither religion in general nor distinct religious traditions in particular' (idem).

new quest for collective (religious) identity, which might be explained by the vacuum created by the collapse of an anti-religious ideology. The Court has to take seriously concerns such as those voiced by eight Member States[102] as third party interveners before the Grand Chamber in the case *Lautsi v Italy*:

> They pointed out that there was a huge diversity of Church-State arrangements in Europe and that more than half the population of Europe lived in non-secular States. ... States should not have to divest themselves of part of their cultural identity simply because that identity was of religious origin. The position adopted by the Chamber was not an expression of the pluralism manifest in the Convention system, but an expression of the values of a secular State. To extend it to the whole of Europe would represent the 'Americanisation' of Europe in that a single and unique rule and a rigid separation of Church and State would be binding on everyone.
>
> In their submission, favouring secularism was a political position that, whilst respectable, was not neutral.[103]

Different State models – a completely open secular pluralist model[104] and a model implicitly or explicitly based on common (religious) traditions – coexist in Europe. In both models individual human rights can be in danger: either fervent believers or convinced atheists can be outsiders. The Court's task is nothing more and nothing less but to help them to feel fully integrated in whatever model they live in.

---

102 Armenia, Bulgaria, Cyprus, the Russian Federation, Greece, Lithuania, Malta and the Republic of San Marino.

103 *Lautsi v Italy* (GC) (n 7), para 47.

104 It may be questionable if any model is really devoid of any link to religion. It suffices to point to the fact that even accepting Sunday as a holiday is not 'neutral'.

CHAPTER 7

Le système interaméricain des droits de l'homme face aux religions

Laurence Burgorgue-Larsen

Libérale et foncièrement protectrice, telle pourrait être synthétisée l'approche du système interaméricain des droits de l'homme face aux religions. Il suffit de remonter le temps, à l'époque créatrice tant du panaméricanisme institutionnel que de l'humanisme juridique. *1948* et *1969*, sont en effet les deux dates historiques qui voient émerger et consacrer, à travers des textes d'inégale portée, la liberté de religion dans l'univers interaméricain.

1948. *Bogotá, Colombie*. La capitale abrite la IXème Conférence internationale américaine dont l'objet est de jeter les bases institutionnelles d'un panaméricanisme longtemps rêvé. Alors que le pays vit un moment dramatique, le *Bogotazo*, marqué par l'assassinat de celui qui était présenté comme le vainqueur des prochaines élections présidentielles, Juan Roa Sierra ; alors que les manifestants envahissent l'enceinte qui abrite la Conférence panaméricaine (*i.e.*, le *Capitolio*), la *Déclaration américaine des droits et devoirs de l'homme*, réussit à être adoptée le 2 mai 1948 – sept mois avant que les Nations Unies ne proclament le 10 décembre la Déclaration universelle des droits de l'homme – tandis que la Charte de l'Organisation des Etats Américains (ci-après OEA) voyait également le jour[1].

L'article III de la Déclaration américaine (Droit à la liberté de religion et de culte) affirme que « Toute personne a le droit de professer librement une croyance religieuse, de la manifester et de la pratiquer en public ou en privé »[2]. Il convient de le lire de façon combinée avec l'article II (Droit d'égalité devant la loi) qui affirme que « Toutes les personnes, sans distinction de race, de sexe, de langue, de religion ou autre, sont égales devant la loi et ont les droits et les devoirs consacrés dans cette déclaration ». Quant à la Charte de l'OEA, les

1 La Charte de l'OEA ne consacre pas de disposition spécifique à la religion. Son article 3§1 affirme plus généralement et logiquement que les Etats membres reconnaissent les droits humains fondamentaux (sans plus de précisions) et s'engagent à les respecter sans discrimination.

2 L'article III dans sa version originelle se lit ainsi : « *Toda persona tiene el derecho de profesar libremente una creencia religiosa y de manifestarle y practicarla en publico y en privado.* »

 | DOI:10.1163/9789004349155_008

Etats entendent « réaffirmer » des principes parmi lesquels on découvre, à l'article 3 *j.*) que « Les Etats américains proclament les droits fondamentaux de la personne humaine sans aucune distinction de race, de nationalité, de religion ou de sexe », tandis que l'article 45 *a.*) du même texte est une profession de foi des Etats qui s'engagent à faire tout leur possible afin que les êtres humains puissent avoir droit « au bien-être matériel et à leur épanouissement spirituel ».

1969. *San José. Costa Rica.* Alors que la Commission interaméricaine des droits de l'homme existe depuis dix ans, créée par une simple résolution des Ministres des affaires extérieures en réunion à Santiago du Chili, dans la foulée de la crise dominicaine et des soubresauts de la révolution cubaine en 1959, les Etats membres de l'OEA décident de créer un véritable système interaméricain de protection des droits[3]. Ils adoptent pour ce faire la *Convention américaine des droits de l'homme* qui instaure une Cour (agissant de façon complémentaire avec la Commission dont l'existence est confirmée) et qui proclame pas moins de vingt-trois droits civils et politiques, parmi lesquels la « liberté de conscience et de religion » à l'article 12[4]. Composé de quatre paragraphes, cet article décline la dimension positive de la liberté (§ 1) et sa dimension négative (§ 2), tandis que le § 3, de façon classique, concerne le régime des limitations susceptibles de lui être apportées. Le quatrième et dernier paragraphe – singularité interaméricaine – garantit le droit des parents d'éduquer leurs enfants selon leurs convictions personnelles, là où la Convention européenne a attendu le premier protocole adopté en 1952 pour affirmer la même chose. Il convient de relier cette disposition à deux autres bases juridiques du texte conventionnel américain : à l'article 1 § 1 tout d'abord, qui mentionne l'obligation des Etats de garantir le plein exercice des droits protégés sans distinction

3 R. K. Goldman, « History and Action : the Inter-American Human Rights System and the Role of the Inter-American Commission on Human Rights », *Human Rights Quarterly*, 31, 2009, pp. 861–862.

4 Il se lit ainsi : « *Article 12. Liberté de conscience et de religion* : 1. Toute personne a *droit* à la liberté de conscience et de religion. Ce droit implique la liberté de *garder* sa religion ou ses croyances, ou de *changer* de religion ou de croyances, ainsi que la liberté *de professer et de répandre sa foi ou ses croyances*, individuellement ou collectivement, en public ou en privé. 2. Nul ne peut être l'objet de *mesures de contrainte* de nature à restreindre sa liberté de garder sa religion ou ses croyances, ou de changer de religion ou de croyances. 3. La liberté de manifester sa religion ou ses croyances ne peut faire l'objet d'autres *restrictions* que celles qui, prévues par la loi, sont nécessaires à la sécurité publique, à la protection de l'ordre, de la santé ou de la morale publics, ou à la sauvegarde des droits ou libertés d'autrui. 4. Les *parents*, et le cas échéant, les tuteurs, ont droit à ce que leurs enfants ou pupilles reçoivent *l'éducation religieuse et morale* conforme à leurs propres convictions. » (Italiques ajoutés)

aucune, notamment au regard de la religion[5] ; à l'article 27 ensuite, qui interdit que les suspensions de droits soient réalisées de façon discriminatoire (notamment sur la base de la religion). Le §2 de cette disposition énumère une liste de onze droits, dont la liberté de religion, qui ne peuvent faire l'objet de suspension en cas « de guerre, de danger public ou dans toute autre situation de crise qui menace l'indépendance ou la sécurité d'un État partie[6].»

On prend la mesure ici que, quelles que soient les époques – 1948 qui voyait la mise en place de l'OEA et l'adoption de la Déclaration américaine ou 1969 qui voyait se concrétiser les efforts des idéalistes par l'adoption du texte interaméricain de protection des droits –, les Etats de l'Hémisphère Sud ont voulu accorder une importance cardinale au principe de non-discrimination au regard de la religion qui, couplé avec le droit de professer, de manifester et de pratiquer sa religion ou ses croyances, lui confère une protection particulièrement ample.

Ceci se confirme quand on entreprend une analyse des textes ultérieurs, adoptés dans le cadre de l'activité de l'organisation panaméricaine : du *protocole de San Salvador*[7] – doté d'une clause de non discrimination religieuse (art. 3) ainsi que des références au nécessaire respect du pluralisme idéologique, de

---

5 Il se lit ainsi : « *Article 1. Obligation d'adopter des mesures de droit interne* : 1. Les États parties s'engagent à respecter les droits et libertés reconnus dans la présente Convention et à en garantir le libre et plein exercice à toute personne relevant de leur compétence, sans aucune distinction fondée sur la race, la couleur, le sexe, la langue, *la religion*, les opinions politiques ou autres, l'origine nationale ou sociale, la situation économique, la naissance ou *toute autre condition sociale*. 2. Aux effets de la présente Convention, tout être humain est une personne. » (Italiques ajoutés)

6 Il se lit ainsi : « *Article 27. Suspension des garanties* : 1. En cas de guerre, de danger public ou dans toute autre situation de crise qui menace l'indépendance ou la sécurité d'un État partie, celui-ci pourra, strictement en fonction des exigences du moment, prendre des mesures qui suspendent les obligations contractées en vertu de la présente Convention, pourvu que ces mesures ne soient pas incompatibles avec les autres obligations imposées par le Droit international et n'entraînent aucune discrimination fondée uniquement sur des considérations de race, de couleur, de sexe, de langue, *de religion* ou d'origine sociale. 2. La disposition précédente n'autorise pas la suspension des droits déterminés dans les articles suivants : 3 (Droit à la reconnaissance de la personnalité juridique) ; 4 (Droit à la vie) ; 5 (Droit à l'intégrité de la personne) ; 6 (Interdiction de l'esclavage et de la servitude) ; 9 (Principe de légalité et de rétroactivité) ; 12 (Liberté de conscience et de religion) ; 17 (Protection de la famille) ; 18 (Droit à un nom) ; 19 (Droit de l'enfant) ; 20 (Droit à une nationalité) ; 23 (Droits politiques). Elle n'autorise pas non plus la suspension des garanties indispensables à la protection des droits susvisés. » (Italiques ajoutés)

7 Protocole à la Convention américaine sur les droits économiques et sociaux adopté à San Salvador le 17 novembre 1988 et entré en vigueur le 16 novembre 1999 après le dépôt du 11ème instrument de ratification.

tolérance et de participation au sein d'une société pluraliste dans le cadre éducatif (art. 13) – à la *Convention interaméricaine pour prévenir, sanctionner et éradiquer la violence contre les femmes*[8] – qui consacre tout à la fois le droit à la liberté de religion (art. 4) et prévoit une clause de non discrimination religieuse (art. 6) – en passant par la *Charte démocratique interaméricaine* (2011) qui pointe, à son article 9, l'importance du respect de la diversité religieuse en tant que valeur qui consolide la démocratie et la citoyenneté ; on prend la mesure de l'extraordinaire richesse du panorama normatif interaméricain. Il démontre à l'envi que l'arsenal juridique est complet et ne se contredit pas : la valorisation de la liberté religieuse y est maximale (étant même un curseur de l'Etat de droit), tandis que toute discrimination fondée sur des critères religieux y est fermement prohibée.

Toutefois, le juriste amoureux du contentieux, l'arrêtiste éperdu d'analyse jurisprudentielle sera particulièrement déçu de découvrir que l'appréhension de cette liberté par la Cour interaméricaine n'a pas été abondante[9]. La moisson contentieuse est maigre. On ne décèle en effet que trois arrêts qui ont *abordé* la question sans déclarer une violation de l'article 12. Une telle rareté contentieuse démontre qu'il n'y a pas, au sein des Amériques, de problèmes structurels graves en la matière comme a pu s'en réjouir le grand juriste mexicain Hector Fix-Zamudio qui fut en outre un des membres de la Cour interaméricaine au début de son fonctionnement. Une autre explication de cette rareté tient au fait que la Commission, et par ricochet la Cour (qui dépend des saisines de la première), s'est logiquement concentrée sur les affaires de violations graves et massives des droits qui ont caractérisé les heures les plus sombres des dictatures latino-américaines. En réalité, les pratiques d'exécutions extra-judiciaires de certains activistes – comme les défenseurs des droits de l'homme et/ou de l'environnement – voire leurs disparitions forcées, incitent la Commission à continuer de se concentrer sur les atteintes au droit à la vie, à la prohibition de la torture, à la liberté et à la sûreté[10]... En tout état de cause, parmi les trois arrêts qui ont à voir avec la liberté de conscience et de religion,

8 Convention interaméricaine pour sanctionner et éradiquer la violence faite aux femmes, adoptée à Belém do Pará au Brésil le 9 juin 1994.

9 F. Arlettaz, « La libertad de religiosa en el sistema interamericano de derechos humanos », *Revista internacional de derechos humanos*, 2011, n° 1, pp. 39–58.

10 Pour des analyses ciblées sur les droits protégeant l'intégrité physique des personnes dans le système interaméricain, voir L. Burgorgue-Larsen, A. Úbeda de Torres, *The American Convention on Human Rights. Case Law and Commentary*, Oxford, OUP, 2011, 886 p. ; C. Medina Quiroga, *The American Convention on Human Rights. Crucial Rights and Their Theory and Practice*, Cambridge, Cambridge University Press, Intersentia, 2016 (2nd ed.), 374 p. T.M. Antkowiak, A. Gonza, *The American Convention on Human Rights. Essential Rights*, Oxford, OUP, 2017, 416 p.

l'un est plus connu que les autres car il est plus directement relié à ce droit ; il a maintes fois débordé les frontières du continent américain pour être commenté ailleurs dans le monde, il s'agit de *La dernière Tentation du Christ c. Chili*, un arrêt du 5 février 2001[11]. Les deux autres arrêts ont été rendus en 2004 et 2005, l'un dans l'affaire du *Massacre Plan de Sanchez c. Guatemala* (29 avril 2004)[12] et l'autre dans l'affaire de la *Communauté Moiwana c. Surinam* (15 juin 2005)[13], et concernent les croyances ancestrales des communautés indiennes.

Il reste toutefois que l'analyse de l'appréhension des atteintes à la religion dans l'Hémisphère Sud prend une autre allure si on s'attèle à l'activité de la Commission interaméricaine. Les nombreuses facettes de ses fonctions permettent en effet de disposer de plus d'éléments On sait qu'elle établit des rapports annuels, des rapports par pays et *last but not least* des rapports dans le cadre de la présentation de « pétitions individuelles », autant de sources non négligeables d'informations. Ces divers documents, dans le cadre de cette étude, ont en effet été importants pour arriver à présenter un état des lieux plus complet et donc plus nourri de la question. Les *rapports* publiés au début des années 1980 – quand nombre d'Etats étaient encore sous la férule de dictatures comme l'Argentine du Général Rafael Videla ou le Cuba du communiste-révolutionnaire Fidel Castro – pointent des politiques discriminatoires à l'endroit des communautés religieuses en général (comme à Cuba) ou de façon plus ciblée à l'endroit des Témoins de Jéhovah (comme en Argentine)[14], au Guatemala[15] ou encore au Paraguay[16]. De même, certaines *pétitions* examinées par la Commission contre le Guatemala (dans l'affaire *Dianne Ortiz*, révélant les atteintes à l'intégrité physique d'une religieuse nord-américaine) ou contre la Bolivie et le Chili – dans les affaires *Alfredo Díaz Bustos*[17] et *Cristián Daniel*

11 Cour IADH, 5 février 2001, Exceptions préliminaires, fond et réparations, *La Dernière tentation du Christ c. Chili*, Série C n°73.

12 Cour IADH, 29 avril 2004, Exceptions préliminaires, fond et réparations, *Massacre Plan de Sanchez c. Guatemala*, Série C n°105.

13 Cour IADH, 15 juin 2005, Exceptions préliminaires, fond et réparations, *Communauté Moiwana c. Surinam*, Série C n°124.

14 Com. IADH, *Testigos de Jehová (Argentina)*, rapport 02/79, 5 mars 1979 (v. rapport publié sur l'Argentine en 1980, ch. X-B).

15 Com. IADH, *La situation des droits de l'homme au Guatemala*, Ch. VI ; OEA/Ser.L/V/II.53 doc. 21, rev. 2.

16 Com. IADH, *Rapport annuel 1979–1980*, Ch. V. Paraguay.

17 Com. IADH, *Alfredo Díaz Bustos c. Bolivie*, rapport n° 52/04, 2004, OEA/Ser/I/V/II.122. doc. 5 rev.1. E. Xavier Gomes, « The Implementation of the Inter-American Norms on Freedom of Religion in the National Legislation of OAS Member States », *BYU Law Review*, vol. 2009, Issue 3, pp. 575–596.

Sahli Vera[18] en matière d'objection de conscience –, permettent là encore d'avoir des éléments supplémentaires pour arriver à discerner la manière dont le système interaméricain fait face aux religions.

Au bout du compte, on peut arriver grâce à ces différents matériaux – qui affectent tous les Etats de l'Hémisphère, *i.e.* ceux qui n'ont pas ratifié la Convention mais qui sont toutefois sous le contrôle de la Commission[19], comme ceux qui se trouvent sous la double obligation de respecter, et la Déclaration, et la Convention[20] – on peut arriver à dégager les grandes lignes de la protection de la liberté de conscience et de religion au sein des Amériques. L'exploration interaméricaine en matière de liberté de religion permettra d'exposer successivement les points saillants relatifs tout à la fois au *contenu* de cette liberté (I), ses *titulaires* (II) et *last but not least*, sa *portée* (III).

1 Le *contenu* de la liberté de conscience et de religion

Une analyse du contenu de la liberté oblige à se pencher, quoique rapidement et de façon non exhaustive, sur le sens des mots (A) afin de voir si les organes de protection ont tiré d'éventuelles conséquences de la dissociation des expressions de « conscience » d'un côté et de « religion » de l'autre, avant d'examiner la place accordée à la liberté éducative des parents au sein même de l'article 12 (B).

1.1 *Le sens des mots*

Que protègent exactement les articles III de la Déclaration et 12 de la Convention américaine ? Qu'est ce que le religieux ? Si les études théoriques de tout type

18 Com. IADH, Fond, 10 mars 2005, *Cristina Daniel Sahli Vera et autres c. Chili*, aff. 12.219, rapport n°43/05.

19 La Commission interaméricaine est en effet la gardienne de la Déclaration américaine des droits et devoirs de l'homme, y compris à l'égard des Etats ayant décidé de ne pas ratifier la Convention et, par voie de conséquence, de ne pas accepter la juridiction de la Cour. Il s'agit des Etats-Unis et du Canada pour l'Amérique du Nord ; de Belize pour l'Amérique centrale et d'Antigua et Barbuda, des Bahamas, de Guyana, de San Kitts et Nevis, de Santa Lucia, de St Vincent et Grenadines pour les autres Etats-îles anglophones des Caraïbes.

20 En ayant ratifié la Convention américaine et accepté la compétence de la Cour. Ces Etats sont, aujourd'hui, au nombre de vingt : Argentine, les Barbades, la Bolivie, le Brésil, le Chili, la Colombie, le Costa Rica, l'Equateur, le Salvador, le Guatemala, Haïti, Honduras, Mexico, Nicaragua, Panamá, Paraguay, Pérou, la République dominicaine, le Suriname et l'Uruguay.

(juridique, philosophique, anthropologique etc..) ont tenté de délimiter ce qui relève de la liberté de conscience et de la liberté religieuse *stricto sensu*, il faut remarquer que l'article III ne consacre que la liberté religieuse *stricto sensu* (*i.e.* professer une croyance religieuse), alors que l'article 12 unit les libertés de conscience et de religion, sans les définir, à l'instar d'ailleurs (en partie) de la Déclaration universelle des droits de l'homme, de la Convention européenne des droits de l'homme et du Pacte international sur les droits civils et politiques.

En effet, ces instruments distinguent, tout en les unissant au sein d'une seule disposition, les libertés de pensée (laquelle intégrerait tout type de croyances, notamment les croyances séculaires), de conscience (laquelle intégrerait tout type de convictions de type éthique sans lien avec la religion *stricto sensu*) et enfin de religion (qui elle engloberait les croyances et convictions religieuses)[21].

Les organes interaméricains de protection ne se sont pas lancés dans une opération de délimitation théorique trop complexe. Les organes quasi judiciaires et judiciaires ne sont pas des théoriciens : il est par trop dangereux de se lier à l'avance les mains. Mieux vaut aborder *in concreto* les affaires quand elles arrivent. C'est le pragmatisme de la fonction judiciaire. Ce qui est sûr, c'est que la Cour, dans l'affaire de la *Dernière Tentation du Christ*, a dûment pointé les deux facettes de la liberté de conscience et de religion, à savoir le religieux d'un côté et le reste (les croyances multiples, qui peuvent aller de l'athéisme à l'agnosticisme en passant par de multiples croyances de type spirituel et/ou culturel).

Il n'est pas inutile à ce stade de rappeler succinctement le contexte qui participa à transmettre à la Cour une affaire de censure cinématographique. La transition démocratique au Chili dans les années 1990 fut marquée par un nombre important de censures *judiciaires* de livres, de pièces de théâtre, d'émissions télévisées et de films. Ces censures – qui furent le fait du juge national – reposaient sur une argumentation marquée par le dogme d'une forte hiérarchisation des droits fondamentaux où le respect du droit à l'honneur primait sur la libre expression[22]. Ce contexte particulier explique que la première

21 On relèvera une exception avec la Charte africaine des droits et devoirs de l'homme et des peuples qui ne mentionne pas, à son article 8, la liberté de pensée puisqu'elle est centrée uniquement sur la liberté de religion.

22 Cela fut parfaitement mis en exergue par Felipe González Morales, ancien membre de la Commission interaméricaine, dans sa thèse de doctorat, *Las transformaciones del sistema interamericano de derechos humanos durante los procesos de democratización de los Estados partes*, Université Carlos III, 2012, pp. 258 et s. Elle a été publiée aux Editions Tirant Lo Blanch en 2013 sous le titre plus générique de *Sistema interamericano de derechos humanos* (495 p.).

affaire de censure que la Cour dût examiner fût chilienne[23]. Contrairement au Conseil de qualification cinématographique chilien qui avait levé l'interdiction de diffusion du film *La Dernière Tentation du Christ* du cinéaste Martin Scorsese, ce furent les autorités judiciaires – la Cour d'appel de Santiago puis la Cour suprême – qui invalidèrent une telle décision et imposèrent la censure de l'œuvre conformément à ce que permettait à l'époque l'article 19.12 de la Constitution chilienne du 24 octobre 1980. L'examen des faits démontre clairement que si la censure fut mise en œuvre, ce ne fut en aucun cas pour respecter la limitation conventionnelle de l'article 13 de la Convention américaine spécifique au domaine – *i.e.* « la protection morale des enfants et adolescents »[24] – mais pour défendre l'image de Jésus Christ mise à mal par l'œuvre cinématographique du cinéaste nord-américain[25]. Ceci rappelé, il est intéressant de souligner que la Cour, au §79 de son arrêt, mentionna ce qu'elle a appelé la « dimension religieuse » de la liberté de conscience et de religion de l'article 12. Et d'affirmer que :

---

23 Cour IDH, 5 février 2001, *La Dernière Tentation du Christ* (*Olmedo Bustos et autres*) *c. Chili*, série C n° 73.

24 Conformément au §4 *in fine* de l'article 13 relatif à la *Liberté de pensée et d'expression.* Afin que le lecteur prenne la mesure de la complexité de l'article 13, il a été pertinent de le reproduire dans son intégralité : « 1. Toute personne a droit à la liberté de pensée et d'expression ; ce droit comprend la liberté de rechercher, de recevoir et de répandre des informations et des idées de toute espèce, sans considération de frontières, que ce soit oralement ou par écrit, sous une forme imprimée ou artistique, ou par tout autre moyen de son choix. 2. L'exercice du droit prévu au paragraphe précédent ne peut être soumis à aucune censure préalable, mais il comporte des responsabilités ultérieures qui, expressément fixées par la loi, sont nécessaires : a) Au respect des droits ou à la réputation d'autrui ; ou b) à la sauvegarde de la sécurité nationale, de l'ordre public, ou de la santé ou de la morale publiques. 3. La liberté d'expression ne peut être restreinte par des voies ou des moyens indirects, notamment par les monopoles d'État ou privés sur le papier journal, les fréquences radioélectriques, les outils ou le matériel de diffusion, ou par toute autre mesure visant à entraver la communication et la circulation des idées et des opinions. 4. Sans préjudice des dispositions du paragraphe 2 ci-dessus, les spectacles publics peuvent être soumis par la loi à la censure, uniquement pour en réglementer l'accès en raison de la *protection morale des enfants et des adolescents.* 5. Sont interdits par la loi toute propagande en faveur de la guerre, tout appel à la haine nationale, raciale ou religieuse, qui constituent des incitations à la violence, ainsi que toute autre action illégale analogue contre toute personne ou tout groupe de personnes déterminées, fondée sur des considérations de race, de couleur, de religion, de langue ou d'origine nationale, ou sur tous autres motifs. »

25 Ibid., §60.e).

> Ce droit est un des ciments de la société démocratique. *Dans sa dimension religieuse*, il constitue un élément transcendant dans la protection des convictions des croyants et de leur forme de vie. (Italiques ajoutés)

Il y aurait donc là, avec cette incise, une délimitation entre ce qui relève du religieux et le reste. La question qui se pose à ce stade est de savoir si l'article 12 a fait l'objet d'une déclaration de violation dans cette affaire, aux côtés de la liberté d'expression (art.13), dont on a vu qu'elle en était au cœur. En fait, si la Commission invoqua la violation de l'article 12, la Cour ne la suivit pas. La première avait estimé qu'elle s'était produite car, en censurant le film, la société dans son ensemble aurait été empêchée d'accéder à une information qui aurait pu permettre à certaines personnes de maintenir, de changer ou de modifier leurs croyances religieuses. La Cour réfuta une telle approche[26], en considérant qu'elle ne disposait d'aucune preuve qui accréditerait le fait que la censure du film *La Dernière Tentation du Christ* ait privé ou affecté d'une quelconque manière le droit de « conserver, changer, professer ou divulguer, en toute liberté, sa religion ou ses croyances[27]. »

Si les indications sur le sens des mots de l'article 12 sont rares, on ne peut pas considérer qu'il en va de même s'agissant de la question éducative et du choix effectué par les parents en matière.

1.2 *La liberté éducative des parents*

Si les travaux préparatoires de la Convention européenne démontrent que les *disputatio* furent à leur zénith quand il s'est agi d'intégrer le droit des parents d'offrir à leurs enfants une instruction conforme à leurs convictions (religieuses ou autres)[28], la rédaction du § 4 de l'article 12 de la Convention

---

26 Ibid., §§63–73.

27 Le §79 dans son intégralité se lit ainsi : « *According to Article 12 of the Convention, the right to freedom of conscience and religion allows everyone to maintain, change, profess and disseminate his religion or beliefs. This right is one of the foundations of democratic society. In its religious dimension, it constitutes a far-reaching element in the protection of the convictions of those who profess a religion and in their way of life. In this case, however, there is no evidence to prove that any of the freedoms embodied in Article 12 of the Convention have been violated. Indeed, the Court understands that the prohibition of the exhibition of the film "The Last Temptation of Christ" did not impair or deprive anyone of their right to maintain, change, profess or disseminate their religion or beliefs with total freedom* ».

28 Il fallut en effet attendre l'adoption du premier protocole pour que ce droit soit consacré dans le champ conventionnel européen (art. 2 du P1).

américaine[29] fut elle aussi l'objet de controverses de dernière minute à l'occasion de la rédaction de la Convention américaine, alors qu'aucune polémique n'avait émaillé les discussions sur la rédaction des autres paragraphes[30].

La première version du texte ne l'incluait pas et il fallut l'intervention du gouvernement chilien – qui mettait en avant le contenu de l'article 18 du Pacte international sur les droits civils et politiques et sa référence à la liberté éducative des parents – afin que la question soit débattue. Du coup, plusieurs délégations se manifestèrent afin de préciser et éclaircir certains points : ainsi de la délégation mexicaine qui mit en avant qu'au Mexique, l'école était laïque ; de la délégation colombienne qui ne voulait pas que l'Etat supporte les frais du droit des parents à ce que leurs enfants reçoivent une éducation religieuse et morale ou encore de la délégation du Honduras qui craignait les répercussions politiques d'une telle mention. Au final toutefois, le § 4 de l'article 12 fut adopté avec une déclaration en bonne et due forme du Mexique – qui était ni plus ni moins qu'une réserve interprétative – qui entendait réitérer son attachement à sa Constitution et au fait qu'il fallait interpréter l'article 12 de façon conforme au texte constitutionnel mexicain.

En tout état de cause, si la jurisprudence de la Cour interaméricaine est muette sur ces questions, on découvre dans certains rapports par pays publiés par la Commission interaméricaine, des éléments intéressants où elle déclara enfreint l'article III de la Déclaration américaine sous cet angle, alors qu'aucune mention du droit des parents d'éduquer leurs enfants selon leurs convictions religieuses ou autres ne s'y trouve[31] (contrairement au libellé de l'article 12 de la Convention américaine).

Ainsi, dans le *Rapport sur la situation des droits de l'homme à Cuba* publié en 1983 – qui était le 7ème rapport sur la situation des droits de l'homme dans ce pays –, la Commission identifia précisément les atteintes au droit des parents d'éduquer leurs enfants librement. En effet, sur la base de l'article 54 de la Constitution cubaine (de 1976), « l'Etat socialiste base l'activité et l'éducation du peuple sur la conception scientifique matérialiste de l'univers ». Ce faisant, il octroie au législateur le pouvoir de règlementer les institutions

29 Il se lit ainsi : « Les *parents*, et le cas échéant, les tuteurs, ont droit à ce que leurs enfants ou pupilles reçoivent *l'éducation religieuse et morale* conforme à leurs propres convictions » (Italiques ajoutés)

30 M. Huaco Palomino, « Artículo 12. Libertad de conciencia y de religión », *Comentario a la Convención americana de derechos humanos*, C. Steiner (dir.), Fondation Konrad Adenauer, 2015, p. 317.

31 L'article III de la Déclaration américaine (Droit à la liberté de religion et de culte) affirme que « Toute personne a le droit de professer librement une croyance religieuse, de la manifester et de la pratiquer en public ou en privé ».

religieuses et de considérer « comme illégal et punissable d'opposer la foi ou les croyances religieuses à la Révolution, à l'éducation ou à l'accomplissement des droits de travailler, de défendre la patrie avec les armes ».

Dans ce contexte, la Commission déclara contraire à la Déclaration américaine la nationalisation en 1961 des écoles privées qui avait entraîné la suppression de l'éducation religieuse ; elle fustigea également la suppression des fêtes religieuses et l'organisation d'activités sportives et de classes d'endoctrinement politique tous les dimanches dans la mesure où cela avait empêché l'assistance aux offices religieux. C'était clairement mettre en avant la violation de la liberté de religion par le régime castriste qui avait interdit l'accès aux églises et avait éliminé l'instruction religieuse du système éducatif[32].

2 Les *titulaires* du droit à la liberté de conscience et de religion

Le premier paragraphe de l'article 12 aborde de façon emblématique la question du *titulaire* du droit en mentionnant que « Toute personne *a droit* à la liberté de conscience et de religion. » Or, couplée avec l'article 1§2 qui précise que par « personne » il faut entendre les « êtres humains », on découvre ici une des importantes singularités du système interaméricain qui dénie aux entités juridiques de tout type la capacité de se prévaloir des droits garantis par la Convention pour présenter des pétitions[33]. Si cette approche a été récemment confirmée par l'avis n° 22 du *22 février 2016*[34], la Cour interaméricaine prit le soin également de confirmer les atténuations jurisprudentielles qu'elle avait été amenée, dans le cadre de sa fonction contentieuse, à forger au fil du temps. Ainsi, les communautés indiennes autochtones, les syndicats, les fédérations et les confédérations de syndicats, ainsi que les personnes physiques qui – comme membres d'entités juridiques – sont en mesure de prouver qu'elles ont été affectées par une mesure litigieuse, sont habilitées à se présenter comme « victimes » devant les organes de protection et à présenter des « pétitions »[35].

---

32 Com. IADH, *La situation des droits de l'homme à Cuba*, 1983, Chapitre IV, § 32 ; OEA/ser/L./V/II.

33 Et ce à l'inverse du système européen et du système universel notamment.

34 Cour IADH, Avis, 26 février 2016, *Reconnaissance des droits aux personnes morales dans le système interaméricain* (interprétation et portée des articles 1§1, 8, 11§2, 13, 16, 31, 24, 25, 29, 30, 44, 46 et 62§3 de la Convention américaine des droits de l'homme ainsi que les articles 8§1a et b. du Protocole de San Salvador), OC 22/16. L'avis fut demandé par le Panamá.

35 Ainsi, les communautés indiennes autochtones ; les syndicats, les fédérations et les confédérations de syndicats, ainsi que les personnes physiques lesquelles, comme membres de personnes morales sont en mesure de prouver qu'elles ont été affectées par une mesure

S'agissant de la liberté de religion, ce sont les premiers et derniers cas de figure qui sont intéressants ici à analyser.

S'agissant du premier point, la jurisprudence sur les communautés indigènes connut *grosso modo* deux importantes étapes. La première permit à la Cour, à partir de l'historique affaire *Awas Tigni* de 2001[36], de connaître les problématiques spécifiques des communautés indiennes, tout en déclarant les violations exclusivement à l'endroit des membres de la Communauté pris individuellement. La deuxième étape démarra onze ans plus tard, avec l'importante affaire du *Peuple indigène Kichwa de Sarayaku,* dans laquelle la Cour interaméricaine, pour la première fois, reconnut comme titulaires des droits protégés par la Convention non seulement les membres de la Communauté, mais la communauté en tant que telle. Avant même ce tournant posant l'exercice « communautaire » de certains droits (dont on peut facilement considérer que la Cour l'appliquera, si elle en a l'opportunité, à l'exercice des « croyances » des communautés indiennes), la jurisprudence de la Cour sur les communautés indigènes avait démontré avec originalité à quel point leurs croyances spirituelles, impliquant notamment un rapport à la terre et d'une manière générale aux éléments naturels, avaient été prises au sérieux[37]. Ceci dit, à aucun moment, l'article 12 de la Convention ne fut au cœur des affaires, mais plutôt l'article 21 sur le droit de propriété.

S'agissant du dernier cas de figure – relatif aux personnes physiques lesquelles, comme membres de personnes morales, seraient en mesure de prouver qu'elles ont été affectées par une mesure litigieuse –, l'activité de la Commission démontre qu'elle a été amenée à prendre en compte la situation personnelle de membres de congrégations religieuses. L'analyse de la portée du droit va permettre d'en faire état.

3 La *portée* du droit à la liberté de conscience et de religion

Avant d'aborder la manière dont les organes de protection ont appréhendé la portée des restrictions au droit à la liberté de conscience et de religion (B), il convient de présenter les obligations imposées aux Etats (A).

litigieuse, sont habilitées à se présenter comme « victimes » devant les organes de protection et à présenter des « pétitions ».

36 Cour IADH, 31 août 2001, Fond, réparations, *Communauté Mayagna (Sumo) Awas Tigni c. Nicaragua,* Série C n° 79.

37 Cour IADH, 4 décembre 1991, *Aloeboetoe c. Suriname,* Série C n° 11.

3.1 *Les obligations des Etats*

Ne pas entraver la liberté de religion est une *obligation négative* élémentaire qui s'impose aux Etats. Or, quand les agents d'un Etat enlèvent, séquestrent, torturent et violent une religieuse, ils contreviennent de façon flagrante à cette obligation. Il s'agit du cas de figure de la célèbre affaire *Dianne Ortiz*, cette religieuse nord-américaine qui, sous prétexte de sa participation à des activités subversives selon les autorités étatiques, avait été l'objet de multiples atteintes à son intégrité physique. Libérée et terrorisée, elle rentra aux Etats-Unis et ne revint plus au Guatemala. La Commission interaméricaine analysa de façon conjointe la violation des articles 12 (religion) et 16 (association) en estimant que son statut de religieuse était « probablement » (la terminologie de la Commission ici n'est pas rigoureuse) à l'origine des attaques perpétrées à son encontre. La terreur qui l'a saisie l'empêcha ultérieurement de continuer ses activités de missionnaire, ce qui entraîna également pour l'organe quasi judiciaire la violation de la liberté d'association. La Commission usa ici de l'esprit de la théorie du *chilling effect*, même si l'expression ne se retrouve pas dans son rapport au fond publié le 16 octobre 1996[38].

Aux côtés des obligations de ne pas faire, les *obligations positives* sont tout aussi majeures. Dans son *Rapport annuel* publié en 2008, la Commission présentant la situation des droits de l'homme au Venezuela, saisit l'occasion pour rappeler à ce pays ses obligations afin de lutter de façon effective contre l'antisémitisme. Plus délicate – et pour tout dire plus intéressante – est la question de savoir si un Etat doit organiser, dans son ordre juridique, un système qui permette d'assurer l'objection de conscience des individus qui ne souhaitent pas effectuer leur service militaire. La question a été traitée à deux reprises. Une première fois contre la Bolivie dans l'affaire *Alfredo Diaz Bustos*. Si, en soi, la pétition était très intéressante – un Témoin de Jéhovah bolivien s'étant plaint devant la Commission interaméricaine de ne pas avoir été exempté de service

---

38 Com. IADH, Fond, 16 octobre 1996, *Dianne Ortiz c. Guatemala*, aff. 10.526, rapport n° 31/96, § 119 : « *Los agentes del Gobierno contravinieron los artículos 12 y 16. Es* probable *que los ataques contra la Hermana Ortiz* hayan tenido como objetivo castigarla y truncar sus actividades religiosas como misionera de la Iglesia *y su labor con los grupos indígenas de Huehuetenango, así como su asociación con miembros del GAM. Además, debido a la vigilancia, amenazas, secuestro, tortura y violación de que fue objeto, regresó a los Estados Unidos para escapar de sus secuestradores y la violencia contra ella y no ha podido regresar a Guatemala por temor. Como resultado, se la ha privado del derecho de ejercer su derecho a la libertad de conciencia y de religión desempeñándose como misionera extranjera de la Iglesia Católica en Guatemala. También se la ha privado del derecho de asociarse con los habitantes de Huehuetenango, la Iglesia de Guatemala y el GAM.* » (Italiques ajoutées)

militaire pour des considérations religieuses –, elle ne permit pas de tirer des conclusions pertinentes en la matière. Elle fit en effet l'objet d'un règlement amiable entre le pétitionnaire et la Commission le *4 juin 2005*, la Bolivie s'engageant en l'espèce à exempter le pétitionnaire de toute obligation militaire.

La deuxième affaire d'objection de conscience est elle plus pertinente pour l'analyse ; elle fut présentée dans l'affaire *Cristián Daniel Sahli Vera et autres c. Chili* et donna lieu à un rapport sur le fond de la Commission en date du *10 mars 2005*[39]. Les pétitionnaires étaient un groupe d'ONG – de Centre pour la Justice et le droit international (CEJIL) en passant par la Corporation des droits du Peuple (CDEPU), pour arriver au Groupe chilien d'objection de conscience « Ni casque, Ni uniforme » – qui avançaient que le Chili avait enfreint les articles 1§1 (Obligation de respecter les droits), 11 (vie privée) et 12 de la Convention pour ne pas avoir adapté sa législation interne aux garanties de la Convention. Le Chili aurait en effet porté préjudice à trois Chiliens qui, une fois fêté leurs 18 ans, durent accomplir leur service militaire obligatoire alors qu'ils avaient invoqué leur objection de conscience en la matière. Le rapport est ici particulièrement fouillé : l'analyse juridique à laquelle se livre la Commission contraste en effet de façon frappante avec l'analyse très pauvre qu'elle avait délivrée sous l'angle de l'article 12 dans l'affaire *Dianne Ortiz*.

Alors que les pétitionnaires se plaçaient sur le terrain des obligations positives, l'Etat et *in fine* la Commission se placèrent, quant à eux, sur le terrain des limitations au droit à la liberté de conscience et de religion. Se livrant à une approche comparée de l'analyse du droit – analysant la jurisprudence du Comité des droits de l'homme avant 2005 et celle de la Commission et de la Cour européennes telle qu'elle découlait de l'arrêt *Thlimmenos*[40], elle considéra – combinant l'analyse de l'article 12 avec l'article 6§3 b) de la

39 Com. IADH, Fond, 10 mars 2005, *Cristina Daniel Sahli Vera et autres c. Chili*, aff. 12.219, rapport n° 43/05.

40 Le passage pertinent se lit ainsi : « § 96. *En los países que no prevén la condición de objetor de conciencia en su legislación, los órganos internacionales de derechos humanos han concluido que no ha habido violación del derecho a la libertad de pensamiento, conciencia o religión.* El sistema europeo *se ha negado a reconocer un derecho a la condición de objetor de conciencia dentro del contexto más amplio del derecho a la libertad de pensamiento, conciencia y religión* (*artículo 9*) *debido a la referencia explícita a los « objetores de conciencia » en el artículo que exceptúa al servicio militar o al servicio sustitutivo de la definición de trabajo forzado o compulsivo* (*artículo 4*(*3*) *de la Convención Europea*). (*note 100 : Se negó específicamente a proceder en tal sentido en el reciente caso*) (*2000*) Thlimmenos (*supra*). *Análogamente*, el Comité de Derechos Humanos *de las Naciones Unidas se ha negado a reconocer un derecho a la condición de objetor de conciencia en los países que no reconocen dicha condición, dentro del derecho a la libertad de conciencia* (*artículo 18*), *debido a la*

Convention – que l'Etat chilien avait le droit de ne pas prévoir dans sa législation une exemption spécifique à l'endroit des objecteurs de conscience et qu'il fallait analyser l'affaire sous le prisme des restrictions ; celles-ci furent en l'espèce analysées comme légitimes (§ 97) : la défense de la sécurité nationale ayant été jugée pertinente[41]...

Pour arriver à cette conclusion, la Commission fournit une interprétation restrictive de l'article 6§3 *b*). Ce dernier – intégré dans la disposition prohibant l'esclavage et la servitude – stipule que : « Ne constitue pas un travail forcé ou obligatoire aux effets du présent article : tout service de caractère militaire et, *dans les pays où l'exemption d'un tel service est accordée aux objecteurs de conscience,* tout service national qui en tient lieu aux termes de la loi ». La Commission considéra qu'il s'agissait d'une disposition qui « de façon non équivoque admettait que l'Etat ne reconnaisse pas les objecteurs de conscience » (§ 98). En affirmant cela, elle s'arrimait aux jurisprudences du Comité des droits de l'homme et de la Cour européenne qui, à l'époque, soutenaient une telle approche.

La question que l'on peut se poser à cet stade est de savoir si une telle argumentation serait maintenue si on a égard à l'évolution respective de la jurisprudence du Comité et de la Cour européenne. Elles ont en effet respectivement

---

referencia explícita a los « objetores de conciencia » en el artículo 8, que prohíbe el trabajo forzado o compulsivo, en los « países en que los objetores de conciencia son reconocidos », dejando, también en este caso, la puerta abierta para que el Estado opte o no por reconocer la condición de objetor de conciencia. El Comité de Derechos Humanos de la ONU ha reconocido el derecho a la condición de objetor de conciencia como derivado del derecho a la libertad de conciencia en los países que han reconocido el derecho en su legislación, pero ha dejado en manos de las autoridades nacionales la determinación de si debe otorgarse o no a una persona la condición de objetor de conciencia, pese a la redacción del Comentario General 22, que establece que « no habrá diferenciación entre los objetores de conciencia sobre la base del carácter de sus creencias particulares ». (Altérations ajoutées)

41 Le § 97 se lit ainsi dans sa version originale : « *La Comisión no ve razón alguna para apartarse de esta jurisprudencia coherente y constante de los órganos internacionales de derechos humanos, que deriva de una interpretación con sentido común del significado claro y normal del texto de los respectivos instrumentos. La Comisión lee el artículo 12 (el derecho a la libertad de conciencia) conjuntamente con el artículo 6(3)(b) de la Convención Americana interpretando que reconocen expresamente el derecho a la condición de objetor de conciencia en los países en que dicha condición está reconocida en su legislación interna. En Chile, la condición de objetor de conciencia no está reconocida en las leyes nacionales, por lo cual el Estado argumenta convincentemente que no está obligado a otorgarla, dado que el artículo 12 de la Convención autoriza expresamente al Estado a limitar el ámbito del derecho por razones de seguridad nacional, habiendo así, por tanto, procedido.* »

intégré l'objection de conscience au sein de l'article 18 du Pacte pour le premier[42] et au sein de l'article 9 de la Convention pour la seconde[43]. Il n'y a, *a priori*, aucune raison d'en douter quand on connaît l'ouverture aux sources extérieures dans la jurisprudence interaméricaine.

3.2 *Les restrictions*

Le paragraphe 3 de l'article 12 donne un aperçu spécifique des restrictions permises en matière de religion. Il se lit ainsi : « La liberté de manifester sa religion ou ses croyances ne peut faire l'objet d'autres restrictions que celles qui, prévues par la loi, sont nécessaires à la sécurité publique, à la protection de l'ordre, de la santé ou de la morale publics, ou à la sauvegarde des droits ou libertés d'autrui. » Une telle formule est classique, elle se retrouve dans nombre de documents internationaux, soit sous forme de clause générale de limitation[44], soit, comme en l'espèce, sous forme de clause *ad hoc* rattachée à un droit précis, suivant en cela l'approche de la Convention européenne.

Les quelques éléments que l'on peut titrer des pétitions individuelles examinées par la Commission interaméricaine, ainsi que de ses constatations sur la situation des droits de l'homme au sein de certains pays, laissent à voir une grande fermeté dans la condamnation des restrictions qui, en réalité, la plupart du temps ont vidé de sa substance l'exercice d'une religion, qui plus est quand ces restrictions sont appliquées de façon discriminatoire. Ceci dit, le lecteur avide d'analyses circonstanciées et fines sur la notion de restriction, de substance ou d'essence d'un droit, sera amplement déçu. Les approches juridiques sont minimalistes quand il s'agit des rapports de la Commission.

Dans l'affaire des *Témoins de Jéhovah c. Argentine* (aff. 2137) – résolue le *18 novembre 1978* lors de la 45ème période de session ordinaire –, la Commission déclara la violation de plusieurs dispositions de la Déclaration américaine : le droit à l'intégrité et à la sécurité, le droit à l'éducation, le droit d'association, le droit de protection contre toute détention arbitraire et *last but not least* le droit de liberté de religion de l'article III. Le gouvernement de Rafael Videla avait en effet adopté un décret en date du 31 août 1976 qui ordonnait la fermeture de tous les lieux de cultes des Témoins de Jéhovah à travers le pays. La motivation du décret soutenait qu'il s'agissait d'une secte dont les principes étaient contraires aux intérêts de la nation, aux institutions de l'Etat et aux préceptes fondamentaux des lois

42 Com. DH, 3 novembre 2006, *Yeo-Bum Yoon et Myung-Jin Cho c. Corée*.

43 Cour EDH, 7 juillet 2011, *Bayatyan c. Arménie*.

44 C'est le cas de la Déclaration universelle des droits de l'homme, de la Charte africaine des droits et devoirs de l'homme et des peuples ou encore de la Charte des droits fondamentaux de l'Union européenne.

nationales[45]. Dans la foulée de la mise en œuvre du décret, en plus de la fermeture de tous leurs centres de foi, des Témoins de Jéhovah furent arrêtés, les enfants pratiquants se virent refuser l'accès aux écoles publiques et leurs parents perdirent leur emploi … Moyennant une résolution adoptée un an plus tard, le 15 mars 1979, la Commission exhortait le gouvernement argentin d'abroger le décret de 1976 et de cesser les persécutions à l'encontre des Témoins de Jéhovah …

La même politique de restriction absolue (autrement dit affectant l'essence même du droit) et discriminatoire (ciblée sur une seule communauté religieuse) fut également à l'œuvre dans une dictature voisine et « amie » de la dictature argentine, celle du gouvernement paraguayen, en 1978 ; elle se manifesta également au *Guatemala,* la Commission relevant dans son rapport spécial sur ce pays, adopté en 1981, les mêmes manifestations de persécutions discriminatoires à l'endroit de cette communauté religieuse[46] et ce, avant le coup d'Etat du 23 mars 1982 d'Efraín Ríos Montt.

Toujours à cette époque, au début des années 80, on découvre également, en prenant connaissance de la publication du rapport annuel de la Commission interaméricaine, faisant le point sur le respect des droits de l'homme au *Paraguay* – alors qu'une visite *in loco* avait constamment été refusée aux membres de la Commission menée par son président Tom J. Farer –, on découvre donc une formule quelque peu alambiquée (au point 10) selon laquelle : « La liberté religieuse souffre de restrictions dans la mesure où comme il a été indiqué dans des rapports antérieurs, la personnalité juridique a été retirée au Témoin de Jehovah et ne lui a pas été restituée, ce qui l'empêche d'exercer une quelconque activité. Cependant, la Commission considère en général qu'au Paraguay, la tolérance religieuse existe »[47]… On avouera être décontenancé par ce qui apparaît presque comme une contradiction *in adjecto.* A la décharge de la Commission, en lisant l'intégralité du rapport, on

---

45 Com. IADH, *affaire Témoins de Jéhovah c. Argentine,* Antecedentes, § 1: « *La secta en cuestión sostiene principios contrarios al carácter nacional, a las instituciones básicas del Estado y a los preceptos fundamentales de esta legislación. La libertad de cultos consagrada en los Artículos 14 y 20 de la Constitución Nacional, por supuesto, se ve a sí misma limitada en el sentido de que las ideas religiosas no deben implicar la violación de las leyes o el atentado contra el orden público, la seguridad nacional, la moral o las buenas costumbres.* »

46 Com. IADH, *La situation des droits de l'homme au Guatemala,* Ch. VI ; OEA/Ser.L/V/II.53 doc. 21, rev. 2), session du 13 octobre de 1981.

47 Com. IADH, *Rapport annuel 1979–1980,* Ch. V. Paraguay, « *La libertad religiosa y de cultos adolece de restricciones por cuanto, como se ha expresado en informes anteriores, a la congregación religiosa Testigos de Jehová se le retiró la personalidad jurídica y no le ha sido restablecida, no permitiéndosele realizar ningún tipo de actividad. No obstante, la Comisión considera que, en general, en Paraguay existe tolerancia religiosa.* »

mesure que ce qui était tout simplement vital à l'époque, c'était plutôt l'état de siège et les atteintes graves au droit à la vie par la dictature au Paraguay.

4 Conclusion

Si la sécularité des sociétés occidentales ne cesse d'être bousculée par l'irruption du fait religieux ; si ce dernier a depuis longtemps dépassé le seul for intérieur[48] – démontrant la force des revendications identitaires qu'il véhicule notamment en Europe[49] –, ce mouvement identitaire qui a consécutivement drainé une forte judiciarisation de l'irruption du fait religieux au sein des sociétés[50] n'a pas de manifestation équivalente au sein des Amériques. Le contexte sociologique n'est pas le même et explique cet état de fait. Jusqu'à quand ?

48 Avoir des convictions ne suffit plus, il faut pouvoir les manifester à tout moment et en tout lieu, y compris en dehors des espaces réservés à cet effet (les églises, les mosquées, les synagogues, les temples etc ...).

49 Au-delà de l'espace public (Cour EDH, Gde Ch., 1er juillet 2014, *S.A.S c. France*; Cour EDH, 11 juillet 2017, *Dakir c. Belgique* ; Cour EDH, 11 juillet 2017, *Belcacemi et Oussar c. Belgique*), ce sont les entreprises (Cour EDH, 15 janvier 2013, *Eweida c. Royaume-Uni* ; CJUE, 14 mars 2017, *G4S Secure Solutions et Bougnaoui*, aff. C157/15 et C188/15), les universités (Cour EDH, Gde Ch., 10 novembre 2005, *Leyla Sahin c. Turquie*) ou encore les écoles (Cour EDH, 4 décembre 2008, *Dogru c. France*; Cour EDH, 15 février 2001, *Dhalab c. Suisse*; Cour EDH, 10 janvier 2017, *Osmanoğlu et Kocabaş c. Suisse*) qui sont les théâtres (publics, professionnels, éducatifs) de la volonté, tantôt d'afficher son appartenance religieuse, tantôt de mettre en œuvre des pratiques considérées comme y étant consubstantiellement reliées.

50 Dans ce contexte délicat, la politique jurisprudentielle de la Cour européenne est assurément marquée par une valorisation des « choix de société » des Etats face aux volontés individuelles, qu'il s'agisse de la volonté d'afficher une pratique radicale de sa religion dans l'espace public (*affaires SAS, Dakir et Belcacemi et Oussar précitées*), ou de celle d'interdire à des enfants de suivre des cours mixtes de natation (*affaire Osmanoglu et Kocabas*).

PART 4

Protection of Religion in International Law

CHAPTER 8

La liberté de religion : marge d'appréciation et mesures positives des Etats

Christoph Grabenwarter

1 Introduction

Le titre de cette contribution fait allusion à deux notions de la théorie des droits de l'homme au niveau européen et ce, dans le domaine de la liberté de religion. A ce propos, je parlerai ici uniquement de la Convention européenne des droits de l'homme (Convention EDH) et de la jurisprudence récente de la Cour européenne des droits de l'homme (Cour EDH).

Les mesures positives correspondent souvent à des obligations positives qui constituent une part de plus en plus importante de presque toutes les garanties de la Convention EDH, article 9 inclus. Elles sont aujourd'hui bien établies dans la jurisprudence de la Cour de Strasbourg, mais certaines peuvent aller au-delà des obligations dérivées de la Convention.

La marge d'appréciation des Etat membres est également bien établie dans la jurisprudence. Elle n'est toutefois ni une théorie, ni une doctrine, mais plutôt un instrument pour régler l'intensité du contrôle des mesures des Etats membres.

Dans la première partie de ce texte, j'aimerais tout d'abord reprendre les grandes lignes de la jurisprudence sur la marge d'appréciation. Je démontrerai ensuite, d'une part, quelle catégorie de cas relatifs à la liberté de religion est susceptible d'un contrôle plus strict et, d'autre part, dans quels cas la Cour de Strasbourg exerce un contrôle plus restreint. Dans la deuxième partie, je discuterai l'importance de l'histoire et de la situation constitutionnelle d'un Etat membre. Il faut en particulier prendre en compte les relations entre les individus confrontés à la religion et aux Eglises en cas de mesures positives.

2 La marge d'appréciation des Etats en général

Même si la marge d'appréciation ne suit pas de théorie, l'analyse de la jurisprudence fait apparaître des critères selon lesquels on peut constater une base commune en ce qui concerne l'intensité du contrôle.

 | DOI:10.1163/9789004349155_009

En général, les critères souvent présents dans la littérature sont essentiellement les suivants[1] :

- le pluralisme des solutions nationales, c'est-à-dire l'existence ou la non-existence d'un standard européen ;
- la qualité des autorités nationales qui sont intervenues pendant la procédure nationale ;
- la qualité de la procédure et surtout des raisons données en faveur d'une certaine décision ;
- la portée de la garantie concernée ;
- le fait qu'il s'agisse d'une situation concernant seulement la relation entre un individu et l'Etat ou bien une situation de droits opposés entre deux ou plusieurs individus pour laquelle il faut trouver un équilibre entre les intérêts opposés.

Le but n'est pas ici de discuter tous les critères. C'est pourquoi je me concentrerai plutôt sur les deux derniers, premièrement, la portée de la garantie – c'est-à-dire la question de savoir s'il y a des spécificités en ce qui concerne la liberté de religion – et deuxièmement, la question des mesures positives, incluant les relations entre les personnes privées, les questions de *Drittwirkung* et celles des obligations positives.

3 La liberté de religion – une garantie à contrôle limité ?

En premier lieu, on pourrait se demander si, en soi, la liberté d'expression exige un contrôle réduit de la Cour de Strasbourg ou bien, au contraire, si elle demande un contrôle plus strict. Une analyse de la jurisprudence récente montre que ce n'est ni l'une, ni l'autre.

Il existe manifestement des arrêts de la Cour qui militent en faveur d'un contrôle restreint. Il s'agit alors souvent de requêtes introduites par des individus s'appuyant soit sur l'article 9 de la Convention EDH en tant qu'il protège la liberté dite « négative », soit sur l'article 8 de la Convention EDH. Ce sont des affaires portant surtout sur la relation entre l'Etat et l'Eglise ou entre l'Etat

1 C. Grabenwarter, « Kontrolldichte des Grund- und Menschenrechtsschutzes in mehrpoligen Rechtsverhältnissen », *EuGRZ*, 2006, pp. 490–491 ; E. Brems, « The Margin of Appreciation Doctrine in the Case-Law of the European Court of Human Rights », *ZaöRV*, 1996, p. 240 ; J. Kratochvíl, « The Inflation of the Margin of Appreciation by the European Court of Human Rights », *Netherlands Quarterly of Human Rights*, 2011, p. 324.

et d'autres religions ; elles concernent en premier lieu la liberté corporative des Eglises, et la question de leur autonomie dans les affaires internes, comme l'élection d'un évêque ou d'autres dirigeants religieux, comme l'a exprimé la Cour par exemple dans l'affaire *Hashan et Tchaouch*[2]. A ce propos, peu importe dans ce contexte que ce soit l'Eglise elle-même qui est la requérante ou bien un membre ou employé de l'Eglise ou d'une autre communauté religieuse. On peut y compter des affaires portant sur les relations de l'Eglise avec ses employés si on regarde l'ensemble des affaires décidées – *Obst*[3], *Siebenhaar*[4], *Fernandez Martinez*[5], et pas uniquement l'affaire *Schüth* pour laquelle la Cour a conclu à une violation[6].

Dans le même cadre, il faut mentionner les affaires concernant le financement des Eglises. Ce sont alors souvent des requêtes introduites par des particuliers, fondées sur les articles 8 et 9 de la Convention EDH (éventuellement combinés avec l'article 14 de la Convention EDH) affirmant que le montant voire le système en lui-même constitue une violation. De nouveau, il existe de bonnes raisons pour un contrôle restreint comme la Cour l'a déjà exercé dans l'affaire *Wasmuth* contre l'Allemagne qui concernait le système allemand de collecte des contributions directement avec l'impôt sur le revenu[7]. Dans le même sens, la Cour a conclu que le système de contribution spéciale pour les couples de confession différentes en Allemagne ne constitue pas une violation de l'article 9 de la Convention EDH[8].

De plus, il faut mentionner les affaires portant sur la présence de l'Eglise ou d'une religion et sur ses rites dans la vie quotidienne et publique. De nouveau, ce sont souvent des particuliers qui portent plainte au titre de la liberté de religion – positive ou négative. Je fais ici référence à l'arrêt *Buscarini* de 1999 concernant l'obligation des parlementaires de prêter serment en utilisant une formule comportant une référence à des textes religieux[9]. Un autre exemple a trait aux préceptes alimentaires fondés sur des règles religieuses[10].

Par ailleurs, nous constatons un contrôle plus strict en ce qui concerne l'établissement des religions et de leur statut juridique. Malgré une référence

---

2 Arrêt de la Cour EDH, *Hassan et Tchaouch c. la Bulgarie*, 26 octobre 2000, n° 30985/96.

3 Arrêt de la Cour EDH, *Obst c. l'Allemagne*, 23 septembre 2010, n° 425/03.

4 Arrêt de la Cour EDH, *Siebenhaar c. l'Allemagne*, 3 février 2011, n° 18136/02.

5 Arrêt de la Cour EDH (GC), *Fernandez Martinez c. l'Espagne*, 12 juin 2014, n° 56030/07.

6 Arrêt de la Cour EDH, *Schüth c. l'Allemagne*, 23 septembre 2010, n° 1620/03.

7 Arrêt de la Cour EDH, *Wasmuth c. l'Allemagne*, 17 février 2011, n° 12884/03.

8 Arrêt de la Cour EDH, *Klein et autres c. l'Allemagne*, 6 avril 2017, n° 10138/11 et autres.

9 Arrêt de la Cour EDH, *Buscarini et autres c. le Saint-Marin*, 18 février 1999, n° 24645/94.

10 Arrêt de la Cour EDH, *Cha'are Shalom Ve Tsedek c. la France*, 27 juin 2000, n° 27417/95.

constante à la marge d'appréciation, la Cour examine les conditions sous lesquelles un mouvement religieux peut éventuellement obtenir un certain statut afin de donner la possibilité à ses fidèles d'exercer ensemble leur liberté de religion. L'affaire de l'*Eglise Métropolitaine de Bessarabie* contre la Moldavie[11] et celle des *Témoins de Jéhovas* contre l'Autriche[12] en sont des exemples pertinents.

Toutes ces affaires portaient également, plus ou moins directement, sur les droits des Eglises ou d'autres religions. S'agissant des droits individuels, la Cour fait régulièrement référence à la marge d'appréciation, le contrôle étant pourtant plus strict, même si le résultat est finalement souvent une non-violation. Un cas de figure important est celui des règles d'habillement dans des institutions publiques soit les universités, soit les écoles, soit l'armée[13]. Le cas *S.A.S.* contre la France[14], qui ne concerne pas une institution particulière mais les lieux publics en général, est un cas spécifique sur lequel je reviendrai à la fin de l'analyse.

4 Mesures positives et obligations positives

Comme annoncé précédemment, la deuxième partie du texte est consacrée aux mesures positives prises par l'État dans le cadre de l'exercice de ses obligations positives découlant des garanties de la Convention EDH.

4.1 *Première thèse : il n'existe pas de différence décisive entre les situations de l'ingérence et des obligations positives.*

Je commence ici par discuter des situations des obligations positives classiques avec, comme point de départ, les affaires de droit du travail, plus précisément des requêtes introduites par des personnes qui ne sont pas employées par des Eglises mais par des entreprises privées et qui, pour cette raison, ne peuvent pas manifester ou pratiquer leur religion au travail. Tandis que la Cour et surtout l'ancienne Commission des droits de l'homme ont conclu à l'absence d'ingérence au motif que l'employé pouvait démissionner de ses fonctions,

11 Arrêt de la Cour EDH, *Eglise métropolitaine de Bessarabie et autres c. la Moldavie*, 13 décembre 2001, n° 45701/99.

12 Arrêt de la Cour EDH, *Religionsgemeinschaft der Zeugen Jehovas et autres c. l'Autriche*, 31 juillet 2008, n° 40825/98.

13 Arrêt de la Cour EDH, *Dahlab c. la Suisse*, 15 février 2001, n° 42393/98 ; arrêt de la Cour EDH, *Leyla Sahin c. la Turquie*, 10 novembre 2005, n° 44774/98 ; Arrêt de la Cour EDH, *Kurtulmuş c. la Turquie*, 24 janvier 2006, n° 65500/01 ; arrêt de la Cour EDH, *Dogru et Kervanci c. la France*, 4 décembre 2008, n° 27058/05, 31645/04.

14 Arrêt de la Cour EDH, *S.A.S c. la France*, 1er juillet 2014 (GC), n° 43835/11.

celle-ci exerce un contrôle plus strict en ce qui concerne des sanctions professionnelles imposées aux employés. Bien que la Cour fasse référence à la marge d'appréciation et aux obligations positives, le contrôle est bien strict. Je fais allusion par exemple à l'affaire *Eweida et autres* pour laquelle on peut constater que la Cour examine de manière détaillée les cas séparés de Mme Eiweida, agent d'enregistrement de British Airways, et de Mme Chaplin, infirmière dans un hôpital public, avant de conclure à une violation dans le premier cas et à une justification de l'ingérence pour des raisons de santé publique dans le cas de Mme Chaplin[15].

4.2 *Marge d'appréciation plus étendue dans le champ de protection de la paix religieuse*

L'Etat doit régler les relations entre les diverses Eglises et communautés religieuses et il doit aussi protéger les Eglises et leurs fidèles contre les attaques motivées par des raisons religieuses ou politiques. Cette obligation découle souvent des constitutions nationales, mais elle est également fondée sur la Convention elle-même, reflétée par les buts légitimes de sécurité publique et de protection de l'ordre dans l'article 9 paragraphe 2 de la Convention EDH. Il existe divers systèmes nationaux, souvent déterminés par l'histoire de chaque pays.

Dans l'affaire de l'*Eglise Métropolitaine de Bessarabie*[16], le gouvernement moldave s'est appuyé sur ces objectifs, mais il est allé trop loin. En revanche, dans l'affaire *Karaahmed*[17], les autorités bulgares ne sont pas allées assez loin dans la protection, face à des manifestants hostiles, des fidèles participant à la prière du vendredi dans une mosquée, et ce malgré des informations précises à disposition des autorités.

4.3 *Les mesures positives au-delà des obligations positives*

Revenons à la relation Etat-Eglise, cette fois-ci afin d'analyser l'importance des relations historiques dans l'argumentation de la Cour. En principe, l'Etat doit être neutre et impartial en définissant le cadre de l'exercice de la religion par les fidèles des diverses Eglises et communautés religieuses sans juger le contenu de leur croyances[18].

15 Arrêt de la Cour EDH, *Eweida et autres c. le Royaume-Uni*, 15 janvier 2013, n° 48420/10 et autres, § 110.

16 Arrêt de la Cour EDH, *Eglise métropolitaine de Bessarabie et autres c. la Moldavie*, 13 décembre 2001, n° 45701/99.

17 Arrêt de la Cour EDH, *Karaahmed* c. *la Bulgarie*, 24 février 2015, n° 30587/13.

18 Arrêt de la Cour EDH, *Religionsgemeinschaft der Zeugen Jehovas et autres c. l'Autriche*, 31 juillet 2008, n° 40825/98 ; arrêt de la Cour EDH, *Verein der Freunde der Christengemeinschaft et autres c. l'Autriche*, 26 février 2009, n° 76581/01.

Le thème que j'aimerais discuter dans cette partie est celui des mesures positives décidées par l'Etat pour faciliter l'exercice des fonctions des Eglises, parfois dans une sorte de coopération, allant jusqu'à un système d'une Eglise d'Etat comme par exemple dans les pays scandinaves. La Cour accepte un double système d'enregistrement prévoyant deux groupes d'Eglises ; parmi eux, un groupe d'Eglises jouit d'un statut d'Eglise à part entière, ce qui induit le droit à des privilèges[19]. Parmi ces privilèges, on trouve surtout des subventions, des avantages fiscaux ou des donations fiscalement avantageuses. Un tel système peut en soi relever de la marge d'appréciation des Etats. L'argument central est de nature historique : comme l'a affirmé la Cour dans l'affaire *Magyar Kereszteny Mennonita,* tout régime de la sorte se rattache normalement à la tradition historique et constitutionnelle des pays qui s'en sont dotés, et un système fondé sur une Eglise d'Etat doit être considéré comme compatible avec l'article 9 de la Convention EDH[20], en particulier s'il procède d'une situation antérieure à la ratification de la Convention EDH[21].

La Cour observe que la liberté de manifester sa religion ou ses croyances en vertu de l'article 9 de la Convention EDH ne confère pas aux associations requérantes ou à leurs membres un droit de s'assurer un financement additionnel sur le budget de l'État[22] ; cela dit, elle implique d'examiner avec la plus grande minutie les subventions octroyées de manière différente à diverses communautés religieuses – et donc, indirectement, à diverses religions[23].

La Cour a reconnu en particulier que les privilèges obtenus par des sociétés religieuses, notamment dans le domaine fiscal, facilitent la poursuite de buts religieux[24] et qu'il existe donc une obligation incombant aux autorités de l'Etat, en vertu de l'article 9 de la Convention EDH, de demeurer neutre dans l'exercice de leurs pouvoirs[25] lorsqu'il s'agit d'allouer ce type de ressources et d'octroyer de pareils privilèges. Dès lors que, pour remplir les obligations positives qui découlent des articles 9 et 11 de la Convention EDH, l'Etat décide volontairement d'accorder à des organisations religieuses un droit à des subventions et à d'autres avantages, les mesures qu'il prend pour octroyer de tels

19 Arrêt de la Cour EDH, *Magyar Kereszteny Mennonita Egyhaz et autres c. la Hongrie*, 8 avril 2014, n° 70945/11 et autres, § 98 (« subventions et ... donations fiscales »).

20 Arrêt de la Cour EDH, *Magyar Kereszteny Mennonita Egyhaz et autres c. la Hongrie*, 8 avril 2014, n° 70945/11 et autres.

21 Arrêt de la Cour EDH, *Darby c. la Suède*, 23 octobre 1990, n° 11581/85.

22 Arrêt de la Cour EDH, *Asatrúarfélagid c. l'Islande*, 18 septembre 2012, n° 22897/08, § 31.

23 Arrêt de la Cour EDH, *Gorzelik et autres c. la Pologne*, 17 février 2004, n° 44158/98.

24 Arrêt de la Cour EDH, *Association Les Témoins de Jéhovah c. la France*, 30 juin 2011, n° 8916/05, § 49 et §§ 52–53.

25 Arrêt de la Cour EDH, *Religionsgemeinschaft der Zeugen Jehovas et autres c. l'Autriche*, 31 juillet 2008, n° 40825/98, § 92.

avantages ne doivent pas revêtir de caractère discriminatoire[26]. Si l'Etat décide de réduire ou de retirer certains bénéfices accordés à des organisations religieuses, pareille mesure ne doit pas davantage être discriminatoire[27].

Le choix de la forme de coopération avec les diverses communautés religieuses, notamment du fait que celles-ci diffèrent largement les unes des autres en ce qui concerne leur organisation, leur nombre d'adhérents et les activités qui découlent de leurs enseignements respectifs doit être laissé à la considération des Etats eux-mêmes. Ceci est encore plus important lorsqu'il s'agit de tâches publiques et sociétales assumées par les communautés religieuses, mais qui n'ont pas de lien direct avec leur vie spirituelle. Les Etats jouissent, d'après la Cour, d'une certaine marge d'appréciation concernant l'organisation de leurs relations avec les communautés religieuses. A cet égard, la Cour prend note du contexte particulier des relations entre l'Etat et les Eglises dans chaque Etat[28]. Mais lorsqu'il choisit des partenaires à des fins d'externalisation de tâches d'intérêt public, l'Etat ne doit opérer aucune discrimination entre les communautés religieuses. Le principe de neutralité exige de fonder le choix des partenaires sur des critères fiables tels que leurs capacités matérielles ou d'autres critères semblables. Une discrimination pour des raisons de religion doit être évitée[29]. La liberté des Etats membres sur ces questions devrait s'étendre à la possibilité de modifier ce type de privilèges par le biais de mesures législatives. Néanmoins, la neutralité et l'impartialité doivent être assurées dans tous les cas[30].

Dans l'affaire *Magyar Kereszteny*, la Cour observe tout d'abord qu'en vertu du droit hongrois, les Eglises incorporées bénéficient d'un traitement préférentiel, en particulier dans le domaine de la fiscalité et des subventions. Les avantages obtenus par ces institutions sont substantiels et les aident à assumer des activités religieuses en raison de leur forme organisationnelle spécifique. L'Etat a outrepassé sa marge d'appréciation en ce qui concerne les formes de coopération avec les différentes confessions : la suppression de certains

---

26 Arrêt de la Cour EDH (GC), *E.B. c. la France*, 22 janvier 2008, n° 43546/02, §§ 48–49 ; arrêt de la Cour EDH, *Savez crkava « Riječ života » et autres c. la Croatie*, 9 décembre 2010, n° 7798/08, § 58.

27 Arrêt de la Cour EDH, *Magyar Kereszteny Mennonita Egyhaz et autres c. la Hongrie*, 8 avril 2014, n° 70945/11 et autres, § 107.

28 Arrêt de la Cour EDH, *Magyar Kereszteny Mennonita Egyhaz et autres c. la Hongrie*, 8 avril 2014, n° 70945/11 et autres, § 108.

29 Arrêt de la Cour EDH, *Magyar Kereszteny Mennonita Egyhaz et autres c. la Hongrie*, 8 avril 2014, n° 70945/11 et autres, § 109.

30 Arrêt de la Cour EDH, *Magyar Kereszteny Mennonita Egyhaz et autres c. la Hongrie*, 8 avril 2014, n° 70945/11 et autres, § 111.

avantages (résultant du refus de réenregistrer des Eglises et de la perte consécutive du statut d'Eglise incorporée) concernait seulement certaines congrégations, dont les communautés requérantes. Certes, il semble que celles-ci ne remplissaient pas les critères cumulatifs établis par le législateur, notamment le nombre minimum d'adhérents et la durée minimum d'existence. Ces critères auraient mis toutefois les communautés requérantes, dont certaines sont nouvelles et/ou de petite taille, dans une situation désavantageuse, au mépris des exigences de neutralité et d'impartialité. Quant à la condition relevant de la durée d'existence des groupes religieux, la Cour admet que la fixation d'une période minimale raisonnable peut être nécessaire dans le cas de groupes religieux nouvellement établis et inconnus. Mais cette condition est difficile à justifier dans le cas de groupes religieux instaurés lorsque les restrictions sur la vie confessionnelle ont été levées après la fin du régime communiste en Hongrie et que les autorités compétentes devraient à présent connaître, même s'ils ne remplissent pas tout à fait les critères requis quant à la durée d'existence. A cet égard, la Cour prend note du point de vue de la Commission de Venise selon laquelle les durées fixées étaient excessives[31].

Une appréciation tout à fait parallèle figure dans l'arrêt *Izzetin Dogan* contre la Turquie du 26 avril 2016. Là encore, la Cour accepte – en principe – pour l'islam, le système turc du Diyanet (Présidence des affaires religieuses), qui privilégie cette religion, et des règles différentes pour les autres communautés religieuses. Néanmoins, le refus de reconnaissance du caractère cultuel de la confession alévie a eu pour effet de nier l'existence autonome de la communauté alévie et a mis ses membres dans l'impossibilité d'utiliser, en toute conformité avec la législation en vigueur, leurs lieux de culte (*cemevi*) et certains titres relatifs à leurs ministres (*dede*). Par conséquent, en l'absence de motifs pertinents et suffisants, l'Etat défendeur a outrepassé sa marge d'appréciation[32].

En conclusion, en ce qui concerne les mesures positives comme part des relations Etat- Eglise, l'Etat dispose d'une marge d'appréciation plus étendue. En même temps, ce contrôle est suivi d'un contrôle de discrimination qui se réfère aux éléments suivants : l'organisation de l'Eglise, la coopération avec l'Etat et le financement. Dans ce contexte, la Cour soutient que ces questions sont étroitement liées à l'histoire et aux traditions du pays concerné.

---

31 Arrêt de la Cour EDH, *Magyar Kereszteny Mennonita Egyhaz et autres c. la Hongrie*, 8 avril 2014, n° 70945/11, § 111.

32 Arrêt de la Cour EDH (GC), *Izzettin Dogan et autres c. la Turquie*, 26 avril 2016, n° 62649/10, § 135.

4.4 *Au-delà des privilèges et de la paix religieuse : la tolérance dans une société influence la marge d'appréciation*

Avant de conclure, j'aimerais mentionner un argument que l'on trouve dans le paragraphe 74 de l'arrêt *Lautsi* de la Grande Chambre de la Cour EDH sur le crucifix dans les écoles italiennes[33]. Dans ce paragraphe, la Cour ajoute un dernier argument (« en outre ») que l'on peut très bien comprendre comme un argument en faveur d'une marge d'appréciation étendue. D'après la Cour, les effets de la visibilité accrue du christianisme dans l'espace scolaire méritent d'être encore relativisés au vu des éléments suivants :

- La présence des crucifix n'est pas associée à un enseignement obligatoire du christianisme [34] ;
- L'Etat ouvre parallèlement l'espace scolaire à d'autres religions. Le gouvernement indique ainsi notamment que le port par les élèves du voile islamique et d'autres symboles et tenues vestimentaires à connotation religieuse n'est pas prohibé, que des aménagements sont prévus pour faciliter la conciliation de la scolarisation et des pratiques religieuses non majoritaires, que le début et la fin du Ramadan sont « souvent fêtés » dans les écoles et qu'un enseignement religieux facultatif peut être mis en place dans les établissement pour « toutes confessions religieuses reconnues » [35] ;
- Rien n'indique que les autorités se montrent intolérantes à l'égard des élèves adeptes d'autres religions, non croyants ou tenants de convictions philosophiques qui ne se rattachent pas à une religion ;
- La présence du crucifix dans les salles de classe n'a pas contribué au développement de pratiques d'enseignement présentant une connotation prosélyte, pas plus que les élèves ne se sont trouvés confrontés à un enseignant qui, dans l'exercice de ses fonctions, se serait appuyé de manière tendancieuse sur cette présence[36].

Au vu de ces constatations, on peut déduire de ces arguments l'interprétation suivante : dans un système de pluralisme de religions qui donne un espace similaire à toutes les confessions souhaitant une telle présence, la marge d'appréciation est plus étendue lorsque l'Etat offre ou bien prévoit une telle présence à la religion de la majorité de la population.

---

33 Arrêt de la Cour EDH, *Lautsi et autres c. l'Italie*, 18 mars 2011, n° 30814/06, § 74.

34 Arrêt de la Cour EDH, *Hasan et Eylem Zengin c. la Turquie*, 9 octobre 2007, n° 1448/04, § 33.

35 Arrêt de la Cour EDH (GC), *Lautsi et autres c. l'Italie*, 18 mars 2011, n° 30814/06, §§ 39 et 74.

36 Arrêt de la Cour EDH (GC), *Lautsi et autres c. l'Italie*, 18 mars 2011, n° 30814/06, § 74.

5 S.A.S., la burqa et le « vivre ensemble »

Cette observation m'amène à la remarque finale qui porte sur l'affaire S.A.S.[37]. La conclusion proposée devrait conduire à un contrôle plus strict dans un système fondé sur le principe de laïcité comme en France. Mais la lecture des paragraphes 129, 153 et 154 de l'arrêt en particulier montre au contraire un contrôle restreint.

La Cour rappelle le rôle fondamentalement subsidiaire du mécanisme de la Convention EDH. Elle souligne que les autorités nationales jouissent d'une légitimité démocratique directe et se trouvent en principe mieux placées que le juge international pour se prononcer sur les besoins et contextes locaux. Il y a donc lieu d'accorder une importance particulière au rôle du décideur national. Selon la Cour, cela vaut surtout pour les cas dans lesquels les rapports entre l'Etat et les religions sont en jeu. Il faudrait donc accorder une marge d'appréciation aux Etats pour décider si et dans quelle mesure une restriction au droit de manifester sa religion ou ses convictions est « nécessaire ». La Cour devrait également prendre en considération le consensus et les valeurs communes qui se dégagent de la pratique des Etats parties à la Convention EDH[38].

La Cour admet qu'en interdisant à chacun de revêtir dans l'espace public une tenue destinée à dissimuler son visage, l'Etat restreint d'une certaine façon le champ du pluralisme, dans la mesure où l'interdiction fait obstacle à ce que certaines femmes expriment leur personnalité et leurs convictions en portant le voile intégral en public.

L'argumentation suivante dans les observations du gouvernement français me semble être un point décisif : pour le gouvernement, il s'agit de répondre à une pratique qu'il juge incompatible, dans la société française, avec les modalités de la communication sociale et, plus largement, du « vivre ensemble ». Selon le gouvernement, la France entend protéger une modalité d'interaction entre les individus, essentielle à ses yeux pour l'expression non seulement du pluralisme, mais aussi de la tolérance et de l'esprit d'ouverture, sans lesquels il n'y a pas de société démocratique[39]. Cette argumentation conduit la Cour à la conclusion que la question de l'acceptation ou non du port du voile intégral dans l'espace public constitue « un choix de société »[40].

37 Arrêt de la Cour EDH (GC), *S.A.S c. la France*, 1er juillet 2014, n° 43835/11.
38 Arrêt de la Cour EDH (GC), *S.A.S. c. la France*, 1er juillet 2014, n° 43835/11, § 129.
39 Arrêt de la Cour EDH (GC), *S.A.S. c. la France*, 1er juillet 2014, n° 43835/11, § 153.
40 Arrêt de la Cour EDH (GC), *S.A.S. c. la France*, 1er juillet 2014, n° 43835/11, § 153.

La Cour constate que dans un tel cas de figure, elle se doit de faire preuve de réserve dans l'exercice de son contrôle européen dès lors qu'il la conduit à évaluer un arbitrage effectué selon des modalités démocratiques au sein de la société dans l'Etat membre. Elle répète son argument que lorsque des questions de politique générale, sur lesquelles de profondes divergences peuvent raisonnablement exister dans un Etat démocratique, sont en jeu, il y aurait lieu d'accorder une importance particulière au rôle du décideur national[41].

En concordance avec l'opinion dissidente de juge Nußberger sur ce point, il ne me semble, dans tous les cas, pas adéquat d'invoquer le but légitime de la protection des droits d'autrui au sens de l'article 9 paragraphe 2 de la Convention EDH pour justifier le motif indiqué par la France, le dit « vivre ensemble »[42].

Il faut plutôt souligner que les arguments présentés ici ne se rapportent pas au champ de la liberté de religion. Même si on peut déduire de quelques parties de l'arrêt que l'argument du « vivre ensemble » est d'abord un argument en faveur des droits d'autrui et ensuite une question d'obligations positives – compensant vraisemblablement la liberté de religion positive avec la liberté de religion négative (le droit de ne pas être confronté à la burqa ou au niqab) – l'argumentation porte en réalité sur la protection de l'ordre public et de la sûreté publique[43]. On doit notamment se demander quelle relation peut être perçue entre les droits d'autrui et les exigences fondamentales, définies par le gouvernement français par la France, du « vivre ensemble » dans la société française. Les mesures prises par l'Etat français sont orientées vers la protection des intérêts publics. Ainsi, elles ne peuvent pas être justifiées par un recours aux intérêts privés[44].

Il est en outre, pour plusieurs raisons, douteux que la Cour exerce vraiment le contrôle minutieux qu'elle annonce dans l'arrêt lui-même[45]. L'interdiction du port du voile intégral est assortie de sanctions pénales. Cela a sans doute un impact tangible sur les intéressées. La Cour admet qu'il est en effet compréhensible qu'être poursuivies pour avoir dissimulé son visage dans l'espace public

41 Arrêt de la Cour EDH (GC), *S.A.S. c. la France*, 1er juillet 2014, n° 43835/11, § 154.

42 C. Grabenwarter, K. Struth, « Das französische Verbot der Vollverschleierung – Absolutes Verbot der Gesichtsverhüllung zur Wahrung der ,Minimalanforderungen des Lebens in einer Gesellschaft' », *EuGRZ*, 2015, pp. 2 et s.

43 C. Grabenwarter / K. Struth, « Das französische Verbot der Vollverschleierung », *op. cit.*, 2015, p. 2.

44 *Id.*, p. 4.

45 Arrêt de la Cour EDH (GC), *S.A.S. c. la France*, 1er juillet 2014, n° 43835/11, § 122.

représente un traumatisme pour les femmes qui ont fait le choix de porter le voile intégral pour des raisons tenant à leurs convictions. D'après la Cour, il faut cependant prendre en compte le fait que les sanctions retenues par le législateur français figurent parmi les plus légères qu'il puisse envisager et que la loi ménage en outre la possibilité pour le juge de prononcer en même temps ou à la place l'obligation d'accomplir un stage de citoyenneté[46]. A mon avis, la Cour ne donne ici pas assez de poids à l'aspect de *chilling effect* des mesures qu'elle a toujours pris en compte – notamment dans les affaires concernant la liberté d'expression, les droits personnels et les symboles – quelle que soit la gravité de la peine[47]. Bien sûr, cette appréciation pourrait changer si en réalité la loi n'était pas exécutée.

De plus, la Cour semble ignorer la gravité et l'intensité de son ingérence dans les droits personnels des femmes concernées[48]. La Cour souligne à cet égard qu'elle est consciente du fait que la prohibition critiquée pèse pour l'essentiel sur les femmes musulmanes qui souhaitent porter le voile intégral. Cependant, elle attache une grande importance au fait que cette interdiction n'est pas explicitement fondée sur la connotation religieuse des habits visés mais sur le seul fait qu'ils dissimulent le visage. Cela distinguerait l'affaire *S.A.S.* des autres cas relatifs aux prescriptions vestimentaires religieuses[49]. Les arguments de la Cour confirment qu'elle a bien conscience que l'interdiction concerne très largement les femmes musulmanes. Néanmoins, elle se réfère à la neutralité formelle de la loi française. Ce faisant, elle reprend trop simplement l'argument fallacieux du gouvernement selon lequel la loi est formulée de façon neutre[50].

---

46 Arrêt de la Cour EDH (GC), *S.A.S. c. la France*, 1er juillet 2014, n° 43835/11, § 152.

47 Arrêt de la Cour EDH, *Amihalachioaie c. la Moldavie*, 20 avril 2004, n° 60115/00, § 38 ; arrêt de la Cour EDH, *Paturel c. la France*, 22 décembre 2005, n° 54968/00, §§ 49 et. s. ; arrêt de la Cour EDH, *Brasilier c. la France*, 11 avril 2006, n° 71343/01, § 43 ; arrêt de la Cour EDH, *Reznik c. la Russie*, 4 avril 2013, n° 4977/05, § 50 ; arrêt de la Cour EDH, *Goodwin c. le Royaume-Uni*, 27 mars 1996, n° 17488/90, § 39 ; arrêt de la Cour EDH, *Barthold c. l'Allemagne*, 25 mars 1985, n° 8734/79, § 58 ; arrêt de la Cour EDH (GC), *Jersild c. le Danemark*, 23 septembre 1994, n° 15890/89, §§ 30 et. s. ; arrêt de la Cour EDH, *Wizerkaniuk c. la Pologne*, 5 juillet 2011, n° 18990/05, §§ 68 et s.

48 C. Grabenwarter, K. Struth, « Das französische Verbot der Vollverschleierung », *op. cit.*, p. 5.

49 Arrêt de la Cour EDH (GC), *S.A.S. c. la France*, 1er juillet 2014, n° 43835/11, § 151.

50 C. Grabenwarter, K. Struth, « Das französische Verbot der Vollverschleierung », *op. cit.*, p. 5; cf. Loi n° 2010–1192 du 11 octobre 2010 interdisant la dissimulation du visage dans l'espace public (1), JUSX1011390L (https://www.legifrance.gouv.fr/eli/loi/2010/10/11/JUSX1011390L/jo/texte) : « Article 1 : Nul ne peut, dans l'espace public, porter une tenue destinée à dissimuler son visage. Article 2 : I. – Pour l'application de l'article 1er, l'espace

Par ailleurs, il faut avouer qu'un Etat doit disposer d'une marge pour évaluer les développements dans sa société. C'est pourquoi l'appréciation de la nécessité d'une interdiction du port de la burqa pourrait varier selon l'époque. En cas de tensions sévères dans la société, une interdiction pourrait alors être perçue différemment[51].

De plus, l'annonce d'un contrôle strict au début de l'examen de la proportionnalité ne correspond pas aux réflexions qui se trouvent dans le point suivant de l'arrêt et qui sont résumées ci-dessus. Comme la requérante est une personne privée qui veut porter le voile intégral dans l'espace public, les rapports entre l'Etat et la religion ne sont pas directement concernés. Il ne s'agit pas des employés de l'Etat ou des institutions publiques. La jurisprudence sur la relation entre l'Etat et la religion n'est donc pas applicable et le recours de la Cour à cette jurisprudence n'est alors pas tout à fait adéquat. La différence entre le cas *S.A.S.* et d'autres affaires, qui concernent spécifiquement les rapports entre l'Etat et la religion, auraient dû peser en faveur d'une restriction de la marge d'appréciation. Les raisons qui justifient l'extension de celle-ci ne sont pas valables dans le cas de l'arrêt *S.A.S.* En effet, ce cas ne concerne pas en priorité la façon de l'Etat d'organiser ses relations avec les communautés religieuses. Ceci serait plutôt un argument pour l'extension de la marge d'appréciation de l'Etat. L'argument se référant au système fondé sur le principe de laïcité ne vaut pas ici, contrairement aux cas de figures mentionnés plus haut[52].

6 Conclusion

La liberté de religion est, comme la plupart des droits de la Convention européenne des droits de l'homme, soumise à un contrôle variable de la part de la

---

public est constitué des voies publiques ainsi que des lieux ouverts au public ou affectés à un service public. II. – L'interdiction prévue à l'article 1er ne s'applique pas si la tenue est prescrite ou autorisée par des dispositions législatives ou réglementaires, si elle est justifiée par des raisons de santé ou des motifs professionnels, ou si elle s'inscrit dans le cadre de pratiques sportives, de fêtes ou de manifestations artistiques ou traditionnelles. (…) Article 4 : Après la section 1 bis du chapitre V du titre II du livre II du code pénal, il est inséré une section 1 ter ainsi rédigée : « Section 1 ter » De la dissimulation forcée du visage « Art. 225-4-10.-Le fait pour toute personne d'imposer à une ou plusieurs autres personnes de dissimuler leur visage par menace, violence, contrainte, abus d'autorité ou abus de pouvoir, en raison de leur sexe, est puni d'un an d'emprisonnement et de 30 000 € d'amende. Lorsque le fait est commis au préjudice d'un mineur, les peines sont portées à deux ans d'emprisonnement et à 60 000 € d'amende »

51 *Id.*, p. 6.

52 *Id.*, « Das französische Verbot der Vollverschleierung », *op. cit.*, p. 7.

Cour européenne. Il n'y a pas, en effet, de règle générale définissant une marge d'appréciation étendue dans les affaires religieuses ou « quasi religieuses ». Ce n'est pas la liberté de religion en soi qui demande un certain contrôle, ce sont plutôt des situations particulières où le contrôle est plus restreint et d'autres, où l'examen est plus détaillé, laissant une marge de manœuvre plus restreinte aux Etats.

Ainsi, l'analyse des arrêts récents de la Cour montre que le contrôle est plus strict lorsqu'il s'agit de la protection des minorités religieuses vis-à-vis de la majorité ou bien des ingérences directes de la part des autorités nationales. En revanche, l'Etat jouit d'une marge d'appréciation plus étendue lorsqu'il s'agit des mesures positives. Les Etats peuvent accorder un certain soutien à des religions en particulier sans en discriminer d'autres. Les Etats ont ainsi la possibilité de prévoir des mesures différentes qui ne sont souvent pas motivées par des considérations relatives aux droits de l'homme mais par les relations particulières entre l'Etat et certaines religions, notamment certaines églises, qui ont souvent été fondées au cours de l'histoire de l'Etat concerné. Il existe ici de bons arguments pour un contrôle restreint, mais ceux-ci ne portent pas sur la liberté de religion.

CHAPTER 9

Religious Profiling, Statistical Discrimination and the Fight against Terrorism in Public International Law

Antje von Ungern-Sternberg

1 Introduction

The concept of 'religious profiling' became widely publicized during the 2016 presidential campaign in the United States. Then-candidate Donald Trump, responding to a deadly mass shooting in California by Islamic State sympathizers, called for 'a total and complete shutdown of Muslims entering the United States until our country's representatives can figure out what the hell is going on'.[1] Once in office, the newly appointed U.S. president lived up to his words and immediately issued an executive order banning individuals from seven predominantly Muslim countries from entering the United States.[2] Given constitutional challenges, that order, dubbed the 'Muslim ban,' was later revised and replaced by a new executive order that accounts for several legal objections,[3] but still bars immigration from six Muslims countries.[4] This is a very

1 Jenna Johnson 'Trump calls for 'total and complete shutdown of Muslims entering the United States'' (*Washington Post*, 7 December 2015) <www.washingtonpost.com/news/post-politics/wp/2015/12/07/donald-trump-calls-for-total-and-complete-shutdown-of-muslims-entering-the-united-states/?utm_term=.51cc2c7a4bbd> all webpages were accessed 10 April 2017.

2 Executive Order 13769 'Protecting the Nation from Foreign Terrorist Entry into the United States'. <www.whitehouse.gov/the-press-office/2017/01/27/executive-order-protecting-nation-foreign-terrorist-entry-united-states>.

3 Executive Order 13769 was successfully challenged in Court (overview at <www.clearinghouse.net/results.php?searchSpecialCollection=44>) based on considerations of due process and religious rights, see only State of Washington v Trump, US Court of Appeals 9th Circuit, Order of 9 February, 2017 No 17-35105 <www.ca9.uscourts.gov/>.

4 Executive Order 'Protecting The Nation From Foreign Terrorist Entry Into The United States'<www.whitehouse.gov/the-press-office/2017/03/06/executive-order-protecting-nation-foreign-terrorist-entry-united-states>. By the time this chapter was finished, the second order was also (temporarily) halted, see State of Hawai'i and Elshikh v Trump, US District Court of Hawai'i, Order of March 15, 2017 No. 17-00050 DKW-KSC <www.nytimes.com/interactive/2017/03/15/us/politics/document-Order.html>.

 | DOI:10.1163/9789004349155_010

visible and *blunt* form of religious profiling; it exemplifies a situation in which authorities act on the inference that a particular adherent of a certain religion – Islam – is more likely to engage in criminal or terrorist behaviour than an adherent of any another religion.

However, other forms of religious profiling have existed in the United States and other countries long before the Muslim ban. In 2011, reporters uncovered that the New York City Police Department ('NYPD') engaged in a surveillance and mapping programme that targeted only Muslims. The NYPD sent undercover officers to Muslim neighbourhoods and mosques to record conversations, report on daily activities and monitor sermons, with the goals of developing a database of where Muslims worked and lived and detecting 'reactionary' speech and actions.[5] Governmental terrorist watch lists provide another example of profiling. In the United States, individuals listed on the FBI's so-called 'No-Fly List' (cataloguing more the 100,000 names) are prevented from flying into, within, or out of the United States.[6] Travellers listed on the so-called 'Selectee List' must undergo additional security checks.[7] The criteria for being put on these lists are undisclosed. While individuals are placed on the No-Fly List because of a 'reasonable suspicion that the individuals are known or suspected terrorists based on the totality of the information reviewed',[8] one must assume that being Muslim is one

5 Nuzhat Chowdhury, 'I Spy (But Only On You): Raza v. City of New York, The Civil Rights Disaster of Religious & Ethnic-Based Surveillance, and the National Security Excuse' (2014–2015) 46 Columbia Human Rights Law Review 278, 279f; see also Faiza Patel and Michael Price, 'Settlement of NYPD Muslim Surveillance Lawsuits: A Platform for Better Oversight' (*Just Security,* 14 January 2016) <www.justsecurity.org/28811/>; Michael Price 'A Broken Playbook: The NYPD Targeted Muslims in Over 95-Percent of Investigations That Broke Surveillance Rules' (*Just Security,* 23 September 2016) <www.justsecurity.org/33132/>; David Kimball-Stanley, 'Settling for More: The NYPD's New Oversight Deal' (*LAWFARE,* 8 March 2017) <lawfareblog.com/settling-more-nypds-new-oversight-deal>.

6 In the beginning, the list was undisclosed and the fact of being listed unknown to the individuals affected. Now, the list is published and updated online, displaying the full name, physical traits and other details of the listed persons (!) <www.no-fly-list.com/>.

7 For an overview, see Justin Florence, 'Making the No Fly List Fly: A Due Process Model for Terrorist Watchlists' (2006) 115 The Yale Law Journal 2148, 2152ff; Eric Hedlund, 'Good Intentions, Bad Results, and Ineffective Redress: The Story of the No Fly And Selectee Lists and Suggestions for Change' (2014) 79 Journal of Air Law and Commerce 597, 601ff; Dan Lowe, 'The Flap with No Fly – Does the No Fly List Violate Privacy and Due Process Constitutional Protections?' (2015) 92 University of Detroit Mercy Law Review 157, 158ff; cf *Latif v Holder* [2014] 969 F. Supp. 2d 1293, 1296ff (D. Or.).

8 *Latif v Holder* (n 7) 1297; cf the US National Counterterrorism Center's March 2013 Wachtlisting Guidance, p 51 – a document disclosed by The Intercept <https://theintercept.com/document/2014/07/23/march-2013-watchlisting-guidance/>.

of the risk factors that constitute the profile of a suspected terrorist.[9] Religion may also be used as a criterion in a dragnet search for Muslim 'sleepers' as a final German example illustrates. Immediately after 9/11, the German police asked public registration offices, immigration authorities and universities to submit personal data of all male students born between 1960 and 1983 (including religious affiliation, if possible) in order to establish a database of male Muslim students originating from certain, predominantly Muslim countries.[10]

These three examples illustrate an important tension. On the one hand, singling out Muslims for surveillance, travel bans, special security checks, or dragnet searches raises the problem of equality (in addition, of course, to the infringements of specific freedoms in question, such as privacy[11] or the right to travel).[12] On the other hand, if a certain danger, such as terrorism, is sufficiently linked to a religion since its perpetrators are Islamists, for example, this might allow authorities to use religious affiliation as a shortcut to identify suspects. This chapter will examine whether the phenomenon of 'religious profiling' is legal under public international law. This chapter will first address conceptual (2.) and normative (3.) aspects before finally confronting the specific question of religious discrimination (4.).

2 The Conceptual Setting: Racial or Religious Profiling and Statistical Discrimination

Does religious profiling violate equality rights? This depends, of course, on the practice covered by the expression 'religious profiling'. And here, both terminological and conceptual issues arise.

9 cf Scott J Upright, 'Suspicionless Border Seizures of Electronic Files: The Overextension of the Border Search Exception to the Fourth Amendment' (2009) 51 William and Mary Law Review 291, 292ff; Reginald C Wisenbaker, 'Muslim Community Reparations' (2015) 2 Savannah Law Review 391, 408ff. That religious affiliation is taken into account, can also be interfered from the official Wachtlisting Guidance (n 8) at page 10, which points to the constitutional protection of the free exercise of religion by the First Amendment. However, this guarantee, according to the Watchlisting Guidance, only outlaws that an individual is included based on the First Amendment protected activity 'alone,' leaving room for a profile based on religion and other factors (not to mention the assumption that the First Amendment does not extend to non-US persons outside the United States).

10 cf German Federal Constitutional Court BVerfGE 115, 320 (322ff).

11 cf German Federal Constitutional Court BVerfGE 115, 320 (341ff).

12 cf *Latif v Holder* (n 7) 1301ff.

2.1 *Racial and Religious Profiling*

'Religious profiling' is a *pejorative* expression implying illegality.[13] It is a modification of the more widely known expression 'racial profiling' which is used to describe U.S. police practices that target African Americans, based on the presumption that there is a disproportionately high involvement of African Americans in drug-related crime. Police stops and searches of African Americans have become a strongly criticised example of state sponsored racial harassment and discrimination in the United States.[14] The expression 'racial profiling' also refers to similar methods applied in other areas of law (such as parole sentencing)[15] and other regions of the world (for example the stop-and-search practice of the French police[16] or behind-the-border controls by German immigration authorities).[17] Today, not only 'driving while black' but also 'flying while Muslim' may get individuals into trouble – and the expression 'religious profiling' equally refers to illegal forms of harassment and discrimination.[18]

The notion of 'racial profiling,' however, has disadvantages. It covers only a very specific form of discrimination and, more importantly, implies a binary distinction between illegal racial profiling and the lawful fight against crime based on a suspect's description. According to this latter concept, it is generally acknowledged that police account for a suspect's characteristics (for example, the

13 Deborah A Ramirez, Jennifer Hoopes, and Tara Lai Quinlan, 'Defining Racial Profiling in a Post-September 11 World' (2003) 40 American Criminal Law Review 1195; Kevin R Johnson, 'Racial Profiling After September 11: The Department of Justice's 2003 Guidelines' (2004) 50 Loyola Law Review 67, 69; Wisenbaker (n 9) 391.

14 Frederick Schauer, *Profiles, Probabilities, and Stereotypes* (Belknap Press 2003) 155ff; Bernard E Harcourt, *Against Prediction – Profiling, Policing and Punishing in an Actuarial Age* (University of Chicago Press 2006) ch 7; Gregory M. Lipper, 'Racial Profiling' (2001) 38 Harvard Journal on Legislation 551; Albert W Alschuler, 'Racial Profiling and the Constitution' (2002) The University of Chicago Legal Forum 163; Samuel R Gross and Debra Livingston, 'Racial Profiling Under Attack' (2002) 102 Columbia Law Review 1413; Stephen J Ellman, 'Racial Profiling and Terrorism' (2003) 22 New York Law School Journal of International and Comparative Law 305; Ramirez et al (n 13); R Richard Banks, 'Racial Profiling and Antiterrorism Efforts' (2003–2004) 89 Cornell Law Review 1201.

15 Harcourt (n 14) ch 1.

16 Open Society Institute, Profiling Minorities – A Study of Stop-and-Search Practic es in Paris (New York 2009) <www.opensocietyfoundations.org/reports/profiling -minorities-study-stop-and-search-practices-paris>.

17 Oberverwaltungsgericht Koblenz (Higher Administrative Court), decision of 21 April 2016, Az 7 A 11108/14; Alexander Tischbirek and Tim Wihl, 'Verfassungswidrigkeit des "Racial Profiling"' (2013) 68 Juristenzeitung 219.

18 Ramirez et al (n 13) 1196; Wisenbaker (n 9) 431.

perpetrator characteristics eyewitnesses at a bank robbery may describe to police could be 'young, female, and white'), so that the police may narrow their investigation to search for individuals matching a particular age, gender, and ethnic background only.[19] But it is not easy to draw a clear line between racial or religious profiling and reliance on suspect description. How narrow and how reliable must the description be? This is a particularly difficult question in the context of crime prevention (as opposed to retroactive prosecution).[20] For instance, does general evidence that Islamists are planning terrorist attacks on public events like football matches or Christmas markets justify specific investigations targeted at Muslims, even though the terrorist threat is not very specific? In this context, it seems helpful to resort to other criteria such as proportionality to draw the line between the illegal targeting of Muslims and legal law enforcement. Moreover, the use of statistical correlations between members of certain groups (defined by sex, age, or behavioural patterns) and certain risks is a generally accepted phenomenon found in many other areas of life, including insurance or finance companies' risk assessments. Considering racial or religious profiling in this bigger context is useful in distinguishing lawful from unlawful uses of statistical correlation, and specifying the particular harms of racial and religious profiling.

2.2 *Statistical Discrimination*

I will therefore use the broader and neutral notion of statistical discrimination coined by economists. Statistical discrimination characterises an economically sensible strategy to cope with information deficits. If information is unavailable (for example, information about the insurance risk of a particular insuree), it is reasonable to use a proxy, that is, to take into account that there are statistical correlations between members of a particular group (for example, women) and certain properties (for example, longer life expectancy).[21]

19 Court of Appeals 221 F.3d 329 (2nd Cir. 2000); Gross and Livingston (n 14) 1415; Ellman (n 14) 306 fn 4; Ramirez et al (n 13) 1206; cf also Banks, 'Racial Profiling and Antiterrorism Efforts' (n 14) 1203ff; Open Society Institute (n 14) 20.

20 Lucas McMillen, 'Eye on Islam: Judicial Scrutiny along the Religious Profiling/Suspect Description Reliance Spectrum' (2006–2007) 4 University of St. Thomas Law Journal 114; very critical due to the similarities of racial profiling and suspect description reliance R Richard Banks, 'Race-Based Suspect Selection and Colorblind Equal Protection Doctrine and Discourse' (2000–2001) 48 University of California Law Review 1075.

21 Gary S Becker, *The Economics of Discrimination* (first published 1957, University of Chicago Press 1971); Edmund S Phelps, 'The Statistical Theory of Racism and Sexism' (1972) 62 The American Economic Review 659; Gabriele Britz, *Einzelfallgerechtigkeit versus Generalisierung: Verfassungsrechtliche Grenzen statistischer Diskriminierung*, (Mohr Siebeck 2008) 15ff.

In short, and to illustrate with this example, it makes economic sense to have higher life insurance premiums for women than for men since women, on average, live longer than men. The resulting difference in treatment of men and women is called statistical discrimination. A similar reasoning applies to fighting crime. Assume, for example, that the data of tax fraud cases reveals that these criminal offences are predominantly committed by men, for example by male dentists or male restaurant owners. If the tax authorities design software that selects a certain percentage of tax returns for closer examination, it would make economic sense to concentrate on examining male dentists' and restaurant owners' tax returns, as they statistically are more likely to have discrepancies. The *normative* question is, of course, whether this statistical discrimination is lawful or whether it violates equality rights.

'Statistical discrimination' is distinct from two other forms of discrimination related to statistics. Statistics are also used to reveal 'indirect' discrimination, that is, to prove that a facially neutral treatment puts members of a particular group at a particular disadvantage. One well-known example of this phenomenon involves working conditions that discriminate against part-time workers. If the statistics of the workforce reveal that part-time workers are predominantly female, the conditions thus indirectly discriminate against women.[22] Statistics are also used to justify 'affirmative action' or 'positive' discrimination. If statistics show, for instance, that certain ethnic groups are considerably underrepresented in public sector employment or at universities, this might justify preferential access (i.e. positive discrimination) for members of these groups.[23] *Statistical discrimination*, however, implies direct, not indirect discrimination.[24] It is meant to overcome a lack of information, not to remedy existing inequalities as affirmative action intends.

---

22 cf Case 170/84 *Bilka* [1986] ECR 1607, paras 24–31; cf also US Supreme Court *Griggs v Duke Power Co.* 401 U.S. 424 (1971): high school diploma requirements rendering ineligible a 'markedly disproportionate number' of Afro-Americans for employment as indirect discrimination.

23 cf the debate about preferential high school admission for minorities in the United States: US Supreme Court *Regents of Univ of California v Bakke*, 438 U.S. 265 (1978); *Grutter v Bollinger* 539 U.S. 306 (2003); *Fisher v University of Texas (I)* 133 S. Ct. 2411 (2013); *Fisher v University of Texas (II)* 136 S. Ct. 2198 (2016); cf Case C-450/93 *Kalanke* [1995] ECR I-3051; Case C-409/95 *Marschall* [1997] ECR I-6363 on affirmative action in favour of female employees in the public sector.

24 Indirect forms of discrimination could also be based on statistical correlations, cf Britz (n 21) 51ff. However, the point of statistical discrimination is that it may justify direct forms of discriminations, which is much more difficult than justifying indirect forms of discrimination.

Furthermore, the statistics themselves also differ. Indirect or positive discrimination is linked to descriptive statistics that simply depict numbers and percentages; for example, the proportion of part-time employees taken from the female and from the male workforce respectively, or the proportion of successful high-school applicants taken from different ethnic backgrounds. Statistical discrimination, however, is based on inference statistics. This method uses samples with certain properties (such as a sample of deceased men and women who reached a certain age) in order to make propositions about a population at large based on probability calculations (for example, about the life expectancy of men and women in general).[25]

Therefore, inference statistics only produces probabilities, not certainty, and it is only as good as the assumptions and models it rests upon. Consequently, if lawyers want to justify statistical discrimination, then they must also consider questions of statistical methodology. Some examples can highlight this point. First, statistical discrimination has to be based on actual statistical findings, not on 'gut feelings' or 'common sense' notions unrelated to empirical data. It was shown, for example, that airport searches of suspected drug couriers by the U.S. Customs Service predominantly targeted African-American women, which can be explained either by outright racial hostility or by a mistaken, unfounded belief linking drug smuggling to a certain ethnicity or sex.[26] Second, stereotypes or biases can distort even probability calculations based on empirical facts and established methodology. Actuarial findings of a higher female life expectancy might, for example, rely on an out-dated hypothesis that women lead healthier lifestyles.[27] More generally, the operation of algorithm-based probability calculations might not only be based on pre-existing biases, but also be shaped by emergent biases in the on-going process.[28] A researcher in the United States found,

25 Michael O Finkelstein and Bruce Levin, *Statistics for Lawyers* (3rd edn, Springer 2015) 159ff; Abdul Quader Miah, *Applied Statistics for Social and Management Sciences* (Springer 2016) 101ff.

26 Schauer (n 14) 175–81.

27 See AG Kokott's attack on sex-based discrimination by insurance companies, arguing that factors such as economic conditions and lifestyle habits might contribute considerably to life expectancy and that female and male lifestyle habits have assimilated: '[B]oth women and men nowadays engage in demanding and sometimes extremely stressful professional activities, members of both sexes consume a not inconsiderable amount of stimulants and even the kind and extent of sporting activities practised by people cannot from the outset be linked to one or other of the sexes.' Case C-236/09 *Test-Achats* [2010] ECR 2011 I-773, Opinion of AG Kokott, para 63.

28 Batya Friedman and Helen Nissenbaum, 'Bias in Computer Systems' (1996) 14 ACM Transactions on Information Systems 330.

for example, that if she conducted a Google search of a traditionally African-American name, very often a private company's ad offering to reveal the person's arrest and criminal record after payment of a fee appeared. If she conducted a Google search of a white name, the ad did not appear, even if the company's database contained records of the white, but not of the African-American, name in question.[29] Since the advertisement algorithm is secret, it is unclear whether this result is caused by the company's assumption that Google users are particularly interested in the arrest and crime records of African-Americans or whether it is actually caused by the users of Google who are particularly interested in the arrest and crime records of African-Americans. In both scenarios, the either assumed or effective bias of Google users leads to discriminating results.[30] Implicit stereotypes or biases may also disfavour African-Americans in the algorithm-based prediction of recidivism, an instrument used in situations from sentencing to parole determinations in the United States. The factors relevant for assessing the risk are not ethnicity itself, but factors highly corresponding with it (eg education level, employment, criminal records of family and friends). The algorithm itself is undisclosed. A recent study revealed that the prediction produces different results for black and white defendants, clearly disfavouring black defendants.[31] Third, law enforcement activities based on statistical interference may also produce a distorting effect, since scrutinizing the targeted group of suspects more closely than the rest of the population yields results that are no longer representative.[32]

In sum, statistical discrimination is defined as unequal treatment based on criteria such as race, sex, age or religion, which relies on the statistical probability that members of a group defined by the proxy (e.g. race, sex, age or religion)

29 Latanya Sweeney, 'Discrimination in Online Ad Delivery', (2013) 56 Communications of the ACM 44.

30 Similarly, a study that showed that significantly fewer women than men were shown online ads promising them help getting jobs paying more than $200,000, Byron Spice, 'Questioning the Fairness of Targeting Ads Online' (*Carnegie Mellon University News*, 7 July 2015) <www.cmu.edu/news/stories/archives/2015/july/online-ads-research.html> which may also result from the preferences of the advertisers or the users.

31 Julia Angwin, Jeff Larson, Surya Mattu and Lauren Kirchner, 'Machine Bias. There's software used across the country to predict future criminals. And its biased against blacks'. (*ProPublica*, 23 May 2016) <www.propublica.org/article/machine-bias-risk-assessments-in-criminal-sentencing> The ProPublica analysis of data from Broward County, Fla., shows that 'blacks are almost twice as likely as whites to be labeled a higher risk but not actually reoffend' whereas whites 'are much more likely than blacks to be labeled lower risk but go on to commit other crimes'.

32 Harcourt (n 14) ch 5.

possess certain properties (eg higher risk of committing or having committed a crime, higher life expectancy).[33] What's more, it can be presumed that religion is one factor amongst many that constitute the profile of a suspected Islamist terrorist.[34] Thus, the question is whether this form of statistical discrimination based on religion is legal.

3 Legal Setting: Non-Discrimination Guarantees and the Fight Against Terrorism in International Law

Can direct discrimination ever be justified even if it is based on classification criteria such as race, sex or religion? In that regard, international law accounts for binding anti-discrimination standards, while strengthening the legitimate interest to fight international terrorism.

3.1 *Anti-Discrimination Guarantees*

Article 26 of the International Covenant on Civil and Political Rights (ICCPR),[35] Article 14 of the European Convention on Human Rights (ECHR),[36] and Article 3 of the 1951 Convention Relating to the Status of Refugees (Refugee Convention) each establish anti-discrimination guarantees, amongst others. These guarantees generally apply in cases of unequal treatment, provided that the cases fall within the scope of the provisions. First, with regard to extraterritorial antiterrorism efforts, the territorial scope might be in dispute. The treaties stipulate that human rights have to be guaranteed by the state parties to all individuals 'within [*their*] territory and subject to [*their*] jurisdiction' (Article 2 (1) ICCPR) or to everyone 'within their jurisdiction' (Article 1 ECHR).[37] Thus, some states reject the extraterritorial application of human rights in favour of non-citizens,

33 cf Britz (n 21) 9.

34 cf the possible profile of a terrorist described by Schauer (n 14) 186: 'gender (male), ethnicity (Middle Eastern), demeanour (nervous), frequent flyer membership (no), date of ticket purchase (last minute), form of purchase (cash), use of travel agent (no), type of luggage (carry-on), which could easily be modified by including religion (Muslim)'.

35 See also Article 2 (1) ICCPR.

36 The other regional human right treaties contain similar provisions, cf Art. 1 (1), 14 American Convention on Human Rights; Art. 2, 3 African Charter on Human and Peoples' Rights; Art. 2 (1), 9 Arab Charter on Human Rights.

37 Notably Art. 2 (1) ICCPR (n 35) 'to all individuals within its territory and subject to its jurisdiction' and Art. 1 ECHR 'The High Contracting Parties shall secure to everyone within their jurisdiction the rights and freedoms defined in Section I of this Convention'.

for example in favour of aliens wishing to enter a state from abroad.[38] It seems, however, more compelling to rely on a broader reading of 'jurisdiction',[39] which would imply that travel or flight bans for aliens wishing to enter a state from abroad were covered by the territorial scope of the non-discrimination guarantees.[40] Second, the personal scope might also be limited. Apart from the narrow understanding of extraterritorial 'jurisdiction' (extending merely to a state's own nationals), Article 26 ICCPR and Article 14 ECHR cover all individuals regardless of their nationality, whereas only refugees qualify for the anti-discrimination guarantees of the Refugee Convention.[41] Finally, the material scope of these guarantees also differs. Article 14 ECHR restricts non-discrimination to the enjoyment of convention rights and does not prohibit discrimination as such.[42] Thus, it must be established that anti-terrorism measures fall within the ambit of a convention right; the right to privacy, for example, which protects against surveillance, stops, and searches (Article 8 ECHR)[43] or the right to free movement within and out of a state party (Article 2 Protocol 4) which does not,

38 For a detailed account and criticism of this view, see Marko Milanovic, *Extraterritorial Application of Human Rights Treaties: Law, Principles, and Policy* (OUP 2013).

39 With respect to Art. 2 (1) ICCPR, the clause 'within its territory and subject to its jurisdiction' must be read, in light of the treaty's object and purpose, to demand the exercise of *either* territorial or jurisdictional sovereignty, see *Palestinian Wall*, Advisory Opinion [2004] ICJ Rep. 136, para 109; Human Rights Committee *López Burgos v Uruguay* [1981] Communication no 56/79, paras 12.2–12.3; *Montero v Uruguay* [1981] Communication no 106/81, para 5. A narrow reading of 'jurisdiction' means, for example, that only effective, overall, and normative power and control qualifies, for example in situations of occupation, see Samantha Besson, 'The Extraterritoriality of the European Convention on Human Rights: Why Human Rights Depend on Jurisdiction and What Jurisdiction Amounts to' (2012) 25 Leiden Journal of International Law 857; a broad reading could mean any factual power a state exercises over a territory or a person, see Milanovic (n 38).

40 The main arguments for this outcome have to be developed elsewhere. In short, the requirement of 'jurisdiction' is meant to guarantee a relationship of responsibility between the individual as a right holder and the state party as a duty bearer (and to delimit areas of responsibility of different state parties), not to grant unfettered state sovereignty for extraterritorial acts. However, the scope of extraterritorial human rights might differ from human rights protected within a state's territory, This could imply, for example, excluding positive obligations to protect social rights or accepting a large margin of appreciation with respect to foreign affairs (including immigration).

41 As defined in Art. 1 1951 Refugee Convention and Art. 1 (2) 1967 Protocol.

42 Art. 1 of Protocol No. 12 contains a general prohibition of discrimination. However, the protocol has only been ratified by ten states so far.

43 *Gillan and Quinton v UK* App no 4158/05 (ECtHR, 12 January 2010) paras 61–65.

however, entail a right of entry to a convention state. Similarly, Article 3 of the 1951 Refugee Convention is limited to the non-discriminatory application of this convention. As a result, international anti-discrimination law accounts for binding standards governing statistical discrimination, even if it might sometimes be difficult to establish jurisdiction for extraterritorial acts (ICCPR, ECHR) or if the guarantees are restricted to certain areas of law (ECHR, Refugee Convention).

As a general rule, the anti-discrimination guarantees prohibit unequal treatment based on religion unless such treatment is justified. Two aspects of this rule merit further consideration. The guarantees may be triggered not only by *direct* forms of unequal treatment based on religion (prohibited by Article 26 ICCPR, Article 14 ECHR, Art. 3 Refugee Convention), but also by *indirect* forms. Targeting potential Islamist terrorists, may, after all, imply measures directed at individuals of Arab/Middle-Eastern ethnicity or nationality (which are often more visible than religious affiliation). If these measures have an exclusive or disparately adverse impact on Muslims, they qualify as indirect forms of unequal treatment, a concept recognized by both the ICCPR's Human Rights Committee[44] and the European Court of Human Rights.[45] This also works the other way round: if an ethnic group (ie Arab, Middle-Eastern) is partly congruent with a religious group (since ethnic Arabs are often Muslims), members of these groups can challenge anti-terrorism measures based on guarantees outlawing race discrimination, such as those of the Convention on the Elimination of All Forms of Racial Discrimination (CERD).[46]

The second aspect concerns the structure of anti-discrimination rights. It is established that unequal treatment does not automatically amount to discrimination, but that indirect[47] and direct forms of unequal treatment can be justified. According to the Human Rights Committee, differentiation does not constitute discrimination, 'if the criteria for such differentiation are reasonable and objective and if the aim is to achieve a purpose which is legitimate

44 Human Rights Committee, *Cecilia Derksen v Netherlands* [2004] Communication no 976/2001 UN Doc CCPR/C/80/D/976/2001, para 9.3.

45 *Orsus v Croatia* (GC) App no 15766/03 ECHR 2010-II 247, para 150.

46 The advantage being that those guarantees tend to be broader and more widespread than other antidiscrimination guarantees; see, for example, the protection of Jews, Sikhs, and Muslims (from a certain ethnical background) by the UK Race Relations Act 1976, House of Lords *Mandla (Sewa Singh) v Dowell Lee* [1983] 2 AC 548 (565, 569). Note, however, that the guarantees of CERD do not extend to the discrimination of foreign nationals (Art. 1 (2), (3) CERD).

47 *Cecilia Derksen v Netherlands* (n 44) para 9.3; *Orsus v Croatia* (n 45) para 150.

under the Covenant'.[48] The European Court of Human Rights holds that 'the principle of equality of treatment is violated if the distinction has no objective and reasonable justification'.[49] However, justification must pass strict scrutiny if unequal treatment is based on a suspect classification such as race[50] or gender.[51] The standard for different treatment on grounds of religion is less clear. It speaks in favour of strict scrutiny, acknowledging that ethnicity and religious affiliation often are inseparably intertwined (as the example of Arab and Middle-Eastern Muslims shows). Moreover, religious freedom expressly protects religious affiliation and religious exercise (Article 18 ICCPR, Article 9 ECHR), which corresponds with a particular need to protect religious minorities. However, race and gender differ from religion. Religious affiliation and exercise (as opposed to race or gender) imply some form of choice and thus some form of responsibility. Furthermore, religiously motivated behaviour may conflict with individual rights or the common good, which justifies differential treatment. Thus, unequal treatment based on religion must also pass some form of stricter scrutiny, but is easier to justify than discrimination based on race or sex.[52]

48 General Comment 18 (Thirty-seventh session, 1989) para 13; cf Human Rights Committee *Lecraft v Spain* [2009] Communication no 1493/2006, para 7.4; cf Sarah Joseph and Melissa Castan, *The International Covenant on Civil and Political Rights: Cases, Materials, and Commentary* (3rd edn, OUP 2013) para 23.48.

49 *Linguistic Case v Belgium* App no 1474/62 (1968) Series A no 5, para 10.

50 The ECtHR holds that difference in treatment which is based exclusively or to a decisive extent on a person's ethnic origin in general is not capable of being objectively justified (*Timishev v Russia* App no 55762/00 ECHR 2005-XII 169, para. 58; *D.H. v the Czech Republic* (GC) App no 57325/00 ECHR 2007-IV 241, para 176); similarly *Lecraft v Spain* (n 48) para 7.4.

51 Under the ECHR, different treatment based on sex has to be justified by 'compelling reasons,' *van Raalte v the Netherlands* App no 20060/92 (ECtHR, 21 February 1997) para 42; the Human Rights Committee is equally reluctant to accept different treatment based on sex, cf *Aumeeruddy-Cziffra v Mauritius* [1981] Communication no 35/1978 UN Doc CCPR/C/12/D/35/1978, para 9.2 (b) 2 (II) 3; *Broeks v Netherlands* [1990] Communication no 172/1984 UN Doc CCPR/C/29/D/172/1984, paras 13–16; *Müller and Engelhard v Namibia* [2002] Communication no 919/2000 UN Doc CCPR/C/74/D/919/2000, paras 6.7-6.8.

52 cf ECtHR, *Savez Crkava 'Rijec Zivota' v Croatia* App no 7798/08 (judgment of 9 December 2010) para 88: 'particular scrutiny'; ECtHR, *Church of Jesus Christ of Latter-Day Saints v UK* App no 7552/09 (judgment of 4 March 2017) para 33: 'certain margin of appreciation'; Human Rights Committee *Foin v France* [1999] Communication no 666/1995 UN Doc CCPR/C/67/D/666/1995, para 10.3; *Waldman v Canada* [1999] Communication no 694/1996 UN Doc CCPR/C/67/D/694/1996, paras 10.5-10.6.

3.2 *Conflicting Interests: The Fight against Terrorism*

In any event, differential treatment can be justified, in principle, by the counterbalancing interest to fight terrorism. At the international level, the fight against terrorism is endorsed by a multitude of UN Security Council resolutions[53] and by international treaties.[54] Two aspects of these international documents are worth mentioning. First, the Security Council expressly recommends the use of profiling mechanisms. One of its recent resolutions, Resolution 2178 (2014) on foreign terrorist fighters, encourages the member states 'to employ evidence-based traveller risk assessment and screening procedures including collection and analysis of travel data'.[55] Thus, the Security Council seems to share the assumption that data based risk-assessment and profiling methods provide an effective means to detect suspects. Second, this resolution does not, however, call for a suspension of anti-discrimination rights. The relevant UN resolutions and treaties emphasise that anti-discrimination guarantees must be respected, and the Security Council resolution on foreign fighters explicitly denounces, 'profiling based on stereotypes founded on grounds of discrimination prohibited by international law'.[56] Furthermore, the perceived link

53 cf <www.un.org/sc/ctc/resources/security-council/>, eg UNSC Res 1373 (2001) UN Doc S/RES/1373, Res 1540 (2004) UN Doc S/RES/1540, Res 1624 (2005) UN Doc S/RES/1624 or Res 2178 (2014) UN Doc S/RES/2178.

54 cf <www.un.org/sc/ctc/resources/international-legal-instruments/>, eg the International Convention for the Suppression of the Financing of Terrorism (1999/2002) UNTS 2178, 197, or the International Convention for the Suppression of Acts of Nuclear Terrorism (2005/2007) UNTS 2445, 89.

55 UNSC Res 2178 (2014) 77CERDminal justice system, No. (n 53) para 2; cf Resolution 2309 (2016) on aviation security calling upon the member states to ensure 'that effective, risk-based measures are in place at the airports within their jurisdiction, including through enhancing screening, security checks, and facility security, to detect and deter terrorist attacks against civil aviation and to review and assess such measures regularly and thoroughly to ensure that they reflect the ever-evolving threat picture and are in accordance with ICAO standards and recommended practices' (UN Doc S/RES/2309, para 6 lit a); Resolution 1624 (2005) on the prohibition of incitement to commit terrorist acts calling upon all states to 'enhanc[e] terrorist screening and passenger security procedures' (n 53, para 2).

56 UNSC Res 2178 (2014) (n 53) para 2; cf Res 1624 (2005) (n 53) para 3 'effort to prevent the indiscriminate targeting of different religions and cultures'; for a general commitments to antidiscrimination guarantees see, eg, Res 2309 (2016) (n 55) para 2; Art. 15 International Convention for the Suppression of the Financing of Terrorism; Art. 16 International Convention for the Suppression of Acts of Nuclear Terrorism. The UN General Assembly urges states 'while countering terrorism … not to resort to profiling based on stereotypes founded on grounds of discrimination prohibited by international law, including on racial, ethnic and/or religious grounds,' UNGA Res 68/178 (28 January 2014) UN Doc A/RES/68/178, para 6 lit n.

between terrorism and religion is challenged in a more general manner, as states are called upon not to associate terrorism with a certain religion[57] and not to accept if terrorists try to justify their acts by religious considerations.[58]

4 Standards for Statistical Discrimination: How to Reconcile Religious Discrimination and the Fight Against Terrorism

Based on these conceptual and legal clarifications, this chapter can now approach two specific problems of statistical discrimination: Which forms of statistical discrimination trigger the need for justification? (4.1); and which considerations determine the justification of statistical discrimination? (4.2).

4.1 *Statistical Discrimination and the Need for Justification*

Statistical discrimination is problematic even if the suspect criterion (race, sex, religion) is only *one* criterion among many. This needs to be emphasised because corresponding statements by human rights bodies could be misunderstood. Dealing with racial profiling, the Committee on the Elimination of Racial Discrimination (CERD) for example, regarding racial profiling, states that interrogations, arrests and searches must not be based 'solely' on a person's race or ethnicity.[59] In a similar manner, the Human Rights Committee found that singling out a rail traveller for a police check 'solely on the ground of her racial characteristics' amounted to discrimination under Article 26 ICCPR.[60] Similar outcomes and rulings by the ECHR[61] imply that statistical discrimination which either exclusively or predominantly relies on race as a proxy for criminal behaviour is illegal and cannot be justified. If one rephrases this categorical outcome in terms of proportionality, which governs the justification of unequal treatment,[62] two aspects are important to highlight. First,

57 For example UNSC Res 2178 (2014) (n 53), preamble 'Emphasising that terrorism cannot and should not be associated with any religion, nationality or civilization'.

58 For example Art. 6 International Convention for the Suppression of the Financing of Terrorism; Art. 6 International Convention for the Suppression of Acts of Nuclear Terrorism.

59 CERD, General recommendation XXXI on the prevention of racial discrimination in the administration and functioning of the criminal justice system, No 20 UN Doc HRI/GEN/1/Rev.9 (Vol. II) p 306.

60 *Lecraft v Spain* (n 48) para 7.4.

61 *Timeshev v Russia* (n 50) para 58; *D.H. v the Czech Republic* (n 50) para 176.

62 Joseph and Castan (n 48) para 23.48; *Chassagnou v France* (GC) App no 25088/94 ECHR 1999-III 21, para 91; *Orsus v Croatia* (n 45) para 150.

associating a certain race or ethnicity with criminal behaviour has a particularly degrading effect. Second, the legitimate aim to fight crime can be reached more effectively by resorting to a refined profile of possible suspects instead of relying (solely or effectively) on the blunt criterion of race.

The wording of this jurisprudence, however, does not imply that all *other* forms of profiling, such as those based on a multitude of criteria, are legal. In other words, though no-fly lists or security checks rely on many factors, such as a person's police record, professional background, travel destinations places of residence, network of friends and family, once an individual's Muslim affiliation becomes a factor, the guarantee of non-discrimination on religious grounds is triggered. This reading stems from the wording and the purpose of the anti-discrimination guarantee. Being singled out for additional checks or sanctions as a Muslim traveller (or a male taxpayer in the context of tax fraud risk assessment) inflicts a direct disadvantage based on a suspect criterion, even if this result is reached by a more complex process based on multiple factors.[63]

4.2 *Justifying Statistical Discrimination*

Since *any* form of statistical discrimination based on suspect criteria such as race, gender, or religion needs a justification, the question remains whether the fight against terrorism may amount to such a justification. In general, justification requires that differential treatment is a proportionate means of achieving a legitimate aim and has to withstand strict scrutiny if suspect criteria apply.[64] The following section suggests that some considerations are common to all instances of statistical discrimination. It deals first with the specific harms of statistical discrimination, and then with alternative means to cope with information deficits.

4.2.1 Three Harms of Statistical Discrimination

Proportionality implies striking a balance between the legitimate aims pursued, such as national or international security, and the human right to non-discrimination. When legal orders face the threat of terrorism, they justly attach great importance to security concerns, including the particularly pressing need to prevent future terrorist acts, as well as the need to investigate and

63 Generally Schauer (n 14) 183–190; cf the full quote from CERD's General recommendation XXXI (n 59) rejecting 'any profiling which exposes [a person defined on grounds of race] to greater suspicion'.

64 n 48–52, 62.

punish past terrorist acts. It is therefore crucial to specify the possible harms of statistical discrimination in order to enable a meaningful balancing exercise.

The harms caused by statistical discrimination are at least threefold. First, statistical discrimination can be over inclusive.[65] Age rules, for example, which prevent pilots over age sixty from flying or which bar minors from voting are over inclusive. They are meant to exclude persons unfit to fly a plane or to participate in political acts, but they also affect perfectly healthy and capable eighty-year-old pilots or politically educated and responsible minors. These rules are considered justified for practical or normative reasons. It would be too cumbersome to regularly check the health of all airline pilots and it would contravene core elements of democracy, such as strict voting equality, if governments required voters to pass a maturity test. (Age rules also affect everybody equally over a lifetime, which makes them more acceptable than discrimination on grounds of race, gender or religion.)

In the context of criminal profiling, over inclusiveness means that law enforcement authorities single out possible perpetrators for investigation, prosecution or other police measures, but many of the targets are neither suspect nor dangerous. Consequently, reducing the degree of over inclusiveness can mitigate its harm. An example taken from health standards for blood donations may illustrate this point. In many countries, homosexual men are not allowed to donate blood because of a high risk of HIV-infection. In this context, the European Court of Justice (ECJ) examined a corresponding French rule governed by E.U. anti-discrimination laws. According to the ECJ, proportionality implied narrowing down the group of risk donors as far as possible according the donor's current sexual behaviour, such as the stability of a relationship or using sexual protection instead of relying on a broader criterion, like past homosexual relations.[66] The urge to avoid over inclusiveness also explains why the binary model[67] distinguishes illegal racial profiling based on an overbroad proxy for crime and legal description of a particular crime and a particular suspect.

Second, statistical discrimination leads to specific disadvantages, ranging from a mere inconvenience to the denial of fundamental rights. Targeted online advertising (responding to a web user's profile) is usually less burdensome than unfavourable health insurance terms (responding to an insuree's risk profile) or unfavourable lending terms (responding to a borrower's credit score).[68] Religious profiling also results in different outcomes, as some

65 cf Schauer (n 14) 108ff; Britz (n 21) 113ff.

66 Case C-528/13 *Léger* [2015] EU:C:2015:288 paras 65–68.

67 See section 2.1.

68 Britz (n 21) 75ff, 97ff.

individuals may consider additional identity or security checks for travellers a mere inconvenience. But Muslims on the American No-Fly List, for example, face grave consequences of being named on that list; they are effectively barred from travelling long distance. Some of them are unable to enter the United States from abroad, pursue their profession, reunite with their families, or go on a pilgrimage to Mecca.[69] Generally speaking, curtailing a right or a legally protected interest is more problematic than other negative consequences. Interestingly, a U.S. District Court dealing with the No-Fly List recently found that international airplane travel is not a mere convenience, but a right.[70] Other interests are not protected as such, for example the intention to travel, study or work abroad, because state sovereignty encompasses sovereign visa and immigration policies.

Due to the specific disadvantage they cause, some forms of statistical discrimination are absolutely prohibited. The ECJ, for example, ruled that European anti-discrimination law requires insurance companies to provide unisex premiums and benefits,[71] thereby categorically outlawing higher health and life insurance premiums for women.[72] Similarly absolute limits exist for criminal profiling. This chapter submits that, in the fight against crime, severe restrictions of rights, such as criminal punishment, imprisonment, or travel bans (sanctions as opposed to investigative measures), can never be justified based on statistical risks correlating with ethnicity, gender or religion. An individual's criminal responsibility or 'dangerousness' must justify those rights restrictions. The notion of individual responsibility and guilt is well established in criminal law,[73] thus inhibiting collective punishment.[74] But restrictions of important liberties beyond criminal punishment, like imprisonment or travel bans, also have to be based on an individual assessment of a person's 'dangerousness,'

69 See Florence (n 7) 2159ff; Hedlund (n 7) 610–11.

70 *Latif v Holder* (n 7) 1296ff.

71 Case C-236/09 *Test-Achats* [2011] ECR I-773, paras 15ff.

72 Britz (n 21) 106ff, 110ff.

73 This might be stated expressly (cf Art. 25 Rome Statute of the International Criminal Court) or even couched in constitutional terms (cf German Federal Constitutional Court BVerfGE 20, 323 (332ff) on 'nulla poena sine culpa'), and follows generally from established principles such as the presumption of innocence until guilt is proven (Art. 14 (2) ICCPR; Art. 2 (2) ECHR; Anthony Duff, 'Theories of Criminal Law' [2013] Stanford Encyclopedia of Philosophy <https://plato.stanford.edu/>, para 2).

74 Outlawed specifically under humanitarian law, cf Art. 50 Hague Regulations, Art. 87, para 3 Third Geneva Convention 1949; Art. 33, para 1 Fourth Geneva Convention 1949; collective punishment must not be mistaken for criminal corporate liability which rests on attribution of individual acts to a particular corporation.

and not on statistical risks related to race, gender or religion. If the core guarantees of anti-discrimination law and important freedoms are at stake, only an individual assessment can justify these sanctions.[75] In contrast, investigative measures based on a statistical risk assessment, such as additional checks, surveillance, or dragnet searches, do not appear disproportionate as such though they do entail specific losses of privacy. Moreover, they may produce distortive effects. If a certain group determined by race, gender or religion is specifically targeted by law enforcement agencies, this might result in sanctions which are no longer evenly distributed among all groups of society (in relation to their respective crime rates), but rather to an overrepresentation of the targeted group, which might lead to a vicious circle of more investigation and more sanctions.[76] However, it still appears possible that security concerns justify the use of proxies for further investigations, as long as privacy rights are respected and distorting effects avoided.

Finally, statistical discrimination can lead to the degradation of a particular group by visibly linking the group to a certain risk. Risk assessment in itself is not necessarily degrading. Women's on-average longer lifespans, while considered a risk to insurance companies, does not stigmatise women. But racial and religious profiling in the fight against crime illustrates the degrading effects of statistical discrimination. It affects minorities whose members already typically suffer from discrimination. Furthermore, linking members of a minority to criminal activities (drug offences, terrorism) reinforces existing prejudices and negative stereotypes. In this situation, every measure directed against a member of the group – stops and searches, identity and security checks, denials of transport – can stigmatise the targeted individual as well as the whole group, for the measure signifies and publicly displays that these individuals are linked to criminal activities from which the majority has to be protected. Yet some measures are more degrading than others. Targeting individuals on account of their affiliation with a particularly dangerous religious group (eg Scientology, radical Salafists) is less problematic than targeting individuals based on a mixture of race, origin or religion (eg Arab Muslims) because specific religious groups, as opposed to race and origin, may be linked to particular teachings that incite risk, such as the brainwashing of adherents, or violent

75 cf the procedural right to a legal remedy (Art. 2 (3) ICCPR; Art. 13 ECHR) which enables calling for such a justification; a comparable idea can be found in Art. 22 (2) General Data Protection Regulation 2016/679/EU: 'The data subject shall have the right not to be subject to a decision based solely on automated processing, including profiling, which produces legal effects concerning him or her or similarly significantly affects him or her'.

76 Harcourt (n 14) ch 5.

acts against 'infidels'. Linking a group to serious crime (drug offences, terrorism) is more stigmatising than linking it to risks resulting from the distribution of different ethnicities around the globe (ie the statistical correlation between immigration law offences and a foreign ethnicity; the higher risk that aliens/travellers from certain geographic are infected with a contagious or transmittable disease such as HIV.[77])

4.2.2 Three Ways to Cope with a Lack of Information

Proportionality is not only determined by the harms of statistical discrimination, but also by possible alternative means to overcome a lack of information. If law enforcement authorities have to rely on a proxy, targeting Arab Muslims, for example, because detailed information about terrorists is lacking, other strategies might better reconcile the conflicting interests of equality and security.

First, gathering more information may reduce an information deficit. Again, the rules barring homosexuals from blood donations[78] make this point clear. If medical tests could identify which of the donated blood samples were infected, unequal treatment of homosexuals would no longer be necessary (and would therefore be disproportionate).[79] Similarly, health or life insurance companies could rely on detailed accounts of their insurees' medical records, living habits or even genetic predisposition instead of using gender as a factor in their risk calculations. This solution obviously comes at a price – privacy. In the context of criminal profiling, another problem arises; additional information is either not easily available, or the proper investigative measure (such as security checks, surveillance, dragnet investigation) is, in itself, in dispute.

Second, equality and security interests could be reconciled by distributing the existing burdens more equally, that is, by burdening everybody or resorting to randomisation. The former seems useful if the stakes are high, but it requires many resources and affects many people. A prime example of this is found in airport security lines, where every passenger must undergo a security check at the airport before boarding their aircrafts in order to prevent

77 This was not taken into account – with respect to immigration controls – by the Human Rights Committee *Lecraft v Spain* (n 48) para 7.4, or by the Oberverwaltungsgericht Koblenz (Higher Administrative Court), decision of 21 April 2016, Az. 7 A 11108/14, paras 103ff; on the risk of disease transmission cf Case C-528/13 *Léger* [2014] EU:C:2014:2112, Opinion of AG Mengozzi, para 60.

78 See section 4.2.1.

79 This was the first argument emphasised by the ECJ in *Léger* [2015] (n 66) paras 59–64 (for the second argument see n 66).

individuals from bringing explosives aboard. Random analysis, on the other hand, is a useful tool to distribute an equal risk of burden if the stakes are not as high. Randomised tax audits, for example, could deter potential offenders from committing tax fraud.[80] Randomisation may also enhance the effectiveness of law enforcement since offenders who anticipate the profiling and act accordingly cannot manipulate it. In our context, for example, speculating that Muslim Arab men are Islamist terrorists is misleading once French or German women (who conceal their religious affiliation) also commit terror acts.

Third, law enforcement authorities may act based on a 'suspect description,' ie properties of an individual suspect, instead of probabilistic generalisations. This reconciles conflicting interests because it enables the fight against crime by restricting it to suspect targets. However, as noted above, it is not clear what 'suspicion' exactly means.[81] Is it sufficient to know that Islamists are planning terrorist attacks without possessing any information concerning the possible perpetrators, their networks, means, possible date, place, or victims? Here, general considerations of proportionality can help to determine the adequate degree of suspicion. If the stakes are high, a more general suspicion, such as the threat of terrorist attacks on planes or public places, can be sufficient to justify investigative measures like additional security checks or dragnet searches based on statistical probabilities regarding religious affiliation. However, in other situations, even a more specific suspicion might not justify such a measure. For example, if less intrusive means are available, collection of more information or randomisation for instance, and if the stakes are lower and the harm is disproportionately high (in the context of 'mere' tax fraud, for example), then a more specific suspicion might not justify such a measure.

In sum, the distinction between criminal profiling and suspect description reliance can also be explained by considerations of proportionality. A narrow description of possible suspects avoids over inclusiveness and generally restricts law enforcement measures. This chapter argues, however, that a proportionality approach is more adequate. A proportionality approach is more sophisticated because it includes all aspects relevant to the task of balancing, helps distinguish different degrees of suspicion, and conforms to Article 26 ICCPR and Article 14 ECHR.

80 Schauer (n 14) 160ff; generally favouring randomisation over profiling Harcourt (n 14).

81 N 19.

5 Conclusion

This chapter qualifies the phenomenon of religious profiling, eg law enforcement measures based on probabilistic generalisations about religious affiliation, not in terms of the binary concept of racial criminal profiling, but rather as an example of the more general phenomenon of statistical discrimination. Assessed in the light of international non-discrimination guarantees, notably Article 26 ICCPR and Article 14 ECHR, every form of unequal treatment on grounds of religion must be justified, even if religion constitutes only one factor among a multitude of factors making up the profile of a suspected terrorist. The fight against terrorism, which is recognised as a legitimate aim in international law, may, in principle, justify profiling measures if they are proportionate. The corresponding considerations of proportionality are structured by the properties of statistical discrimination. As a result, 'religious profiling' can be justified in narrow circumstances – circumstances that might typically also qualify as 'suspect description reliance'. However, the proportionality approach is more comprehensive and hence more adequate.

CHAPTER 10

La protection de l'héritage culturel religieux en droit international

Claas Friedrich Germelmann

1 Introduction

L'héritage culturel, et notamment l'héritage culturel religieux, se trouve dans un état de menace permanent. Les crises diverses de nos jours exercent une influence multiple, mais en somme pernicieuse, sur les biens et les valeurs qui forment l'ensemble de ce qu'on décrit par le terme « héritage » ou « patrimoine » culturel[1]. Les formes des menaces sont aussi riches que les lieux où elles adviennent de sorte qu'aujourd'hui, la question des zones de sécurité (« *safe haven* ») fait partie de la discussion internationale des archéologues et des institutions ayant vocation à protéger les biens culturels[2].

Pendant les dernières années, peu de mois sont passés sans qu'on ne puisse lire des nouvelles sur des atteintes étatiques, quasi étatiques ou privées aux établissements religieux ou à la pratique de la religion. Les atteintes pendant les temps de conflit armé international ou interne sont certes les plus visibles[3]. Les attaques des groupes terroristes sont parmi les raisons les plus évidentes de la perte d'innombrables trésors culturels et religieux, notamment dans les pays arabes et africains. La lutte contre l'organisation criminelle du prétendu « État islamique » n'a pas réussi à conserver des bâtiments sacrés qui furent les victimes d'une idéologie abracadabrantesque dans les derniers jours même d'une bataille[4]. Pourtant, on peut aller plus loin. A part les destructions dans les conflits, les persécutions et discriminations actives en raison de la religion

1 Sur la terminologie *infra* 2.1.

2 Voir les « ILA Guidelines for the Establishment and Conduct of Safe Havens for Cultural Material », *IJCP*, 16 (2009), p. 371 ; K. Engelhardt, « Safe Haven für gefährdete Kulturgüter », *in* K. Odendahl, P.J. Weber (dir.), *Kulturgüterschutz-Kunstrecht-Kulturrecht. Festschrift für Kurt Siehr*, Nomos, 2010, p. 55.

3 Voir le titre très juste de V. Négri (dir.), *Le patrimoine culturel, cible des conflits armés – De la guerre espagnole aux guerres du 21ème siècle*, Bruylant, 2014.

4 Voir l'exemple récent de la grande mosquée al-Nouri à Mossoul qui fut détruite le 21 juin 2017 par les troupes d'occupation du soi-disant « État islamique » peu de jours avant leur défaite et retraite.

 | DOI:10.1163/9789004349155_011

en temps de guerre aussi bien que de paix peuvent également s'avérer fatales non seulement pour les personnes concernées, mais aussi pour leur héritage religieux. Cela se manifeste le plus clairement dans les situations qui décident les personnes et les groupes discriminés et poursuivis à abandonner leurs lieux d'origine et, en même temps, leurs bâtiments sacrés qui, par la suite, sont souvent livrés à la déchéance et à la destruction.

Le patrimoine culturel religieux est donc pris pour cible dans maints conflits politiques. Partant de ce diagnostic, plusieurs questions se posent sur le plan du droit international, la plus centrale étant de savoir si le droit international contient des dispositions relatives à une forme « d'abri » efficace pour le patrimoine culturel religieux et s'il existe des mécanismes suffisants pour garantir la protection de ce qu'on comprend par la notion d'héritage culturel religieux.

2 La religion et l'héritage culturel : la dimension juridique de la terminologie

Les aspects juridiques, toutefois, sont tellement divers que ce bref essai ne peut envisager que quelques-uns d'entre eux. L'accent central de cette recherche se portera sur le droit international qui essaie de combattre le danger de la destruction et de l'éradication de l'héritage culturel religieux. Elle n'enquête pas forcément sur l'enlèvement des objets à vocation religieuse bien qu'il ne soit pas rare que l'on rencontre les deux dangers ensemble[5]. Ils font toutefois objet de règles internationales spécifiques[6]. Alors que le déplacement des biens culturels qu'on observe notamment en temps de guerre civile ou internationale pose un péril imminent pour la sauvegarde du patrimoine, le danger de la destruction semble être encore plus fondamental et visible de nos jours.

Même en ce qui concerne la destruction des biens culturels, les implications juridiques sont diverses. Elles touchent, d'un côté, à la tâche de l'État de garantir la liberté religieuse individuelle. La raison se trouve dans le fait que l'héritage culturel religieux est indispensable pour exercer la religion[7]. Cela regarde les objets cultuels et les bâtiments sacrés aussi bien que les coutumes, les traditions et les enseignements religieux qui sont à la base de l'exercice complet et non perturbé de la liberté religieuse et qui, seuls, la rendent possible.

5 Voir R. O'Keefe, *The Protection of Cultural Property in Armed Conflict*, Cambridge University Press, 2006, pp. 1 ss.

6 Voir, en détail, I. Stamatoudi, *Cultural Property Law and Restitution. A Commentary to International Conventions and European Union Law*, E. Elgar, 2011.

7 Voir, en plus de détail, *infra* 3.1.

A part ce caractère individuel, l'héritage culturel religieux revêt en même temps une dimension collective. Elle est encore plus visible que dans le cas de la liberté religieuse qui, elle aussi, possède des éléments collectifs[8]. L'héritage culturel à vocation religieuse ou, comme on pourrait dire, « l'héritage cultuel », ne consiste pas en premier lieu en des confessions individuelles, mais s'appuie sur les traditions et les acquis des communautés religieuses[9]. On ne peut donc pas concevoir un héritage culturel religieux sans avoir recours à la dimension collective de l'exercice de la religion.

2.1 *Les biens culturels, les traditions religieuses et leur rôle comme « héritage culturel »*

Les deux dimensions de l'héritage culturel religieux possèdent une signification dans le champ du droit interne[10] aussi bien que du droit international. En dépit de son importance et des dangers évidents, la signification de « l'héritage culturel » dans le contexte du droit international est loin d'être définie d'une façon claire et sans équivoque[11]. Cela rend difficile de créer et d'appliquer un régime efficace pour la protection de ce qu'on peut à juste titre nommer une des bases de la civilisation dans le monde entier.

Le sens ordinaire de « l'héritage culturel religieux » comprend les institutions et les biens qui ont une signification traditionnelle pour la pratique religieuse comme par exemple les églises ou les objets d'art à vocation religieuse, ainsi que les pratiques et les traditions elles-mêmes qui forment les cultes religieux. Naturellement, la signification de tous ces éléments diffère selon les cultes divers qui existent de par le monde. Or, l'importance des éléments s'avère fort différente selon les communautés de fidèles[12]. Tandis que pour certains cultes, la valeur des objets matériels s'efface devant les textes écrits ou non écrits ou

---

8 Voir CCPR General Comment n° 22 : Article 18 (Freedom of Thought, Conscience or Religion), 30 juill. 1993, CCPR/C/21/Rev.1/Add.4, § 1; CEDH, Gr. Ch., 26 oct. 2000, n° 30985/96, *Hassan et Tchaouch c. Bulgarie*, § 62, CEDH 2000-XI.

9 Sur cette nature intergénérationnelle qui nécessite une obligation de préservation, voir P. Häberle, « National-verfassungsstaatlicher und universaler Kulturgüterschutz – ein Textstufenvergleich », *in* F. Fechner, T. Oppermann, L.V. Prott (dir.), *Prinzipien des Kulturgüterschutzes*, Duncker & Humblot, 1996, pp. 91, 107-108.

10 Du point de vue du droit constitutionnel comparé, voir P. Häberle, « National-verfassungsstaatlicher und universaler Kulturgüterschutz ... », *op. cit.*, 1996, p. 91.

11 Voir, pour une discussion plus approfondie, C.F. Germelmann, *Kultur und staatliches Handeln*, Mohr Siebeck, 2013, pp. 582 ss.

12 CCPR General Comment n° 22 : Article 18 (Freedom of Thought, Conscience or Religion), 30 juill. 1993, CCPR/C/21/Rev.1/Add.4, § 4.

des rites immatériels, pour d'autres, les lieux de cultes, soit des bâtiments, soit des sites naturels, ou les objets rituels ont une importance suprême.

La notion d'« héritage » au sens du droit international doit réunir toutes ces différences et se comprend donc de manière extrêmement large. Elle rassemble différents biens matériels aussi bien que des aspects immatériels, selon les traditions et les cultes respectifs. Au surplus, elle contient l'héritage du passé aussi bien que les traditions de la foi qui sont vécues jusqu'à nos jours. Cette conception est une prémisse inévitable afin de rendre efficace la protection de l'héritage culturel religieux par la voie du droit international. Bien que les difficultés de la définition augmentent avec le pluralisme croissant de la conception de la religion en droit international, il ne faut, *a priori*, exclure aucun bien matériel ou immatériel qu'une religion regarde comme essentiel.

Il est pourtant nécessaire d'établir deux limites. D'abord, il est évident que l'héritage ne couvre pas toutes les convictions et pratiques qui sont protégées par la liberté religieuse individuelle, mais seulement celles qui revêtent une pertinence pour la collectivité des fidèles. Bien qu'un héritage puisse être décidément individuel, l'héritage « culturel » présuppose une relation avec la communauté, la société ou, le cas échéant, la nation. Ensuite, le fait qu'une pratique ou une tradition fassent partie de l'héritage culturel ne les rend pas sacro-saintes du point de vue des droits de l'homme individuels qui peuvent entrer en conflit avec elles. Dans ces cas-là, une balance entre la sauvegarde des éléments de l'héritage culturel et les droits de l'homme concernés doit être établie selon les mécanismes pertinents des instruments internationaux[13].

2.2 *L'héritage culturel religieux et le patrimoine culturel du monde*

Outre son importance pour l'exercice de la religion, l'héritage culturel religieux possède une importance distincte pour l'héritage esthétique du monde. La religion étant un aspect traditionnel de la culture, les bâtiments et objets à vocation religieuse de même que les textes et les compositions musicales ecclésiastiques ont eu une influence indéniable sur le développement des arts dans le passé. Il s'ensuit que beaucoup d'entre eux ne font pas seulement partie de l'héritage « spirituel », mais également de l'héritage culturel laïc. Il y a donc des parties de l'héritage culturel religieux qui ne s'épuisent pas dans leur fonction spirituelle ou cultuelle, mais qui, au surplus, créent des relations avec la culture et l'auto-perception des nations dans leur intégralité[14]. Cela est souvent le cas pour les objets du passé dont l'usage cultuel a diminué ou disparu,

13 Voir, par ex., pour le prosélytisme, CEDH, 25 mai 1993, nº 14307/88, *Kokkinakis c. Grèce*.

14 Un exemple classique est la dispute entre la Grèce et le Royaume-Uni concernant les frises du Parthénon qui, aujourd'hui, n'ont qu'une valeur artistique (bien que suprême).

de même que pour les bâtiments, objets et biens immatériels dont la valeur artistique surpasse leur seule signification pour les rites spirituels.

De là, la question se pose de savoir si le terme « héritage » représente un équivalent du terme traditionnel du « patrimoine ». Les textes internationaux offrent une réponse peu éclairante. La vaste majorité se sert du terme « patrimoine culturel mondial », même si ce concept n'a jamais été sans équivoque[15]. C'est le cas pour les conventions de l'UNESCO comme la Convention concernant la protection du patrimoine mondial culturel et naturel de 1972[16] ou la Convention pour la sauvegarde du patrimoine culturel immatériel de 2003[17]. La Convention de La Haye pour la protection des biens culturels en cas de conflit armé de 1954[18] qui se concentre sur les objets mobiliers et immobiliers prend une approche pareille. Une certaine divergence se laisse constater dans les traités européens. Tandis que le préambule de la Charte des droits fondamentaux de l'Union européenne parle du « patrimoine », l'article 167 TFUE met en relief « l'héritage culturel commun ». Même si l'on pourrait attribuer au terme « héritage » un contenu plus large et peut-être plus abstrait, il semble justifié de traiter les termes « héritage » et « patrimoine » comme des synonymes aux fins de la protection des biens et des valeurs culturels et religieux. Ce qui importe, c'est que les textes internationaux eux aussi montrent de façon claire que l'intention sous-jacente à ces normes internationales consiste à attribuer au terme une portée large[19] et, de cette manière, à protéger non seulement des objets, mais aussi des traditions et les biens immatériels qui forment la religion et la foi.

3 Le système imparfait du droit international pour la protection de l'héritage culturel religieux

L'histoire de la destruction des biens culturels est aussi ancienne que l'histoire des conflits humains. La situation n'est pas plus favorable pour l'héritage à

Il en est de même pour les demandes régulières de restitution de la part de l'Égypte ou de la Turquie relatives à des objets d'art qui, dans l'antiquité, servaient des buts religieux.

15 Voir par ex. L.V. Prott, P.J. O'Keefe, « 'Cultural Heritage' or 'Cultural Property' » ?, *IJCP*, 1 (1992), p. 307 ; B. Genius-Devime, *Bedeutung und Grenzen des Erbes der Menschheit im völkerrechtlichen Kulturgüterschutz*, Nomos, 1997, pp. 167 ss., 337 ss.; I. Stamatoudi, *Cultural Property Law and Restitution*, *op. cit.*, pp. 6 ss.

16 *RTNU*, vol. 1037, p. 173.

17 *RTNU*, vol. 2368, p. 49.

18 *RTNU*, vol. 249, p. 217.

19 Voir C.F. Germelmann, *Kultur und staatliches Handeln*, *op. cit.*, pp. 582 ss., avec les références de la discussion.

vocation religieuse. Des atteintes pernicieuses sont commises pendant la paix aussi bien que pendant les conflits armés. En général, il est possible de les catégoriser en deux groupes. D'abord, il existe des actes intentionnels qui nuisent à l'intégrité du patrimoine culturel et qui ont souvent pour but de détruire ou de subjuguer une communauté religieuse ou nationale. Jusqu'à nos jours, on rencontre des exemples d'expulsions et de dévastations dans les conflits du Proche-Orient qui sont motivées par des antagonismes politiques et religieux. Pendant la guerre en ex- Yougoslavie, il en fut de même avec maints crimes de guerre qui furent commis dans le but de déplacer et de déraciner des groupes ethniques et religieux[20].

L'histoire connaît également maints exemples de destructions qui se caractérisent plutôt comme des dommages collatéraux à des combats ou à la négligence de l'État vis-à-vis des biens culturels. Les exemples du passé sont aussi nombreux que ceux du droit international moderne[21]. Selon l'historiographie classique[22], l'ancienne bibliothèque d'Alexandrie subit un destin pire encore que, plusieurs siècles plus tard, le Parthénon de l'acropole d'Athènes. La destruction de la bibliothèque de Louvain par les troupes allemandes pendant la Première Guerre mondiale est un des rares cas où un traité de paix[23] a formellement établi une obligation de compensation en nature en attribuant à l'université de Louvain des livres des bibliothèques allemandes. Dans d'autres situations, une reconstruction complète ou partielle des édifices ou des œuvres d'art dévastés pendant la guerre fut entreprise par les communautés concernées elles-mêmes, avec un soutien international ou sans[24]. Les problèmes juridiques de l'art spolié ou confisqué relèvent d'un autre ensemble de questions sans qu'ils puissent être tranchés dans le contexte présent[25] puisqu'ils ne concernent pas la destruction, mais l'enlèvement des biens culturels.

20 Voir, par ex., F. Lenzerini, « Suppressing and Remedying Offences against Culture », *in* A. Vrdoljak (ed.), *The Cultural Dimension of Human Rights*, Oxford University Press, 2013, pp. 240, 250-251 ; Y. Dinstein, *The Conduct of Hostilities under the Law of International Armed Conflict*, Cambridge University Press, 3ème éd., 2016, p. 203.

21 Voir C. de Visscher, « La protection internationale des objets d'art et des monuments historiques », *RDILC*, 1935, p. 246.

22 Plutarque, *Vies parallèles : Vie de César*, § 49.

23 Art. 247 du Traité de Versailles.

24 Voir exposé parfois critique de D. Viejo-Rose, « Identité et mémoire d'après-guerre. La destruction et la reconstruction du patrimoine culturel en Espagne et en Bosnie », *in* V. Négri (dir.), *Le patrimoine culturel, cible des conflits armés*, *op. cit.*, p. 101.

25 Voir, sur ce sujet, M. Anton, *Illegaler Kulturgüterverkehr*, De Gruyter, 2010, pp. 273 ss.

3.1 *La protection de l'héritage culturel religieux par la voie des droits de l'homme*

Comme il a été déjà souligné, la protection de l'héritage culturel religieux est étroitement liée à la protection des droits de l'homme. Elle est la base de l'exercice de la liberté religieuse. Même si cette liberté couvre en premier lieu les convictions et les confessions religieuses individuelles et se rapporte donc à des pensées et des expressions immatérielles[26], l'héritage culturel peut gagner une importance particulière pour la pratique des rites qui est protégée en tant que droit fondamental. Il n'existe aucun doute que la destruction et l'éradication de l'héritage culturel religieux d'une communauté par les organes étatiques viole la liberté religieuse de la communauté et celle de ses membres[27]. La garantie fondamentale reconnue par l'article 9 de la Convention européenne des droits de l'homme se retrouve, de manière parallèle, dans l'article 18 du Pacte international relatif aux droits civils et politiques[28].

A part cette dimension prédominante liée à la liberté religieuse, l'identification avec l'héritage culturel peut être en outre l'expression des droits de la personnalité. Cela est valable notamment pour les biens religieux matériels ou immatériels dotés d'une importance marquée pour la confession qui forme une partie intégrale et importante de la personnalité humaine[29].

Une relation étroite entre l'héritage culturel et le droit de la personnalité peut exister de manière pareille lorsqu'il s'agit d'objets et de traditions dont l'influence religieuse s'est plutôt évanouie. Même l'identification personnelle avec un culte traditionnel des ancêtres peut avoir une influence sur le droit de la personnalité. Cela se justifie par le fait que l'héritage culturel religieux peut jouer un rôle déterminant dans une société ou un groupe social[30], ce qui le mène à exercer une influence marquée sur la personnalité humaine. La

26 Voir, en général, F. Sudre, *Droit européen et international des droits de l'homme*, PUF, 12ème éd., 2015, § 524.

27 Sur la dimension collective, voir CEDH, Gr. Ch., 26 oct. 2000, n° 30985/96, *Hassan et Tchaouch c. Bulgarie*, § 62, CEDH 2000-XI ; CEDH, 13 déc. 2001, n° 45701/99, *Eglise métropolitaine de Bessarabie et autres c. Moldova*, § 114 ; CCPR General Comment n° 22 : Article 18 (Freedom of Thought, Conscience or Religion), 30 juill. 1993, CCPR/C/21/Rev.1/Add.4, § 4.

28 CCPR General Comment n° 22 : Article 18 (Freedom of Thought, Conscience or Religion), 30 juill. 1993, CCPR/C/21/Rev.1/Add.4, § 1.

29 CEDH, 20 sept. 1994, n° 13470/87, *Otto-Preminger-Institut c. Autriche*, § 47 ; CEDH, 13 déc. 2001, n° 45701/99, *Eglise métropolitaine de Bessarabie et autres c. Moldova*, § 114.

30 Pour des exemples des premières nations des Amériques voir A. Delpuech, « Dimensions anthropologiques, culturelles et économiques du patrimoine archéologique », *in* V. Négri (dir.), *Le patrimoine archéologique et son droit*, Bruylant, 2015, p. 15.

culture en général, aussi bien que son patrimoine, sont des éléments constitutifs du développement de la personnalité humaine individuelle[31]. Ils restent des points de repère comme les règles et les acquis de la civilisation[32]. A cause de cette influence sur la personnalité, il est possible d'établir une relation entre l'héritage culturel qui touche à la liberté de religion et la dignité humaine. Si la destruction des biens matériels et immatériels à vocation religieuse porte atteinte à un aspect fondamental de la personnalité humaine, il peut en être de même pour la dignité humaine qui est à la base de tous les droits de la personnalité[33]. Même si une violation du droit suprême de la dignité humaine n'est établie que lorsqu'il y a une qualité spécifiquement grave et arbitraire de l'acte de l'État[34], cette relation marque l'importance et la valeur du patrimoine culturel pour les droits de l'homme.

La relation entre l'héritage culturel religieux et les droits de l'homme regarde donc le champ des droits individuels. Cela signifie, d'une part, qu'il appartient aux individus de s'en prévaloir et, d'autre part, qu'ils disposent de la liberté d'y renoncer s'ils jugent le rôle de l'héritage culturel religieux insignifiant pour leurs personnalités individuelles. Cette conséquence découle de la structure des droits de l'homme et pourrait réduire l'efficacité de la protection de l'héritage culturel. Vue son importance globale pour l'existence et la cohésion du groupe social et de la société, il est pourtant impératif qu'en plus de la dimension individuelle, l'identité culturelle forme un droit collectif qui soit reconnu

---

31 Le rôle des droits culturels est déjà reconnu dans l'article 22 de la Déclaration universelle des droits de l'homme : « Toute personne, en tant que membre de la société, a droit à la sécurité sociale ; elle est fondée à obtenir la satisfaction des droits économiques, sociaux et culturels indispensables à sa dignité et au libre développement de sa personnalité, grâce à l'effort national et à la coopération internationale, compte tenu de l'organisation et des ressources de chaque pays. » Voir également A. Kerdoun, « La place des droits économiques, sociaux et culturels dans le droit international des droits de l'homme », *RTDH*, 87 (2011), p. 499, 506 ; P. Meyer-Bisch, « Du 'droit au patrimoine' : l'approche innovante des articles 1 et 2 de la Convention de Faro », in *Le patrimoine et au-delà*, Conseil de l'Europe, 2009, p. 65, 66.

32 Voir, pour une discussion plus approfondie, M. Bidault, *La protection internationale des droits culturels*, Bruylant, 2009, pp. 215 ss.

33 J.-F. Renucci, *Droit européen des droits de l'homme*, LGDJ, 2ème éd. 2012, § 1 ; F. Sudre, *Droit européen et international des droits de l'homme*, *op. cit.*, § 127. Pour la Convention européenne des droits de l'homme voir CEDH, 29 avr. 2002, nº 2346/02, *Pretty c. Royaume-Uni*, § 65, CEDH 2002-III : « La dignité et la liberté de l'homme sont l'essence même de la Convention. »

34 Dans ce sens J. Bröhmer, « Menschenwürde, Freiheit der Person und Freizügigkeit », *in* D. Merten, H.-J. Papier (dir.), *Handbuch der Grundrechte in Deutschland und Europa*, tome VI/1, C.F. Müller, 2010, § 139 nº 42.

dans différents pactes sur la protection des minorités[35]. Lorsqu'il s'agit des traditions et des rites, ces droits collectifs jouent un rôle crucial. Les conflits avec la libre décision de l'individu de ne pas adhérer à une religion doivent être résolus selon les mécanismes reconnus qui accordent une liberté négative de religion à chacun[36].

Le fondement de l'héritage culturel religieux dans les droits de l'homme a pour conséquence que les obligations des États s'alignent sur les directives des conventions pertinentes. Outre les obligations de respecter les droits de l'homme, cela peut, le cas échéant, aboutir à des obligations positives[37] de protéger activement l'héritage culturel religieux en tant qu'il forme une base indispensable à l'exercice des libertés fondamentales.

3.2 *La protection de l'héritage culturel par le droit international général et par le droit international des conflits armés*

La protection de l'héritage culturel fait l'objet de plusieurs conventions internationales spécifiques. Tandis que les conventions du droit international humanitaire mettent en relief la protection des biens culturels mobiliers et immobiliers en les excluant du cercle des objectifs militaires admissibles, les conventions modernes du droit international général font valoir de manière plus prononcée la protection du patrimoine intangible.

La protection des objets non militaires par le droit international humanitaire traditionnel[38] est située dans le contexte des normes relatives à la protection

35 Voir, par ex., l'article 27 du Pacte international relatif aux droits civils et politiques de 1966 : « Dans les Etats où il existe des minorités ethniques, religieuses ou linguistiques, les personnes appartenant à ces minorités ne peuvent être privées du droit d'avoir, en commun avec les autres membres de leur groupe, leur propre vie culturelle, de professer et de pratiquer leur propre religion, ou d'employer leur propre langue. » Il en est de même pour la Convention-cadre pour la protection des minorités nationales du Conseil de l'Europe de 1995, STE n° 157. Voir en général D. Szymczak, « Droits culturels », *Jurisclasseur*, Fasc. 1220, 2007, §§ 25 ss., 60 ss.

36 J.-F. Renucci, *Droit européen des droits de l'homme*, *op. cit.*, § 207 ; F. Sudre, *Droit européen et international des droits de l'homme*, *op. cit.*, § 525 ; CCPR General Comment n° 22 : Article 18 (Freedom of Thought, Conscience or Religion), 30 juill. 1993, CCPR/C/21/Rev.1/Add.4, § 2.

37 Pour la Convention européenne des droits de l'homme, voir en général, F. Sudre, *Droit européen et international des droits de l'homme*, *op. cit.*, §§ 159 ss. ; K. Hajiyev, « The Evolution of Positive Obligations under the European Convention on Human Rights », *in* D. Spielmann, M. Tsirli, P. Voyatzis (dir.), *La Convention européenne des droits de l'homme, un instrument vivant – Mélanges en l'honneur de Christos L. Rozakis*, Bruylant, 2011, p. 207.

38 Voir C. de Visscher, « La protection internationale des objets d'art et des monuments historiques », *RDILC*, 1935, pp. 246, 256 ss.

des personnes civiles ce qui la mène donc proche aux droits de l'homme. C'est le cas, respectivement, pour l'article 52 du Premier et l'article 16 du Deuxième Protocole additionnel de 1977[39] aux Conventions de Genève de 1949. Pour protéger les biens culturels et spirituels, le droit de la guerre défend de les traiter en objectifs militaires légitimes s'ils ne sont pas utilisés abusivement eux-mêmes à des fins militaires[40].

La protection du patrimoine dans le droit international général moderne, en revanche, suit le concept d'un patrimoine global qui appartient à l'humanité entière et qui surpasse la seule protection des monuments qui forme l'objet de la Convention de l'UNESCO de 1972 concernant la protection de patrimoine mondial culturel et naturel. La protection des biens intangibles fut introduite par la Convention de l'UNESCO de 2003 pour la sauvegarde du patrimoine culturel immatériel qui, pourtant, ne contient pas de règles spécifiques pour le patrimoine culturel religieux[41].

L'accent mis sur le patrimoine commun de l'humanité, toutefois, n'exclut en aucun cas qu'il existe un effet protecteur individuel qui soit en même temps axé sur la protection des droits de l'homme[42]. C'est la conséquence du parallélisme des deux catégories de normes[43]. Pourtant, il serait désirable que le droit international moderne rende plus visible cette combinaison d'objectifs.

3.2.1 Les obligations des Etats

La réalité de la protection du patrimoine culturel par le droit international est plus sombre que l'acquis normatif ne le laisse croire. Les destructions

---

39 *RTNU*, vol. 1125, p. 3, 609.

40 Les exceptions sont très rares. Voir Y. Dinstein, *The Conduct of Hostilities under the Law of International Armed Conflict, op. cit.*, pp. 210-214.

41 Voir les définitions à l'article 2 de la Convention qui ne mentionnent pas explicitement les éléments du patrimoine spirituel, mais qui ne les excluent pas non plus, ce que montrent les listes établies en conformité avec les articles 16 et 17 de la Convention. Voir aussi la Convention de l'UNESCO sur la protection et la promotion de la diversité des expressions culturelles de 2005.

42 Voir, pour plus de détails, C.F. Germelmann, « Kulturelles Erbe als Menschenrecht ? », *DÖV*, 2015, p. 853. Sur la discussion en général voir par ex. P. Meyer-Bisch (dir.), *Les droits culturels – une catégorie sous-développée de droits de l'homme*, Editions universitaires, 1993 ; *id.*, « Le droit à la propriété culturelle, un droit individuel et commun », in *Avancées et confins actuels des droits de l'homme. Mélanges offerts à Silvio Marcus Helmons*, Bruylant, 2003, p. 243 ; J. Ringelheim, *Diversité culturelle et droits de l'homme*, Bruylant, 2006 ; M. Bidault, *La protection internationale des droits culturels*, Bruylant, 2009.

43 Voir aussi U. Leanza, « Conflitti simmetrici, conflitti asimmetrici e protezione dei beni culturali », in *Le grandi opere. Studi in onore di Vincenzo Starace*, Editoriale scientifica, tome I, 2008, p. 483.

intentionnelles ou collatérales des monuments et des sites culturels en temps de guerre aussi bien que la dégradation du patrimoine par une politique d'infrastructures inadéquate des Etats en sont la preuve.

3.2.1.1 *Le champ d'application des conventions*

Il y a à cela plusieurs raisons d'ordre juridique, la première étant les champs d'application restreints de beaucoup de conventions internationales. Tel est le cas du système des listes selon la Convention sur le patrimoine mondial de 1972, mais il vaut aussi pour les conventions du droit humanitaire[44]. La plupart d'entre eux ne protègent que quelques biens culturels sélectionnés et, de surcroît, ne lient pas tous les Etats.

Bien que la Convention de La Haye pour la protection des biens culturels en cas de conflit armé de 1954 ait été ratifiée par plus de 120 Etats, son Deuxième Protocole de 1999, qui a introduit l'instrument de la « protection renforcée »[45] pour améliorer le système déficitaire de la Convention de 1954, n'a pas connu un succès comparable et, jusqu'aujourd'hui, il n'a été ratifié que par 72 Etats. Mêmes les deux Protocoles additionnels de 1977 aux Conventions de Genève de 1949, qui renforcent la protection des biens culturels en temps de guerre en interdisant « tout acte d'hostilité dirigé contre les monuments historiques, les œuvres d'art ou les lieux de culte qui constituent le patrimoine culturel ou spirituel des peuples »[46], ne lient pas l'ensemble des Etats[47]. Le champ d'application matériel desdites conventions se confine aux biens tels qu'ils sont définis par l'article premier de la Convention de La Haye de 1954[48] et donc seulement

44 Voir la comparaison chez M. Frigo, « Le patrimoine culturel en danger et la responsabilité des Etats », *in* V. Négri (dir.), *Le patrimoine culturel, cible des conflits armés*, *op. cit.*, p. 137.

45 Chapitre 3 du Deuxième Protocole.

46 Article 53 du Protocole I et article 16 du Protocole II.

47 Le Protocole I a été ratifié par 174 États, le Protocole II par 168 États.

48 « Aux fins de la présente Convention, sont considérés comme biens culturels, quels que soient leur origine ou leur propriétaire :

a) les biens meubles ou immeubles, qui présentent une grande importance pour le patrimoine culturel des peuples, tels que les monuments d'architecture, d'art ou d'histoire, religieux ou laïques, les sites archéologiques, les ensembles de constructions qui, en tant que tels, présentent un intérêt historique ou artistique, les œuvres d'art, les manuscrits, livres et autres objets d'intérêt artistique, historique ou archéologique, ainsi que les collections scientifiques et les collections importantes de livres, d'archives ou de reproductions des biens définis ci-dessus ;

b) les édifices dont la destination principale et effective est de conserver ou d'exposer les biens culturels meubles définis à l'alinéa a, tels que les musées, les grandes

au patrimoine matériel qui, de plus, doit revêtir une valeur particulièrement élevée[49].

En ce qui concerne le patrimoine immatériel culturel et religieux, les conventions du droit humanitaire ne contiennent que des règles qui exercent au mieux une force protectrice indirecte. Elles découlent des obligations générales au profit de la population civile, comme dans la IVème Convention de Genève et les Protocoles additionnels de 1977, mais elles ne sont pas capables de créer un concept adéquat pour protéger l'intégralité de l'héritage immatériel. Au contraire, ce sont les conflits armés civils et internationaux qui sont responsables d'une dégradation de la diversité culturelle consécutive à des persécutions et à la fuite de groupes de population. Tandis que la convention de l'UNESCO pour la sauvegarde du patrimoine culturel immatériel de 2003, dont les règles sont alignées sur le temps de paix[50], rencontrera des difficultés de s'imposer dans les conflits armés[51], les normes internationales humanitaires ne parlent pas expressément des biens immatériels. Cela s'explique par l'époque et le contexte de leur conclusion. Malgré une pratique pertinente des États dans les années passées, il n'est pas envisageable non plus qu'il existe un corpus de règles coutumières qui puisse remplir cette lacune[52].

---

bibliothèques, les dépôts d'archives, ainsi que les refuges destinés à abriter, en cas de conflit armé, les biens culturels meubles définis à l'alinéa a ;

c) les centres comprenant un nombre considérable de biens culturels qui sont définis aux alinéas a et b, dits 'centres monumentaux'. »

Les Protocoles additionnels de 1977 aux Conventions de Genève y ajoutent de manière expresse les « lieux de cultes » qui font partie du « patrimoine culturel ou spirituel des peuples ».

49 Y. Dinstein, *The Conduct of Hostilities under the Law of International Armed Conflict, op. cit.*, pp. 207, 212.

50 Articles 18 (programmes, projets et activités de sauvegarde du patrimoine culturel immatériel) et 19 à 24 (assistance internationale) de la Convention. Bien que les mesures continuent pendant les temps de conflit armé, la Convention n'établit pas de régime exprès pour ces cas-là.

51 L'article 3 de la Convention de 2003 ne précise pas la relation entre celle-ci et les instruments du droit humanitaire. Les droits fondamentaux garantissent une protection complémentaire ; voir I. Bantekas, L. Oette, *International Human Rights Law and Practice*, Cambridge University Press, 2ème éd., 2016, pp. 658-659.

52 Voir sur le droit coutumier de la protection du patrimoine F. Francioni, « La protezione internazionale dei beni culturali : un diritto consuetudinario in formazione ? », in *Studi in onore di Vincenzo Starace, op. cit.*, p. 303.

3.2.1.2 *Le problème de la mise en œuvre des obligations de protection*

La seconde question, et peut-être la plus ardente dans le droit international du patrimoine culturel, est celle de la mise en œuvre, c'est-à-dire celle du destinataire et de la rigidité des obligations de protection. Les conventions pour la sauvegarde du patrimoine s'adressent principalement aux Etats. La convention de 1972 oblige les Etats membres à veiller sur le patrimoine sur leur territoire. La Convention de La Haye de 1954 leur interdit d'y porter atteinte pendant les conflits armés. Son Deuxième Protocole de 1999 précise ces obligations. D'autres conventions, comme celle sur la sauvegarde du patrimoine culturel immatériel de 2003, lient également les États. Il en est de même pour les conventions du Conseil de l'Europe, comme celle de Grenade de 1985 pour la sauvegarde du patrimoine architectural de l'Europe[53] et celle de La Valette de 1992 pour la protection du patrimoine archéologique[54].

En dépit de la force contraignante des obligations, toutes ces règles internationales souffrent du caractère classique du droit international traditionnel qui se confine à des mécanismes d'exécution plutôt faibles vis-à-vis des obligations des Etats. C'est vrai pour les conventions du droit humanitaire, ainsi que pour les conventions de protection du patrimoine matériel et immatériel. Bien qu'il existe des mécanismes de protection, comme des listes sous la surveillance des comités intergouvernementaux des conventions de 1972 et de 2003, les règles n'ont une chance réelle de s'appliquer que lorsque les Etats disposent d'une vue favorable sur le patrimoine culturel aussi bien que des fonds suffisants pour prendre des mesures actives de préservation. Même dans cette hypothèse, pourtant, aucune garantie n'existe en droit international pour empêcher que le droit interne ne demeure en contradiction avec les obligations de l'État sur le plan international[55]. A plusieurs occasions, le comité de la Convention du patrimoine mondial de 1972 fut obligé de prendre des mesures contre des Etats développés qui, normalement, considèrent la protection du patrimoine comme

53 STE n° 121.

54 STE n° 143.

55 C'est le cas pour quelques législations des *Länder* allemands en matière de protection des monuments. Dans un cas récent, la transposition des obligations internationales de l'Allemagne sur le patrimoine archéologique dans le droit interne fut jugée insuffisante par la Cour administrative fédérale. La législation interne du *Land* de Saxe-Anhalt n'était pas en conformité avec la Convention de La Valette et donc le droit international ne pouvait pas prévaloir. Voir Bundesverwaltungsgericht, 13 déc. 2010, n° 7 B 64/10, *NVwZ*, 2011, 752.

un but important[56]. En tout cas, les mécanismes de sanction s'avèrent aussi sous-développés que les mécanismes de coopération et les fonds déterminés à aider les Etats les moins capables dont les ressources sont limitées[57]. Dans beaucoup de situations, donc, les mécanismes des obligations conventionnelles ne mènent pas à une protection efficace.

En temps de guerre, la protection est plus faible encore. Les règles de la Convention de La Haye pour la protection des biens culturels en cas de conflit armé de 1954 aussi bien que son Deuxième Protocole de 1999 s'efforcent d'y remédier. Dans ce but, le Deuxième Protocole exclut la nécessité militaire impérative au sens de l'article 4, paragraphe 2, de la Convention de 1954 comme base justificative pour les atteintes aux biens culturels. Pourtant, les dispositions laissent subsister des lacunes et ne prévoient pas de système complet pour protéger même les biens matériels les plus précieux[58]. A part le fait que l'adhésion à ces deux instruments de droit international est loin d'être universelle[59], dans de nombreux conflits internes, les dévastations des sites sont le fait de groupes terroristes ou militants que l'Etat lui-même ne peut plus contrôler. Dans ces situations-ci, l'efficacité des conventions est également prise en défaut. Les sanctions contre les Etats ne peuvent aboutir à rien, car ils ne sont plus à même de poursuivre les crimes et de faire cesser les destructions. Les instruments et les mécanismes d'exécution des conventions classiques sont donc loin d'être satisfaisants.

Une question difficile dans ce contexte consiste à savoir s'il existe, en droit international général, hors droits de l'homme[60], des obligations positives des Etats ou de la communauté internationale, voire peut-être des Nations Unies, de prévenir ou de mitiger les atteintes au patrimoine culturel religieux. Bien que des points de départ existent dans le droit international contemporain, les directives des Conventions de l'UNESCO de 1972 et de 2003 concernant l'assistance internationale[61] restent incomplètes parce qu'elles n'englobent que le patrimoine figurant sur la liste du Comité intergouvernemental et ne créent pas d'obligations suffisamment

56 Même si l'exemple ne se trouve évidemment pas dans le champ du patrimoine culturel religieux, l'histoire déplorable de la dite « *Waldschlösschenbrücke* » à Dresde restera longtemps dans les mémoires.

57 Voir A. Ciampi, « Identifying and Effectively Protecting Cultural Heritage », *RDI*, 2014, pp. 699, 711 ss.

58 Voir la règle beaucoup plus restrictive de l'article 6 du Deuxième Protocole.

59 *Supra* 3.2.1.1.

60 *Supra* 3.1.

61 Articles 6, 7, 19 à 26 de la Convention de 1972 et articles 19 à 24 de la Convention de 2003.

fortes et concrètes pour Etats *ut singuli*[62], autres que de l'Etat où le bien culturel est situé ou présent[63]. Les mesures de précautions prévues par le Deuxième Protocole de la Convention de La Haye pour la protection des biens culturels en cas de conflit armé[64] font naître des doutes quant à leur efficacité. Bien qu'il aborde, d'une manière générale, des mesures d'assistance internationale, leur champ d'application reste restreint et leur contenu, juridiquement vague[65].

Les discussions sur une obligation positive d'intervention militaire sous la forme d'une « responsabilité de protéger » se sont avérées peu fertiles[66]. Même dans les situations de génocide ou en cas de crimes contre l'humanité,

---

62 Voir notamment l'article 6, paragraphe 2, de la Convention des 1972 : « Les Etats parties s'engagent en conséquence, et conformément aux dispositions de la présente convention, à apporter leur concours à l'identification, à la protection, à la conservation et à la mise en valeur du patrimoine culturel et naturel visé aux paragraphes 2 et 4 de l'article 11 si l'Etat sur le territoire duquel il est situé le demande. » L'article 19, paragraphe 2, de la Convention de 2003 est encore plus souple : « Sans préjudice des dispositions de leur législation nationale et de leurs droit et pratiques coutumiers, les Etats parties reconnaissent que la sauvegarde du patrimoine culturel immatériel est dans l'intérêt général de l'humanité et s'engagent, à cette fin, à coopérer aux niveaux bilatéral, sous-régional, régional et international. »

63 Voir les articles 4 et 5 de la Convention de 1972 et les articles 11 à 15 de la Convention de 2003.

64 Selon l'article 5 du Deuxième Protocole, elles comprennent « l'établissement d'inventaires, la planification de mesures d'urgence pour assurer la protection des biens contre les risques d'incendie ou d'écroulement des bâtiments, la préparation de l'enlèvement des biens culturels meubles ou la fourniture d'une protection in situ adéquate ».

65 « Article 31 Coopération internationale : Dans les cas de violations graves du présent Protocole, les Parties s'engagent à agir, tant conjointement, par l'intermédiaire du Comité, que séparément, en coopération avec l'UNESCO et l'Organisation des Nations Unies et en conformité avec la Charte des Nations Unies. »« Article 32 Assistance internationale :

1. Une Partie peut demander au Comité une assistance internationale en faveur de biens culturels sous protection renforcée ainsi qu'une assistance pour l'élaboration, la mise au point ou l'application des lois, dispositions administratives et mesures visées à l'article 10.
2. Une partie au conflit qui n'est pas Partie au présent Protocole mais qui accepte et applique ses dispositions, comme prévu au paragraphe 2 de l'article 3, peut demander au Comité une assistance internationale appropriée.
3. Le Comité adopte des dispositions régissant la présentation des demandes d'assistance internationale et définit les formes que peut prendre cette assistance.
4. Les Parties sont encouragées à fournir toutes formes d'assistance technique, par l'intermédiaire du Comité, aux Parties ou parties au conflit qui en font la demande. »

66 Voir l'idée avancée par C. Bories, *Le patrimoine culturel en droit international*, Pedone, 2011, pp. 345-346.

le concept n'a pas été accepté dans la pratique internationale comme un titre juridique valable pour justifier l'usage des moyens militaires[67]. Il est évident que seul le système des interventions prévu par le droit de l'ONU pourrait justifier des actions militaires dans une situation de menace du patrimoine. Cette approche est soulignée par la règle décidée de l'article 22, paragraphe 5, du Deuxième Protocole de la Convention de La Haye de 1954. Du point de vue légal, une activité des Nations Unies ne paraît pas inconcevable car un danger pour l'héritage culturel et notamment pour l'héritage culturel religieux peut représenter une « menace contre la paix » au sens de l'article 39 de la Charte des Nations Unies[68]. La connexion entre l'héritage culturel religieux et les droits de l'homme établie *supra* pourrait éventuellement développer des effets sur le plan politique, de sorte que la justification d'une intervention de la part de la communauté internationale pourra devenir plus convaincante.

Des obligations positives des Etats, agissant à titre individuel, peuvent en outre s'imposer par la voie de la dimension positive des droits de l'homme et aller au-delà des obligations restrictives des conventions. En ce qui concerne la sauvegarde *in situ*, les limites de l'application territoriale sont déterminantes[69] qui, normalement, s'opposeront à une intervention de la part des Etats tiers. Cela se trouve confirmé par l'article 22, paragraphe 2, du Deuxième Protocole de la Convention de La Haye de 1954 qui exclut toute situation de « tensions internes » ou de « troubles intérieurs » de son champ d'application. Néanmoins, le fait qu'il s'agisse d'une question de droits de l'homme protégés par le droit international place les manquements étatiques hors du domaine purement interne même s'il ne s'agit pas des biens culturels qui font déjà l'objet d'une convention spécifique. Il est de plus concevable que, par le truchement des droits de l'homme, la protection du patrimoine culturel religieux devienne une obligation *erga omnes*[70].

67 Voir L. Boisson de Chazournes, L. Condorelli, « De la 'responsabilité de protéger', ou d'une nouvelle parure pour une notion déjà bien établie », *RGDIP*, 2006, p. 11 ; P. Hilpold, « The Duty to Protect and the Reform of the United Nations – A New Step in the Development of International Law? », *MPUNYB*, 10 (2006), p. 35.

68 La menace peut également se présenter sous la forme d'une « agression armée » au sens de l'article 51 de la Charte ONU et donc déclencher le droit de légitime défense.

69 Voir sur ces limites en droit international, G. Giacca, *Economic, Social, and Cultural Rights in Armed Conflict*, Oxford University Press, 2014, pp. 108 ss. ; F. Sudre, *Droit européen et international des droits de l'homme*, *op. cit.*, § 209.

70 Voir dans ce contexte, U. Leanza, « Il rafforzamento della tutela internazionale del patrimonio culturale in tempo di guerra nel nuovo diritto dei conflitti armati », in *Studi di diritto internazionale in onore di Gaetano Arangio-Ruiz*, Editoriale scientifica, tome III, 2004, pp. 2037, 2052-2053 ; pour les droits de l'homme, voir I. Bantekas, L. Oette, *International Human Rights Law and Practice*, *op. cit.*, p. 70.

A part cela, une obligation de soutien qui commence par des aides financières, qui contienne un échange de savoir, qui renforce les capacités des pays et qui puisse même aboutir à une conception des zones de sécurité (« *safe haven* ») pour les biens culturels menacés semble possible et ajouterait une dimension concrète à la conception du patrimoine de l'humanité entière[71]. Certes, dans la situation actuelle, il paraît difficile de déduire une telle obligation directement du droit international général ou bien des droits de l'homme. Cependant, la dimension que les droits de l'homme ajoutent au droit contemporain de l'héritage culturel religieux est une raison forte pour avancer et, ainsi, développer des normes nouvelles et fiables afin de créer une responsabilité et un cadre juridique clairs pour les mesures de soutien de la part des Etats tiers, ce qui améliorerait la protection de l'héritage culturel religieux partout dans le monde.

3.2.2 Les obligations des individus et l'impact du droit international pénal

En comparaison avec les engagements internationaux des États, il est encore plus difficile d'établir des obligations pour des individus. Cela semble pourtant de plus en plus important à l'époque moderne où les frontières entre les branches étatiques et privées deviennent floues. Des acteurs privés menacent le patrimoine culturel de différentes manières qui ne sont guère moins redoutables que les mesures étatiques.

Parmi les menaces les plus évidentes dans le domaine de l'héritage culturel religieux figurent les atteintes pendant des conflits armés présentant ou non un caractère international. La destruction des bâtiments et la tentative d'éradiquer des traditions spirituelles dont les auteurs sont ou bien des organes étatiques ou bien des organisations terroristes et criminelles privées ou quasi étatiques se répètent avec une triste régularité. Les règles internationales établissant une responsabilité individuelle ne sont pas encore très efficaces. Il existe pourtant des exceptions importantes en droit pénal international[72]. Après la guerre en ex-Yougoslavie, le Tribunal pénal a condamné quelques-uns des responsables de destructions de biens culturels[73]. De façon

71 Voir également C. Bories, *Le patrimoine culturel en droit international*, *op. cit.*, pp. 316 ss.

72 Voir V. Mainetti, « De Nuremberg à La Haye : L'émergence des crimes contre la culture et la pratique des tribunaux internationaux », *in* V. Négri (dir.), *Le patrimoine culturel, cible des conflits armés*, *op. cit.*, p. 151 ; C. Ehlert, *Prosecuting the Destruction of Cultural Property in International Criminal Law. With a Case Study on the Khmer Rouge's Destruction of Cambodia's Heritage*, Martinus Nijhoff, 2014.

73 Pour les cas du Tribunal pénal international pour l'ex-Yougoslavie, voir G.D. Solis, *The Law of Armed Conflict. International Humanitarian Law in War*, Cambridge University Press, 2ème éd., 2016, pp. 724-731.

plus englobante, l'article 8 du Statut de Rome de la Cour pénale internationale définit comme crime de guerre « [l]e fait de diriger intentionnellement des attaques contre des bâtiments consacrés à la religion, à l'enseignement, à l'art, à la science [… et contre] des monuments historiques ». De cette manière, la norme met les atteintes à l'héritage culturel et religieux sur le même plan que les atteintes aux hôpitaux et aux lieux de soin pour des malades ou des blessés. La pertinence de cette norme a été récemment confirmée dans l'affaire *Al-Mahdi*[74]. La Cour pénale internationale a condamné à neuf ans d'emprisonnement un terroriste qui était responsable pour la destruction de dix lieux religieux à Tombouctou. Il ne paraît pas exclu d'étendre la répression pénale internationale à la destruction du patrimoine culturel religieux en temps de paix si, par une lecture inspirée des droits de l'homme, on peut la considérer comme une persécution représentant un crime contre l'humanité au sens de l'article 7 du Statut de Rome.

A part les dispositions du droit international pénal, il incombe aux Etats de prévoir des règles qui soient suffisamment efficaces pour prévenir des dommages irréparables au patrimoine culturel religieux. Cela comprend des normes de droit criminel interne pour des individus comme le prescrit l'article 15, paragraphe 2, du Deuxième Protocole de la Convention de La Haye de 1954 pour les infractions commises pendant des conflits armés.

Dans cette relation, l'influence du droit international est plutôt indirecte mais pas forcément moins importante. D'une part, il oblige les Etats à agir et traite une omission comme une infraction. D'autre part, si le droit international établit un lien étroit entre la sauvegarde du patrimoine matériel et immatériel religieux et les droits de l'homme suprêmes – comme la liberté religieuse, les droits de la personnalité et, en fin de compte, la dignité humaine –, il prédétermine en même temps la valeur juridique éminente de celui-là. Une conviction religieuse ou idéologique divergente ou la conception d'une liberté négative de religion ne peut jamais justifier, en droit international, la destruction ou l'éradication d'un patrimoine culturel religieux d'un autre groupe ou d'une autre communauté. C'est une des leçons majeures de la décision *Al-Mahdi* même si elle n'établit pas – et ne pouvait pas forcément établir – de manière expresse une relation entre le droit international pénal et les droits de l'homme. Les seules limites légitimes pour l'héritage culturel religieux sont donc les droits fondamentaux de l'individu qui sont protégés par le droit international même

74 CPI, 27 sept. 2016, n° ICC-01/12-01/15, *Le Procureur c. Ahmad Faqi Al-Mahdi*, Jugement portant condamnation ; 17 août 2017, n° ICC-01/12-01/15, *Le Procureur c. Ahmad Faqi Al-Mahdi*, Ordonnance de réparation.

envers les coutumes traditionnelles, mais qui ne justifient pas une lutte disproportionnée contre le patrimoine spirituel entier[75].

4 Conclusions

Il résulte clairement de ce parcours bref du droit international que, bien qu'il existe des mécanismes de protection, ceux-ci ne sont pas de nature à résoudre tous les problèmes contemporains du patrimoine culturel. En premier lieu, ce sont les règles positives du droit international, et notamment celles des conventions, qui sont défaillantes parce qu'elles sont à la fois trop étriquées pour ce qui est de leur champ d'application et trop faibles pour ce qui concerne leur mise en œuvre. Enserrées dans de nombreuses limites, elles ne sont guère adaptées à garantir une sauvegarde fiable du patrimoine. En tant que protecteur de l'héritage culturel religieux, le droit international contemporain ne montre pas seulement des faiblesses dans les situations extrêmes comme dans les conflits armés nationaux et internationaux ; il n'est pas non plus en mesure d'assurer que les Etats accomplissent leurs obligations en ce qui concerne la sauvegarde du patrimoine matériel et immatériel en temps de paix[76]. Les mécanismes exécutoires des conventions de l'UNESCO sont si faibles qu'ils n'ont même pas pu prévenir des infractions de la part d'Etats membres qui n'ont pourtant pas une attitude hostile envers des obligations internationales. Le droit de la protection des biens culturels est peut-être exemplaire d'un problème basique et insoluble : l'exécution du droit international.

Néanmoins, c'est au niveau des obligations des Etats dans les conventions où il faut commencer pour améliorer le système de protection de l'héritage culturel et religieux. Bien que les mécanismes de contrôle de la mise en œuvre revêtent une faiblesse structurelle, la force protectrice des normes serait accrue si elles étaient à la fois plus exactes et plus larges dans leur champ d'application. Cela regarde la discussion sur l'établissement des « sphères de sécurité » pour les biens culturels pendant les temps de crise aussi bien que

75 Dans ces cas, il incombe aux Etats de protéger la liberté religieuse individuelle, mais également de prévenir des atteintes exagérées contre la religion elle-même. Voir, dans le contexte européen, CEDH, 20 sept. 1994, nº 13470/87, *Otto-Preminger-Institut c. Autriche*, § 47 ; J.-F. Renucci, *Droit européen des droits de l'homme*, *op. cit.*, § 206 ; I. Bantekas, L. Oette, *International Human Rights Law and Practice*, *op. cit.*, p. 394.

76 Voir, sur les différents besoins de protection des biens culturels matériels et immatériels, L. Lankarani, « La notion de dispersion en droit international des patrimoines culturels (immatériel, naturel et mondial) », *JDI*, 2011, p. 283.

l'amélioration de la protection de l'héritage immatériel. Pourtant, il ne faut pas ignorer que la situation actuelle du droit international et des relations internationales ne s'avère pas très favorable à la conclusion de nouveaux accords établissant un système cohérent d'obligations étatiques dans cette matière.

Néanmoins, il n'est pas admissible de s'arrêter devant une telle constatation. Comme il a été démontré, l'héritage culturel religieux a une signification éminente pour l'exercice des droits fondamentaux. Il faut donc rechercher les chemins les plus prometteurs en matière de droit international pour protéger le patrimoine culturel religieux et pour identifier les instruments à améliorer afin d'arriver à une protection plus efficace. Le renforcement des institutions internationales et des fonds monétaires pour aider les Etats en crise à préserver leurs trésors est sûrement une possibilité viable. De même, il est souvent nécessaire d'améliorer les structures nationales avec l'aide internationale. Toutefois, cela ne résout qu'une partie des problèmes et a ses limites comme le montrent différents exemples où une négligence de la part de l'Etat est à l'origine d'une détérioration de la situation du patrimoine. Trop souvent, une omission ou une faute dans le droit interne empêche l'Etat d'honorer ses obligations internationales.

Une voie alternative, qui a pourtant aussi ses limites, pourrait consister en l'extension de la responsabilité individuelle par le droit international. Dans l'état de droit actuel, cette approche paraît seulement possible dans le contexte du droit international pénal et donc en premier lieu dans les situations des conflits armés. Néanmoins, la décision *Al-Mahdi* de la Cour pénale internationale représente un pas important dans la direction d'une protection efficace des biens culturels en temps de guerre. Elle se justifie par les règles détaillées du Statut de la Cour qui certes ne sont pas identiques à ceux des tribunaux que le Conseil de sécurité des Nations Unies peut ériger[77]. Or, la décision de la Cour pénale internationale est de nature à influencer non seulement la jurisprudence des autres juridictions, mais aussi, par le biais de l'article 38, paragraphe 1, alinéa *d*, du Statut de la Cour internationale de Justice, le développement du droit international. Au surplus, la décision rappelle qu'il incombe aux Etats de créer des normes pénales efficaces pour les infractions contre le patrimoine culturel dans leur droit interne. Dans les situations de conflits armés qui, trop souvent, minent les règles et les mécanismes protecteurs du droit international, l'expansion de la responsabilité personnelle et criminelle est forcément le chemin le plus prometteur.

77 Voir CPI, 27 sept. 2016, nº ICC-01/12-01/15, *Le Procureur c. Ahmad Faqi Al-Mahdi*, Jugement portant condamnation, paragraphe 16.

Pour combler les lacunes dans le contexte de la protection internationale de l'héritage culturel religieux, l'approfondissement cohérent et systématique des relations entre l'héritage culturel et les droits de l'homme paraît inévitable. Tous les deux sont indivisibles : rendre plus efficace la protection de l'héritage culturel signifie également protéger les droits de l'homme. Il semble donc être cohérent d'appliquer les concepts des obligations positives des États. Cela amènerait à développer une obligation fondée sur les droits fondamentaux internationaux de prendre des mesures positives efficaces pour protéger l'héritage culturel religieux. La communauté internationale aussi bien que les Etats eux-mêmes seraient appelés à veiller sur ce droit spécifique comme sur les droits de l'homme internationalement protégés en général et ils ne s'y heurteraient pas au principe de l'interdiction d'intervenir dans les affaires internes. Au contraire, le lien entre les droits fondamentaux internationaux et le patrimoine culturel, que les traités déclarent comme celui de l'humanité entière[78], nécessite des mesures positives également de la part de la communauté internationale. C'est juste la combinaison des deux bases juridiques qui mène à une véritable responsabilité internationale. Les règles et les conditions précises pourtant, attendent toujours d'être écrites, la pratique internationale quant à elle étant faible.

Le résultat général est donc ambigu. Malgré toutes les tentatives bien intentionnées, la protection internationale de l'héritage culturel reste une tâche difficile, en apparence quasi insurmontable. L'internationaliste ressemble donc un peu à Sisyphe. Mais, comme nous tous le savons, celui-ci est un homme heureux[79].

---

78 Voir notamment les préambules des Conventions de l'UNESCO de 1972 sur la protection du patrimoine mondial culturel et naturel et de 2003 sur la sauvegarde du patrimoine culturel immatériel.

79 A. Camus, *Le mythe de Sisyphe*, 1942 : « La lutte elle-même vers les sommets suffit à remplir un cœur d'homme. Il faut imaginer Sisyphe heureux. »

PART 5

Religious Beliefs and Freedom of Expression

CHAPTER 11

Blasphemy and Hate Speech: Clarifications of International Human Rights Law Standards

Eleni Polymenopoulou

1 Introduction

Controversies such as the publication of the cartoons mocking the Prophet by the Danish journal *Jyllands Posten* in 2006, as well as the bloodshed in the *Charlie Hebdo* offices in Paris in early 2015 sparked immense reactions by the public. The incidents were followed by increased philosophical and political turmoil and discussion in different media platforms. For a while, the world seemed split in two: those *who were Charlies* and those who *were not* – in other words, those in favour and those against publication of religiously offensive speech.

Law held only a minimal part of these debates. International human rights standards in particular, albeit pertinent, have been generally overshadowed by questions of an ethical and socio-political nature, including questions of religious tolerance, the rise of extremism, multicultural policies and the role of the arts in contemporary societies. What one may naturally wonder therefore is whether a legal response, apart from being an indicator of a society's social standards, is actually useful in providing remedies to such situations – as well as preventing them from happening in the future.

The answer to this question is positive. Law does offer solutions to complex situations, and does so in its very prestigious role of a 'regulator' of human behaviour. This however does not entail that these solutions may be offered at a normative or legislative level. As long as one accepts that most rights may be limited in some situations, and that not only 'sticks and stones' but equally words may break bones, a consideration of the concrete facts of each distinct case is always necessary. Terminology issues, exceptions and tests such as 'necessity' and 'proportionality', along with core values of liberal and democratic societies, including human dignity and pluralism, are all part of the vocabulary of the Judge who is called to decide on a specific case: should a society tolerate one or the other form of speech? Is it legitimate under international human rights law to allow prosecutions or even civil claims against the authors of a blasphemous work – be it a novel, or an artwork? Or on the

 | DOI:10.1163/9789004349155_012

contrary, be it that expression (perhaps in particular artistic freedom) should be free from all limitations? This chapter attempts to answer these questions, focusing on the 'grey area' between blasphemy and hate speech. It seeks to clarify the legitimate limits of expression that may be offending to either the divine or a specific segment of the population under the current interpretation of international human rights standards. In the view of providing a clear overview on the protection of such speech, it examines the approach of universal human rights bodies, such as the Human Rights Committee and the Committee on Elimination of Racial Discrimination ('CERD'). The chapter however does not address all possible solutions to a 'clash' between expression and religions. National and regional approaches to the matter in particular including the jurisprudence of the European Court of Human Rights and that of the Inter-American Court of Human Rights fall outside its scope. Likewise, spiritual and religious approaches to the topic of blasphemy, including religious offences under Islamic law (*Sharia*) as well as Muslim state practices, are not part of the analysis.[1]

The chapter is divided in two parts. In the first part, it discusses the international legal framework, with a particular focus on international mechanisms and standards set by the relevant UN instruments and Committees. In the second part, it explains challenges related to the enforcement of those standards, providing relevant illustrations from United Nations' ('UN') debates.

2 International Standards on Freedom of Speech, Hate Speech and Blasphemy

2.1 *Standards set by the ICCPR and the ICERD*

At the international level, freedom of expression is guaranteed by the 'International Covenant on Civil and Political Rights' ('ICCPR'). Article 19 paragraph 2 of the ICCPR specifies that protection encompasses all kinds of expression,[2] while article 20 provides for restricting grounds, prohibiting 'propaganda of war' and obliging States to impose laws banning 'any advocacy of

1 But see Irmgard Marboe, 'Freedom of Expression – Theory and Practice in the Islamic Realm', in this volume, chapter 12.

2 Article 19 paragraph 2 provides that the right to freedom of expression 'shall include freedom to seek, receive and impart information and ideas of all kinds, regardless of frontiers, either orally, in writing or in print, in the form of art, or through any other media of his choice'.

national, racial or religious hatred that constitutes incitement to discrimination, hostility or violence'.[3] A similar provision that compels States to legislate on the matter of hate speech exists also in article 4 (a) of the International Convention on the Elimination of All Forms of Racial Discrimination ('ICERD') that prohibits 'all dissemination of ideas based on racial superiority or hatred' as well as any 'incitement to racial discrimination' and 'all acts of violence or incitement to such acts'. [4]

Both provisions therefore (article 4 of the ICERD and article 20 of the ICCPR) are applicable in hate speech matters. Yet, they set distinct conditions in the determination of what constitutes impugned speech. The most obvious differences are the following two. First, hate speech that is not linked to 'discrimination, hostility or violence' may be outlawed by the ICERD but not under the ICCPR. Second, religious hate speech (as long as it incites to violence and discrimination) is punishable under the ICCPR but not under the ICERD. Hence cartoons that would be published in a wide-circulation magazine portraying the Prophet as a terrorist for instance (as those published in Jyllands Posten in 2005 and in Charlie Hebdo in 2015), while not punishable by law under the ICERD, would be most likely breaching ICCPR standards. The reason would not be that the cartoons are 'derogatory or blasphemous to Islam' (in terms of international human rights law this would obviously be an invalid point).[5] but rather, that they advance publicly the view that all Muslims are related in one way or another to terrorism, therefore inciting the public to 'discrimination, hostility or violence' against them.

In contrast, the ICERD leaves religious discrimination, intolerance and hatred outside its protective scope. The general stance of the ICERD Committee ('CERD') on the matter to date has typically been to punish discrimination and intolerance against religious minorities only when 'intersectionality' is

3 Article 20 of the ICCPR provides that '[a]ny propaganda for war … [and a]ny advocacy of national, racial or religious hatred that constitutes incitement to discrimination, hostility or violence shall be prohibited by law'.

4 Article 4 (a) of the ICERD provides that 'States parties … (a) shall declare an offence punishable by law all dissemination of ideas based on racial superiority or hatred, incitement to racial discrimination, as well as all acts of violence or incitement to such acts against any race or group of persons of another colour or ethnic origin, and also the provision of any assistance to racist activities, including the financing thereof'.

5 See eg Article19, *Response to publication of Charlie Hebdo cartoons and distribution of Innocence of Muslims video,* (*Article19*, 20 September 2012) <https://www.article19.org/resources/article-19-response-publication-charlie-hebdo-cartoons-distribution-innocence-muslims-video/> accessed 30 May 2017.

demonstrated, protecting therefore religious minorities only insofar as they identify as *both* religious *and* racial. This would be 'double' or 'aggravated' discrimination according to the Committee.[6]

2.1.1 Largo Sensu Approach to 'Race'

Two recent trends have had an impact on this situation, amounting to a certain conflation between the notions of race and religion. The first is the *largo sensu* approach to the notion of race, including the pressing claims to include religious minorities (specifically Muslim minorities) within the protective scope of the ICERD. This has been most visible in the 2002 recommendation of the Council of Europe's 'European Commission against Racism and Intolerance' (ECRI) in which religious discrimination is included among the grounds indicating racism, as well as the more recent work of the CERD.[7] It is also precisely why there needs to be 'a more concentrated debate on what our laws on freedom of expression are designed to achieve', as Keane points out.[8] The second is the interpretation of current human rights standards posed by the ICERD in

6 On 'intersectionalities' between race, gender and religion see generally, see Patrick Thornberry, *The International Convention on the Elimination of All Forms of Racial Discrimination: A Commentary* (OUP 2016), chapter 6. Also, Nazila Ghanea, 'Intersectionality and the spectrum of racist hate speech: Proposals to the UN Committee on the Elimination of Racial Discrimination' (2013) 35 Human Rights Quarterly 935; Nazila Ghanea, 'Religious or Minority? Examining the Realisation of International Stadards in Relation to Religious Minorities in the Middle East' (2008) 36 Religion, State and Society 303; David Keane, 'Addressing the Aggravated Meeting Points of Race and Religion' (2006) 6 University of Maryland Law Journal of Race, Religion, Gender and Class 367, 367 (fn 2) and 370 (citing Abdelfattah Amor and arguing that 'ICERD represents the primary legal basis for addressing aggravated discrimination'); Patrick Thornberry, 'Confronting Racial Discrimination: A CERD Perspective' (2005) 5 Human Rights Law Review 239, 258–59; Stephanie Berry, 'Bringing Muslim Minorities within the International Convention on the Elimination of All Forms of Racial Discrimination: Square Peg in a Round Hole?' (2011) 11 Human Rights Law Review 423, 431 (citing several CERD monitoring State reports observing the rise of 'Islamophobia' in Northern European states).

7 ECRI, General policy recommendation no 7 on national legislation to combat racism and racial discrimination, 13 December 2002, CRI(2003)8, p 5: '"racism" shall mean the belief that a ground such as race, colour, language, religion, nationality or national or ethnic origin justifies contempt for a person or a group of persons, or the notion of superiority of a person or a group of persons' (footnote omitted). Also, Berry (n 6) 423; Thornberry, (n 5) 259 (noting already in 2005 that 'the Committee may in future need to engage in specifically focused work on the religion/race intersection, especially in light of phenomena of Islamophobia ...').

8 David Keane, 'Cartoon Violence and Freedom of Expression' (2008) 30 Human Rights Quarterly 845, 875.

a way that encompasses religious discrimination. This would recompense for the absence of a Convention encompassing *religious intolerance*.[9] By way of indication, the five experts of the HRC Intergovernmental Working Group on the effective implementation of the Durban Declaration and Programme of Action, back in 2007 considered that international standards are a priori adequate and sufficient to combat *religious* hate speech.[10] In contrast, in its 2015 session, the HRC 'Ad Hoc Committee on the Elaboration of Complementary Standards' accepted – although not without debate – that additional standards are needed.[11]

In practice, the question of the intersection between race and religion is extremely complex. Hence, although incidents of religious hatred (especially anti-Semitic) have contributed to the inception of the ICERD,[12] the protection of religious minorities still lacks explicit legal basis in the that instrument.[13] In addition, many States have not exactly embraced hate speech standards posed by the ICCPR and the ICERD. The declarations and reservations to both instruments are indicative – to date seventeen in respect of article 20 of the ICCPR and nineteen as regards article 4 of the ICERD. These declarations and reservations do not only emanate from States that typically do not accept any

---

9 On the drafting history of the ICERD and the abandoning of the idea of the 'Religion' Convention (initiated along the Race Convention), see Keane, 'Aggravated Meeting Points of Race and Religion' (n 6) 386ff citing also Donna Sullivan, 'Advancing the Freedom of Religion or Belief through the UN Declaration on the Elimination of Religious Intolerance and Discrimination' (1988) 82 American Journal of International Law 487; generally, David Keane & Annapurna Waughray (eds), *50 Years of the International Convention on the Elimination of All Forms of Racial Discrimination 1965: A Living Instrument* (Manchester University Press, 2017); Natan Lerner, *The UN Convention on the Elimination of All Forms of Racial Discrimination* (Brill 2014).

10 Intergovernmental Working Group on the effective implementation of the Durban Declaration and Programme of Action (established by Commission on Human Rights resolution 2002/68), *Report on the study by the five experts on the content and scope of substantive gaps in the existing international instruments to combat racism, racial discrimination, xenophobia and related* intolerance, 27 August 2007, UN Doc A/HRC/4/WG.3/6P 39, para 130 (discussing religious intolerance and hate after 9/11).

11 Ad Hoc Committee on the Elaboration of Complementary Standards, 'Racism, racial discrimination, xenophobia and related forms of intolerance: follow-up to and implementation of the Durban Declaration and Programme of Action', 30 January 2015, UN Doc A/HRC/28/81, para 143.

12 Lerner (n 9); Keane 'Cartoon Violence and Freedom of Expression'(n 8).

13 See however Keane, 'Aggravated Meeting Points of Race and Religion' (n 6) arguing that this legal basis could be article 5 of the ICERD.

obligations whatsoever,[14] but also from States that refuse to lower their freedom of expression standards (Finland);[15] those that consider that the limitation of speech for reasons of 'public order' are adequate (Australia and the UK); or simply that additional anti-discrimination legislation is not necessary (France).

2.1.2 Protection against 'Latent Racism'

Religious hate speech set aside, on all other counts the ICERD imposes a threshold of restrictions much higher than that of the ICCPR. This is because, first, it applies to all *ideas* rather than to *advocacy* – suffices therefore their mere dissemination. Second, there is no need to establish the linkage with 'discrimination, hostility or violence' as in the ICCPR. Third, for a complaint to reach the CERD, there is no strict requirement that each individual belonging to a racial or ethnic group establishes that they are a victim of hate speech, neither that the violation is already happening. Organizations therefore, have also standing before the CERD, and this even in the case of their 'potential victimhood', as otherwise according to the CERD 'the reference to 'groups of individuals' would be [rendered] meaningless'.[16]

This means that ideas and any form of expression should be punished not only when they are publically and obviously discriminating, or inciting to racist crimes,[17] but also when generally enhancing negative or diminishing stereotypes, and this even when expressed in private or to a small public. Ideas expressed in racist jokes, films or cartoons for instance, rather than

14 The US for instance 'does not accept any obligation under [the ICERD], in particular under articles 4 and 7 to restrict' individual freedom of speech, expression and association and declares that 'article 20 [ICCPR] does not authorize or require legislation or other action by the United States that would restrict the right of free speech and association'. See UN treaty collection, *Declarations and Reservations to the ICCPR,* available at https://treaties.un.org/pages/ViewDetails.aspx?src=TREATY&mtdsg_no=IV-4&chapter=4&clang=_en (ICCPR) and https://treaties.un.org/Pages/ViewDetails.aspx?src=TREATY&mtdsg_no=IV-2-a&chapter=4&clang=_en (ICERD).

15 The hesitation of States vis-à-vis the limits imposed by the ICERD may be also seen in the reference to the (freedom of expression provisions) of the Universal Declaration within the text of article 4 of the ICERD.

16 Eg CERD, *The Jewish Community of Oslo et al v Norway* [2005] Communication no 30/2003, UN Doc CERD/C/67/D/30/2003, para 7.4 and 8.4 (case in which the Norwegian Supreme court found that the penalization of approval of Nazism would be incompatible with freedom of speech standards).

17 Eg CERD, *Mohammed Hassan Gelle v Denmark* [2006] Communication no 34/2004, UN Doc CERD/C/68/D/34/2004.

merely considered as 'bad humour' could be punishable under the ICERD. For instance, the ICERD standards, general assertions such as 'Arab and Turkish populations do not integrate themselves' and 'the Turks are conquering Germany ... through a higher birth rate' could give rise to a prosecution: in a 2013 case, concerning an interview with former right-wing politician, Mr. Sarrazin, that was published in a medium-circulation magazine in Germany and contained claims against the integration of Turkish and Arab populations,[18] the Committee found a violation of the ICERD. More specifically, it found that this type of speech was 'impugned speech' under article 4 (a), which enhanced racial prejudice and referred to an identifiable group of ethnic origin 'in a derogatory and discriminatory' way;[19] and that the responding State ought to have undertaken an effective investigation as to whether such ideas 'amounted to dissemination of ideas based upon racial superiority or hatred'.[20] It therefore embraced the view of the petitioners, according to whom this type of expression was 'latent racism'[21] which ought to be outlawed in liberal societies.

By the same token, a cartoon representing the Italian earthquake victims as 'pasta dishes',[22] or a survey that would represent the Greeks as silly and lazy,[23] could also be considered a type of expression that could be give rise to a successful prosecution by national authorities according to the ICERD – provided of course that one can prove that such types of expression refer to these populations in a 'derogatory and discriminatory' way.

---

18 CERD, *TBB-Turkish Union in Berlin/Brandenburg v Germany* [2013] Communication no 48/2010 UN Doc CERD/C/82/D/48/2010, paras 7.1–8.3 (attacked under article 4 (a) of the ICERD by members of a Turkish Union of Berlin). For case law of the committee prior 2011, see Berry (n 6).

19 *TBB-Turkish Union in Berlin/Brandenburg* (n 18) para 2.1.

20 ibid, para 12.7–12.8.

21 ibid, para 4.5.

22 Rozina Sini, 'Charlie Hebdo Italy earthquake cartoon sparks anger' (*BBC news*, 2 September 2016) <www.bbc.com/news/world-europe-37260217> accessed 30 May 2017.

23 By way of illustration, see Alex Andreou, 'Exploding the myth of the feckless, lazy Greeks' (*Newstatesman*, 18 May 2012) <www.newstatesman.com/blogs/world-affairs/2012/05/exploding-myth-feckless-lazy-greeks> accessed 18 October 2016; J.S., 'Stereotypes of Europe: Greeks say they are the hardest-working European nation' (*The Economist*, 30 May 2012) <www.economist.com/blogs/graphicdetail/2012/05/greeks-say-they-are-hardest-working-european-nation?fb_ref=scn/fb_ec/stereotypes_of_europe&fb_source=home_multiline> accessed 18 October 2016.

2.2 *Protection of Religious Beliefs against Offences?*

2.2.1 Impossibility of a Prêt-a-Porter Solution

It follows from the analysis above that protection against hate speech including religious intolerance and hatred goes uncontested in international human rights law. The protection of religious sensibilities against offences however does not. Contrary to hate speech, there is nothing explicit in the ICCPR or the ICERD or any other international instrument that allows to give a forthright 'yes or no' answer to the question of allowing the offence of religious beliefs to be or not be considered a legitimate breach of freedom of speech. Only minimal soft law exists on the matter. For instance, the conclusions of the Rabat plan of action, adopted following an expert meeting initiated by the OHCHR in 2012,[24] provides that 'under international human rights standards ... expression labelled as "hate speech" can be restricted [*inter alia*] under article 18 and 19 of the ICCPR', i.e. the religious freedom provision of the ICCPR.[25] Blasphemy in particular, an offence rooted in the Ancient testament and heired also to classical Islam, has found its way in law through States' religious traditions and identities. Blasphemy laws and other offences that entail criminal punishment therefore are endorsed in approximately one third of the UN member States – although a minority among Council of Europe member states.[26] Specifically in the Muslim world there exists a general religious obligation not to challenge Sharia law, which is enforced by religious courts to Muslims and non-Muslims alike.[27] Likewise, they are common in African and Asian States as well as in

---

24 By way of illustration, see OHCHR 'Expert seminar on the links between articles 19 and 20 of the International Covenant on Civil and Political Rights', Geneva, 2–3 October 2008.

25 *Rabat Plan of Action on the prohibition of advocacy of national, racial or religious hatred that constitutes incitement to discrimination, hostility or violence,* Conclusions and recommendations emanating from the four regional expert workshops organised by OHCHR and adopted by experts in Rabat, Morocco (2012) para 14.

26 European Commission For Democracy Through Law (Venice Commission), *On The Relationship Between Freedom Of Expression And Freedom Of Religion: The Issue Of Regulation And Prosecution Of Blasphemy, Religious Insult And Incitement To Religious Hatred*, Strasbourg, 23 October 2008, CDL-AD(2008)026, at 8 (noting that 'blasphemy is an offence in only a minority of member States: Austria, Denmark, Finland, Greece, Italy, Liechtenstein, the Netherlands, San Marino').

27 See, Eleni Polymenopoulou, 'A Thousand Ways to Kiss the Earth: Artistic Freedom, Cultural Heritage and Islamic Extremism' (2015) 17 Rutgers Journal of Law and Religion 39, 61–62; Intisar Rabb, 'Negotiating Speech in Islamic Law and Politics' in Anver Emon et al (eds), *Islamic law and international human rights law* (OUP 2012) 146ff; Kamran Hashemi, *Religious legal traditions, international human rights law and Muslim states* (Brill 2008) 31; and generally Abdullah Saeed and Hassan Saeed, *Freedom of religion, apostasy and Islam* (Routledge 2004) 37f.

the so-called Western world, particularly in States where religion holds a powerful status in the public sphere. In those cases, punishments are perhaps not as severe as in Sharia compliant States, but still harsh and active.[28] By way of illustration, in Greece, blasphemy is a criminal offence punished by three years of imprisonment and to date actively prosecuted.[29]

The extent to which blasphemy is considered problematic for one or another national order is certainly different. As Parliamentary Assembly of the Council of Europe ('PACE') Resolution 1510 stipulates, 'what is likely to cause substantial offence to persons of a particular religious persuasion will vary significantly from time to time and from place to place'.[30] Two situations may be distinguished here. The first situation arises by accepting that blasphemy laws (or other national laws prohibiting insults and lack of reverence to a certain religion) are part of a State's public morality or public order. Indeed, article 19 paragraph 3 of the ICCPR poses numerous limitations to freedom of expression, allowing this freedom to be balanced against other rights and public interests, including on the grounds of offence to public morals.[31] This is especially true in those States that maintain an official religion. As Cox puts it, when religion is 'inextricably linked with a nation's public morality, then it is difficult to see why this justification for restricting speech could not apply, at least in theory, to "irreligious" speech'.[32]

The second situation arises when religious freedom (an already 'broad' right, encompassing the protection of 'theistic, non-theistic and atheistic beliefs, as well as the right not to profess any religion or belief' and 'not limited in its application to traditional religions or to religions and beliefs with institutional characteristics'),[33] is interpreted in a way that includes a 'negative' protection

28 Eg Article 282 of the Greek Criminal Code (providing for punishments of 3 years of imprisonment).

29 Article 182 of the Greek Criminal Code. Eg, Hellenic Ligue of Human Rights, 'Arrest of a 27 year old for mocking a late monk of the Greek Orthodox Church', 2012, <www.hlhr.gr/en/arrest-27-year-mocking-late-monk-greek-orthodox-church/> accessed 29 October 2016.

30 PACE Resolution 1510 (2006) *on Freedom of expression and respect for religious beliefs*, para 11.

31 Article 19 paragraph 3 provides that '[t]he exercise of [the right to freedom of expression] carries with it special duties and responsibilities. It may therefore be subject to certain restrictions, but these shall only be such as are provided by law and are necessary. (a) For respect of the rights or reputations of others; (b) For the protection of national security or of public order (ordre public), or of public health or morals'.

32 Neville Cox, 'Irreligious beliefs' (2016) 16 Human Rights Law Review 195, 203.

33 Human Rights Committee, General comment 22, *The right to freedom of thought, conscience and religion* (Art. 18) 48th session, 1993, UN Doc CCPR/C/21/Rev.1/Add.4, para 4.

against offences of one's sensibilities. Religious freedom in those cases would be perceived as an ultra-protective right that would serve as a limitation to freedom of expression under the 'right of others' limitative clause of article 19 paragraph 3 (which warrants that 'the exercise of [the right to freedom of expression] ... may be subject to certain restrictions ... for protection of the rights of others'). The right not to be offended would therefore stem directly from article 18 of the ICCPR on religious freedom, allowing therefore for a virtual 'clash' between freedom of expression and religious freedom.

2.2.2 The Approach of Human Rights Bodies

In some instances, the ECtHR has accepted that sensibilities may by protected under article 9 of the European Convention on Human Rights. This approach of the Court has not gone without criticism, and indeed has raised fierce doctrinal debates.[34] Hence, while maintaining on numerous occasions that pluralism, broadmindedness and tolerance are hallmarks of a democratic society; that freedom of expression encompasses opinions that 'offend, shock or disturb the State or any sector of the population',[35] and that all restrictions to freedom of expression ought be construed *narrowly* and in accordance with the principle of proportionality; [36] it has equally found that 'an obligation to avoid as far as possible expressions that are gratuitously offensive to others ... and which therefore do not contribute to any form of public debate capable of furthering progress in human affairs'.[37] Consequently, and as a matter of principle, in the view of the Court 'it may be considered necessary to punish improper attacks on objects of religious veneration'.[38]

At the universal level – despite the fact that international instruments contain explicit hate speech restrictions – these views adopted by the European

34 By way of example, Ilias Trispiotis, 'The Duty to Respect Religious Feelings: Insights from European Human Rights Law' (2013) 19(3) Columbia Journal of European Law 499, 545 (arguing that bans against offensive speech are justified only when the link between the offence and public disorder are sufficiently clear); George Letsas, 'Is there a right not to be offended in one's religious beliefs' in Zucca and Ungureanu (eds), *Law, State and Religion in the new Europe: Debates and Dilemmas* (CUP 2012) 239–60 (finding that States should not value the protection of religious feelings as much as free speech).

35 *Handyside v UK* App no 5493/72, (1976) Series A no 24, para 49.

36 See by way of example, *Steel and Morris v UK* App no 68416/01 ECHR 2005-II 1, para 87; *Pedersen and Baadsgaard v Denmark* App no 49017/99 ECHR 2004-XI 105.

37 Eg *İ.A. v Turkey* App no 42571/98 ECHR 2005-VIII 235, para 24; *Otto-Preminger-Institut v Austria* App no 13470/87 (1994) Series A no 295-A, para 49; *Wingrove v UK* App no 17419/90 ECHR 1996-V, para 42.

38 *I.A. v Turkey* (n 37) para 24.

Court could only with difficulty be sustained. The UN Human Rights Committee has clarified in both its comments and jurisprudence that religious restrictions to freedom of expression are not legitimate, while even the banning of hate speech should be compatible with the strict 'tests' posed by article 19, ie legality, necessity and proportionality. More specifically, the Committee has found the protection afforded to freedom of expression in article 19 paragraph 2 to encompass speech that is 'deeply offensive', and equally, that the ICCPR hate speech provision (article 20) should always be read in conjunction with the strict conditions laid down in article 19 paragraph 3 of the ICCPR on freedom of expression.[39] In its last general comment on freedom of expression in particular, the Committee has flagged that 'since any restriction on freedom of expression constitutes a serious curtailment of human rights, it is not compatible with the Covenant for a restriction to be enshrined in traditional, religious or other such customary law'.[40] Similarly, and in relation to States maintaining an official religion or where religion holds a privileged status, it has noted that persons opposing it shall be free to exercise not only their religious freedom, but also their other rights granted by the ICCPR (including therefore the right to freedom of expression).[41] Likewise, the CERD's general comment no 35 on hate speech stipulates that, contrary to 'stereotyping and stigmatization of members of protected groups', 'criticism of religious leaders or commentary on religious doctrine or tenets of faith' should not be prohibited or punished.[42] And in a much more straightforward way, the Rabat outcome declaration, supported by the Office of the High Commissioner for Human Rights, has affirmed a 'right to criticise' and even ridicule a religion.[43]

---

39 Human Rights Committee, General Comment 11, *Prohibition of propaganda for war and inciting national, racial or religious hatred* (Art. 20), 19th session, 1983, para 2; Human Rights Committee, *Ross v Canada* [2000] Communication no 736/1997 UN Doc CCPR/C/70/D/736/1997; also generally, Jeroen Temperman, *Religious Hatred and International Law: The Prohibition of Incitement to violence and discrimination* (CUP 2015) and, Hannes Cannie and Dirk Voorhoof, 'Abuse clause and freedom of expression in the European Human Rights Convention: an added value for democracy and human rights protection?' (2011) 29 Netherlands Quarterly for Human Rights 54, 80.

40 Human Rights Committee, General comment 34, Freedoms of opinion and expression,(Art. 19), 102nd session 2011, UN Doc CCPR/C/GC/34, para 24.

41 ibid, para 10.

42 CERD, General recommendation 35, 83rd session, 2013 UN Doc CERD/C/GC/35, para 6.

43 Rabat plan of action (n 25) para 19.

3 Challenges Related to Enforcement of Freedom of Expression Standards

The permissibility of limitations against freedom of expression according to the ICCPR as well as the extraordinary variety and prevalence of national solutions to 'clashes' between religion and expression has had an impact on the enforcement of the international human rights standards on freedom of speech. Two examples may serve as illustrations of this observation. The first is the question of defining terns such as hate, incitement and advocacy. The second is the purely political debate that has taken place within the UN Human Rights Council and the UN General Assembly for a decade, known as the 'defamation of religions' debate.

3.1 *Blurry Limits between 'Incitement to Hatred' and Offences to Religious Beliefs*

At many instances the limits between offending one's beliefs and incitement to or advocacy of hatred (hate speech) are extremely blurry. In fact the content of both incitement to hatred and religious intolerance offences in national laws may differ substantially. This has an impact on the national implementation of international standards, inhibiting at the same time the task of the Judge, who is ultimately the one in position to rule on a specific case. As the Rabat outcome declaration flags

> the terminology relating to offences on incitement to national, racial or religious hatred varies in the different countries and is increasingly rather vague while new categories of restrictions or limitations to freedom of expression are being incorporated in national legislation ... The broader the definition of incitement to hatred is in domestic legislation, the more it opens the door for arbitrary application of these laws.[44]

The definition of 'hate speech' on the one hand stems from the relevant indications in article 20 of the ICCPR and 4 of the ICERD (that prohibit advocacy of hatred and incitement to hatred and discrimination respectively). In its general comment no 35, issued in 2013, the CERD notes that the 'lack of explicit reference [of the term hate speech in the ICERD] has not impeded the Committee from identifying and naming hate speech phenomena and exploring the relationship between speech practices and the standards of

44 Rabat plan of action (n 25) para 15.

the Convention'.[45] This however provides only superficial understanding of what 'hate' or 'incitement' or 'advocacy' may actually consist of. An additional attempt to clarify the term was undertaken in a series of workshops and expert seminars and meetings organized at the initiative of the Office of the High Commissioner for Human Rights (OHCHR) and with the participation of a number of NGOs.[46] One of the first meetings organized in 2009 at the initiative of the organization on freedom of expression ARTICLE 19 amounted to the *Camden Principles* on freedom of expression. These principles clarify that the terms 'hatred' and 'hostility' refer to 'intense and irrational emotions of opprobrium, enmity and detestation towards the target group'.[47] Likewise, at the same meeting it was suggested that 'the term "advocacy" is to be understood as requiring an intention to promote hatred publicly …'; and that 'incitement' refers to statements which create an imminent risk of discrimination, hostility or violence.[48] Drawing from the findings of these workshops, CERD's general comment no 35 also suggests definitions, for instance that 'incitement characteristically seeks to influence others to engage in certain forms of conduct, including the commission of crime, through advocacy or threats', taking in particular into account also 'the intention of the speaker, and the imminent risk or likelihood' as well as other elements.[49]

Definitions on blasphemy and religious defamation on the other hand are more ambiguous given that they concern a primarily religious offence – the prohibition of uttering certain words,[50] or in the largest sense, being disrespectful for religious scripts, persons and symbols.[51] The more relevant

45 CERD (n 42) para 6.

46 Final Expert Workshop on the Prohibition of Incitement to national, racial or religious hatred. See also, OHCHR, *Striking a balance between freedom of expression and the prohibition of incitement to hatred* 23 October 2012 <www.ohchr.org/EN/NewsEvents/Pages/Strikingabalancebetweenfreedomofexpression.aspx> accessed 19 October 2016.

47 ARTICLE_19, *The Camden Principles on Freedom of Expression and Equality, Principle 12: Incitement to hatred* (2009) section 1 (I–IV).

48 ibid. This latter suggestion was also the view of the Special Rapporteurs on religious freedom and the Special Rapporteurs on discrimination and intolerance. See the Report of the Special Rapporteur on freedom of religion or belief, Asma Jahangir, and the Special Rapporteur on contemporary forms of racism, racial discrimination, xenophobia and related intolerance, Doudou Diène, UN Doc A/HRC/2/3, 20 September 2006, para 47.

49 CERD (n 42) paras 15–16. See on this comment, Tarlach McGonagle, 'General Recommendation No. 35 on Combating Racist Hate Speech' in David Keane and Annapurna Waughray (n 9).

50 Dartevelle Patrice et al (eds), *Blasphèmes et libertés* (Cerf 1993) 11.

51 ibid 12.

formulation is that given by UN political bodies in the so-called 'defamation of religions' resolutions that will be discussed in the next section. Some of these resolutions define 'defamation of religions' as negative stereotyping of racial and religious groups, including also religious profiling and linking terrorism with Islam after 9/11. Others make a distinction between blasphemy and defamation,[52] although again, may associate 'defamation of religion' to other offences, such as attacks to religious symbols.[53] Many of them equally make the assumption that defamation of religions 'lead[s] to a restriction on the freedom of religion'.[54]

At many instances international bodies have attempted to clarify the link between 'defamation of religions' (i.e. blasphemy), hate speech and religious intolerance.[55] The PACE in particular has stipulated in a series of Resolution on freedom of expression and religious hatred that 'any democratic society must permit open debate on matters relating to religion and religious beliefs' and that 'blasphemy, as an insult to a religion, should not be deemed a criminal offence'.[56] In other words, taking offence for hurting one's religious feelings should not amount to the initiation of prosecutions, and a fortiori not to imprisonment as, in the wording of the Council of Europe's Committee of Ministers, 'the imposition of criminal sanctions generally constitutes a serious interference with' freedom of expression.[57] Virtually all human rights bodies have flagged up at one point or another that the right to freedom of expression is the rule and its limitations are only exceptional. This is not only the view of the ECtHR, as discussed above. The CERD too, in its general comment 35, provides for numerous 'exceptions' to incitement to hatred in favour of freedom of speech – considering for instance that 'the expression of ideas and opinions made in the context of academic debates, political engagement or similar activity, and without incitement to hatred, contempt, violence or

52 Eg HRC Res 13/16, 25 March 2010, UN Doc A/HRC/RES/13/16, at para 2, stating that Member States 'Expresses deep concern at the negative stereotyping and defamation of religions and manifestations of intolerance and discrimination'.

53 Eg Commission on Human Rights, Res 2005/3, UN Doc E/CN.4/RES/2005/3, paras 3–5.

54 Eg UN HRC Res 13/16 (n 52) Preamble.

55 See eg Defamation of religions and global efforts to combat racism: anti-Semitism, Christianophobia and Islamophobia UN Doc E/CN.4/2005/18/Add.4.

56 PACE, Resolution 1577 (2007) *on Blasphemy, religious insults and hate speech against persons on grounds of their religion* paras 2–4; likewise, Resolution 1510 (n 30) at 2.

57 Council of Europe (CoE) Committee of Ministers, *Recommendation No R (97) 20 on 'hate speech',* adopted on 30 October 1997, Principle 5.

discrimination, should be regarded as legitimate exercises of the right to freedom of expression, even when such ideas are controversial'.[58]

3.2 *The Defamation of Religions' Debate and its Ramifications on Freedom of Speech Standards*

Starting in 1999, at the initiative of Pakistan, the Organization of the Islamic Conference (an organization aligning 57 Muslim-majority States presided by Turkey and sieging in Jeddah, Saudi Arabia) has been pressuring to blur the limits between religious defamation and incitement to hatred. With this objective, a number of Human Rights Council ('HRC') and General Assembly ('GA') resolutions were voted on the prohibition of 'defamation of religions', specifically the defamation of Islam.[59] Part of the debate on religious defamation coincided with the two UN meetings and plans of action that the UN initiated in order to combat racism, xenophobia, intolerance and discrimination that took place in Durban, South Africa (Durban I and Durban II-Review Conference). It is in the first Durban Declaration (and Plan of Action) that the participant member states observed 'the emergence of increased negative stereotyping, hostile acts and violence against [religious] communities because of their religious beliefs and their ethnic or so-called racial origin',[60] attempting in a way to diminish the gap between racial and religious hatred in terms of international standards. This may also be the reason why they were initially given some legitimacy among non-OIC States (most of them were backed by all OIC member States, as well as by African, Asian and some Latin American member States).

A superficial reading of these resolutions would give the impression that they were a step forward in addressing these issues in multicultural societies. Their aim however was rather more alarming – namely to create an 'international offense for defaming or insulting Islam',[61] outlawing even the mere criticism of it.

58 CERD (n 42) para 25.

59 By way of illustration, see the last resolutions passed in 2009 and 2010: UNGA Res 64/156, UN Doc A/RES/64/156 (18 December 2009) 'Combating Defamation of Religions'; UN HRC Res 10/22 (26 March 2009) 'Combating Defamation of Religions', UN Doc A/HRC/RES/10/22; UNGA Res 65/224, UN Doc A/RES/65/224 (21 December 2010) 'Combating Defamation of Religions'; UN HRC Res 13/16, (n 52).

60 World Conference against Racism, Racial Discrimination, Xenophobia and Related Intolerance, Durban Declaration of 8 September 2001, UN Doc A/CONF.189/12, paras 59–60.

61 Javaid Rehman and Stephanie Berry, 'Is "Defamation of Religions" Passé? The United Nations, Organisation of Islamic Cooperation, and Islamic State Practices: Lessons From Pakistan' (2012) 44 George Washington International Law Review 431, 433.

Indeed, the intention to alter current human rights standards has been clear from the outset: first, all resolutions associate the 'defamation of religions' with Islam, 9/11 and the situation of Muslim minorities in particular in many parts of the world,[62] therefore blurring the notions of blasphemy and incitement to (religious) hatred. Second, the resolutions specifically instructed both Special Rapporteurs and the High Commissioner for Human Rights to report on the matter, but also, to examine the 'implications [of defamation of religions] for article 20, paragraph 2, of ICCPR'.[63] This would give leeway to national legislators in the view of maintaining the status of national blasphemy laws as criminal offences in the name of anti-hate speech laws, allowing violations against religious minorities to continue. Fortunately, from 2011 onwards and following the changes in the HRC leadership, no such resolution was passed.

It appears nonetheless that despite this shift at the international level, pressure from specific member States has continued.[64] In addition, the ramifications of the 'defamation of religions' debate may have had an impact on the approach of the treaty bodies towards the subject of blasphemy and the offence of sensibilities. The Human Rights Committee in particular has not yet fully clarified its stance vis-à-vis the legitimacy of blasphemy laws. In general comment 22 with respect to the interpretation of article 18 of the ICCPR (on freedom of thought, conscience or religion) it clarified that measures taken according to article 20 of the ICCPR (on hate speech) are 'important safeguards' against religious minorities violations.[65] In the following General Comment, however, on freedom of expression that was issued in 2011, the question of blasphemy appeared more challenging. The draft prepared by the Committee stipulates in a straightforward way that 'States parties should repeal criminal law provisions on blasphemy', adding also that this prohibition must be applied within the

62 See by way of example, UN HRC Res 13/16 (n 52), 'stressing the need to effectively combat defamation of all religions and incitement to religious hatred in general and against Islam and Muslims in particular'.

63 HRC Dec. 1/107 on incitement to racial and religious hatred and the promotion of tolerance and subsequent report A/HRC/2/3 (n 48) para 49.

64 UNGA Res 70/140, *A global call for concrete action for the total elimination of racism, racial discrimination, xenophobia and related* intolerance, 14 December 2015, UN Doc A/RES/70/140, para 5; UNGA Res 68/151, *Global efforts for the total elimination of racism, racial discrimination, xenophobia and related intolerance*, 18 December 2013, UN Doc A/RES/68/151, para 5. In contrast, see UN Resolution *United against racism, racial discrimination, xenophobia and related intolerance,* 16 September 2011, A/66/L.2. Also, Rehman and Berry (n 61).

65 Human Rights Committee (n 33) para 9.

limits to freedom of expression as set in Article 19 of the ICCPR.[66] The final text adopted however adopted a different formulation, providing for an exception to the permissibility of blasphemy laws in favour of hate speech: 'prohibitions of displays of lack of respect for a religion or other belief system, including blasphemy laws, are incompatible with the Covenant, except in the specific circumstances envisaged in article 20, paragraph 2, of the Covenant'.[67] This addition (which is also one found in the Camden Principles of 2011[68] but not in the subsequent Rabat plan of action) suggests that blasphemy laws, in the view of the Committee are compatible with the Covenant when they amount to hate speech. This situation could arise, for instance, when blasphemy is accompanied by negative stereotyping and profound reject of a religion – as in the case of the cartoons portraying the Prophet Mohammed as a terrorist, as in the case of the *Danish cartoons*. As a result, although legitimately the comment also notes that 'it would not be permissible for such prohibitions to be used to prevent or punish criticism of religious leaders or commentary on religious doctrine and tenets of faith',[69] there is no clear indication that blasphemy laws should be repealed. As a result, the confusion between hate speech, the offence of religious ideas and incitement to hatred against religious minorities remains.

4 Conclusion

The present chapter examined the fine line between blasphemy and hate speech. While it found that blasphemy laws are incompatible with human rights standards, it equally found that according to the current interpretation of human rights law by international bodies, expression may be legitimately restricted when offences related to religion breach hate speech standards. In addition, the chapter also discussed terminology issues that are crucial to the application and enforcement of human rights standards. In this respect it observed that there is no one acceptable definition of either hate speech or blasphemy. This means therefore first, that criticism of religion is *a priori* only

66 Human Rights Committee, Draft general comment 34, 25 January 2010, UN Doc CCPR/C/GC/34/CRP.5 para 50.

67 UN Human Rights Committee (n 40) para 48.

68 Camden Principles (n 47), Principle 12, under 12.3: 'States should not prohibit criticism directed at, or debate about, particular ideas, beliefs or ideologies, or religions or religious institutions, unless such expression constitutes hate speech as defined by Principle'.

69 Rabat plan of action (n 25) at para 23.

legitimate under international human rights law and second, that it ultimately falls upon the judiciary to decide on a specific case.

This however raises the issue of consistency among different orders (or even different international human rights bodies), a problem that is aggravated by the fact that religious defamation has been associated to Islamophobia and 'personal' offences, such as negative stereotyping of religious minorities.

Two solutions may be suggested therefore. The first refers to the clarification of human rights standards: there needs to be a distinction between criticism directed to a religious dogma as such (a criticism therefore of ideas), and criticism of the adherents of a religion, as a group (criticism therefore of persons). From the two categories, only the latter is in need of punishment. A punishment of any criticism of religion (ie of an idea) is incompatible with the idea of freedom itself, liberalism, let alone democracy and religious pluralism. This is also the view of international human rights bodies as well as civil society actors.[70] By way of illustration, in their joint report in 2006, the two Special rapporteurs on religion and xenophobia respectively, noting the 'confusion between a racist statement and an act of defamation of religion',[71] have clarified cases of 'clashes' between freedom of expression and freedom of religion, explaining that 'as such, the right to freedom of religion or belief, as enshrined in relevant international legal standards, does not include the right to have a religion or belief that is free from criticism or ridicule ... Defamation of religions may offend people ... but it does not necessarily or at least directly result in a violation of ... their right to freedom of religion'.[72] As for cases when law should intervene, the Council of Europe recommendation 1805 (2007) seems more pertinent: 'national law should only penalise expressions about

70 By way of illustration, see, Report of the United Nations High Commissioner for Human Rights, *Rights of persons belonging to national or ethnic, religious and linguistic minorities,* 17 December 2014, UN Doc A/HRC/28/27, paras 44–47 (concerning the visit of the Special Rapporteur in Pakistan). Likewise, Farida Shaheed, Farida Shaheed, *Report of the Special Rapporteur In The Field Of Cultural Rights*, UN Doc A/HRC/23/34 (14 March 2013) paras 47–8 (recalling that 'prohibitions of displays of lack of respect for a religion or other belief system, including blasphemy laws, are incompatible with the [ICCPR], except in the specific circumstances envisaged in article 20, paragraph 2, of the Covenant' and that 'Blasphemy laws have a stifling impact on the enjoyment of freedom of religion or belief and impede a healthy dialogue and debate about religion').

71 A/HRC/2/3, (n 47) para 49 (adding that 'the elements that constitute a racist statement are not the same as those that constitute a statement defaming a religion. To this extent, the legal measures, and in particular the criminal measures, adopted by national legal systems to fight racism may not necessarily be applicable to defamation of religion').

72 ibid, para 36–37.

religious matters which intentionally and severely disturb public order and call for public violence'.[73]

The second solution suggests a more thoughtful approach to those virtual 'clashes' between freedom of expression and religious beliefs and would allow to seek alternative ways of raising responsibility both among authors of offensive expressions and among believers. This is however a long-term approach. As the Venice Commission once flagged,

> a responsible exercise of the right to freedom of expression should endeavor to respect the right to respect for religious beliefs or convictions of others. In this and other areas, sensible self-censorship could help to strike a balance between freedom of expression and ethical behaviour. Refraining from uttering certain statements can be perfectly acceptable when it is done in order not to hurt gratuitously the feelings of other persons, whereas it is obviously unacceptable when it is done out of fear of violent reactions.[74]

73 PACE Recommendation 1805 (2007), *Blasphemy, religious insults and hate speech against persons on grounds of their religion* para 15.

74 Venice Commission Report (n 26) para 83.

CHAPTER 12

Freedom of Expression: Theory and Practice in the Islamic Realm

Irmgard Marboe

1 Introduction

Freedom of expression is one of the most contentious issues in the discussion about the compatibility of Islam and human rights.[1] The specific controversy arises out of the fact that Islam does not only set out religious, ethical, and moral values, but also a normative system, the Islamic Sharia, which is deemed to regulate society as a whole, including the relationship with non-believers as well as international relations. Several states have adopted the Sharia as 'a' or 'the' source of law in their constitutions. Sharia would then qualify as 'national law' which must not be in contravention of international law, including international human rights law. However, this hierarchy is not self-evident.

This becomes apparent in the formulation of the right to freedom of expression in Article 22 of the Cairo Declaration of Human Rights in Islam of 1990, which is an important referential document for the Organization of Islamic Cooperation (OIC) and its recently established Independent Permanent Human Rights Commission (IPHRC):[2]

1 See, for example, Abdullahi Ahmed An-Na'im, 'The Contingent Universality of Human Rights: The Case of Freedom of Expression in African and Islamic Contexts' (1997) 11 *Emory International Law Review* 29–66; Niaz A. Shah, 'Freedom of Religion: Koranic and Human Rights Perspectives' (2005) 1 and 2 *Asia-Pacific Journal on Human Rights and the Law* 69; Mohamed Azam Mohamed Adil, 'Restrictions in Freedom of Religion in Malaysia: A Conceptual Analysis with Special Reference to the Law of Apostasy' (2007) 4(2) *Muslim World Journal of Human Rights* 1; Abdullah Saeed, 'Introduction', in Abdullah Saeed (ed), *Islam and Human Rights. Key Issues in the Debates* (Edward Elgar, Cheltenham 2012), vol I, xvi.

2 The IPHRC was established on the basis of Article 15 of the revised Charter of 2008 of the Organization of Islamic Cooperation (OIC) in 2011. Its basis of work includes, amongst others, the Cairo Declaration of Human Rights in Islam of 1990. However, it is notable that the Council of Ministers of the OIC at its 42nd Meeting in May 2015 requested the IPHRC to review the Cairo Declaration against existing universal human rights instruments and make suggestions for its improvement, if and where necessary. See Resolution No 1/42-Legal, Follow-Up and Coordination of Action in the Field of Human Rights, OIC/CFM-42/2015/LEG/DR.RES.1, 27–28 May 2015, para 12.

 | DOI:10.1163/9789004349155_013

(a) Everyone shall have the right to express his opinion freely in such manner as would not be contrary to the principles of the Sharia.
(b) Everyone shall have the right to advocate what is right, and propagate what is good, and warn against what is wrong and evil according to the norms of Islamic Sharia.
(c) Information is a vital necessity to society. It may not be exploited or misused in such a way as may violate sanctities and the dignity of Prophets, undermine moral and ethical values or disintegrate, corrupt or harm society or weaken its faith.
(d) It is not permitted to excite nationalistic or doctrinal hatred or to do anything that may be an incitement to any form or racial discrimination.

This provision differs considerably from the formulation of the right to freedom of expression in international human rights documents.[3] Especially the broad prohibition of anything 'contrary to the principles of the Sharia' appears problematic, as it is well known that Islamic Sharia is interpreted and applied in different countries in many different ways. Who decides which speech is contrary to the Sharia?

Against this background it is worth reiterating that the Islamic Sharia does not represent a monolithic block or a fully-fledged, clearly confined legal system. On the contrary, it is a complex body of religious, moral, and legal norms that has developed over centuries. The split between Sunni and Shia Islam occurred early in history, and several different schools within each of them emerged. The prominent author *Ann Elizabeth Mayer* keeps emphasizing that it is not possible to talk about the compatibility or not of 'Islam' and human rights, but that it is necessary to accept that there are many different 'Islams'.[4]

In view of this, it is understandable that the cursory statements by the European Court of Human Rights in *Refah Partisi*, 'that sharia, which faithfully

3 See, for example, Article 19 ICCPR: 1. Everyone shall have the right to hold opinions without interference. 2. Everyone shall have the right to freedom of expression; this right shall include freedom to seek, receive and impart information and ideas of all kinds, regardless of frontiers, either orally, in writing or in print, in the form of art, or through any other media of his choice.3. The exercise of the rights provided for in paragraph 2 of this article carries with it special duties and responsibilities. It may therefore be subject to certain restrictions, but these shall only be such as are provided by law and are necessary: (a) For respect of the rights or reputations of others; (b) For the protection of national security or of public order (ordre public), or of public health or morals.

4 Ann Elizabeth Mayer, 'General Remarks on Human Rights and Islam in the Middle East' in Hatem Elliesie (ed) *Islam and Human Rights* (Peter Lang, Frankfurt et al 2010) 219.

reflects the dogmas and divine rules laid down by religion, is stable and invariable' and that 'pluralism in the political sphere or the constant evolution of public freedoms have no place in it'[5] have created fierce criticism.[6]

The purpose of the present chapter is to discuss the ways in which 'freedom of expression' is reflected in existing interpretations of Islamic Sharia. It will recall the discussion which emerged after the publication of the cartoons of the Prophet Mohammad in the Danish newspaper *Jyllands Posten* in 2005 and the appalling terrorist attacks against the offices of the French magazine *Charlie Hebdo* in France in 2015.[7] First, it will analyze, in theory, whether there are approaches and methodologies to support the 'freedom of expression' under Islamic law. On this basis, the chapter will then address the practice of Muslim states in this respect.

2 Some Theory on Islamic Sharia and Freedom of Expression

One of the reasons for the alleged tension between Islamic law and human rights law originates from the misconception about Islamic law being wholly divine and immutable, which usually arises from the non-distinction between the sources and methods of Islamic law.[8] The primary sources of the Islamic Sharia are the Quran, the revelations of the Prophet Mohammad (between 610

---

5 *Refah Partisi (The Welfare Party) and Others v Turkey* (GC), App Nos 41340/98, 41342/98, 41343/98 and 41244/98. ECHR 2003-II 267, para 123; see also Chamber Judgment of 31 July 2001, para 72.

6 Three of the seven judges in the Chamber decisions dissented. To the Grand Chamber judgment two judges issued a joint concurring opinion and one judge a separate concurring opinion. See also the criticism in academic commentary, for example, by Kevin Boyle, 'Human Rights, Religion and Democracy: The Refah Party Case', (2004) 1 *Essex Human Rights Review* 1, 3, 12 ff; Melanie Reed, 'Western Democracy and Islamic Tradition: The Application of Shari'a in a Modern World' (2004) 19 *American University International Law Review* 485, 487; Peter Danchin, 'Islam in the Secular *Nomos* of the European Court of Human Rights' (2011) 32 *Michigan Journal of International Law* 663, 699.

7 The ILA Committee on Islamic Law and International Law dedicated its reports of 2012, 2014 and 2016 to the issue of Islamic law and the rule of law, with a particular focus on the freedom of expression. These reports are available at <www.ila-hq.org/index.php/committees> accessed 11 September 2017. The results of the work of the ILA Committee are also reflected in a book co-authored by the three Co-Rapporteurs of the Committee. See Hossein Esmaeili, Irmgard Marboe, and Javaid Rehman, *The Rule of Law, Freedom of Expression and Islamic Law* (Hart Publishing, Oxford and Portland, Oregon 2017).

8 Mashood Baderin, 'Establishing Areas of Common Ground between Islamic Law and International Human Rights' (2001) 5 *The International Journal of Human Rights* 72, 75.

until 632),[9] and the Sunna, the acts and deeds with regard to spiritual and temporal questions which are compiled in *hadiths*.[10] Of these two primary sources, only the words of the Quran are considered as divine and immutable. They are regarded as the exact revealed words of God upon which the concept of legality is based.[11] The Sunna, translated as 'tradition', already indicates the need for interpretation which, as done by the prophet himself, is also considered as a source of law, albeit with some difference. Not all *hadiths* are considered as equally authentic and credible, so that the chain of transmission (*isnad*) has to be proven and is subject to challenge.[12]

As not all cases could be solved by use of these two sources, further sources or methods of interpretation were needed. The doctrine of *ijtihad* (legal reasoning) was developed from which the principles of *ijma* (legal consensus) and *quias* (legal analogy) emerged. These two principles are usually considered as secondary sources of Islamic law.[13] However, they are the product of human reasoning which can be regarded as an indication of the recognition of human reasoning in the Islamic legal theory from the earliest period of Islam.[14]

The process of understanding, interpreting and explaining Islamic law is called *fiqh* (understanding). Usually, *fiqh* is translated as 'Islamic jurisprudence'.[15] As such, it is not divine and immutable but subject to change and reinterpretation. Whether this is possible until today or whether the 'closing of the gates of ijtihad' by the end of the tenth century put an end to it, is a matter of controversy between the different schools of Islamic law.[16] All four Sunni schools, the Hanafi, Shaafi, Maliki and Hanbali schools of law, as well as

9 ibid, 76; see also Mathias Rohe, *Islamic Law in Past and Present* (Brill, Leiden 2015) 61–66.

10 Rohe (n 9) 66–73.

11 In the words of Mashood Baderin, the Quran represent the 'basic norm' in Islamic law, the 'grundnorm', as Hans Kelsen calls it in his pure theory of law, or the 'ultimate rule of recognition' in Hart's concept of law. See Baderin, 'Common Ground' (n 8) 76.

12 Raj Bhala, *Understanding Islamic Law: Shari'a* (Lexis Nexis, New Providence, NJ 2011) 307–309.

13 Baderin, 'Common Ground' (n 8) 77; Bhala (n 12) 288–290.

14 Baderin, 'Common Ground' (n 8) 77.

15 Rohe (n 9) 55; Bhala (n 12) 288.

16 According to the doctrine of the 'closing of the gates of ijtihad' emerging in the 13th century, new cases must be solved on the basis of *taqulid* (imitation, conformism) being restricted to the application of the legal findings of the jurists as recorded in the treatises of the established schools of jurisprudence. Baderin, 'Common Ground' (n 8) 78; on this discussion see also Ziba Mir-Hosseini, 'How the Door of Ijtihad Was Opened and Closed: A Comparative Analysis of Recent Family Law Reforms in Iran and Morocco' (2007) 64 *Washington and Lee Law Review* 1499–1511.

the Shia schools accept the two secondary sources of law in principle, but they accord them different value.[17]

It is characteristic for Islamic Sharia that it is not only concerned with questions which in a Western realm would be regarded as legal questions, but also with religious and moral questions.[18] It is a normative system addressed to all Muslims around the world, regardless where they reside, to provide guidance for them to live in accordance with religious and moral principles. Whether these are also transformed into legally binding and enforceable laws remains the decision of the respective worldly authority.[19] If a state decides to choose one of the various possible interpretations of the primary or secondary sources of Islamic law for application within its jurisdiction, the problem of safeguarding other opinions and the freedom of expression arises.[20]

2.1 *Rules and Principles of Islamic Law Supporting Freedom of Expression*

The treatises on Islamic jurisprudence (*fiqh*) do not treat freedom of speech and expression in the same manner as it is done in modern constitutional discourse.[21] Consequently, the relevant information on this theme is rather scattered and the discussion of the freedom of expression under Islamic law has remained relatively underdeveloped.[22] In the following, some doctrines and concepts which have been highlighted by Islamic scholars in support of the freedom of expression shall be discussed. They include the concept of *hisbah* (the principle of commanding good and forbidding evil) and the Quranic principle of *shura* (consultation) which encourage or presuppose the exchange of information and ideas amongst citizens. Finally, references to freedom of religion and the confirmation of pluralism in the primary sources of Sharia shall be highlighted.

17 See Bhala (n 12) 289–290,317–322.

18 In the system of Islamic sharia, the categories of obligations are distinguished between obligations to God (*ibadat*) and obligations in interpersonal relationships (*muamalat*). See Rohe (n 9) 15.

19 Nisrine Abiad, *Sharia, Muslim States and International Human Rights Obligations: A Comparative Study* (British Institute of International and Comparative Law, London 2008) 32–34; Irmgard Marboe, 'Promoting the Rule of Law: UN, OIC and ILA Initiatives Approaching Islamic Law' in Marie-Luisa Frick and Andreas Müller (eds), *Islam and International Law* (Brill Martinus Nijhoff 2013) 184, 190–191.

20 Abiad (n 19); Abdullahi Ahmed An-Na'im, *Islam and the Secular State* (Harvard University Press, Cambridge, MA 2008) 4–7.

21 Mohammad Kamali, *Freedom of Expression* (Islamic Texts Society, Cambridge 1997) 27.

22 Esmaeili et al (n 7) 11.

2.1.1 The Doctrine of *hisbah*

According to Kamali, the Quranic principle of *hisbah* takes for granted the basic freedom of individuals to formulate and express their own opinions.[23] Even though Islamic law does not put an emphasis on individual rights, but rather on individual duties and obligations towards society and the state,[24] this does not mean that rights of the individual are not existent. Kamali advances a change of perspectives that leads to the understanding of rights as the inherent and logical counterparts of duties.[25]

The core of the concept of *hisbah* is 'commanding good and forbidding evil'.[26] On the one hand, this is regarded as the religious and ethical foundation of governmental power. On the other hand, it may also be seen as an entitlement of citizens to speak and act in pursuit of what in their judgement seems good and condemn any evil which they see being committed.[27] According to Kamali, 'without freedom of expression, it would be inconceivable to command good or to forbid evil'.[28] He refers to a *hadith* which says that, 'if [anyone] sees something evil, he should set it right with his hand; if he is unable to do so, then with his tongue, and if he is unable to do even that, then (let him denounce it) in his heart. But this is the weakest form of faith'.[29]

The principle of *hisbah* is expressed in several verses of the Quran. According to verse 104 of sura 3, 'there should be from among you a community of people (*ummah*) who call others to good and enjoin others to right conduct and forbid what is wrong'.[30] Another verse provides that 'you are the best community of people who command good and forbid others from committing evil and wrong conducts'.[31]

It is notable that Kamali refers to this doctrine as one to encourage individual freedom. Telling others what to do or not to do could also be considered as exactly the opposite. It may therefore overstretch the potential of the doctrine of *hisbah* to see in it an encouragement of open exchange of views and opinions in Muslim societies and a basis for voicing criticism

---

23 Kamali, *Freedom of Expression* (n 21) 28.

24 Ann Elizabeth Mayer, *Islam and Human Rights* (5th edn, Westview Press 2013) 48–55.

25 Kamali, *Freedom of Expression* (n 21) 27–28; see also Mohammad Kamali, 'Fundamental Rights of the Individual: An Analysis of *Haqq* (Right) in Islamic Law', (1993) 33 The American Journal of Islamic Social Sciences 340, 341.

26 Kamali, *Freedom of Expression* (n 21) 28.

27 ibid.

28 ibid, 28.

29 Muslim, *Mukhtasar Sahih Muslim,* 16, *Hadith* no. 34.

30 The Quran 3: 104.

31 The Quran 3: 110, see also 3: 114; 7: 157; 9: 71; 9: 12; 22: 41.

against the government. Indeed, in practice it is often used for the opposite purpose, namely for curbing individual freedoms, including the freedom of expression.[32] In Saudi Arabia, *hisbah* is institutionalised as the Commission for the Promotion of Virtue and the Prevention of Vice, a religious police, which enforces Sharia law, particularly in the public sphere.[33] In Iran, legislation regulates the principle of *hisbah* through the Act for Protection of those Who Command Virtue and Forbid Vices.[34] In Egypt, the principle of *hisbah* is included in the regulations governing Sharia courts.[35]

It follows that the principle of *hisbah* has some potential for promoting individual rights and freedoms, including the freedom of expression but needs to be developed further in that direction.

2.1.2 Consultation (*Shura*)

The principle of *shura*, or consultation, frequently appears in the debates on the compatibility of Islam with democracy.[36] The Arabic term *shura* means picking and selecting the best thing, but also taking or giving one's opinion with due care and deliberation.[37] The Islamic Sharia refers to the need for consultation in the decision making of rulers and also encourages consultation in private affairs. Verse 159 of sura 3 is generally regarded as pertinent to the political decision-making process:

32 Esmaeili et al (n 7) 123–124.

33 ibid; see also Killian Clarke, 'A Modernization Paradox: Saudi Arabia's Divided Society', (2007) 30 *Harvard International Review* 30–33.

34 Esmaeili et al (n 7) 123–124; see also Fae Chubin, 'When My Virtue Defends Your Borders: Political Justification of Nation and Order Through the Rhetorical Production of Womanhood in the 1979 Islamic Revolution of Iran' (2014) 42 *Women's Studies International Forum* 44–55.

35 See Articles 89 and 110 of the Decree-Law No 78 on the Organization of the Sharia Courts and their Proceedings, Official Gazette No 53 of 20 May 1931; see Nora Alim and Nadjma Yassari, 'Between Procedure and Substance: a Review of Law Making in Egypt' in Nadjma Yassari (ed), *Changing God's Law: The Dynamics of Middle Eastern Family Law* (Routledge Abingdon, Oxon 2016) 113, 120.

36 Uriya Shavit, 'Is *Shura* a Muslim Form of Democracy? Roots and Systemization of a Polemic' (2010) 46 *Middle Eastern Studies* 349–374; Ann Black, Hossein Esmaeili, and Nadirsyah Hosen, *Modern Perspectives on Islamic Law* (Edward Elgar 2013) 43–44.

37 Gamil Mohammed El-Gindy, 'The Shura and Human Rights in Islamic Law. The Relevance of Democracy' in Eugene Cotran and May Yamani (eds), *The Rule of Law in the Middle East and the Islamic World. Human Rights and the Judicial Process* (NY, IB Tauris, 2000) 164–169.

> And by the Mercy of Allah, you dealt with them gently. And had you been severe and harsh-hearted, they would have broken away from about you; so pass over (their faults), and ask (Allah's) Forgiveness for them; and consult them in the affairs. Then when you have taken a decision, put your trust in Allah, certainly, Allah loves those who put their trust (in Him).[38]

Furthermore, sura 42 is entirely dedicated to the topic of consultation, as its title 'Surah Ash-Shurah' indicates. The need for consultation is highlighted together with two of the five pillars of Islam, the declaration of faith (*shahada*), the prayer (*salat*) and alms-giving (*zakat*), which, according to Muslim scholars,[39] is evidence for its distinct significance:

> And those who answer the Call of their Lord [i.e. to believe that He is the only One Lord (Allah), and to worship none but Him Alone], and perform *As-Salat* (*Iqamat-as-Salat*), and who (conduct) their affairs by mutual consultation, and who spend of what We have bestowed on them.[40]

Some scholars see a confirmation of the freedom of expression and consultation in combination with education in the first four verses of sura 55:

> 1. The Most Beneficent (Allah)!
> 2. Has taught (you mankind) the Qur'an (by His Mercy).
> 3. He created man.
> 4. He taught him eloquent speech.[41]

Another verse praises those who listen to different views and make their own judgment as the 'people of wisdom':

> '[Give the good news to] [t]hose who listen [to different views and perspectives (*qawl*), and follow the best of [those views] ... [that] those are the ones whom God has guided, and those are the ones who are indeed people of wisdom (*ulul al-bab*)'.[42]

---

38 Quran 3:159.

39 Kamali, *Freedom of Expression* (n 21) 41; Esmaeili et al (n 7) 125.

40 Quran 42:38.

41 Quran 55:1–4; see Mashood Baderin, *International Human Rights and Islamic Law* (OUP 2003) 126–129; Esmaeili et al (n 7) 121.

42 Quran 39:17–18.

Also in the Sunna, references to the importance of consultations are found. One of the Prophet's companions is narrated to have said: 'I have not seen anyone more diligent in consulting his companions than the prophet himself'.[43]

The reformist movements at the end of the 19th century led by al-Afghani and Muhammad Abdhu[44] argued that the true, original Islam practices by the prophet and his four righteous successors did not contradict modernity and rationalism. Most importantly, they introduced the idea that the principle of *shura* rejects tyranny.[45] Their intention was to prove that some Western ideas and institutions are originally Muslim so that it would be possible to adopt them. Abduh emphasized that implementing *shura* was an Islamic obligation rather than an imitation of foreigners.[46]

Abd al-Rahman al-Kawakibi elaborated that Islam was based on the foundations of democratic government and that Muslims only had to return to its true nature, that of equality, fraternity and consultation, in order to overcome tyranny.[47] He argued against 'foreign liberals' who claimed that the reason for tyranny in Muslim societies was their religious devoutness. The most influential of Abduh's students and an important link between his ideas to those of the Muslim Brothers, Muhammad Rashid Rida, also utilized *shura* in rejecting the idea that religion is an enemy of democracy.[48]

---

43 Al-Tirmidhi, *Sunan al-Tirmidhi,* IV, 213; see Esmaeili et al (n 7) 126.

44 Jamal al-Din al-Afghani (1838–97) and Muhammad Abduh (1849–1905) both argued that Islam was inherently rational and needed not be abandoned in the face of modernity and the encroachment of Western scientific and cultural thought. They argued that it was possible to demonstrate the authenticity of Islamic teachings and their relevance within an Islamic society. See Abba Idris Adam, 'Islamic Civilization in the Face of Modernity: the Case of Jamal al-Din al-Afghani (1838–97) and Muhammad Abduh', Proceeding of the 2nd International Conference on Social Sciences Research ICSSR 2014, 9–10 June 2014, 594–599.

45 Shavit (n 36) 350.

46 ibid.

47 Abd al-Rahman al-Kawakibi (1855–1902) was a Syrian pioneer of Arab nationalism and a student of Muhammad Abduh. He advocated a return to the original purity of Islam, claiming that alien concepts and distortions such as mysticism, fatalism, sectarian divisions, and imitation had led to ignorance and submission to stagnant theologians and despotic rulers who suppressed freedoms, promoted false religion, and corrupted the moral, social, educational, and financial systems of the Muslim nation, as exemplified by the Ottoman Empire. He advocated Arab independence and an elected Arab caliph with limited powers as the basis for the revival of Islam. See John L. Esposito (ed), The Oxford Dictionary of Islam (OUP, published online 2003).

48 Shavit (n 36) 352–353. Muhammad Rashid Rida, (1865–1935) viewed European dominance over Muslims as a result of Muslim weakness due to a lack of mastery over the

However, this development was distorted by political developments starting in the 1970s. The idea that a Western 'cultural attack' or 'ideological attack' aimed at shattering Muslim identity as part of a plan to re-conquer Muslim territory was reflected in academic writing.[49] As a result, some Western democratic norms and institutions were embraced, but others were rejected. On the one hand, it was accepted that the people should elect its political leadership and hold it accountable; basic freedoms – such as freedom of speech and freedom of association for the opposition – should be guaranteed.[50] On the other hand, Islamists cautioned against blind imitation of the West and stressed that Allah's laws must not be questioned, that sovereignty was reserved for Him only, and that personal freedoms end where they contradict Islam's teachings.[51]

In view of the above it can be concluded that the concept of *shura* is generally only advisory in nature.[52] There is still significant doubt whether it paves the way for real democracy.[53] Yet, while the significance of the *shura* for the purpose of establishing democracy may still be open to debate, the prominence of this concept in Islamic legal sources and in Muslim scholarly writings may serve as an indication that freedom of speech and expression as the prerequisite for consultation is not alien to the Islamic Sharia.[54]

2.1.3 Freedom of Religion and Pluralism

The most relevant restriction on the freedom of expression in the Islamic realm and prominently evidenced in the incidents of the Danish cartoons and the attacks on Charlie Hebdo, stems from the prohibition of apostasy (*ridda,*

sciences, an inability to form organized political institutions, and a lack of restrictions on the power of government. See John L. Esposito (ed), The Oxford Dictionary of Islam (OUP, published online 2003).

49 The foundations of the concept that exposes an 'organized Western cultural attack' on the Muslim world in other than militaristic means were first laid by Muhammad Rashid Rida and were later developed by Hasan al-Banna. In the 1960s they were popularized by the Egyptian journalist Muhammad Jalal Kishk in a series of books, and since the 1970s they have been a common thread in Arab Islamist writings on the West. Shavit (n 36) 352, 371.

50 Shavit (n 36) 352–353.

51 ibid, 353.

52 Sayyid Abul A 'la Maududi, 'The Political Theory of Islam' in Mansoor Moaddel and Kamran Talattof (eds) *Modernist and Fundamentalist Debates in Islam* (Palgrave Macmillan 2000) 263–271.

53 Black et al (n 36) 44.

54 Kamali, *Freedom of Expression* (n 21) 41; Esmaeili et al (n 7) 125.

irtidad) and blasphemy (*sabb*).[55] The subject of freedom of religion under the Islamic Sharia has several dimensions. As Sarwar points out, it concerns (1) Muslims renouncing their faith, (2) Muslims being able to practice their faith as Muslims in a way they consider appropriate, and (3) the free practice of religion in a pluralist society in which other freedoms, in particular the freedom of expression, are equally guaranteed.[56]

While the prohibitions of apostasy and blasphemy in the Islamic Sharia are prominent, the Quran also contains numerous references to freedom of religion and pluralism. Without going into the details, only some significant provisions shall be outlined. One of the important verses relating to freedom of religion in the Quran is sura 2, verse 256 which declares:

> There is no compulsion in religion: true guidance has become distinct from error, so whoever rejects (taghut) false gods and believes in God has grasped the firmest hand-hold, one that will never break. God is all hearing, all knowing.[57]

In sura 18, verse 29, the Quran confirms the free decision to believe in a rather clear wording: 'And say, "The truth is from your Lord, so whoever wills – let him believe; and whoever wills – let him disbelieve."'[58]

Another important verse of the Quran, which maintains freedoms of religion and thought, is sura 10, verse 99. It rejects attempts by the prophet to compel people against their will to believe in Allah: 'And had your Lord willed, those on earth would have believed, all of them together. So, will you (O Muhammad) then compel mankind, until they become believers'.[59]

In addition it is worth highlighting that the entire sura 109 of the Quran which is dedicated to the 'Non-believers' (*Al-kafirun*) seems to contain a clear confirmation of the freedom of religion at least for the adherents of other religions. The sura only consists of five verses, but they all appear to unequivocally encourage tolerance and pluralism.

55 See Javaid Rehman, 'The Shari'ah, International Human Rights Law and the Right to Hold Opinions and Free Expression: After Bilour's Fatwa', in Marie-Luisa Frick and Andreas Müller (eds), *Islam and International Law* (Brill Martinus Nijhoff 2013) 244.

56 Malik Imtiaz Swarwar, 'Freedom of Religion and Expression: A "Rule of Law" Perspective' in Anver Emon, Mark Ellis and Benjamin Glahn (eds), *Islamic Law and International Human Rights Law* (OUP 2012) 247.

57 Quran 2:256.

58 Quran 18:29.

59 Quran 10:99.

1. Say (O Muhammad) to these Mushrikun and Kafirun: "O Al-Kafirun (disbelievers in Allah, in His Oneness, in His Angels, in His Books, in His Messengers, in the Day of Resurrection, and in Al-Qadar, etc.)!
2. I worship not that which you worship,
3. Nor will you worship that which I worship.
4. And I shall not worship that which you are worshipping.
5. Nor will you worship that which I worship.
6. To you be your religion, and to me my religion (Islamic Monotheism).[60]

The acceptance of more than one religion and their peaceful living together is present in several other Quranic verses. One of the most frequently quoted is sura 5, 48:

> If Allah willed, He would have made you one nation, but that (He) may test you in what He has given you; so strive as in a race in good deeds. The return of you (all) is to Allah; then He will inform you about that in which you used to differ.[61]

The formulation 'Si Dieu avait voulu …' has become a key phrase describing the spirit of dialogue present in Islam which encourages respect for different beliefs, in particular in francophone Christian-Islamic relations.[62] It is understood as an encouragement of peaceful competition between the religions in their striving for the good, as opposed to other verses in the Quran which encourage fighting against and even killing the 'unbelievers'.

2.2 *Principles of Islamic Sharia Challenging Freedom of Expression*

The rules, concepts, and principles used to limit the freedom of expression in Islamic Sharia are not only concerned with the protection of religion or believers, but also with other aims. Restricting freedom of expression is most frequently a tool to limit criticism against political leaders and to maintain power. The discussion in the following will be limited to reasons based in the Islamic Sharia under the sources explained above.

60 Quran 109:1–6.

61 Quran 5:48.

62 Cheikh Mohamed Nokkari, 'Multi Confessionnalisme et Citoyenneté en Islam' (2007) 23 *Annales de Philosophie et des Sciences Humaines* 225, 230; Kamel Meziti, '« Si Dieu l'avait voulu … » Vivre en harmonie avec l'autre, avec ses différences …', Publications du Groupe de Recherches Islamo-Chrétien, 22 March 2012, <gric-international.org/2012/publications-du-gric/gric-de-paris/si-dieu-lavait-voulu-vivre-en-harmonie-avec-lautre-avec-ses-differences/> accessed 11. September 2017.

2.2.1 Apostasy amd Blasphemy in Islamic Law

The most disturbing instances of limitation of the freedom of expression are usually based on the crimes of apostasy (*ridda, irtidad*) and blasphemy (*sabb*).[63] Under Islamic Sharia, apostasy is a criminal offence. Whether it belongs to the so-called *hudud* crimes which are regarded as crimes against God and defined in the Quran with severe and fixed punishment, is subject to some divergence of opinion.[64] The undisputed *hudud* crimes are theft, adultery, false accusation of adultery (slander), and brigandage, for which the Quran proscribes the punishment which the judge cannot abrogate or change.[65] Crimes for which there are no specified penalties in the Quran or Sunna are categorized as *tazir* crimes for which the ruler or the judge enjoys discretion. In their determination whether an act is punishable and by which punishment they can consider the public interest and changing conditions and times.[66]

The central Quranic verse about apostasy does not contain a concrete punishment, as is the case with other *hudud* crimes, but refers to 'hellfire' deferring the punishment to the hereafter:

> And whosoever of you turns back from his religion and dies as a disbeliever, then his deeds will be lost in this life and in the hereafter, and they will be the dwellers of the fire. They will abide therein forever.[67]

Nevertheless, many scholars consider apostasy as a *hadd*[68] crime.[69] Furthermore, the punishment for apostasy is generally deemed to be the death

63 Abdullah Saeed and Hassan Saeed, *Freedom of Religion, Apostasy and Islam* (Ashgate, Aldershot et al 2004) 35–39; Shah (n 1).

64 See Saeed and Saeed (n 63) 56; Ahmad Abd al-Aziz al-Alfi, 'Punishment in Islamic Criminal Law' in Cherif Bassiouni (ed), *The Islamic Criminal Justice System* (Oceana 1982) 227; Christoph Zehetgruber, *Islamisches Strafrecht versus europäische Werteordnung* (Facultas Wien 2010) 68; Abdullahi Ahmed An-Na'im, *Towards an Islamic Reformation: Civil Liberties, Human Rights, and International Law* (Syracuse University Press 1990) 108–109.

65 These punishments are hand amputation for theft (Quran 5:41), death penalty for armed robbery (5:32), 100 lashes for adultery (24:2), and 80 lashes for slander (24:4). Other crimes which are sometimes included in this group are the drinking of alcohol, apostasy and rebellion. See Rohe (n 9) 155–177.

66 al-Aziz al-Alfi (n 64) 227; Zehetgruber (n 64) 71; Black et al (n 36) 270.

67 Quran 2:217; see also 3:86–91; 16:106–109.

68 *Hadd* is the singular of *hudud*.

69 Muhammad Salim al'Awwa, 'The Basis of Islamic Penal Legislation' in Cherif Bassiouni (ed), *The Islamic Criminal Justice System* (Oceana, London 1982) 127; Aly Aly Mansour, 'Hudud Crimes' in ibid, 195, 197; Zehetgruber (n 64) 115 ff.

penalty.[70] The basis of this opinion is a *hadith* according to which the prophet ordered the killing of those who changed their religion.[71] Another well-known *hadith* reports that the prophet said:

> Allah's Apostle never killed anyone except in one of the following three situations: (1) A person who has killed somebody unjustly, was killed ..., (2) a married person who committed illegal sexual intercourse, and (3) a man who fought against Allah and his Apostle about orders of the prophet to kill those who fought against Allah and his apostle.[72]

These three grounds legitimizing the death penalty go beyond the Quran and enlarge it also for adultery which, according to the Quran, must be punished by 100 lashes.[73] However, this *hadith* seems to be broadly accepted as authentic and authoritative and thus as widening the scope of the death penalty.[74] In addition, there is even an alleged consensus (*ijma*) with respect to the death penalty for apostates.[75]

Whether blasphemy is classified under the same principles, depends on the interpretation of what constitutes apostasy. In view of the purpose of the criminalization of apostasy, the crime cannot be committed by non-Muslims.[76] However, in a broader understanding, apostasy addresses not only Muslims

70 See Saeed and Saeed (n 63) 51–68; Salim al'Awwa (n 69) 166; Mansour (n 69) 195, 197.

71 According to a prominent hadith, the prophet said: 'If somebody discards his religion, kill him'. It is recorded in the hadith collection by Muhammad al-Bukhari, 52:260. The collection by Muhammad al-Bukhari (died in 870) is highly authoritative in the Muslim world as the most authentic collection of reports of the sunnah of the prophet Muhammad. It contains over 7500 hadith in 97 books. A translation provided by Muhammad Muhsin Khan is available online at <https://sunnah.com/bukhari>. See critically Shah (n 1) 74–80.

72 See Bukhari 83:37. Other hadiths also support the death penalty for apostasy, see Bukhari 9:85, 9:58, 84:57. See <https://sunnah.com/bukhari>.

73 See above (n 65).

74 Even An-Na'im Concedes that the death penalty for apostates is firmly rooted in the Islamic sharia by this *hadiths* and others in the sunnah. Abdullahi An-Na'im, *Islamic Reformation* (n 64) 109.

75 See Salim al'Awwa, Islamic Penal Legislation, above n 69, 166 with references to Muslim scholars who support this opinion, such as Ibn Rushd, Ibn Qudama, and Al-Shawkani; see also Safia Safwat, 'Crimes and Punishments under Various Schools of Shari'ah: A comparative overview' in Tahir Mahmood et al (eds), *Criminal Law in Islam and the Muslim World – A Comparative Perspective* (Institute of Objective Studies 1996) 56, 81.

76 Zehetgruber (n 64) 121.

changing their religion, but also denying principles of the Islamic Sharia.[77] In this wider sense it also encompasses insulting or ridiculing the prophet Muhammad, insulting or ridiculing the Quran or the Sunna, or otherwise undermining God's names or rules.[78] Such a broad definition does not only address actions and omission of Muslims but paves the way for criminalising non-Muslims as well. Under this interpretation of Islamic Sharia, apostasy and blasphemy are regarded as the same offence so that blasphemy committed by non-Muslims is also punishable by death. Blasphemy alone can still be a *tazir* crime which appertains to the discretion of the ruler or the judge, but may also involve severe punishments.[79]

The different Sunni and Shia schools of Islamic law have different approaches in their dealing with apostasy and blasphemy. Some of them differentiate between Muslims and non-Muslims and make also a difference whether the offender is man or a woman.[80] Generally, repentance is a way to escape punishment, except for the specific acts, such as reviling the prophet.[81] The diversity of opinions in Islamic scholarship shows the variety of possible solutions and, notably, the absence of any *ijma* (consensus) on the issue.

Modern scholars highlight that the harsh punishment in classical Islamic law must be understood in the context of the social and political situation and circumstances during the lifetime of the prophet.[82] In the early years of Islam, the Muslim community was involved in numerous fights with other tribes and felt constantly threatened. In such a situation, it was important to keep the community together and uphold solidarity. Apostasy under these circumstances was in some way equivalent to high treason in the modern nation state.[83] In this political context, a person either belonged to the community of believers or to the unbelievers who were at war with Muslims.[84] An apostate was perceived to have automatically joined the non-Muslim side, becoming part of the enemy ranks and using apostasy as a means to attack and inflict harm on the Muslim community.[85] As such, the severe punishment in the hadith of the prophet served a specific political purpose. It is not impossible that

77 Esmaeili et al (n 7) 128; Saeed and Saeed (n 63).

78 Rohe (n 9) 174–175.

79 ibid, 175.

80 Black et al (n 36) 269–270.

81 Rohe (n 9) 174.

82 See for many others Saeed and Saeed (n 36) 66–68; Black et al (n 36) 270; Shah (n 1) 77–80; Baderin, *Human Rights* (n 41) 124; An-Na'im, *Islamic Reformation* (n 64) 111.

83 See Black et al (n 36) 270–271; Wael B. Hallaq, *Sharia: Theory, Practice, Transformations* (CUP 2009) 319.

84 Saeed and Saeed (n 63) 31–33.

85 ibid.

the feeling of being constantly under attack by others is, until today, used as an implicit justification for the treatment of apostates as traitors.

According to another line of argument, Islamic law must be understood as a coherent system free of contradictions and that, in view of the numerous allegations to freedom of religion and pluralism in both the Quran and the Sunna, the punishment of apostasy and blasphemy cannot be upheld.[86]

In view of the existing divergence of opinion in Islamic scholarship about apostasy under Islamic law, it can be concluded that it is not possible to identify which legal rules or practices of a state are in accordance with Islamic law. Muslim states are not compelled by the Sharia to provide any punishment, not to mention harsh corporal punishment or the death penalty, for blasphemy or apostasy. If they do so, it is a deliberate choice of the political power to follow one of the possible interpretations of Islamic law.

2.2.2 Other Restrictions on the Freedom of Speech

Apart from apostasy with its special significance under Islamic jurisprudence as discussed above, Islamic law contains also other restrictions and limitations on the freedom of expression. Similar to modern common law and civil law, they relate to defamation, insults, and sedition. The crimes of slanderous accusation (*qadhf*), sedition (*fitnah*), insult (*sabb*) and cursing (*l'an*), attribution of lies or calumny (*iftira*) and the labelling of others as disbelievers (*tafkfir*) are based in the Islamic Sharia and can restrict freedom of expression.[87] Most of these crimes fall under the category of *tazir*, so that the rulers have discretion to enact laws to regulate them. As they are not subject to strict provisions for punishment in the Quran or Sunna, it should not be a problem for states to respect international human rights standards in their national laws.

The exception is slanderous accusation (*qadhf*). As mentioned above, false accusation of adultery is categorized as a *hadd* crime.[88] It is a Quranic offence which provides a specific punishment for those who accuse others of having committed adultery (*zina*) without providing sufficient evidence for their claim, namely 80 lashes:

> And those who accuse chaste women, and produce not four witnesses, flog them with eighty stripes, and reject their testimony forever, they indeed are the *Fasiqun* (liars, rebellious, disobedient to Allah).[89]

86 An-Na'im, *Islamic Reformation* (n 64) 109–111; An-Na'im, 'Contingent Universality' (n 1) 42.

87 Kamali, *Freedom of Expression* (n 21) 166–167; Esmaeili et al (n 7) 123–133.

88 See n 65.

89 Quran 24:4.

In addition to the corporal punishment, the crime also entails the removal of the ability to testify in legal procedures for lifetime as well as punishment in the thereafter.[90]

The offence of *qadhf* can be seen as a 'neutralising' counterpart of the *hadd* crime of adultery (*zina*) which must be punished by 100 lashes according to the Quran, and even by death penalty according to the Sunna.[91] As such, it can serve as a protection from unfounded accusations, in particular through the need to present four witnesses, which is also necessary to prove *zina*. In both cases, the evidence required seems to be prohibitive. As a result, both *hudud* crimes should never be applicable. However, practice has shown that the evidentiary requirement of the four witnesses has been used against women in Pakistan and Somalia who were raped, but could not show four witnesses.[92]

Besides these more than problematic forms of application, the offence of *qadhf* has a more general purpose of promoting virtue and chastity in the Muslim society. As a peculiarity it should be mentioned that the wife of the prophet, Aisha, has herself reportedly been accused of adultery.[93] As four witnesses were not available, the prophet himself inflicted the punishment upon the slanderers.[94]

The inclusion of defamation in the group of *hudud* crimes has created a culture that goes beyond the limit of law.[95] Making accusations, labelling people, or insulting other people for inchastity and sexual misbehaving is taken very seriously in Muslim societies. Expressions involving accusations of unchastity and foul language involving sexual allegations are not tolerated. In Western countries, while the use of foul sexual language is not welcome, it is generally not legally prohibited. The seriousness of the *hadd* crime of slander might be an additional explanation why the reaction to Salman Rushdie, when he used some sexual language in relation to the prophet Mohammed and his wives, was fierce.

90 Quran 24:19 and 24:23.

91 See already n 65.

92 Rohe (n 9) 161.

93 Al' Awwa (n 69) 137.

94 It was three men, *Hassan bin Thabit, Mistah bin Athatha,* and *Himna bin Jahsh.* See Zehetgruber (n 64) 87.

95 Esmaeili et al (n 7) 133.

3 Freedom of Expression in the Practice of Muslim States

The status of freedom of expression in the Middle East and the wider Muslim world is a serious concern from a human rights perspective.[96] Even though constitutions and other legal documents may provide for some protection of human rights, restrictions on freedom of expression are widespread and significant in practice. Surveys about freedom of the press put the Middle East and North Africa together with some other Muslim countries amongst the regions and countries where freedom of expression is significantly restricted.[97]

In the following, the practice of Islamic states with regard to the freedom of expression will be addressed, first, on the basis of their ratification of international human rights conventions and, secondly, at the example of some high profile international cases. The term 'Islamic states' will be understood as states which are members of the Organisation of Islamic Cooperation (OIC) which understands itself as 'the collective voice of the Muslim world'.[98]

3.1 *Ratification of International Human Rights Conventions by Muslim States*

A survey about the ratifications of international human rights conventions by OIC members shows that almost all member states of the OIC have ratified core international human rights treaties, most importantly the two UN Covenants of 1966 (ICCPR and ICESCR), the Convention on the Elimination of all Forms of Discrimination Against Women of 1979 (CEDAW), the Convention Against Torture of 1984 (CAT), and the Convention of the Rights of the Child (CRC).[99] As regards the lodging of reservation, the picture is heterogeneous. Some states have not lodged any reservations, but most states have lodged some, at least to some of the conventions. With regard to the issue of freedom of expression, reservations against the ICCPR are of particular interest.

96 Rehman, 'Right to Hold Opinions' (n 55) 261–265; Javaid Rehman and Stephanie Berry, 'Is "Defamation of Religions" Passé? The United Nations, Organisation of Islamic Cooperation, and Islamic Practices: Lessons from Pakistan', (2012) 44 *George Washington International Law Review* 431–472; Esmaeili et al (n 7) 115.

97 Esmaeili et al, ibid; Jennifer Dunham, *Press Freedom 2015: The Battle of the Dominant Message,* Freedom House (2016), see <https://freedomhouse.org/report/freedom-press/freedom-press-2016> accessed 11 September 2017; see also Reporters Without Borders, *2017 World Press Freedom Index*, see <https://rsf.org/en/ranking> accessed 11 September 2017.

98 See the self-description of the Organisation of Islamic Cooperation at the website of the United Nations, <www.oicun.org/2/23/> accessed 11 September 2017.

99 See the table in Appendix II in Esmaeili et al (n 7) 217–227.

In addition, numerous reservations lodged with respect to the CEDAW and the CRC are also relevant as they also contain the right to freedom of expression.[100]

Most OIC member states have ratified the ICCPR, with the important exception of Malaysia, Oman, Qatar, Saudi Arabia, and the United Arab Emirates.[101] The remaining states have ratified it, mostly without any reservation. Those states which have made reservations rarely refer to the Islamic Sharia explicitly, with Bahrain, Kuwait and Mauretania being the notable exceptions.[102] The Maldives ratified in 2006 with a reservation to Article 18 (freedom of religion) with respect to the Constitution of the Maldives. Pakistan ratified the ICCPR in 2010 with a number of explicit reservations referring to numerous Articles, including articles 18 and 19, but withdrew them all in 2011 so that it is now bound by it without any reservation.[103]

While CRC is known to be the most widely ratified human rights treaty, also CEDAW is ratified by almost all member states of the OIC, with the exception of Iran, Somalia, and Sudan. However, the reservations to CEDAW and CRC are relatively explicit with respect to the safeguarding of the principles of the Islamic Sharia or national law. Broad reservations referring to the Islamic Sharia have been lodged by Afghanistan, Brunei-Darussalam, Egypt, Iran, Kuwait, Malaysia, Maldives, Mauretania, Oman, Qatar, Saudi Arabia, Somalia, Syria, and the United Arab Emirates, to either one or to both of these conventions.[104]

This current picture is the result of political, historical and legal struggles over the years in the Middle East and the Muslim world. Yet, it provides only a very superficial impression on the real situation of human rights in the respective countries. What matters is, of course, the implementation of the respective rights at the national legal level. From this perspective, ratification

---

100 Articles 2 and 3 CEDAW; Articles 12 and 13 CRC.

101 To this list is to be added Brunei-Darussalam, which has not ratified it, either, and lodged general reservations referring to Islam and Islamic law to CEDAW and CRC.

102 Bahrain declared, in 2006, with respect to Article 3, 18 and 23, that it interprets them as 'not affecting in any way the prescriptions of the Islamic Shariah'. Kuwait, in 1996, referred to Islamic law with respect to Article 23. Mauretania, in 2004, declared that 'while accepting the provisions set out in article 18 concerning freedom of thought, conscience and religion, declares that their application shall be without prejudice to the Islamic Shariah'.

103 See Javaid Rehman, 'Adjudicating the Rights of Sexual Minorities in the Muslim World' in James Graan and Christopher Waters (eds), *Adjudicating International Human Rights. Essays in Honour of Sany Ghandhi* (Brill Nijhoff 2015) 119, 129. However, Pakistan has not yet ratified the First Optional Protocol which would allow individual complaints procedures.

104 See Esmaeili et al (n 7) 217–227.

is only a starting point.[105] In addition, broad Sharia reservations raise suspicions as to the real intentions of the state parties and, furthermore, do not provide any insight into the reasoning behind reservations or the scope of their effect.[106] However, that most OIC member states have ratified most of the human rights treaties is an important fact. What is still missing is an increased acceptance by Muslim states of monitoring bodies with a strong mandate to investigate human rights violations, be it at the international level with the individual complaints procedure before UN committees. At the regional level of the OIC, the Independent Permanent Human Rights Commission (IPHRC), established in 2011, has mainly an advisory function and cannot receive individual complaints.

3.2 *Political Practice with Regard to Freedom of Expression*

Controversies about the freedom of expression and Islam are today not limited to the national level, but have international repercussions. One of the first high-profile cases was the execution of Mahmoud Muhammad Taha for the crime of apostasy in Sudan on 18 January 1985.[107] Taha was the author of a book entitled 'The Second Message of Islam' in which he developed a theory of legal interpretation of the Quran.[108] He distinguished between the sections of the Quran which were revealed to the prophet Muhammad in Mecca (610 to 622) and those which were revealed to him in Medina thereafter until 629. According to Taha, the former dealt with the core principles of the Islamic religion, while the latter were more concerned with the organisation of the community in Medina and have merely a political nature. For the interpretation of the Quran, this means, according to Taha, that the older verses are more important and representative of the Islamic message than the newer ones. Taha's interpretation contradicted the prevailing doctrine that in case of contradiction, later verses should prevail in accordance with the principle of 'abrogation' (*naskh*). Based on this doctrine, Taha opposed the introduction of traditional Islamic law by Gaafar Nimeiry, President of Sudan, in 1983,

105 Abiad (n 19) 98.

106 ibid, 82.

107 His most prominent student, Abdullahi Ahmed An-Na'im, is still living in exile in the United States, working as a professor at Emory University in Atlanta, Georgia. See his reflections on the topic of freedom of expression in Islam, for example, in An-Na'im, 'The Islamic Law of Apostasy and Its Modern Applicability: A Case from the Sudan' (1986) 16 *Religion* 197–224; An-Na'im, *Islamic Reformation* (n 64) 34 ff.

108 Mahmoud Muhammad Taha, *The Second Message of Islam* (*Contemporary Issues in the Middle East*) (Abdullahi Ahmed An-Na'im tr, Syracuse University Press 1996).

which precipitated the Second Sudanese Civil War. The government of Sudan persecuted Taha for apostasy, and sentenced him to death based on the *hadd* of *irtidad*. The court argued that Taha was guilty for 'heresy, opposing application of Islamic law, disturbing public security, provoking opposition against the government, and re-establishing a banned political party'.[109] There is no doubt that Taha was executed primarily for political reasons, but the fact that his prosecution and execution were based on the crime of apostasy remains a disturbing fact both for the Muslim world and elsewhere. Shortly after the execution of Taha, Gaafar Nimeiry had to resign and went into exile in Egypt. Sudan ratified the ICCPR and the ICESCR in 1986 as a political signal which, however, failed to have the expected long-lasting results.

The second high-profile case involving Islamic law and blasphemy was the Salman Rushdie affair, triggered by the publication of the novel 'The Satanic Verses' in 1988.[110] The title refers to a legend of the Prophet Mohammad, when a few verses were supposedly spoken by him as part of the Quran, and then withdrawn on the grounds that the devil had sent them to deceive Mohammad into thinking they came from God. They permitted prayer to three pre-Islamic Meccan goddesses, which represented a violation of monotheism. Furthermore, the name of Aisha, the wife of Mohammad, was used for a fanatical Indian girl who leads her village on a fatal pilgrimage. Moreover, the brothel of the city of Jahilia was staffed by prostitutes with the same names as Muhammad's other wives. The publication of the book caused violent demonstrations in several Muslim countries. It was banned in 13 countries with large Muslim communities, including India, South Africa, Thailand, and Venezuela. In a Fatwa of 14 February 1989, Ayatollah Khomeini of Iran required Salman Rushdie's execution. A bounty was offered for Rushdie's death, and he was forced to live under police protection for several years. The UK broke diplomatic relations with Iran in 1989 and re-assumed them only in 1998. Even though the Fatwa was criticised by many Muslim scholars, including by the Al-Azhar University, as a verdict without trial and proper legal procedure and, actually, without jurisdiction, the Salman Rushdie affair divides the Muslim world and the West until today. The bounty for Rushdie's death has been reiterated and confirmed in the

109 Declan O'Sullivan, 'The Death Sentence for Mahmoud Muhammad Taha: Misuse of the Sudanese Legal System and Islamic Shari'a Law?' (2001) 5 *International Journal of Human Rights* 45, 53–54; Mohamed Mahmoud, 'Mahmud Muhammad Taha and the Rise and Demise of the Jumhuri Movement' (2001) 23 *New Political Science* 65–88.

110 See for a detailed collection of facts Daniel Pipes, *The Rushdie Affair* (2nd edn, Transaction Publishers, New Brunswick 2009); see also Abdulrazak Gurnah (ed), *The Cambridge Companion to Salman Rushdie* (CUP 2007).

past years and is currently more than 3.5 Million USD, the most recent increase having been announced in February 2016.[111]

The cartoons controversy of the Danish Newspaper, *Jyllands-Posten*, of 2005 was of a different nature. This time, it was not Muslim thinkers and authors who were accused of apostasy and blasphemy, but Western journalists whose publication of the cartoons in a Danish Newspaper was regarded as blasphemous. A severe foreign policy crisis ensued.[112] Many Muslim countries and Islamic societies boycotted Danish and Norwegian products. There were also numerous death threats and violent incidents including a car bomb explosion outside the Danish embassy in Islamabad, Pakistan, killing eight people. The murders of twelve people at the site of the French satirical newspaper, *Charlie Hebdo*, in 2015 is another tragic culmination of violence rooted in the controversy over freedom of expression in relation to Islam.[113]

These high-profile cases challenging the freedom of expression against sensitivities of adherents of the religion of Islam show the still existing split on the interpretation of norms which almost 70 years ago were considered to be 'universal'.

4 Conclusion

The concept of the freedom of expression is contentious in the Islamic world. The criteria set out in international human rights instruments are only rudimentarily mirrored in the system of the Islamic Sharia. The complexity of the problem is connected to the broad spectrum of possible interpretations. A solution would be to distinguish between norms stemming from primary and secondary sources of Islamic law, including their interpretation by Islamic jurisprudence (*fiqh*), and their adoption and application by states. This would allow putting the state practice under scrutiny, both from the perspective of religious leaders and from the perspective of international law. The decisions taken by governments could then be subject to an assessment of their

111 Alison Flood, 'PEN Condemns Increased Fatwa Bounty on Salman Rushdie' *The Guardian* (2 March 2016).

112 Anshuman Mondal, *Islam and Controversy: The Politics of Free Speech After Rushdie* (Palgrave Macmillan 2014) 147–166.

113 See Jeroen Temperman and Andras Koltay (eds), *Blasphemy and Freedom of Expression: Comparative, Theoretical and Historical Reflections after the Charlie Hebdo Massacre* (CUP 2017).

compatibility with norms they have voluntarily accepted, most importantly by ratifying international human rights conventions.

Another problem is the lack of effective international monitoring institutions with a mandate to investigate incidents of human rights violations. The member states of the OIC are reluctant to accept the individual complaints procedure in the UN system. The same is true with regard to the newly created IPHRC of the OIC. This new body could, in principle, help to develop a supranational interpretation of what the 'principles of the Sharia' could be. At the moment, however, it does not have the mandate to investigate human rights violations and act in a comparable manner as European or American regional human right bodies,[114] as its current function is mainly advisory.[115] In view of the above the prospects that this situation will change in the near future are not promising.

114 See Marie Juul Petersen, *Islamic or Universal Human Rights? The OIC's Independent Permanent Human Rights Commission* (The Danish Institute for Human Rights 2012) 22; Turan Kayaoglu, *The OIC's Independent Permanent Human Rights Commission: An Early Assessment* (The Danish Institute for Human Rights 2015) 18–19.

115 See Chapter IV, Articles 12–17 of the IPHRC Statute.

CHAPTER 13

Is Religion a Threat to Human Rights? Or is It the Other Way Around?

Defending Individual Autonomy in the ECtHR's Jurisprudence on Freedom of Religion

Paulo Pinto de Albuquerque and Andrea Scoseria Katz

1 Introduction

A foundational value under the European Convention on Human Rights, freedom of religion is itself both a positive right enshrined in Article 9 of the Convention and an important guarantor of democratic values in pluralist societies.[1] Article 9 para 1 ECHR protects the right of all individuals to freedom of thought, conscience, and religion, and to free religious exercise, which includes the freedom to change religion or beliefs and to manifest religion or belief, whether in public or private, individually or collectively, and through worship, teaching, practice and observance. Article 9 para 2 ECHR provides that limitations upon religious rights must be both prescribed by law and 'necessary in a democratic society in the interests of public safety, for the protection of public order, health or morals, or for the protection of the rights and freedoms of others'.

Article 9 ECHR protects both beliefs and practices. Beliefs, to warrant Article 9 protection, require a certain level of cogency, seriousness, cohesion and importance. At the same time, protected beliefs include a wide range of opinions and convictions.[2] These include: Alevism,[3] Buddhism,[4] Christian

1 M Todd Parker, 'The Freedom to Manifest Religious Belief: An Analysis of the Necessity Clauses of the ICCPR and ECHR' (2007) 17 Duke Journal of Comparative and International Law 91 (describing the freedom of religion as part of the 'core' of most conceptions of human rights).

2 Not all opinions or convictions necessarily fall within the scope of the provision, and the term "practice" as employed in Article 9, 1 does not cover each act which is motivated or influenced by a religion or belief (*Pretty v UK* App no 2346/02 ECHR 2002-III 155, para 82).

3 *Sinan Isik v Turkey* App no 21924/05 ECHR 2010-I 317; *Cumhuriyetçi Eğitim Ve Kültür Merkezi Vakfi v Turkey* App no 32093/10 (ECtHR, judgment of 2 December 2014).

4 *Jakóbski v Poland* App no 18429/06 (ECtHR, judgment of 7 December 2010).

© KONINKLIJKE BRILL NV, LEIDEN, 2018 | DOI:10.1163/9789004349155_014 denominations;[5] various forms of Hinduism;[6] Islam;[7] Judaism;[8] Sikhism;[9] Taoism;[10] and many new or relatively new religions[11] as well as some non-religious philosophies.[12] Protected practices, meanwhile, fall under one of two categories: *forum internum*, concerning matters of the individual conscience or individual action, such as the freedom to hold or not to hold a belief, or to practise or not practise a religion.[13] *Forum externum* refers to institutional or

5 *Sviato-Mykhailivska Parafiya v Ukraine* App no 77703/01 (ECtHR, judgment of 14 June 2007); *Savez crkava "Rijec zivota" and others v Croatia* App no 7798/08 (ECtHR, judgment of 9 December 2010).

6 *Gatis Kovaļkovs v Latvia* App no 35021/05 (ECtHR, decision of 31 January 2012).

7 *Hasan and Chaouch v Bulgaria* (GC) App no 30985/96 ECHR 2000-XI 117; *Leyla Şahin v Turkey* (GC) App no 44774/98 ECHR 2005-XI 115.

8 *Cha'are Shalom Ve Tsedek v France* (GC) App no 27417/95 ECHR 2000-VII 231; *Francesco Sessa v Italy* App no 28790/08 (ECtHR, judgment of 3 April 2012).

9 *Phull v France* (decision) App no 35735/03 ECHR 2005-I 409; *Jasvir Singh v France* App no 25463/08 (ECtHR, decision of 30 June 2009).

10 *X v UK* App no 6886/75 (Commission Decision, 18 Mai 1976).

11 These include Aumism (*Association des Chevaliers du Lotus d'Or v France* App no 50615/07 (ECtHR, judgment of 31 Janurary 2013)), the Bhagwan Shree Rajneesh movement, also known as Osho (*Leela Förderkreis e.V. and others v Germany* App no 58911/00 (ECtHR, judgment of 6 November 2008)), Mormonism (*The Church of Jesus Christ of Latter-Day Saints v UK* App no7552/09 (ECtHR, judgment of 4 March 2014)), Raelianism (*F L v France* App no 61162/00 (ECtHR, decision of 3 November 2005)), Neo-Paganism (Ásatrúarfélagið *v Iceland* App no 22897/08 (ECtHR, decision of 18 September 2012)); Sainto Daime (*Franklin-Beentjes and CEFLU-Luz da Floresta v the Netherlands* App no 28167/07 (ECtHR, decision of 6 May 2014)), and Jehovah's Witnesses (*Religionsgemeinschaft der Zeugen Jehovas and others v Austria* App no 40825/98 (ECtHR, judgment of 31 July 2008); *Jehovah's Witnesses of Moscow and others v Russia* App no 302/02 (ECtHR, judgment of 10 June 2010)).

12 These include pacifism (*Arrowsmith v UK* App no 7050/75 (1977) 8 DR 123); principled objection to military service (*Bayatyan v Armenia* (GC) App no 23459/03 ECHR 2011-IV 1); veganism (*W v UK* App no 18187/91 (Commission Decision, 10 February 1993)); opposition to abortion (*Knudsen v Norway* App no 11045/84 (Commission Decision, 8 March 1985)); and the conviction that marriage is a lifelong union between a man and a woman and rejection of homosexual unions (*Eweida and others v UK* App nos 48420/10, 36516/10, 51671/10, 59842/10 (ECtHR, judgment of 15 January 2013)). It is not clear that the protections of Article 9 include activities of an entirely profit-making nature, however (*Company X v Switzerland* App no 7865/77 (1979) 16 DR 86); *Kustannus OY Vapaa Ajattelija AB and Others v Finland* App no 20471/92 (Commission Decision, 15 April 1996); *Church of Scientology and Others v Sweden* App no 8282/78 (1980) 21 DR 109. To the contrary, see *Cumhuriyetçi Eğitim Ve Kültür Merkezi Vakfı* (n 3).

13 *Kokkinakis v Greece* App no 14307/88 (ECtHR, judgment of 25 May 1993), para 31; *Buscarini and others v San Marino* (GC) App no 24645/94 ECHR 1999-I 605, para 34.

collective dimensions of religious exercise; under its auspices fall claims of religious adherents related to the space, time, and institutional facilities required to practice a religion, as well as activities related to dissemination of that religion.

The right to free exercise of religion stands in a complex relationship with the panoply of human rights protected under the Convention more generally. Religious exercise can be beneficial to human rights, an important source of rights-enhancing norms as well as a powerful vehicle for educating and mobilizing people in the name of rights. Consider, for instance, the Christian roots of the concept of human dignity,[14] the imprint of the Christian philosopher Jacques Maritain upon the Universal Declaration of Human Rights, or the role of African American churches in the American civil rights movement,[15] respectively.

At the same time, unconstrained religious exercise may threaten or impinge upon human rights, as for instance, when religious norms are opposed to the values of the State or the Convention,[16] or where beliefs are imposed upon others by coercion.[17] Conversely, the exercise of other freedoms may threaten religion, as, say, when the free expression of ideas strikes believers as blasphemous and offensive.[18]

Accordingly, Article 9 ECHR contemplates a number of permissible limitations upon religious freedom, and in principle, member States are granted a margin of appreciation in deciding whether and to what extent a restriction on the right to manifest one's religion and beliefs is 'necessary'.[19]

---

14 Samuel Moyn, *Christian Human Rights* (University of Pennsylvenia Press 2015).

15 Sarah Azaransky, *This Worldwide Struggle: Religion and the International Roots of the Civil Rights Movement* (OUP 2017).

16 *Khan v UK* App no 11579/85 (Commission Decision, 7 July 1986); *S.A.S. v France* (GC) App no 43835/11 ECHR 2014-III 341, para 153.

17 *Jehovah's Witnesses of Moscow* (n 11) para 119; *Larissis and others v Greece* App no 23372/94 (ECtHR, judgment of 24 February 1998), para 45.

18 See, among many authorities, *Otto-Preminger-Institut v Austria* App no 13470/87 (1994) Series A no 295-A, para 47; *Wingrove v UK* App no 17419/90 ECHR 1996-V; *İ.A. v Turkey* App no 42571/98 ECHR 2005-VIII 235; *Giniewski v France* App no 64016/00 ECHR 2006-I 277; *Klein v Slovakia* App no 72208/01 (ECtHR, judgment of 31 October 2006); see also *X. Ltd. and Y. v the UK* App no 8710/79 (1982) 28 DR 77. At the same time, the right to religious freedom without interference does not guarantee a right to bring legal proceedings against those who offend the sensitivities of an individual or group (*Dubowska and Skup v Poland* App nos 33490/96, 34055/96 (Commission Decision, 18 April 1997); *Choudhury v UK* App no 17439/90 (Commission Decision, 5 March 1991); *Ben El Mahi and others v Denmark* (decision) App no 5853/06 ECHR 2006-XV 365).

19 Several limitations upon permissible manifestations of religious belief are possible under the Convention. First, not every act motivated, inspired, or influenced by religious belief constitutes a manifestation of religion or belief entitled to Article 9's protections.

Where religion and human rights stand in an oppositional relationship, the Court, in its review, will seek to ensure that the two competing rights are protected as far as is possible by the governing organs of a member State; that an appropriate legal framework to ensure these rights is established and applied in practice; and that a fair balance is struck among the competing rights.[20] When a right such as the freedom of religion comes into conflict with another Convention right, these must be balanced against each other.[21]

In such cases, the member State and, if necessary, the European Court of Human Rights (ECtHR) must balance the two opposing rights in such a way as to respect the importance of both. This is far from a simple task. In addition to maintaining an eye to the particularities of the individual case and differences in member States' traditions and values, the Court must avoid the pitfalls of casuistic, situation-specific 'balancing' of rights, which has been criticized as an unprincipled mode of decision-making.[22] Balancing can leave large questions unanswered, and may be opaque in its reasoning. Insofar as it leaves behind little in the way of a precedential trail, it is difficult for lower courts to apply and leaves these with little incentives toward self-discipline and consistency. This chapter explores these theoretical concerns by examining the case law of the ECtHR in cases where human rights and religion stand in conflict.

Our analysis suggests a certain asymmetry. Where religious intolerance is a threat to human rights – as found in cases concerning political extremism and extradition, in particular – we find that the Court has offered broad protection for the values of democracy and individual freedom. Where, on the

---

To count as such, the act in question must be intimately linked to the religion or belief and must be sincere (*X v UK* App no 7291/75 (1977) 11 DR 55). Secondly, interference with such a manifestation may be justified if the religious act is incompatible with the key principles underlying the Convention, as in the case of polygamous or underage marriage or a flagrant breach of gender equality (*Khan* (n 16)), or where religious beliefs are imposed upon believers by force or coercion (*Larissis* (n 17) para 45). Thirdly, the State may limit speech and expression in pursuit of the legitimate aims provided in Article 9 para 2.

20 *Karaahmend v Bulgaria* App no 30587/13 (ECtHR, judgment of 24 February 2015), paras 91–96.

21 Nicholas Bratza, 'The 'Precious Asset': Freedom of Religion Under the European Convention on Human Rights' (2012) 14 Ecclestiastical Law Journal, 256; Françoise Tulkens, 'Freedom of Religion under the European Convention on Human Rights: A Precious Asset' (2015) 2014 BYU Law Review 509, 522.

22 Jürgen Habermas, *Between Facts and Norms* (William Rehg tr, 2nd edn, Polity 1996) 256–259.

other hand, religious freedom comes under threat as a result of the exercise of other rights – as typified in cases on freedom of assembly of religious groups, and freedom of religious expression through the wearing of symbols or clothing – the Court has charted a path of judicial minimalism that, to some, has proven unsatisfactory.[23] This chapter argues that a more robust understanding of religious claims as constitutive of individual autonomy on the part of the religious believer might yield a jurisprudence at once more regular, principled, and just.

2 Religion as a Threat to Human Rights: Extremist Political Parties and Extradition

Article 9 ECHR protects religious freedom against threats from individuals, as well as from politics and society. Yet freedom can be limited in the pursuit of one of the following ends: the protection of public safety, public order, health or morals, or the protection of the rights and freedoms of others.[24] An important, and increasingly common, site of such limitations is in States' responses to perceived threats to the societal and political order in the form of extremist religious parties.

In the well-known case of *Refah Partisi v Turkey*,[25] the Court upheld the severest of limitations upon a religious political party's free exercise, made in the name of the Convention values of democratic pluralism and tolerance. In 1998, the Constitutional Court of Turkey had allowed the Turkish authorities to ban the Islamist Refah Partisi (Welfare Party), the largest in Parliament, on the grounds that its platform and activities violated the constitutional principles of secularism and separation of church and state. The party's assets were confiscated, and many of its members were forced to leave Parliament and were banned from founding or joining any other political party for five years.

23 Ian Leigh, 'Damned if they do, Damned if they don't: the European Court of Human Rights and the Protection of Religion from Attack' (2011) 17 Res Publica 55 (arguing that embellishment and over-emphasis of freedom of religion; excessive use of the margin of appreciation; and the devaluing of some forms of offensive speech plague the Court's jurisprudence on religiously offensive expression).

24 In contrast to Articles 8 para 2, 10 para 2 and 11 para 2 of the Convention and Article 2 para 3 of Protocol No. 4, 'national security' is not included among the aims listed in Article 9 para 2. This omission is not accidental, in consequence of which no national security interest can authorize a State to dictate what a person believes (*Nolan and K. v Russia* App no 2512/04 (ECtHR, judgment of 12 February 2009), para 73).

25 (GC) App nos 41340/98, 41342/98, 41343/98, 41344/98 ECHR 2003-II 267.

Upon review of the case, the ECtHR upheld the ban. It considered the interference upon party members' rights a lawful exercise of the State's power to pursue the legitimate aims of Article 9 ECHR, in this case protecting public safety, defending rights and freedoms, and preventing disorder or crime. Furthermore, reasoned the Court, the ban had responded to a 'pressing social need': preventing the enactment of policies violative of Convention rights and freedoms, a distinct possibility given Refah's numerical strength in Parliament at the time of its dissolution. Party leaders had espoused proposals to refound the Turkish state on sharia law, as well as to introduce different legal regimes for individuals of different religions. And although it was not clear that the party itself endorsed violence, the fact that party leaders had not distanced themselves from members who had publicly called for the use of force to bring about political change justified the Turkish authorities' uncompromising response to that perceived threat. Finally, the interference had been proportional, as not all Refah members had been forced out of office, and the prohibition on political activities imposed on party leaders had been temporary.

The judgment did not fail to earn its share of controversy and criticism,[26] but it articulated the core principles grounding the Court's review of contested religious exercise by political parties: legal and religious pluralism and tolerance as foundational values of a democratic society; the importance of respect for constitutional principles, such as that of secularism; and an emphasis on context, namely the historical and cultural experience of a State – in this case, Turkey's history of struggles against Islamic fundamentalism – as important factors in assessing the lawfulness of a limitation upon free exercise by a religious party.[27]

Under the Court's jurisprudence concerning threats to individuals as a result of religion, of particular importance has been the assertion of the extraterritorial protection of Convention rights in cases where individuals are faced with a risk of persecution as a result of deportation. In several emblematic cases, we find a coherent and uniform body of cases that articulates clear principles of review.

In *N.K. v France*[28] and *Singh and others v Belgium*,[29] the Court found a violation in the proposed deportation of applicants who faced the risk of

26 Christopher Moe, 'Refah Partisi (the Welfare Party) and Others v Turkey' (2003) vol 6 no 1 *The International Journal of Not-for-Profit Law.*

27 The European Court of Human Rights has heard nine cases against Turkey concerning political party bans by Turkey's Constitutional Court; a violation was found in all but *Refah Partisi* (n 26). See, also, *Staatkundig Gereformeerde Partij v the Netherlands* App no 58369/10 (ECtHR, decision of 10 July 2012), para 71.

28 App no 7974/11 (ECtHR, judgment of 19 December 2013).

29 App no 33210/11 (ECtHR, judgment of 2 October 2012).

ill-treatment in their native countries. In both instances, applicants' petitions for asylum had been dismissed on the basis of a cursory review of the provided materials. The Court found that authorities had failed to make an effort to verify the authenticity of the materials, and to assess the real risk of ill-treatment that the applicants faced.

The landmark case *F.G. v Sweden*[30] expanded upon these cases, reiterating that where there were substantial grounds to believe that a potential deportee, if expelled, would face a real risk of ill-treatment in their native country, a Convention State was bound to not expel that person. The applicant was an Iranian national facing deportation to Iran by Swedish authorities and who, as a converted Christian and a political activist against the regime, was in fear for his life. The Swedish authorities found the man's potential risk of ill-treatment as an activist to be insufficient to stay his deportation, and did not examine the level of risk he faced in Iran as a converted Christian in light of the fact that the man, alleging that his religious faith was a 'private' matter, had not invoked his recent religious conversion as ground for asylum. The Court, however, considered that the Swedish authorities had failed to discharge their duty to assess the level of risk faced by the applicant. The applicant's reluctance to invoke his religious conversion as a ground for asylum notwithstanding, in view of the well-known risk to Christians living in Iran, it was incumbent upon Swedish authorities to carry out an investigation as to whether the individual faced risk as a member of a particular group systematically exposed to ill-treatment in the destination country. Accordingly, the Court found a violation of Articles 2 and 3 ECHR in the proposed deportation.

Emerging from these cases were several important principles related to the rights of individuals facing persecution by intolerant religious majorities. First, authorities could not reject documentary evidence submitted by asylum seekers without any prior verification of its authenticity. Secondly, as concerned the substantiation of an applicant's risk of ill-treatment, in consideration of the absolute nature of the rights guaranteed under Articles 2 and 3 of the Convention, and the position of vulnerability in which asylum seekers find themselves, where a Contracting State was made aware of facts relating to an individual that could expose him or her to a risk of ill-treatment upon returning to their native country, State authorities were obligated to carry out, of their own motion, an assessment of that risk. This applied in particular to situations where the national authorities were made aware of the fact that the asylum seeker could, plausibly, be a member of a religious or other group systematically exposed to a practice of ill-treatment.

30 ECtHR (GC), App no 43611/11 ECHR 2016.

3 Human Rights as a Threat to Religious Freedom: Assembly and Symbols

Under Article 9 of the Convention, all individuals have a right to publicly manifest their religious faith, whether alone or in community with others. One way in which many do so is by meeting in order to worship in the manner prescribed by their religion.[31] The right to freedom of assembly for purposes of religious worship can conflict with the rights of others. In such cases, the State may have to strike a balance in weighing competing rights of religious expression with other general rights held by individuals of the broader public.

Article 9 ECHR does not bestow a right for individuals to gather to manifest their religious beliefs wherever they wish,[32] and as provided by Article 9 para 2 ECHR, freedom of worship can be limited by Convention States in the pursuit of certain legitimate aims (the protection of public order and the rights of the people, among others). Such interferences have taken the form of the dissolution of a religious organisation; the interruption of meetings by the police; the denial of legal authorisation, recognition or approval of a religious group that seeks to assemble; and the interference by the State in an intra-denominational dispute.

By and large, where the right of religious worship comes into conflict with the rights of others, the ECtHR has resolved such conflicts by the balancing method.[33] For instance, in *Karaahmed* (n 20), a group of protestors, incited by leaders of a right-wing political party, disrupted a public prayer held at the Sofia Mosque, insulting and violently assaulting the worshippers. The Court found a violation of Article 9 ECHR (taken in conjunction with Article 11 ECHR, providing for the right to free assembly), determining that the Bulgarian police had failed to minimize the conflict and risk of violence, and therefore had not struck a 'fair balance' between respecting the respective rights of the demonstrators and the worshippers (para 107).

31 *Cyprus v Turkey* (GC) App no 25781/94 ECHR 2001 IV 1, paras 243–246.

32 *Pavlides and Georgakis v Turkey* App nos 9130/09, 9143/09 (ECtHR, decision of 2 July 2013), para 29.

33 Other such cases include *Jehovah's Witnesses of Moscow* (n 11) para 99–103; *Biblical Centre of the Chuvash Republic v Russia* App no 33203/08 (ECtHR, judgment of 12 June 2014), para 52; *Boychev and others v Bulgaria* App no 77185/01(ECtHR, judgment of 27 January 2011); *Metropolitan Church of Bessarabia and others v Moldova* App no 45701/99 ECHR 2001-XII 81; *Vergos v Greece* App no 65501/01 (ECtHR, judgment of 24 June 2004); *Holy Synod of the Bulgarian Orthodox Church and others v Bulgaria* App nos 412/03, 35677/04 (ECtHR, judgment of 16 September 2010),para 157.

The result of *Karaahmed* (n 20) appears beyond dispute; the Court concluded based on video evidence that the police had made minimal efforts to control the demonstration (paras 84, 105). However, the case still exemplifies rights balancing's potential lack of transparency: in this instance, as in many others, the guiding rationale for a judgment, namely the conclusion that Bulgarian authorities failed to ensure that 'proper consideration was given to how to strike [an] appropriate balance' (para 107) between the rights of the worshippers and the demonstrators, is rather opaque.

Of even greater concern is the possibility that balancing has been used as a way to avoid conflicts with Convention States in cases even where a broader, more principled decision-making rationale is called for. In *Krupko v Russia,*[34] applicants challenged a decision by the Russian police to break up an annual Jehovah's Witnesses celebration held in the assembly hall of the Agricultural Academy of Moscow. In that case, the Court sidestepped the issue of the lawfulness of the interference, finding a violation on the narrow grounds that, even granting authorities' concern that the Jehovah's Witnesses had failed to secure proper authorization for their gathering, the police's intervention had, in any case, clearly not been 'necessary in a democratic society' where less invasive remedies were possible (para 56). The Court did not go so far as to declare that Russia's Religions Act, which required certain groups to seek prior authorization of their meetings, even when conducted indoors, was unlawful. Yet the prior authorization requirement was not only unique among Convention States and under international law, which protects without limitations, the right of religious groups to hold indoor meetings but the statute had also recently been declared unconstitutional by the Russian Constitutional Court on the same grounds.[35]

In cases involving the more radical interference of the dissolution of an existing religious organisations, the Court has also adopted a narrow rationale emphasizing, not systemic flaws in domestic legal frameworks on religious freedom, but procedural missteps by the relevant authorities. In a case involving the dissolution of the Moscow Jehovah's Witness community, the Court found that the allegations made by authorities against the community to justify the dissolution were unsupported by evidence, or instead concerned quite normal manifestations of freedom of religion. Further, the legal framework concerning religious associations had failed to provide for any sanction less drastic than dissolution (*Jehovah's Witnesses of Moscow* (n 11) paras 114, 159).

34 App no 26587/07 (ECtHR, judgment of 26 June 2014).

35 See the concurring opinion of Judge Pinto de Albuquerque in *Krupko* (n 35).

In another case, the dissolution of a religious group had been allegedly motivated by that group's failure to secure legal authorisation and to comply with certain health and safety requirements. However, the Court noted, the applicant group had not been given any prior warning which would have enabled it to bring its conduct in compliance with health requirements, and further, the dissolution was not foreseeable, as domestic jurisprudence suggested that the organisation in question did not require special authorisation (*Biblical Centre of the Chuvash Republic* (n 34) paras 57–60). In both of these cases, the criteria employed by the Court – prior notice, leniency of sanctions, a lack of 'necessity' for the measures – failed to address core questions of the scope of the right of assembly in a religious context.[36] After all, it is one thing to find that the action of police forces was disproportional; quite another to say that the State lacks the power to criminalize peaceful religious gatherings.

Another way that individuals of faith choose to communicate their belief is through the wearing of religious clothing or symbols, an action which is therefore protected by Article 9 para 1 ECHR (*Eweida* (n 12) para 89). As with other manifestations of the right to religious freedom, the right to wear religious clothing and symbols is not absolute.[37]

The Court's case-law purports to treat differently three different realms in which religious adherents may wear symbols to manifest their faith: the public space; schools and universities; and the workplace. The distinction is justified on the grounds that the aims of the State in these respective realms may differ,

36 Making a similar critique, see the concurring opinion of Judge Pinto de Albuquerque in *Krupko* (n 35).

37 For instance, the bodies of the Convention have always refused to acknowledge the merits of complaints where the freedom to wear religiously associated items of clothing has been limited by security concerns. This has included dismissals of applications by: a Sikh fined for refusing to remove his turban in order to comply with a regulation requiring motorcyclists to wear a crash helmet (*X v UK* App no 7992/77 (1978) 14 DR 234); a Sikh obligated to remove his turban when passing the walk-through scanners at the airport (*Phull* (n 9)); an applicant requesting a visa required to remove her veil for an identity check (*El Morsli v France* App no 15585/06 (ECtHR, decision of 4 March 2008)); applicants obligated to appear bare-headed in identity photographs for official documents (*Karaduman v Turkey* App no 16278/90 (1993) 74 DR 93; *Arac v Turkey* App no 39573/11 (ECtHR, decision of 15 April 2014); *Mann Singh v France* App no 24479/07 (ECtHR, decision of 13 November 2008)). Likewise, the Court has refused to recognise the right to conscientious objection to taxation, even where motivated by protected faiths such as Quakerism (*C. v UK* App no 11882/85 (Commission Decision, 7 October 1987)) and opposition to abortion (*Bouessel du Bourg v France* App no 20747/92 (Commission Decision, 18 February 1992)).

as well as its duties. For instance, the State may require public servants to show discretion in manifesting their faith in the name of protecting the principles of secularism. The same may be true in the case of public school teachers, in view of the susceptibility of children.

In one seminal case, *Ahmet Arslan and others v Turkey,*[38] the Court found a violation in the criminal conviction of a religious group on the basis of legislation banning the wearing of certain types of religious costumes in public places. The Court agreed that the aims of the legislation – ensuring compliance with the secular democratic principles underpinning the Turkish republic, and protecting public security, order, and the freedoms of others – were legitimate. Yet it found that criminal sanctions vis-à-vis such aims had not been necessary: the prohibition had been directed at, not public servants, but ordinary citizens, and had targeted clothing worn not in specific public establishments, but throughout the public space. Furthermore, there was little evidence to suggest that the applicants, in wearing a specific type of clothing, had constituted a threat to public order or engaged in proselytism on passers-by in the streets.

Conversely, in a similar much-discussed case, *S.A.S.* (n 16), the Court upheld a French ban on wearing in public of clothing intended to cover the face (therefore including the burqa and the niqab). Distinguishing *Arslan* (n 39), it noted that the full-face Islamic veil was unique in entirely concealing the face, and accepted the French government's argument that, as the face plays an important role in human interaction and the open interpersonal relationships that constitute community life in society, the veil could be perceived as raising a barrier against others, and thereby breaching the right of all to live together in a space of socialisation. In this connection, the Court considered that the ban could be upheld as necessary to ensure the 'protection of the rights and freedoms of others' (n 16 para 140).

In the case of religious symbols being displayed public educational institutions such as primary schools and universities, the Court's case-law describes two different categories depending on whether the applicant demanding the right to wear religious clothing is a teacher or a student. As individuals, teachers qualify for protection of Article 9 of the Convention; at the same time, as public servants they have a duty to refrain from ostentatiously expressing their religious beliefs in public.[39] The Court places great importance on the possible proselytising effect that religious clothing or symbols may have on pupils, particularly in virtue of pupils' age and susceptibility. For instance, the Court

38 App no 41135/98 (ECtHR, judgment of 23 February 2010).

39 *Kurtumulus v Turkey* App no 65500/01 ECHR 2006-II 297; *Karaduman v Turkey* App no 16278/90 (1993) 74 DR 93.

upheld a prohibition on a State primary school teacher wearing an Islamic headscarf in the performance of her teaching duties. The Court reasoned that the headscarf was 'hard to square with the principle of gender equality' and 'the message of tolerance, respect for others and, above all, equality and non-discrimination that all teachers in a democratic society must convey to their pupils'. Furthermore, the Court felt, the headscarf constituted a 'powerful external symbol' capable having a persuasive effect upon young students: 'it cannot be denied outright that the wearing of a headscarf might have some kind of proselytising effect'.[40]

At the same time, the plethora of cases in which bans on students wearing religious symbols – most commonly, the Islamic headscarf or the Sikh turban – have been upheld suggests that distinctions among wearers of the religious symbol play little role in the Court's case-law in practice. In these cases, the guiding rationale has been, not the fear of proselytism by an authority figure, but rather the State's margin of appreciation to preserve the constitutional principle of secularism in public institutions of learning (*Leyla Şahin* (n 7)).[41]

As for the wearing of religious clothing in the workplace, the Court has generally upheld the prerogative of the employer to ensure and protect workplace order by dismissal of an employee who chooses to manifest his or her religious faith. A commercial company may legitimately impose a dress code on its employees in order to protect a specific commercial image; this interest, however, must be balanced against the individual's right to manifest his or her religion.[42] The Court found a violation of Article 9 ECHR where a private company dismissed an employee for refusing to conceal the Christian cross she wore, while certain other symbols of other religions (turban or hijab) were

40 *Dahlab v Switzerland* App no 42393/98 ECHR 2001-V 447.

41 See, also, *Köse and others v Turkey* (decision) App no 26625/02 ECHR 2006-II 339; *Dogru v France* App no 27058/05 (ECtHR, judgment of 4 December 2008); *Kervanci v France* App no 31645/04 (ECtHR, judgment of 4 December 2008); *Gamaleddyn v France* App no 18527/08 (ECtHR, decision of 30 June 2009); *Aktas v France* App no 43563/08 (ECtHR, decision of 6 June 2011); *Ranjit Singh v France* App no 27561/08 (ECtHR, decision of 6 June 2011); *Jasvir Singh v. France* App no 25463/08 (ECtHR, decision of 6 June 2011).

42 A recent decision by the ECJ held that an internal company rule prohibiting the visible wearing of any political, philosophical, or religious sign does not constitute direct discrimination on the basis of religion. At the same time, an employer could not invoke the wishes of a customer in no longer being served by a employee wearing an Islamic headscarf as a reason to dismiss said employee (Cases C-157/15, *Achbita, Centrum voor Gelijkheid van kansen en voor racismebestrijding v. G4S Secure Solutions* (ECJ, 14 March 2017) and C-188/15 *Bougnaoui and Association de défense des droits de l'homme* (ADDH) *v. Micropole Univers* (ECJ, 14 March 2017)).

authorised (*Eweida* (n 12) para 94). In the same case, however, the Court found no violation in a case where a nurse working in a geriatric ward was transferred for refusing to remove the cross she wore on a chain around her neck. In the particular instance, the Court accepted that the prohibition had had a legitimate aim, namely to avoid the risk that a disturbed patient might seize and pull the chain (*Eweida* (n 12) para 98–100).[43]

The duties of public servants or the fear of improper proselytism are often invoked as criteria guiding judgments in this realm. At the same time, the Court's condoning of restrictions upon the full veil in the public sphere, religious headgear worn by students in schools, and the headscarf in the workplace (although, with exceptions, not the cross) suggests that, not State values nor individual autonomy, but rather, the margin of appreciation, deployed in unpredictable or unprincipled ways, may be driving the Court's jurisprudence in this regard.

As evidenced by this quick survey of the Court's jurisprudence in the particular realm of cases where religious exercise is construed as a threat to human rights, it is difficult to find a coherent rationale to explain these results. We suggest that, here, an excessive solicitude for State claims alleging threats to the general public by particular forms of religious worship, whether gatherings or the wearing of symbols, may be at work.

In the final section, we conclude by proposing that an autonomy-enhancing principle would be a more parsimonious, principled, and ultimately fair criterion for assessing religious freedom claims, both in the context of groups of individuals seeking to worship in community and individuals manifesting their faith by wearing religious symbols or clothing.

4 Conclusion

The jurisprudence of the ECtHR in cases involving the conflict between religious expression and other human rights has been, so to speak, a mixed bag. Whereas protection of human rights against religious threats has been robust, the reverse cannot quite be claimed. Where the rights of religious believers have been threatened by the State or by the broader public, the Court has favoured either narrow proportionality analysis over clear, categorical statements of the principles that justify limitations upon the right of assembly, or a selective and superficial treatment of individual autonomy that downplays the

43 See, also, *Ebrahimian v France* App no 64846/11 ECHR 2016.

centrality of the manifestation of belief to the speaker and overemphasizes the broader public's suggestibility to persuasion by the content of those symbols. In both contexts, the effect has been to exaggerate the potential 'threat' to public order and morals posed by manifestations of religious belief.

At the same time, under the principle of subsidiarity built into the Convention system, domestic courts are the 'first line' of rights defence.[44] Furthermore, great deference by the Court is necessary when a State claims a threat to its order (*Refah Partisi* (n 26) para 102). Yet a mechanically applied practice of deference is unable to distinguish the 'imminent' danger posed by religious actors in *Refah Partisi* (n 26) from the negligible one of those in *Krupko* (n 35). In so doing, the Court has, we argue, demonstrated an excessive deference to State-initiated claims that manifestations of religious belief – through peaceful assembly and symbols – may pose threats to public 'order'.

Here we propose that in the realm of Article 9 jurisprudence involving competing rights, a criterion of jurisprudence that takes seriously and prioritizes *individual autonomy* would be, not only most consistent with the principles and values of the Convention, but also possible to implement in a way that is consistent, parsimonious, and fair. We briefly articulate what form this rationale might take, and suggest several benefits to its adoption.

The protection of individual autonomy as the main criterion for analysis of Article 9 cases involving freedom of religious assembly and expression already underpins some of the cases we have discussed. For instance, considerations of the autonomy of religious believers appear, too, in the Court's protection of the right 'to try to convince one's neighbour' as an essential element of religious freedom (*Kokkinakis* (n 13) para 31) for the religious speaker, even while it protects the listener from 'improper' or coercive proselytism (the application of improper pressure in order to induce the listener to accept the beliefs of the faith in question, by offering material or social advantage, or exploiting power differentials, for example) (*Larissis* (n 17) para 45).

And while the Court, in the much-discussed full-veil case, *S.A.S*, explicitly rejected the idea that the aim of the ban had been related to women's

44 Hersch Lauterpacht, one of the forefathers of the European Convention, argued that the Court's jurisdiction would be of a "residuary character," with domestic courts the first and main line of rights protection. The Court's first president, Lord McNair, averred similarly that the ECtHR no more than "crowns the edifice" that is the larger system of domestic courts interpreting and applying Convention law. Eirik Bjorge, *Domestic Application of the ECHR: Courts as Faithful Trustees* (OUP 2015), at 1. See, also, Kanstantsin Dzehtsiarou et al (eds), *Human Rights Law in Europe: The Influence, Overlaps and Contradictions of the EU and the ECHR* (Taylor and Francis 2014).

autonomy, the dissenting opinion pointed out that by the French authorities' own admission, the ban had clearly been motivated by a fear of paternalism:

> The first report 'on the wearing of the full-face veil on national territory', by a French parliamentary commission, saw in the veil 'a symbol of a form of subservience' .... The explanatory memorandum to the French bill referred to its 'symbolic and dehumanising violence' ... The full-face veil was also linked to the 'self-confinement of any individual who cuts himself off from others whilst living among them'. Women who wear such clothing have been described as 'effaced' from the public space ...[45]

As the French parliamentary reports made plain, the ban on the full-face veil had its origins in concerns that women, firstly, could not autonomously choose to wear the garment in view of oppressive cultural structures, and secondly, that the wearing of the veil per se excluded the wearer from full participation in society.

At the same time, if the autonomy principle underpins some of the Court's Article 9 jurisprudence, it has been inconsistently applied, frequently giving way to the margin of appreciation with little discernible explanation as to when or why the latter principle should take precedence. In *Krupko* (n 35), as noted, the Court found a violation on grounds of necessity in a democratic society, but left untouched a law which departed from international practice and which had already been declared unconstitutional by the Russian Constitutional Court.[46] In other cases, symbols are sometimes treated as if they possessed their own content and meaning; sometimes not. For instance, while the Court has held that crucifixes in public classrooms did not necessarily 'encourage the development of teaching practices with a proselytising tendency', in cases involving Islamic symbols like the headscarf in the classroom, the Court has accepted that these symbols *per se* may have a 'proselytising effect' or may be 'hard to square' with Convention values like gender equality, tolerance, and non-discrimination.[47]

---

45 ECHR, *S.A.S. v France* (n 16), para 6.

46 As the dissenting opinion in *Krupko* pointed out, the right to assemble indoors is guaranteed without any limitations in many European countries (eg, Czechoslovakia, Denmark, Germany, Greece, Italy, and Spain).

47 *Lautsi and others v Italy* (GC) App no 30814/06 ECHR 2011-III 61, para 74; *Dahlab* (n 41); *Leyla Şahin* (n 7). It is worth recalling that the Court has, on repeated occasions, stated that the State's role as the 'neutral and impartial organiser' of the exercise of various religions, faiths and beliefs, and its 'duty of neutrality and impartiality' are incompatible with the power to assess the legitimacy of religious beliefs or the ways in which those beliefs are expressed; see *Hasan and Chaouch* (n 7) para 76; *Leyla Şahin* (n 7) para 107.

We submit that in the context of religious freedom, a flawed theory of individual autonomy is at work. On the one hand, this jurisprudence routinely conceives of the listener or witness to manifestations of religious belief as implausibly susceptible to conversion, all the while exaggerating the inherent 'proselytising effect' that religious symbols have in context. On the other side, insufficient recognition has been granted to the centrality to individual identity that religious claims have for the speaker. As a result, the Court has sometimes granted excessive credence to arguments advanced by States that demonize such displays as a violation of 'public order'.[48]

In this regard, we would propose that a more realistic treatment of autonomy in these cases would partly mitigate these problems. Such an approach:

- Conceives of manifestations of religious belief as involving far weightier autonomy claims for the speaker than for the listener/observers. Consequentially, a claim about the right of the 'public' to not be exposed to an offensive practice (the wearing of the veil, the witnessing of a demonstration) must be met with caution;
- Does not treat ordinary expressions of religious belief as improper intrusions upon the listener, or upon the public more broadly, except insofar as these involve 'improper' or coercive means. The Court's jurisprudence on proselytism is a guide here: ordinary attempts 'to try to convince one's neighbour' are protected under the Convention except where these involve the application of pressure, the offering of material or social advantage, or the exploitation of power differentials, and so forth (*Kokkinakis* (n 13) para 31; *Larissis* (n 17) para 45);
- Limits claims by the State that religious symbols are per se a disruption of 'public order' or a violation of secularism (the State would enjoy a greater margin of appreciation in the context of public spaces, where the wearer is a public servant, or where the State can prove a disruption or threat); and
- Avoids, to the extent possible, inquiries into the content of a symbol, for instance in attempting to remedy 'symbolic' violence. In this regard, allegations of the 'proselytising effect' of symbols should be supported with evidence.

A host of complex jurisprudential questions will remain unresolved by this exercise. Religious expression, whether in the staging of a public prayer or

48 This appears to be more the case in the case of symbols and clothing than in the context of religious assembly (contrast, for instance, *Dahlab* (n 41) and *Karaahmed* (n 20)).

the wearing of a turban, necessarily comprises both collective and individual dimensions which must be reconciled. The question of whether individual autonomy is best realized through state intervention or abstention will endure, as will situational decisions about reconciling multiple competing interests.

At the same time, the Court must refrain from upholding State-imposed sanctions that, under the guise of concerns for public order or proselytism, criminalize practices that a majority finds merely distasteful. A manifestation of religious belief may not be limited merely on the grounds that it is 'perceived as strange by many of those who observe it' (*S.A.S.* (n 16) para 120). In light of the critique presented here of the Court's jurisprudence in two contested realms of freedom of religious exercise, a more robust and realistic account of individual autonomy would better account for claims of religious freedom and the significance they hold for people of faith, resulting in a jurisprudence that is more principled, reasoned, and just.

PART 6

Religion and Other Individual Rights

CHAPTER 14

Discrimination in the Name of Religion in Employment and Occupation: An ILO Perspective

Ninon Colneric

1 Introduction

In 1998, the International Labour Organization (ILO) adopted the Declaration on Fundamental Principles and Rights at Work.[1] It states that, in freely joining the ILO, all Member States have endorsed the principles and rights set out in its Constitution and in the Declaration of Philadelphia. These principles and rights have been expressed in the form of specific rights and obligations in conventions recognized as fundamental both inside and outside the Organization. The Declaration concludes that the Member States have to respect and promote principles and rights in four categories, whether or not they have ratified the relevant conventions. One of these categories is the elimination of discrimination in respect of employment and occupation.

This matter is covered by ILO Convention No. 111 of 1958 concerning discrimination in respect of employment and occupation.[2] The fact that this convention was included in the core conventions of the ILO underlines its importance.

The cornerstones of Convention No. 111 are a definition of the term 'discrimination'[3] and an obligation to pursue a national policy designed to promote equality of opportunity and treatment in respect of employment and occupation, with a view to eliminating any discrimination in respect thereof.[4]

Article 1(1)(a) of Convention No. 111 defines the term 'discrimination' with reference to a number of criteria, among them 'religion'.[5] The term

1 <www.ilo.org/declaration/thedeclaration/textdeclaration/lang--en/index.htm> accessed 2 February 2017.

2 Discrimination (Employment and Occupation) Convention, 1958 (No. 111), 362 UNTS 31, adopted 25 June 1958, entered into force 15 June 1960 <www.ilo.org/dyn/normlex/en/f?p=NORMLEXPUB:12100:0::NO::P12100_ILO_CODE:C111> accessed 2 February 2017.

3 Article 1 of Convention No. 111.

4 Article 2 of Convention No. 111.

5 The non-authoritative German translation published in the Bundesgesetzblatt (BGBl. 1961 II, 97, 98) translates 'religion' as 'Glaubensbekenntnis,' which has a slightly different connotation

 | DOI:10.1163/9789004349155_015

'discrimination' includes any distinction, exclusion or preference made on the basis of one of the listed criteria, which has the effect of nullifying or impairing equality of opportunity or treatment in employment or occupation. According to Article 1(3) of the convention, the term 'employment and occupation' includes access to vocational training, access to employment and to particular occupations, and terms and conditions of employment.[6]

This chapter shall focus on the provision of the convention that defines what does not constitute discrimination. Article 1(2) of the convention provides: 'Any distinction, exclusion or preference in respect of a particular job based on the inherent requirements thereof shall not be deemed to be discrimination'.

As this part of the book is about the relation between religion and other individual rights, my chapter shall mainly discuss to what extent religion can be invoked to curtail individual rights of others; it deals with discrimination in the name of religion. Discrimination on the basis of religion is only covered insofar as the source of this discrimination is another religion.

The problem of discrimination in the name of religion is particularly acute in Germany where the churches and their organizations are the second largest employer after the public service.[7]

2 The Discrimination (Employment and Occupation) Convention, 1958 (No. 111)

Several bodies of the ILO have expressed their opinion about the interpretation of Convention No. 111 in the framework of the ILO supervisory system.[8] In 1988, the ILO Committee of Experts on the Application of Conventions and Recommendations (in the following referred to as 'Committee of Experts') published a general survey about equality of treatment in employment

---

because it refers to the act of confessing. However, only the English and French versions of the text of Convention No. 111 are authoritative (Article 14 of Convention No. 111).

6 The non-authoritative German translation published in the Bundesgesetzblatt (BGBl. 1961 II, 97, 98) translates 'access' in a somewhat misleading way as 'Zulassung' as if it were a matter of an administrative decision.

7 Burkhard Schäfers, 'Engagiert, aber nicht bibeltreu' (*ZEIT ONLINE*, 22 November 2014) <www.zeit.de/gesellschaft/zeitgeschehen/2014-11/kirche-arbeitsrecht-arbeitgeber-homosexualitaet> accessed 2 February 2017.

8 The ILO supervisory system is explained here <www.ilo.org/global/about-the-ilo/how-the-ilo-works/ilo-supervisory-system-mechanism/lang--en/index.htm> accessed 2 February 2017.

and occupation.[9] In 1996, it presented a special, much shorter survey on Convention No. 111.[10] One of its objectives was to provide the ILO with an educational tool for promotional activities in relation to the Convention. In interpreting Convention No. 111, the Committee of Experts has consistently referred to these two reports. They are also major points of reference in the General Survey on the fundamental Conventions concerning rights at work in light of the ILO Declaration on Social Justice for a Fair Globalization (2008), presented in 2012.[11]

When dealing with religion, the ILO supervisory bodies sometimes make reference to case-law concerning other grounds of discrimination, in particular political opinion. For this reason, this chapter will also include some material related to other grounds of discrimination.

The following picture emerges from the various documents produced by the ILO supervisory system:

The scope of Convention No. 111 is very broad, extending to all sectors of activity and covering employment both in the public and private sectors.[12] As the Committee of Experts put it in the General Survey of 1988, '[p]rotection against discrimination in employment and occupation should not be limited by a restrictive definition of employment. No employment and no occupation is excluded from the scope of the Convention, which covers all workers'.[13]

The term 'religion' has to be given a broad meaning. Thus the Committee of Experts criticized the discrimination of the free-masons and of organizations whose constitutions imply atheism in the Islamic Republic of Iran.[14]

9 Equality in Employment and Occupation, General Survey by the Committee of Experts on the Application of Conventions and Recommendations, International Labour Conference, 75th Session, Report III (Part 4B), Geneva 1988. Paras 47–53 deal with religion, paras 125–133 with inherent requirements of a particular job.

10 Equality in Employment and Occupation, Special Survey on Equality in Employment and Occupation in respect of Convention N. 111 by the Committee of Experts on the Application of Conventions and Recommendations, International Labour Conference, 83rd Session, Report III (Part 4B), Geneva 1996. Paras 41–42 deal with religion, paras 118–122 with inherent requirements of a particular job.

11 Report of the Committee of Experts on the Application of Conventions and Recommendations, International Labour Conference, 101st Session, Report III (Part 1B), Geneva 2012. Paras 798–801 deal with religion, paras 827–831 with distinctions, exclusion or preferences bases on inherent requirements.

12 Special Survey (n 10) para 79.

13 General Survey, 1988 (n 9) para 88.

14 ibid, para 50.

It also noted that the risk of discrimination often arises from the absence of religious beliefs.[15]

On the other hand, the Committee of Experts consistently stressed that Article 1(2) of Convention No. 111, which deals with inherent requirements of a particular job, must be interpreted restrictively.[16] It is considered as an exception.[17]

Article 1(2) of Convention No. 111 is composed of two elements: on the one hand, the concept of 'a particular job' and, on the other hand, the term 'inherent requirements'.

Regarding the first element, the Committee of Experts stated:

> It appears from the preparatory work and the text of the Convention as ultimately adopted, that the concept of 'a particular job' refers to a specific and definable job, function or task. Any limitation within the context of this exception must be required by the characteristics of the particular job, and be in proportion to its inherent requirements. Certain criteria may be brought to bear as inherent requirements of a particular job, but they may not be applied to all jobs in a given occupation or sector of activity, … without coming into conflict with the principle of equality of opportunity and treatment in occupation and employment.[18]

A narrow interpretation of the term 'a particular job' was also adopted by the ILO Commission of Inquiry appointed in proceedings against the Federal Republic of Germany because of the so-called Radicals Decree. The inquiry concerned discrimination on the basis of political opinion. One feature of the report is also of major interest in the context of discrimination on the basis of religion: The Commission of Inquiry drew the attention to an inadequacy of the German translation of Article 1(2) of Convention No. 111. 'A particular job' had been translated as 'eine bestimmte Beschäftigung'. The Commission of Inquiry noted that the expression 'eine bestimmte Beschäftigung' is capable of referring not merely to 'a particular job' but to a broader sector of employment.

15 Special Survey (n 10) para 41.

16 ibid, para 118; General Survey, 1988, (n 9) para 125 ('The exception allowed for in Article 1 paragraph 2, of the Convention, must be interpreted strictly, so as not to result in undue limitation of the protection which the Convention is intended to provide.')

17 General Survey, 1988, (n 9) para 125; Special Survey (n 10) para 118.

18 General Survey, 1988, (n 9) para 126. See also Special Survey (n 10) para 119, and General Survey, 2012, (n 11) para 828.

It recapitulated the history of the provision and concluded that the exception relates to specific posts, work or functions. [19]

Not only the element 'a particular job' but also the element 'inherent requirements' must be interpreted restrictively. In 1958, the Employer's members submitted a subamendment to insert after the words 'inherent requirements of the job' the words 'or the particular circumstances under which the job is being performed'. The Conference Committee rejected it.[20]

In the case concerning the Radicals Decree, the Commission of Inquiry held: 'The word "inherent," which is used in the English text, is defined in the Oxford English Dictionary in the following terms: "existing in something as a permanent attribute or quality; forming an element, especially an essential element, of something; intrinsic, essential." A corresponding idea is expressed by the words used in the French text ("qualifications exigées"). … Accordingly, any limitation which it is sought to bring within the scope of the exception provided for in Article 1, paragraph 2, must be necessary because of the very nature of the job in question. The notion of "necessity" is widely resorted to in international human rights instruments as a criterion restricting exceptions to the rights recognised therein'.[21]

It implies the principle of proportionality already briefly mentioned above. The Commission of Inquiry dealing with the Radicals Decree spelled this out in detail:

> Moreover, in considering whether a particular limitation can be justified as necessary, it is not sufficient to address only the question whether circumstances exist in which action may be called for to meet a purpose for which limitations are authorised by the provision in question. One must also consider whether the form and extent of the measures actually provided for or taken are commensurate with the exigencies of the situation. In other words, the limitation must be proportionate to the aim pursued.[22]

---

19 Report of the Commission of Inquiry appointed under Art. 26 of the ILO Constitution to examine the observance by the Federal Republic of Germany of Convention No. 111, ILO Official Bulletin, Volume LXXX, 1987, Series B, Supplement 1, para 530.

20 Report of the committee set up to examine the representation presented by the Norwegian Federation of Trade Unions (LO) under article 24 of the Constitution alleging non-observance of the Discrimination (Employment and Occupation) Convention, 1958 (No. 111) by Norway, para 22.

21 Report of the Commission of Inquiry (n 19) para 531.

22 ibid.

According to the Committee of Experts,

> [r]estrictions for a narrow range of jobs associated with particular religious or political institutions or non-profit organizations and organizations specifically promoting the well-being of an ethnic group may be acceptable. Criteria such as political opinion, national extraction and religion may be taken into account as inherent requirements of certain posts involving special responsibilities. However, the inherent requirements of the particular job must still be evaluated in the light of the actual bearing of the tasks performed on the institution's or organization's objective.[23]

More specifically, the Committee of Experts stated that

> [p]olitical opinions may in certain limited circumstances constitute a bona fide qualification for certain senior administrative posts, for example in those involving special responsibilities for the development of government. However, it is essential that this not be carried beyond certain limits – to be evaluated on a case-by-case basis ....[24]

Insofar as national provisions restrict jobs associated with a particular religion to persons of that religion, this exclusion cannot be applied to all work performed for a religious organization (such as building maintenance).[25]

In its General Survey of 2012, the Committee of Experts concluded: 'There are very few instances where the grounds listed in the Convention actually constitute inherent requirements of the job'.[26]

An example from the case-law of the ILO supervisory bodies is a complaint by the Norwegian Federation of Trade Unions relating to § 55A of the Norwegian Worker Protection and Working Environment Act. A committee of the ILO Governing Body had to deal with the question of whether this provision was compatible with Convention No. 111.

When this provision was adopted, both the Government and a parliamentary majority considered that, for example, in institutions with a Christian objective, the administration of such institutions would have a right to demand information of applicants regarding their Christian faith, even if the

23 General Survey, 2012, (n 11) para 831.

24 Special Survey (n 10) para 122.

25 ibid, para 121.

26 General Survey, 2012, (n 11) para 830.

application applied to positions as cleaners, kitchen assistants, caretakers, etc.[27] The committee of the Governing Body regarded § 55A as incompatible with Convention No. 111.[28] It would accord with Article 1(2) of the Convention if, in regard to advertisements for Christian kindergarten and private school teachers, information on one's views on life, etc. could only be required of personnel who are to teach the philosophy of life in question.[29]

Another example from the work of the ILO supervisory bodies are the critical remarks of the Committee of Experts on the Anti-Discrimination Act of Slovakia. Under this Act, different treatment on the basis of sex or religion by registered churches, religious societies and other legal entities, whose activities are based on religion or belief, was not held to be discriminatory when relating to employment by or to carrying out activities for such organizations. The Committee of Experts recommended that this provision be interpreted strictly and limited solely to particular jobs based on the inherent requirements thereof.[30] Subsequently, the Slovakian Government explained that this concerns persons specifically performing activities of the clergy. The Committee of Experts asked the Slovakian Government to monitor the application of the provision concerned so as to ensure that, in practice, it is strictly limited to particular jobs based on the inherent requirements thereof.[31] Meanwhile, the text of the respective provision has been changed.[32] I shall come back to this later on.

3 Comparison with EU Legislation

It is noteworthy that the protection against discrimination in the name of religion provided by ILO Convention No. 111 is more comprehensive than that conferred by EU legislation.

27 Report of the committee set up to examine the representation presented by the Norwegian Federation of Trade Unions (LO) under article 24 of the Constitution alleging non-observance of the Discrimination (Employment and Occupation) Convention, 1958 (No. 111) by Norway, para 12.

28 ibid, paras 27 and 32.

29 ibid, para 27.

30 Direct Request (CEACR) – adopted 2007, published 97th ILC session (2008).

31 Direct Request (CEACR) – adopted 2009, published 99th ILC session (2010); Direct Request (CEACR) – adopted 2011, published 101st ILC session (2012).

32 European network of legal experts in gender equality and non-discrimination, Country report Non-discrimination Slovakia 2015, 80 <http://ec.europa.eu/justice/discrimination/files/ad_2014_country_reports/2015-sk-country_report_nd_final.pdf> accessed 8 June 2017.

This is the effect of Article 4 of the Council Directive 2000/78/EC of 27 November 2000 establishing a general framework for equal treatment in employment and occupation.[33] The Directive deals with occupational requirements which Member States may admit. Its Article 4 comprises two paragraphs. The first is of general application, the second deals with religious organizations.

Pursuant to paragraph 1, Member States may provide that a difference of treatment which is based on a characteristic related to any of the grounds covered by the Directive shall not constitute discrimination where, by reason of the nature of the particular occupational activities concerned or of the context in which they are carried out, such a characteristic constitutes a genuine and determining occupational requirement, provided that the objective is legitimate and the requirement is proportionate. As stated above, in 1958, the ILO Conference Committee had rejected the employer's attempt to insert after the words 'inherent requirements of the job' the words 'or the particular circumstances under which the job is being performed' into Article 1(2) of Convention No. 111.[34] At EU level, the essence of that formula reappears, thus broadening the scope of exceptions which, under EU law, are permitted.

Article 4(2) of the Framework Directive opens the door to exceptions even further. It has to be seen in the light of the Declaration No. 11 on the status of churches and non-confessional organizations, annexed to the Final Act of the Amsterdam Treaty of 1997. This so-called Amsterdam Declaration on Churches can be mainly traced back to the German chancellor Helmut Kohl.[35] It reads:

> The European Union respects and does not prejudice the status under national law of churches and religious associations or communities in the Member States.
>
> The European Union equally respects the status of philosophical and non-confessional organisations.[36]

33 OJ L303/16.

34 See n 20.

35 Frauke Gebert, 'The Role Of Religion In the European Union' (2014) 6 <http://eu.bilgi.edu.tr/media/uploads/2014/06/30/The_Role_Of_Religion_In_the_European_Union_by_Frauke_Gebert.pdf> accessed 2 February 2017.

36 Declaration No. 11 on the status of churches and non-confessional organiations, [1997] OJ C340/133; now Article 17(1) and (2) Treaty on the Functioning of the European Union.

The German Basic Law is an instance of national law granting a special status to churches. On the one hand, it contains provisions interdicting discrimination because of religious opinions[37] and conferring freedom of faith and conscience.[38] On the other hand, it contains an article which integrates provisions about religious denominations of the Weimar Constitution of 1919 into the Basic Law,[39] among them this clause: 'Religious societies shall regulate and administer their affairs independently within the limits of the law that applies to all'.[40]

The Framework Directive refers to the Amsterdam Declaration on Churches in its 24th recital. Germany, which had already forced through this declaration, successfully pressed for adding a special paragraph on churches to Article 4 of the Framework Directive.[41] It deals specifically with occupational activities within churches and other public or private organizations the ethos of which is based on religion or belief. In relation to such activities, Member States may maintain national legislation – or provide for future legislation incorporating national practices existing at the date of adoption of this Directive – pursuant to which a difference of treatment based on a person's religion or belief shall not constitute discrimination where, by reason of the nature of these activities or of the context in which they are carried out, a person's religion or belief constitute a genuine, legitimate and justified occupational requirement, having regard to the organization's ethos. The next sentence provides, among other things, that this difference of treatment shall be implemented taking account of Member States' constitutional provisions and principles.

In its implementing legislation, Germany put the right to self-determination of the religious community concerned and the nature of the particular activity on an equal footing.[42] The EU Commission launched an infringement procedure. The case was closed because Germany and the EU Commission agreed that the problem could be solved by interpretation in conformity with the Framework Directive.[43]

37 Article 3(3) of the Basic Law.

38 Article 4 of the Basic Law.

39 Article 140 of the Basic Law.

40 Article 137(3)(1) of the Weimar Constitution.

41 Gerhard Czermak, *Religions- und Weltanschauungsrecht* (Springer 2008) 260.

42 Article 9 of the Allgemeines Gleichbehandlungsgesetz (General Act on Equal Treatment) of 14 August 2006, BGBL. 2006 I, 1897.

43 Ingrid Matthäus-Maier, 'Die Kirchen auf dem "Dritten Weg"' (2012) 1 MIZ <www.miz-online.de/node/343> accessed 2 February 2017.

The problem of non-conformity with ILO Convention No. 111 remains. In a milder form it also exists in Slovakia. This country reacted to the criticism of the ILO Committee of Experts by adopting a legislation more in line with Article 1(2) of the Convention. However, the exception created for employers with an ethos based on religion or belief does not only refer to 'the nature of occupational activities' but alternatively to 'the context in which they are carried out', [44] thus following the model of Article 4 of the Framework Directive.

4 Comparison with the ECHR

To conclude, let me cast a glance at the case-law of the European Court of Human Rights (ECtHR). In the case *Schüth v Germany*,[45] the applicant was an organist and choirmaster who had been dismissed by a Catholic parish church because he had left his wife and lived with another partner. The ECtHR held that there had been a violation of Article 8 of the Convention for the Protection of Human Rights and Fundamental Freedoms, which confers the right to respect for private and family life. In its reasoning, the ECtHR stated: 'Whilst it is true that, under the Convention, an employer whose ethos is based on religion or on a philosophical belief may impose specific duties of loyalty on its employees, a decision to dismiss based on a breach of such duty cannot be subjected, on the basis of the employer's right of autonomy, only to a limited judicial scrutiny exercised by the relevant domestic employment tribunal without having regard to the nature of the post in question and without properly balancing the interests involved in accordance with the principle of proportionality'.[46] The Court pointed out that Germany's transposition of the Framework Directive into its domestic law was subject, in relation to certain points, of a complaint by the European Commission on comparable grounds.[47]

This case-law is entirely in line with Art. 1(2) of ILO Convention No. 111.

44 European Commission, European network of legal experts in gender equality and non-discrimination, 'Country report Non-discrimination Slovakia 2015', p 80 <http://ec.europa.eu/justice/discrimination/files/ad_2014_country_reports/2015-sk-country_report_nd_final.pdf> accessed 24 October 2017.

45 App no 1620/03 ECHR 2010-V 397.

46 ibid, para 69.

47 ibid, para 70.

5 Conclusion

To sum up: We are faced with two different ways of dealing with religion in the framework of anti-discrimination law. One way is to treat religion just as other possible grounds for discrimination. This is the path adopted by ILO Convention No. 111 and also by the European Convention on Human Rights. The other way is to create special rights for the churches and comparable organization which give additional weight to their interests. This is the path adopted by the German legislation and, under its impact, to a lesser extent also by EU legislation. It is time to recall the obligations under Convention No. 111. It strictly limits the instances where religion can be invoked to curtail individual rights of others. However, unfortunately, Germany has used its political weight to water this approach down at the level of the EU.

CHAPTER 15

Religion et droits des femmes : le concordat n'aura pas lieu

Sophie Grosbon

> La compatibilité entre … la liberté de pratiquer une religion, un culte ou un rite, et les droits fondamentaux de la femme en tant que droits universels, pose … un problème essentiel. Le problème provient du fait que certaines pratiques préjudiciables à la santé, ou au statut juridique, ou de manière générale à la condition de la femme sont revendiquées par des personnes ou des communautés ou encore des Etats qui exercent ces pratiques ou les perçoivent comme une composante de la liberté de religion et comme une obligation religieuse à laquelle, eux et leurs ancêtres, se sont soumis depuis des temps immémoriaux et qui semblent à leurs yeux étrangères à toute question de protection universelle des droits des femmes. L'universalité des droits de la femme en tant que personne humaine nous entraîne ainsi dans un débat classique mais toujours d'actualité : celui de l'universalité des droits de l'homme et de la femme, en particulier face aux spécificités culturelles[1].

La question des relations entre religion et droits des femmes relève d'un débat classique mais par ailleurs tout à fait symptomatique des tensions qui traversent tant la philosophie que le droit international des droits de l'Homme : confrontation entre liberté individuelle et ordre moral quand les droits des femmes sont limités par des impératifs religieux[2] ; conflit entre liberté individuelle et

1 Rapport soumis par M. Abdelfattah Amor, Rapporteur spécial, conformément à la résolution 2001/42 de la Commission des droits de l'Homme, *Etude sur la liberté de religion ou de conviction et la condition de la femme au regard de la religion et des traditions*, E/CN.4/2002/73/Add.2, § 3.

2 V. *Infra* : les multiples réserves à la Convention sur l'élimination de toutes les formes de discrimination à l'égard des femmes justifiées par le respect de la Charia (CEDAW/SP/2010/2) ; « Les positions prises par le Saint-Siège » au cours de la 4ème Conférence mondiale sur les femmes « à l'égard des méthodes de planification de la famille que l'Eglise catholique considère comme moralement inacceptables », à savoir « le recours à la contraception », « l'emploi de préservatif », même « comme moyen de lutter contre l'infection par le VIH/sida » (A/CONF.177/20/Rev.1, p. 171).

 | DOI:10.1163/9789004349155_016

ordre public quand la liberté religieuse des femmes est restreinte au nom de celui-ci[3] ou si l'on admet que l'égalité des sexes puisse être en soi un ordre public[4] ; opposition entre liberté et égalité, ou plus précisément entre liberté individuelle et égalité des sexes[5], voire antagonisme entre liberté individuelle et émancipation collective[6] ; lutte entre universalisme et relativisme culturel, puisque, sur la scène internationale, c'est principalement au sujet des droits des femmes qu'interviennent les critiques les plus vives à l'encontre d'une protection des droits de l'Homme « occidentalo-centrée » et insensible à la diversité[7].

3 V. par exemple, Cour EDH, déc., 24 janvier 2006, *Şefika Köse et 93 autres c. Turquie*, n° 26625/02 : interdiction du port du voile islamique au sein d'un établissement scolaire justifiée notamment au nom de la protection de l'ordre ; Cour EDH, déc., 30 juin 2009, *Tuba Aktas c. France*, n° 43563/08 : à propos de l'interdiction du port de signes religieux ostensibles dans les établissements scolaires publics.

4 A rapprocher de : Cour EDH, Grande chambre, 1er juillet 2014, *S.A.S c. France*, n° 43835/11 : l'interdiction de se dissimuler le visage dans l'espace public est justifiée au nom de la préservation des conditions du « vivre ensemble ».

5 Cour EDH, déc., 15 février 2001, *Lucia Dahlab*, n° 42393/98 : il semble « difficile de concilier le port du foulard islamique avec le message … d'égalité [des sexes] et de non-discrimination que dans une démocratie tout enseignant doit transmettre à ses élèves » ; Cour EDH, déc., 10 juillet 2012, *Staatkundig Gereformeerde Partij*, n° 58369/10 : la liberté de religion ne peut justifier qu'un parti politique au nom d'une interprétation rigoriste du rôle attribué aux deux sexes par la Bible interdise aux femmes d'être candidates aux élections sur ses listes.

6 A rapprocher de : Cour EDH, Grande chambre, 10 novembre 2005, *Leyla Sahin c. Turquie*, n° 44774/98, §§ 113–115 : sur l'interdiction du foulard islamique dans les universités turques, la Cour relève l'impact que peut avoir le port de ce symbole, perçu comme une obligation religieuse, sur celles qui ne le portent pas.

7 V. l'intervention de l'Arabie Saoudite lors des négociations de la Convention sur l'élimination de toutes les formes de discrimination à l'égard des femmes, A/C.3/32/SR.20, § 54–57 : « en prenant l'initiative de la Décennie des Nations Unies pour la femme, les puissances occidentales surtout ont cherché à imposer leur conception de la femme et de son rôle social à d'autres cultures qui ne veulent pas nécessairement suivre l'exemple de pays où la révolution industrielle a bouleversé la société et détruit en particulier la famille » ; Déclaration de Gro Harlem Brundtland, Première ministre de Norvège à la suite de la 4ème Conférence mondiale sur les femmes, A/CONF.177/20/Rev.1, p. 235 : « nous avons eu un débat difficile sur le point de savoir comment la Conférence devait définir les droits fondamentaux de la femme. Comme s'il pouvait y avoir une série de droits fondamentaux pour l'homme et une autre, plus restreinte, pour la femme. J'ai même entendu cette réflexion de la part d'un pays que je ne nommerai pas : 'En fait, l'Occident chercher à imposer son modèle culturel comme modèle international'. C'est faux : aujourd'hui, la plupart des pays défendent avec force leur propre culture ; et l'on respecte, et l'on comprend

De nombreuses instances internationales en charge des droits de l'Homme ont donc été confrontées à la question de la conciliation entre religion et égalité des sexes[8]. Dans le cadre de l'ONU, s'il existe depuis 1946 une Commission de la condition de la femme[9], c'est à partir de la moitié de années soixante-dix que la question de l'émancipation féminine figure réellement à l'agenda international. 1975 est consacré « Année internationale de la femme », initiative ayant vocation à intensifier les actions en faveur de l'égalité des sexes et de la contribution des femmes au développement et à la paix[10]. Apogée médiatique de ce projet, la première Conférence mondiale sur les femmes se tient à Mexico. Elle impulse la proclamation de la « Décennie pour la femme » (1976–1985)[11] et sera suivie jusqu'en 1995 de trois autres conférences, espace-temps de mobilisation de la communauté internationale réunissant représentants des gouvernements, organisations internationales et société civile transnationale. Ces conférences s'achèvent par l'adoption d'une déclaration, d'un plan d'action et de résolutions, textes de *soft law*, censés témoigner d'une appréhension commune des problématiques et d'une volonté partagée de fédérer les énergies au niveau international, régional, national et local en vue de réaliser les objectifs énoncés. Sous l'impulsion de la Commission de la condition de la femme et grâce à l'élan de la Conférence de Mexico, l'Assemblée générale des Nations Unies adopte le 18 décembre 1979, la Convention sur l'élimination de toutes les formes de discrimination à l'égard des femmes (Convention EDEF)[12], premier traité catégoriel et généraliste déclinant l'égale jouissance des droits

mieux que jamais, la valeur des autres cultures et des autres religions. Mais la véritable question n'est pas là. Il y a des limites aux pratiques que les pays peuvent espérer voir accepter, ou approuver, par la communauté internationale, même lorsque ces pratiques ont de profondes racines culturelles. C'est là qu'interviennent les droits de l'Homme ».

8 V. par exemple récemment : Rapporteuse spéciale dans le domaine des droits culturels au Conseil des droits de l'Homme, « Les conséquences du fondamentalisme et de l'extrémisme sur l'exercice des droits culturels », 2017, A/HRC/34/56, « Les droits culturels des femmes », 2012, A/67/287 ; Groupe de travail chargé de la question de la discrimination à l'égard des femmes dans la législation et dans la pratique auprès du Conseil des droits de l'Homme, « Discrimination dans la vie culturelle et familiale », 2015, A/HRC/29/40 ; Rapporteur spécial sur la liberté de religion et de conviction, « Liberté de religion et de conviction et égalité entre hommes et femmes », 2013, A/68/290 ; CDH, « Observation générale n° 28 « Egalité des droits entre hommes et femmes », 2000, HRI/GEN/1/Rev.9, vol. I, § 13, § 21, § 28, § 32.

9 Résolution 11(II) ECOSOC.

10 Résolution 3010 (XXVII) AGNU, 18 décembre 1972.

11 Résolution 3520 (XXX) AGNU, 15 décembre 1975.

12 Résolution 34/180.

fondamentaux entre les femmes et les hommes dans tous les domaines civils, politiques, économiques, sociaux et culturels[13]. Le Comité pour l'élimination des discriminations à l'égard des femmes veille depuis 1982 au respect de la Convention par les Etats parties[14]. Ces deux espaces de consécration des droits des femmes auraient pu être superbement ignorés des Etats qui, au nom de la diversité culturelle et/ou religieuse, sont réticents à accepter ce qu'ils considèrent comme une appréhension occidentale, individualiste ou libertaire de l'égalité des sexes. Il n'en est rien. Plus de cent trente Etats sont représentés à la première Conférence sur les femmes, cent quatre-vingt dix à la dernière[15]. Avec cent quatre-vingt-neuf Etats parties, la Convention sur l'élimination de la discrimination faite aux femmes est devenue le deuxième traité de droit de l'Homme le plus ratifié. Or, l'investissement quasi universel au sein de ces forums n'en a pas fait spécialement le lieu d'une réflexion constructive sur une éventuelle conciliation entre revendications féministes et religieuses. Guerre des sexes et guerre de religion ont bien eu lieu, mais dans une temporalité différée. Passées sous silence au début de la Décennie de la femme, les tensions sont montées en puissance lors des conférences à tel point que la dynamique est aujourd'hui paralysée (1). Face à une convention fortement contestée lors des processus de négociation et de ratification, le Comité pour l'élimination de la discrimination à l'égard des femmes tente désormais, afin d'éviter tout affrontement stérile, une stratégie de l'apaisement (2).

1 Montée en puissance des tensions

Mexico 1975, Copenhague 1980, Nairobi 1985, Beijing 1995, hasard ou convergence des agendas onusiens, les grandes conférences mondiales sur les femmes sont généralement précédées de sommets internationaux sur la population – à Bucarest en 1974, Mexico en 1984 et au Caire en 1994. Lors de la première décennie de cette période, les revendications des pays en voie

13 S. Grosbon, « Splendeur et misère de la Convention sur l'élimination de toutes les formes de discrimination à l'égard des femmes », in *La Convention pour l'élimination des discrimination à l'égard des femmes,* D. Roman (dir.), Pedone, 2014, pp. 19–47.

14 B. Delzangles et M. Möschel, « Le Comité pour l'élimination des discriminations à l'égard des femmes : trente ans d'activités en faveur des femmes », in *La Convention pour l'élimination des discriminations à l'égard des femmes,* D. Roman (dir.), Pedone, 2014, pp. 49–80.

15 133 Etats représentés à la Conférence de Mexico, 145 à Copenhague, 157 à Nairobi, 190 à Beijing.

de développement en faveur du nouvel ordre économique international[16] ou contre l'Etat d'Israël réussissent à jeter le voile sur les oppositions latentes entre pressions féministes et religieuses (1.1). Au cours de la deuxième décennie, l'affirmation croissante d'un droit des femmes à maîtriser leur fécondité fait éclater au grand jour les antagonismes et irréductibles hostilités (1.2).

1.1 *Indifférence réelle ou supposée*

La première Conférence mondiale sur les femmes se tient à Mexico du 19 juin au 2 juillet 1975 et se concentre sur l'égalité, le développement et la paix. Le rapport final suggère que les questions religieuses n'ont pas été soulevées[17]. Prolongeant les avancées des Conférences internationales sur les droits de l'Homme de Téhéran (1968)[18] et sur la population de Bucarest (1974)[19], le rapport final insiste itérativement sur le droit de chaque couple et de chaque personne « de décider librement et en toute responsabilité d'avoir ou non des enfants ainsi que de déterminer leur nombre et l'espacement de leurs naissances, et d'avoir l'information, l'instruction et les moyens nécessaires à cette fin » ; l'exercice de ce droit est considéré comme « essentiel pour la réalisation de l'égalité véritable entre les sexes » et indispensable pour bénéficier des autres réformes émancipatrices ; l'accès aux renseignements et aux moyens d'exercer ce droit devrait s'effectuer « par l'intermédiaire d'un système institutionnalisé »[20]. Ce sont donc bien les prémisses d'un droit d'accès à la contraception qui

---

16 Résolution 3202 (S-VI) AGNU du 1er mai 1974.

17 Une seule référence marginale à la religion figure dans le rapport (Plan d'action mondial en vue de la réalisation des objectifs de l'année internationale de la femme, § 118, E/CONF.66/34, p. 31).

18 Acte final de la Conférence internationale des droits de l'Homme, 1968, A/CONF.32/41, Résolution XVIII : « les couples ont le droit fondamental de décider librement et en toute responsabilité du nombre d'enfants qu'ils veulent avoir et du moment de leur naissance, et aussi le droit d'être suffisamment instruits et informés de ces questions ». Il s'agit donc d'un droit des couples et non des individus, d'un « accès à l'information et non à la contraception », du « choix du nombre de naissances sans mentionner la possibilité de refuser toute naissance » (B. Marques-Pereira et F. Raes, « Les droits reproductifs comme droits humains : une perspective internationale », in *Corps de femmes, sexualité et contrôle social*, M.-T. Coenen (dir.), De Boeck Université, 2002, p. 21).

19 Rapport de la Conférence mondiale des Nations Unies sur la population, 1974, A/CONF.60/19, § 14*f* : le droit de décider du nombre et de l'espacement des naissances devient un droit des individus et s'y ajoute le droit de « bénéficier de services adéquats en la matière ».

20 Déclaration de Mexico de 1975 sur l'égalité des femmes et leur contribution au développement de la paix, § 12 ; Plan d'action mondial, *op. cit.*, § 19, §§ 136–137, §§ 142–143, Résolutions n° 15 et n° 17, E/CONF.66/34.

semblent se profiler à Mexico, dont le plan d'action recommande d'ailleurs la mise au point de « moyens de contraception et de limitation des naissances qui soient à la fois efficaces et compatibles avec les valeurs culturelles prévalant dans les différentes sociétés »[21], la conjonction de ces deux adjectifs relativisant d'emblée la portée de certaines méthodes contraceptives purement naturelles. Si les discussions sur la planification familiale ont pu être longues[22], elles semblent avoir été beaucoup moins controversées qu'à la Conférence sur la population de Bucarest qui avait vu s'opposer certains Etats occidentaux prônant une régulation des naissances nécessaire au développement à certains pays du sud appuyés par le Saint-Siège pour qui les questions démographiques étaient liées à une répartition inégale des richesses et le développement, le meilleur contraceptif[23]. Plus généralement, à Mexico, aucun Etat ne conteste frontalement les objectifs retenus pourtant ambitieux en matière d'égalité des sexes et d'émancipation des femmes. Trois Etats traditionnellement catholiques (Argentine, Irlande, Pérou) insistent sur la souveraineté étatique en matière démographique pour nuancer le droit individuel à la planification familiale. Deux Etats seulement (Inde et Egypte) invoquent la tradition ou la culture pour contester les unions consensuelles, l'enseignement mixte ou les normes relatives au mariage, alors même que parallèlement dans le cadre des négociations relatives à la Convention sur l'élimination de la discrimination faite aux femmes, l'égalité dans les rapports maritaux et familiaux est âprement discutée (*Infra*). Finalement, il n'y a guère que le Koweit et le Saint-Siège qui expriment des réticences fondées sur la religion, en des termes néanmoins extrêmement mesurés : le premier affirme, obscur, accepter le texte « dans un esprit de compromis » sans abandonner pour autant ses « convictions » ; le second conteste le droit des individus à la planification familiale, mais non celui des couples[24].

Cinq ans après les rencontres de Mexico, la deuxième Conférence mondiale de la décennie des Nations Unies pour la femme se déroule à Copenhague du 14 au 30 juillet 1980. Elle garde pour thèmes principaux l'égalité, le développement et la paix mais précise trois sous-thèmes prioritaires : l'emploi, la santé

21 Plan d'action mondial, *op. cit.*, § 143. Les plans d'action régionaux, de manière plus confidentielle, font explicitement référence à la « distribution de moyens contraceptifs » (E/CONF.66/34, p. 70).

22 E/CONF.66/34, p. 192.

23 A. Sauvy, « La Conférence mondiale de la population à Bucarest. Le Centre démographique ONU-Roumanie », *Population*, 1974, vol. 29, n° 6, p. 1009.

24 E/CONF.66/34, pp. 55–59.

et l'enseignement[25]. A nouveau, le rapport final comporte peu de références à la religion[26]. En revanche, le droit à la planification familiale s'étoffe : il devient un droit des femmes, et non plus des individus ou des couples, de décider du nombre de leurs enfants et de l'espacement des naissances, un « droit à une maternité voulue, responsable et désirée », soutenu par l'élaboration de programmes de planification familiale utilisant « des méthodes sûres et acceptables de contrôle de la fécondité » et visant à réduire la mortalité en cas de risques élevés tels que les « grossesses trop rapprochées » ou « la fréquence et le danger d'avortements illégaux »[27]. Il devient dès lors difficile d'exécuter ce programme d'action sans reconnaître l'accès à la contraception, voire à l'avortement. Quelques Etats traditionnellement catholiques (Argentine, Equateur, Irlande), le Saint-Siège et le Pakistan ne s'y trompent pas et émettent une réserve à ce sujet[28]. La première résolution adoptée lors de la Conférence porte d'ailleurs sur la planification familiale et invite les gouvernements à prendre « toutes les mesures appropriées » « afin de dispenser l'information, l'éducation et les moyens nécessaires » à l'exercice du droit de chacun de décider de la taille de sa famille. Portée par certains pays en voie de développement, elle sera en revanche contestée par six Etats d'Amérique Latine, la Roumanie et le Saint-Siège[29]. Plus généralement, ce dernier s'abstiendra lors du vote du Programme d'action dans son ensemble en contestant la trop faible attention portée au rôle de la femme dans la cellule familiale et à la responsabilité mutuelle des deux sexes en matière de parenté ouvrant « la porte à l'utilisation aveugle de méthodes de planification familiale attentatoires à la dignité humaine »[30]. Quant au Pakistan, c'est en tant que « pays islamique » qu'il prévient que, même si la Conférence promeut la Convention sur l'élimination

25 Rapport de la Conférence mondiale pour la décennie des Nations Unies pour la femme : égalité, développement, paix, 1980.

26 Participation des groupes religieux à l'exécution du programme d'action ; Attention particulière aux attitudes religieuses différentes des migrantes à l'égard des soins de santé (Programme d'action pour la seconde moitié de la Décennie pour la femme, § 100 et § 205 *h*) ; critique de la publicité commerciale surestimant les valeurs matérialistes d'une civilisation étrangère aux traditions religieuses (Résumé du débat général, § 85), E/CONF.94/35.

27 Programme d'action, *op. cit.*, § 146 et § 211.

28 E/CONF.94/35, p. 240. Le Pakistan et le Saint-Siège émettent également une réserve à l'encontre de l'incitation faite aux ONG d'œuvrer à l'acceptation de la planification familiale et de l'éducation sexuelle.

29 E/CONF.94/35, p. 72, pp. 178–179.

30 E/CONF.94/35, pp. 237–238.

de la discrimination à l'égard des femmes, il émet des réserves sur certains de ses articles[31]. Mais, quoique ces deux Etats semblent ainsi témoigner en creux d'une idéologie incompatible avec le principe de non-discrimination, les critiques à l'égard du Programme d'action paraissent circonscrites tant sur le plan géographique que matériel. Pourtant, celui-ci n'hésite pas à réitérer l'engagement en faveur de l'égalité des sexes dans tous les domaines, notamment en matière familiale[32].

Il faut cependant souligner qu'à Mexico comme Copenhague, ce ne sont visiblement pas les droits des femmes qui ont accaparé l'attention des Etats. Les pays en voie de développement ne cessent de défendre l'idée que la condition inégale des femmes résulte davantage de facteurs géopolitiques liés au colonialisme et à l'ordre économique international injuste que de facteurs culturels et certains utilisent la Conférence comme une tribune pour fustiger le « sionisme » d'Israël[33]. Ce sont donc principalement les Etats occidentaux et Israël qui s'opposeront ou s'abstiendront lors de l'adoption des rapports des Conférences par l'Assemblée générale des Nations Unies[34]. A la troisième Conférence mondiale chargée d'examiner et d'évaluer les résultats de la décennie des Nations Unies pour la femme, qui se déroule à Nairobi du 15 au 26 juillet 1985, des critiques identiques relatives à l'instrumentalisation des débats par certains pays en voie de développement à des fins de politique internationale générale se feront entendre. Pourtant, les Stratégies prospectives d'action pour la promotion de la femme adoptées afin de faciliter la réalisation des objectifs de la Décennie sont

31 E/CONF.94/35, p. 184.

32 Programme d'action, *op. cit.*, § 59.

33 Déclaration de Mexico, *op. cit.*, §§ 23–26, Résolutions n° 32, p. 132 (E/CONF.66/34) ; Programme d'action de Copenhague, *op. cit.*, § 5, § 12 et § 41 et p. 162. Ce discours peut trouver appui auprès de certaines délégations féministes du Sud pour qui, face aux graves inégalités économiques liées au « néo-colonialisme et à l'impérialisme des sociétés occidentales », les préoccupations « des féministes du Nord, à savoir l'accès à une carrière professionnelle, à des postes de responsabilité ou encore la question du choix de disposer de son corps » peuvent paraître « des revendications de luxe » (F. Ramdani, « Les organisations féministes américaines à l'ONU : un exemple de diplomatie citoyenne », *Politique Américaine*, 2016, n° 27, p. 92).

34 AGNU, A/PV.2441 du 15 décembre 1975, pp. 1433–1443 : 107 voix pour, 1 contre (Israël) et 26 abstentions à l'adoption du rapport de Mexico. Lors de la Conférence de Copenhague, le programme d'action a été adopté avec 94 voix pour, 4 contre (Australie, Canada, Etats Unis, Israël) et 22 abstentions (E/CONF.94/35, pp. 228–239), à l'AGNU avec 132 voix pour, 3 contre (Canada, Etats Unis, Israël) et 9 abstentions (A/35/PV.92 du 11 décembre 1980, pp. 1768–1769).

approuvées par consensus[35], alors même que ce texte gagne considérablement en consistance et en précision quant au statut des femmes. Les relations entre mouvements féministes et revendications religieuses commencent à se tendre, mais c'est surtout dix ans plus tard à la Conférence de Beijing qu'elles témoigneront d'une irréductible hostilité.

1.2 *Irréductible hostilité*

Sous l'impulsion de la Conférence internationale sur la population de Mexico en 1984, la troisième Conférence sur les femmes de Nairobi en 1985 proclame le droit fondamental des femmes de contrôler leur fécondité[36]. Le choix du nombre et de l'espacement des naissances s'exerce désormais « en pleine connaissance de cause » et non plus « en toute responsabilité » : Il ne dépend plus du bien-être des enfants et de la communauté, mais des femmes, de leur accès aux « informations sur les contraceptifs » et de méthodes et médicaments anticonceptionnels de qualité. A cet égard, à Nairobi, on abandonne la référence à la planification naturelle qui figurait encore un an auparavant à Mexico[37]. Mais l'avortement, contesté lors de la Conférence sur la population[38], n'est pas évoqué par les Stratégies d'action pour la promotion de la femme. En revanche, elles citent, dès le premier paragraphe et pour la première fois au sein d'un rapport d'une conférence internationale sur les femmes, les facteurs religieux parmi les entraves à la promotion de la condition féminine[39]. Le camp des contestataires commence alors à s'étendre. A Mexico en 1984, l'Arabie Saoudite remet en cause la totalité des paragraphes relatifs à l'amélioration de la condition féminine et à la non-discrimination[40] ; le Saint-Siège refuse de s'associer au consensus en raison de la légitimité accordée aux rapports sexuels hors mariage et à certaines méthodes de planification familiale « moralement inacceptables »[41]. A Nairobi, l'Irlande conteste le droit au divorce, le Maroc et les Emirats arabes unis, l'égalité juridique des époux devant le mariage, le

35 Rapport de la Conférence mondiale chargée d'examiner et d'évaluer les résultats de la décennie des Nations Unies pour la femme : égalité, développement, paix, 1985, A/CONF.116/28/Rev.1, pp. 160–175.

36 Déclaration de la Conférence internationale sur la population, 1984, E/CONF.76.19, § 17 ; Stratégies prospectives d'action de Nairobi, A/CONF.116/28/Rev.1, § 29.

37 Stratégies prospectives d'action de Nairobi, A/CONF.116/28/Rev.1, §§ 156–159 ; Recommandation n° 25 concernant la poursuite de l'exécution du plan d'action mondial sur la population, E/CONF.76.19.

38 E/CONF.76/19, pp. 61–62, §§ 72–75, pp. 82–83, §§ 172–177.

39 Stratégies prospectives d'action de Nairobi, A/CONF.116/28/Rev.1, § 1.

40 E/CONF.76/19, p. 83, § 178.

41 E/CONF.76/19, p. 82, § 172.

divorce et la garde des enfants ainsi que la non-discrimination à l'égard des mères célibataires, alors même que pour la première fois dans une conférence sur les femmes, les droits de celles-là sont reconnus « sans préjudice des traditions religieuses »[42]. Pendant le débat pourtant, plusieurs pays traditionnellement musulmans insistent sur la mauvaise interprétation des enseignements de l'Islam qui proclamerait vraiment l'égalité des droits et des devoirs des deux sexes[43]. Quant au Saint-Siège, il émet de « sérieuses réserves » aux Stratégies de Nairobi, en critiquant notamment l'absence de références aux qualités proprement féminines et aux aspects religieux de l'épanouissement humain, l'idéologie de la liberté sexuelle ainsi que certaines méthodes de planification familiale promues par de « puissantes institutions » qui menacent l'unicité du couple et « les valeurs culturelles des pays du tiers monde, notamment la sainte vitalité et la joie de vivre de leurs familles »[44]. La critique n'est pas anodine, car elle appuie les accusations de certains pays en voie de développement contre les politiques antinatalistes promues par les Etats-Unis notamment et qui auraient conduit à la distribution de contraceptifs mais également à des stérilisations volontaires ou forcées[45]. La critique du néomalthusianisme permet alors de contester la liberté reproductive des femmes.

La Conférence internationale sur la population et le développement qui se déroule au Caire du 5 au 13 septembre 1994 rompt avec la tendance à instrumentaliser le corps des femmes et leur fécondité à des fins démographiques. Son Programme d'action consacre un chapitre entier à « l'égalité entre les sexes et la promotion de la femme », ainsi qu'un long chapitre aux « droits et santé en matière de reproduction ». Il insiste particulièrement sur l'importance du choix des individus, « le but des politiques démographiques est désormais de donner à tous l'accès à des connaissances et à des méthodes contraceptives variées »[46]. Les « droits en matière de procréation correspondent à certains droits de l'Homme » reconnus au niveau onusien et « fruit d'un consensus ». Ils reposent sur le droit de décider du nombre et de l'espacement des naissances, de disposer des informations nécessaires pour ce faire, de prendre des décisions en matière de procréation sans être en butte à la discrimination,

42 Stratégies prospectives d'action de Nairobi, A/CONF.116/28/Rev.1, § 74.

43 A/CONF.116/28/Rev.1, p. 126.

44 A/CONF.116/28/Rev.1, pp. 161–162.

45 V. A. Gautier, C. Grenier-Torres, « Controverses autour des droits reproductifs et sexuels », *Autrepart*, 2014/2, n° 70, pp. 5–6 ; A. Gautier, « Les politiques de planification familiale dans les pays en voie de développement : du malthusianisme au féminisme ? », *Lien social et Politiques*, 2002, n° 47, pp. 67–81.

46 A. Gautier, C. Grenier-Torres, *op. cit.*, p. 7.

à la coercition ou à la violence et sur le droit d'accéder à la meilleure santé en matière de sexualité et de reproduction[47]. La santé sexuelle s'émancipe donc de sa tutelle procréative et moralisatrice. Elle vise en effet la capacité à « mener une vie sexuelle satisfaisante », c'est-à-dire « à améliorer la qualité de la vie et des relations interpersonnelles, et non à se borner à dispenser conseils et soins relatifs à la procréation et aux maladies sexuellement transmissibles ». La santé reproductive concerne la capacité et la liberté de toute personne de procréer « aussi souvent ou aussi peu souvent qu'elle le désire », en utilisant les méthodes de régulation des naissances de son choix, pour autant que celles-ci « ne soient pas contraires à la loi »[48]. Et c'est naturellement ici que le bât blesse : tout d'abord parce que, contrairement à ce que souhaitent les féministes, l'avortement n'est reconnu ni comme un droit au niveau international, ni comme une « méthode de planification familiale ». Son autorisation ou non relève du droit national. Cependant, même en cas d'interdiction, les femmes doivent être traitées avec compréhension et soins en cas de complications[49]. Ensuite, pour la première fois lors d'une conférence sur la population, le Programme d'action ne cesse de répéter que sa mise en œuvre respectera les différentes valeurs religieuses, éthiques et culturelles[50].

Un an après la Conférence du Caire, s'ouvre à Beijing la quatrième Conférence mondiale sur les femmes, du 4 au 15 septembre 1995. Le rapport final témoigne d'une forte irruption de la question religieuse au cœur de la rencontre internationale et de négociations acharnées entre les Etats soumis aux pressions et au contrôle des groupes féministes ou religieux. Dans la lignée de la Conférence de Vienne sur les droits de l'Homme de 1993, le Programme d'action confirme le caractère irrécusable de l'universalité des droits de l'Homme en dépit de la diversité culturelle et religieuse[51]. Il combat la violence faite aux femmes fondée sur des pratiques religieuses en les liant généralement à des comportements extrémistes[52]. Il exige la non-discrimination entre hommes et femmes dans la jouissance des droits fondamentaux sans distinction fondée sur la religion[53]. Toutefois, sauf en ce qui concerne les filles qui ne doivent

47 Rapport de la Conférence internationale sur la population et le développement, 1994, A/CONF.171/13/Rev.1, Programme d'action, § 7.3.

48 Programme d'action, § 7.2.

49 Programme d'action, § 8.25.

50 A/CONF.171/13/Rev.1, Programme d'action, § 1.11, § 1.15, Préambule du chapitre II.

51 Rapport de la 4ème Conférence mondiale sur les femmes, 1995, A/CONF.177/20/Rev.1, Programme d'action, §§ 9–10.

52 Programme d'action, §§ 118, 124, 224

53 Déclaration, § 32, Programme d'action, §§ 46, 225, 232, 276.

pas être discriminées par des pratiques religieuses, cette proposition est ambiguë : elle peut finalement chercher à protéger la liberté de religion des populations minoritaires tout autant que la condition des femmes au regard de la religion.

D'ailleurs, pour la première fois au sein d'une conférence mondiale sur les femmes, les documents insistent sur la liberté de religion et sur la contribution positive de celle-ci à la satisfaction des besoins spirituels des individus. Seul l'extrémisme *peut* exercer – et non exerce – « un effet négatif sur les femmes »; « La prise en compte et le strict respect des diverses valeurs religieuses et éthiques ... des individus et de leurs communautés devraient aider les femmes à jouir pleinement de leurs droits fondamentaux »[54], reste à savoir s'il s'agit d'une supposition, d'une prescription ou d'une affirmation, ce qui change profondément le sens de la proposition. En revanche, le Programme d'action consacre de longs développements aux droits sexuels et génésiques qui prolongent les résultats du Programme d'action du Caire en précisant notamment avec éclat le droit fondamental des femmes d'être maîtresses de leur sexualité et en demandant la dépénalisation de l'avortement[55].

Du Caire à Beijing, la contestation religieuse s'installe et ce sont les mêmes Etats qui vont s'opposer aux droits des femmes parfois de manière conservatrice, parfois de manière régressive par rapport à ce qu'ils avaient accepté au cours des précédentes conférences et ce, malgré les concessions faites en matière de diversité religieuse et culturelle[56]. « En d'autres termes, à partir des années 1990, les luttes d'influence ne reposent plus sur un nouvel ordre économique mondial, mais sur un nouvel ordre idéologique culturel qui gravite autour des droits des femmes »[57]. Ainsi, une dizaine d'Etat d'Amérique Latine et Malte contestent la reconnaissance implicite de l'homosexualité et l'avortement. Sur ce point, la plupart ne se fonde pas explicitement sur des valeurs religieuses, mais sur la Convention interaméricaine des droits de l'Homme qui protège le droit à la vie dès la conception. Cependant, le Salvador précise au Caire que les pays latino-américains « étant pour l'essentiel chrétiens », ils considèrent que « la vie est donnée par le Créateur et ne peut être interrompue

54 Déclaration, § 12, Programme d'action, § 9, § 24.

55 Programme d'action, §§ 96 et 106 *k*.

56 A/CONF.171/13/Rev.1, pp. 129–145 ; A/CONF.177/20/Rev.1, pp. 162–184. V. D. Couture, « Droits des femmes et religions : Analyse de quelques discours islamiques et catholiques », *Sciences Religieuses,* 2003, vol. 32, n° 1–2, pp. 5–18 ; D. Otto, « Holding up Half the Sky, but for Whose Benefit? A critical Analysis of the Fourth World Conference on Women », *Australian Feminist Law Journal* 1996, n° 6, pp. 7–28.

57 F. Ramdani, *op. cit.,* p. 94.

sauf motif valable »[58]. Une dizaine d'Etats se joignent, au nom de la religion musulmane, à ces critiques et y ajoutent parfois la condamnation des rapports sexuels extra-conjugaux et de l'égalité successorale. L'Iran et la Libye contestent au Caire l'ensemble du chapitre relatif à l'égalité des sexes et à la promotion de la femme. Certains de ces Etats catholiques ou musulmans rappellent qu'ils n'appliqueront les Programmes d'action que sous réserve d'une compatibilité avec les valeurs religieuses de leur pays. Le Saint-Siège fustige l'individualisme libertaire, la liberté sexuelle, l'avortement, l'homosexualité, les rapports extra-conjugaux, la contraception et l'égalitarisme qui fait fit de la complémentarité des sexes. A l'inverse, à Beijing, Israël, les Etats-Unis et l'Afrique du Sud regrettent l'absence de consécration explicite du droit de déterminer son orientation sexuelle.

A l'occasion de la journée internationale de la femme, le 8 mars 2012, le Président de l'Assemblée générale et le Secrétaire général des Nations Unies se prononcent en faveur de la tenue d'une 5ème Conférence mondiale sur les femmes en 2015[59]. Cependant, la crainte qu'un tel événement soit l'occasion d'une régression plus que d'une progression des droits des femmes n'est pas de nature à inciter à soutenir le projet. Les résultats de la Conférence de Beijing sont donc depuis vingt ans examinés dans un cadre onusien plus institutionnel et moins médiatique, notamment au sein de la Commission de la condition de la femme[60]. Le Comité pour l'élimination des discriminations à l'égard des femmes demande également régulièrement aux Etats Parties à la Convention EDEF de mettre en œuvre le Programme d'action de Beijing. Echaudé par les oppositions entre droits des femmes et diversité religieuse, il semble parfois jouer la stratégie de l'apaisement, afin de conserver, dans la mesure du possible, l'intégrité de la Convention.

2 Stratégie de l'apaisement

La Convention sur l'élimination de toutes les formes de discrimination à l'égard des femmes a été adoptée après sept ans d'âpres négociations durant lesquelles les Etats musulmans se sont opposés à d'autres Etats, principalement occidentaux, sur le rôle des religions et des femmes dans la société, sur

58 A/CONF.171/13/Rev.1, p 130.

59 Communiqué de presse, SG/SM/14148-AG/SM/1388-FEM/1903: http://www.un.org/press/fr/2012/SGSM14148.doc.htm.

60 Résolution 59/1 de la CCF, Déclaration politique proclamée à l'occasion du 20ème anniversaire de la 4ème Conférence mondiale sur les femmes.

les droits individuels et sur le principe d'égalité des sexes[61], divergences idéologiques que l'acceptation quasi universelle de la Convention ne parvient pas à dissimuler (2.1). Afin d'éviter un affrontement indépassable qui n'apporterait rien à la cause des femmes, le Comité pour l'élimination de la discrimination à l'égard des femmes cherche à maintenir un dialogue entre impératifs religieux et féministes, en utilisant la voie de l'interprétation compatible (2.2).

2.1 *Conflit ouvert*

Lors des négociations de la Convention, certains Etats contestent la rédaction ou la formulation d'articles qu'ils estiment incompatibles avec le respect de la religion musulmane. Sont notamment concernées les dispositions relatives à l'abrogation des coutumes ou pratiques discriminantes (article 2 *f*), aux droits égaux en matière de nationalité et de transmission de celle-ci aux enfants (article 9), à la liberté de circulation des femmes (article 15 § 4), aux droits égaux en matière maritale et familiale (article 16)[62]. Plus généralement, certains Etats critiquent l'égalité des sexes au nom de la complémentarité et du rôle maternel de la femme[63]. Toutefois, leurs amendements seront systématiquement rejetés par une majorité d'Etats négociateurs. Le jour de l'adoption de la Convention, certains Etats musulmans exigent un vote séparé sur les articles concernant les droits égaux au cours du mariage et de sa dissolution (article 16 § 1 *c*) et en matière de transmission de la nationalité aux enfants (article 9 § 2). Ils seront à nouveau mis en minorité et la Convention, adoptée avec 130 voix pour, 11 abstentions et aucune opposition. Parmi les Etats abstentionnistes, seul le Maroc exprime clairement un désaccord de fond : il critique l'« extrémisme » de la Convention qui ne constitue pas « une juste balance entre tous les systèmes juridiques prévalant » et qui impose les vues d'« un continent déterminé »[64].

61 L.A. Rehof, *Guide to the travaux préparatoires of the United Nations Convention on the Elimination of all Forms of Discrimination against Women,* Boston, M. Nijhoff Publishers, 1993, p. 2. Nous n'avons pas trouvé au sein des travaux préparatoires d'oppositions aux dispositions de la Convention explicitement justifiées par le respect d'autres religions.

62 L.A. Rehof, *op. cit.,* p. 54, pp. 59–60, p. 104, p. 167, pp. 170–186 : parmi les droits maritaux et familiaux, les dispositions les plus contestées au nom de l'Islam sont celles relatives à la dissolution du mariage (article 16 § 1 *c*) et aux droits égaux des parents pour les questions se rapportant à leurs enfants « quel que soit leur état matrimonial » (article 16 § 1 *d*), cette référence pouvant être comprise comme légitimant l'adultère ou à tout le moins les relations extra-conjugales.

63 V. les observations du Maroc, A/C.3/34/SR.70, §§ 28–31 ; les observations de l'Arabie Saoudite, A/C.3/32/SR.20, §§ 54–57.

64 A/34/PV.107: les Etats abstentionnistes sont le Bangladesh, le Brésil, les Comores, Djibouti, Haïti, le Mali, la Mauritanie, le Mexique, le Maroc, l'Arabie Saoudite et le Sénégal.

Le texte adopté par l'Assemblée générale des Nations Unies privilégie donc les impératifs d'égalité des sexes sur les prescriptions religieuses. Seules deux dispositions ont été abandonnées au profit de la spécificité musulmane : l'égalité des droits en matière d'héritage a été écartée, ce qui constitue un retour en arrière par rapport à la Déclaration sur l'élimination de la discrimination à l'égard des femmes du 7 novembre 1967[65] ; l'égalité entre les enfants légitimes et naturels a été combattue au nom de l'interdiction islamique de l'adultère et non défendue par les féministes qui ne voyaient pas directement le rapport avec l'objet de la Convention[66]. Hormis ces deux dispositions, la Convention ne renonce à aucune de ses ambitions : elle décline la non-discrimination dans tous les domaines civils, politiques, économiques, sociaux et culturels (articles 2 et 3) ; mais elle va également « plus loin » que les autres instruments de droits de l'Homme existants jusqu'ici « car elle tient compte de l'influence que la culture et les traditions exercent sur les comportements et les mentalités de la collectivité, restreignant considérablement l'exercice par les femmes de leurs droits fondamentaux »[67]. Elle ne traite jamais explicitement de religion, mais exige l'abrogation des coutumes ou pratiques discriminatoires (article 2 *f*) et « l'élimination des préjugés et de pratiques coutumières, ou de tout autre type, qui sont fondés sur l'idée de l'infériorité ou de la supériorité de l'un ou l'autre sexe ou d'un rôle stéréotypé des hommes et des femmes » (article 5 § 1). Elle consacre pour la première fois conventionnellement le droit de « décider librement et en toute connaissance de cause du nombre et de l'espacement des naissances et d'avoir accès aux informations, à l'éducation et aux moyens nécessaires » pour « exercer ces droits » (article 16 § 1 *e*). Parallèlement, elle ne mentionne pas la liberté de religion et évite ainsi les injonctions contradictoires entre liberté et égalité. Pourtant, parallèlement, la Convention, qui se concentre sur la déclinaison de l'égale jouissance des droits fondamentaux, en oublie les oppressions majoritairement subies par les femmes et notamment l'interdiction des violences. Elle ne réaffirme pas les droits intangibles, le droit à la vie, l'interdiction de la torture et de l'esclavage et ignore donc les mutilations génitales, les lapidations, les infanticides de fillettes ou autres pratiques traditionnelles préjudiciables, souvent justifiées par des coutumes culturelles et/ou religieuses[68].

65 M.A. Freeman, « Article 16 », in *The UN Convention on the Elimination of all forms of Discrimination against Women, a Commentary*, M. Freeman, C. Chinkin, B. Rudolf (dir.), Oxford University Press, 2012, p. 414.

66 L.A. Rehof, *op. cit.*, pp. 184–186.

67 CEDEF, « Recommandation générale n° 21, Egalité dans le mariage et les rapports familiaux », 1994, A/49/38, § 3.

68 S. Grosbon, *op. cit.*, pp. 36–37.

Ainsi rédigée et malgré l'absence de vote négatif lors de son adoption par l'Assemblée générale, la Convention ne fait pas consensus. La plupart des Etats musulmans n'y adhéreront que dans les années quatre-vingt-dix, voire dans les années deux mille. Le Saint-Siège, l'Iran, la Somalie, le Soudan, les Tonga, les Palaos et les Etats-Unis ne sont toujours pas parties à la Convention, alors qu'ils ont accepté de ratifier d'autres traités de protection des droits de l'Homme. Mais surtout, plus d'un tiers des Etats parties ont émis des réserves, limitant la portée de leur engagement conventionnel, et la plupart de celles-ci sont fondées sur le respect de prescriptions religieuses ou de dispositions nationales inspirées de celles-là. Ainsi, au Royaume-Uni, la Convention ne s'appliquera pas aux questions concernant les confessions ou les ordres religieux. En Israël, les différentes communautés ne se verront imposer ni la nomination de femmes-juges au sein des tribunaux religieux en dépit de l'article 7 (égal accès à la vie publique), ni la modification des lois relatives à l'état des personnes contraires à l'article 16 (égalité dans les rapports maritaux et familiaux). A Singapour, les lois personnelles et religieuses des différentes communautés primeront sur les articles 2 (principe général de non-discrimination) et 16. Une vingtaine d'Etats ont émis des réserves en se fondant sur la Charia, parfois à l'encontre de la Convention dans son ensemble, parfois à l'encontre de ses articles 2, 16, 9 (droits égaux relatifs à la nationalité) ou 15 (capacité juridique et liberté de circulation)[69]. Des objections ont été formulées à l'égard des réserves « Charia » considérées comme incompatibles avec l'objet et le but de la Convention. Mais le régime de l'objection s'applique mal au droit international des droits de l'Homme, parce qu'il aboutit à priver l'individu de droits conventionnels sans que l'Etat réservataire n'en subisse la moindre conséquence négative[70]. Un certain nombre d'Etats ont alors indiqué, dans un élan plus humaniste que juridique, que leur objection n'empêcherait pas l'entrée en vigueur de la Convention *dans son intégralité* dans leurs relations bilatérales avec les Etats concernés, déniant ainsi tout effet à la réserve contestée[71]. Le Comité pour l'élimination de la discrimination à l'égard des femmes s'est également rapidement préoccupé des nombreuses réserves conventionnelles. D'une manière générale, dans son contrôle du respect de la Convention, il tente dans la mesure du possible de rechercher s'il existe une interprétation

69 Nations Unies, Collection des traités : <https://treaties.un.org/Pages/ViewDetails.aspx?src=TREATY&mtdsg_no=IV-8&chapter=4&clang=_fr#EndDec>.

70 O. de Frouville, *L'intangibilité des droits de l'Homme en droit international*, Paris, Pedone, 2004, p. 299 et p. 407.

71 S. Grosbon, *op. cit.*, pp. 45–46.

compatible permettant aux droits des femmes et aux prescriptions religieuses de coexister sans confrontation.

2.2 *L'interprétation compatible*

La technique de l'interprétation compatible consiste à rechercher une interprétation permettant de concilier l'application de deux normes potentiellement conflictuelles. Plusieurs stratégies du Comité EDEF cherchent ainsi à éviter l'opposition entre les dispositions de la Convention et les impératifs religieux. Il s'agit tout d'abord d'un positionnement prudent sur la question éminemment conflictuelle de l'avortement. Le Comité ne déduit pas du droit de décider librement et en toute connaissance de cause du nombre et de l'espacement des naissances (article 16 § 1 *e*) un droit à l'autonomie personnelle des femmes en matière d'interruption volontaire de grossesse. Il tente simplement d'inciter les Etats à accepter plus libéralement cette pratique contraceptive en adaptant ses exigences aux réalités culturelles et aux politiques nationales[72]. Il exige au minimum la dépénalisation de l'avortement et son autorisation dans les hypothèses de viol, inceste, danger pour la santé ou la vie de la mère, malformation fœtale grave. Afin de réduire la pratique de l'avortement comme méthode de planification familiale, il demande, sans ambages pour les sensibilités religieuses, d'accroître l'accès à des méthodes de contraception modernes et abordables[73].

Sur la question également controversée du port du voile, le Comité EDEF reste également prudent. Alors que selon le Comité des droits de l'Homme, l'interdiction des signes religieux ostensibles dans les établissements scolaires publics et de la dissimulation du visage dans l'espace public « portent atteinte à la liberté de manifester sa religion » et « affectent particulièrement les personnes appartenant à certaines religions et les filles »[74], le Comité EDEF demande à l'Etat de mener une étude exhaustive pour déterminer l'impact de la première interdiction sur le droit des filles à

72 D. Roman, « Le corps des femmes. Autonomie et intégrité corporelles dans la Convention », in *La Convention pour l'élimination des discriminations à l'égard des femmes*, D. Roman (dir.), Pedone, 2014, pp. 190–191.

73 Comité EDEF, « Recommandation générale n° 24, Les femmes et la santé », 1999, A/54/38/Rev.1, chap. I, § 31 *c*) ; En 2016, les observations finales du Comité EDEF sur le Bengladesh, CEDAW/C/BGD/CO/8, §§ 34–35 ; l'Argentine, CEDAW/C/ARG/CO/7, §§ 32–35 ; le Burundi, CEDAW/C/BDI/CO/5–6, §§ 38–39 ; Trinidad & Tobago, CEDAW/C/TTO/CO/4–7 ; l'Uruguay, CEDAW/C/URY/CO/8–9, §§ 35–36 ; Grèce, 2013, CEDAW/C/GRC/CO/7, § 31 *a*.

74 CDH, Observations finales sur la France, 2015, CCPR/C/FRA/CO/5, § 22.

l'éducation et leur insertion dans toutes les sphères de la société et d'indiquer les mesures pour remédier à un éventuel constat négatif. Il n'évoque pas du tout la deuxième interdiction, mais précise qu'il faut combattre la discrimination contre les femmes de minorités religieuses et renforcer la capacité et la volonté de vivre harmonieusement ensemble[75], objectif qui avait justement, aux yeux de la Cour européenne des droits de l'Homme, justifié l'interdiction[76].

Afin d'éviter la confrontation entre impératifs religieux et non discriminatoires, le Comité va délibérément interpréter certaines pratiques comme relevant de traditions culturelles et ignorer leur éventuelle origine confessionnelle[77]. Il peut alors exhorter les Etats « à considérer la culture comme un élément dynamique du tissu social du pays et de la vie en société, qui peut par conséquent évoluer »[78], contrairement à une prescription religieuse brandie comme immuable et intemporelle.

Enfin, le Comité recommande régulièrement que les Etats prennent modèle sur « l'expérience de pays dotés de systèmes religieux et juridiques similaires et ayant réussi à adapter leur législation interne » aux exigences de la Convention[79]. Critique à l'égard des systèmes de justice pluriels (coexistence de mécanismes judiciaires civils, religieux, coutumiers ou communautaires) qui bien souvent perpétuent les normes sociales discriminatoires, le Comité précise qu'il existe une série de modèles favorisant leur harmonisation avec la Convention afin de réduire au minimum les conflits de normes et de garantir aux femmes l'accès à la justice[80]. Face aux pratiques traditionnelles préjudiciables, il recommande l'organisation de débats publics mobilisant notamment les communautés religieuses et diffusant les expériences culturelles positives des « communautés ayant une histoire semblable » et qui ont réussi à éliminer

---

75 CEDEF, Observations finales sur la France, 2016, CEDAW/C/FRA/CO/7–8, § 33 et § 19.

76 Cour EDH, Grande chambre, 1er juillet 2014, *S.A.S c. France,* n° 43835/11.

77 CEDEF, « Recommandation générale n° 19, Violences à l'égard des femmes », 1992, A/47/38 : insistance sur les pratiques traditionnelles et culturelles violentes telles que l'excision, les mariages forcées, la préférence pour les enfants mâles, sans jamais évoquer les éventuels aspects religieux.

78 Observations finales sur le Mozambique, 2007, CEDAW/C/MOZ/CO/2 ; R. Holtmaat, « Article 5 », in *The UN Convention on the Elimination of all forms of Discrimination against Women, a Commentary,* M. Freeman, C. Chinkin, B. Rudolf (dir.), Oxford University Press, 2012, p. 150 et p. 155.

79 CEDEF, « Recommandation générale n° 29, Conséquences économiques du mariage, et des liens familiaux et de leur dissolution », 2013, CEDAW/C/GC/29, § 55.

80 CEDEF, « Recommandation générale n° 33, Accès des femmes à la justice », CEDAW/C/GC/33, § 63.

ces coutumes néfastes[81]. Pour préparer l'opinion à de telles réformes, l'Etat devrait nouer des partenariats avec des organismes religieux de recherche juridique et des organisations non gouvernementales féministes ou féminines. Plus généralement, il devrait inciter les autorités religieuses à lutter contre les pratiques préjudiciables fondées sur des « croyances culturelles profondément ancrées », à véhiculer une image favorable des femmes et à lutter contre les stéréotypes et les attitudes patriarcales[82].

Pour autant, l'interprétation compatible ne peut fonctionner que tant que les normes potentiellement en conflit ne sont pas fondamentalement inconciliables. Ainsi, le Comité affirme que la Convention EDEF l'emporte sur les lois coutumières, traditionnelles ou religieuses qui tolèrent les pratiques préjudiciables telles que les mutilations génitales, le mariage forcé, la polygamie, les crimes dits d'honneur et la violence relative à la dot et que les réserves tendant à relativiser le droit de vivre à l'abri de tels actes sont incompatibles avec l'objet et le but de la Convention[83]. Plus précisément, il estime illicites les réserves générales[84], et notamment celles qui conditionnent le respect de la Convention ou de certains de ses articles à leur compatibilité avec la Charia sans préciser les impératifs religieux visés. Il est en effet impossible de connaître la portée de l'engagement étatique à la lecture de ces réserves, ce d'autant plus que les exégèses des textes religieux peuvent varier considérablement et que les Etats concernés n'ont visiblement pas la même interprétation des rapports de compatibilité entre les dispositions de la Convention et le droit islamique. Les tentatives du Comité EDEF de mener des études sur le statut des femmes en vertu des lois musulmanes, qui auraient permis de mieux identifier la portée de telles réserves, furent rapidement abandonnées devant les accusations d'islamophobie dont elles firent les frais au sein du Conseil économique et social[85]. Le Comité précise alors que les réserves à l'article 2 (principe général de non-discrimination) et à l'article 16 (droits égaux en matière maritale et

81 CEDEF et CDE, « Recommandation générale/Observation générale conjointe, Les pratiques préjudiciables », CEDAW/C/GC/31/CRC/C/GC/18, 2014, § 81.

82 CEDEF, Observations finales sur Singapour, 2007, CEDAW/C/SGP/CO/3, § 16 ; Ouganda, 2010, CEDAW/C/UGA/CO/7, § 22 ; Yémen, 2009, CEDAW/C/YEM/CO/6, § 15 ; Russie, 2015, CEDAW/C/RUS/CO/8, § 20.

83 CEDEF et CDE, « Recommandation générale/Observation générale conjointe, Les pratiques préjudiciables », *op. cit.*, § 55 et § 14.

84 Examen des directives générales concernant l'établissement des rapports initiaux, A/50/38, p. 147, § 8 c).

85 J. Connors, « Article 28 », in *The UN Convention on the Elimination of all forms of Discrimination against Women, a Commentary*, M. Freeman, C. Chinkin, B. Rudolf (eds.), Oxford University Press, 2012, p. 582.

familiale) portent sur des dispositions conventionnelles essentielles et sont à ce titre incompatibles avec l'objet et le but du traité. A ses yeux, « les réserves à l'article 16, qu'elles soient formulés pour des motifs nationaux, coutumiers, religieux ou culturels » sont « illicites »[86]. Une telle affirmation ne saurait totalement convaincre : ce n'est pas l'essentialité de tel ou tel droit, mais le contenu de la réserve qui permet d'en apprécier la licéité. Si celle-ci nie la substance du droit protégé, la réserve sera incompatible avec l'objet et le but du traité. Si elle ne fait qu'en réglementer l'exercice, elle pourra être autorisée[87]. Mais pour le Comité, « l'inégalité entre les membres de la famille sous-tend toutes les autres formes de discrimination que subissent les femmes et est souvent justifiée au moyen d'arguments idéologiques ou au nom de la tradition et de la culture »[88]. Ainsi, « quels que soient le système juridique, la religion ou la tradition du pays, les femmes doivent, dans la loi et dans les faits, être traitées dans la famille selon les principes d'égalité et de justice consacrés par l'article 2 de la Convention »[89]. Les traditions familiales qui constituent par ailleurs des pratiques préjudiciables, telles que la polygamie ou le mariage forcé, doivent naturellement être interdites. Mais en outre, le Comité critique également sévèrement les lois et coutumes relatives au statut personnel, qui varient selon l'appartenance ethnique ou religieuse de l'individu et qui perpétuent les discriminations. Par une interprétation téléologique, il estime également que les discriminations en matière de succession sont contraires à la Convention[90]. Plus généralement, en matière de liens maritaux et familiaux, il souligne que « ni des pratiques traditionnelles, religieuses ou culturelles ni des lois et politiques nationales incompatibles ne sauraient justifier des violations des dispositions de la Convention »[91].

En déterminant lui-même les normes qu'il considère irréconciliables avec les exigences conventionnelles, le Comité pose les limites de sa tolérance. Sa stratégie semble parfois porter ses fruits : si les réserves religieuses semblent

86 Déclaration sur les réserves à la Convention EDEF, 1998, A/53/38/Rev.I, pp. 49–52, § 6, § 8, § 17.

87 O. de Frouville, *op. cit.*, p. 299 et p. 302. Ainsi, en refusant que le droit à des moyens nécessaires pour décider librement du nombre de naissances (article 16 § 1 *e*) impose la légalisation de l'avortement, les réserves maltaise et monégasque ne font vraisemblablement qu'en réglementer l'exercice (CEDAW/SP/2010/2).

88 CEDEF, « Recommandation générale n° 29 », *op. cit.,*, § 2.

89 CEDEF, « Recommandation générale n° 21 », *op. cit.*, § 13.

90 CEDEF, « Recommandation générale n° 29 », *op. cit.*, §§ 10-14 ; CEDEF, « Recommandation générale n° 21 », *op. cit.*, § 28 et § 35.

91 Déclaration sur les réserves à la Convention EDEF, 1998, A/53/38/Rev.I, pp. 49–52, § 17.

les plus tenaces et si un Etat (les Maldives) a illicitement étendu la portée de la sienne, d'autres commencent à les retirer soit partiellement soit totalement[92] et tant la Palestine que le Sud Soudan viennent de ratifier la Convention sans réserve. L'optimisme ne saurait pourtant être de mise, et le 8 mars 2017, le Comité épaulé de la Rapporteuse spéciale sur les violences à l'égard des femmes et par le Groupe de travail chargé de la question de la discrimination à l'égard des femmes dans la législation et dans la pratique lançaient encore à la communauté internationale :

> not only is the advancement of women taking a very long time and full equality far from a global reality, but today women's hard fought achievements face the risk of reversal. An unprecedented pushback has been launched across regions by an alliance of conservative political ideologies and religious traditionalism. This pushback happens both in established democracies and countries in transition ... Women's human rights are fundamental rights which cannot be subordinated to cultural, religious or political considerations. We say to the women of the world – stand up and push forward[93].

---

92 J. Connors, « Article 28 », *op. cit.*, p. 591–595 : En 1991, le Malawi a retiré sa réserve selon laquelle il n'était pas lié par les dispositions de la Convention exigeant l'abolition immédiate des coutumes et pratiques traditionnelles discriminatoires. En 2004, le Lesotho a retiré sa réserve selon laquelle aucune obligation de la Convention ne s'applique aux affaires d'ordre religieux. Le 8 avril 2011, le Maroc a notifié sa levée des réserves aux articles 9 § 2 et 16 de la Convention. Le 17 avril 2014, la Tunisie a levé toutes ses réserves. Elle maintient tout de même sa déclaration interprétative subordonnant l'application de la Convention à l'article 1er de sa Constitution, qui fait référence à l'Islam.

93 International Women's Day Statement by United Nations Women's Human Rights Experts, « Elimination of discrimination against women – an unfinished agenda » : <www.ohchr.org/FR/NewsEvents/Pages/DisplayNews.aspx?NewsID=21302&LangID=E>.

CHAPTER 16

Religious Freedom and Parental Rights in a Pluralist Society

Dagmar Richter

1 Introduction

This chapter deals with a dilemma challenging the fundaments of an open and free society: Must a state tolerate parental wishes to keep children away, for religious reasons, from the impacts of individualism and pluralism? By guaranteeing religious freedom and parental rights, the state acts in conformity with human rights as interpreted in the light of the principles of pluralism and broadmindedness. However, it is exactly this kind of tolerance, by which it may undermine the preconditions of its own existence.[1] Religious freedom and parental rights can be put to good use but also abused in order to advise children against the values of the democratic *Rechtsstaat* including pluralism, individual rights and respect of others, and in favor of collectivism, subordination and authoritarian leadership. While the liberal conception of education seeks to enable children to freely develop their own personality in order to take individual choices in their future lives, traditional religious communities seek to form a certain religious background from the very beginning of a person's life in order to strengthen and perpetuate collectivism. Whilst religious 'imprinting' may be even essential for the preservation of a religion, freedom from such imprinting seems to be vital for the preservation of a democratic culture. Additionally, religious 'imprinting' can be considered incompatible with the possible right of the child to

1 cf Ernst-Wolfgang Böckenförde, *Staat, Gesellschaft, Freiheit* (Suhrkamp 1976) 60: 'Der freiheitliche, säkularisierte Staat lebt von Voraussetzungen, die er selbst nicht garantieren kann' [The liberal and secularized State subsists on preconditions it cannot guarantee itself]. Previously, Justice Learned Hand, 'The Spirit of Liberty. Address on 21 May 1944 in New York's Central Park' (*Digital History* 2016, ID 1199) <www.digitalhistory.uh.edu/disp_textbook.cfm?smtID=3&psid=1199> accessed 12 July 2017: '... Liberty lies in the hearts of men and women; when it dies there, no constitution, no law, no court can save it; ...'.

 | DOI:10.1163/9789004349155_017

remain uninfluenced by religious upbringing,[2] respectively the child's 'right to an open future'.[3]

The article will discuss the problem with regard to the European Convention on Human Rights (ECHR) and the First Protocol Additional (AP 1) to it, which are both binding upon France and Germany.[4] The Convention system does not only guarantee certain human rights but also creates a 'European public order'[5] defining the human rights standards of the 'espace européen' with respect to the Council of Europe and, indirectly, to the European Union.[6] According to the concept of the Convention being a 'living instrument' Convention rights must always be interpreted in a way that is named as 'dynamic-evolutionary'.[7] Legal change will be considered by the Strasbourg Court depending on the degree of conformity of state practice among the States Parties.[8] The more conformity there is the more open the Court will be with regard to the adaptation of its jurisprudence to new developments. Yet, culturally sensitive issues and in particular those of religious importance are among the least likely to show such conformity.

2 Understanding Article 2 of the Protocol – Parental Rights Within the ECHR System

2.1 *The Interrelationship of Parental Rights and Other Convention Rights*

Where cases show educational as well as religious implications, both the right to education (Article 2 AP 1) and the freedom of religion (Article 9 ECHR) apply. Both provisions are interrelated and re-enforcing each other. As the

2 See Heiner Bielefeldt, 'The Liberty of Parents to Ensure the Religious and Moral Education of Their Children' in Heiner Bielefeldt, Nazila Ghanea and Michael Wiener (eds), *Freedom of Religion or Belief, An International Law Commentary* (OUP 2016) 205, 215–219.

3 Joel Feinberg, 'The Child's Right to an Open Future' in William Aiken and Hugh LaFollette (eds), *Whose Child? Children's Rights, Parental Authority, and State Power* (Rowman and Littlefield 1980); Claudia Mills, 'The Child's Right to an Open Future?' (2003) 34 Journal of Social Philosophy 499, 501.

4 See CoE Treaty Office <www.coe.int/en/web/conventions/full-list/-/conventions/> accessed 12 July 2017.

5 See eg, *Cyprus v Turkey* (ECtHR GC) App no 25781/94 ECHR 2001-IV 1, para 78.

6 See Article 6 (3) TEU and Article 52 (3) Charter of Fundamental Rights.

7 *Tyrer v The UK* App no 5856/72 (ECtHR, 1978) Series A no 26, para 31.

8 Extensively, eg, *Buzadji v The Republic of Moldova* (GC) App no 23755/07 (ECtHR, 5 July 2016), paras 45–60, 92f. For State practice in European countries see Anders Sjöborg and Hans-Georg Ziebertz (eds), *Religion, Education and Human Rights* (Springer 2017)

European Court of Human Rights (ECtHR) has put it, 'the provisions of the Convention and Protocol must be read as a whole'.[9] Yet, the Court does not only seek to maintain consistency between Article 2 AP 1 and all other Convention rights but also refers to the 'general spirit' of the Convention which it considers 'an instrument designed to maintain and promote the ideals and values of a democratic society'.[10] This spirit is considered a pluralist one, including religious beliefs.[11]

2.2 *The Two Sentences of Article 2 AP 1 – Delimitating the Rights and Duties of Parents, Children and the State*

Parental rights can easily touch upon the rights of others, in particular the human rights of children, the competence of the State to organize the educational system, and even the rights of religious communities.[12] However, this does not mean that Article 2 AP 1 may be invoked by Religious Communities, as only individuals can be victims of a violation of the right to education.[13] Being considered an '*empowerment right*'[14] the latter entails a right to being educated oneself but not to educate anybody else.

According to the Court the first sentence ('*No person shall be denied the right to education*') does not guarantee a right to a specific form of school education but no more than the right of access to educational institutions *existing at a given time*. This right calls for regulation by the State, which may vary in time and place.[15]

9 ECtHR, *Kjeldsen, Busk Madsen and Pedersen v Denmark* App no 5095/71 (1976) Series A no 23, para 53. For further details below 2.3.

10 *Kjeldsen, Busk Madsen and Pedersen* (n 9) para 53.

11 Below 2.2.

12 See Bielefeldt (n 2) 206.

13 *Savez Crkava 'Riječ života' and Others v Croatia* App no 7798/08 (ECtHR, 9 December 2010), para 125: Also *Karnell and Hardt v Sweden* App no 4733/71 (Commission Decision, 19 July 1971). With regard to Article 18 CCPR, Human Rights Committee, *Erkki Hartikainen v Finland* [1978] Communication no 40/1978, para 3. Joana Cismas, *Religious Actors and International Law* (OUP 2014) 114–119, considers the principle of the evolving capacities of the child (cf Article 5 Convention on the Rights of the Child) to be the reason for excluding churches from claiming educational rights.

14 Committee on Economic, Social and Cultural Rights, General Comment 13, Article 13 (21st session, 1999) UN Doc E/C.12/1999/10, para 1.

15 *Case Relating to Certain Aspects of the Laws on the Use of Languages in Education in Belgium v Belgium* App nos 1474/62 et al (ECtHR, 1968) Series A no 6, para 7. See also *Bulski v Poland* App nos 46254/99, 31888/02 (ECtHR, decision of 30 November 2004).

The second sentence (‘*In the exercise of any functions which it assumes in relation to education and to teaching, the State shall …*’) acknowledges the exercise of state functions in relation to education and to teaching, in particular the State's competence to organize and regulate the operation of educational institutions. Accordingly, the setting and planning of the curriculum (including expediency) fall within the competence of the Contracting States.[16] It ‘may legitimately vary according to the country and the era’.[17]

It is only on this basis that the endmost part of the second sentence of Article 2 AP 1 establishes a duty of the Convention States to respect parents' religious convictions (‘*…the State shall respect the right of parents to ensure such education and teaching in conformity with their own religious and philosophical convictions*’). This duty is broad and covers all functions assumed by the state. It includes, in particular, a proper treatment of (religious) minorities, as the provision aims at safeguarding *pluralism*, which the ECtHR holds to be essential for the preservation of a democratic society.[18] On the one hand, Article 2 AP 1 does not guarantee an absolute right to have children educated in accordance with parents' religious and philosophical convictions, but only a right to *respect* for those convictions.[19] On the other hand, ‘respect’ means more than ‘acknowledge’ or ‘take into account’. It even implies ‘some positive obligations’,[20] and cannot be overridden by the alleged necessity of striking a balance between the conflicting views involved.[21]

16 *Kjeldsen, Busk Madsen and Pedersen* (n 9) para 53.

17 *Lautsi and Others v Italy* (GC) App no 30814/06 (ECtHR, 18 March 2011), para 62.

18 *Kjeldsen, Busk Madsen and Pedersen* (n 9) para 50. Also *B N and S N v Sweden* App no 17678/91 (Commission Decision, 30 June 1993); *Konrad v Germany* (decision) App no 35504/03, ECHR 2006-XIII 355; *Folgerø and Others v Norway* (GC) App no 15472/02 ECHR 2007-III 51, para 84 (f).

19 See eg, *Family H v The UK* App no 10233/83 (EComHR, 1983) 37 DR 105.

20 Not including the establishment of certain forms of schools. See before with n 15. See also *Ingrid Jordebo Foundation of Christian Schools and Ingrid Jordebo v Sweden* App no 11533/85 (EComHR, 1987) 51 DR 125, para 4.2.

21 *Campbell and Cosans v The UK* App nos 7511/76, 7743/76 (ECtHR, 1982) Series A no 48, para 37: ‘As is confirmed by the fact that, in the course of the drafting of Article 2 (P1-2), the words “have regard to” were replaced by the word “respect” (see documents cdh [67] 2, at 163) the latter word means more than “acknowledge” or “taken into account”; in addition to a primarily negative undertaking, it implies some positive obligation on the part of the State …. This being so, the duty to respect parental convictions in this sphere cannot be overridden by the alleged necessity of striking a balance between the conflicting views involved, nor …’.

Regarding Article 2 AP 1 it is crucial for a proper understanding to consider the inter-relationship between the first sentence and the second sentence. As both sentences relate to public and private teaching, the existence of private schools does not dispense a State Party from its obligation to safeguard pluralism in public schools. Rather the two sentences of Article 2 AP 1 must be read in the light of each other. Accordingly, parental rights correspond to parental responsibilities. What is more, the parental right (2nd sentence) is held to be a mere 'adjunct' of the fundamental right to education (1st sentence),[22] as Article 2 constitutes a whole that is dominated by its first sentence.[23] It is only in the discharge of this responsibility to their children that parents may require the state to respect their religious and philosophical convictions. Consequently, parents must not refuse a child's right to education on the basis of their convictions.[24]

2.3 *Interpreting 'Religious Convictions' in the Light of the Convention*

Article 2 AP 1 guaranteeing respect of the rights of parents with regard to religious convictions in matters of education must be deemed *lex specialis* with regard to Article 9 ECHR (freedom of religion).[25] However, both sentences of Article 2 AP 1 must not only be interpreted in the light of each other but also in the light of Articles 8, 9, 10 ECHR.[26] Additionally, one has to resort to Articles 8 to 10 ECHR in order to determine the range of religious convictions to be protected under Article 2 AP 1.[27] The ECtHR seems to equate 'conviction' (Article 2 AP 1) to the term of 'belief' (Article 9 ECHR), but clearly distinguishes the words 'opinions' and 'ideas' (Article 10 ECHR) from 'convictions': Whereas any kind of spontaneous non-sense idea can be protected by the freedom of speech and information, the term of religious 'convictions' is limited to denote 'views that attain a certain level of cogency, seriousness, cohesion and importance'.[28]

22 *Kjeldsen, Busk Madsen and Pedersen* (n 9) para 52.

23 *Campbell and Cosans* (n 21) paras 36, 40.

24 *Konrad* (n 18). See also section 3.1.

25 *Lautsi and Others* (n 17) para 59. C Grabenwarter and K Pabel, *Europäische Menschenrechtskonvention* (6th edn, Beck 2016) 355–356 (ch 22, para 100).

26 *Kjeldsen, Busk Madsen and Pedersen* (n 9) para 52; *Efstratiou v Greece* App no 24095/94 (ECtHR, 18 December 1996), para 26.

27 cf *Kjeldsen, Busk Madsen and Pedersen* (n 9) para 52; *Efstratiou* (n 26) para 26.

28 *Efstratiou* (n 26) para 26, with further references.

3 Case Law of the European Court of Human Rights

3.1 *The Relationship between Parental Rights and the Child's Right to Education*

As mentioned before, the parents' right to respect with regard to religious convictions (Article 2 AP 1, 2nd sentence) is considered by the ECtHR a mere 'adjunct' of the child's fundamental right to education (1st sentence). Yet, the obligation to respect parental convictions cannot be overridden by the alleged necessity of striking a balance between the conflicting views involved in the respective case.[29] Both statements taken together point to the conclusion that *respect in principle cannot be relativized.* The decisive question, however, remains whether a certain conviction qualifies for being respected.

The ECtHR has answered this question in its *Campbell and Cosans* judgment dealing with 'philosophical convictions'. As the Court found, Article 2 AP 1 pertains to convictions

> as are worthy of respect in a 'democratic society' ... and are not incompatible with human dignity; in addition, they must not conflict with the fundamental right of the child to education, the whole of Article 2 (P1-2) being dominated by its first sentence ...[30]

This statement was further elaborated in the case of *Konrad v Germany* (2006), where the applicant parents for religious reasons rejected the attendance by their children of any type of common school.[31] Sharing the German Government's view the ECtHR found this claim to endanger the children's right to education:

> It is on to this fundamental right that is grafted the right of parents to respect for their religious and philosophical convictions ... Therefore, respect is only due to convictions on the part of the parents which do not conflict with the child's right to education, the whole of Article 2 of Protocol No. 1 being dominated by its first sentence ... This means that parents may not refuse a child's right to education on the basis of their convictions ...[32]

---

29 Above section 2.2.

30 *Campbell and Cosans* (n 21) para 36.

31 For further details see section 3.5.

32 *Konrad* (n 18) referring to *B N and S N* (n 18).

This statement, at first view, reminds us of a circular argument: Whereas the duty to respect parental convictions cannot be overridden, the latter is totally subject to the child's right to education which, however, is to be guaranteed by the state on the basis of the State Party's competence to organize and regulate the operation of its educational institutions. In order to prevent the parental right from losing relevance, the State Party must not compete with parents in imparting religious contents to children when exercising its competence. Rather it is subject to restrictions which have been elaborated by the ECtHR.[33]

3.2 *Religious Instruction in State Schools?*

In the case of *Kjeldsen, Busk Madsen and Pedersen v Denmark* (1976), where a State Church was still in place, the ECtHR acknowledged in principle that the Convention states may insert religious instruction into the curricula for public schools. At the same time it defined intransigent limits of such instruction:

> In particular, the second sentence of Article 2 of the Protocol ... does not prevent States from imparting through teaching or education information or knowledge of a directly or indirectly religious or philosophical kind. It does not even permit parents to object to the integration of such teaching or education in the school curriculum, for otherwise all institutionalised teaching would run the risk of proving impracticable. ...
>
> The second sentence of Article 2 ... implies on the other hand that the State ... must take care that information or knowledge included in the curriculum is conveyed in an objective, critical and pluralistic manner. The State is forbidden to pursue an aim of indoctrination that might be considered as not respecting parents' religious and philosophical convictions. That is the limit that must not be exceeded.[34]

Although the Court has never given a clear definition of the notion of indoctrination, the judgment seems to differentiate: 'Information or knowledge' in particular must be conveyed 'in an objective, critical and pluralistic manner', whereas all forms of teaching – including religious instruction – must fulfil the requirement that they would not amount to indoctrination. Accordingly, one can conclude that 'information or knowledge' is subject to a higher standard of scrutiny referring to 'objectivity' rather than the absence of 'indoctrination'.

33 *Below* section 3.2.

34 *Kjeldsen, Busk Madsen and Pedersen* (n 9) para 53.

In the *Folgerø* case (2007) the Grand Chamber (GC) of the ECtHR extended the notion of knowledge to religious issues by stating that Article 2 AP 1 'does not embody any right for parents that their child be kept ignorant about religion and philosophy in their education'. It further clarified that knowledge about a certain religion such as, eg, Christianity may even represent a greater part of the Curriculum than knowledge about other religions if that religion has played a special role in the national history and tradition of the respondent state (Norway). The Court found that putting more emphasis to such a religion could not of its own be viewed as a departure from the principles of pluralism and objectivity amounting to indoctrination but rather must be regarded as falling within the respondent State's margin of appreciation in planning and setting the curriculum.[35]

Apparently, the ECtHR interprets the States' obligation to offer religious teaching 'in an objective, critical and pluralistic manner' in a way that ultimately includes a differentiating approach. Though the Court has not propagated any form of unequal treatment of religions, but rather accepts that religions being of different importance to the history and tradition of the pertinent State may be treated differently. With that differentiation the Court started to put greater emphasis to the identity concerns of states facing rapid increases in multi-culturalism.

In contrast, the ECtHR formulated more caveats in the case of *Hasan and Zengin v Turkey* (2008) by establishing a two-tier mode of examination. According to this the Court did not only examine whether the content-matter of the contested subject was taught in an objective, critical and pluralist manner. Additionally, it sought to learn whether appropriate provisions have been introduced in the educational system to ensure that parents' convictions are respected.[36] This additional requirement may be due to the fact that this case did not involve any identity concerns on the majority's side but rather related to the assimilation of a religious minority group to the majority religion.

3.3 *Religious Symbols in State Schools*

In the case of *Lautsi and Others v Italy* (2011) the Grand Chamber of the ECtHR extended the prohibition of 'indoctrination' to the display of religious symbols. Whereas the Chamber previously had considered the crucifix to be a 'powerful external symbol' of Catholicism violating the negative right to remain free from symbols placed in a situation from which dissenters cannot extract

35 *Folgerø and Others* (n 18) para 89.

36 *Hasan and Eylem Zengin v Turkey* App no 1448/04 (ECtHR, 9 October 2007), para 57.

themselves,[37] the Grand Chamber turned the outcome of the judgment into the opposite.[38]

The Grand Chamber emphasized that the decision whether or not to perpetuate a tradition falls in principle within the margin of appreciation of the respondent state. The Court had to respect such decisions, including the place a state accords to religion, provided that this would not lead to a form of indoctrination. The decision whether crucifixes should be present in the classrooms was held by the Court, in principle, to fall within the margin of appreciation, all the more as there was no European consensus. Though it conceded that the Crucifixes conferred preponderant visibility to the country's majority religion, it did not find this in itself sufficient to be viewed as a 'departure from the principles of pluralism and objectivity amounting to indoctrination'.[39] Referring to its *Folgerø* and *Zengin* judgments the Court, again, acknowledged the importance of the history and tradition of the state concerned. The Court continued to argue that the crucifix, 'furthermore', were an 'essentially passive symbol', which 'cannot be deemed to have an influence on pupils comparable to that of didactic speech or participation in religious activities'.[40] Even though the principle of neutrality was held applicable, the Court denied the existence of a violation of parental rights, because the exposition of crucifixes was not associated with compulsory teaching about Christianity and the school environment was opened up in parallel to other religions.[41]

This is not the place to take up the vivid discussion on this judgment. The Court has been criticized, eg, for retreating before ferocious national criticism, declaring 'respect' to be a matter of consensus, poor reasoning, etc.[42] What matters here is the approach the Court has taken up by relating to the absence of indoctrination. Ultimately, the Grand Chamber started to distinguish 'didactic speech' from 'non-didactic speech', respectively active teaching from the display of 'passive symbols'. Yet, we do not learn about the source from which the Grand Chamber obtained its knowledge on the influences of symbols on juvenile minds. Additionally, the GC started to confuse objectivity with

37 *Lautsi and Others* (n 17) paras 54–56.

38 *Lautsi and Others* (n 17) paras 57–77.

39 *Lautsi and Others* (n 17) para 71.

40 *Lautsi and Others* (n 17) para 72.

41 *Lautsi and Others* (n 17) paras 72, 74.

42 See eg, Lorenzo Zucca, 'A Comment on Lautsi' (*EJIL Talk*, 19 March 2011) <www.ejiltalk.org/a-comment-on-lautsi/#more-3161> accessed 16 July 2017. Pointing to the 'dilemma' Lori G. Beaman, 'Battles Over Symbols: The "Religion" of the Minority Versus the "Culture" of the Majority' (2012–13) 28 Journal of Law and Religion 67.

indoctrination by speaking of a 'departure from the principles of pluralism and objectivity amounting to indoctrination'. That sounds as if a lack of objectivity in itself would not be relevant to the assessment of 'respect'. According to the GC's *Lautsi* judgment the prohibition of 'indoctrination' seems to have become a super-criterion which superimposes all other criteria such as in particular 'objectivity' and 'neutrality'.

3.4 *Exemption Arrangements*

3.4.1 Necessity of Exemption in Accordance With International Human Rights Standards

As Convention States remain free to determine their relationship to religious communities, they can choose, e.g., to maintain a traditional State Church system and embed activities and doctrines affiliated to it in the curriculum for public schools. In these instances a special exemption arrangement is needed, because the competence of a State to freely determine its relationship to certain churches does not dispense it of its human rights obligations from the Convention as in particular its duty to protect the rights of religious dissenters including parental rights. It is characteristic of these cases that the ultimate question is not whether the teaching amounts to indoctrination but whether a system of exemption can neutralize inevitable impacts on religious dissenters. The pertinent international human rights standard has been formulated by the UN Human Rights Committee in its General Comment no. 22 as follows:

(1) Article 18 (4) CCPR on parental rights permits public school instruction in subjects such as the general history of religions and ethics if it is given in a neutral and objective way.
(2) Public education that includes instruction in a particular religion or belief is inconsistent with Article 18 (4) CCPR unless provision is made for non-discriminatory exemptions or alternatives that would accommodate the wishes of parents and guardians.[43]

The Committee on Economic, Social and Cultural Rights has replicated this standard in a slightly modified way. Within the first rule (1) the term 'neutral' was replaced by 'unbiased'.[44] Additionally, instruction in subjects such as the general history of religions and ethics must not only be given in an unbiased

43 Human Rights Committee, General Comment 22, Article 18 (48th session, 1993) UN Doc CCPR/C/21/Rev.1/Add.4, para 6.

44 For further details on the meaning of these terms below section 4.4.1.

and objective way but, additionally, must be 'respectful of the freedoms of opinion, conscience and expression'.[45]

According to what is named here the '*two alternatives approach*' states can choose between two alternatives leaving them the choice to uphold close relations with a state church. If a state, however, chooses this option it must exempt dissenters from obligatory school attendance so far. Accordingly, the International Consultative Conference on School Education in Relation to Freedom of Religion or Belief, Tolerance and Non-Discrimination has proclaimed a 'right not to receive religious instruction inconsistent with his or her conviction'.[46] The jurisprudence of the ECtHR must be considered against this background.

3.4.2 Requirements Relating to the Exemption Arrangement

In the *Folgerø* case[47] the ECtHR held that the mere existence of an exemption regime cannot compensate the burdens put upon dissenters, unless the conditions to gain such exemption would be reasonable. The complainants, who were members of the Norwegian Humanist Association, objected to the fact that their children were exposed to the subject of 'Christianity, religion and philosophy', which formed part of the curriculum of Norwegian public schools. Even though it was mainly designed to give knowledge and insight and not to serve as a tool for religious preaching, pupils should be given 'a Christian and moral education'. Children of parents who were not members of the Church of Norway, upon the parents' request, could be exempted in whole or in part from lessons on the Christian faith.

The ECtHR found that inherent in the condition to give reasonable grounds for exemption was a risk that the parents might feel compelled to disclose to the school authorities intimate aspects of their own religious and philosophical convictions. This situation was aggravated by the fact that the legal system lacked predictable conditions for exemption. Assuming a 'risk of undue exposure of their private life' the Court came to the conclusion that the refusal to grant exemption from the relevant subject gave rise to a violation of Article 2 AP 1.[48]

45 *General Comment 13* (n 14). Commenting on the reasons for the modification, Bielefeldt (n 2), 210.

46 Consultative Conference on School Education in Relation to Freedom of Religion or Belief, Tolerance and Non-Discrimination '*Final Document of the Meeting in Madrid from 23 to 25 November 2001*', E/CN.4/2002/73 Appendix, sub 4 (Commission on Human Rights, 14 March 2002).

47 *Folgerø and Others* (n 18).

48 *Folgerø and Others* (n 18) paras 98–102.

Three years earlier the Human Rights Committee (HRC) had decided on a similar (or even identical[49]) complaint that was lodged by some other sets of parents facing the same situation. In *Leirvåg and Others v Norway* (2004)[50] the HRC referred to the principles established by General Comment No 22, according to which instruction in a particular religion is inconsistent with Article 18 para 4 CCPR 'unless provision is made for non-discriminatory exemptions or alternatives that would accommodate the wishes of parents or guardians'.[51] Applying this standard the HRC found that a system of partial exemption imposed a considerable burden on parents, insofar as it required them to give reasons for exempting their children without being informed on what kind of reasons would be accepted. Additionally, the scheme of the subject relating to the Christian religion did not ensure that education of religious knowledge and religious practice would be separated in a way that could make the exemption scheme practicable. The children could be exposed to loyalty conflicts whilst their parents had no means to ensure that their children would not be exposed to religious ideas. For all of this Article 18 para 4 CCPR was held to be violated.[52]

It becomes apparent from this that the ECtHR in *Folgerø* made an effort to adapt its findings to the HRC source in order to avoid contradictory interpretations by two human rights treaty bodies concerning practically 'the same matter'.[53] Both treaty bodies pointed out that an Education Act, even if it contains a clear preference for a certain religion, can be considered as complying with the human rights of dissenters, if such preference will be neutralized by a practicable and reasonable system of exemption. However, both cases were characterized by the fact that the respective laws and regulations lacked predictable conditions for exemption. Accordingly, there was no need to get involved in the difficult question whether and how the transfer of religious knowledge and the conveyance of religion can be distinguished from each other.

---

49 Both Article 35 para 2 (b) of the Convention and Article 5 para 2 (a) of the Optional Protocol of the United Nations Covenant on Civil and Political Rights seek to prevent two different international organs from providing different or even contradictory interpretations concerning 'the same matter'. See Separate Opinion of Judges Zupančič and Borrego Borrego, sub 2, Appendix to *Folgerø and Others* (n 18).

50 Human Rights Committee, *Leirvåg and Others v Norway* [2004] Communication no 1155/2003, UN Doc CCPR/C/82/D/1155/2003.

51 *General Comment 22* (n 43).

52 cf, in contrast, *Erkki Hartikainen* (n 13): no violation, as alternative course of instruction is given in a neutral and objective way.

53 See n 49.

3.4.3 Exemption from Obligatory Sex Education?

In the case of *Kjeldsen, Busk Madsen and Pedersen v Denmark* (1976) the ECtHR decided on whether parents for religious reasons could claim exemption of their children from obligatory (integrated) sex education in public schools. Examining the legislation in dispute the Court found that it in no way amounted to an 'attempt at indoctrination aimed at advocating a specific kind of sexual behaviour'. Regarding the risk of sex education probably being applied in an abusive manner, the Court made it clear that the competent authorities (including schools and teachers) 'have a duty to take the utmost care to see to it that parents' religious and philosophical convictions are not disregarded at this level by carelessness, lack of judgment or misplaced proselytism'. It also pointed out that teaching in sex-related subjects in schools would not affect the right of parents to enlighten and advise their children according to their own beliefs.[54]

This argumentation reveals the firm belief by the Court that any kind of subject – except religious instruction – can be taught in a neutral and objective way and, accordingly, may be taught without any possibility of exemption. Apparently, it took a hard line against any form of 'opting-out from knowledge': Neither should parents be entitled to dissociate their children for various religious reasons from certain subjects or parts of it. Nor should schools get entangled in a situation where constant negotiations with parents on the details of the curricula and their implementation would be needed. However, school authorities remain obliged not to exceed the limit of 'indoctrination' and, additionally, to handle 'critical' issues such as sex education with the utmost care. According to the *Kjeldsen* judgment 'indoctrination' does not necessarily imply a religious tendency but can also be present if the taking of a certain position is being advised in 'critical' secular contexts.

3.4.4 Exemption from Participation in School Activities Outside of School

In the cases of *Efstratiou* and *Valsamis* (1996)[55] the applicants were Jehovah's Witnesses who adhered to pacifism, e.g., by refusing to take part in any events with military overtones. Their children were punished by school authorities for failure to take part in the celebration of the National Day which is commemorated with school and military parades, both passing off outside of school but usually not at the same time and place.

54 *Kjeldsen, Busk Madsen and Pedersen* (n 9) paras 53–54.

55 *Efstratiou*(n 26); *Valsamis v Greece* App no 21787/93 (ECtHR, 18 December 1996).

Although the ECtHR conceded to be 'surprised that pupils can be required on pain of suspension from school ... to parade outside the school precincts on a holiday', it could discern 'nothing, either in the purpose of the parade or in the arrangements for it, which could offend the applicants' pacifist convictions to an extent prohibited by the second sentence of Article 2 of Protocol No. 1'.[56] The Court argued that such commemorations of national events serve, 'in their way', both pacifist objectives and the public interest. Even the presence of military representatives at some of the parades did not in itself alter the nature of the parades. Once more, the Court seemed satisfied with the fact that parents, despite of the obligation to join the parade, remain the right 'to enlighten and advise' their children in conformity with their religious convictions.

These judgments cannot be considered convincing, because it is not the Court's task to replace the parents' perception of the symbolism and character of the school parades by its own perception. As Judges *Thór Vilhjálmsson* and *Jambrek* rightly observed in their joint dissenting opinion, it is for the Court to accept such perceptions unless they are obviously unfounded. The crucial point here relates to the fact that the pupils were impelled to commonly deliver, outside of school, a specific political message (neither neutral nor objective) to the public. Whereas it may be doubted whether obligatory parading in a nationalist manner is compatible at all with the concept of a pluralist society, exemption for religious reasons must be granted, if parents can plausibly maintain that such public confession contradicts to their religious convictions.

3.5 *Home Schooling for Religious Reasons?*

Requesting authorization to educate one's children at home challenges the very essence of public education, which lies in its social dimension. Whereas some of the Convention states as, eg, Scandinavian states are quite liberal in that respect, other states as, eg, Germany refuse, as a matter of principle, to any form of home schooling.[57] As no uniform European practice exists, a relatively wide margin of appreciation has to be left to the Convention states.[58]

Even in Scandinavian states home schooling has been refused occasionally, eg, with regard to the last three forms of the compulsory school because

---

56 *Efstratiou* (n 26) para 32; *Valsamis* (n 55) para 31.

57 Sceptical on the comprehensive ban, however, Julian von Lucius, *Homeschooling* (Nomos 2017).

58 Above section 1.

of 'increasing specialization of the education' and 'increasing emphasis on social training',[59] or with regard to a lack of teaching capacity on the parents' side.[60] Such cases had already been dealt with by the former European Commission of Human Rights which considered the requirement of social training, ie the 'obligation to go to school with other children in order to learn how to establish social contacts … inherent in any system of compulsory schooling' and not going 'outside what is common practice in Contracting States'.[61]

In the case of *Konrad v Germany* (2006), where adherents to the 'Philadelphia School' movement were refused to remove their children from public school, the ECtHR assessed the legal situation in Germany accordingly:

> In the present case, the Court notes that the German authorities and courts … mainly stressed the fact that not only the acquisition of knowledge but also integration into and first experiences of society are important goals in primary-school education. … The Court considers that this presumption is not erroneous and falls within the Contracting States' margin of appreciation … The Federal Constitutional Court stressed the general interest of society in avoiding the emergence of parallel societies based on separate philosophical convictions and the importance of integrating minorities into society. The Court regards this as being in accordance with its own case-law on the importance of pluralism for democracy …[62]

It can be derived from this formulation that the Court explicitly acknowledges the general interest of society in *avoiding the emergence of parallel societies* as being in accordance with its own case-law on the importance of pluralism for democracy. However, it avoids committing itself to a certain position. Qualifying the German position as to be 'not erroneous' the Court leaves it to the Convention states to decide on whether a total prohibition of homeschooling would be mandatory or not in order to retain pluralism.

---

59 See, eg, *B N and S N* (n 18).

60 See, eg, *Family H* (n 19).

61 *B N and S N* (n 18).

62 *Konrad* (n 18). The complaint was rejected as manifestly ill-founded. See also *Willi, Anna and David Dojan v Germany* App no 319/08 (ECtHR, 13 September 2011), relating to claims for partial exemptions.

4 Conclusions

4.1 *Parental Rights and the Freedom of Religion*

There is only a limited role for the freedom of religion (Article 9 ECHR) with regard to parental rights. Usually, the Court confines itself to Article 2 AP 1 (Parental Rights) stating that 'no separate issue arises under Article 9 of the Convention'.[63] This conforms to the fact that Article 2 AP 1 is the more specific right (*lex specialis*) in cases, where parents' religious convictions conflict with state action in the field of school education.[64] Furthermore, it is common practice of the Court not to engage in any examination of any other rights unless a clearly distinct issue remains to be examined. Although the Court continues to maintain that Article 2 AP 1 must be interpreted 'in the light of' Article 9 ECHR,[65] no practical consequences follow from this in most of the cases. The unwillingness of the Court to refer to the freedom of religion may be explained by the fact that Article 2 AP 1 implies a system of rules balancing the rights of the child, the parents and the competences of the state,[66] while Article 9 (2) ECHR requires limitations to be necessary in a democratic society, which has a potential to strengthen the parents' position.

However, there is one exception: If the Court relates to the 'duty of neutrality and impartiality' or the state's duty to actively maintain tolerance between opposing groups, it explicitly reads the second sentence of Article 2 AP 1 in the light of Article 9 ECHR considering the fact that the latter includes the freedom not to belong to a religion (negative freedom).[67] Thus the role of the freedom of religion can be described as supplementary in a selective rather than a material sense.

4.2 *The Impact of Rising Multiculturalism in European Societies On the Interpretation of Article 2 AP 1*

Formerly, conflicts arose mainly between a state (majority) religion and certain parental (minority) convictions. Those conflicts could be solved by granting exemptions, whilst disputes in that context related to the question on whether

63 *Lautsi and Others* (n 17) para 77. See also *Folgerø and Others* (n 18) para 105, where the Court refused to engage in an additional examination of Article 14 ECHR in conjunction with Article 9 ECHR and Article 2 AP 1, after a violation of Article 2 AP 1 (alone) had been denied.

64 Above section 2.1.

65 Above section 2.3.

66 Above section 2.2.

67 *Lautsi and Others* (n 17) para 60.

the conditions to gain exemption were reasonable.[68] The problem associated with exemptions, however, is that they can isolate a child from his or her class community. In today's multi-religious societies the environment has changed fundamentally and so have the conflict lines. The typical conflict of today does not root in the fact that adherents of a minority religion or non-believers are being exposed to any form of religious instruction in public schools. Rather, religious groups of a fundamentalist kind (including Christians) seek to escape from public education in order to keep their children away from 'libertarian' and multi-cultural influences. This intention militates to the integrating function of schools, which has been perceived to be ever more important in states with multi-religious societies, including European states with a growing number of immigrants and their descendants.[69]

In such instances public schools have a greater responsibility to impart ethical and religious knowledge to all children in order to avoid the emergence of radicalism and parallel societies. Consequently, exemption claims seem more likely to fail.[70] It is in line with this fundamental change that the European Court of Human Rights explicitly denies to the parents any right to keep their children away from religious knowledge concerning doctrines and rites of other religions or beliefs.[71] Respecting the situation of former majority or even homogeneous societies claiming a 'right' to preserve their respective cultural identities,[72] it even accepts that the Convention states may reserve a greater part of the Curriculum to the religion traditionally dominant, because this kind of preference 'cannot ... of its own be viewed as a departure from

68 Above section 3.4.

69 See CoE Parliamentary Assembly Resolution 2163 (2017) on the protection of the rights of parents and children belonging to religious minorities.

70 See, with regard to Germany, Stefan Huster, 'Gleichheit statt Freiheit: Die Verschiebung der Argumentationsgewichte im Religionsverfassungsrecht unter Bedingungen des Pluralismus' in Hans-Michael Heinig and Christian Walter (eds), *Religionsverfassungsrechtliche Spannungsfelder* (Mohr Tübingen 2015) 203, 214. Huster speaks of a 'Tendenzwende' (reversal of a tendency) from a liberal exemption practice of the courts to a much more restrictive practice.

71 cf *Konrad* (n 18). Above section 3.5.

72 See Dagmar Richter, 'Die Verteidigung tradierter Rechtsräume als Schranke der Religionsfreiheit' in M Breuer et al (eds), *Der Staat im Recht. Festschrift für [Essays in Honour of] Eckart Klein* (Duncker und Humblot 2013), 1263–1288; and 'Die neuen Konflikte um Kulturräume. Zur Bewahrung kultureller Identität im post-terriorialen Zeitalter' in K Odendahl and T Giegerich (eds), *Räume im Völker- und Europarecht* (Duncker und Humblot 2014), 71–104.

the principles of pluralism and objectivity amounting to indoctrination'.[73] The magic term for handling today's conflict hence is 'indoctrination'.

4.3 *The Limited Functionality of the 'Indoctrination Formula'*

What is called here the 'indoctrination formula' has already been applied by the Court in the *Kjeldsen* judgment (1976).[74] However, the prohibition of indoctrination constituting 'the limit that must not be exceeded' has changed its function in the course of time. In *Kjeldsen* the Court explained that, e.g., advocating a specific kind of sexual behaviour can constitute indoctrination, but not so confronting children of a proper age with knowledge on sexuality. Indoctrination stands here for implanting a certain doctrine (or behaviour) in the context of a religiously sensitive issue. In contrast, the Court argues in *Folgerø* (2007) and *Lautsi* (2011) that the conveyance of knowledge about religion, even with a clear preponderance of Christianity, or the display of Christian Crucifixes 'cannot of its own be viewed as a departure from the principles of pluralism and objectivity amounting to indoctrination'.[75] Indoctrination stands here for an extremely intrusive type of action, possibly departing from objectivity but – having regard to the respective majority traditions – not too much.

Applying the formula of 'no indoctrination – no problem' the Court avoids weighing of interests and striking a fair balance with respect to conflicting rights. It ultimately equates 'respect' with 'prohibition of indoctrination' resp. 'not associated with compulsory teaching',[76] despite of the fact that a person can be deprived of 'respect' even if neither indoctrination nor compulsion is at stake. Accordingly, there is no indication in the norm that any behavior short of indoctrination or compulsion would automatically be respectful under Article 2 AP 1. Referring to a prohibition of indoctrination the Court drifts away from the standard of objectivity, because biased or non-objective forms of instruction or practices can fall short of indoctrination. E.g., the Crucifix being exposed in class-rooms can be considered not to 'indoctrinate' children – but it clearly is not objective. After all, one has to conclude that the indoctrination formula considerably narrows the scope of application of respect for parental convictions. It is not suitable at all where exemption claims relate to any form of non-intellectual activities such as, e.g., the display of symbols or the

73 *Folgerø and Others* (n 18) para 89. Relating to the Italian 'Crucifix tradition', *Lautsi and Others* (n 17) para 68, 71.

74 *Kjeldsen, Busk Madsen and Pedersen* (n 9) paras 53–54.

75 Above 4.2, with references.

76 *Lautsi and Others* (n 17) para 74, adding the readiness to open up the school environment to other religions.

participation in sports lessons.[77] as we shall never find any symbol or sports exercise *ipso facto* having the capacity to indoctrinate minds.

4.4 *Categorizing Impacts on Religious Convictions*

Ensuring respect for parental convictions is not an end in itself. It is designed in order to serve the child's best interest and must neither compromise the child's right to education nor contribute to keeping a child off the impacts of pluralism and making him or her part of a 'parallel society'. However, the parents' right to 'respect' must keep its proper function to protect children from any form of school education that, due to the family's religious convictions, causes conflicts or isolates a child within the school class.

The ECtHR jurisprudence seems to lack a systematic approach relating to the particularities of the various types of religious conflicts in schools: Some parents do not want teachers to present Darwin's theses, others do not want their girls to participate in co-educative swimming lessons, and still others feel disrespected because their children are offered pork for lunch. There is a need to better adapt the limits of respect for parents' religious and philosophical convictions to the distinct types of impacts on children.

4.4.1 Intellectual Impacts – The Principle of Objectivity As An Alternative

As concerns the contents of teaching or 'didactic speech'[78] (*intellectual impacts*) the *principle of objectivity* can provide for adequate solutions without being compromised by the indoctrination formula: As shown before, parents have no right to keep their children away from age-appropriate forms of the reception of knowledge.[79] Conveying 'knowledge' can be described as presenting a subject matter including information on other religions in concordance with the principle of objectivity. The qualitative criteria for objectivity are 'respect

---

77 For the dispute on the question whether Muslim girls must participate in obligatory swimming lessons at public schools see *Burkini* [11 September 2013] BVerwG (German Federal Administrative Court), NVwZ 2014, 81. Commenting on this, eg, Arnd Uhle, Integration durch Schule. Die Urteile des BVerwG in den Verfahren 'Burkini' und 'Krabat' (6 C 25/12 und 6 C 12/12) [2014] NVwZ 541. The ECtHR has not yet decided on this issue.

78 cf *Lautsi and Others* (n 17) para 72.

79 Above 3.4.3. For the so-called 'Bildungserziehung' [Knowledge education] see Christine Langenfeld, 'Das Elternrecht im Schulwesen' in O Dörr, R Grote and T Marauhn (eds) *EMRK/GG. Konkordanzkommentar* (2nd edn, Mohr Siebeck 2013), 1661 (ch 24, para 22); respecting Germany, Langenfeld, *Integration und kulturelle Identität zugewanderter Minderheiten in der Bundesrepublik Deutschland – eine Untersuchung am Beispiel des allgemeinbildenden Schulwesens* (Mohr Siebeck 2001), 413f.

for plurality of convictions in classes and schools, as also the dictates of scientific neutrality inherent in any educative function, which constitute the essential guarantees of such instruction'.[80] According to this, instruction must not, e.g., convey a historically negative image of a certain religion or resort to 'value judgments'.

It is true that it often will be a subject of controversy whether a teacher has reported on a certain subject matter in an objective way. However, a deminimis approach can help to handle this problem and provide for the practicability needed in order to ensure the proper functioning of every-day school life. According to this approach, the absence of objectivity amounts to disrespect of the parents' convictions only if it is attached with some importance, discriminates against a certain religion or shows a consistent pattern of value judging. It must also be considered that a teacher can be entitled to inform children of his or her personal views on a certain subject matter, given that the personal character of such views is revealed to the children in an age-appropriate manner and the conveyance of such views would not amount to indoctrination. Hence, the notion of 'indoctrination' remains to be helpful in this specific and limited context – but should be discarded in all other instances. Strengthening the child's right not to be prevented from any kind of age-appropriate knowledge and, under certain circumstances, learn about the teacher's personal views can be considered a core aspect of the children's 'right to an open future'.[81]

If a state does not adhere to the principle of neutrality but to a *state-church system* by preferring a certain religion, it may introduce religious instruction into the curricula for public schools. However, under these circumstances dissenters have a right to have their children exempted from such lessons ('*two alternatives approach*')[82]. The conditions for gaining exemption must be reasonable and, in particular, respect the parents' right not to reveal their personal convictions to the authorities.[83]

4.4.2 Non-intellectual Impacts – The Need for Scientific Evidence

Non-intellectual impacts on the parents' religious convictions such as, e.g., the display of certain symbols in schools, the ingredients of the lunch menu or the

80 Study on 'Racial discrimination, religious intolerance and education' by Special Rapporteur of the Commission on Human Rights on religious intolerance Abdelfattah Amor [3 May 2001] UN Doc A/CONF.189/PC.2/22, para 53.

81 Above section 1.

82 Above section 3.4.1.

83 Above section 3.4.2.

participation of the children in certain exercise like co-educative swimming lessons, co-educative learning in general, teaching by either female or male teachers, school outings, etc., must be treated differently. Although the parents' right to respect is not subject to limitation,[84] the decisive question will be what would be respectful in a certain situation.[85] For this purpose the parents' and the children's rights as well as legitimate public interests relating to education have to be balanced whilst considering the fact that the child's right to education must not be compromised. Retaining parents the right to enlighten and advise their children in private[86] cannot be of any importance in this context, because Article 2 AP 1 requires respect in the field of public education. It is not appropriate to declare a religious symbol like the Crucifix to represent an 'essentially passive symbol', which could not be deemed 'to have an influence on pupils comparable to that of didactic speech or participation in religious activities',[87] – because this exactly has to be proved. What form of respect is to be considered imperative, must be determined on grounds of socio-scientific expertise revealing the actual impacts on juvenile minds of the respective facts or actions. *Informed impact* alone leads to informed decisions serving the child's best interest, in accordance with the parents' rights to respect.

84 Above section 2.2.

85 cf *Lautsi and Others* (n 17) para 61: '… the requirements of the notion of "respect" … vary considerably from case to case, given the diversity of the practices followed and the situations obtaining in the Contracting States'.

86 See, however, *Kjeldsen, Busk Madsen and Pedersen* (n 9) para 54; *Valsamis* (n 55) para 31; *Lautsi and Others* (n 17) para 75.

87 *Lautsi and Others* (n 17) para 72.

PART 7

Conclusions

CHAPTER 17

Les influences réciproques entre religion(s) et droit international

Emmanuel Decaux

Il y a une part d'inconscience à faire des conclusions, surtout sur un tel sujet, car il est toujours délicat de parler de religion pour un simple juriste, d'autant que dans son propos d'accueil le professeur Jörg Fritzsche, doyen de l'Université hôte, a fait monter les enchères en annonçant de « *good conclusions* ». Mais ce qui me rassure est de partager cette responsabilité avec le professeur Christian Walter, qui restituera la trame intime des propos très riches de ce colloque, alors que je me contenterai d'une approche extérieure du sujet, en m'excusant auprès des différents intervenants qui ont nourri ma réflexion, sans que je puisse les citer nommément.

Et comme cela a été souligné dès l'ouverture par le professeur Robert Uerpmann-Wittzack, il est encore plus risqué de parler de la religion, *a fortiori* des religions, comme on ne le sait que trop à Ratisbonne. Je me souviens de débats entre les experts de la Sous-Commission des droits de l'homme des Nations Unies, à propos de ce qui est fort improprement qualifié de « crime d'honneur ». Notre collègue pakistanais, M. Sattar, s'indignait de ce qu'il appelait plus justement un « *hideous crime* » en souhaitant une consultation officielle de dignitaires religieux pour dissiper les interprétations erronées de la Sharia, tandis que l'experte marocaine, Mme Warzazi, recommandait de dénoncer les violations des droits de l'homme en évitant surtout de se mêler de religion.

Cette réticence naturelle est encore plus forte pour un juriste français, marqué par une vieille tradition de dualisme, qui a débouché sur la notion de laïcité[1], aujourd'hui consacrée dans la Constitution qui affirme dès les premiers mots de l'article 1er que « *la France une République indivisible, laïque, démocratique et sociale* », avant de préciser « *qu'elle assure l'égalité devant la loi de tous les citoyens sans distinction d'origine, de race ou de religion. Elle respecte toutes les croyances* ». Mais l'émergence de l'Etat-Nation,

1 E. Tawil, *Laïcité de l'Etat et liberté de l'Eglise*, Artège, 2013. Cf. également l'œuvre classique d'E. Poulat, et notamment *Notre laïcité publique*, Berg, 2003.

 | DOI:10.1163/9789004349155_018

sous l'influence des légistes du royaume, est marquée par la double affirmation du roi de France face au pape et à l'empereur. A cet égard, la signature du concordat de 1516 par le roi François Ier, dans une position de force face à la papauté, marque l'importance des « libertés gallicanes » farouchement défendues par les Parlements jusqu'à la fin de l'Ancien Régime. Depuis l'échec sanglant de la « constitution civile du clergé » lors de la Révolution française[2] et, plus encore, depuis la rupture du concordat de 1801 et la loi de Séparation de 1905, il n'y a plus à proprement parler d'« Eglise de France », mais bien une « Eglise en France »[3]. Dans un tel contexte, il peut sembler étrange de voir les pouvoirs publics chercher à mettre en place un « Islam de France »[4], sur le modèle du Grand Sanhédrin de 1807 convoqué par Napoléon visant tout à la fois à émanciper, moderniser et contrôler le judaïsme en France. Encore aujourd'hui, chaque samedi, une « prière pour la République » est prononcée dans toutes les synagogues de France, comme l'a rappelé récemment le grand rabbin de France Haïm Korsia[5].

C'est ce temps long de l'histoire qu'il faut avoir à l'esprit lorsqu'on aborde un tel sujet, où le passé et le présent ne cessent de s'entremêler. Lorsque le pape François se rend à Lund, le 1er novembre 2016, à l'invitation de l'Eglise luthérienne de Suède, c'est pour marquer le 500ème anniversaire de la Réforme et du geste de Luther affichant ses « 95 thèses » sur la porte de la chapelle du château de Wittenberg en 1517. Lorsque le pape François, le 12 février 2016, fait escale à La Havane sur sa route vers New York, pour rencontrer Kyrill, le patriarche de Moscou, en territoire « neutre », c'est un geste sans précédent depuis le schisme de 1054. Derrière les césures religieuses apparaissent des fractures géopolitiques, héritées de la division de l'Empire romain, que l'on retrouve dans les conflits de l'après-guerre froide, dans les Balkans comme en Ukraine. Sans parler des enjeux historiques de la question d'Orient et du statut de la Terre sainte, marqués par les souvenirs des croisades et l'antagonisme

2 Cf. deux œuvres remarquables parues à des dates critiques : Edgar Quinet, *La Révolution*, 1865, (rééd., Belin, 1987) et Pierre de la Gorce, *Histoire religieuse de la Révolution française*, 5 vol. Plon, 1909–1923.

3 Sur cette distinction, cf. Mgr Claude Dagens, *Survie ou métamorphose ? L'avenir du catholicisme en France*, Edition de l'atelier, 2015. Le conseil permanent de la Conférence des évêques de France a publié en octobre 2016, à la veille des élections présidentielles, un document de travail adressé « à tous les habitants de notre pays », *Dans un monde qui change, retrouver le sens de la politique*.

4 Pour une excellente mise en perspective, cf. M. Arkoun (dir.), *Histoire de l'Islam et des musulmans en France du Moyen Age à nos jours*, Albin Michel, 2006.

5 *Le Figaro*, 21 février 2017.

des grandes religions monothéistes[6]. On pourrait en dire autant des relations actuelles de l'Eglise et de la Chine qui s'inscrivent dans une longue histoire culturelle où les jésuites ont joué un rôle de premier plan, depuis Matteo Ricci jusqu'à Teilhard de Chardin[7].

Encore faut-il garder à l'esprit que la religion, avec sa dimension transcendante, sa relation intime au sacré, sa vocation universelle, est irréductible aux analyses juridiques ou géopolitiques, par définition limitées dans l'espace et le temps. De ce point, de vue la religion est tout sauf un « fait » ...

Autrement dit, dès le départ il faut bien reconnaître que la dialectique droit et religion est bancale, en raison même de cette dissymétrie de leur essence. Notre colloque est organisé autour de deux notions, de deux pôles, « *la religion et le droit international* », appartenant à des ordres différents – pour parler comme Pascal – et tellement complexes qu'ils sont difficiles à cerner, et encore plus à articuler.

1 Les frontières de la dialectique

A tout le moins, son intitulé invite à nous interroger sur ce que « dit » la religion du droit international, comment elle l'influence, et ce que « dit » le droit international de la religion, comment il l'encadre ...

Mais au préalable il faut s'interroger sur les contours des deux termes ...

1 / Nous parlons du droit international et non de l'histoire diplomatique, ou des relations internationales, même si les frontières sont perméables. Un colloque de la Sorbonne, qui vient d'être publié en 2016, est consacré justement au thème « Diplomatie et religion »[8], dans une perspective française, qu'il s'agisse du rétablissement des relations diplomatiques avec le Vatican en 1921, ou du rôle des « congrégations religieuses » à travers le monde. Curieusement ce sont plus les historiens qui s'intéressent à cette problématique que les politistes, l'analyse des relations internationales, qu'elle soit fondée sur la *realpolitik,* à l'image de Raymond Aron[9], ou sur une lecture économique de type

6 Cf. G. Israël, *Jérusalem la sainte*, Odile Jacob, 2001. Et pour une nouvelle approche historiographique, V. Lemire, *Jérusalem 1900, la ville sainte à l'âge des possibles*, Armand Colin, 2016.

7 Benoit Vermander, *Les jésuites et la Chine. De Matteo Ricci à nos jours*, Lessius, 2012.

8 *Diplomatie et religion*, sous la direction de G. Ferragu et de F. Michel, Publications de la Sorbonne, 2016.

9 Même si la dimension idéologique du conflit est-ouest est très présente dans son œuvre, avec l'accent mis sur la liberté comme facteur historique.

marxiste, n'intégrant que de manière marginale les facteurs idéologiques ou les influences morales, les « forces de l'esprit »[10].

C'est dire si, après la chute du mur de Berlin, la nouvelle grille de lecture des relations internationales de Samuel Huntington fondée sur le « choc des civilisations »[11] a marqué un tournant radical. En réaction à ces thèses, de nombreuses initiatives ont cherché à promouvoir le « dialogue des civilisations ». Déjà, à l'occasion du Millénaire, le Secrétaire général avait invité l'ensemble des « leaders religieux et spirituels » à un Sommet organisé à New York, ce qui constituait une première aux Nations Unies. Le discours d'ouverture de Kofi Annan, prononcé le 20 août 2000, reste un vibrant appel contre la haine et l'intolérance, opposant l'ombre et la lumière pour souligner la contribution des religions à la paix. Ce faisant, il reprenait à son compte l'inspiration profonde de Dag Hammarskjöld : « *The United Nations stands outside – necessarily outside – all confessions, but it is, nevertheless, an instrument of faith. As such it is inspired by what unites and not by what divides the great religions of the world* »[12].

La neutralité religieuse qui a présidé à la mise en place du système des Nations Unies ne traduit pas seulement l'hostilité des régimes totalitaires pratiquant un « athéisme d'Etat », elle reflète la volonté de transcender les différences entre les peuples pour « proclamer à nouveau notre foi dans les droits de l'homme et la valeur de la personne humaine, dans l'égalité de droit des hommes et des femmes, ainsi que des nations, grandes et petites », comme l'affirme d'emblée le préambule de la Charte. En utilisant le mot « foi », la Charte vise-t-elle une nouvelle « religion civile » venant remplacer les vieux cultes, ou cherche-t-elle un dénominateur commun à toutes les croyances et à toutes les

10 Chez les juristes français, Marcel Merle fait figure de pionnier avec ses travaux de *Sociologie des relations internationales*, Dalloz, 1974, dans le prolongement de son recueil *Pacifisme et internationalisme*, collection U, Armand Colin, 1966, auquel répond celui de Marcel Prélot, *Le libéralisme catholique*, Armand Colin, 1969. Cette césure entre l'histoire religieuse et l'étude des relations internationales est d'autant plus curieuse, que toute une école d'historiens, comme Jean-Baptiste Duroselle, André Latreille et René Rémond, était très marquée par l'influence catholique. Cf. notamment le témoignage d'A. Latreille in *De Gaulle, la Libération et l'Eglise catholique*, Le Cerf, 1978.

11 *The Clash of Civilizations and the Remaking of World Order*, Simon & Shuster, 1996 (trad. fr. *Le Choc de civilisations*, Odile Jacob, 1997).

12 *To Speak for the World, Speeches and Statements by Dag Hammarsköld*, Atlantis, 2005, p. 60. On ne retrouve plus le discours de Kofi Annan de 2000 sur le site des Nations Unies, mais il est en ligne sur internet comme des déclarations plus récentes sur « *Religion, Pluralism and Démocracy* », publiées par la Fondation Kofi Annan, www.kofiannanfoundation.org.

convictions ? Pendant toute la période de la guerre froide, il a été impossible de répondre à cette question, mais la « coexistence pacifique » a permis le retour de cette problématique, dès les années soixante tandis que le Concile Vatican II favorisait un dialogue avec le Monde. Dès 1963, dans l'Encyclique *Pacem in terris*, le pape Jean XXIII écrivait qu'« un des actes les plus importants accomplis par l'ONU a été la Déclaration universelle des droits de l'homme », en y voyant « un pas vers l'établissement d'une organisation politico-juridique de la communauté mondiale » (§ 114).

Aujourd'hui, la religion est de plus en plus conçue comme un élément de *soft power* pour les Etats, comme c'était déjà le cas dans le passé, notamment au XIXème siècle, avec l'action des missions étrangères et la protection des minorités religieuses. C'est devenu un élément de la politique juridique extérieure, notamment pour les Etats-Unis avec le rapport annuel du Département d'Etat sur la liberté religieuse, y compris en faveur des sectes, qui a trouvé son prolongement international avec la création de trois représentants personnels du président en exercice de l'OSCE, en charge de lutter pour l'un contre l'antisémitisme, pour l'autre contre l'islamophobie et le troisième contre l'intolérance et la discrimination à l'égard des Chrétiens et des membres d'autres religions. De même, la Russie de Poutine affiche son soutien au patriarcat de Moscou, illustré par la construction d'une nouvelle cathédrale orthodoxe au pied de la Tour Eiffel, complexe cultuel et culturel édifié aux frais du gouvernement russe et bénéficiant des immunités diplomatiques pour échapper à toute saisie par un tribunal arbitral. Dans les enceintes internationales, à l'ONU comme au Conseil de l'Europe, la Russie se veut le meilleur défenseur des « valeurs traditionnelles » à l'encontre des droits de l'homme, en dénonçant la décadence morale de l'Occident.

Dans le même temps, la multiplication des conflits et des crises ayant une dimension inter-religieuse ou intra-religieuse impliquait de nouveaux outils d'analyse. A cet égard, on peut noter qu'à côté du poste de conseiller aux affaires religieuses du Quai d'Orsay – poste créé en 1920 au moment du rétablissement des relations diplomatiques avec le Saint-Siège et occupé notamment par Louis Canet, pendant l'entre-deux-guerres –, c'est seulement en 2009 qu'un « pôle religions » a été créé au sein de la direction de la prospective en 2009 puis de la direction générale de la mondialisation, confiée à Joseph Maïla, avant de disparaître en 2012 avec l'alternance politique et l'arrivée de Laurent Fabius à la tête du Quai d'Orsay.

L'enjeu était pourtant de taille, en intégrant la dimension religieuse aux analyses stratégiques, notamment au Moyen-Orient, qu'il s'agisse du conflit israélo-palestinien ou de l'antagonisme entre shiites et sunnites, sans parler des tensions dans le sous-continent indien et le sud-est asiatique, ces crises historiques servant de toile de fond à la montée du terrorisme islamiste qui touche tous les continents. Ainsi, lorsque le président Hollande prépare son dernier voyage officiel en Asie, c'est notamment pour se rendre en Indonésie, qu'il présente comme « un des pays les plus peuplés au monde, qui compte le plus grand nombre de musulmans au monde ; avec un islam qui a toujours été conçu comme une ouverture et une tolérance »[13].

2/ Cet élargissement des préoccupations, au-delà des relations historiques avec le Saint-Siège, se traduit aussi dans l'autre volet de notre colloque. Vaste programme, d'autant que l'intitulé vise *la religion* et non les religions, encore moins les seules institutions religieuses, ou les droits individuels et collectifs... S'agit-il d'une religion abstraite, de la quintessence de la « religion », dans une analyse dérivée du catéchisme positiviste d'Auguste Comte, ou des religions telles qu'elles existent, les « grandes religions » ? Là encore le droit trouve ses limites entre mystique et politique.

A cet égard, on peut constater que le *Dictionnaire Salmon* n'a pas d'entrée propre au mot « religion », mais vise la « liberté de religion » en partant de l'article 18 de la Déclaration universelle. On notera qu'il n'y a pas non plus d'entrée de référence spécifique aux « minorités religieuses » dans l'entrée sur les minorités. Mais on retrouve tout le vocabulaire lié à l'Eglise catholique : « Cité du Vatican » et « Saint-Siège », « concordats » et « nonciatures », avec toute la gamme des « nonces », « pro-nonces », « inter-nonces », des « légats », « légats a latere », etc. Il faut faire une place à part au vocabulaire des conventions de Genève, avec le terme « aumônier » qui apparaît dès 1864, puis celui de « personnel religieux », utilisés tous deux sans discrimination.

A l'évidence, pour des raisons tenant tout à la fois à l'histoire et au droit, lorsque les internationalistes évoquent la religion, c'est essentiellement au regard du statut *sui generis* du Saint-Siège. Ainsi, Georges Bry, dans un « appendice » sur les « rapports internationaux », présente-t-il la situation indéterminée « de la papauté en droit international », au lendemain de l'unification italienne[14]. Si un auteur comme Bluntschli se réfère aux « Eglises chrétiennes », c'est pour noter qu'elles ne sont pas des « personnes internationales ... car elles ne sont pas les représentants ni les garants du droit international », tout en ajoutant aussitôt qu'elles sont des « personnes analogues aux Etats », entretenant avec eux « des rapports qui ont plus ou moins de ressemblance avec les relations des Etats entre eux », mais une note visant le concile de Vatican I de 1870 montre bien qu'il s'agit avant tout de l'Eglise catholique[15].

13 Discours pour le Nouvel An chinois, cité par *le Journal du dimanche*, 26 février 2017.

14 *Précis élémentaire de droit international public*, Larose, 1901, p. 406.

15 *Le Droit international codifié*, Traduction de Lardy, 1881, p. 69, § 26.

Plus près de nous, Mme Bastid décrit la situation du Saint-Siège, dans une partie portant sur les « entités non étatiques relevant du droit international », en notant que les accords de Latran de 1929 sont un simple traité bilatéral alors que le statut de l'Eglise est universel[16]. Mais c'est sans doute Paul Reuter qui décrit avec le plus d'acuité l'originalité de l'Eglise catholique dans les « relations transnationales », lorsqu'il souligne que « La seule institution par essence transnationale qui ait déjà pu conquérir une personnalité internationale qui lui permet de traiter directement avec les Etats et sur le même plan qu'eux est l'Eglise catholique : encore s'agit-il d'une situation tout à fait particulière ... »[17]. Et de conclure que le statut international du Saint-Siège, « cas particulier complexe et important », ne peut être compris que dans une perspective historique[18].

La liste des cours de l'Académie de La Haye est elle-même un bon indicateur des évolutions intellectuelles du XXème siècle, à travers la place donnée à la religion par la doctrine, avec un contraste très net entre la période de l'entre-deux-guerres, celle des années soixante-soixante-dix, et la période actuelle.

Dès la deuxième année, en 1924, le cours d'un juriste tchèque, Antoine Hobza, évoque des « questions de droit international concernant les religions » (vol. 5). En 1925, c'est le pasteur Boegner, une grande figure du protestantisme français, qui consacre un cours à « L'influence de la Réforme sur le développement du droit international », tandis que l'académicien Georges Goyau – un « cardinal vert » – traite de « L'Eglise catholique et le droit des gens » (vol. 6). On retrouve les mêmes auteurs en 1929, avec « La condition internationale des missions catholiques » (vol. 26) et « les missions protestantes et le droit international » (vol. 29).

Dépassant ce double parallélisme, il revient à un certain Joseph Müller[19] de traiter en 1930 de « L'œuvre de toutes les confessions chrétiennes (Eglises) pour la paix internationale » (vol. 31), tandis qu'en 1933 un cours classique évoque « Les théologiens espagnols du XVIème siècle et l'école moderne du droit international » (vol. 43). On retrouve l'actualité avec le R.P. Yves de la Brière, un jésuite qui fait un cours sur « la condition juridique de la Cité du Vatican » (vol. 33) à l'occasion des accords de Latran conclus en 1929. En 1938,

16 *Cours de droit international public*, Les cours du droit, polycopié, 1976–1977, p. 920.

17 *Institutions et relations internationales* (avec J. Combacau), PUF, 1980, p. 54.

18 *Id.*, p. 115.

19 Ce curieux juriste, vice-consul d'Equateur en Bavière, se faisait appeler Muller-Azua et avait publié à Berlin en 1927 un ouvrage sur « L'œuvre pacificatrice de l'Eglise pendant les 3 derniers siècles », sujet légèrement élargi qu'il présente – sans fausse modestie – comme le premier cours sur « la religion et la paix ».

le R.P. de la Brière fera un autre cours sur « le droit concordataire dans la nouvelle Europe » (vol. 63).

Après la guerre, on voit apparaître pour la première fois en 1949 un élargissement des perspectives, avec un cours sur « La conception de l'Etat et de l'ordre légal dans l'Islam » (vol. 75). Il faudrait aussi mentionner les différends cours de droit international privé sur les statuts confessionnels. On retrouve encore des sujets classiques avec un cours en anglais sur le droit concordataire en 1961 (vol. 104), ou « L'ordre souverain de Malte » (vol. 163) en 1979.

Mais l'Académie semble soucieuse de se livrer à un panorama systématique des grandes traditions religieuses ou philosophiques, avec « Hinduism and International Law » en 1966 (vol. 117), puis en 1967 « The Principles of International Law in the Light of Confucian Doctrine » et « The Principles of International Law in Buddist Doctrine » (vol. 120). Il faudra cependant attendre encore dix ans pour le cours de Prosper Weil sur « Le judaïsme et le développement du droit international » (vol. 151) en 1976, encadré par deux cours plus brefs de H. de Riedmatten sur « Le catholicisme et le développement du droit international » et de P.H. Kooijmans sur « Protestantism and the Development of International Law » (vol. 152).

Paradoxalement, le « retour du religieux » depuis le tournant des années quatre-vingt-dix, au cœur des enjeux de la paix et de la guerre, ne s'est pas traduit par de nouveaux cours, sans doute parce que le thème est trop sensible, en faisant écho au « choc des civilisations », mais aussi trop subtil pour entrer dans les catégories du droit international. C'est bien le sens de ce colloque, me semble-t-il. Sans pouvoir reprendre ce qui a été dit et fort bien dit par les différents intervenants, je voudrais revenir à la dialectique qui est au cœur du sujet, en m'efforçant d'éclairer des aspects négligés, faute de temps[20].

Il y a un discours des religions sur le droit et sur la société internationale, mais il faut distinguer les convergences intellectuelles, les influences mutuelles voire les effets de miroir, autrement dit les « sources matérielles » du droit international et les « sources formelles ». Il faudrait aussi prendre en compte la diversité des « parties prenantes », des différents acteurs, avant envisager l'interaction des normes, lorsque les religions ne sont plus seulement des sujets mais des objets du droit international ….

20 Cf. le colloque organisé le 13 octobre 2016 par le CEDIN de Nanterre, sur « Religion et Droit international », qui avec le même titre avait une tout autre structure, avec un volet important consacré au « droit international vu par les religions » avant d'esquisser une nouvelle typologie des «entités confessionnelles internationales ».

2 La dualité des sources

1/ S'agissant des sources matérielles, les exemples abondent, même s'ils s'inscrivent dans une temporalité différente.

La référence a pu être directe, comme dans le cas de la « Sainte Alliance », conclue le 26 septembre 1815 entre l'empereur d'Autriche, le roi de Prusse et l'empereur de Russie – trois souverains de dénominations religieuses différentes – qui invoquent « La Très Sainte et Indivisible Trinité » pour fonder « leurs rapports mutuels sur les vérités sublimes que nous enseigne l'éternelle religion du Dieu sauveur », en considérant que « les préceptes de cette religion sainte, préceptes de justice, de charité et de paix » ne relèvent pas seulement de la vie privée mais doivent dicter l'ordre politique[21]. On sait ce qu'il en est advenu pour « le bonheur des nations trop longtemps agitées ». Ces références ont perduré tout pendant le XIXème siècle, comme avec le traité de Paris de 1856 ou le traité de Berlin de 1878 dont le préambule commence par ces mots « au nom de Dieu tout puissant ». Il en va de même pour des traités bilatéraux sur les sujets les plus divers, comme le traité de navigation conclu en 1858 entre le Pérou et le Brésil[22].

L'influence est le plus souvent indirecte. On peut penser au renouveau des analyses sur la « guerre juste » et à la Responsabilité de protéger. De même s'agissant de la paix, de la non-violence et de la légitime défense, du droit humanitaire, des armes « licites » et du désarmement nucléaire, il y a un discours proprement religieux qui est au cœur de la « doctrine sociale » de l'Eglise. L'Eglise catholique a pu elle-même évoluer profondément dans sa doctrine, comme au sujet des droits de l'homme ou de l'interdiction de la peine de mort.

Un dernier exemple est celui de l'encyclique *Laudato si*, qui a eu une influence indéniable sur la mobilisation collective en faveur de la CoP 21 : « le pape peut être utile » comme l'aurait dit le président français. La France n'a d'ailleurs pas hésité à organiser une réunion de dignitaires religieux au Conseil économique, social et environnemental (CESE), à l'initiative de Nicolas Hulot – qui avait multiplié les visites à Rome et annoncé lui-même une « encyclique verte » – en invitant le cardinal Turkson qui était alors à la tête du Conseil pontifical Justice et Paix avant de devenir, signe des temps, le responsable d'un nouveau dicastère consacré au développement intégral.

---

21 Cf. texte dans le recueil de M. Kerautet, *Les Grands traités de l'Empire (1810–1815). Documents diplomatiques du Consulat et de l'Empire*, tome 3, Nouveau Monde éditions/fondation Napoléon, 2004, p. 266.

22 Bry, *Précis élémentaire de droit international public*, Larose, 1901, p. 345.

L'effort pour mesurer une influence directe des autres grandes religions est beaucoup plus difficile, faute d'une centralité comparable à celle de l'Eglise catholique, mais on peut se référer à la belle anthologie de Jeanne Hersch qui, lorsqu'elle était à la tête de la division de la philosophie de l'UNESCO, avait recensé dans une « anthologie mondiale de la liberté » des grands textes de toutes les traditions religieuses ou philosophiques[23]. De même, un autre ouvrage parrainé par l'UNESCO sur *Les dimensions internationales du droit humanitaire,* s'est efforcé de trouver les soubassements des « idées humanitaires » dans toutes les traditions culturelles[24]. Force est de souligner qu'il s'agit de tentatives *ex post* visant à consolider l'universalité des grands principes, plus qu'une analyse de l'influence *ex ante* des différents courants recensés sur l'émergence d'une « conscience publique » pour reprendre la formule de la clause de Martens.

2/ Mais pour le positiviste, seules les sources formelles importent. Historiquement, la diplomatie romaine a été un modèle, avec une influence indéniable sur le droit des relations diplomatiques, jusqu'à la codification de Vienne, comme sur le droit des traités, y compris dans le principe de « bonne foi ».

Le « *treaty making power* » du Saint-Siège est double, en visant les intérêts spirituels de l'Eglise, avec en particulier les concordats, mais aussi les intérêts matériels de la Papauté. Ainsi un traité d'extradition entre la France et les Etats pontificaux avait été signé en 1859. On retrouve aujourd'hui cette dualité entre les accords conclus par le Saint-Siège « en son nom et au nom de l'Etat de la Cité du Vatican », comme l'accord sur la lutte contre la corruption conclu avec les Etats-Unis en 2015.

Mais la distinction juridique est parfois tenue, si ce n'est artificielle, s'agissant des engagements multilatéraux signés par le Saint-Siège, depuis la signature en 1952 de la convention de Genève sur les réfugiés. C'est le cas des traités universels relatifs aux droits de l'homme ratifiés par le Saint-Siège, comme la Convention contre la discrimination raciale en 1969, la Convention sur les droits de l'enfant en 1990, et ses deux protocoles en 2001, la Convention contre la torture en 2002. La ratification est le plus souvent assortie d'une déclaration soulignant le « soutien moral » du Saint-Siège qui s'engage « au nom de la Cité du Vatican », en tenant compte de la « nature particulière de cet Etat ». Ainsi, selon la déclaration faite lors de l'adhésion à la Convention contre la torture : « C'est dans cet esprit que le Saint Siège entend

23 *Le droit d'être un homme*, J.C. Lattès/Unesco, 1968.

24 *Les dimensions internationales du droit humanitaire,* Pedone, Institut Henry Dunant, UNESCO, 1986.

apporter son soutien moral et sa collaboration à la communauté internationale, afin de contribuer à l'élimination du recours à la torture. En adhérant à la Convention au nom de l'Etat de la Cité du Vatican, le Saint-Siège s'engage à l'appliquer dans la mesure où cela est compatible, en pratique, avec la nature particulière de cet Etat »[25].

Il est impossible d'entrer dans le débat technique sur la portée des traités relatifs aux droits de l'homme, né à l'occasion des récentes observations finales du Comité contre la torture et du Comité des droits de l'enfant sur les rapports présentés par le Saint-Siège[26]. Mais, à l'évidence, un strict dédoublement fonctionnel fondé sur une fiction juridique, minerait l'exemplarité morale que le Saint-Siège entend défendre. Le recours aux notions juridiques de « sphère d'influence » ou de « *due diligence* », mises en œuvre dans l'obligation de « respecter et de faire respecter les droits garantis, ou de « contrôle effectif », en matière d'application extraterritoriale des traités, répondraient mieux à la nature propre du Saint-Siège, sans pour autant remettre en cause les immunités qui fondent son indépendance absolue à l'égard des autres Etats.

Une contribution trop méconnue du Saint-Siège est son rôle actif dans le règlement des différends, à travers les bons offices ou la médiation. C'est une bulle du pape Alexandre VI qui a fixé la frontière entre les possessions espagnoles et portugaises en Amérique latine. On se souvient de la médiation officielle dans l'affaire du canal de Beagle, à la suite de la sentence arbitrale entre le Chili et l'Argentine[27].

Mais de manière tout aussi discrète, le Vatican a joué un rôle d'intermédiaire dans le récent rapprochement entre les Etats-Unis et Cuba, rôle salué tant par Raul Castro que par Barack Obama … L'appui du Saint-Siège n'a pas été négligeable dans l'accord négocié à Cuba entre la Colombie et les FARC, comme en témoigne la présence du secrétaire d'Etat, le cardinal Parolin, pour la signature des accords de paix le 26 septembre 2016, à Bogota. De même, la diplomatie vaticane s'est efforcée de contribuer à la solution de la crise politique au Venezuela, à l'occasion d'une visite du secrétaire pour les relations avec les

25 La version française du bureau des traités comportant un mastic, le texte a été corrigé au regard de la version anglaise.

26 Cf. le 2ème rapport en vertu de la Convention des droits de l'enfant, CRC/C/VAT/2, ainsi que les observations finales du Comité, CRC/C/VAT/CO/2 et les « *comments* » présentés en anglais par le Saint-Siège à la suite de ces échanges sur le site du OHCHR. Pour le 1er rapport devant le CAT, la séquence est plus structurée, CAT/C/VAT/1 et CAT/C/VAT/CO/1 avec un additif donnant une cote officielle aux « *comments* », CAT/C/VAT/CO/1/Add.1.

27 Alain Brouillet, « La médiation du Saint-Siège dans le différend entre l'Argentine et le Chili sur la zone australe », *AFDI*, 1979, pp. 47–73.

Etats, Mgr Gallagher. Ces bons offices prennent parfois l'appui d'une conférence épiscopale en liaison étroite avec le nonce, comme dans la tentative en cours de sortie de crise en République démocratique du Congo.

D'autres efforts restent sans doute plus symboliques, comme la réunion, à l'initiative du pape François, du président de la République israélienne Simon Pérès et du président palestinien Mahmoud Abbas, dans les jardins du Vatican le 8 juin 2014 en vue d'une « prière pour la paix ».

3 La pluralité des acteurs

Mettre l'accent sur les sujets de droit, c'est privilégier l'Eglise catholique, de par sa mission universelle et sa structure centralisée, encore plus manifeste après la perte de sa souveraineté temporelle, à la suite de la réunification italienne en 1870 et de la conclusion des Accords de Latran en 1929, apportant un terme à la « question romaine ».

Les autres survivances historiques sont d'une portée beaucoup plus modeste, comme l'Ordre de Malte, dépourvu de toute assise territoriale depuis les guerres napoléoniennes, mais qui conserve un droit de légation au bénéfice de ses œuvres humanitaires. L'intervention directe du pape dans une crise interne à « l'Ordre souverain », a été décrite en des termes anachroniques par un canoniste américain : « *Under international law, what we are seeing is effectively the annexion of one country by another* »[28].

1/ Le Statut du Saint-Siège, comme « sujet primaire » du droit international, reste unique. Rien ne l'exprime mieux que les premiers mots prononcés par Paul VI, devant l'Assemblée générale des Nations Unies, en 1965, lors du 20ème anniversaire de l'Organisation, en rappelant aux Etats souverains qu'il

> n'est investi … que d'une minuscule et quasi symbolique souveraineté temporelle : le minimum nécessaire pour être libre d'exercer sa mission spirituelle et assurer ceux qui traitent avec lui qu'il est indépendant de toute souveraineté de ce monde. Il n'a aucune puissance temporelle, aucune ambition d'entrer avec (eux) en compétition.

Depuis lors, tous les papes ont tenu à venir s'exprimer devant l'Assemblée générale, soulignant la convergence entre les buts et principes de la Charte et les idéaux de l'Eglise contemporaine. En 2015, pour le 50ème anniversaire du

28 *Times*, 26 janvier 2017.

discours de Paul VI, le pape François a prononcé un discours qui fait largement écho à celui de son prédécesseur. On peut toutefois relever une note plus pessimiste sur l'efficacité du système international, là où Paul VI saluait « la belle construction juridique internationale de l'ONU » et encourageait la codification du droit international ...

Le Saint-Siège, qui a obtenu le statut d'observateur auprès des Nations Unies en 1964, n'a pas souhaité devenir un Etat membre en 2004, au moment où la Suisse adhérait à l'Organisation. Cette décision de principe de rester simple « observateur » est liée à la volonté de préserver la neutralité du Saint-Siège, même si ce dernier ne se prive pas d'intervenir par la voix de son représentant dans toutes les enceintes onusiennes, y compris le Conseil de sécurité.

Un tournant important a été marqué par la présence du Saint-Siège à la CSCE, en tant qu'Etat participant, sur un pied d'égalité avec les autres Etats participants, dans le prolongement de l'*Ostpolitik* lancée au tournant des années soixante-dix par le cardinal Casaroli, le secrétaire d'Etat du Vatican. A ce titre, il est signataire de l'Acte final de Helsinki aux côtés des chefs d'Etat et de gouvernement des autres Etats participants. La diplomatie du Saint-Siège a été particulièrement active dans ce contexte de coexistence pacifique, mettant en avant les principes fondamentaux et les garanties concrètes de la liberté religieuse dans le document final de la réunion des suites de Vienne en 1989.

Paradoxalement, la situation du Saint-Siège est plus complexe au regard des organisations européennes. Ce n'est pas le lieu de revenir sur le débat autour des « racines religieuses » de l'Europe, si ce n'est pour remarquer que la Charte de Nice reprend les formules prudentes du préambule du Statut du Conseil de l'Europe, jugé à l'époque l'incarnation de « l'Europe vaticane ». Le Saint-Siège est devenu Etat observateur du Conseil de l'Europe en 1970 après avoir adhéré à la Charte culturelle européenne dès 1962 [29]

A défaut d'être reconnu comme « sujet primaire », à l'instar du Saint-Siège, quel est le statut international des autres grandes religions ? Parfois un Etat se fait le porte-parole attitré d'un culte, à rebours du dédoublement qui est à la base du sécularisme contemporain. C'était toute l'ambiguïté de l'Etat d'Israël, tout à la fois Etat juif et démocratie moderne, de plus en plus isolé malgré le soutien américain.

La représentation de l'Islam quant à elle est minée par la rivalité entre les monarchies sunnites face à l'Iran shiite et à ses alliés. Mais leurs responsables politiques et leurs diplomates n'hésitent pas à commencer leurs discours

---

29 Mais le Saint-Siège n'a adhéré qu'à une demi-douzaine de conventions européennes, dans des domaines techniques comme la reconnaissance des diplômes universitaires ou la télévision transfrontière.

onusiens par une invocation religieuse. En pratique, c'est l'Organisation de la coopération islamique (OCI) – instituée en 2011 à la suite de l'Organisation de la Conférence islamique fondée en 1969 [30] – qui, en tant qu'organisation régionale, souvent relayée par la Ligue arabe et les groupes régionaux, se fait le porte-parole du monde musulman, aussi bien sur le terrain des prises de position politiques – à travers la multiplication des mises en cause d'Israël qui fait l'objet d'un point permanent de l'ordre du jour du Conseil des droits de l'homme, mais est également visée par de nombreuses sessions extraordinaires – que des thèses religieuses, notamment sur la question de l'islamophobie et de la diffamation des religions. Parfois, les compromis de langage sont trouvés entre les Etats-Unis et le Pakistan, au détriment de la conception européenne de la liberté de conscience, qui implique le droit de ne pas avoir ou de changer de religion.

2/ Mais au-delà de la représentation des religions en tant que telles, dans leur dimension politique, il faudrait faire place à une myriade d'ONG d'inspiration religieuse plus ou moins affichée, très présentes dans le champ de la coopération internationale et de l'action humanitaire.

Les études de sociologie religieuse en la matière restent un champ d'exploration[31]. On se contentera de quelques pistes, trop sommaires, à défaut d'inventaire systématique. Il est encore plus difficile d'évaluer l'impact et l'originalité de ces mouvements, leur force d'entraînement au-delà de leur valeur de témoignage. Les plus actifs s'insèrent harmonieusement dans des coalitions d'ONG mobilisées sur des sujets thématiques ou des crises géographiques. Mais il faudrait aussi prendre en compte les limites que leur impose une stricte adhésion à la doctrine religieuse – et notamment à la doctrine officielle de l'Eglise catholique, s'agissant du respect de la vie, comme l'illustre encore la crise de l'Ordre de Malte.

Parfois, ce sont des ordres religieux qui sont relayés par des ONG, comme *Franciscans International*, auxquels les dominicains sont associés, avec leur présence sur le terrain depuis des siècles, ou des fédérations d'œuvres catholiques, comme le Bureau international catholique de l'enfance créé en 1948 (BICE). La dimension œcuménique peut-être mise en avant comme avec l'Action des chrétiens contre la torture (ACAT) tandis que l'inspiration religieuse est laissée

30 Hasan Moinuddin, *The Charter of the Islamic Conference. The Legal and Economic Framework*, Clarendon Press, 1987.

31 Cf. les travaux de S.-H. Trigeaud, depuis sa thèse *Devenir mormon : la fabrication communautaire de l'individu*, Presses Universitaires de Rennes 2013, et notamment son enquête de terrain avec J. Carrette, *Religious NGOs at the United Nations in New York and Geneva*, Université du Kent, 2013.

au second plan, pour ATD Quart-Monde, même si l'ONG reste très marquée par son fondateur, le père Joseph Wresinski. Il faudrait aussi mentionner toutes les ONG de terrain, souvent liées aux épiscopats locaux, et rattachées à Caritas International, comme en Amérique latine, en Afrique et en Asie.

Il y a également une tradition protestante ancienne, comme dans le cas des Quakers, très actifs sur certaines problématiques de droits de l'homme depuis l'interdiction de l'esclavage jusqu'à l'objection de conscience, ou plus récentes comme la CIMADE, qui a eu un rôle historique pendant la dernière guerre avant de trouver son prolongement dans l'accueil des réfugiés et des migrants. Le Conseil œcuménique des Eglises qui a été fondé en 1948 sert souvent de point de ralliement aux ONG à Genève.

Un mouvement religieux comme les Bahaïs est également très présent et respecté dans le monde des droits de l'homme, pour alerter l'opinion publique sur les persécutions subies par leurs coreligionnaires en Iran. En revanche, une minorité musulmane comme les Halévis n'est pas représentée auprès des organisations internationales, même si elle a introduit des recours devant la Cour européenne des droits de l'homme contre les discriminations imposées par la Turquie. Un mouvement bouddhiste, comme Soka Gaccai, accrédité comme ONG depuis 1983[32], est également très impliqué à Genève dans les problématiques liées au droit à l'éducation.

Un cas limite est celui des « sectes », parfois accréditées sur un pied d'égalité, comme au sein de l'OSCE ou de l'UNESCO, où les Raëliens ont trouvé une tribune pour prôner le clonage extra-territorial. Les Etats se trouvent à front renversés, lorsque les Etats-Unis attachent dans leurs rapports officiels la lutte anti-sectes menée par la France ou l'Allemagne[33], tandis que la « Mission interministérielle de lutte contre les sectes » (MILS) établissait sans beaucoup de discernement une coopération étroite avec son homologue chinois.

Des ONG d'inspiration religieuses sont parfois aussi très proches des revendications des Etats et peuvent paraître relayer leurs thèses, en adoptant des positions radicales. Parfois sous un intitulé neutre, on est en présence de véritables GONGOs, lançant des campagnes de diffamation. A cet égard le fonctionnement du Comité des ONG lors de sa dernière session, tenue en février 2017, à New York, est un caricatural révélateur du jeu politique des Etats.

32 Un rapport parlementaire sur les sectes publié en 1999 par Jean-Pierre Brard (AN n° 1687) mettait en cause nommément ce mouvement.

33 *International Religious Freedom Report*, publié chaque année par le Département d'Etat, en vertu de l'International Religious Freedom Act de 1998. Pour le rapport de 2016, cf. www.state.gov/religiousfreedomreport/.

Si la *Social Service Agency of the Protestant Church in Germany* voit son statut reporté, c'est parce que le représentant de la Chine l'interroge sur sa position à l'égard du Tibet. *Pax Christi International, International Catholic Peace Movement* (Suisse) a eu grand tort de faire « une comparaison entre la Chine et Taïwan » dans un rapport. L'ONG *Presbyterian Women in the Presbyterian Church* (USA) se voit reprocher « d'avoir cité sur son site internet le 'séparatiste' Dalaï Lama ». Et c'est le Pakistan qui demande à *Coptic Solidarity* (Etats-Unis) comment elle recoupe ses informations. L'Iran, qui questionne le *World Jewish Congress* (Etats-Unis) sur « la condition de l'autonomisation de la femme », et les Etats-Unis, qui demanderont lors de la même séance à *l'Iman Khomeini Relief Foundation* (Iran) quelle est son action en faveur des LGBT. La Turquie demande quelles sont « les organisations interconfessionnelles qui sont partenaires de *Christian Conference of Asia* (Thaïlande). De son côté, l'*Islamic African Relief Agency* du Soudan tout comme *Muslim Aid* (Royaume-Uni) sont questionnées par la nouvelle administration américaine. L'*European Muslim League* (Suisse) est interrogée par Israël sur les propos antisémites de son président.

Le « dysfonctionnement » du Comité des ONG – qui ne concerne pas seulement les ONG d'inspiration religieuse, mais est beaucoup plus général – est tel que les diplomates eux-mêmes finissent par s'impatienter : le dossier de la branche néerlandaise de *Pax Christi* sur lequel s'interrogent la Russie, le Burundi et l'Afrique du Sud a déjà été repoussé 5 fois ... Le record revient sans doute à *Christian Solidarity Worldwide* dont le statut est repoussé depuis 14 sessions, après plus de 80 questions : « En toute bonne foi, s'est emporté le Royaume-Uni, quelle question peut-on encore poser à une ONG qui a respecté tous les critères du Comité ? Nous ne comprenons pas, a-t-il avoué, ce qui se cache derrière ces questions ... »[34].

4 L'interaction des normes

Les relations entre droit religieux et droit international ne vont pas de soi. D'un côté, il y a la vieille tentation de subordonner le « droit humain », un droit fait par les hommes pour les hommes, au « droit divin », qui subsiste dans les théocraties. De l'autre, la reconnaissance de deux sphères indépendantes, le droit canonique et le droit de la communauté politique, n'empêche pas les interférences, avec les risques de conflit de juridictions et de conflit de normes[35].

---

34 ECOSOC/6812, ONG/845, 3 février 2017.

35 Cf. l'arrêt *Pellegrini c. Italie*, rendu le 20 juillet 2001 par la Cour européenne des droits de l'homme qui, à travers la question de l'*exequatur*, vise indirectement la procédure devant le tribunal romain de la Sainte Rote.

Mais le plus souvent, c'est le droit positif qui se présente en position de surplomb, pour déterminer l'encadrement juridique des religions, quitte à reconnaître leur domaine d'autonomie. Sur le plan international, en prenant un peu de recul, au risque de simplifier un sujet particulièrement complexe, on peut distinguer une approche juridique, fondée sur le « droit dur » et une approche diplomatique, passant par le droit déclaratoire.

1/ L'approche juridique est ancrée dans le droit international des droits de l'homme, qui consacre sans ambiguïté la liberté religieuse dans sa dimension individuelle et collective, visant tout à la fois les personnes – les fidèles ou les « infidèles » – que les institutions.

La problématique est bien connue, à travers les débats sur la liberté de religion, qui sont éclairés par les travaux préparatoires de la Déclaration universelle et des deux Pactes[36]. La liberté religieuse, c'est d'abord la liberté de conscience, c'est-à-dire la liberté de croire ou de ne pas croire, tout comme la liberté de changer de religion. L'absence de convention spécifique sur la liberté religieuse, faute d'accord possible sur ces principes ou sur les notions d'apostasie ou de blasphème, traduit bien l'impasse où se trouvent les Nations Unies. En 1981, l'Assemblée générale a adopté une Déclaration sur l'élimination de toutes les formes d'intolérance et de discrimination fondée sur la religion ou la conviction qui se borne à noter que « nul ne subira de contrainte pouvant porter atteinte à sa liberté d'avoir une religion ou une conviction de son choix ». Il faut souligner les efforts d'Abelfattah Amor, - en tant que rapporteur spécial de la Commission des droits de l'homme - pour donner toute leur portée à ces principes, qui se retrouvent dans l'observation générale n° 22 du Comité des droits de l'homme sur l'article 18 *Liberté de pensée, de conscience et de conviction*, adoptée en 1993. De manière significative, l'intitulé du mandat de rapporteur spécial sur l'intolérance religieuse, institué en 1986, a été modifié en 2000 pour devenir celui de rapporteur spécial sur la liberté de religion et de conviction[37].

L'affaire Salman Rushdie avait brutalement illustré cette contradiction fondamentale[38], qui trouve son prolongement dans de la crise des caricatures danoises et avec l'attentat terroriste contre *Charlie Hebdo*. Il ne s'agit plus de

36 Cf. William Schabas, *The Universal Declaration of Human Rights. The travaux préparatoires*, 3 vol., Cambridge University Press, 2013 ; Marc Bossuyt, *The 'travaux préparatoires' of the International Covenant on Civil and Political Rights*, Nijhoff, 1987.

37 Ce mandat a été renouvelé en 2016 par la résolution 31/16 du Conseil des droits de l'homme.

38 S. Szurek *et al.*, *L'affaire Salman Rushdie, dossier d'un différend international*, collection du CEDIN, Montchrestien, 1999.

respecter ou de faire respecter la liberté de conscience ou la liberté artistique face aux Etats, mettant en jeu les notions de tolérance et de pluralisme, mais d'imposer le « respect » absolu de la religion à travers ses prophètes, ses rites ou ses symboles, y compris par la violence au mépris des droits individuels comme de la compétence des Etats.

Faute d'une convention spécifique visant à sanctionner le blasphème ou le sacrilège, par le biais de l'islamophobie ou de la « diffamation des religions », c'est la recherche de « normes complémentaires » à la Convention contre la discrimination raciale qui a prévalu, avec la mise en place d'un groupe de travail du Conseil des droits de l'homme dont les travaux ne progressent guère. Dans le même temps, le mandat du rapporteur spécial sur la liberté d'expression a été recadré pour prendre en compte les « abus » de cette liberté ... Le débat n'est plus entre des droits de l'homme qui doivent être conciliés, mais dans la subordination des droits de l'homme à des devoirs envers la divinité.

Dans ce débat, un volet est négligé, et c'est celui de la protection des minorités religieuses, malgré les dispositions de l'article 27 du Pacte sur les droits civil et politiques. On se trouve sans doute à la charnière de l'approche collective et de l'approche institutionnelle, avec la difficulté pour l'Etat de garantir le pluralisme religieux et surtout de trancher les conflits au sein d'une même confession[39].

Mais la dimension religieuse va bien au-delà, dans le respect dû aux morts que la jurisprudence internationale n'a abordé que récemment, y compris à travers une conception très large de la famille pour les peuples autochtones incluant les ancêtres. Il en va de même des exigences culturelles de matière de restitution des « restes » de victimes de disparitions forcées, en présence d'un chaman. L'accès sans discrimination à un cimetière a également fait l'objet d'une jurisprudence européenne visant les Etats de l'ex-Yougoslavie et en particulier la Bosnie-Herzégovine. Enfin, on ne saurait oublier que la convention contre le génocide de 1948 vise la destruction « en tout ou en partie, d'un groupe ... religieux ... comme tel ». Définition reprise dans le Statut de Rome ...

2/ L'approche institutionnelle est également très riche ; pas plus que le droit interne, le droit international ne peut ignorer les religions, même si c'est pour affronter les mêmes défis opposant neutralité des pouvoirs publics ou « religions établies », voire religion d'Etat. Parfois le pluralisme prend la forme d'une tolérance des religions minoritaires, limitativement répertoriées.

---

39 Pour tous ces aspects, cf. la thèse récente de J.-P. Schouppe, *La dimension institutionnelle de la liberté religieuse dans la jurisprudence de la Cour européenne des droits de l'homme*, Pedone, 2015.

Le traité de Lisbonne, après les débats sans fin sur son préambule, se borne à introduire un article 17 dans le TFUE en semblant marcher sur des œufs, pour ne fâcher personne, au risque de décevoir tout le monde :

> 1. L'Union respecte et ne préjuge pas du statut dont bénéficient, en vertu du droit national, les églises et les associations ou communautés religieuses dans les Etats membres.
> 2. L'Union respecte également le statut dont bénéficient, en vertu du droit national, les organisations philosophiques et non confessionnelles.
> 3. Reconnaissant leur identité et leur contribution spécifique, l'Union maintient un dialogue ouvert, transparent et régulier avec ces églises et organisations.

Les organisations internationales sont dans une situation encore plus floue, tiraillées entre des forces contradictoires. L'UNESCO qui s'en était tenu pendant longtemps à la protection des « biens religieux », en tant que composante du patrimoine culturel, voit ces enjeux devenir éminemment politiques, qu'il s'agisse des fouilles archéologiques dans la vieille ville de Jérusalem – à commencer par l'usage de noms religieux (mur des lamentations, esplanade du Temple …) dans ses résolutions – ou des destructions systématiques de biens culturels, comme les Bouddhas de Banyan, les mausolées de Tombouctou, les ruines de Palmyre qui sont le fait d'acteurs non étatiques … Les conventions de La Haye sur la protection des biens culturels en temps de conflit armé trouvent difficilement à s'appliquer, et l'UNESCO a dû se borner à faire une déclaration pour condamner la destruction des Bouddhas. La notion de « puissance protectrice » trouve également ses limites dans ces conflits asymétriques où la terreur se fait iconoclaste.

L'ONU a pris le relai des initiatives déjà anciennes de Federico Mayor pour développer une « culture de la paix », lorsqu'il était directeur général de l'UNESCO, en lançant « l'Année du dialogue des civilisations » proclamée pour 2001. A la suite du rapport d'un panel de haut niveau où siégeaient des personnalités comme Richard von Weizsacker, Jacques Delors, Amartya Sen ou le théologien Hans Küng, un « *programme mondial du dialogue des civilisations* » a été adopté par l'Assemblée générale le 9 novembre 2001 (res. 56/6), dans un contexte de crise marqué, coup sur coup, par l'échec de la Conférence mondiale sur le racisme de Durban conclue le 9 septembre et par les attentats terroristes du 11 septembre ….

Face à ce contretemps, il faudra attendre 2005 pour voir dans une perspective très différente, le lancement par l'Espagne et la Turquie, d'une « Alliance des civilisations » dotée d'un comité présidé par Federico Mayor. Les diverses initiatives se brouillent, non sans arrière-pensées évidentes. Ainsi, la résolution 65/5 adoptée le 20 octobre 2010 prévoit la création d'une « semaine mondiale de l'harmonie interconfessionnelle » qui a lieu chaque année, au début février, en se référant dans ses considérants aussi bien à « la promotion de la compréhension, de l'harmonie et de la coopération culturelles et religieuses » (rés. 58/128) ou à « la promotion du dialogue, de l'entente et de la coopération entre les religions et les cultures au service de la paix » (rés. 64/81) qu'à « l'élimination de toutes les formes d'intolérance et de discrimination fondées sur la religion ou la conviction » (rés. 64/164)[40].

La résolution 65/5 utilise des mots rarement entendus dans les enceintes internationales, pour « engage[r] tous les Etats qui souhaitent le faire à appuyer la diffusion dans les églises, mosquées, synagogues, temples et autres lieux de culte de la planète, du message d'harmonie interconfessionnelle et de bonne volonté fondé sur l'amour de Dieu et du prochain, ou sur l'amour du bien et du prochain, chacun selon les traditions ou convictions religieuses qui lui sont propres » (§ 3).

Alors que le programme de 2001 ne mentionnait le mot « religion » qu'une seule fois, il s'agit désormais d'un « dialogue des cultures, des civilisations et des religions », d'une mobilisation étatique pour « l'harmonie interconfessionnelle », avec toute l'ambiguïté que cela implique. Les Etats européens, notamment la France, se trouvent en porte-à-faux à l'égard de telles initiatives où les Etats tendent à parler au nom si ce n'est à la place des religions, à monopoliser, voire à instrumentaliser, ce dialogue entre « hommes de bonne volonté » dans une enceinte interétatique, revenant à la logique *ejus regio, cujus religio,* le principe de la paix d'Augsbourg de 1555, au risque de renforcer des identités religieuses antagonistes.

Dans ces conditions, de telles initiatives, en contradiction avec les principes de liberté religieuse, qui sont à la base du droit international des droits de l'homme, paraissent pour le moins suspectes au moment où les religions apprenaient à dialoguer directement entre elles, de manière beaucoup plus informelle mais libre, avec les « rencontres interreligieuses » d'Assise, lancées par le pape Jean-Paul II dès 1986, dont le 30ème anniversaire a été célébré le 20 septembre 2016, à l'invitation de la communauté Sant'Egidio. De même, sur le plan bilatéral, le Conseil pontifical pour le dialogue interreligieux, présidé

40 Sur les débats piégés concernant la « diffamation des religions », cf. notre étude, « Les débats sur la liberté religieuse, le blasphème et le droit des minorités religieuses au Conseil des droits de l'homme des Nations Unies », in *Le dialoguel interculturel et interreligieux à l'heure de la mondialisation,* sous la direction de C. Grannec, O. Landron et S.-H. Trigeaud, Parole et silence, 2014.

par le cardinal Jean-Louis Tauran, et la commission du dialogue d'Al-Azhar, se sont réunis au Caire en février 2017 pour un séminaire sur « la lutte contre le fanatisme, l'extrémisme et la violence au nom de la religion », à la suite de la visite à Rome du grand iman d'Al-Azhar le 23mai 2016, après plusieurs années de froid[41].

On se trouve en présence de réalités contradictoires, avec une asymétrie structurelle entre forces transnationales et relations interétatiques que seul le statut historique du Saint-Siège permet de dépasser par une fiction juridique, là où les autres courants religieux se trouvent placés sous la dépendance ou la protection d'un Etat. Cet antagonisme est au cœur des négociations délicates entre l'Eglise catholique, désireuse de témoigner de son universalité, et la République populaire de Chine, soucieuse de contrôler une « église patriotique ».

Ces relations transnationales qui viennent doubler les relations interétatiques marquent bien la nature plurielle de la société internationale. René-Jean Dupuy s'était inspiré de Saint-Augustin pour évoquer la double nature de la « communauté internationale », opposant la cité des hommes et la « cité de Dieu ». La distinction de ces deux sphères, fondée sur l'évangélique « Rendez à César ce qui est à César et Rendez à Dieu ce qui est à Dieu », est à la base du sécularisme moderne qui est la condition même de la liberté de conscience. Mais le défi demeure entier pour qui veut passer de la morale individuelle à la « morale internationale » ou, pour reprendre la formule fameuse de Max Weber, de l'éthique de la conviction à l'éthique de la responsabilité. Le processus de « civilisation » des relations internationales reste fragile et les acquis du droit international sont eux-mêmes contestés par la violence.

Une image symbolique marque cette dialectique permanente. La salle du Conseil de la SdN, au Palais des Nations, à Genève, est ornée d'une fresque de José-Maria Sert qui est un hommage à l'Ecole de Salamanque, à travers la figure de Francisco de Vitoria. Au moment de la conquête des Indes et de la découverte un « nouveau monde », les théologiens espagnols se sont interrogés sur la nature humaine, en fondant le droit international moderne. Bartolomé de Las Casas, un autre dominicain espagnol, devenu évêque du Chiapas, s'est fait le défenseur des Indiens. Quatre siècles plus tard, le préambule de la Charte des Nations Unies entend « préserver les générations futures du fléau de la guerre qui deux fois en l'espace d'une vie humaine a infligé à l'humanité d'indicibles souffrances ». L'appel à la conscience universelle qui est au cœur du droit international trouve tout son sens face à la violence du monde.

41 *La Croix*, 22 février 2017.

CHAPTER 18

Religion and International Law: Strengthening and Enhancing a Comparative Approach

Christian Walter

The usual legal discourse in Western democracies views religion as a social phenomenon, which, like many other social phenomena, is subject to regulation by law in a neutral and secular manner.* This is also the overall perspective which international law takes on the subject, notably when it comes to freedom of religion and non-discrimination on religious grounds as human rights. Nevertheless, religion bears certain characteristics which distinguish it from other social phenomena, which are also subject to legal regulation. In a first step, I briefly develop these characteristics and explain why they are important for the further legal analysis (1). The second part of these conclusions then summarizes the most relevant points made in the preceding chapters regarding the regulation of religion by international law (2). In a third step, I reverse the perspective and look at religion not as a subject for regulation by international law, but rather as a factor which has shaped and continues to shape international law as it currently stands. Again, the main points of the preceding chapters are summarized (3). The overall conclusion is that the subject of religion can only be dealt with properly in a comparative perspective (4).

1 Specific Characteristics of Religion

When analyzing the relationship between law and religion, it is important to take into account certain characteristics of religion, which make it a special subject for regulation. For the analysis provided for in these conclusions, religion's claim for a normative regulation of social behaviour deserves specific attention since it competes with a similar claim made by the state (1.1). Furthermore, religion is only partially accessible to determination by administrative organs and courts. For this reason, the self-determination by the

* The following remarks were presented orally at the Conference. They have been kept basically in their structure and content, but references have been added to the papers as they are now printed in this volume.

 | DOI:10.1163/9789004349155_019

individual bearer of rights of the content of his or her religious convictions is of crucial importance (1.2).

1.1 *Competing Claims for the Normative Regulation of Social Behaviour*

The most important among these characteristics is that many religions – just like law – set up normative codes, which aim at the regulation of social behaviour. In that sense, they are competitors to the claim of exclusive regulation usually associated with the state. Depending on the historical development of a given legal order, the autonomous regulatory role of religion or religious institutions is present to a larger or lesser degree.

In consequence, the respective claims for regulation by the state (or more generally: by public power) and by religions need delimitation. However, no simple hierarchy can be established given the fact that each religion and the state operate within their respective normative systems. However, it is precisely the historical background of the development of the principle of state sovereignty in the religious civil wars of the 16th and 17th centuries, which illustrates why, in case of conflicting norms, the ultimate decision must remain with the public power represented by the state. Competing religious claims and convictions can only be dealt with in a neutral and impartial manner, when the decisions on such issues are taken by institutions which are not themselves religiously bound. Therefore, a system in which the entire legal order is made subject to an interpretation according to the requirements of a specific religion (i.e. where the public power and its institutions operate within and under a specific religious framework) – as is the case under Art. 4 of the Constitution of Iran[1] – is structurally unable to provide for freedom of religion.

At the same time, any determination on the part of the state of what a specific religion requires from its members would automatically infringe upon their freedom of religion. For that reason, the self-determination of religious convictions by the religious communities concerned must be ensured to the extent possible. It ensues that the second crucial element for the analysis is the principle of self-determination, which shall now be briefly addressed.

1.2 *Self-Determination as a Necessary Element of Freedom of Religion*

A second important characteristic of religion is that, in contrast to most other fundamental rights, the state and its organs are unable to define the

1 'All civil, penal financial, economic, administrative, cultural, military, political, and other laws and regulations must be based on Islamic criteria. This principle applies absolutely and generally to all articles of the Constitution as well as to all other laws and regulations, and the fuqaha' of the Guardian Council are judges in this matter'.

exact scope of the guarantees.[2] This is because any definition of what constitutes a religion, or which rites it requires its members to observe, potentially infringes upon the free exercise of religious beliefs. Hence, the application of freedom of religion, whether at the national or the international level, must on the one side respect the autonomous determination by each religion of what it considers to constitute its 'belief'. At the same time, the role of the state as supreme public power requires its institutions to be the final arbiter in any legal dispute. Under such conditions, balancing may become a difficult exercise – a matter which is highlighted in a number of contributions, most notably in the analyses of international jurisprudence and practice presented by *Ludovic Hennebel,*[3] *Angelika Nußberger*[4] and *Laurence Bourgorgue-Larsen*.[5] The overall approach followed in that regard is that in order to establish a certain conviction or behaviour as religious, it is sufficient that the religious background is plausibly argued. If that is the case, freedom of religion becomes applicable and any restriction needs to be justified under the restriction clauses.

2 Regulation of Religion by International Law

As a social phenomenon, religion takes place in concrete societies with existing national legal orders. Hence, religion is not only regulated by international law but first, and foremost, by norms of national law. This has two important consequences, which are well reflected in the current volume: The first concerns the relationship between national and international law (2.1), and the second the necessity of a comparative approach (2.2). In addition to these two consequences, the regulation of religion, both at the national and the international level, is confronted with a number of norm collisions, which require balanced and nuanced solutions (2.3).

2 See with regard to the practice at the level of the UN, Ludovic Hennebel, 'Les organes de protection des droits de l'homme des Nations Unies face à la religion', in this volume, chapter 5, section 2.1.

3 Hennebel (n 2).

4 Angelika Nußberger, 'The European Court of Human Rights and Freedom of Religion', in this volume, chapter 6.

5 Laurence Bourgorgue-Larsen, 'Le système interaméricain des droits de l'homme face aux religions', in this volume, chapter 7.

2.1 *Relationship between National and International Law – a Specific Role for the Concept of Margin of Appreciation in the Context of Disputes Involving Religion*

The impact of international law on the domestic legal orders is, of course, a perennial subject for international lawyers, beyond the specific issue of freedom of religion. However, it is of specific relevance precisely in the context of conflicts involving religion for two reasons, which have already been mentioned. The first is the historical influence of religious traditions and affiliations on many national legal orders. This raises the question of uniformity and diversity in the area, and whether and to what extent international law needs to be specifically considerate to the role of religion in a given domestic order. The second reason is a general aspect of human rights protection at the international level. At least with regard to states, which possess a developed and sophisticated domestic system of human rights protection, the general question arises under which conditions international institutions may replace the national legal decision by their own assessment of the situation.

Both of these questions are dealt with under the concept of margin of appreciation. In fact, notably the European Court of Human Rights in its jurisprudence grants a specifically broad margin of appreciation in the area of religion because the domestic systems of balancing the relations between state and religion are quite diverse even among the members of the Council of Europe. This aspect was the decisive argument for the Grand Chamber to overturn the Chamber decision in the famous *Lautsi* case concerning crucifixes in the classrooms of Italian public schools.[6] The contribution by *Christoph Grabenwarter* analyzes the function of the margin of appreciation also in the broader context of positive obligations.[7] In this contribution, he convincingly retraces the general jurisprudence of the Court concerning the member states' margin of appreciation and concludes that, for that matter, the distinction between positive and negative obligations has practically lost its significance. The result is that other factors, notably the coherence or divergence among the Member States, become more important. A necessary consequence of this is the need for a comparative approach.

6 *Lautsi and Others v Italy* (GC) App no 30814/06 (ECtHR, 18 March 2011); see also Dagmar Richter, 'Religious Freedom and Parental Rights in a Pluralist Society', in this volume, chapter 16, section 3.3.

7 Christoph Grabenwarter, 'La liberté de religion: marge d'appréciation et mesures positives des Etats', in this volume, chapter 8, passim.

2.2 *The Necessity of a Comparative Approach*

As the preceding section already indicated, an international law perspective on religion necessarily requires a comparative approach. There are two reasons for this necessity. The first has just been mentioned and is closely related to the concept of margin of appreciation. Since the scope of the margin of appreciation varies according to whether or not there is a common ground among the member states, the analysis must start by establishing the respective domestic approaches to religion. This is in fact not only the approach followed by the European Court of Human Rights but also confirmed by a similar practice at the Inter-American and the universal level, where the respective religious and cultural context is also of crucial importance for the analysis.[8]

The second factor, which contributes to the necessity of a comparative approach, must be seen in the fact that most legal controversies concerning religion are dealt with under a human rights perspective. Hence, the normative toolbox of international lawyers is very similar to the one used in national law. In consequence, many legal questions arising with regard to religion are the same in international law and in national (constitutional) law. This is very well reflected in almost all contributions in this volume and concerns both, the substantive issues in dispute (i.e. religiously motivated clothing and food prescriptions,[9] blasphemy and freedom of expression,[10] apostasy and freedom of religion,[11] the rights of parents,[12] the legal position of religious organizations,[13] etc.) and the structural concepts applied (e.g. the extension of the scope of application of freedom of religion,[14] questions of interference and justification,[15] including the issue of balancing with competing human rights positions such as freedom of expression[16] or parental rights,[17] problems of

8 Hennebel (n 2) and Burgorgue-Larsen (n 5).

9 Hennebel (n 2), sections 2.3 and 2.4.

10 Eleni Polymenopoulou, 'Blasphemy and Hate Speech: Clarifications of International Human Rights Law Standards', in this volume, chapter 11; Hennebel (n 2), section 2.8.

11 Nathalie Bernard-Maugiron, 'Liberté religieuse en islam', in this volume, chapter 4; Hennebel (n 2), section 2.7.

12 Richter (n 6); Burgorgue-Larsen (n 5), section 1.2.

13 Hennebel (n 2), section 2.2.

14 Burgorgue-Larsen (n 5), sections 2 and 3.

15 Henebel (n 2); Burgorgue-Larsen (n 5), 3.2.; Nußberger (n 4), section 3.3.

16 Polymenopoulou (n 9); Irmgard Marboe 'Freedom of Expression – Theory and Practice in the Islamic Realm', in this volume, chapter 12; Pinto de Albuquerque and Scoseria Katz, 'Is Religion a Threat to Human Rights? Or is it the Other Way Around?', in this volume, chapter 13.

17 Richter (n 6).

discrimination on grounds of religion[18] etc.). For the comparative perspective this implies that the comparison should not be limited to comparing different national approaches but needs to be extended to the concepts and principles applied by international institutions on the level of international law as well.

2.3 *Norm-collisions with Regard to Religion*

A field, which is particularly apt for comparing approaches and solutions in the different national and international settings, are norm-collisions between freedom of religion and other human rights guarantees. In fact, many chapters in this book reveal such norm-collisions and how they are approached, the issue being most pointedly addressed in the contribution by Pinto and Katz with the question of whether religion is a threat to (other) human rights.[19]

2.3.1 Religion and Freedom of Expression

In the area of reconciling religion and freedom of expression a number of different approaches are presented in this book. A good example of a broad comparative approach is the chapter by *Irmgard Marboe* on freedom of expression in Islamic Law. Here, different concepts and approaches to human rights law become visible, when the inherent limitation of freedom of expression by religious predeterminations is analyzed.[20] In fact, the chapter examines the Islamic concept of freedom of expression, i.e. the human right as conceived *within* a religiously determined legal order. The contribution by *Eleni Polymenopoulou* underlines a different approach to the same issue. Under the Convention against Racial Discrimination certain contents of opinions may be categorized as discriminatory. This is particularly true if, under a broad concept of race, religion is assimilated to race, and critical opinions on certain religions are then perceived as discriminating against the adherents of these religions. Whether the Committee against Racial Discrimination took sufficiently into account the right to freedom of expression in the *Sarrazin*-case,[21] is a matter on which one may have different views. Irrespective of possible divergent views on the reasoning and the outcome, the *Sarrazin*-case underlines from an analytical point of view the difficulties which arise where specialized human

---

18 Antje von Ungern-Sternberg, 'Religious Profiling, Statistical Discrimination and the Fight against Terrorism in Public International Law', in this volume, chapter 9; Ninon Colneric, 'Discrimination in the Name of Religion in Employment and Occupation – An ILO Perspective', in this volume, chapter 14; Hennebel (n 2), section 2.6.

19 Pinto de Albuquerque and Scoseria Katz (n 16).

20 Marboe (n 16), section 2.

21 Polymenopoulou (n 9), section 2.1.2.

rights regimes are set up for specific human rights and tend to develop an agenda for 'their' human rights. Where issues of balancing are concerned, a lot depends on who is entrusted with the final decision.

2.3.2 Freedom of Religion and Family Rights

Another area with a strong necessity for balancing competing individual human rights positions concerns the various rights involved in family law disputes. Here, we are not only confronted with a substantive problem that requires balancing, but also with the institutional question of whether and to what extent such disputes may be solved by religious institutions on the basis of religiously determined family law. This is a question, which mainly arises in the context of Jewish law and Islamic law but also reaches the state courts in European countries via the application of foreign law and foreign decisions in the context of private law cooperation. Beyond specific problems, there exists a general necessity to inquire into the conditions under which the state may leave jurisdictional tasks such as marriage, divorce and other family law issues, to the decision of religious institutions. While there are good arguments to assume that deference to religious institutions in such matters is not as such incompatible with the requirements of religious freedom, there are equally strong arguments for a positive obligation on the part of the states, who accept such a system, to provide for secular alternatives for those who are unable to accept the jurisdiction of religious institutions because of their own religious convictions.

2.3.3 Questions of Equality and Non-Discrimination

A third area, which deserves specific attention with regard to the issue of balancing concerns equality and non-discrimination. When it comes to employment with religiously affiliated employers, such as churches or church-run institutions, various questions of discrimination may arise. To what extent can religious convictions be made part of the employment conditions and under which circumstances may a violation of religious prescriptions result in the termination of the labor relations? These issues often require either taking into account freedom of religion on both sides or they require a balancing with other human rights such as the right to marriage, which – according to the convincing jurisprudence of the European Court of Human Rights – is not a right that can only be exercised once in a lifetime. With regard to the Catholic Church this has given rise to disputes which have also reached the European Court of Human Rights and which have been addressed in the contribution by *Christoph Grabenwarter*. Furthermore, such disputes open a completely different field of international law, in so far as ILO conventions on labour standards may also apply. As the chapter by *Ninon Colneric* shows, one can follow different approaches to the matter.[22] Under the ILO conventions and the European Convention on Human Rights the issue is dealt with as a question of freedom of religion and non-discrimination. National systems, such as the German regulations of the Weimar Constitution may follow a different approach. However, if one looks at the outcome of the more recent case-law of the Strasbourg Court, the conceptual differences, although undeniably existent, do not seem to make too much of a difference as far as the result is concerned.

3 Religion as a Factor Influencing International law

Regarding religion as a factor influencing international law, two different aspects may be distinguished, which are present throughout a number of chapters in this book: On the one side, certain legal concepts and institutions have – at least in part – been shaped by religious convictions (3.1). Secondly, a number of actors on the international sphere are religiously affiliated. In order to achieve a better understanding of freedom of religion on the international sphere, these influences need to be taken into consideration.

3.1 *Concepts and Institutions*

It has often been said that many concepts and principles of international law have a background in religion or have been/are influenced by religious convictions. The most prominent candidate in that regard is human dignity, which has also been referred to explicitly as a religiously influenced concept in some chapters of this book.[23] The contribution by *Ludovic Hennebel* takes issue with the position that human rights have their roots in religion and emphazises – rightly – that there are secular sources as well which need to be taken into account. However, one need not go as far as to claim that international human rights law 'is a law without God',[24] in order to raise awareness for the decisive point, namely that when interpreting such provisions in the secular international legal order, recourse to religion and religious convictions is not an option. In other words: A distinction needs to be made between the analysis of legal

22 Colneric (n 18).

23 Pinto de Albuquerque and Scoseria Katz (n 16), section 1; Hennebel (n 2), text preceding section 1.

24 Hennebel (n 2), text preceding section 1.

concepts and institutions with the aim of developing a better understanding of how they came about and how and why they developed into a certain direction on the one hand, and their interpretation and application in positive law on the other. While the contribution of religion deserves a necessary and important place in the former, it would run against the duties of religious neutrality and impartiality to determine the interpretation and application of human rights based on religious convictions.

It follows from the preceding distinction, that – again – the focus must be on a comparative analysis. In order to discover open or hidden influences of religion on certain concepts developed in the area of human rights, they need to be analyzed in a comparative perspective in order to shed light on such influences. The contribution by *Irmgard Marboe* is a good example in that regard since it shows to what extent freedom of expression and notably its scope of protection are dependent on the (religious) context in which this fundamental right operates.[25] The overall problem is also strongly (and inevitably) present throughout the chapter by *Sophie Grosbon* concerning the relationship between religion and gender equality.[26]

3.2 *Actors*

International Law is mainly concerned with the relations between independent states. Usually, religion is not the decisive factor, which motivates the behaviour of these actors. However, it cannot be overlooked that some states have a clear religious foundation in their constitutions. Such religious foundations may – also from a legal point of view – influence their actions in the international arena. Furthermore, as the example of the Organization of the Islamic Cooperation (OIC) shows, religion may also be a basis for the construction of political alliances resulting in the creation of more or less formal international organizations. Finally, there are certain actors with a clear religious foundation, the Holy See being the most obvious traditional example in that regard, which is subject to a comprehensive analysis in the chapter by *Jean-Pierre Schouppe*.[27]

25 Marboe (n 16).

26 Sophie Grosbon, 'Religion et droits des femmes: le concordat n'aura pas lieu', in this volume, chapter 15, passim.

27 Jean-Pierre Schouppe, 'Le Saint Siège en tant que sujet et acteur de droit international', in this volume, chapter 3, passim; see also Emmanuel Decaux, 'Les influences réciproques entre religion(s) et droit international', in this volume, chapter 17.

4 The Way Ahead: Enhancing the Comparative Approach to Religion in International Law

The overall conclusion which may be drawn from the conference and the preceding chapters in this book is, that the comparative approach towards religion needs to be strengthened and enhanced. It promises a better understanding not only of the roots of freedom of religion and human rights in general, but it also provides for a deeper insight into most of the current conflicts involving religion, both internationally and at the domestic level. The comparative approach will have different dimensions: First, and for lawyers most obviously, it relates to different solutions to similar problems in different legal orders, including the approaches taken in international law.[28] Secondly, the comparison must also include religious positions on human rights issues such as freedom of expression, blasphemy, parental rights, or gender equality, to name just a few of the ones treated in this book.

---

28 See above, section 2.2.